The Palgrave Handbook of Humour, History, and Methodology

Daniel Derrin • Hannah Burrows
Editors

# The Palgrave Handbook of Humour, History, and Methodology

*Editors*
Daniel Derrin
Department of English Studies
Durham University
Durham, UK

Hannah Burrows
Department of History
University of Aberdeen
Aberdeen, UK

ISBN 978-3-030-56645-6        ISBN 978-3-030-56646-3   (eBook)
https://doi.org/10.1007/978-3-030-56646-3

© The Editor(s) (if applicable) and The Author(s), under exclusive licence to Springer Nature Switzerland AG 2020
This work is subject to copyright. All rights are solely and exclusively licensed by the Publisher, whether the whole or part of the material is concerned, specifically the rights of translation, reprinting, reuse of illustrations, recitation, broadcasting, reproduction on microfilms or in any other physical way, and transmission or information storage and retrieval, electronic adaptation, computer software, or by similar or dissimilar methodology now known or hereafter developed.
The use of general descriptive names, registered names, trademarks, service marks, etc. in this publication does not imply, even in the absence of a specific statement, that such names are exempt from the relevant protective laws and regulations and therefore free for general use.
The publisher, the authors and the editors are safe to assume that the advice and information in this book are believed to be true and accurate at the date of publication. Neither the publisher nor the authors or the editors give a warranty, expressed or implied, with respect to the material contained herein or for any errors or omissions that may have been made. The publisher remains neutral with regard to jurisdictional claims in published maps and institutional affiliations.

Cover illustration: John Potter / Alamy Stock Photo

This Palgrave Macmillan imprint is published by the registered company Springer Nature Switzerland AG.
The registered company address is: Gewerbestrasse 11, 6330 Cham, Switzerland

# Foreword

This book is a carefully considered and curated study of humour and the past. Far from being assembled in haste, it has had a long gestation. Given its rich variety of topics and the expertise involved, that is not surprising—co-ordinating such a multi-talented team might challenge any editorial team. However, Daniel Derrin and Hannah Burrows have proved their organisational skill time and again during this developmental period. Together, they have staged not one but four collaboratories and panel presentations to explore resources and possible collaborations, launched and maintained a website (https://humoursofthepast.wordpress.com/), and administered a research grant to support the whole. For those authors lucky enough to attend sessions at the University of Aberdeen in 2015 and 2016, at Trinity College Dublin in 2016 and at Durham University in 2017, meeting and discussing face to face moved the book forward, providing inspiration, a vital critique and wonderful memories.

The real reason for cautious preparation is neither length nor number of authors: it is meeting the demands of the methodological challenges that this book is designed to address. For those who have watched the project from its inception, therefore, the book forms the end product of extended and deliberate discussion about how best to tackle this serious—if amusing—subject. It is not at all straightforward to approach texts and practices from times past and across many different languages and cultures, and to focus upon their nexus with humour further complicates the task. Humour is largely a modern concept and remains quite ill-defined, even in English-speaking cultures. Importantly, it is innately ambiguous, a potential trap for the unwary scholar in any age. Until very recently, cultural historians were loath to include humour in their remit, even when studying the so-called emotions of the past.

While much has been achieved since the first pioneering conference dedicated to the cultural history of humour, convened in Amsterdam in 1994, methodologies and terminologies have remained unclear. This is despite the rapid development of humour studies itself, a field that bridges across many disciplines, from neuroanatomy and psychology to linguistics and performance art and politics. Indeed, looking back over the last quarter-century, it seems to me that cultural history and humour studies tended to remain in largely separate camps with little intellectual exchange. In 2013, I was invited to contribute to a University of Cambridge seminar on the history of the emotions, teaching a section titled 'Humour and Laughter'. Coming from a humour studies background, I welcomed the decision to include both terms, but found it difficult to identify either as an emotion. When I asked my (cultural historian) colleagues for clarity, they told me they regarded laughter as the emotion, humour as the cause.

From the stance of humour studies, however, laughter is a multi-valent form of human behaviour that can signal many things—amusement, certainly, but also nervous embarrassment, surprise, even antagonistic sarcasm and disparagement. Laughter may be fake, concealing all manner of non-humorous inner feelings (psychologists term this non-Duchenne laughter, and it induces quite different feelings in its audience than does true Duchenne laughter). Seen this way, laughter is not itself an emotion, but can be allied to a very wide range of emotions, including humour. When allied to humour, then it stands to it as weeping does to its own possible range of emotions, from grief to joy.

Humour on the other hand cannot be limited to being an emotion. It certainly can be what Wallace Chafe calls 'the feeling of non-seriousness' (*The Importance of Not Being Earnest*, 2007) that characterises amusement, but the word is also used variously to denote the stimulus to being amused or the creation of a humourist or comedian, and to describe a range of experiences and responsive behaviour that includes laughter and smiling. It has become a convenient umbrella term that sums up a very wide range of humour-related phenomena and, as such, has spread around the world, and has been adopted as a modernising neologism into languages such as Japanese and Chinese.

But is humour an emotion? The question of whether humour (in the general sense) is purely a cognitive or an affective experience has plagued humour studies from its inception in linguistic studies. Recently, however, neuroanatomy (using MRI scans) has convincingly demonstrated that in response to humour, the human brain activates both cognitive and affective pathways, and does so in a complex sequence. Distinguished by nanoseconds, several distinct neural steps occur for a human subject exposed to a humour stimulus: first comes recognition of something as humorous (i.e. not serious, a kind of recognition of a play-frame), then comes comprehension or decoding (what might be called 'getting it') and finally come the responses to it (possibly including laughter and smiling). While these steps are sequential, their outcomes are far from inevitably positive. For example, a humour recipient may recognise that something is intended as humour—and may even respond to it with signs of acceptance—but still may not like it nor enjoy the process. By the same token, enjoyment of the humour does not always require full comprehension, let alone a grasp of the hidden structures of topic/s, target/s and structural devices employed, nor possession of the specialist knowledge required for decoding humour's incongruities, ambiguities and wordplays. Consciousness of why something is funny is not required in order to find it amusing—or only humour scholars would ever laugh. For many reasons, therefore, it is well-nigh impossible to separate the cognitive and affective elements of humour.

If these complexities exist for present-day humour and laughter, how much more must they apply to other cultural periods in the past? Many languages possess their own terms for words relating to humour, including its forms and purposes, and the social conventions surrounding the use of humour and laughter vary enormously between cultures and also within cultures, even today. All this presents formidable barriers preventing an easy application of contemporary concepts, theories and assumptions about where to find humour and how to approach it. Rising admirably to the challenge posed by such methodological difficulties, the editors and authors alike have nevertheless managed here to present a book designed to help others as well as to offer its own insights.

The book's structure guides the reader first through issues of theory and method, and then through case studies capitalising on detailed knowledge of periods and texts, linking historical material with particular theoretical approaches. Interestingly for me at least, this illuminates not only the source material but the general utility of the theory, whether traditional or modern. Daniel Derrin refers to this as 'conceptual grafting', a way to get around some of the problems that arise when trying to apply in specific historical contexts typically universalising 'theories of humour'. As far as I am aware, this is the first book to adopt such an approach, first discussing the limits of what is possible in identifying and accessing humour that is located in the past, and then linking a range of modern theories and techniques to specific texts and their cultural milieux. As such, I believe it marks an important step forward in constructive interchange between humour studies and cultural history, and justifies the book's title of 'Handbook'.

For full measure, the third part of the book puts this approach to a practical test. Several chapters investigate what happens when an informed application of theory and expert knowledge is carried into translating and interpreting past texts and images for modern audiences. Is the humour workable? What are the difficulties that arise? How do modern audiences respond to the humour? Does the superficial meaning of the humour only translate, or can its deeper significance or worldview pass from its original age to the present?

Throughout the book, the editors have ensured that it deals meticulously with the past widespread tendency in both humour studies and cultural history to conflate laughter and humour, reaching for precision in the terms and descriptions used across all chapters. Authors distinguish between benign and corrective (malicious) humour—and there is plenty of malice in some of the texts and interpersonal remarks here analysed! In other places, the humour considered is benign and uplifting, linked to religious insight. The principal argument made by all the specialists across their separate fields is that studying humour in past texts, images and records is rewarding in and of itself, for a number of reasons.

Firstly, looking for such humour is often a pioneering effort: it is surprising how often in the past scholars have completely overlooked it. Treating the past with too much reverence can do it as much disservice as studying it too superficially. Secondly, searching for humour puts our knowledge of the past to the test, showing how demanding it is to peer at images and passages that look suspiciously odd and to be confident of one's interpretation of them as humour. This is not a task for the faint-hearted. Thirdly, however, the task reminds us not only of the distance between our own contemporary culture and that of the past, but also of some of the closeness that exists between the past and the present. While today's comic practices and theoretical approaches of course vary from those of the past, they also have surprising similarities. Despite the lack of direct equivalence of terms in many periods and languages, some of the studies reveal the sense of a shared experience of humour and of being amused. When we see Erasmus's *Folly* recommending laughter as a way of discreetly passing over tensions between married couples and avoiding divorce, we immediately recognise the insight. From that early modern world, it is just a step to Harvard University in the 1930s and the beginnings of personality assessment, when Gordon Allport chose to include in his instruments a test for sense of humour as an indicator of maturity and good mental health.

I am proud to recall that the first steps towards this book can be traced to Australia. The Australasian Humour Studies Network (AHSN), now hosted by the University of Sydney, was founded on a wave of interest in studying humour that was generated by the 8th Conference of the International Society for Humor Studies at the University of New South Wales in 1996. The AHSN has assembled each year since then to exchange papers and strengthen each other's belief that their topics, far from being simple and easy as many colleagues in the academy suppose, are in fact highly demanding. I and others in Australia and New Zealand have had the honour of providing a meeting ground for this group. During some of those events, the editors first explored the possibility of this project. After that, as they say, the rest is history. It seems only appropriate that I salute them in this foreword as they encourage exploration of the challenges involved in appreciating historical humour. It is my belief that their book will play an important part in assisting the future achievements of humour scholars.

Sydney, Australia
Jessica Milner Davis

# ACKNOWLEDGEMENTS

We wish to thank Jessica Milner Davis for her unfailing support in this endeavour from the very beginning. The Arts and Humanities Research Council (Project Reference: AH/N008987/1) generously funded the *Humours of the Past (HOP)* project, which led to this volume and for that we are very grateful. A grant from the *Principal's Interdisciplinary Fund* at the University of Aberdeen helped us crucially at an early stage. Thanks also to the members of the HOP project's steering group who helped us plan and organise conferences.

Among them, we wish to single out the following individuals to whom we are sincerely grateful for their help as members of the editorial board for this volume. Many thanks to each of you for your advice and input.

- Giulia Baccini
- Ron Stewart
- Conal Condren
- Delia Chiaro
- Jessica Milner Davis

# CONTENTS

| | | |
|---|---|---:|
| **Part I** | **Preliminaries: Terms and Theories** | 1 |
| 1 | **Introduction**<br>Daniel Derrin | 3 |
| 2 | **The Study of Past Humour: Historicity and the Limits of Method**<br>Conal Condren | 19 |
| 3 | **No Sense of Humour? 'Humour' Words in Old Norse**<br>Hannah Burrows | 43 |
| 4 | **Rewriting Laughter in Early Modern Europe**<br>Lucy Rayfield | 71 |
| 5 | **The Humour of Humours: Comedy Theory and Eighteenth-Century Histories of Emotions**<br>Rebecca Tierney-Hynes | 93 |
| 6 | **Bergson's Theory of the Comic and Its Applicability to Sixteenth-Century Japanese Comedy**<br>Jessica Milner Davis | 109 |
| 7 | **Comic Character and Counter-Violation: Critiquing Benign Violation Theory**<br>Daniel Derrin | 133 |
| 8 | **Humour and Religion: New Directions?**<br>Richard A. Gardner | 151 |

xii  CONTENTS

**Part II  Case Studies**                                                    173

9  **Visual Humour on Greek Vases (550–350 BC): Three
   Approaches to the Ambivalence of Ugliness in Popular Culture**  175
   Alexandre G. Mitchell

10  **Approaching Jokes and Jestbooks in Premodern China**        201
    Giulia Baccini

11  **Testing the Limits of Pirandello's *Umorismo*: A Case Study
    Based on *Xiaolin Guangji***                                  221
    Antonio Leggieri

12  **The Monsters That Laugh Back: Humour as a Rhetorical
    Apophasis in Medieval Monstrology**                           239
    Rafał Borysławski

13  **Medieval Jokes in Serious Contexts: Speaking Humour to
    Power**                                                       257
    Martha Bayless

14  **'Lightness and Maistrye': Herod, Humour, and Temptation in
    Early English Drama**                                         275
    Jamie Beckett

15  **Embodied Laughter: Rabelais and the Medical Humanities**    293
    Alison Williams

16  **Naïve Parody in Rabelais**                                  313
    John Parkin

17  **'By God's Arse': Genre, Humour and Religion in William
    Wager's Moral Interludes**                                    325
    Lieke Stelling

18  **Romantic Irony: Problems of Interpretation in Schlegel and
    Carlyle**                                                     341
    Giles Whiteley

19  **Unlocking Verbal-Visual Puns in Late-Nineteenth-Century
    Japanese Cartoons**                                           361
    Ronald Stewart

CONTENTS xiii

**20 Popular Humour in Nordic Jesting Songs of the Nineteenth and Twentieth Centuries: Danish Recordings of Oral Song Tradition** 383
Lene Halskov Hansen

**21 Spanish Flu: The First Modern Case of Viral Humour?** 405
Nikita Lobanov

**Part III Humour of the Past in the Present** 429

**22 Translating Humour in *The Song of Roland*** 431
John DuVal

**23 Intercultural and Interartistic Transfers of Shandean Humour in the Twentieth and Twenty-First Centuries** 443
Yen-Mai Tran-Gervat

**24 *The Scholars, Chronique indiscrète* or *Neoficial'naja istorija?* The Challenge of Translating Eighteenth-Century Chinese Irony and Grotesque for Contemporary Western Audiences** 459
Anna Di Toro

**25 Putting Humour on Display** 481
Laurence Grove

**26 Building *The Old Joke Archive*** 499
Bob Nicholson and Mark Hall

**Index** 515

# Notes on Contributors

**Giulia Baccini,** PhD, is Assistant Professor of Premodern Chinese literature and Classical Chinese at Ca' Foscari University of Venice. Her principal research interests lie in Early Medieval Chinese literature (220–581 AD), in particular, non-canonical literary production, entertaining literature and practices linked to it. She is also interested in the diachronic study of joke-books as a 'genre' in the pre-modern period. Among her publications related to humour, she has published 'Forest of Laughter and Traditional Chinese Jestbooks', *Encyclopedia of Humor Studies* (2014) and with Maddalena Barenghi, 'The Witty Courtiers, Memoir 66' (*Guji liezhuan*), *The Grand Scribe's Records* (2019).

**Martha Bayless** is Professor of English and Director of the Folklore and Public Culture Program at the University of Oregon, USA, where she specializes in medieval popular culture, including humour, food, and games. Her books include *Parody in the Middle Ages: The Latin Tradition*, *Fifteen Medieval Latin Parodies*, and the forthcoming *Humour and Literature in Culture: The Middle Ages*. She also is the editor of *A Cultural History of Comedy in the Middle Ages*.

**Jamie Beckett** is a research impact officer at Coventry University. He holds a doctorate from Durham University, undertaken as part of the Arts and Humanities Research Council (AHRC) project 'Records of Early English Drama: North East' within the Department of English Studies. His thesis sought to complicate preconceptions about the role of laughter in early biblical performances, considering the vitality of humour and audience response in the 'mystery plays' of York and the Towneley MS. With interdisciplinary research interests in late medieval urban societies, civic performance, visual cultures, and popular devotion, his publications include articles for *Medieval English Theatre* and *European Medieval Drama*.

**Rafał Borysławski** is an Associate Professor in the Institute of Literary Studies, University of Silesia, Poland. His research focuses chiefly on Old

## xvi NOTES ON CONTRIBUTORS

English literature as well as on the questions of medieval culture associated with the field of socio-cultural history. He has published a book on the idea of enigmaticity in Old English literature and numerous papers discussing Old English philosophical and cultural outlooks, Middle English romances and fabliaux, and medieval visual culture.

**Hannah Burrows** is Senior Lecturer in Scandinavian Studies at the University of Aberdeen. Her research interests range widely across Old Norse literature and culture. She has edited and translated the Old Norse riddle corpus for the Skaldic Poetry of the Scandinavian Middle Ages series, and her publications include articles on the relationship between the riddles and Norse mythological poetry.

**Conal Condren** is an Emeritus Scientia Professor at the University of New South Wales and honorary professor at the Institute of Advanced Studies in the Humanities, University of Queensland. He is a Fellow of the Australian Academy of the Humanities and of the Social Sciences in Australia. He is a member of both Clare Hall and Churchill College, Cambridge. His main research interests are in intellectual history, historical semantics and method, specifically focused on early modern Europe. Among his books are *The Status and Appraisal of Classic Texts* (1985), *Argument and Authority in Early Modern England* (2006), *Hobbes, The Scriblerians and the History of Philosophy* (2011), and *Political Vocabularies* (2017). He is working on a volume of essays on the study of humour.

**Jessica Milner Davis,** PhD, FRSN, is a member of Clare Hall, Cambridge; a research associate at the University of Sydney and at Brunel University London's Centre for Comedy Studies Research; and co-ordinates the Australasian Humour Studies Network (AHSN). She is a past president of the International Society for Humor Studies (ISHS) and in 2018 received the ISHS Lifetime Achievement Award for her interdisciplinary research and publications on humour and laughter.

**Daniel Derrin** is an honorary research fellow in the Department of English Studies at Durham University. Prior to research and teaching fellowships at Durham, he was the S. Ernest Sprott Fellow for 2014–2015 (University of Melbourne), and an Associate Investigator for the Australian Research Council's Centre for the History of Emotions (2013–2015). He is the author of *Rhetoric and the Familiar in Francis Bacon and John Donne* (2013) and of *Humour and Renaissance Culture: 1500–1660* (forthcoming, 2022), as well as co-editor with A.D. Cousins of *Shakespeare and the Soliloquy in Early Modern English Drama* (2018) and of *Alexander Pope in the Reign of Queen Anne: Reconsiderations of His Early Career* (2020).

**Anna Di Toro** studied Chinese and Russian language and literature in Beijing and Moscow and obtained her PhD in Rome. She teaches Chinese Language and Literature at Università per Stranieri di Siena. Her research is centred on Sino-Russian cultural relations, European sinology, and translation of Chinese literature. Among her publications are *La percezione della Russia in Cina tra XVII e XVIII sec.*, Roma, Nuova Cultura, 2012; Wang Zhenhe, *Rosa Rosa amore mio* (adaptation, notes and Introduction by A. Di Toro), Roma, Orientalia, 2014; 'Antonio Montucci e la sinologia europea tra '700 e '800', in *Di padre in figlio. Antonio ed Enrico Montucci senesi europei*, ed. by D. Cherubini, Milano, Franco Angeli, 2018, pp. 19–40; 'The Kitajskaja grammatika (1835) and Bičurin's ideas on the "mechanism" of Chinese between European and Chinese grammatical traditions', *HEL*, 2019, pp. 57–77. She is working on an Italian translation of the Qing novel *Rulin waishi*.

**John DuVal,** a holder of the James E. and Ellen Wadley Roper Chair of Creative Writing/Translation, 2014 through 2018, and Professor of English and Literary Translation at the University of Arkansas, has published 13 books so far. He received a National Endowment for the Arts award for his translation of the thirteenth-century French verse play, *Greenwood Follies*, and two awards from the Academy of American Poets for his translations of twentieth-century Romanesco poetry (the Harold Morton Landon Award for his translation of Cesare Pascarella's *The Discovery of America;* and the Raiziss/de Palchi Award in Translation for his *Tales of Trilussa*). His latest books are *Interpreting a Continent: Voices of Colonial America*, co-authored with his daughter Kathleen; *The Song of Roland*, which was a finalist for the PEN-USA Award in Literary Translation; and *Esteban: Sixteenth-Century African Explorer of North America*, co-authored with Kathleen DuVal (forthcoming, 2021).

**Richard A. Gardner** is an Emeritus Professor at Sophia University in Tokyo where he taught religion and comparative culture, was Dean of the Faculty of Liberal Arts, and served as the co-editor of *Monumenta Nipponica*. Among the topics he has published on are the reaction to Aum Shinrikyô, Japanese noh theater, and religion and humour. He also served as the editor of the Japanese translation of Lauren Artress' *Walking a Sacred Path* and edited *Between Religion and the Study of Religion: Towards New Forms of Human Community*, a book that has appeared only in Japanese and is centered on introducing the thought of the historian of religion Charles H. Long to a wider audience.

**Laurence Grove** is Professor of French and Text/Image Studies and Director of the Stirling Maxwell Centre for the Study of Text/Image Cultures at the University of Glasgow. His research focuses on historical aspects of text/image forms, and in particular *bande dessinée*. He is President of the International Bande Dessinée Society. Grove (also known as Billy) has authored (in full, jointly or as editor) 12 books, including *Comics in French* (Berghahn, 2010 and 2013) and approximately 60 chapters or articles. He co-curated the *Comic Invention* exhibition (The Hunterian, Glasgow, 2016; Clydebank Museum, 2017) and *Frank Quitely: The Art of Comics*

xviii NOTES ON CONTRIBUTORS

(Kelvingrove, Glasgow, 2017) and has long-term hopes of seeing a National Comics Centre for Scotland.

**Mark Hall** is Lecturer in Computing and Communications at the Open University in the UK. His primary research focus is on improving access to our cultural heritage through digital means, in particular for non-expert users. He has an established track-record developing web-based digital humanities applications, covering a variety of aspects such as digitising medieval documents, exploring digital museum collections online, and transcribing and annotating text. He leads the development of the Old Joke Archive—the world's first purpose-built digital repository of historical jests.

**Lene Halskov Hansen** is an archivist and researcher at the Danish Folklore Archives, the Royal Danish Library. Her research explores traditional Danish/Nordic ballads, song performance, the use and meaning of songs and singing, humour, chain dance, and folk music movements in the 1970s–1980s. Among her publications in those areas are *Ballader og kædedans. To perspektiver på dansk folkevisekultur* (Ballads and chain dance. Two aspects of Danish folk song culture), Copenhagen, 2015, and 'Ironi og forvirring i 1800-tallet' (Irony and confusion in the nineteenth Century). In *En aldeles egen och förträfflig National-Musik*, ed. by Märta Ramsten and Gunnar Ternhag, Uppsala, 2015. She is a member of the Nordic research network for vocal folk music (NoFoVoFo).

**Antonio Leggieri** is a PhD candidate in Chinese Literature at the University of Salento, in co-supervisorship with the University of Vienna. He has a background in translation and interpreting, two professions that he still pursues alongside academic research. He lived in Beijing from 2012 to 2016, where he first came into contact with the jokes that he presents in this volume. His interests include comparative literature and comparative poetics, late-imperial Chinese literature (in particular, jestbooks, narrative, and drama), Chinese/Italian translation and translation history. His articles in English, Italian, and Chinese have appeared in influential journals, and he has translated two collections of Chinese short stories into Italian, which were published in 2018 and 2019, respectively. He is based in Taiwan, where he first came for a short research visit at National Taiwan University and ended up staying because of the Covid-19 pandemic.

**Nikita Lobanov** is a PhD candidate in the Department of Interpreting and Translation at the University of Bologna, Forlì. His research is focused on the use of humour online by the radical right movements in the UK following the Brexit referendum, the evolution of memes as units of culture throughout time, and the link with hate crimes that occur on the ground. He has presented papers on humour at several international conferences, most recently, for example, at the International Congress on Verbal Humor, Universidad de Alicante, 2019.

**Alexandre G. Mitchell** (D.Phil Oxon 2002) is the director of Expressum (https://www.expressum.eu), a Brussels-based translation company specialising in scientific translation (antiquity and medieval fields) from French to English. He is a scientific collaborator at the University of Fribourg. *Greek Vase Painting and the Origins of Visual Humour* (2009, 2012, and 2013) is an essential book in the study of visual humour. He writes in the fields of Greek vase painting, the history of medicine, and the reception of antiquity (https://www.alexmitchell.net).

**Bob Nicholson** is a Reader in History and Digital Humanities at Edge Hill University in the UK. He works on the history of nineteenth-century popular culture, with a particular focus on periodicals, comedy, sport, gender, transatlantic relations, and digital archives. His research project explores cultures of joke telling in Victorian Britain. Alongside Mark Hall, he curates and leads the development of The Old Joke Archive—the world's first purpose-built digital repository of historical jests.

**John Parkin** is Emeritus Professor of French Literary Studies at University of Bristol, where he taught French literature and language for 39 years having previously studied at the universities of Oxford and Glasgow. He has written books on Rabelais, Marguerite de Navarre, and Henry Miller, as well as investigated various aspects of the theory and practice of humour. He now lives in Bristol in retirement with Eileen, his wife of 48 years.

**Lucy Rayfield** is a Research Associate in French at St Benet's Hall, University of Oxford, and Lecturer in Modern Languages (French and Italian) at the University of Bristol. From 2019 to 2020 she was the Modern Humanities Research Association (MHRA) Research Fellow at the Centre for the Study of the Renaissance, University of Warwick. Rayfield is the author of *Poetics, Performance and Politics in French and Italian Renaissance Comedy* (2021) and has written articles and chapters on poetics, festival culture, and rivalry in early modern France and Italy. Her new research project concerns the role of Italian propaganda in the French Wars of Religion, with a particular focus on satirical, subversive, and multilingual responses to the conflict.

**Lieke Stelling** is Assistant Professor of English at Utrecht University. She is the author of *Religious Conversion in Early Modern English Drama* (2019), which was shortlisted for the Shakespeare's Globe Book Award 2020, and coeditor of *The Turn of the Soul: Representations of Religious Conversion in Early Modern Art and Literature* (2012). Other publications include 'Recent Studies in Religious Conversion' (*English Literary Renaissance*, 2017) and '"Leaving Their Humours to the Word Mongers of Mallice": Mocking Polemic in *Tarltons Newes Out of Purgatorie* (1590) and Two Contemporary Responses' (*Shakespeare Jahrbuch*, 2018). Her book-length project, *Faith in Jest*, is on humour and religion in the literature of the English Reformation.

xx NOTES ON CONTRIBUTORS

**Ronald Stewart** teaches in the Department of Sociology of Daito Bunka University, Japan. He has published his research work on political cartoons and Japanese manga history in both English and Japanese. Stewart's most recent paper in English, co-authored with Khin Wee Chen and Robert Phiddian, is the chapter 'Towards a Discipline of Political Cartoon Studies: Mapping the Field' in *Satire and Politics: The Interplay of Heritage and Practice* (Palgrave, 2017). He planned, co-curated, and translated the Japanese political cartoon exhibition, *The Other Manga: It Bites*, held at RMIT University in 2019. Stewart serves on the board of the Japan Society for Studies in Cartoons and Comics and is the review editor for their journal *Manga Kenkyū*. He also sits on the board of Saitama Municipal Cartoon Museum's Kitazawa Rakuten Society devoted to Japan's first career cartoonist.

**Rebecca Tierney-Hynes** is a lecturer in the Department of English at the University of Edinburgh. She is the author of *Novel Minds: Philosophers and Romance Readers, 1680–1740* (2012) and articles on eighteenth-century novels in *ECS*, *SEL* and *The Eighteenth Century*. Her work on comedy is funded by a Leverhulme Research Fellowship. Recent or forthcoming articles on eighteenth-century drama and on political celebrity include essays in *SECC*, *Textual Practice*, and *Genre*, and essays for the collections *Intimacy and Celebrity in Eighteenth-Century Culture* and *Making Stars: Biography and Eighteenth-Century Celebrity*.

**Yen-Mai Tran-Gervat** is Senior Lecturer (*Maître de conférences*) in Comparative Literature at Université Sorbonne-Nouvelle (Paris). Her research in humour focuses on Early Modern European literature (England, France, and Spain): parody, burlesque, and comic fiction in the seventeenth and eighteenth centuries; translations and adaptations of early modern humorous works in later periods; early theories of humour. She is a member of the International Society for Humor Studies (ISHS) and of the Humours of the Past (HOP) network. She chairs the French society for humour studies called Réseau Interdisciplinaire de Recherches sur l'Humour (RIRH), which she co-founded in 2017.

**Giles Whiteley** is Associate Professor of English Literature at Stockholm University. He has published widely on nineteenth-century literature and is the author of four monographs, most recently *The Aesthetics of Space in Nineteenth-Century Literature, 1843–1907* (2020). His projects include editing Walter Pater's novel *Marius the Epicurean* for Oxford University Press and writing a monograph on humour and culture in the nineteenth century for Routledge.

**Alison Williams** is Associate Professor of French at Swansea University. She has published on medieval and Renaissance literature, including articles and book chapters on *Le Roman de Renart*, *Fouke le FitzWaryn*, and Rabelais, and a monograph on tricksters and pranksters in French and German pre-modern literature (2000). She has a particular interest in the interdisciplinary medical humanities and has presented several conference papers on the connection of medieval and Renaissance literature to the field, including papers on Marie de France and Rabelais.

# LIST OF FIGURES

Fig. 6.1 Shigeyama Shigeru (b. 1975, left) as Tarō Kaja and Shigeyama Dōji (now Sennojō, b. 1983, right) as Jirō Kaja in a 13 January 2013 performance of *Busu* at the Kongō Nō Theatre, Kyoto. (Photo by Uesugi Haruka, reproduced courtesy of Shigeyama Kyōgenkai Jimukyoku) 117

Fig. 6.2 Shigeyama Dōji (now Sennojō, b. 1983, left) as Jirō Kaja and Shigeyama Shigeru (b. 1975, right) as Tarō Kaja in a 13 January 2013 performance of *Busu* at the Kongō Nō Theatre, Kyoto. (Photo by Uesugi Haruka, reproduced courtesy of Shigeyama Kyōgenkai Jimukyoku) 118

Fig. 6.3 Graphic representation of four basic comic plots types, showing the directions taken by the dramatic narrative in each. (Milner Davis, *Farce*, 7) 119

Fig. 9.1 178

Fig. 9.2 179

Fig. 9.3 180

Fig. 9.4 181

Fig. 9.5 182

Fig. 9.6 184

Fig. 9.7 185

Fig. 9.8 186

Fig. 9.9 187

Fig. 9.10 188

Fig. 9.11 189

Fig. 9.12 192

Fig. 9.13 193

Fig. 9.14 193

Fig. 19.1 363

Fig. 19.2 364

Fig. 19.3 *Maru-maru Chinbun*, issue no. 175 (25 August 1885) cover. (Personal collection of the author) 367

xxiii

xxiv  LIST OF FIGURES

Fig. 19.4  Untitled cartoon by Honda Kinkichirō (*Maru-maru Chinbun*, 31 August 1878). (Reprinted with the permission of the National Diet Library, Japan)  374

Fig. 19.5  376

Fig. 20.1  Percy Grainger is instructing crofter Jens Peter Jensen on how to sing into the funnel of the phonograph while Evald Tang Kristensen is ready to transcribe the lyrics, 1922. (Photo: H. P. Hansen. Danish Folklore Archives, The Royal Danish Library)  387

Fig. 20.2  Ane Jensen (1865–1932), 1925. (Photo: Percy Grainger. Danish Folklore Archives, The Royal Danish Library)  390

Fig. 20.3  Mette Marie Jensdatter (Mette Skrædder, 1809–1895), 1895. 'A strong memory, a living imagination and a natural, poetic talent'— that is how Kristensen characterised her. Kristensen, *Gamle kildevæld*, 62. (Photo: Peter Olsen. Danish Folklore Archives, The Royal Danish Library)  396

Fig. 25.1  George Morrow. 'How the Cubist, by a Mere Alteration of Titles, Achieved a Ready Sale of Unmarketable Pictures'. *Punch* (October 14, 1914), 32  483

Fig. 25.2  *Glasgow Looking Glass*. No. 1, June 11, 1825, front cover. Glasgow University Library  485

Fig. 25.3  *Comic Invention*. Hunterian Art Gallery, Glasgow. March 18 to July 17, 2016. Display panel for 'The World's First Comic' section  487

Fig. 25.4  Sha Nazir. *Two Hipsters in the Car*. 2015. Poster for *Comic Invention*  489

Fig. 25.5  *Comic Invention*. Hunterian Art Gallery, Glasgow. March 18 to July 17, 2016. Design plan  490

Fig. 25.6  *Comic Invention*. Hunterian Art Gallery, Glasgow. March 18 to July 17, 2016. A system of podia allows the juxtaposition of a comics timeline with contemporary works by Frank Quitely that share the same themes. Centre-left is the series of six engravings for William Hogarth's A Harlot's Progress (1732)  490

Fig. 25.7  *Comic Invention*. Hunterian Art Gallery, Glasgow. March 18 to July 17, 2016. The 'Culture of Comics' section  491

Fig. 25.8  Frank Quitely. *Frank Quitely: The Art of Comics*. 2017. Exhibition Poster  493

Fig. 25.9  Christine Borland. *To Be Set and Sown in the Garden*. 2001. University of Glasgow  495

Fig. 26.1  A nineteenth-century dialogue joke with metadata  510

# LIST OF TABLES

Table 20.1 Recordings from *Viser på Valse* mentioned in this chapter. *The Types of the Scandinavian Medieval Ballad* (TSB) classification numbers have been added 387

Table 20.2 The singers on *Viser på Valse* mentioned in this chapter, and the year the song/ballad was recorded 388

PART I

# Preliminaries: Terms and Theories

CHAPTER 1

# Introduction

*Daniel Derrin*

## LEAR'S FOOL'S JESTS

Consider, for a moment, the jests of the fool in Shakespeare's *King Lear*. To what extent can we say we are dealing with 'humour' when we encounter the jests while reading the play or watching a performance of it? Before returning to that question, here are three examples of the fool's jests. Each of them can be found in both major versions of the play: the first Quarto text of 1607–1608 and the Folio text of 1623.[1] The fool, of course, makes many other jests than just these three.

At 1.4, the fool has barely made his requested entrance before he is threatened with whipping. In response, he ramps up his critical edge, constructing an acerbic little family allegory involving a seemingly comic image of inverted domestic order: 'Truth's a dog that must to kennel; he must be whipped out, when the Lady Brach [Bitch] may stand by the fire and stink' (1.4.109–111). 'Truth' could be taken to refer to banished Cordelia, and 'Lady Brach' to refer to Lear's two other daughters, Goneril and Regan, though 'truth' might also refer to the true wisdom that the seeming 'fool' cannot help speaking, even when, as a faithful dog, he is whipped out to the kennel now that Lady Brach, the misogynistic image of disorder (and of desire), has taken pride of place at the fire.

Here is another, a few lines further on. The fool offers Lear a purportedly entertaining riddle: 'Nuncle, give me an egg and I'll give thee two crowns'; pursuing entertainment, the old king responds: 'What two crowns shall they be?' (1.4.148–50). The fool quickly provides a punchline-like answer:

D. Derrin (✉)
Department of English Studies, Durham University, Durham, UK
e-mail: daniel.derrin@durham.ac.uk

© The Author(s), under exclusive license to Springer Nature
Switzerland AG 2020
D. Derrin, H. Burrows (eds.), *The Palgrave Handbook of Humour, History, and Methodology*, https://doi.org/10.1007/978-3-030-56646-3_1

Why, after I have cut the egg i'the middle and eat up the meat, the two crowns of the egg. When thou clovest thy crown i'the middle and gav'st away both parts, thou bor'st thine ass on thy back o'er the dirt. Thou hadst little wit in thy bald crown when thou gav'st thy golden one away. If I speak like myself in this, let him be whipped that first finds it so. (1.4.151–7)

The riddling link between egg 'crowns' and golden ones is transposed here onto another image of Lear's silliness from the 'fool's' perspective: bearing one's ass on one's back. Shakespeare has invoked an old comic jest about a man who ends up carrying his ass on his own back to the market in an attempt to placate people he meets on the way: 'the moral', as Foakes puts it, 'is that in trying to please all [the man] pleases no one'.[2]

Finally, here is the amusing little image the fool creates at a moment when Lear is filled with intense anger. He has witnessed his new servant in the stocks and is now being ignored by his daughter Regan and son-in-law, the Duke of Cornwall, who are apparently too busy within to come out and speak with him. In his indignation he calls out: 'my heart! My rising heart! But down!' (2.2.310—following the Folio text). In reply, the fool creates an amusing image of an unorthodox cook—not quite severe enough to achieve her own ends—followed by an equally ludicrous image of a man tending to a horse:

Cry to it [i.e. to his heart], nuncle, as the cockney did to the eels when she put 'em i'the paste [pastry] alive: she knapped 'em o'the coxcombs [heads] with a stick, and cried 'Down, wantons, down!' 'Twas her brother that in pure kindness to his horse buttered his hay. (2.2.311–315)

The 'cockney' is absurdly kind to her foodstuffs—she indulges the wanton eels as if they were impetuous, amorous youths; her 'brother' is, likewise, absurdly kind to his horse: buttering the hay will probably make it go hungry! Just so, the fool implies, Lear has been absurdly kind to his daughters (and rather stupid) in giving away his authority and then getting into a huff about its inevitable effects.

In order to take the fool's jesting as an instance of 'historical humour' do we need to be able to recognise it as 'funny'? The jests I've described are not likely to be experienced now as *very* funny in themselves, unless made so with additional elements of absurdity and surprise in performance, though the eel pastry example is perhaps the more obviously comical among them. Furthermore, the wider context of the play gives the jests an unmistakable bitterness. As the play goes on, Lear experiences more deeply the effects of his lost authority, and out in the blowing winds of the great storm, the fool fights a losing battle labouring 'to outjest' Lear's 'heart-struck injuries' (3.1.16–7). And yet, to experience the fool's jests as not-particularly-funny is not the same thing as to deny that they are a kind of 'humour', for surely it is possible to see that humour is operating in a historical context without having to enjoy it intensely as such oneself.

What does it mean, then, to identify and account for 'humour' in a historically-removed cultural context, when the emotional or cognitive force it might once have had has diminished? What are the problems involved in doing so, especially considering that the evolution of the English term 'humour', with its peculiar descriptive capaciousness and its difference from related terms in other languages, is relatively modern? The problems are many: identification, establishing function, coherence of research object, the insufficiency of existing humour concepts and theories, subjective involvement, and so on. It is the aim of this volume to begin the task of mapping and confronting such problems self-consciously, as the field of historical humour studies takes shape. As a way into a fuller discussion of the book's aims and critical context, I want to return to the jests of Lear's fool and explore some of the problems involved in using some modern 'humour theories' to engage with the jests mentioned above as 'humour'.

Of course, it must be conceded that one can engage critically with Lear's fool's jesting in other ways than thinking of its status as humour. First, jests and jesting scenes in Renaissance plays have been seen as fulfilling a dramatic purpose. For instance, witty jesting is often understood in the context of tragedy, regrettably, as simply a kind of 'comic relief'.[3] In the context of comedy, jesting has been, for instance, modelled as a representational proxy for the 'erotic heat' driving the plot.[4] But witty jesting in Renaissance plays has also been understood more broadly in terms of the wider jesting culture of the period and its contexts, for instance in connection with the practices of sociability and cultures of courtesy.[5] In addition, scholars have explored other broader patterns, such as the way jesting culture itself could confront social categories by producing a 'counterhegemonic discourse' or, irrespective of their supposed funniness, could develop a 'transformative potential' through their form of word play.[6] Lear's fool's jesting specifically has been seen as a manifestation of Erasmus's ironic character *stultitia* (Folly) from *Praise of Folly*, as well as a kind of 'language game' playing with sense in nonsense.[7]

Those options, however, as useful as they are for investigating the broader context of jesting culture in Shakespeare's time, do not really address what it means to speak of the jests as a historically-specific kind of humour. It is not unreasonable to ask that question considering the cultural importance of the category, 'humour', as it has developed across modernity and the powerful assumption in contemporary humour theory that the category signifies a kind of pattern, if not quite a unity, across varied phenomena.

## Using Humour Theories

The fact that Shakespeare signals that the fool's speech is 'jesting'—he labours to 'out-jest'—perhaps cues the expectation that we will find humour in it but if the jests do not seem 'funny' then how do we know that it is humour? Likewise, a further contextual clue might well be that so much of the fool's jesting is bawdy: Lady Brach is perhaps a bitch in heat and the eels, quite obviously, are meant to be sexually evocative. But the extent to which sexually playful language is amusing is quite subjective, so again, on what grounds is it reasonable to describe what we are dealing with as 'humour'?

One of the most prominent of all recent humour theories, the 'General Theory of Verbal Humor' (GTVH) offers a way of addressing that problem of subjective recognition. By applying two of its core concepts, we might try to coordinate the jests in relation to what is more familiar from modern jokes. The GTVH is in fact one stage of a continually evolving theory of verbal humour based on the core idea of script opposition: first, the SSTH (Semantic Script-based Theory of Humor), then the GTVH (General Theory of Verbal Humor), and now a much more elaborate development of the same framework, the OSTH (Ontological Semantic Theory of Humor).[8]

The first core concept is that of 'Script Opposition', first developed by Victor Raskin to distinguish 'humor-carrying' from non-'humor-carrying' texts.[9] It posits that: (1) 'the text of a joke is always fully or in part compatible with two distinct scripts' and (2) 'the two scripts are opposed to each other in a special way'; a 'script' is a sequence of events in a situation understood (cognitively) as 'a chunk of structured semantic information'.[10] Scripts coexisting in a joke text might oppose one another in the following ways, for instance, by embodying: actual reality versus a non-actual situation, a normal versus abnormal situation, or possible versus impossible.[11] The joke text 'how many [so-and-sos—insert preferred target group] does it take to screw in a light bulb: one to hold the light bulb and four to turn the table he's standing on' holds in opposition an ordinary script of the process of efficiently screwing in lightbulbs and an imagined, abnormally stupid or inefficient way of doing so. Getting the joke means perceiving the presence of both opposing scripts, a perception often triggered by a punchline. GTHV added more to this script-based view of verbal humour: in particular, the 'Logical Mechanism' by which the joke text puts forward opposing scripts. One logical mechanism is the reversal of 'figure' and 'ground'; others include the creation of false analogies, 'false priming' or leading down the 'garden path', and the exploitation of ambiguity or homonymy.[12] The logical mechanism of the joke about screwing in lightbulbs is the reversal of figure (bulb and hand screwing it) and ground (the stable environment of the table stood on).[13] The GTVH describes several other aspects of the variance of verbal humour (i.e. of jokes) but script opposition and logical mechanism have tended to be seen as central.

Do those concepts help in approaching Lear's fool's jests as humour? In the Lady Brach example, one could perhaps say that one script is the scenario of a disordered domestic space, in which the faithful dog 'truth' is cast outside because the bitch hound 'Lady Brach' now stinks by the fireside, and that the other script is the disordered political state, figured in this domestic disorder, from the fool's perspective. But are those scripts opposed, such that the logical mechanism is a notionally false analogy between dogs and humans? Then again, perhaps the key opposition is not between different levels of metaphorical reference (dogs and humans) but between scripts of order and disorder. Is the

1 INTRODUCTION 7

Lady stinking because she is in heat? One might then ask how that affects the interpretation. Is a class contrast relevant—she is, after all, a 'Lady'? Or is her stinking a figuration of the falseness that leads to truth's whipping? It is a difficult case, virtually spawning possible script oppositions.

Things are perhaps more straightforward in the others. In the egg and crowns example, the fool's words make the script of cutting an egg and the script of severing the kingdom that the play's audience has just witnessed seem compatible though opposed in the sense that the unrealistic analogy between 'crowns' is a bit of a stretch. In the eel pie image, an ordinary real script of cooking with eels that need to be dead is opposed by an unrealistic script in which the cook does not want to kill them but nevertheless expects the wanton things to comply. The logical mechanism is not exactly a figure-ground reversal but it shares something of the same the dumb-way-to-do-something 'logic' with the lightbulb-screwing joke in that both create an image of wasted energy.

The GTVH concepts, then, can, where it seems possible to apply them, be a helpful way of confirming the suspicion that a particular textual example from a historical context involves 'humour', but to apply the theory here involves the suggestion that at least some 'jests' are just like 'jokes'. This sort of equation across time and cultural space, however, is something that historians usually have reasons not to do. In this case, the verbal form of a 'joke' with its generic elements and expectations is relatively modern despite the etymological derivation from Latin *iocus*, and 'jests' have not always been conceived as something laughable, ridiculous, or amusing.[14]

If the GTVH provides at least some measure of humour as a discernible pattern in verbal texts across divergent times and places, what it cannot and was never intended to provide is, nevertheless, equally significant for cultural history. It is unable to deal with the problem of what sort of emotional effects and intentions humour implies. This is obviously important in the context of Lear's fool because the jests are part of a dramatic context in which characters are interacting intentionally and emotionally. GTVH is not actually interested in the question of what rhetorical effects humour might have nor how one could think of its emotional import (except in so far as that can be coded by 'scripts'). It relegates these issues to the sphere of 'special theories', such as those 'attempting to deal with the alleged communicative goals of humor'.[15] Yet grappling with specific historical contexts almost always requires a way of thinking about effects and intentions precisely because the 'humour' is not being grasped in a verbal time vacuum but being contextually situated.

Mikhail Bakhtin's justly famous book *Rabelais and his World* does present a conceptual model of humour's effects and intentionality. Bakhtin suggested that Rabelais's kind of humour could be situated within a (changing) social structure shaped by the opposition of popular and official impulses: (popular) humour exemplified by carnival has its liberalising function and effects in relation to the weight of (official) seriousness. However, Bakhtin grasps these effects in the abstract and at the level of the social. As has been pointed out, when actual historical contexts are addressed, Bakhtin's abstract conception of social structure can break down.[16] One can certainly situate Lear's fool's jesting and the historical context of court jesters with reference to Bakhtin's concepts though that would be to create an analysis of social structure, not of what Shakespeare represents the fool as doing with humour. The fool uses humour in a socially licensed way, certainly, and much of his humour involves the 'bodily lower stratum', to use Bakhtin's famous phrase. One can construct a certain sense of the effects of the fool's humour in these terms but Shakespeare invites the recognition that the fool's aims are scuppered as things go on and that the limited effect of his humour is a part of the play's meaning: his labour to 'outjest' Lear's 'heart-struck injuries' dramatically disintegrates after act three.

A very different kind of humour theory provides a more psychologically relevant insight. The concept of humour as consisting of 'benign violations' suggests that: 'three conditions are jointly necessary and sufficient for eliciting humor: A situation must be appraised as a violation, a situation must be appraised as benign, and these two appraisals must occur together'.[17] The term 'appraised' signals that it is psychological experience, not linguistic or visual form, that matters here. The 'violations' envisaged are violations of norms: moral, physical, linguistic, and social. Benignity is a condition that can be variously meaningful depending on who is doing the appraising. Thus, what makes the lightbulb joke (and its target group) funny is that it (and they) violate the norms of efficiency and intelligence, which are so significant in ordinary social life. It is simultaneously benign in part because the violation includes a built-in psychological distance: no one actually does or perhaps even could screw in lightbulbs that way. More significantly, however, the theory suggests that the joke will probably not be funny to a member of the target group because it will not seem so benign to them. The theory of benign violations, then, gives an explanation of why some things are 'humour' to some and not to others: benignity conditions shift with the person concerned. Any joke will be funny to us only if we value the norm it violates and at the same time feel relatively unthreatened by that violation. The implication of this theoretical conception is that when people laugh together at the same thing, they are sharing both the norm that is violated *as well as* a sense of the violation's relative benignity, a sense of psychological distance. Much more attention is given to this theory and its antecedents in Chap. 7 of this volume.

So what of the fool's jests? Lady Brach offers an image of violated (patriarchal) order (domestic and political), the egg and crowns of Lear's violation of political wisdom, and the eel pie of common sense. There are various ways in which we might describe the differing benignity conditions (and thus the jests' funniness) for various participants: for the fool, for Lear himself, for Shakespeare's first early modern audiences, for audiences in our own time, and for us as historians of humour. In the first two cases—the fool and Lear himself—the descriptions we come up with would probably explain, from the perspective of benign violation theory, why the fool's humour seems so strained. There is little that is benign in the world of *King Lear*. What the play represents through the fool's jesting is a failed humour, a limping rhetoric. The fool attempts to generate a shared perspective with Lear by means of his humour: a shared perspective on true wisdom violated by the king's folly. But the pain of the violation cannot be tempered with psychological distance. Lear's reply to the desperately strained 'Lady Brach' jest is emphatically lacking in benignity: 'a pestilent gall to me' (1.4.112), he replies, and he may at once be responding to the image of his family and to the fool's jesting in general (the 'truth'). At 1.5.11–13, the fool exhorts him 'I prithee be merry', and Lear's immediate response 'Ha, ha, ha' may signal a kind of laughter, but any it implies quickly dissolves: the eel pie and buttered hay jests elicit no response.

Benign violation theory gives a useful conceptual framework within which to explore this rhetorical interpretation of the fool's humour but its application generates new problems, specifically around the terminology of 'norm'. The term captures the normative or ideological perspective from which people enjoy humour by means of the suggestion that it is the violation of that perspective which structures the experience of humour. But if the fool's jests violate 'norms' why does Lear seem largely unmoved by them? Do not norms have a claim on everyone? It had been as normal for Lear in his kingly state to ignore everybody else's norms, and now, out of that state, the continuation of his attitude becomes a painful delusion. The point here is not that benign violation theory's terminology is incoherent but that it is put under strain when an historical context remote from modern western (arguably also, modern American) society makes us ask whose values actually are the 'norm'.

Furthermore, if the jests' larger rhetorical purpose is to encourage in Lear a self-awareness of his own laughable folly, from the perspective of the wisdom it violates, is it reasonable to think of that structuring 'wisdom' as a 'norm'? This fool's wisdom isn't shared by everybody and an early modern fool's usual point is to show that wisdom is rare. The discourse of wisdom versus folly is itself 'normative' in the period but the ideological perspectives that might count as wisdom, especially for people in positions of privilege, were multiplicitous. The very power of Erasmus's biblical wisdom/folly paradox is its perspectival variability after all. The fool produces the idea that Lear violates how-things-ought-to-be but isn't his apprehension of how-things-ought-to-be subject not merely to class but also to the imagination? 'Norm' is a term pushed to its limit here. Any temptation to use the term 'value' in place of 'norm' when applying the benign violation concept to this historically-removed context also raises the problem of terminological anachronism. Shakespeare and his contemporaries never spoke of 'norms' or 'values'. These terms carry emphatically modern assumptions about how the world works and what it is, which makes it reasonable to doubt the extent to which they allow us to situate historically-remote humour such as the fool's jests. Nothing has been said here of Freud's conception of savings on psychic energy or Bergson's of comic rigidity because, in this particular case, they seem of less use than those I have discussed.[18]

## The Volume's Aims

The case of Lear's fool's jesting cannot signal all the problems generated by attempts to understand a historically-distant humour context. It is merely a helpful example demonstrating what is by now perhaps palpably clear: that grappling with a case of historical humour by applying appropriate modern theories of 'humour' generates methodological problems. This volume tackles that fact. It aims to encourage a self-conscious exploration of the methodological problems and challenges that arise from studying humour in specific historical contexts and across cultural history as the field of historical humour studies takes shape. This, of course, includes the issues of identification, subjectivity of viewpoint, coherence of the object of study, terminological strain, and so on, which have already been mentioned. The book does this in three different ways: by addressing theories themselves, by addressing the needs of specific case studies, and by addressing the challenges of presenting historical humour to contemporary audiences through various forms of transfer.

There have long been individual cultural histories of fools and fooling, of festivals and festivity, of laughter in ancient Greece and Rome, and so on, but it is only relatively recently that a disciplinary convergence of 'humour studies' and 'history' itself has started to emerge. Their different disciplinary assumptions have barely begun to clash. Jan Bremmer and Herman Roodenburg's excellent collection of essays, *A Cultural History of Humour*, offered, in 1997, a range of essays investigating humour in specific cultural contexts, and pointed to the changing history of discourse about humour, as well as the history of the word 'humour' in English together with related terms in modern European languages. Bremmer and Roodenburg defined 'humour' broadly as 'any message [...] intended to produce a smile or a laugh', in order 'to pose questions of interest to cultural historians: who transmits what humour in which way to whom, where and when?'[19] Allied to that concern with humour's specific historical situatedness, its rhetorical facts, was their interest in a history of humour itself. Drawing on the work of Keith Thomas and Peter Burke, Bremmer and Roodenburg emphasised the broad idea of a cultural shift in what counted as humour across the seventeenth and eighteenth centuries, a shift in which traditional forms of humour dissolved and were displaced by a new kind of polite decorum; the shift, of course, closely accords with Norbert Elias's ideas about the effects of the 'civilising process'.[20] They thereby drew attention to a broad-brush picture of the process in which 'polite and folk humour had grown apart', a process with 'a legacy that would persist for a long time' creating historiographical gaps that 'we are still trying to fill'.[21]

The implied call to fill a historiographical gap has been answered with several collections of essays since then. This includes works on specific periods such as Halsall's collection *Humour, History and Politics in Late Antiquity and the Early Middle Ages* (2002) and Knights and Morton's *The Power of Laughter and Satire in Early Modern Britain* (2017), as well as works more broadly conceived, such as Korte and Lechner's *History and Humour: British and American*

*Perspectives* (2013) together with Cheauré and Nohejl's *Humour and Laughter in History: Transcultural Perspectives* (2014). These works have sought to make humour a part of the discipline of history and have documented some of the reasons for the neglect: for Halsall, what was needed was 'a generation of historians who not only saw that history has its funny side but also, conversely, that humour and its past uses are, themselves, serious subjects'.[22]

Existing studies of humour in history and of the history of humour spanning multiple historical contexts have acknowledged some of the theoretical and methodological problems but have not placed them centre stage. By contrast, works focused intently on specific cultural contexts have tended to address methodological problems more deeply.[23] Bremmer and Roodenburg identify the relative modernity of the universalised concept of 'humour' but their collection largely confines itself to the tasks of building a cultural history and documenting some of the humour 'messages' across time that invited laughing and smiling. Knights and Morton adapt the language of humour theory including the big three signifiers—superiority, incongruity, and relief—to show how early modern thinking about laughter specifically can be categorised with those and other terms, and how the consequently historicised categories are relevant to early modern contexts. By and large, scholarly work bringing humour studies and history together has critiqued the universalising concept of 'humour' by establishing the complicated cultural history of what has counted as humour across time and how it has been thought of differently.[24] That work has, of course, been necessary. *The Palgrave Handbook of Humour, History, and Methodology*, however, is designed to push the question of method further, creating a map of the difficulties, not just the topics, that are involved in this intersection of disciplines, and encouraging further exploration at a time when new books on specific contexts within the cultural history of humour are appearing rapidly. Its disciplinary aims are twofold: to encourage a humour-studies scholarship—as it stands, predominantly produced by psychologists, sociologists, folklorists, linguists and computer scientists—that really confronts the problems presented by historical examples and by historicist critique and also to encourage histories of humour that generate new theoretical perspectives.

In terms of humour-studies scholarship, one obvious tendency is especially important. That is the tendency to proceed (even if with a caveat or two) as if 'humour' was an unproblematic universal category. Historical examples and their cultural distance, however, force the issue of whether there is a universal thing labelable as 'humour', operating across time; it is a question that 'humour-studies' scholars, who tend to work primarily with the relatively stable genre of modern jokes, are understandably reluctant to explore beyond a certain point. Rather, the assumption tends to be that there is a universal category that manifests itself variously through 'modes' or 'types'. That assumption is both made and queried across the different chapters within this volume.[25] The need to confront the historical instability of the signifier as defining the object of study at the same time as making use of it is one of the core methodological problems that humour-studies scholarship faces, and it is brought into sharp relief by historically-distant examples.

One way around this problem in historical terms has been just to treat 'humour' as a large umbrella category that allows us to pull together into synoptic vision (minimally articulated) a range of quite different historical phenomena: jests, smiling, laughter, puns, jokes, comic characters, games and play, popular entertainment, and so on. Westbrook and Chao's recent *Humour in the Arts: New Perspectives* (2018) makes productive use of this approach, emphasising humour less as an aesthetic pattern and more as a mode of reading, a strategic window onto changing cultural dynamics across periods. The historiographical strengths of this procedure are clear but, as in the case of out-and-out historicist scepticism about 'humour' as a useful category, the cost is that a sense of the coherence of research 'object' across time and space and across cultural phenomena is necessarily thinned out. This volume presupposes that the category is both meaningful and problematic. Is it possible to generate new apprehensions of cross-temporal patterns concerning humour as an object of study and at the same time avoid treating 'humour' as an unproblematic universal?

A further tendency within humour-studies scholarship has been to overuse ad infinitum the standard three labels—superiority, incongruity, and relief—for humour historiography. Those three labels have come to signal actual theories of humour—however hazily apprehended: one can easily find the suggestion that there exists, so to speak, 'the superiority theory', 'the incongruity theory', and 'the relief theory'. Those labels often function in effect as explanations of humour: we laugh because we feel superiority, because we perceive incongruity, or because something is being released. As such, the three categories have deeply influenced attempts to grapple with the history of humour. Yet, as John Morreall, who has himself used the three categories across several books, reminds us, a concept like 'superiority theory' is a term 'meant to capture one feature shared by accounts of laughter that differ in other respects [...] it is not [...] a name adopted by a group of thinkers consciously participating in a tradition'.[26] And so with the other two. The three labels, explanatory as they are, are most helpfully understood as terms for categorising the similarities between various theoretical apprehensions of past thinkers. Standard connections, for instance, are these: Aristotle, Thomas Hobbes, and Bergson (superiority); Kant and the GTVH (incongruity); Freud and Bakhtin (relief). Several chapters in this volume are invested in showing why one or more of the labels are unhelpful in their respective contexts.[27] Elliott Oring has offered some useful critiques of humour theories typically categorised in this way, especially those of incongruity and relief, though with reference primarily to modern jokes.[28] This volume uses more distant historical examples to do related critical work.[29]

One of the significant problems created by too easily relying on such meta-theories is that the reliance can imply ideological commitments that muddy the waters of historical understanding. Alfie Bown helpfully emphasises laughter's 'key role in forming ideology', something that a belief in laughter as liberation, for instance, might obscure.[30] The broad idea that laughter liberates, as exemplified by Bakhtin, is perhaps not quite the same thing as 'the relief theory' exactly, but it helps make the point. Gurevich's critique of Bakhtin, mentioned above, suggested that Bakhtin's vision of liberation in the medieval carnivalesque was a perspective shaped by his position in Stalinist Russia.[31] One might go further and suggest that it says as much about Bakhtin's context as it does about medieval Europe. And what about superiority? Can the expectation that premodern humour often involves a 'laughter of superiority', together with our modern moral distaste for it, affect what we see? The ideological commitments tied up with our preferred ways of viewing (and theorising) historical humour have to be confronted.

The volume also aims to encourage new methodological thinking that gets around some of the problems posed by historically-distant examples. The modern universalising theories of humour—for example, Freud's and Bergson's, the GTVH, the theory of benign violation, as well as Pirandello's concept of the Opposite, the notion of Discovering False Beliefs, Appropriate Incongruity and others—have reasonably been a starting point for historical humour case studies. Here though, we are not just asking how the details of specific case studies test the limits of one or more such universalising theories, but also what theoretical formulations those case studies individually call for.

What counts as a theory is of course contested. The GTVH and its new incarnation the OSTH is a 'theory' in a restricted sense. Its creators make clear that their theory is not simply an explanation but 'a set of statements' creating a generalisation about a series of facts within a clearly defined purview; it is explicit about its premises and goals and carries with it stated methods of falsification and evaluation.[32] Most if not all contributors to this volume use 'theory' in a slightly different, less restricted sense: as an articulable perspective on a set of historical details that generates specific understanding because of its particular shape. The creators of GTVH/OSTH contrast their capacity to generate 'real knowledge' in the form of generalisations about 'more than one particular fact' with the apprehensions of those 'who like to address individual facts, discuss all the details about them, and not care about generalizing their observations'.[33] However, the discipline of history (in its historicist form) requires us to consider the peculiarities of individual facts and phenomena: what makes them uniquely situated in their own time and place. Though this does not mean we are uninterested in larger generalisations: for instance, how a specific case study might be seen together with others as related instances of larger patterns, within and beyond their own temporal context. The envisioning of larger patterns in this sense is theory from an historian's disciplinary angle. The GTVH/OSTH is admirably precise in its notion of 'theory' because it sharply restricts its 'purview' to verbal humour in the form of joke texts and its goal to computerised recognition. But as historians we cannot restrict our purview so sharply because we are not merely trying to understand the aesthetic form of humour that has existed in the past but its emotional power, its rhetorical meaning in context, and its manifestation of social structure.

Approaches to contemporary humour developed within Social Science and Psychology engage with these factors too—obviously; the point is simply that for historians these factors become centrally important and difficult when the unique historical shape of a specific context is most divergent from what is modern and familiar. For all that, historians too are seeking coordinated understanding across a range of historical 'facts', a level of generalisation, that is to say.

Furthermore, the very questions we ask shape what we require a theory to do and this affects our perception of its usefulness. This is itself a methodological issue since the types of questions we are asking as historians of humour are various. Readers will perhaps have perceived that my own interest in the rhetorical meaning of Lear's fool's jests within the context of the play itself has shaped my discussion of the limits of the theories I mentioned. Benign violation theory has a stronger attraction than the GTVH with respect to the question of humour as rhetoric because it provides a more relevant perspective.

At the same time, it has its stated limits and some modification of it is necessary in respect of the problems generated by anachronistic terms. Taking an established humour theory and grafting onto it other ideas or concepts is one way to deal with such limits. That is an approach I take in Chap. 7. Other chapters generate theoretical innovation differently by exploring the relevance of concepts in related areas: the aesthetics of ugliness (Mitchell); apophasis (Borysławski); medical humanities (Williams); affect theory (Tierney-Hynes); and translation studies (Tran-Gervat). John Parkin develops his own ideas about 'naïve parody'. This handbook offers some suggestions for theoretical innovation.

Its primary purpose, however, is to explore methodological problems. Accordingly, it is arranged in three parts. A preliminary section grapples with some fundamental issues: Conal Condren and Hannah Burrows variously explore problems of language and terminology; Lucy Rayfield and Rebecca Tierney-Hynes address the complexities involved in grappling with histories of humour theory even just in specific periods. The two centrally important periods they explore, respectively, are: the early modern (in which ancient ideas about laughter and the ridiculous were vigorously discussed) and the eighteenth century (in which uses and meanings of the word 'humour' developed rapidly). The following three preliminary chapters evaluate specific theoretical formulations from a historical perspective: the ideas of Henri Bergson, the theory of benign violation, and broader formulations of the relationship between humour and religion. The largest section of the book, however, is a series of case studies of historical humour ranging widely in time and place. Each chapter in this section exposes problems involved in its own specific context. However, while in some chapters emphasis is placed on the way a specific context challenges an existing theoretical formulation (Leggieri and Beckett), in other chapters emphasis is placed on what is methodologically useful/necessary therein (Mitchell, Baccini, Borysławski, Bayless, Williams, Parkin, Stelling, Whiteley, Stewart, Hansen, and Lobanov). Yet past humour is not just read. It is also presented, and different issues arise in that context. The third and final section of the volume, therefore, presents six chapters dealing with the challenges and stakes involved in presenting historical humour to contemporary or near-contemporary audiences through translation and curation. Each of those contributions shows what can happen to historically-distant humour by means of its new forms of presentation and how the problems can be and have been managed.

Finally, a note about coverage. The aim of the volume has been comprehensiveness and variety concerning the types of methodological challenge encountered, not comprehensiveness of topic. It could never have been possible to cover every historical-temporal ground or cultural-linguistic situation. The volume has taken the shape it has partly as a result of its emergence from the conferences of the Humours of the Past (HOP) Network—generously funded by the UK's Arts and Humanities Research Council—which were designed to explore humour, history, and methodology.[34] At those memorably enjoyable meetings, many of the essays herein were first presented. My hope is that the attempt to begin mapping out the theoretical issues involved in humour history through those conferences and in this volume will continue in present and future studies within this exciting interdisciplinary field.

## NOTES

1. Reference here is to the text and line numbers of the third Arden edition of the play edited by R.A. Foakes, who provides a conflated text (of Q and F) leaning toward F's readings. Citations from the play are given in brackets following quotes.
2. See Shakespeare, *King Lear*, 200. For the text of the old jest as Shakespeare might have encountered it see Zall, 289–90, where it appears as number 59 of *Tales and Quick Answers* (c.1535).
3. Hornback, English Clown Tradition, 12–13. Hornback points to the specifically 'neoclassical' character of the category 'comic relief'.
4. Greenblatt, *Shakespearean Negotiations*, 86–93.
5. See for instance, O'Callaghan, *The English Wits*, and Withington, 'Tumbled into the Dirt'.
6. For the former, see Brown, *Better a Shrew*, 16; for the latter, see Smyth, 'Divines into Dry Vines', 69–70.
7. For the former, see Kaiser, *Praisers of Folly*, 99; for the latter, see Gatti, 'Nonsense and liberty'.
8. For SSTH, the seminal work is Raskin, *Semantic mechanisms*; for GTVH, Attardo and Raskin, 'Script theory revis(it)ed'; for, OSTH, Raskin, et al., 'How to Understand'.
9. Raskin, et al., 'How to Understand', 288.
10. Attardo and Raskin, 'Script theory revis(it)ed', 307–8.
11. Ibid., 308. These oppositions can be described at different levels of abstraction.
12. These are mentioned in Attardo and Raskin, 'Script theory revis(it)ed' 303–7; for further elaboration see Attardo, et al., 'Script Oppositions and Logical Mechanisms' and for an extended critique, see Oring, 'Oppositions, Overlaps, and Ontologies'.

16    D. DERRIN

13. Attardo and Raskin, 'Script theory revis(it)ed', 303.
14. The OED traces it to the late seventeenth century. On jests and humour, see the helpful discussion in Smyth, 'Divines into Dry Vines', 59–62.
15. Attardo and Raskin, 'Script theory revis(it)ed', 330–31.
16. See Gurevich, 'Bakhtin and his Theory', 55–6.
17. McGraw and Warren, 'Benign Violations', 1142.
18. Freud's concepts were developed in 'The Joke', and Bergson's in 'Laughter'.
19. Bremmer and Roodenburg, *A Cultural History*, 1.
20. Ibid., 7–8.
21. Ibid.
22. Halsall, *Humour, History and Politics*, 2.
23. Examples include: Chey and Milner Davis, 'Humour in Chinese Life and Culture'; Beard, 'Laughter in Ancient Rome'; Halliwell, 'Greek Laughter'.
24. A very helpful review of a range of recent work on humour and cultural history can be found in the introduction to Westbrook and Chao, 'Humour in the Arts'.
25. For a skeptical approach, see in particular Conal Condren's chapter herein.
26. Morreall, *Comic Relief*, 6. For another discussion of the problems labelling historical thinkers as theorists of 'superiority', see Lintott, 'Superiority in Humor Theory'.
27. Lucy Rayfield, for instance, shows that, with respect to early modern theory about laughter and the ridiculous, the three categories are insufficient to account for the complexity of thought on the topic in this period.
28. See Oring, 'Joking Asides', especially 1–99.
29. See, for instance, Jamie Beckett's chapter herein.
30. Bown, *In the Event of Laughter*, 24.
31. Gurevich, 'Bakhtin and his Theory', 58.
32. Raskin, et al., 'How to Understand', 286–7.
33. Ibid., 286.
34. The HOP Network's blog can be found at https://humoursofthepast.wordpress.com/.

## BIBLIOGRAPHY

Attardo, Salvatore and Victor Raskin. 'Script Theory Revis(it)ed: Joke Similarity and Joke Representation Model'. *Humor: International Journal of Humor Research* 4, no.3/4 (1991): 293–347.

Attardo, Salvatore, Christian F. Hempelmann and Sarah Di Maio. 'Script Oppositions and Logical Mechanisms: Modeling Incongruities and Their Resolutions'. *Humor: International Journal of Humor Research* 15, no.1 (2002): 3–46.

Bakhtin, Mikhail. *Rabelais and His World*. Translated by Helene Iswolsky. Bloomington: Indiana University Press, 1984.

Beard, Mary. *Laughter in Ancient Rome: On Joking, Tickling, and Cracking Up*. Berkeley: University of California Press, 2014.

Bergson, Henri. *Laughter: An Essay on the Meaning of the Comic*. Translated by Cloudesley Brereton and Fred Rothwell. Mineola: Dover, 2005.

Bown, Alfie. *In the Event of Laughter: Psychoanalysis, Literature and Comedy*. New York: Bloomsbury, 2019.

Bremmer, Jan and Herman Roodenburg, eds. *A Cultural History of Humour: From Antiquity to the Present Day*. Cambridge: Polity Press, 1997.

Brown, Pamela Allen. *Better a Shrew than a Sheep: Women, Drama, and the Culture of Jest in Early Modern England*. Ithaca and London: Cornell University Press, 2003.

Cheauré, Elisabeth and Regine Nohejl, eds. *Humour and Laughter in History: Transcultural Perspectives*. Bielefeld: Transcript Verlag, 2014.

Chey, Jocelyn and Jessica Milner Davis, eds. *Humour in Chinese Life and Letters: Classical and Traditional Approaches*. Hong Kong: Hong Kong University Press, 2011.

Freud, Sigmund. *The Joke and its Relation to the Unconscious*. Translated by Joyce Crick. London: Penguin, 2002.

Gatti, Hilary. 'Nonsense and Liberty: The Language Games of the Fool in Shakespeare's King Lear'. In *Nonsense and other Senses: Regulated Absurdity in Literature*, edited by Elisabetta Tarantino and Carlo Caruso, 147–60. Newcastle Upon Tyne: Cambridge Scholars Publishing, 2009.

Greenblatt, Stephen. *Shakespearean Negotiations: The Circulation of Social Energy in Renaissance England*. Oxford: Clarendon, 1988.

Gurevich, Aaron. 'Bakhtin and his Theory of Carnival'. In *A Cultural History of Humour: From Antiquity to the Present Day*, edited by Jan Bremmer and Herman Roodenburg, 54–60. Cambridge: Polity Press, 1997.

Halliwell, Stephen. *Greek Laughter: A Study of Cultural Psychology from Homer to Early Christianity*. Cambridge: Cambridge University Press, 2008.

Halsall, Guy, ed. *Humour, History and Politics in Late Antiquity and the Early Middle Ages*. Cambridge: Cambridge University Press, 2002.

Hornback, Robert. *The English Clown Tradition from the Middle Ages to Shakespeare*. Cambridge: D.S. Brewer, 2009.

Kaiser, Walter. *Praisers of Folly: Erasmus, Rabelais, Shakespeare*. Cambridge, MA: Harvard University Press, 1963.

Knights, Mark and Adam Morton, eds. *The Power of Laughter and Satire in Early Modern Britain: Political and Religious Culture, 1500–1820*. Woodbridge: Boydell Press, 2017.

Korte, Barbara and Doris Lechner, eds. *History and Humour: British and American Perspectives*. Bielefeld: Transcript Verlag, 2013.

Lintott, Sheila. 'Superiority in Humor Theory'. *The Journal of Aesthetics and Art Criticism* 74, no. 4 (2016): 347–358.

Morreall, John. *Comic Relief: A Comprehensive Philosophy of Humor*. Malden: Wiley-Blackwell, 2009.

O'Callaghan, Michelle. *The English Wits: Literature and Sociability in Early Modern England*. Cambridge: Cambridge University Press, 2007.

Oring, Elliott. *Joking Asides: The Theory, Analysis, and Aesthetics of Humor*. Logan: Utah State University Press, 2016.

Oring, Elliot. 'Oppositions, Overlaps, and Ontologies: The general Theory of Verbal Humor Revisited'. *Humor: International Journal of Humor Research* 32, no.2 (2019): 151–170.

Raskin, Victor. *Semantic Mechanisms of Humor*. Dordrecht: Reidel, 1985.

Raskin, Victor, Christian F. Hempelmann and Julia M. Taylor. 'How to Understand and Assess a Theory: The Evolution of the SSTH into the GTVH and Now into the OSTH'. *Journal of Literary Theory* 3, no.2 (2009): 285–312.

Shakespeare, William. *King Lear*. Edited by R.A. Foakes. *Arden Third Edition*. London: Methuen, 1997.

Smyth, Adam. '"Divines into dry Vines": forms of Jesting in Renaissance England'. In *Formal matters: Reading the materials of English Renaissance literature*, edited by Allison K. Deutermann and András Kiséry, 55–72. Manchester: Manchester University Press, 2013.

Westbrook, Vivienne and Shun-liang Chao, eds. *Humour in the Arts: New Perspectives.* New York: Routledge, 2019.

Withington, Phil. 'Tumbled into the Dirt: Wit and Incivility in Early Modern England'. *Journal of Historical Pragmatics* 12 (2011): 156–77.

Zall, P.M., ed. *A Hundred Merry Tales and Other English Jestbooks of the Fifteenth and Sixteenth Centuries.* Lincoln: University of Nebraska Press, 1963.

CHAPTER 2

# The Study of Past Humour: Historicity and the Limits of Method

*Conal Condren*

## The Problem of Universality

G. B. Milner's taxonomic coinage, *Homo ridens*, encourages the belief that a sense of humour, evidenced in laughter, is a defining characteristic of *Homo sapiens*.[1] The universalist proposition can almost be put syllogistically: laughter signifies humour, laughter is universal, and therefore humour is also. Thus Bremmer and Roodenberg, who reject a formally universalist position, nevertheless hold that a large-scale history of humour is possible because humour is found in whatever is intended to make us laugh or smile.[2] Even this cake-and-eat-it universalism is problematic, so I want to shift the angle of approach.

In his reformulation of Leibniz's law of identity, the logician David Wiggins argues that designating two things *a* and *b* as the same presupposes a general classifier under which they can be subsumed: thus *a* and *b* are the same both being instances, or expressions of *H* (in this case humour). But if *H* can subsume *a* and *~a*, *b* and *~b*, assertions as to sameness are empty and the classification may be close to meaningless.[3] In this light, it is not enough to treat *H* (humour) with an open-ended generality, attributing to it a diversity of forms, for that is to beg the question of what is it we are actually talking about.[4] The postulation of humour as a concept somehow independent of language only

---

My thanks to Dr Hannah Burrows and Dr Daniel Derrin, for the invitation to give this paper in Durham, July 2017, to the other discussants and to Dr Marguerite Wells, Dr Mark Rolfe and Averil Condren.

---

C. Condren (✉)
University of New South Wales, Sydney, NSW, Australia

© The Author(s), under exclusive license to Springer Nature Switzerland AG 2020
D. Derrin, H. Burrows (eds.), *The Palgrave Handbook of Humour, History, and Methodology*, https://doi.org/10.1007/978-3-030-56646-3_2

disguises the evasion. To draw on Michael Reddy's analysis of the family of metaphors commonly used to rationalise this bifurcation: once seen as a reified concept, humour becomes something to be packaged, conveyed and revealed, and relatively undamaged, in multi-lingual contexts: hence it can be thought to be stable but have different forms.[5] If taken for granted as part of a conceptual realm, humour might even be inferred from the absence of linguistic dressing; laughter is evidence enough. This propositional circularity may amount to little more than a euphemistic way of accommodating the world to the semantics of our own tongue; more clearly, it is a means of avoiding the conspicuous absence of humour or a direct equivalent for it in most languages for most of their recorded histories.

Even restricting ourselves to English, the word humour looks less than conceptually stable. Consider the following partial descriptors in its ambit: wit, farce, absurdity, jokiness, playfulness, satire, comedy, levity, the nonsensical, the wry, the whimsical and ironic. It is through use of such a field of words operating conceptually—that is, being used at varying levels of formality to organise, assess and discriminate, that we identify something putatively as humorous. From such a sprawling terrain diverging accounts readily sprout, such as Michael Billig's 'three great theories' of humour—incongruity, release and superiority, each of which captures something of the uncertain reach of humour.[6] The instability of humour itself partly derives from its associated terms, such as play and nonsense sometimes operating beyond the humorous. Certainly, something has to be posited as lying beyond the humorous for the very idea of it to have meaningful discrimination; but this delineating domain of what is usually designated the serious, is neither straightforward nor decisive. Seriousness can be a dimension of a joke, and since antiquity traditions of *serio ludere* writing would appear systematically to have violated a firm distinction between the serious and humorous—if that is, *ludere*, to mock, involves humour. The phrase is invariably translated as if it must: through the humorous say what is serious. It is to affirm the universality of humour by sleight of hand and to avoid a question that needs addressing.

Only from around the early eighteenth century has humour been used as the general classifier we now rely on and through which claims as to universality are made.[7] The Earl of Shaftesbury used it casually in much this way, treating raillery as a kind of humour.[8] Much before then, however, there was no single expression with humour's modern function.[9] And to project this back into the more distant past, redescribing surviving evidence to accord with a universality thesis, is itself distorting. This is especially so if humour and laughter are treated much as an asymmetric unity: all laughter expresses humour, although not all humour occasions laughter.[10] Such unexamined preconceptions help explain why theories of laughter before the eighteenth century can be treated as theories of humour. Historically speaking, that is precisely what should not be taken for granted. The case of Hobbes and 'superiority theory' will be discussed by way of conclusion.

As Daniel Wickberg points out, the now familiar notion of a sense of humour appears as a characteristic of individuals only relatively recently.[11] It is the result of a complex and highly contingent history, involving an expansion in the range of the word sense; and the separation of humour from humoral medical theory, in which, on the cusp of the seventeenth century, the humours (vital fluids) had come to refer to the temperamental types they were believed to help explain. In fact, the Latin literature suggests that there was little reliance on the explanatory power of the humours[12]; but as humoral theory was popularised, the humours became associated both with stable character and with changing moods.

Only, Wickberg argues, after humour became a discursive construct, an erratic process during the seventeenth century, occurring in tandem with the gradual abandonment of humoral theory, were the conditions in place for people to begin talking about a sense of humour. This locution capitalises on sense as awareness or appreciation and so presupposes self-consciousness about humour: one can hardly unknowingly have a sense of humour. The expression is also part of a linguistic chain reaction. *Humorist* becomes a person intentionally writing or performing in a humorous vein and ceases to designate someone who is risible or unduly subject to an imbalance of the humours. In French *humoriste* as peevish still carries the older meaning. The adverbial form *humourously* was shifted away from the capriciousness of humoral imbalance, to refer to conduct that might befit someone trying to amuse. And a sense of humour required the contrastive adjectival neologism *humourless* also seeming to date from the mid-nineteenth century.[13] Keeping such now submerged linguistic shifts in mind, it seems naïve to assume that all languages will have an equivalent expression for what has become humour's classificatory reach. Indeed, in the eighteenth century, the French regarded its generalised standing as specifically English and were slow to accept it; and *sens de l'humor* can still be taken to refer to something characteristically English. And in French now, the English loan word *humor* is given greater intension than in English, by being distinguished from *humeur*, as variable mood or disposition.

Classical Greek gave us comedy but had no word for the modern humour, and so Demotic has taken it as a loan word ($\chi\iota o\upsilon\mu o\rho$) around which related terms are gathered, most without obvious classical roots. Whether or not the ground was prepared by its Latin antecedent, the English humour has proved a remarkably successful export. It, and the phrase a sense of humour, is now found in most European languages, though in fewer Asian and African ones. It is not in Korean, but is in Mandarin (from c.1924) and (presumably via Dutch) in Indonesian and Javanese. It is also in Maori, but seems not to have been taken up in Indigenous Australian languages exposed to English.[14]

The evidence of language raises an obvious question: if humour is the universal attribute so often assumed, why has it taken so long for this to be recognised, and why was the process of discovery apparently so ad hoc and Anglo-centric, possibly being carried in the baggage of trade and imperial expansion? In this light, the entailed self-consciousness of having a sense of humour becomes problematic if the requisite conceptual vocabulary through which self-awareness can be expressed has been absent for so long among so many peoples.

Part of the answer may lie in the dominance of psychology in the modern academic study of humour, a discipline geared to universal traits, proclivities, motivations and pathologies that discovered the analytic and explanatory value of humour from the late nineteenth century. Part may lie in the globalisation of the English language and the parochialism that can result from taking for granted successfully adopted words, or from their reification, their apotheosised status in a distinct conceptual realm. This can then be used to explain away, or rationalise, discordances between languages, and be posited as the content that other tongues more or less adequately convey. Such mechanisms of accommodating the world to English can disguise the fact that humour's attendant field of terms does not map neatly on to other languages, as only passing reference to French intimates. The point is reinforced if we move beyond Europe.

Japanese has the loan words *faasu, komedi*, and the general humour as *yumoa* added to Indigenous terms in its associational field, such as *u-itto* largely cognate with wit. Not all languages have a specific, dedicated term for pun—the Italian *bisticcio*, for example, does punning double duty in also meaning an altercation, and so the periphrastic *gioco di parole* can be used. In contrast, Japanese has a number of words for the single English pun. Moreover, as Marguerite Wells has shown, the Japanese *füshi*, the term closest to *satire*, is often at odds with English use. This, beyond questions of transient specificity that so often dog the study of satire, helps explain why British and Japanese satire can be mutually impenetrable.[15] It is for such reasons that translation is by degrees approximate, a matter in Umberto Eco's expression of 'negotiation' between cultures—a point Roman Jacobsen stressed many years ago with respect to puns, translating them can be a matter of 'creative transposition'.[16]

The implication is that when we claim or assume a universality for humour, or a sense of humour, we can show that our own vocabulary organised around the word can impose some sort of order on the alien, and even that since the nineteenth century, many other languages have followed suit, becoming a little more like English; but it is uncertain that we are eliciting what is independently common to all, let alone what always has been. In post-Kantian terms, it is less a matter of ontology, what there is, than epistemology, how and through what conceptual vocabulary we seek to understand. But a familiarity with the point is long-standing. As Indira Ghose has also concluded, things are not inherently funny.[17]

The differentia of what we now call humour vary, leaving us with a universality that is best seen as a matter of family resemblance between overlapping notions and configurations of vocabulary justifying the reliance on humour as a loose classifier. Sometimes it is valuable in enabling interconnections within and analysis of evidence; sometimes it is harmless as a shorthand; but it is also potentially misleading when, as an analytic tool it is projected as being in or underlying the evidence.[18] Rather, then, than taking humour as a given in historical analysis or a variably manifesting universal, it might seem that what is needed are methodologically secure criteria for determining the limits of the word's classificatory usefulness.

## METHOD, GENEALOGY, SEMANTIC CONTINUITY AND CHANGE

Preliminaries aside, I want to stress the limitations of methodology by sketching some of the problems touching context, intentionality and reception that can derail the historical study of 'humour'. I will do so mainly with brief illustration from early modern England, concluding with a single case—Thomas Hobbes on laughter. There are, however, two caveats.

First, not all encounters with previous humour need be historical. Engagement can be a creative enrichment of an inheritance ensuring vitality and expressing contemporary tastes and priorities. Yet, as Daniel McKee has stressed in discussing the wit of Japanese surimono print poetry, connoisseurship, appreciation by our own standards and historicity should not to be confused.[19] The second caveat arises from the instrumentalist character of methodology, taken here as the formulation of the procedural rules furthering a given activity. As historical writing varies in its discursive rigidity, so methodological considerations will have uneven sway. If history is just genealogy, writing about the past insofar as it relates to the present, there is greater methodological tolerance than if it aspires to the historicist rigors of attempting to eradicate anachronism and myth-making.

Certainly not all genealogy can be mistaken for history. The formulaic 14-generation Anglo-Saxon pedigree, probably modelled on the lineage of Jesus (Matt 1. 1–17), was what the archaeologist Sam Newton has called an adjustable 'tally' of names assembled for the purposes of propaganda and negotiation.[20] But albeit modified by some desire to understand the past as such, genealogy is driven by the blandishments of relevance. It thus requires principles of evidence selection, predication and narrative construction that engage either in a critical or in a celebratory fashion with the here and now. To do so it often involves redescribing evidence through salient modern terminology. All these requirements compromise the historicist imperatives designed to minimise the distorting presence of the present in the past. Throughout I shall assume a fairly historicist austerity. If the identification of past humour depends upon the use of a conceptual field of terms in its ambit, insufficient awareness of change can be a means of inadvertent genealogical re-shaping, to the extent of myth-making. This can occur by nothing more sophisticated than simply taking Plato's or Aristotle's reflections of comedy and laughter as theories of humour.

Where, in contrast we have the reassurance of semantic continuity, for example, in the word satire, overlooking shifts in meaning can have a similarly distorting effect. A word may have, as C. S. Lewis argued, a 'dangerous sense', in that our meaning might make sense of the evidence, but the usage might actually have been only subordinate or absent at the time of writing.[21] Since the 1960s satire has become entrenched in the lexicon of humour. But over the *longue durée* it has focused overwhelmingly on moral and political critique and never amounted to the relative tidiness of a 'literary genre'—a genealogical convenience cut from poetics to fit the nineteenth-century discipline of English Literature.

John Donne's first satire (c. 1595) begins 'Away thou fondling motley humourist'.[22] Formally this is to quash expectations that the satire has anything to do with what we call humour, but such expectations would not have been strong, a point suggested by the distinction made in Donne's day between satire and comic satire, and by Donne's usage of 'humorist', designating the risable, even despicable. A 100 years later, a dictionary definition had deemed satire to be any discourse of sharp reproof.[23] No humorist motley or otherwise in sight. To paraphrase T. J. Mathias, satire was neither pleasant nor desirable but a necessity for public order, often seeming severe.[24] Hence, Jane Austen's reference to Mr. Darcy's satirical eye; it was not humour twinkling, but a generally censorious demeanour that, as she remarked, might generate fear.[25]

Similarly with laughter: though referring to precisely the same ubiquitous physiological contortions of the face with accompanying decibels, it has had a decidedly messy history if one considers questions of function, expression, meaning and register. As I have indicated, for the historian to take it as evidence of a sense of humour is a case of *petitio principi*—and contradicts what people have previously thought laughter expressed.

I think we can identify six broad, often entangled patterns of usage evidenced certainly from 1500 to 1800. First, was what I shall call rhetorical laughter, held to be expressive, not of humour, but of contempt. There is, wrote George Puttenham, something indecent about laughter, even when justified.[26] He discusses only the propriety of laughing at, so much was laughter associated with aggressive rhetoric, a response to be stimulated usually by demeaning and isolating a victim. No man, wrote Samuel Butler, fully laughs without showing his teeth.[27] Unsurprisingly Jesus was held never to have laughed, neither according to Cicero should the wise man, and instructed Lord Chesterfield, neither should the gentleman. The smile expressed love, the laugh disdain.[28]

This understanding, now generally gathered under the rubric of 'superiority theory', attracted most attention in antiquity and in early modern Europe[29]; and because the provocation of rhetorical laughter was censorious, it helped form a contingent association with the moral indignation of satire: satire might stimulate laughter not because it was funny, but because it was damaging. Such laughter, however, could also be the hallmark of a philosophical posture towards the human condition as a whole, foreclosing on any sense of superiority. This was the laughter of Democritus, and, via Lucian to be adopted by Erasmus, More, then Robert Burton. It contrasted with the perspective of Heraclitus whose compassion for the world made him weep for it—a contrastive *topos* popularised by Montaigne.[30]

Secondly, there was what has been called festive laughter. This has been explored largely through the later theories of Bakhtin and the carnivalesque.[31] There is an allegorical quality to Bakhtin's theories in that they may tell us as much or more about alienation in the USSR than they do about the world to which they were formally applied.[32] Despite the dangers of relying on Bakhtin, the festive was important from antiquity, some of the earliest examples coming not from the oppressed whose subversive laughter was the whistling of a safety valve controlled by an elite (the Bakhtinian image); but rather, as Noel Malcolm has pointed out, from within and for elite circles themselves.[33] But either way, it is not easily or necessarily distinguished from aggressive laughter. Rhetorical laughter is overwhelmingly about purpose, it might infuse any situation. The festive tells us more about where, who and when—social framing—than it does about purpose, though it could be justified as releasing inner tensions, as the physical act released air from the lungs. A highly ritualised tradition of festive laughter has been identified in Japan by Goh Abe. In seven Shinto festivals, the rights to hold hospitable laughing occasions, *Warai-kō*, have been handed down within selected families for hundreds of years.[34] Such evidence indicates that the festive may take on a dangerous sense as it is stretched to accommodate occasions for laughter in very different cultures.

Third, in his commentary on Aristotle's *Poetics* (1570), Ludovico Castelvetro discusses spontaneous laughter of the sort that might be generated by the unexpected meeting of old friends.[35] There is, fourth, the much studied laughter associated with 'gallows humour' as a mode of coping with immediate horror, such as the apocryphal punning wit of Cicero to his executioner: there is nothing proper in what you are doing but make a proper job of it.

Fifth, there was also what we might see as the laughter, or rather mirth of Christian rejoicing. For John Straight, merriment amounted to a Christian office or spiritual duty.[36] The office might, as it did for Isaac Barrow, stretch to sanctioning innocent jollity and good fellowship. These associations, now making the relationship between humour and laughter seem self-evident, only gradually assumed the prominence they now have.[37] This suggests that laughter's register might vary, that although a general descriptor for a physical act, and perhaps sometimes operating as a synecdoche for what we retrospectively classify as humour, it might also be redescribed as mirth or rejoicing when it was to be sanctioned under the aegis of good humour, that is benign character. In commending 'merriment', 'jollity', 'rejoicing' 'cheerfulness' and 'gladness', Straight never once mentions laughter. It may have been displaced to be implicit in what he dismissed as 'hellish' as opposed to 'holy joy'.[38] Barrow referred to laughter only passingly in his concern with jesting, foolishness and facetiousness.[39] There is then, the danger of focusing on what may not always have been the most important word or a word so laden with negative connotations that it might be avoided. Sixth, and in contrast, Robert Burton in *The Anatomy of Melancholy* gives considerable attention to remedial laughter. This activity could have been much as Hobbes regarded singing, something to be practiced for the sake of the lungs and if done badly, kept well clear of innocent by-standers.

Overall, the tumbled modes and dynamism of laughter and its largely uncharted semantics make its study intricate. The facile appeal of *Homo ridens*, and the easy presumption that laughter evidences a sense of humour, requires discounting the ambiguities and indeterminacies we need to confront in identifying the ends it might have served.

The inclination now, for example, is to laugh with Falstaff. Andrew Bradley treated him as a figure of blissful, rejoicing humour, revelling in a freedom to be celebrated. This image is still commonplace.[40] Enjoying him is a matter of connoisseurship in McKee's sense; but historically speaking, Falstaff was an image of cowardice and corruption, at one, as Dover Wilson argued, with the forces of iniquity in the miracle plays and well known in Shakespeare's day as a representation of evil to be enjoyed because it would be overcome.[41] The antimasques that preceded the court masque performances of the seventeenth century continued the tradition. It is, I think, unlikely that Shakespeare would have expected very much sympathy for Falstaff when he was rejected by young King Henry; even less that the rejection expressed any authorial ambivalence towards Henry. To have embraced Falstaff, would have signalled complicity in corruption and incipient tyranny, as Shakespeare makes abundantly clear. In act 5 of *Henry IV, Part II*, Falstaff is prepared to steal horses in order to rush to Henry that his own de facto rule of cronyism and revenge might begin. The confusion of our enjoyment of a riotous character with historicity, arises through misunderstanding the resonances of laughter; and it helps misread the dramatic point of Falstaff's fall from grace. It announced the emergence of heroic virtue from the counterpoint between East Cheap and a malfunctioning court.

There are, then, problems enough where the lexicon of humour is semantically stable; but with a new word come others. Initially, wit had referred to qualities in the ambit of consciousness and intelligence, but by the end of the sixteenth century, its range was being extended to encompass laughter in its rhetorical mode. Thus, Falstaff claims, early in act 1 scene 2 of *Henry IV, Part II*, that nothing 'tends to laughter more than I invent, or is invented on me. I am not only witty in myself, but the cause that wit is in other men'. In effect, I laugh at them because they deserve it.

Wit then gradually came to embrace the sort of deft utterance that creates a shock of amusement. It is thus cognate with what laughter often indicates—surprise and delight; and by the latish seventeenth century, it is personified in people called wits, those who can be expected to amuse in such an elegant fashion. In *MacFlecknoe*, (1678/82) Dryden made the point relentlessly against the hapless Shadwell, heir apparent to the kingdom of dullness and stupidity, the enemies of wit, (lines 199–202). Often the point of evoking wit was to deploy its antonyms—as Cowley put it in his short poem 'On Wit' (1656), only by negatives could it be defined. This, however, hardly stabilised a precise meaning, especially in relation to the similarly variable humour. Sometimes they were opposed, as when Dryden distinguished the refinements of wit from the vulgarities of humour; sometimes, as Congreve remarked, they were taken as much the same[42]; Margaret Cavendish bundles together wit, humour and satire as virtues characteristic of her husband's plays.[43] In such reflections we have humour as a discursive construct and by the eighteenth century, a general classifier, pre-conditions for forming the notion of a sense of humour.

Thus far my point has been to stress the gradual process of change that sees important meanings eventually established in the ambit of humour and that help illustrate that word's own shift to an encompassing category; but in such processes older patterns of use might survive. Such continuity hardly makes the historian's task easy; and other than by warning of the possibilities, methodology can give little help.

I suspect wit's early modern uses on the cusp of what we call the humorous may have been occasioned by direct or vicarious familiarity with Castiglione's *Il cortegiano*, (1528, trans 1561). For central to Castiglione's work was his neologism for a vital quality of lightness of style in aristocratic accomplishment, *sprezzatura*. The extended use for wit, still carrying older meanings of deft intelligence, may have functioned as an attempted translation of *sprezzatura* for which there was only periphrasis in English. Certainly much of the meaning of the Italian overlaps with the newer, seventeenth century connotations of wit that by the early eighteenth century were common-place. How far the word helps clarify and accentuate, as Nietzsche would put it, a name that lets us see what is already before us[44]; and how far wit creates a new licit style of expression, solidifying humour's discursive standing, are possibilities with which the historian needs to consider, but can hardly do so if humour is taken as a universal given. So far I have touched only on problems arising from the immediate semantic context, but if we move beyond that, we confront contextualisation more generally.

## Context and the Idioms of Historiography

Contexts, including traditions of activity, are expressions of Dilthey's notion of the hermeneutic circle, the bi-conditional relationship between general and particular: each is understood in interplay with the other.[45] This requires a distinction between context and background; contexts I take to be only those surroundings that directly elucidate the problematic identity. The distinction is dependent on the sort of enquiry undertaken and so contexts are functions of the questions we ask, less historical realities per se, than historiographical necessities. As contextualisation is a matter of privileging a certain sort of evidence, so contexts are shaped in turn through the changing understanding of what we place within them; and the more detailed the examination of the problematic object, the more contexts it might suggest. If the object of study, such as a joke book, comes directly under the auspices of humour, then it initially suggests a context of the same sort, such as a tradition of joke book production and recycling of jokes, or a *topos* of joking also found in other contemporaneous writings. It may, however, also lead to publishing history, distribution, reading networks, modes of social consolidation and exclusion, even of paper making, type-setting and watermarks, contexts that can rapidly leave the joking aside for changing priorities.[46] Humour can be a key to what lies beyond it.[47] This applies even to something as apparently insulated from broader ramifications as nonsense poetry, a clear tradition of which existed in the early seventeenth century[48]; and this is a hitherto unexplored context for the reception and use of More's *Utopia*, a work whose opaque seriousness is itself a partial function of nonsense—signalled in the pun of the title Utopia, a play on the dipthongs *eu* and *ou* that creates a neologistic homonym quite lost in English.

Yet, conversely, a humorous context can become unexpectedly relevant: consider the case of Haydn's 'Farewell' symphony, (no. 45 F# minor, 1772). When put in a context of its reported performance, the point of its scoring and structure is shown to carry a partially jesting injunction to Haydn's patron Prince Esterhazy that the musicians were homesick. On the autograph, the scoring annotation '*nichts mehr*', (nothing more) refers only to final passages by oboe and horn, but in later copies it applies, seriatim to all but two violins who conclude the work alone; each of the other players having left the stage in turn. Circumstantial evidence points to this having happened on the first performance.[49]

It follows then, both that the non-humorous might be enriched by a context of humour, and humour itself might need to be placed in other surroundings, extending as far as the preconditional patterns of social relationship that make jesting possible.[50] Contextualisation, then, is a necessity of procedure not a panacea; contexts are always porous and can raise as many questions as they answer—they keep the historian in business.

History, as Maitland said, may be a seamless web, but historical writing is not. Independently of contextualisation it involves distinct but easily confused idioms of description, and of analysis and explanation, on which historians rely when described evidence becomes problematic. A historical description requires minimising the imposition of later values, concepts, purposes and vocabulary. But this descriptive integrity might be violated when the historian turns to explanation: modern knowledge of bacteriology needs to be used to explain the Black Death, but not to describe contemporary reactions to the pestilence. Awareness of what W. B. Gallie called the voice changes between idioms is therefore crucial if description and explanation are not to be tumbled in mutually destructive confusion. As he argued, the use of words like 'because' often signal a shift from describing a state of affairs to making it more intelligible.[51] And this brings me to questions of intentionality.

## Aspects of Intentionality

The line between description and explanation can be unclear, and intentionality, and similarly translation help make it so, for they have, as it were, an interstitial modal status. On the one hand, to posit an intention in or behind something created marks a voice change to elicitation. It is a conjectural gloss and may delay a need for formal explanation. In short, given what we take to be a rational artefact, putative intention provides a reason for its being. Yet on the other hand, unlike giving the cause of an outbreak of plague, hypothesising an intention requires conformity to descriptive integrity. Specified intentions cannot historically speaking be anachronistic; and it is for this reason that they are sometimes misconceived as simply being in the evidence to be found, like invisible ink; but they are not, they remain forms of conjectural enhancement and explanatory power. That is, a commitment to the belief that in a play or painting we have a rational artefact entails positing some locus of agency and intentionality, but attributed intentions are conclusions elucidating or decoding it or glosses upon it, not simple discoveries.[52] Universal agreement on the conclusions does not convert them into something else. Statements of intention explicit in a text, have a special meta-status, in providing sign-posts for the reader 'I now intend to show...'. Yet like any other aspect of a text they can generate questions about intentionality—especially if there is discrepancy between stated intention and performance of the sort often intimating humour, through for example, irony or litotes: 'I wouldn't dream of criticizing ...'.

Translation raises overlapping difficulties, involving a voice change and a mediation of the evidence rather than a literal description. It may come close in finding a direct descriptive equivalent for original expression. But often this is not the case, especially insofar as translation of any given word or phrase may involve confronting rather different semantic surroundings and may seek to convey meaning, purpose or intention. Translation is also, though possibly only since the eighteenth century, a process more or less governed by a sense of historical integrity, probably resulting in compromises in cultural negotiation.[53] For as Vives noted in the sixteenth century, once we invoke a notion of an informing purpose, or the meaning of the passage to be translated, the more we might need to compress or elaborate.[54] For Madame Dacier, only an expansive prose translation could capture the inner spirit of Homer's poetry. Thus she rewrote his epics to become part of a genealogy of Christian philosophy.[55] Once more, humour can augment the difficulties involved. Only recently has the homely levity of Hobbes's verse translations of Homer been recognised as deliberately subversive rather than blunderingly inept.[56] Dudley Fitts has illustrated from *The Greek Anthology*, how to convey humour might require abandoning strict replication, even historicity for something closer to contemporary analogy, Jacobsen's 'creative transposition' beyond the problem of the pun.[57]

In most languages puns are to be expected, and they can be notoriously difficult to elucidate even within a single language as it mutates. Not to see Shakespeare's puns, as Coleridge knew, is to lose an aspect of his work. Frankie Rubinstein illustrates the point by recovering the intricacy of the puns on holy, holes and making whole the sole of a shoe in *Julius Caesar*; and Indira Ghose has drawn particular attention to the thematic significance of the complex pun in the title of *Much Ado About Nothing*.[58]

In surimono, according to McKee, puns (specifically *jiguchi*) and the more general word/picture play of *kakekotoba* can form the multidimensional image that unites sound, picture and the calligraphy of its poetic content. These pictorial poems revelled in playful cleverness, designed to amuse the recipient of the riddling gift.[59] But the same sort of punning structure results in a hardly comparable humour in Heartfield's visual and verbal pun on the Nazi slogan *millionen stehen hinter mir*: it is a montage of a saluting Hitler accepting money from a huge figure standing behind him.[60] So a universalist structural shell allows comparison, but does not show a universality of humour itself. Reading the multi-modal can be historically tricky not least as the symbolic resonance may well exceed an author's interest or horizon of awareness; it can make the limits of intentionality difficult to assess.

In the early eighteenth century there was what might seem to have been a nonce controversy about punning: Joseph Addison excoriated it as a false wit.[61] If it defied translation it was only noise. Others addressed the topic, taking his arguments to parodic extremes or directly defending the practice.[62] It is difficult to know what to make of this, partially forced as it was onto the template of debates about the 'ancients' versus the 'moderns' that gave an inflated seriousness to what might have been a series of jests. Indeed the controversy might have been a means by which innocent laughter assumed more prominence in understanding humour. Thomas Sheridan's *Ars Pun-ica* (Dublin, 1719) does not acknowledge these preceding discussions, but it illustrates contextual under-determination and the consequent problems for specifying intentionality. *Ars pun-ica* is thematically Scriblerian. It is a pseudo-philosophical argument reducing punning to rigid rules to maximise and enforce its practice. There are apparently 79 rules, though we are blessed only with 34. Sheridan's work is laden with puns itself, probably all intentional, but to what purpose? How serious was Sheridan in decrying the clarification of language as a form of vulgarising impoverishment because it would eradicate the creative exuberance of punning? Was *Ars pun-ica* just play, a variation on a theme for the joy of ingenuity—illustrating how activities can generate their own momentum to create traditions of endeavour, or does a wider context of language theory complicate matters? For the work is decidedly paradoxical. The aim is to regiment language use in the name of fostering creativity. Sheridan was a theorist of language, and he paraded the philosophical pretensions of the work. The pseudonymous author modestly hopes for a Newton to unify the science; and we are given both physiological and moral definitions of the pun (appropriate to scholastic philosophy). The physiological involves a parody of natural philosophical accounts of muscular movement in laughing[63]: the moral is the final cause of provoking good fellowship through laughter; benign 'Christian' merriment would seem to be ascendant, specifically as laughter, what harmlessly might be re-couched as celebrating a healthy sense of humour. Yet if Sheridan is satirising linguistic purification, and reductive rule-mongering, a Scriblerian *bête noir*, perhaps not. We have a case of plausible contexts complicating a reading of a work that might just have been a belated joke at Addison's expense or elaborated only for the author's amusement.

## The Imponderables of Reception

Studying the reception of a work does not always settle issues of humorous intent, some responses to Sheridan's work were decidedly vicious. That something is accepted as humorous does not mean that the humour is understood. As the Earl of Shaftesbury claimed, defensive raillery is intended not to be.[64] Where humour is unacknowledged, neither does it mean that it has passed unrecognised. Swift remarked that Arbuthnot's *Art of Political Lying* (1712) was too clever to be understood. Was he criticising his friend or denigrating the capacities of the audience? The pamphlet was a Lucianically elaborate and ingenious variation of the logical paradox of the liar. It took the form of a promotional puff for a subscription publication. As no satire had taken this form before, it lacks some obvious contextual sign-posts; although Arbuthnot had earlier played a practical joke on Queen Anne's Ladies in Waiting, getting them to subscribe to a non-existent history of the Ladies in Waiting, detailing who among them had made the best wives. As *Political Lying* is just the bland synopsis of the contents of the first volume there are no obvious clues as to its bogus nature.[65] Nothing is said of the second volume, but incompleteness is itself a Scriblerian characteristic. Did it fool contemporaries? He had the book advertised, but did anyone commit to buying copies of it from the (genuine) coffee houses in which it would be placed? The only known person gulled by the satire was a twentieth-century American literary critic, who regretted the work's loss.[66]

Lack of evidence, however, may also indicate disapprobation. If people did take Swift literally in advocating the Irish eat their children, it is unlikely that they naively thought he meant it, just that he was nasty.[67] Not to see the jest could have been a form of riposte as much as it might have been obtuseness. Conversely, to read in humour where none was intended can be a mode of ridicule. As a curious variation of such refractions of reception, Roger Lund has pointed out that modern French linguistic theory after Barthes—that sees humans imprisoned in the independent free play of linguistic abstractions—was first invented in the eighteenth century as a satiric *reductio* of a preoccupation with nominalisation.[68] A theory invented to be laughed at ends up being taken seriously, like the compositional hoax of the poems of Ern Malley.[69]

Legal constraints may also be relevant factors in recognising or losing a facetious dimension. In both Roman and Common Law, un-malicious intent could be a defence, but it was made vulnerable by the forensic option of assuming that the provocation of laughter expressed hostility and was designed to damage. Nevertheless, plotting humorous responses may be a means of delineating audiences, just as humour within a work may be an attempt to discriminate among them.

## The Case of Hobbes on Laughter

Many of the imponderables I have canvassed can be illustrated by Thomas Hobbes's reflections on laughter. In *The Elements of Law*, 1640, he referred to 'that distortion of the countenance we call LAUGHTER' as the sign of a nameless passion, but the joy and triumph involved, 'hath not hitherto been declared by any'. It is occasioned by what 'must be new and unexpected'. He then called it a 'sudden glory' in our own superiority (or 'vain glory') over another or over our previous selves.[70] In the abbreviated account in *Leviathan*, the claim to the originality of his theory disappears and 'sudden glory' is named as the passion 'which maketh those grimaces called laughter'.[71]

Addison drew attention to Hobbes's initial discussion in 1711 when he considered it curious that a man laughing heartily should be considered not merry, but proud.[72] Since then, Hobbes's reflections have become so well known in the *Leviathan* redaction that its citation seems almost as obligatory as it is misleading in discussing theories of humour in general, and 'superiority theory' in particular. To this Hobbes has been routinely attached, either to epitomise it, or to commend his seminal originality in doing most to invent it from hints in Plato and Aristotle.[73]

To regard his discussions of laughter as advancing 'superiority theory', smacks, in Newton's expression, of genealogical tallying—attaching a prestigious name and a few de-contextualised words to a species of theory we now believe worthy enough for the ornamentation of a pedigree. For although emphasising that a sense of superiority was something humans relish, especially given the discomforts of their natural equality, his theory is not of or about superiority per se. Indeed, his brief discussion embraces what is usually at odds with 'superiority theory' or seems to diminish its explanatory power, namely a capacity for self-mockery. And it concludes, with what would appear to contradict it, recognition of laughter as victimless, the socially affirming merriment Addison overlooked. In Hobbes's emphasis on the new and unexpected, there are even intimations of 'incongruity theory' to which Kant's name is conventionally and arbitrarily affixed, as another big name for the tally; for it was common during the eighteenth century on earlier precedent to invoke incongruity and surprise in explaining laughter—William Preston would applaud Hobbesian theory precisely in these terms.[74] For Hobbes, laughter expressive of a sense of superiority over another was, in short, given as a major, though not the only reason for the sounds and facial signs of human joy, and his emphasis is on the immediate cause of the suddenness in the glory.[75] Hobbes's discussion is offered to illustrate his account of the passions, reduced to the opposing drives of avoidance and attraction, and used to redefine the moral lexicon comprising words such as *glory, courage, love, charity, anger, pity, weeping, lust* as well as *laughter*.[76]

Insofar as Hobbes was attempting to make better philosophical sense of a familiar moral vocabulary, there was no need for the understanding of laughter itself to be innovatory, as Hobbes claimed it was. And historically speaking, as Quentin Skinner has shown, it was not, but was part of a sustained tradition of sophisticated commentary on Aristotle's *Rhetoric* and the widely cited elaborations by Cicero and Quintilian.[77] When Hobbes presented what Skinner says was largely an unacknowledged paraphrase of Quintilian, it may even have been a little old-fashioned and certainly familiar to his audience. Thus what strikes

Skinner as 'especially disingenuous', therefore, are the 'noisy protestations' of originality, serving to show how out of touch Hobbes could be.[78] If context is restricted to a clear tradition of discussing rhetorical laughter, and to the jangling discordances in the reception of Hobbes's work, there the matter might rest.

Yet, if context is augmented, a different intentional possibility takes shape. Certainly Hobbes upset people and was seen as an arrogant, boasting scoffer who did not properly address objections to his philosophy.[79] He was also a man of great wit, and given to mirth that was not always other-directed and aggressive. Yet under-pinning all appears to have been an unshakable sense of his own philosophical significance.

This, however, was more than the conceit of which he was accused. It was part of his conception of philosophy derived from Francis Bacon. In The *Advancement of Learning* (1605), Bacon had urged that to understand nature properly, to create a new philosophy, a new type of philosopher was required.[80] It was a strident claim given the predominantly negative associations of newness and innovation, often synonymous with the destructive change that might stem from arrogance and a tyrannous disposition. Despite vulnerability to attack in such terms, as Richard Serjeantson has shown, philosophers in Bacon's idiom began to emerge; Hobbes, along with Descartes, foremost amongst them, he was a '*novatore*'.[81]

What helped make a true, new philosopher was precisely a disregard of received authority. To paraphrase: everything should be taken back to first reckonings built upon definitions. Reliance upon the word 'of an *Aristotle*, a *Cicero*, or a *Thomas*' is not science but opinion; it makes the words that are wise men's counters, the money of fools.[82] Little wonder Hobbes rarely cited previous writers (especially classical authorities) even when in agreement with them, and that he emphasised his own distinctiveness.[83] His clarion claim at the beginning of *De cive*, from which he never retreated was that in this work he had invented political philosophy.

This begins to cast a different light on his assertion that none had declared laughter properly before him. If he could dismiss Aristotle on most things as dangerously misguided, it was easy to ignore the echoes of earlier laughter theory derived from him.[84] There is a certain irony in the fact that modern authors in wanting an easy genealogy for the 'superiority theory' of laughter that will do double duty as a theory of humour have taken his claim to origination perilously close to face value—relying literally on 'the authority of […] a Thomas'.[85]

More than this, Hobbes's assertion as to his own ground-breaking significance, is in *The Elements* a work of scribal publication, not intended for print. There were many copies, but the audience would have been relatively narrow and cohesive, and stretching from his patron William Cavendish, at whose behest it was written. The two men were close friends, Cavendish had effectively his own court of philosophers, his brother Sir Charles was a distinguished mathematician, and William, now barely clinging to the skirt-tails of his second wife Margaret, ('Mad Meg') another Baconian *novatore*, was a man of parts.

It is also relevant that the ancient writer Lucian was popular in the Cavendish circle. Margaret admits to familiarity with some of his work[86]; the Cavendish protégé Jasper Mayne, also a friend of Hobbes, probably provided the Cavendish sponsored translations she knew.[87] Lucian is one of the few ancients Hobbes treats with respect, even paraphrasing and half quoting (without acknowledgement). The significance is that Lucian was par excellence the philosophical scoffer, ridiculing philosophical authority, the pretension of its schools and the dogmatism of their opinions. His boast was that he had taught the philosophical dialogue to laugh—at philosophy. It is easy to see his appeal for a *novatore*, as a ground-clearing satiric precursor of true philosophy.

Hobbes's immediate audience was of like-minded men of letters; even William and Margaret Cavendish, both apt to feign ignorance of books, would have known something of the literature Hobbes ignores in asserting his own Baconian independence. It is possible, then, that what 'hitherto hath not been declared' about laughter is an in-joke against his own self-image as a philosopher and his dim view of antiquity. Not so much misreading his audience, as hoping to generate that sudden glory amongst them at his own momentary expense through a witty paradox about laughter itself. The novelty and surprise that for Hobbes causes laughter is occasioned by the surprise at a spurious claim to novelty. Such a gesture would have economically illustrated his own recognition that people laugh at themselves, a point that might also have been familiar from Erasmus's famed emphasis on self-mockery in the *Morae encomium*. If we have such a reflexive jest, it is neither pointed nor explicit; and perhaps that too is appropriate, for Hobbes concludes his discussion, possibly again echoing the widely known Erasmus, by noting that to avoid offence laughter should be at generalities, 'abstracted from persons', denuded, in short, of any nastiness, so 'all the company may laugh together'. It is a clear recognition and commendation of innocent merriment as socially affirming, even egalitarian. This is something beyond the reductivism of Hobbes, superiority theorist of laughter/humour. Perhaps the members of his immediate circle did laugh together. And perhaps also this sense of audience explains why the possible joke disappears from *Leviathan*, a work intended for the press and a diversity of undiscerned and, as Hobbes anticipated, often undiscerning reader.

I do not suggest this as a better account than Skinner's; it may well be a case of over-reading, but simply to illustrate the following: that although Ockham's razor encapsulates the logical virtue of explanatory economy, this can be a historiographical vice. Awareness of contextual porosity can have the merit of avoiding over-simplification and can also directly affect specifications of conjectured intentionality. It follows that the more contexts are suggested by a work, the more complicated interpretation becomes. If a humorous dimension potentially exacerbates the situation, it is also the case that the hypothesis of humorous intent may help refine a specification of audience. And I cannot think of a methodological criterion by which such indeterminacies can be settled.

If humour in the past has been under-explored by historians we may, then, have the beginnings of an explanation: humour augments the difficulty of reading. The suspicion of it is enough to destabilise any interpretative comfort zone. As Sir Percy Percy said (*Blackadder Two*, 'Money'), when given a whole afternoon to discover the secrets of alchemy and turn base metal into gold, 'I like a challenge'. So should we all.

## NOTES

1. Milner, 'Towards a Semiotic Theory of Humor', 1–30. *Homo ridens* overlaps with Johan Huizinga's much earlier *Homo ludens*, a seminal study of play in the Middle Ages.
2. Bremmer and Roodenberg, *Cultural History of Humour*, 1.
3. Wiggins, *Identity and Spacio-Temporal Continuity*, at length.
4. See for example, Bremmer and Roodenberg, *Cultural History*, 1.
5. Reddy, 'Conduit Metaphors', 164–201.
6. Billig, *Laughter*, 5; Morreall, ed. *Philosophy of Humor*; Critchley, *Humour*, 2–4 attributing the tripartite classification to Morreall.
7. Bremmer and Roodenberg, *Cultural History*, 1.
8. Anthony Ashley Cooper, Earl of Shaftsbury, 'Sensus Communis' 1.1.
9. See for example, Barrow, *Against Foolish Talking*, 305–28, 306, 312.
10. See, for example, Billig, *Laughter*, at length; Ruch, *Sense of Humor*; Critchley, *Humour*, 2–3.
11. Wickberg, 'Sense of Humour in American Culture', 30–139; for brief but not entirely reliable comments on the pre-history of a sense of humour, see also Ruch, *Sense of Humor*, 1–10.
12. Maclean, *Logic, Signs and Nature*, 241–3.
13. The *OED* gives 1847 as the earliest use, but negative neologisms can precede their positive forms. Words with the *un* prefix provide good examples, see Dixon, *Making New Words*, 77.
14. I have consulted a number of lexicons through the extremely valuable Australian Society for Indigenous Languages (ausil) website. Although all had distinct and variably organised vocabularies of laughter, Walpiri, for example, having different terms for laughing in fun and derisively, none had accommodated humour or has a listed semantic equivalent, including New Tiwi, a simplified version of Tiwi with many English loan words.
15. Wells, 'Satire and Constraint',193–217; see also Wells and Jessica Milner Davis, 'Farce and Satire', 127–52, although the suggestion seems to be that farce does map pretty precisely on the faasu of kyōgen.
16. Eco, *Mouse or Rat*; Jacobson, 'Linguistic Aspects of Translation', 222–239, 238.
17. Ghose, 'Licence to Laugh', 42–3.
18. For further discussion see Attardo, *Linguistic Theories*, 5–7.
19. McKee, *Japanese Poetry Prints:* 9–33, 10–11. I am grateful to Dr. Aoise Stratford for drawing this to my attention.
20. Newton, *Origins of Beowulf*, 55–63.
21. Lewis, *Studies in Words*, 8–13.
22. Donne, 'Satyre I', 129.
23. Bailey, *Universal Etymological Dictionary*.

24. Matthias, *The Pursuits of Literature*, 6–7.
25. Austen, *Pride and Prejudice*, chapter 6.
26. Puttenham, *Arte of English Poesie*, 291.
27. Samuel Butler, quoted in Farley-Hills, *Benevolence of Laughter*, 8.
28. Resnik, 'Risus monasticus', 90–100, 90–1 on John Chrysostom's claim about Jesus; Skinner, 'Hobbes and the Classical Theory of Laughter', 150, 174,
29. For a valuable survey, Skinner, 'Hobbes and the Classical Theory of Laughter', 14—176; see also 'Why Laughing Mattered', 418–47.
30. Montaigne, 'On Democritus and Heraclitus', 219–21; for a valuable discussion, Curtis, 'From Sir Thomas More to Robert Burton', 90–112.
31. Bakhtin, *Rabelais and his world*.
32. Gurevich, 'Bakhtin and his theory of carnival', 54–60.
33. Malcolm, *Origins of English Nonsense*, 117–24.
34. Goh Abe, 'A Ritual Performance of Laughter', 37–50.
35. Castelveltro, *Poetica d'Aristotele*, pt.2, pp.34b-62; Attardo, *Linguistic Theories*, 42.
36. Straight, *Rule of Rejoycing*, 2, 24–5.
37. Barrow, *Against Foolish Talking*, 304–20 writing of innocent jesting and face-tiousness; it is an understanding, specifically of laughter that threads through *The Spectator*; Skinner, 'Hobbes and the Classical Theory of Laughter',162–4; Ghose, 'Licence to Laugh', 43 who both suggest that it gains increased attention from the eighteenth century.
38. Straight, *The Rule of Rejoycing*, 7; Farley-Hills, *Benevolence of Laughter*, 11–12, seems not to notice the absence of reference to laughter.
39. Burrow, *Against Foolish Talking*, 312.
40. Rackin, *Stages of History*, 38–42.
41. Dover Wilson, *Fortunes of Falstaff*, 17–35.
42. Wickberg, 'Sense of Humor', 103–110, 106.
43. Cavendish, *Life*, 202.
44. Nietzsche, *La Gaia scienza*, para 26.
45. Dilthey, *Ideas Concerning a Descriptive and Analytic Psychology; The Understanding of Other Persons*; Makkreel, *Dilthey*, 247–73, esp. 269–71, 333–4.
46. Some of the issues are raised in Brewer, 'Prose Jest-Books', 90–111.
47. Bremmer and Roodenberg, *Cultural History*, 3.
48. Malcolm, *Origins of English Nonsense*.
49. Webster, *Haydn's "Farewell" Symphony*, 1–3, 113–6, for a brilliant analysis: see also Bonds, 'Haydn', 57–91, for the interplay of wit and humor between words and music.
50. Ghose, 'Festive Laughter', at length.
51. Gallie, *Philosophy*, 105–115.
52. Gallie, *Philosophy*, 115 for the historian's causal vocabulary as a matter of glossing a text.
53. On the late emergence of a historical rationale for translation, see Burke, 'Cultures of Translation', 7–38.
54. Vives, *De ratione dicendi*, III, 225–6.
55. Dacier, *Iliade d'Homère*; similarly, it has been argued that the intellectual content of William of Ockham's logic can only be properly revealed through modern notation.

2 THE STUDY OF PAST HUMOUR: HISTORICITY AND THE LIMITS OF METHOD    37

56. Davis, 'Thomas Hobbes's Translations of Homer', 231–55; and especially, Nelson, 'General Introduction'.
57. Fitts, 'The Poetic Nuance', 42–7.
58. Rubinstein, *Dictionary of Shakespeare's Sexual Puns*, x-xiii; Ghose, *Much Ado* 114–17.
59. McKee, *Japanese Poetry Prints*, 12–13,188–90.
60. Rose, *Parody*, 117.
61. Addison, *The Spectator*, 228.
62. Nokes, *John Gay*, 231–3, discussing *God's Revenge Against Punning*, and *A Modest Defence of Punning*, (Swift), a *Defence of the Ancient Art of Punning*, (possibly Arbuthnot); see also, Arbuthnot and Pope, *Memoirs*, 125–8, 262–3.
63. John Bulwer, *Pathomyotomia* (1649) 104–26, cited Kerby-Miller, ed. *Memoirs*, 277; the parodic account in the *Memoirs*, chapter 10, 133, may in some form have been known by Sheridan, via Swift.
64. Shaftesbury, *'Sensus communis'*, 1.2.
65. An exception may be an arithmetical error about the number of chapters— Arbuthnot was probably the foremost mathematician of his generation. But the pamphlet is anonymous and Arbuthnot was notoriously careless about his own writings.
66. Adams, *Bad Mouth*, 43–5.
67. Arbuthnot and Pope, *Memoirs*, 169.
68. Lund, '*Res* and *verba*', 63–78.
69. Lund, '*Res et verba*',63–78; Anderson, *Sons of Clovis*.
70. Hobbes, *Elements of Law*, (1640) pt. 1. Ch. 9. sect. 13, 41–3; 'our previous selves' is a cumbersome, if precise formulation for laughing at ourselves, consequent upon Hobbes's belief that we exist in the present, the past, however recent, being decaying sense.
71. Hobbes, *Leviathan*, vol. 2 ch. 6, 88–9; see also Skinner 'Hobbes and the Classical Theory of Laughter', 147–9.
72. Addison, *Spectator*, April, 1711, 174.
73. Roeckelein, 'Hobbesian Theory', vol. 1, 340–2, is entirely representative; Billig, *Laughter*, 37–56; for a timely critical discussion, Lintott, 'Superiority in Humor Theory', 357–58.
74. Preston, *Essay*, 69–76.
75. In *De cive*, Hobbes very briefly posits a wider range for *gloria* (vain glory) in mentioning laughter, but even this is qualified.
76. Hobbes, *Elements*, pt. 1, chs 9–10, 36–48; Lintott, 'Superiority', 352–6.
77. Skinner, 'Hobbes and the Classical Theory of Laughter', 151.
78. Skinner, 'Hobbes and the Classical Theory of Laughter', 155, 151.
79. Parkin, *The Taming of Leviathan*.
80. Gaukroger, *Francis Bacon*, 101–31.
81. Serjeantson, 'Hobbes, the universities and the history of philosophy', 114–5.
82. Hobbes, *Leviathan*, ch. 4
83. Hobbes, *Leviathan*, 'Review and Conclusion'.
84. Hobbes, *Leviathan*, ch. 46.
85. It is true that he is sometimes seen as part of a lineage, preceded by Plato and Aristotle, for which similar distortions are required, on which see Lintott, 'Superiority' at length; he is nevertheless given an untoward preeminence in keeping with his own assessments.

86. Hutton, 'Science and Satire' 161–78; Cottegnies, 'Utopia, Millenarianism and the Baconian Programme', 71–92, 71–2.
87. Mayne, *Part of Lucian Made English.*

## BIBLIOGRAPHY

Adams, Robert M. *Bad Mouth: Fugitive Papers from the Darkside.* Berkeley: University of California Press, 1977.

Addison, Joseph, and Richard Steele. *The Spectator.* Edited by G. Hill Smith, 4 vols., London: Dent, 1906.

Anderson, Don. *The Sons of Clovis: Ern Malley, Adoré Floupette and a Secret History of Australian Poetry.* Brisbane: University of Queensland Press, 2011.

Arbuthnot John and Pope Alexander. *The Memoirs of the Extraordinary Life, Works and Discoveries of Martinus Scriblerus.* Edited by Charles Kirby-Miller. New York: Oxford University Press, 1988.

Attardo, Salvatore. *Linguistic Theories of Humor.* Berlin: Mouton de Gruyter, 1994.

Austen, Jane. *Pride and Prejudice.* London, 1813.

Bailey, N. *A Universal Etymological Dictionary,* London, 1735.

Bakhtin Mikhail. *Rabelais and his world.* Translated by Helene Iswolsky. Cambridge, Mass.: MIT Press, 1968.

Barrow, Isaac. *Against Foolish Talking and Jesting,* 1678. In *Theological Works.* Oxford: Clarendon Press, 1818, 6 vols. 1, Sermon xiv, 305–28.

Billig, Michael. *Laughter and Ridicule: Towards a Social Critique of Humour.* London: Sage, 2005.

Bonds, Mark Evan. 'Haydn, Laurence Stern and the Origins of Musical Irony'. *The Journal of the American Musicological Society* 44, no.1 (1991): 57–91.

Bremmer, Jan and Herman Roodenberg, eds. *A Cultural History of Humour, From Antiquity to the Present Day.* Cambridge: Polity Press, 1997.

Brewer, Derek. 'Prose Jest-Books Mainly in the Sixteenth to Eighteenth Centuries in England'. In *A Cultural History of Humour, From Antiquity to the Present Day,* edited by Jan Bremmer and Herman Roodenberg, 90–111. Cambridge: Polity Press, 1997.

Burke, Peter. 'Cultures of Translation in Early Modern Europe'. In *Cultural Translation in Early Modern Europe,* edited by P. Burke and R. Po-Chia Hsia, 7–38. Cambridge: Cambridge University Press, 2007.

Castelvetro, Ludovico. *Poetica d'Aristotele vulgarizzat te sposta.* Vienna, 1570.

Cavendish, Margaret. *The Life of the Thrice Noble William Cavendish, Duke of Newcastle* (1667). Edited by C. H. Firth. London: Nimmo, 1886.

Critchley, Simon. *On Humour.* London: Routledge (2002) 2011.

Cooper, Anthony Ashley, Earl of Shaftsbury. 'Sensus Communis: An Essay on The Freedom of Wit and Humour'. In *Characteristicks of Men, Manners, Opinions, Times,* 3 vols. Edited by Douglas Den Uyl, 1, 37–94. Indianapolis: Liberty Fund, 2001.

Cottegnies, Line. 'Utopia, Millenarianism and the Baconian Programme of Margaret Cavendish's *The Blazing World* (1666)'. In *New Worlds Reflected: Travel and Utopia in the Early Modern Period,* edited by Chloë Houston, 71–92. Farnham, U.K.: Ashgate, 2010.

Cowley, Abraham. 'Of wit' (1656). In *The Norton Anthology of English Literature*, edited by M. H. Abrams. New York: Norton, 1986.

Curtis, Catherine. 'From Sir Thomas More to Robert Burton: the laughing philosopher in the early modern period'. In *The Philosopher in early Modern Europe: The nature of a contested identity*, edited by Conal Condren, Stephen Gaukroger and Ian Hunter, 90–112. Cambridge: Cambridge University Press, 2006.

Dacier, Anne. *Iliade d'Homère, Traduite en François avec de Remarques Par Madame Dacier.* Paris, 1699.

Davis, Paul. 'Thomas Hobbes's Translations of Homer: Epic and Anti-Clericalism in the Late Seventeenth Century'. *Seventeenth Century* 12 (1997): 231–55.

Dilthey, Wilhelm. *Ideas Concerning a Descriptive and Analytic Psychology* (1884); *The Understanding of Other Persons and their Expressions of Life,* (1910). Translated by K. L. Heiges and R. M Zaner, respectively. The Hague: Nijhoff, 1977.

Dixon, R. M. M. *Making New Words: Morphological Derivation in English.* Oxford: Oxford University Press, 2014.

Donne, John. *The Poems of John Donne.* Edited by Sir Herbert Grierson. London: Oxford University Press, (1934) 1967.

Dover Wilson, John. *The Fortunes of Falstaff.* Cambridge: Cambridge University Press, 1970.

Eco, Umberto. *Mouse or Rat: Translation as Negotiation.* London: Weidenfeld and Nicolson, 2003.

Farley-Hills, David. *The Benevolence of Laughter.* London: Macmillan, 1974.

Fitts, Dudley. 'The Poetic Nuance'. In *On Translation.* Edited by Reuben Brower, 32–47. Cambridge, MA.: Harvard University Press, 1959.

Gallie, W. B. *Philosophy and the historical Understanding.* London: Chatto and Windus, 1964.

Gaukroger, Stephen. *Francis Bacon, and the Transformation of Early-Modern Philosophy.* Cambridge: Cambridge University Press, 2001.

Ghose, Indira. *Much Ado About Nothing: Language and Writing.* London: Bloomsbury, 2018.

Ghose, Indira. 'Licence to Laugh: Festive Laughter in Twelfth Night'. In *A History of English Laughter: From Beowulf to Beckett and Beyond.* Edited by Manfred Pfister, 35–46. Leiden: Brill, 2002.

Goh, Abe. 'A Ritual Performance of Laughter in Southern Japan'. In *Understanding Humour in Japan,* edited by Milner Davis, 37–50. Detroit Michigan: Wayne State University Press, 2006.

Gurevich, Aaron. 'Bakhtin and his theory of carnival'. In *A Cultural History of Humour.* Edited by Jan Bremmer and Herman Roodenburg, 54–60. Cambridge: Polity Press, 1997.

Hobbes, Thomas. *The Elements of Law,* (1640). Edited by Ferdinand Tönnies. London: Frank Cass, 1969.

Hobbes, Thomas. *Leviathan* (1651). Edited by Noel Malcolm, 3 vols. Oxford: Clarendon Press, 2012.

Hutton, Sarah. 'Science and Satire: The Lucianic Voice of Margaret Cavendish's *Description of a New World Called the Blazing World'.* In *Authorial Conquests,* edited by L. Cottegnies and N. Weitz, 161–78. New Jersey: Fairleigh Dickinson University Press, 2003.

Jacobson, Roman. 'Linguistic Aspects of Translation'. In *On Translation.* Edited by Reuben Brower, 222–239. Cambridge, MA.: Harvard University Press, 1959.

Lewis, C. S. *Studies in Words*. Cambridge: Cambridge University Press, 1976.

Lintott, Sheila. 'Superiority in Humor Theory'. *The Journal of Aesthetics and Art Criticism* 74, no. 4 (2016): 357–58.

Lund, Roger. '*Res* and *verba*: Scriblerian Satire and the Fate of Language'. *Bucknell Review: Science and Literature* 27, no. 2 (1983): 63–78.

Malcolm, Noel. *The Origins of English Nonsense*. London: Fontana, 1997.

Maclean, Ian. *Logic, Signs and Nature in the Renaissance: The Case of Learned Medicine*. Cambridge: Cambridge University Press, 2002.

Makkreel, Rudolf A. *Dilthey: Philosopher of the Human Sciences*. Princeton, N.J.: Princeton University Press, 1975.

Matthias, T. J. *The Pursuits of Literature, A Satirical Poem in Four Dialogues, with notes*. London, (1794) 1808.

Mayne, Jasper. *Part of Lucian Made English from the Original*, (1638) 1663.

McKee, Daniel. *Japanese Poetry Prints: Surimono from the Schoff Collection*. Ithaca and New York: Herbert F Johnson Museum of Art, 2006.

Milner, G. B. 'Towards a Semiotic Theory of Humor and Laughter'. *Semiotica* 5, no.1 (1972): 1–30.

Montaigne, Michel de. *Essays*. Translated by Donald Frame. Stanford: Stanford University Press, (1948) 1958.

Morreall, John, ed. *The Philosophy of Humor*. New York: State University of New York Press, 1986.

Nelson, Eric, ed. *Thomas Hobbes, Translations of Homer*. 2 vols. Oxford: Clarendon Press, 2008.

Newton, Sam. *The Origins of Beowulf*. Woodbridge: Boydell and Brewer, 1993, 2004.

Nietzsche, Frederick. *La Gaia scienza*, (1888) *Werke*, vol.2. Edited by Karl Schlechte. 3 vols. Munich: Hanser. 1967.

Nokes, David. *John Gay: A Profession of Friendship*. Oxford: Oxford University Press, 1995.

Parkin, Jon. *The Taming of Leviathan: The Reception of the Political and Religious Ideas of Hobbes in England, 1640–1700*. Cambridge: Cambridge University Press, 2007.

Preston, William. *An Essay on Ridicule, Wit and Humour*. Transactions of the Royal Irish Academy. Dublin: Pt.1, 69–76. Pt 2, 77–90.

Puttenham, George. *The Arte of English Poesie* (1589). Edited by Gladys Doidge Willcock and Alice Walker. Cambridge: Cambridge University Press, (1936) 1970.

Wiggins, David. *Identity and Spacio-Temporal Continuity*. Oxford: Blackwell, 1988.

Rackin, Phyllis. *Stages of History: Shakespeare's English Chronicles*. New York: Cornell University Press, 1990.

Reddy, Michael. 'Conduit Metaphors'. In *Metaphor and Thought*, edited by Andrew Ortony, 164–201. Cambridge: Cambridge University Press, 1993.

Resnik, I. M. 'Risus monasticus: Laughter and medieval monastic culture'. *Revue Bénédictine* 97, no. 1–2 (1987): 90–100.

Roeckelein, Jon Edward. 'Hobbesian Theory'. In *The Encyclopedia of Humor Studies*, 2 vols., edited by Salvatore Attardo, 1, 340–2. Los Angeles and London: Sage, 2014.

Rose, Margaret. *Parody and Meta-Fiction*. London: Croom Helm, 1979.

Rubinstein, Frankie. *A Dictionary of Shakespeare's Sexual Puns and their Significance*. Basingstoke: Palgrave Macmillan, 1989.

Ruch, Willibald, ed. *The Sense of Humor: Explorations of a Personality Characteristic*. Berlin: Mouton de Gruyter, 1986.

Serjeantson, Richard. 'Hobbes, the universities and the history of philosophy'. In *The Philosopher in early Modern Europe: The nature of a contested identity*, edited by Conal Condren, Stephen Gaukroger and Ian Hunter, 113–139. Cambridge: Cambridge University Press, 2006.

Skinner, Quentin. 'Hobbes and the Classical Theory of Laughter'. In *Visions of Politics (III): Hobbes and Civil Science*, 14–176. Cambridge: Cambridge University Press, 2002.

Skinner, Quentin. 'Why Laughing Mattered in The Renaissance'. *History of Political Thought* 22, no.3 (2001): 418–447.

Straight, John. *The Rule of Rejoycing or a Direction of Mirth*. London, 1671.

Vives, Juan Louis. *De ratione dicendi*. Basil, 1536.

Webster, James. *Haydn's 'Farewell' Symphony and the Idea of Classical Style*. Cambridge: Cambridge University Press, 1991.

Wells, Marguerite. 'Satire and Constraint in Japanese Culture'. In *Understanding Humour in Japan*, edited by Jessica Milner Davis, 193–217. Detroit, Michigan: Wayne State University Press, 2006.

Wells, Marguerite and Jessica Milner Davis. 'Farce and Satire in *Kyōgen*'. In *Understanding Humour in Japan*, edited by Jessica Milner Davis, 127–52. Detroit, Michigan: Wayne State University Press, 2006.

Wickberg, Daniel B. 'The Sense of Humour in American Culture, 1850–1960'. Unpublished PhD Thesis, Yale University, 1993.

CHAPTER 3

# No Sense of Humour? 'Humour' Words in Old Norse

*Hannah Burrows*

As several contributions to this *Handbook* demonstrate, the word 'humour' is fraught with difficulty.[1] Even for native speakers of Modern English, the Modern English word is difficult to define in a way that satisfies everyone. Although it is undoubtedly a useful term, even more problems surface when trying to apply it to historical (and contemporary) contexts in which there is no equivalent native word. Does that absence mean that that culture does not have the concept? The same is true for subtypes of humour such as satire, wit, or farce. Do we project too much onto the subjects of our study if we impose terms that native speakers would not recognise (or be able to translate easily into their own language)?

A simple answer is: not necessarily—and there are many illuminating studies of 'humour' or subtypes of humour in historical contexts that explicate their subject using familiar modern terminology to facilitate communication and analysis. Nonetheless, understanding the ways in which a culture, or a group of language-speakers, categorises its own experience lends another dimension to fully understanding that experience. This chapter examines a range of Old Norse words that relate to the various phenomena we connect with the rubric of 'humour' in English. In doing so it begins to map the shape of Old Norse's 'sense of humour', but also aims to demonstrate the difficulties that can arise both in determining nuanced semantics and in identifying whether or not particular scenarios arising in texts should be thought of as humorous, or

---

H. Burrows (✉)
Department of History, University of Aberdeen, Aberdeen, UK
e-mail: hannah.burrows@abdn.ac.uk

© The Author(s), under exclusive license to Springer Nature
Switzerland AG 2020
D. Derrin, H. Burrows (eds.), *The Palgrave Handbook of Humour, History, and Methodology*, https://doi.org/10.1007/978-3-030-56646-3_3

43

otherwise. For that reason, it is intended that this chapter serves as a case study that can be applied to other languages and cultures, and should not be purely of interest to Old Norse specialists.

Humour's relation to emotion has been a contentious issue. The purpose of this chapter is not to try and settle these debates, even for the historical context on which it focuses, although trying to understand the emotions felt and elicited by agents and targets of humour in the examples that emerge contributes to interpreting the semantic value of the words investigated here. For now it may be observed that the historical study of humour shares a methodological problem with the historical study of emotions: 'emotion', too, is a modern, Anglophone word, expansive in scope and with contentious definition, that is not always easily translatable.[2] It has frequently been pointed out that understanding 'emotion words' in their own context, and not simply translating them into familiar modern terms, is an important step in understanding how those emotions were experienced.[3] The investigation of emotions in historical and cross-cultural perspective has developed various methods to study emotion words, such as the historian Barbara Rosenwein's advocacy of seeking contextual collocations: 'we can be fairly sure a word is an emotion word if it is paired with—or appears as a transformation of—terms of affect known to have been considered as such' or the linguist Anna Wierzbicka's pioneering use of Natural Semantic Metalanguage as a tool.[4] From a cultural history perspective, vocabulary is at the heart of Stephen Halliwell's monumental study *Greek Laughter*, where he is particularly interested in 'cultural self-definition and conflict'.[5]

This study borrows from these various methodologies where appropriate, but its scope, function, and body of research data are different from theirs. There is not room in a single chapter either to exhaustively map all the potential 'humour words' of Old Norse or to analyse each word comprehensively. Instead I wish to sketch out the main contours of the Old Norse vocabulary relating to what we now label as 'humour'. My major resource has been the online *Dictionary of Old Norse Prose* (*ONP*). For any given headword, *ONP* provides 'supporting quotations':[6] instances of that word in its immediate textual context excerpted from the corpus of extant Old Norse prose texts. The citations are selective, not comprehensive:

> so as to present the various semantic and syntactic usages within each signification and to illustrate the headword's occurrence in a variety of genres and cultural settings. *ONP*'s earliest example of each headword (in terms of the age of the manuscript in which it is found) is always included.[7]

The number of citations is thus not a definitive record of all occurrences of any given word, but the editors have been generous in what is included: citations for common words number well into the hundreds. The number of citations also provides a guide to the relative frequency of occurrence of words in comparison to one another.

My examination of each vocabulary item included here conforms to the following structure.[8] The headword, in bold type, heads each entry; I have chosen nominal forms as headwords and follow *ONP*'s orthography. Underneath, the number of *ONP* citations is given, followed by the definition construed by *ONP*. The dictionary is as yet incomplete with regards to definitions; in addition, it construes its definitions separately in Danish, which work is more advanced, and English. Where the English definition is available, that is provided; where it is not, the Danish is given, followed by an English gloss. This is supplemented by the definition given in the older standard *An Icelandic-English Dictionary*, by Richard Cleasby and Guðbrandur Vigfússon (abbreviated here *CV*). (The first edition of this work was published in 1874; the glosses given there are sometimes outdated compared to modern usage.[9]) Next, related words, where extant, are provided in bold: this section includes other parts of speech (verbs, adjectives, adverbs, and other nouns) with the same stem; it does not include compounds, though those are sometimes mentioned in the analysis. Except in instances where *ONP*'s English definition has been completed, only *CV*'s definitions are routinely provided here.

Following the presentation of each word and its definition, I offer some discussion of the item's use in context, based on examples from *ONP*'s supporting quotations. This contextual commentary aims to demonstrate something of the range and nuance of a word and/or differences between members of a word family. Other vocabulary terms are introduced here where relevant (highlighted in bold type), for instance when a quotation includes multiple words of interest and there is not space to analyse them all separately. Contexts that exemplify the phenomenon in question have been prioritised (e.g. examples of 'jokes' or other speech acts or actions). However, as should now be clear, this chapter is not primarily an analysis of the literary or narrative functions of 'humour' in Old Norse literature, nor primarily of how it works.[10] Rather, as stated above, its purpose is to highlight some of the Old Norse vocabulary for items that we might now label as 'humour' or a related term. In doing so it aims to highlight the problems and complexities of translation and interpretation from a linguistic and cultural context in which there are often no easy one-on-one correspondences with Modern English vocabulary and terminology, as well as to show where continuities with Modern English can be found.

**hlátr**, n.
47 citations. *ONP*: 'latter' [laughter]. *CV*: 'laughter'.
*Related words*: **hlæja**, vb. 80 citations. *CV*: 'to laugh'; **hlœgja**, vb. 12 citations. *CV*: 'to make one laugh'; **hlœgi**, 7 citations. *CV*: 'ridicule'; **hlœg(i)liga**, adv. 2 citations. *CV*: 'ridiculously'; **hlœg(i)ligr**, adj. 13 citations. *CV*: 'ridiculous, laughable'.

Though a conflation between laughter and humour has been a persistent hindrance both to historical studies of humour and to humour studies more widely, that their relationship is not simply a straightforward one of effect from a cause is by now widely accepted.[11] Nonetheless, terms for laughter are clearly relevant to a consideration of humour in historical texts, and have already received considerable attention in the context of Old Norse, particularly as part of a literary trope. Due caution as to what textual representations of laughter might signify is expressed by Sif Rikhardsdottir in her recent book *Emotions in Old Norse Literature*. She emphasises that:

> physiological responses are […] misleading when understood as kinetic reactions and need instead to be contextualised and interpreted as a performative gesture. The smile or laughter in this case becomes a signifying token intended not to articulate emotive interiority but to convey a narrative message.[12]

Kirsten Wolf takes a similar approach, but points out that 'nonetheless, one must assume that this literary laughter would seem to have had at least some affinity with the reality of laughter in medieval Iceland for it to be properly understood'.[13] Laughter is often socially performative, and literary laughter, mediated by an author, doubly so. Saga laughter should not be taken as a straightforward indicator of the presence of 'humour', yet neither should the two be separated entirely.

In 1978–1979 M. I. Steblin-Kamenskij differentiated between 'directed' laughter, in which there is a target that is laughed at or ridiculed, and 'non-directed' laughter, where there is no such object.[14] He asserted, somewhat flying in the face of the available evidence, that 'directed' laughter is 'of comparatively recent origin' and thus that any instance of ridicule, satire, mocking and suchlike in Old Norse texts was 'meant to provoke mirth' and to 'have merely entertainment value'.[15] Hugh Magennis, on the other hand, suggested in 1992 that 'scornful laughter is the most characteristic kind of laughter found in Old Norse and other heroic poetry',[16] which Wolf later found also to be true for Old Norse prose, in the most extensive (article-length) treatment of Old Norse laughter to date.[17] Wolf categorises c. 80 instances of laughter in the Sagas of Icelanders into the following groups: an expression of joy or relief, an expression of triumph or scorn, an expression of defiance, a way of camouflaging discomfort, and a reflection of folly. Laughter as an expression of amusement, as a reaction to a joke or something funny, is notably absent here. There is, however, some overlap between amusement and scorn, where a target is made the butt of a joke. Indeed, echoing three of the common 'theories' of or explanations for humour, Wolf reports that 'scornful or mocking laughter […] is often prompted by the juxtaposition of things that do not fit together, and surprise is frequently a condition'.[18]

The Old Norse lexicon does not radically distinguish laughter based on its cause or intention (whether it is 'directed' or 'non-directed'; 'laughing at' or 'laughing with'), in the way that, for example, Latin and Greek can.[19] Nonetheless, it was possible to signal specific types of laughter. **Brigzlanahlátr** is found in a religious text to denote 'scornful laughter' (*ONP*; cf. **brigzli**, 90 citations; *ONP*: (i) 'reproach (for s[ome]th[ing].) (from s[ome]b[od]y), recrimination, denigration, insult'; (ii) 'ignominy, shame, disgrace'; (iii) '(of a person) object of scorn, disgrace (to sby)'). In Old Icelandic law, 'Ef maðr bregðr manne brigzlom' [if someone makes a defamatory statement against someone else], the penalty was lesser outlawry (three years' exile).[20]

Elsewhere, **kaldahlátr** is used in *Njáls saga* during Hildigunnr's efforts to get her kinsman Flosi to avenge the death of her husband: as Flosi negotiates Hildigunnr's intentions, we are told, 'Hildiguðr hló kaldahlátr' [Hildigunnr laughed cold laughter].[21] This is not laughter prompted by amusement, but by bitter determination. **Skellihlátr** (4 citations) does not give any clues to the provocation of the laughter but rather describes its manifestation: roaring laughter.

The compound **athlátr** (9 citations; *ONP*: 'mockery, ridicule') would seem from its form to denote 'targeted' laughter, literally meaning 'at-laughter' or 'towards-laughter'. Rather than denoting a type of physiological behaviour, however, it has a metaphorical application indicating taunting or jeering. For example, one instance from the *Heilagra feðra æfi* [Lives of the Holy Fathers] has St John speak to the devil 'sem med nockurs konar athlatri' [as with certain kinds of *athlátr*].[22] That the *athlátr* can take various forms suggests that it is not physiological but verbal. The related **athlǿgi** (12 citations; *ONP* (i) 'ridicule, derision'; (ii) 'source of amusement, object of derision') functions like English 'laughing stock', as for example in this instance from *Gautreks saga*: 'Þá er [Refr] var ungr, lagðizt hann í elldaskála ok beit hrís ok bǫrk af trjám […] Refr varð frægr mjǫk at ǫngum snotrleik né frama, helldr því at hann gjǫrði sik athlægi annarra sinna hraustra frænda' [When Refr was young he lay by the fire and chewed twigs and bark from trees … Refr became very famous not for any wise acts or distinction, but rather because he made himself a laughing stock (*athlægi*) among his other, more intrepid kinsmen].[23]

The two citations of the adverb **hlǿg(i)liga** (*CV*: 'ridiculously') appear in context to denote amusement rather than derision. *Fagrskinna* relates the aftermath of a battle thought to have taken place c. 985, between a Norwegian force led by Hákon *jarl* [earl] Sigurðarson, and an invading Danish army, on whose behalf the semi-legendary band of mercenaries known as the Jomsvikings are fighting. Though such a battle probably did take place, the saga does not provide an eye-witness account but, like many sagas, blends oral tradition and poetic source-material with authorial licence. The Jomsvikings are known in this text and elsewhere as having a strict code of conduct based around ideals of bravery and strength. We join the story as the victorious Norwegians are executing the surviving Jomsvikings:

> Því næst var einn til hǫggs leiddr ok mælti svá: 'Hrútr!' Þeir spurðu: 'Hví mælir þú svá?' Hann svaraði: 'Mǫrg á hefir af yðrum mǫnnum nefnd verit í dag, ok vil ek því fá hrútinn til'. Þetta þótti mælt hlægiliga ok óhræðiliga. Jarlinn spurði, ef hann vildi grið, ok lézk hann vilja.[24]

> Next thing one was led forward to be struck executed and spoke thus: 'Ram!' They asked, 'Why do you say that?' He answered, 'Many a ewe has been named by your men today, and for this reason I want to give them the ram'. That was

48    H. BURROWS

thought to be said *hlœgiliga* and fearlessly. The *jarl* [Eiríkr, Hákon's son] asked if he would want quarter, and he said he did want that.

Alison Finlay explains the humour succinctly: 'The word *á*, accusative of *ær* "ewe", is also an exclamation, "ow!"'. The young man's pun implies that the Norwegians cried out with pain in the battle'.[25] As badly as this witticism flops in translation, the narratorial comment, 'Þetta þótti mælt hlœgiliga ok óhræði-liga' [That was thought to be said *hlœgiliga* and fearlessly], suggests that the saga compiler had his own problems grappling with historic humour and thought that even his native-speaking audience might fail to be moved by, or even notice, the Jomsviking's joke. Jarl Eiríkr is impressed, however, as he grants the young man his life.[26]

Finlay, the saga's most recent translator, renders the narrative interjection slightly more periphrastically, if more idiomatically in English: 'That was considered a funny and fearless thing to say'.[27] The adverbial construction is difficult to translate literally; to derive the meaning of the adverb from the verb, we would end up with something like: 'That was bravely and "laugh-causingly" said'. The other instance of the same adverb, which occurs in the Flateyjarbók manuscript of *Magnúss saga góða ok Haralds harðráða*, produces a similar result. The saga claims that the Byzantine empress Zoe (lived c. 978–1050) asks for a lock of hair from King Haraldr harðráði of Norway, who at that time is going by the pseudonym Norðbrigt. Norðbrigt/Haraldr replies that to make things equal, she should give him one of her pubic hairs. Again the narrator explains, 'Þetta þotti hlægliga mællt uera og þo diarfliga vid þuilika konu' [This was thought to be 'laugh-causingly' said, and yet boldly, to such a woman].[28] *CV*'s definition seems to me inadequate here: although there is an element of mockery in the humour of both instances, the tone suggested by Finlay's 'funny' is clearly appropriate. There is more than just scorn in these utterances, and the speakers of the 'jokes' are admired for their quick and bold wit and wordplay.

Wolf takes the verb **glotta** (24 citations; *CV*: 'to grin') to be essentially synonymous with *hlæja*.[29] This premise works in terms of an examination of performative gesture and certainly seems to overlap with *hlæja* in terms of its literary function. Old Norse literature's most famous grinner is Skarpheðinn Njálsson of *Njáls saga*, whose unsettling facial expression is notorious for its 'mirthless content'.[30] It commonly appears in the phrase *glotta við tǫnn*, defined by *CV* 'to smile scornfully, sarcastically, so as to shew the teeth'. In *Karlamagnúss saga*, the phrase 'Karlamagnus kongr glotti' [King Charlemagne *glotti*] in the A redaction appears in the B redaction as 'Karlamagnus kongr brosti' [King Charlemagne smiled], suggesting a similarity between the two gestures.[31] Interestingly, however, in a late manuscript of *Gibbons saga*, AM 585c 4to of c. 1700, we find, 'þä glotte dvergr hatt, so bulde j klettunum' [then the dwarf *glotti* ('glotte') loudly, so it echoed in the crags].[32] In this instance there appears to be a vocal element to the gesture. Indeed, other, earlier redactions have 'skeller d(vergr) vpp <og> hlær' [the dwarf kicked up his heels and laughed].[33]

Perhaps physiognomic verisimilitude is less important in the usage of this word than the attitude behind it. As Low concludes, 'in O[ld] I[celandic] *glott* there is none of the warmth of shared amusement; the tone is one of contempt for fools not suffered'.[34]

> **skem(m)tun/skem(m)tan**, n.
> 142 citations. *ONP*: (1) 'underholdning, fornøjelse, tidsfordriv, festivitas, glæde' [entertainment, pleasure, pastime, festivities, joy]; (2) '(om seksuel forlystelse)' [(about sexual amusement)]; (3) 'pragt, overdådighed, herlighed' [splendour, opulence, glory]; (4) 'jubel, jubelråb' [jubiliation, cheer]. *CV*: 'an entertainment; amusement, entertainment'.
> *Related words*: **skemmta**, vb. 83 citations. *CV*: 'to amuse, entertain'; **skemmtanarsamligr**, adj. 2 citations. *CV*: 'amusing'; **skemmtiliga**, adv. 1 citation. *CV*: 'amusingly, pleasantly'; **skemmtiligr**, adj. 38 citations. *CV*: 'amusing, interesting, pleasant'.

*Skemmtan* is related to *skemma*, 'to shorten', giving the sense 'pastime, diversion'. It covers a broad range of entertainments or 'amusements', such as hunting, shooting, wrestling, drinking, feasting, dancing, board games, and story-telling. It is not often connected to humour specifically, although an instance in (most manuscripts of) *Heimskringla* demonstrates it could be used to refer to amusement in that (humorous) sense. The captured jarl Finnr Árnason is offered truce by King Haraldr Sigurðsson, but refuses to accept it '"af hundinum þínum"' ['from a dog like you'].[35] He is asked whether he will accept it from Haraldr's son, Magnús, but replies '"Hvat mun hvelpr sá ráða griðum?"' ['Why would that puppy be offering truces?'].[36] The narrator then states: 'Þá hló konungr ok þótti skemmtan at erta hann' [Then the king laughed and thought it amusing (*skemmtan*) to tease him].[37] Whether it is Finnr's canine-themed responses that the king finds funny, or simply the opportunity to humiliate his opponent, is not clear.

In the Frískók manuscript of *Heimskringla* (AM 45 fol), *gaman* (see below) stands in place of *skemmtan* here, suggesting an overlapping if not (near-) synonymous meaning in this context. Similar variation between manuscripts occurs in a handful of *ONP's* other *skemmtan* citations. The two words are also juxtaposed in a number of instances. While these cases might suggest the words have similar but not identical meanings, precise distinctions are difficult to draw based on the contexts in question, and the terms may instead be collocated for emphasis, for example: '"Segja mun ek þér þriðja æventýr þér til gamans ok skemtanar"' ['I will tell you three romances for your amusement and pleasure'].[38] Further comparison with *gaman* will be made in the discussion of that word, below. The prefix *skemmtanar-* forms several, rarely attested compounds, such as **skemmtanarmaðr** [entertaining man] and **skemmtanarferð** [pleasure trip].

50    H. BURROWS

**gaman**, n.
136 citations. *ONP*: (i) 'fun, amusement, pleasure'; (ii) '(a form of) entertainment (for others), play'; (iii) '(of erotic exploits)'. *CV*: 'game, sport, pleasure, amusement'.
*Related words*: **gamansamligr**, adj. 11 citations. *CV*: 'amusing'; **gamanssamr**, adj. 6 citations. *CV*: 'gamesome, merry'.

Like Modern English 'amusement', *gaman* covers a range of meanings from something that is funny to a diverting entertainment or pastime. An example of the former, more humour-related sense can be found in *Njáls saga*, when the eponymous Njáll gives his friend Gunnarr advice on how to dissolve his kinswoman's marriage by tricking her husband into thinking he is legally inept. Njáll advises Gunnarr initally to make a mess of legal terminology: '"Þá mun Hrútr hlæja ok þykkja gaman at"' ['Then Hrútr will laugh and find amusement in it'].[39] The collocation with *hlæja* [to laugh] (see above) reinforces the interpretation of *gaman* here as suggesting funniness.

By contrast, an instance in *Egils saga* demonstrates the other end of the 'amusement' spectrum, cautioning against uncritically taking the word *gaman* as a possible indicator of the presence of humour: 'var þá mest gaman Egils at ræða við [Þordís]' [It was then the greatest pleasure of Egill's to speak with Þordís]. At this point in the saga, Egill is in his eighties and blind: he takes pleasure in conversing with his stepdaughter, not in laughing at or teasing her.

*Gaman* forms part of a variety of compounds, each rarely attested in the corpus. These include, by way of illustrative examples, **gamanferð** (2 citations; *CV*: 'pleasure trip'); **gamanleikr** (6 citations; *CV*: 'a game'); **gaman(s)vísa** (4 citations; *CV*: 'comic ditty'). Of particular interest is **gamanmál** (3 citations; *CV*: 'merry talk, joking'). Like English 'joking', the word seems to cover a range from 'making jokes' to 'not being serious'.

One instance comes in *Jómsvíkinga saga* to highlight another of the Jomsvikings' fearless responses to Norwegian capture. This young man, who has long golden hair, asks that someone hold it out of the way while he is executed so that it does not become bloodstained. As his executioner strikes, the Jomsviking jerks his head so that the sword instead falls onto the man holding his hair, severing his arms at the elbow. 'En hann sprettr up enn ungi maðr ok bregðr á gamanmál ok mælti: "hverr á sveina", segir hann, "hendr í hári mér?"' [He sprang up, the young man, and took to joking (*gamanmál*) and said, 'To which boy', he says, 'do the hands in my hair belong?'].[40] The lighthearted implications of the word—the Jomsviking is joking rather than being scornful—emphasise his blithe detachment from the horrors of combat.

In an example from *Laxdæla saga*, *gamanmál* rather conveys a lack of seriousness than something actually funny. Two brothers are witnessed plotting what turns out to be an attack, and are asked what they are discussing: '"þat muni hvárki hégómi ne gamanmál, er þit munuð lengstum um tala"'[41] ['it will be neither nonsense nor joking around (*gamanmál*), when you spend so long talking about it'].

## 3 NO SENSE OF HUMOUR? 'HUMOUR' WORDS IN OLD NORSE    51

*Gaman* appears in a variety of phrases, such as **hafa gaman/hafa at gamni/ hafa til gamans** 'to have (as) entertainment', **henda gaman** 'to take pleasure in' and **þykkja gaman** 'to find (something) fun/amusing'. It can indicate that something is to be taken as a joke, that is not seriously, rather than as an insult (or that someone chooses to react in such a way), for instance in *Þorgils saga skarða*. Þorgils has been accused in the strongest possible terms of behaving unmanfully: the word *ragr* is used, a term over which the target had the right to kill with impunity in Icelandic law.[42] Instead of challenging his interlocutor, however, Þorgils says, "'[Hart] þotti [mér] þv at mer kveða [...] ok veit ek, [at] þer var þat gaman, en engi alhvgi, ok þvi tek [ek] þat firir gaman'" ['It seems to me you have spoken harshly, but I know that it was in jest, and not your innermost conviction, and so I will take it as a joke'].[43]

In several texts it is collocated with **gleði** (162 citations; *ONP*: (i) 'happiness, gladness, joy, glee'; (ii) '(in conn. with festivity) merriment, festivity, amusement, entertainment'), for example in the *Norwegian Homily Book*: 'þar er gleði ok gaman með guði siolfum' [in that place is joy and pleasure with God himself].[44] Overall, most instances of the word suggest the broader senses of pleasure and amusement than the specifically humorous. However, *gaman* seems more likely than the similar *skemmtan* (see above) to be used when something is not only fun but funny.

> **leikr**, n.
> 325 citations. *ONP*: (i) 'forlystelse, tidsfordriv, underholdning' [amusement, pastime, entertainment]; (ii) '(om musikalsk tidsfordriv: sang, dans, spil)' [(about musical activities: singing, dancing, playing)]; (iii) 'nydelse, fornøjelse' [enjoyment, pleasure]; (iv) '(item pl. *leikar*) organiseret kampleg, dyst, stævne' [(in plural, *leikar*) organised fight, jousting, contest]; (v) 'konfrontation, kamp, slagsmål' [confrontation, fight, brawl]; (vi) '(om ridderturnering)' [(in relation to knights' tournaments)]; (vii) 'det at lege, (børne)leg' [to play, (children's) play]; (viii) '(om ondskabsfuld leg)' [(in relation to malicious play)]; (ix) '(med seksuel undertone) elskovsleg, flirt' [(with sexual undertones) lovemaking, flirting]; (x) '(om noget der foregår ubesværet, som en leg)' [(in relation to something effortless, like a breeze)]; (xi) 'trolddom, trylleri' [sorcery, magic]; (xii) 'spot, skæmteri, spøg' [mockery, joke, jest]; (xiii) 'forløb, procedure, gerning, handling' [course, procedure, deed, action]. *CV*: 'a game, play, sport'.
> *Related words*: **leika**, vb. 483 citations. *CV*: 'to play, sport'; 'to delude, play a trick on'; 'to perform'; 'to move, swing'; 'to lick, of flame, to catch'; 'to be [...] bewitched'; 'to ill-treat, vex'; in various phrases/forms with specific meaning; **leikandi**, adj. 2 citations. *CV*: 'a sport, jest'; **leikari**, n. 42 citations. *CV*: 'a player, esp. a fiddler, jester'; **leikaraskapr**, n. 4 citations. *CV*: 'scurrility, histrionic manners'; **leikinn**, adj. 15 citations. *CV*: 'playful, gay'.

The number of definitions put forward by *ONP* gives a good indication of the range of this word; the ones most relevant to this chapter are definitions (i) and (xii), and they will be focused on here.

52   H. BURROWS

In the citations under *ONP's* definition i, *leikr* is used in a similar way to *skemmtan* and *gaman* (see above). Indeed, it is several times used in conjunction or interchangeably with *skemmtan* in particular. For instance, in the *Gylfaginning* section of Snorri's *Edda*, Gangleri asks: "'Eða hvat er skemtun einherjanna þá er þeir drekka eigi?'"[45] ['What is the entertainment of the Einherjar [Odin's army] when they are not drinking?']. The response, that they fight, is followed: "'Þat er leikr þeira'" ['That is their pastime'].[46] In four of *ONP's* citations it is collocated with *hlátr* [laughter] (see above), but those cases give a sense of general merriment.

The phrase **gera leik** can imply 'to make a joke (of something or someone)', but it does not necessarily do so. For instance, in *Þorgils saga ok Hafliða*, one Grímr is physically weak and ill-matched in sports against stronger and rougher contenders, for which he receives 'gár ok gys' [derision and mockery].[47] The narrator relates: 'Grímr ræðir, at þeim væri þat lítilmenska at gera hann at athafnarmannin ok gera leika til hans' [Grímr said that it was mean of them to turn him into a laughing stock and make a joke (*gera leika*) of him].[48] Compare, however, the following instance of the phrase in *Bósa saga ok Herrauðs*: 'hirðin hafði soppleik […] ok gerðu þeir nú leik til Bósa' [the kings' men had a ballgame … and they directed the play (*gerðu … leik*) now towards Bósi].[49] There is no element of mockery in the latter instance; the phrase utilises the more common meaning of *leikr* as referring to sport, game, or play.

Other citations highlight the difficulty caused where context is ambiguous. An interesting case occurs in *Bárðar saga Snæfellsáss*. A flock of sheep belonging to the farmer Þorbjǫrn goes missing and cannot be found. Þorbjǫrn asks his father-in-law Skeggi for advice, who replies, "'þat hafa troll tekit einhver, ok hafa huldu yfir; mun þat ekki öðrum vinnast en sonum þínum, at ná því aptr, þvíat til þeirra mun leikr gerr'" ['trolls have taken them and made them hidden; it will be the case that no-one apart from your sons will be able to get them back, because *leikr* will be aimed at them'].[50] For this last clause, containing *leikr*, the standard English translation of the sagas says simply 'this is all aimed at them'.[51] *Leikr* could be translated as 'deed or action' (cf. *ONP* sense xiii), or as 'pastime' (sense i), but the sense 'joke' or 'prank' works equally well if taken as a comment on the trolls' motivation or perspective.

In an instance in *Fóstbrœðra saga*, a search is made of people's trunks to attempt to discover some property that has gone missing. A character called Vegglagr objects to being searched like a thief, to which the response is: "'Þetta er ecki til eins manz leikr gerr, þvi at varar kistvr hafa fyst verið ransakaðar'" ['This *leikr* is not done only to one man, because our chests have been searched with willing permission'].[52] The standard translation of the first clause reads, 'You're not the only one in this […]'.[53] Equally, it could be translated, 'This jest is not done only to one man […]'. Although the situation is taken seriously by all participants, the latter reading subtly changes the tone of the response to a more sarcastic one that acknowledges that all are involved in a game-like situation where the stakes are high and no-one is having much fun. The published translations are not incorrect, but opportunities to consider grim humour in these situations, very much in keeping with the sort of understated black humour found across the saga corpus, are lost in them.

> **glens**, n.
> 28 citations. *ONP*: 'fun, jest, gibing, mockery'; *CV*: 'gibing, fun, a gibe, jest'.
> Related words: **glensa**, vb. 7 citations. *CV*: 'to jest, gibe'; **glensan**, n. 1 citation.
> *CV*: 'gibing'; **glensligr**, adj. 2 citations. *CV*: 'gibing';

*ONP* notes that 'the word covers a wide range of meanings from "innocent fun" to "mockery"'. Interestingly this word often seems to function like 'joke' does in the Modern English phrase 'it was only a joke', when someone is trying to claim or explain that they did not intend offence. Whether or not the actual 'humour' is fun(ny) or malicious often remains ambiguous. For example, in *Heiðarvíga saga*, a woman throws a cushion at her husband 'sua sem með glenzi' [as if it were a joke];[54] the situation rapidly escalates into domestic violence and divorce. A good illustration that the word was used to signal a contrasting intent to mockery comes in an incident from *Óláfs saga Tryggvasonar en mesta* (AM 61 fol), in a passage containing several humour words. The context is that Þorkell *dyðrill* [tail], the uncle of King Óláfr Tryggvason, has been spying on the king, who is known to leave his ship at night without anyone seeing him do so. Þorkell suddenly finds himself seized and thrown into the harbour while wearing expensive clothes, including a fine fur-and-velvet cloak:

> Þá mælti konungr er hann saa at Þorkell leít aa skickiuna. hvat er nv frændi. huart hefir vóknat dydrillinn þinn. Þorkeli þotti hann spotta sik ok suar(aði) engu. en kastaði af ser skickiuni helldr hermiliga. konungr m(ælti). Ver eɴ kátr ok glaðr frændi. þviat ek gerði þetta fyrir glennz ok gaman. en ekki til haðungar við þik.[55]

> Then the king said, when he saw that Þorkell was looking at the cloak, 'What is it now, kinsman? Has your tail got wet?' Þorkell thought he mocked him and did not reply but cast the cloak off rather angrily. The king said, 'Be cheerful and glad again, kinsman, because I did this for fun and amusement, and not out of scorn for you'.

Whether or not we (never mind Þorkell) would class throwing someone into a body of water as 'innocent fun', the word *glens*, here found in conjunction with *gaman* (see above) and opposed to *háðung* (see below), is clearly meant to convey a sense of something lighthearted and funny—'banter' might be a good rendering, with a (purported) intention of 'laughing with' as opposed to 'laughing at'.

The narrator of Flateyjarbók's redaction of *Óláfs saga Tryggvasonar* uses *glens* to point out that potentially malicious words are said jokingly, although again, whether the parties involved really believe the truth of the claims (and therefore whether the jokes are meant to ridicule rather than tease mildly) is left ambiguous. In this instance, a mysterious, well-built red-bearded stranger (who turns out to be the god Þórr [Thor]) comes aboard King Óláfr's ship and begins play-wrestling with the king's men. In addition, 'uæittu huorir ôdrum j glenzse hadulig ord ok athlatr' [they exchanged with each other in fun (*'j glenzse'*) abusive words and ridicule].[56] The episode turns out to be a cautionary tale about failing to recognise demons in attractive guise.

> **fleymingr**, n.
> 11 citations. *ONP*: 'hån, spot, latterliggørelse, sjov'. *CV*: 'jest, sport'.
> *Related words*: **fleymi**, 1 citation. *CV*: 'jest, sport'.

In context, many instances of *fleymingr* carry a sense of mocking one-upmanship and perhaps a satirical tone. In *Íslendinga saga*, the servant of Sighvatr Sturluson's wife Halldóra kills a rival to Sighvatr's household, and we are told, 'Sighvatr hafði miok i fleymingi, oc kallaði svmrvngana odóla, oc ekki radligt at hallda kavpi þeira' [Sighvatr made great sport of it, and said summer-workers to be difficult, and that it was not advisable to buy them].[57] Drawing on stereotypes about temporary itinerant workers, Sighvatr pretends to be critical when in fact the servant did exactly what he had hoped for. His ironic distancing of himself from the killing smugly draws attention to the fact that he has got what he wants but is untouchable for it. (On the other hand, Guðrún Nordal has pointed out that Sighvatr often hides behind jokes or pretends to take things *í fleymingi* (as a joke) 'whenever he is most deeply moved'.[58])

*Laxdæla saga* has a poignant example that suggests people did not react well to being the target of such jesting attitudes. In a sequence of romantic entanglements, Kjartán is gifted a fine headdress by his Norwegian princess lover to give to Guðrún, his childhood sweetheart back in Iceland, as a wedding present. However, his friend Bolli has told Guðrún about Kjártan's relationship with the princess, and she marries him instead. Kjartán turns his attention to Hrefna and gives her the headdress as a bridal gift. Guðrún, realising it was meant for her, is jealous of the headdress and secretly steals and destroys it. Discovering the theft, Kjartán goes to Bolli's household to humiliate them by preventing them from leaving the house for three days. Upon his return, the saga tells us:

> Þá mælti Hrefna ok brosti við: 'þat er mér sannliga sagt, at þit Guðrún munið hafa við talazk, ok svá hefi ek spurt, hversu hon var búin, at hon hefði nú faldit sik við motrinum ok semði einkar vel'. Kjartan svarar ok roðnaði mjǫk við—var mǫnnum auðsynt, at hann reiddisk við, er hon hafði þetta í fleymingi.[59]

> Then Hrefna said with a smile, 'I was reliably informed that you and Guðrún had a chat, and I also heard how she was dressed: that she'd wrapped herself in the headdress and it suited her exceptionally well'. Kjartán answered and went very red—it was obvious to people that he was angry that she made sport of this (*hafði þetta í fleymingi*).

Hrefna is battling with (justified) insecurity that Kjartán still loves Guðrún: her words, disguised as a joke, test her husband, revealing her suspicions about Guðrún's involvement in the disappearance of the headdress and looking for reassurance both that he did not speak to Guðrún and that he is willing to criticise his former sweetheart. For his part, Kjartán's reaction reveals his hidden heartbreak and his inability to emotionally side with Hrefna over Guðrún. Neither of them can take any real amusement in the situation: *fleymingr* captures the bitter irony of this situation in which no-one is happy.

> **háð**, n.
> 42 citations. *ONP*: 'hån, spot' [scorn, mockery, derision]. *CV*: 'scoffing, mocking'.
> *Related words*: **háðsamr**, adj. 4 citations. *CV*: 'scoffing'; **háðsemi**, n. 4 citations. *CV*: 'mockery'; **háðuligr**, adj. 53 citations. *CV*: 'scornful, contemptible'; **háðuliga**, adv. 43 citations. *CV*: 'shamefully'; **háðung**, n. 78 citations. *CV*: 'shame, disgrace'.

Probably the most famous instance of the word *háð* comes in Snorri Sturluson's Prologue to *Heimskringla*, his collection of sagas about the kings of Norway. He aims to dispel doubt about the validity of using poetry composed by the kings' own court praise-poets as reliable sources of history:

> En þat er háttr skálda at lofa þann mest, er þá eru þeir fyrir, en engi myndi þat þora at segja sjálfum honum þau verk hans, er allir þeir, er heyrði, vissi, at hégómi væri ok skrǫk, ok svá sjálfr hann. Þat væri þá háð, en eigi lof.[60]

> It is the habit of poets to praise most the person they are standing before, but no-one would dare to relate to his face deeds that everyone in hearing would know to be falsehoods and inventions, as would he himself. That would then be mockery, and not praise.

Nonetheless, Snorri's nephew Óláfr Þórðarson cites just such a practice that Snorri claims not to exist in his definition of *ironia* [irony] in his *Third Grammatical Treatise*, a work on poetry based on Latin textbooks:

> Jronia gerir gagn-staðlict mál þvi, er hon vill merkia [...] her er oæiginlig framfæring ok liking, þviat lof ær fyrir háði sætt. Þessi figvra ær iafnan sætt i skalldskap.[61]

> Irony gives the opposite meaning to what is denoted [...] here there is improper translation and comparison, because praise is used for mockery. This figure is frequently used in poetry.

Indeed, *háð* often occurs in connection with poetry, but that is less likely to indicate anything inherent about the form of *háð* and more likely because poetry was a key means of communication and entertainment, which tended to be exploited for the purpose of insulting one's rivals. The practice of composing poetic praise in order to mock someone (*til háðungar*, see further below)

56  H. BURROWS

is condemned on penalty of outlawry in *Grágás*, the Icelandic law code used up to c. 1271.[62]

In Modern Icelandic *háð* still means 'irony'.[63] In Old Norse it seems also to have a broader range of meanings, including what we might rather classify as sarcasm, parody, and satire, but it often involves false representations. In *Gunnlaugs saga*, Gunnlaugr comes across a mock-duel in which the participants have been given the names Gunnlaugr and Hrafn (Hrafn is Gunnlaugr's poetic and romantic rival, and the pair had earlier fought a famous but inconclusive duel). The players are said to 'hyggi smátt' [strike weakly] and Gunnlaugr 'fann at hér fylgdi mikit háad ok her var mikit spott at dregit' [found that there was great *háð* and much ridicule was taken from it].[64] The use of both *háð* and *spott* (see below) here suggests they may have had different shades of meaning, and *háð* might best be translated here as parody or even farce.

On the other hand, *háð* is several times collocated with *spott* (see below) or **gabb** (56 citations; *CV*: 'mocking, mockery'), possibly for emphasis rather than for contrast.[65] Where the action or speech act in question is not described, it is not possible to say for sure whether 'mockery' broadly or something more specific is meant; however, when more detailed context is given, a more particular meaning than the dictionaries suggest can be ascertained, denoting a false representation with the intention to mock.

**Háðung** has a still broader range and carries a more emphatically derogatory force. One could prosecute or be prosecuted for it under Icelandic law; in *Grágás*, 'Ef maðr mælir við maɴ háðung eða gerir ýki vm' [if a man speaks with mockery (*háðung*) against someone or makes an exaggeration about him] the penalty is lesser outlawry (three years' exile)].[66] Actions such as shaving someone's hair off, tearing their clothes, making them dirty, or 'allt þat er maðr gørir til haðungar avðrom mann huernge veg er hann feʀ at þvi' [everything that someone does in mockery of another whatever way he goes about it] are subject to full outlawry.[67] There are specific regulations about the composition of poetry: one is not to take offence about a couplet 'nema last mæle se í' [unless there is defamatory speech in it], but if two people conspire together to each compose two lines and put them together, the penalty is full outlawry 'ef löstr er i eða haðung' [if defamation or mockery is in it].[68] Even composing poetry about someone else 'þot eigi se háþung i' [though there is no mockery in it] is subject to either a fine or lesser outlawry, depending on the length of the composition.[69] The penalty is increased to full outlawry if there is *háðung* in it, as is also the case for spreading poetry 'er til haðungar metz' [if it is deemed in mockery].[70] In the later law-code *Járnsíða*, *háðung* is collocated with **heipt/heift** (55 citations; *CV*: 'deadly hatred, spite'), and with **níð** (39 citations; *CV*: 'contumely' [invective, defamation, opprobrium], 'a libel'), a particularly heinous form of insult.[71] It is difficult to draw lines here around what may be considered under the umbrella of 'humour' and what is simply abuse.

**spott**, n.
79 citations. *ONP*: 'drilleri, spot, forhånelse, hån' [teasing, mockery, scoffing, derision, scorn]. *CV*: '"sport", mock, scoff'.
*Related words*: **spotta**, vb. 61 citations. *CV*: 'to mock, make sport of'; **spottsamr**, adj. 4 citations. *CV*: 'mocking, sporting'; **spottsamligr**, adj. 3 citations. *CV*: 'mocking'.

Despite the similarity to Modern English 'sport', the words are not etymologically related; the Scandinavian forms are related to 'spit (upon)', although the Old Norse usage is already metaphorical. The Modern Icelandic means 'mockery, ridicule', with the phrase *hafður að háði og spotti* meaning 'made the butt of jokes'.[72]

In some instances the word is used to describe incidents of trickery or insincerity; fooling or making a fool out of someone. For instance, in *Heimskringla* King Aðalsteinn of England sends a valuable sword by messenger to King Haraldr in Norway, who takes it by the hilt. The messenger immediately responds that Haraldr has, with this gesture, made himself a retainer of Aðalsteinn's. The text comments: 'Haralld konungr skildi þa at þetta var með spotti gert til hans. þviat hann uilldi engis mannz þegn uera' [King Haraldr realised that this was done in mockery (*með spotti gert*) towards him, because he wished to be no man's retainer].[73] In *Fóstbrœðra saga*, the character Þormóðr requests to buy an old, rag-tag and louse-ridden cloak from the vagrant Lusa-Oddi [Oddi Louse]. Thinking there could be no reason for the wealthy merchant Þormóðr to want his cloak and that his request must be insincere, Oddi replies, '"Eigi þarftv at spotta at mer?"' ['Do you have to make fun of me?'].[74] Þormóðr reassures him, '"Eigi er þetta spott"' ['This is not making fun'];[75] he needs the cloak as a disguise.

On other occasions, however, the word has a more inclusive sense. An interesting example in *Íslendinga saga* uses *spott* in connection with the enemies of Snorri Sturluson making fun of his poetry: 'Svndlendingar drogo spott mikit at kvędvm þeim, er Snori hafdi ort vm iarllinn, ok snoro afleiðiz' [The southerners drew great sport from these verses that Snorri had written about the *jarl* and distorted them].[76] An example is given of one of the parodic verses composed in mockery of Snorri, which plays on the words and concepts used in his original poem.

Elsewhere in *Íslendinga saga*, *spott* appears as a catch-all term for various forms of mockery and disparagement performed by one party against a rival: 'Ok her með færðv Breidbælingar Lopt i flimtan, oc gerðo vm hann danza marga oc margskonar spott annat' [The Breiðbælings also taunted Loptr in lampoons (*flimtan*, see below), and made up many dance-lyrics about him and many other kinds of mockery (*spott*)].[77] The word **danz** (25 citations; *ONP*: 'dancing, dance (prob. with singing)'; 'dance-lyric, ballad'] here suggests that comic songs were composed and performed as accompaniment to dancing. *CV* suggests that in this sense *danz* is synonymous with *flimt(an)*, on which see below. Compare **hopp** (10 citations; *ONP* 'dans, lystighed, tant og fjas' [dance, merriment, pleasurable activity]) and **mansǫngr** (8 citations; *CV*: 'love song'),

58    H. BURROWS

which was banned in Icelandic law, and which Edith Marold has comprehensively investigated in connection to obscene and/or offensive songs or dance-ballads.[78]

*Spott* could certainly describe a form of mockery that could be deeply offensive: Guðrún Nordal observes that it is used in all four instances in *Íslendinga saga* 'where serious mockery in poetry becomes a source for conflict'.[79]

> **skaup**, n.
> 16 citations. *ONP*: 'spot, hån' [mockery, ridicule]. *CV*: 'mockery, ridicule'.

Of the many words denoting mockery in Old Norse, *skaup* is highlighted here because its Modern Icelandic form, *skop*, is translated as 'humour'.[80] (The other word so translated, *kímni*, is not attested in Old Norse before 1700 according to *ONP*.) It can securely be understood as having exclusively mocking or derisive force in Old Norse, however. It is frequently collocated with *skǫmm* [shame] and used synonymously or as a variant for *spott* and *fleymingr* (see above). In an instance in *Vatnsdœla saga*, it is contrasted with less malicious forms of humour: 'Þorkell kvað meiri kurteisi at láta gleði ok gamanræður koma í mót beinleika en skaup eða atyrði' [Þorkell said it would be more courteous to meet hospitality with merriment and good cheer rather than with *skaup* or abusive words].[81]

> **flimtun/flimtan** n.
> 7 citations. *ONP*: '(oftest på vers) spot, hån [(most often about verse) mockery, ridicule]'. *CV*: 'a lampooning, quizzing, satire'.
> *Related words*: **flim/flím/flimt/flimtr**, n. 'a lampoon, libel (in verses)' (7 citations); **flimberi**, n. 'a flouter [one who mocks]' (1 citation); **flimska**, n. 'mockery' (1 citation); **flimta**, vb. 'to flout, lampoon' (8 citations); **flimtari**, n. [one who mocks] (1 citation).

As the dictionary definitions suggest, *flim* and *flimtun* refer to mocking verses. They seem to differ from verses that could be described as *háð* in that those verses have double meanings or offer ironic praise in order to highlight the failings of the target, whereas a *flimtun* is straightforwardly critical. In terms of form, the word can describe both short, simple ditties (e.g. *Morkinskinna* st. 21), and sophisticated compositions in complex skaldic metres (e.g. *Egils saga* st. 8).

Although its use as synonymous with *danz* (see above; also *Þórðar saga kakala* ch. 29) suggests an entertaining aspect, it is not always clear whether the translation of 'lampoon' or 'satire', suggesting as it does an element of humour, is accurate in every case.[82] Of course, this difficulty could be a result of modern audiences lacking details necessary to 'get the joke', but in some cases there are few markers or contextual clues to suggest that humour is intended.[83] Take for example an instance in *Njáls saga*. We are introduced to Þórhildr skáldkona [poetess], who is said to be 'orðgífr mikit, ok fór með flimtan' [a word-witch and went about composing *flimtun*s].[84] At a wedding,

## 3 NO SENSE OF HUMOUR? 'HUMOUR' WORDS IN OLD NORSE    59

Þórhildr's husband Þráinn begins eyeing up the teenage daughter of the bride. Þórhildr 'reiðisk' [became angry] and composes the following couplet (*kviðlingr*, see below):

Era gapriplar góðir,
gægir er þér í augum.[85]
Gawpers aren't good; goggling is in your eyes.

At this, Þráinn jumps up and declares himself divorced from her, saying 'vil ek eigi hafa flimtan hennar né fáryrði yfir mér' [I won't have any more of her *flimtun*s or acrimonious words hanging over me].[86] Þráinn insists that he will not stay at the feast while she is present, and Þorhildr leaves (or is sent away). We are then told, 'ok nú sátu menn hverr í sínu rúmi ok drukku ok váru kátir' [and now everyone sat in their own seat and drank and were cheerful]. Intent to critique and to highlight a flaw is apparent in the verse, but whether it is done in a humorous way seems doubtful. The alliteration and wordplay (Þórhildr uses two words not otherwise attested in this form) could suggest humour, but those are both intrinsic features of most Norse poetry and so would not automatically assume a comic effect. Þórðr juxtaposes the word *flimtun* with *fáryrði* [acrimonious words], which has little implication of humour. Furthermore, it appears that no-one present finds the exchange funny; people become 'cheerful' after the incident has died down and the festivities recommence. It should not be assumed, then, that the label *flimtun/flimtan* offers an indication of the presence of satire as we understand it in Modern English.

Compare here **kviðlingr**, n. (21 citations; *CV*: 'a ditty, esp. of a satire or lampoon'), which is sometimes used synonymously with *flimtun*. ONP specifies it as a 'digt bestående af én strofe' [poem comprised of one stanza]. In this case the word describes the form rather than the content: a *kviðlingr* is not necessarily mocking in intent, though in practice, the examples recorded often are so (see the example under *kverskiyrði*).

> **kerski/kerska**, n.
> 8 citations. *ONP*: (1) 'spøg, vittighed' [prank, joke]; (2) 'glæde, lyksalighed' [joy, bliss]. *CV*: 'cheerfulness, mirth, fun'.
> *Related words*: **kerskifimr**, adj. 1 citation. *CV*: 'witty'; **(all-)kerskiligr**, adj. 1 citation. *CV*: 'very sarcastic, biting'; **kerskilæti**, n. 1 citation. Undefined; **kerskimál**, n. 4 citations. *CV*: 'a jest'; **kerskimáll**, adj. 1 citation. *CV*: 'facetious'.

In the Hauksbók redaction of *Hervarar saga ok Heiðreks*, the seventh of eight pieces of advice given to King Heiðrekr by his father is: 'at eiga jamnan kerski við komanda gest' [always to have *kerski* with a newly-arrived guest].[87] To translate *kerski* as 'cheerful conversation' works well here, although as Christopher Tolkien observes, this counsel might have been added to the story to foreshadow a later plot-point in which Heiðrekr gives a poor welcome to the god Óðinn [Odin] in disguise, and later attacks him, for which he is cursed by

60    H. BURROWS

Óðinn.[88] There is a nice double meaning in the choice of word, since in-between these events Óðinn and Heiðrekr compete in a riddle-match. *Kerski*, and the advice, could be equally well understood as the more specific 'always exchange witticisms with a newly-arrived guest'. In this case, there is an indication that a riddle could be classed as *kerski*.

The citation for **kerskiyrði** (1 citation. *CV*: 'jokes' [*lit. kerski*-words]) in *Þorgils saga ok Hafliða*, part of the *Sturlunga saga* collection of so-called contemporary sagas, relates to a tantalising episode containing several humour words. In an account of a wedding feast in Reykjahólar, Iceland, which took place in 1119, people are drinking heavily and 'hverr stingi annan nǫkkuru hnæfilyrði, ok er þó fátt hermt at þeira keskiyrðum í þessari frásögn' [each stings the others with taunting words, but little is reported of their *kerskiyrði* in this account].[89] Although the narrator appears to be holding out on his audience here, some at least of their *kerskiyrði* are recounted, and it is worth quoting more of this episode at length. To provide some necessary context, the wedding is attended by, amongst others, two notable chieftains: the local chieftain Þorgils Oddason and one from another district, Þórðr Þorvaldsson. The guests are seated along two long benches, with Þórðr and his retinue opposite Þorgils and his, which includes a priest named Ingimundr and a man named Óláfr Hildisson, who has been outlawed but given three years to leave the country and is under Þorgils' protection. We learn that Þórðr suffers from various health issues, including a condition that makes it difficult for him to eat meat, and gives him rather bad breath. In what follows, humour words are highlighted in bold on their first occurrence.

> Þess er getit, at Ingimundr prestr laut at sessunaut sínum ok mælti við hann, svá sem hinn spyrði:
>
>> 'Hvaðan kennir þef þenna?      Þórðr andar nú handan'.
>
> Ok verðr at **hlátr** mikill, ok er næsta gerr at þessu **gyss** mikill, ok er því léttir, þá kveðr Þórðr í mot:
>
>> 'Andi es Ingimundar      ekki góðr á bekkjum'.
>
> Ok af þessum **ákǫstum** tekr heldr at grána **gamanit**, ok koma **kviðlingar** við svá. Þá var þetta kveðit til Þórðar:
>
>> 'Rymr i barka          glitar skallinn við
>> ríkismanni,            á goða yðrum'.
>
> Hér hlær Þórðr mjǫk at þessum kveðlingi ok kveðr þegar í móti:
>
>> 'Vaxa blástrar         raunillr gerisk þefr
>> á bekk þaðan           af ropum yðrum'.
>
> Þorgils **brosti** nú at, en lagði aldri til um akǫstin. Ingimundr mælti, at nǫkkur þeira bekkjunauta skyldi sjá í móti við Þórð. Þá var þetta kveðit:

## 3 NO SENSE OF HUMOUR? 'HUMOUR' WORDS IN OLD NORSE   61

| | |
|---|---|
| 'Þat es válítit | Reptir Þórðr |
| þótt vér reptim | Þorvalds sonr, |
| búðunautar | Kjartans sonar |
| af bolakjǫtvi. | af kana sínum'.[90] |

It is mentioned that Ingimundr the priest bowed towards his benchmate and spoke to him as if he'd asked a question:

| | |
|---|---|
| 'Where does this smell come from? | Þórðr breathes now from there'. |

And much laughter arose at this, and the next thing is much mockery is made of it, and when it lightens off Þórðr says this in response:

| | |
|---|---|
| 'Ingimundr's breath | is not good for the bench'. |

And from these taunts the entertainment begins to grow coarse, and ditties came forth. Then this was said to Þórðr:

| | |
|---|---|
| 'Din in the windpipe | the bald head shines at it: |
| of the powerful man; | that of your chieftain [i.e. Þórðr]'. |

Here Þórðr laughs greatly at this ditty and says immediately in response:

| | |
|---|---|
| 'The blasts of breath increase | the smell gets very bad |
| onto the bench from there; | from your belches'. |

Þorgils now smiled at that, but put nothing forward in response to the taunt. Ingimundr said that some other of their benchmates should respond to Þórðr. Then this was said:

| | |
|---|---|
| It is harmless | Þórðr belches – |
| though we belch, | son of Þórvaldr |
| we booth-mates, | son of Kjartan – |
| from beef. | from his food-bowl. |

This latter verse turns out to have been uttered by the outlaw Óláfr Hildisson. Þórðr asks the hosts to send Óláfr away; Þorgils, as the local chieftain, refuses to allow this to happen, saying Þórðr may leave if he wishes but that Óláfr is under his protection. Þórðr and his party leave, to the accompaniment of two more insulting verses being recited, and this departure is thought to be 'íbrosligt' [comical (lit. 'smilable')].[91]

The word *kerskiyrði* in the opening to this exchange signals the presence of a type of 'humour', and the descriptions of laughter suggests that the verses were well received. But what is a modern audience to make of the nature of that humour? Leaving aside the fact that much of the 'humour' described here seems somewhat juvenile ('you stink'), if not merely cruel (given that the taunts

62    H. BURROWS

levelled at Þórðr seem to be true),[92] the dynamics of this encounter are complex, and somewhat obscure. Why does Þórðr take such offence at Óláfr's verse but not before?

We know that poetry was particularly potent because of its memorability and ease of transmission (proven in that verse is what is recorded in the saga, above more prosaic exchanges). We also know that couplets, such as the two exchanged between Þórðr and Ingimundr, are not to be seen as offensive. According to the law at least, Þórðr could perhaps have chosen to take offence at the four-line *kviðlingr*, but he is able to give as good as he gets (cf. the genre of **senna**, or exchange of poetic insults).[93] What is likely to have caused such umbrage in Óláfr's verse is that not only Þórðr but his father and grandfather are named in it. There is no hiding who the verse is about; it brings shame to three generations of his family. Since Þórðr does not immediately know who the author of the verse is, he is unable to retaliate in kind. And finally, Óláfr is of lower social standing than Þórðr and an outlaw (legally, a non-person). To be bested by an inferior would have lowered Þórðr's own status, and honour, considerably.

## CONCLUSIONS

The well-known cliché that there are 50 so-called 'Eskimo' words for snow is controversial,[94] but it barely seems so to conclude in this investigation that there are at least approaching 50 Old Norse words for 'mockery'. Many of these now survive in only one or two citations, and it is impossible here for reasons of space and lack of data to analyse them in further depth. To list just some of those further words—and I restrict myself here to nouns: *ákǫst, dár, dáruskapr, frýja, fyndi, gabb, gár, gletta/glettr, gymbing, gyss, hróp, hæðni, hnæfilyrði, kalls, skalk, skeitun, skelkni, skeypi, skimp, skopun, skǫll, skúti, spé, spýting*. Modern English does not have an adequate vocabulary to be able to translate all these words and their shades of meaning differently: we have to make do, in most cases, with 'mockery'. Then there are words such as *skǫmm* [shame], *skaði* [scathe, harm, damage], *hatr* [hatred, spite, animosity], and the legal category *fullréttisorð* [words requiring full personal compensation], which in English and in contemporary Western contexts we would instinctively be likely to categorise as different from 'humour'; but clear lines are often difficult to demarcate. If even the most heinous insult is delivered in a clever, inventive, and witty way, or is formally recognisable as having a 'joke' structure, it is not humour? If it makes people (if not the target) laugh, is it not humour? And of course, the very obscene or offensive may be found funny precisely *because* it is outrageous or taboo.[95] These issues throw up a methodological problem in a semantic study of 'humour words': what should be included and what should be left out?

Such gradation was a problem for the honour culture of early Scandinavian society, too.[96] Stephen Halliwell writes (of ancient Greece, but the point is transferable):

the need to know how (to try) to distinguish between insults and jokes, together with an awareness of how easily the latter might slip into or be mistaken for the former, was a matter for recurrent unease in a culture where the dynamics of maintaining or losing status (or impugning the status of others), of suffering or avoiding shame (or wielding its public power against others), were so fundamental.[97]

For speakers of Old Norse, in most cases linguistic labels would perhaps not have helped much with this distinction. Manifestations of the speech acts and actions examined in this chapter slide along the scale from benign to malignant; it is not always possible to predict whether a target will be amused or take offence, nor which reaction was intended. Old Icelandic law decreed *brigzli*, *lǫstr*, *níð*, and *háðung* to cross the line, but even then, in many cases these were not particular, clearly defined acts, but depended on whether or not *háðung* (*CV*: 'shame, disgrace') was *intended*, which remained subject to discretion. Society acknowledged that most types of mockery could be done or said 'fyrir glennz ok gaman [eða] til haðungar' [for *glens* and *gaman*, or for *háðung*].[98] A degree of subjectivity, of variable emotional reaction, is acknowledged even in the law. On name-calling, for instance—if someone is given a mocking nickname—the law prescribes a penalty of lesser outlawry 'ef hann vill reiðaz við' [if he (the target) wants to get angry about it].[99]

Certainly, to make something an offence in all senses of the word, legally and emotionally, is to make it a serious matter. However, that such instances are not benign and for that reason are not always found 'funny' is not necessarily to say they should not be considered as forms of 'historical humour'. Take Bremmer and Roodenburg's definition of humour as 'any message [...] intended to produce a smile or a laugh'.[100] Halliwell points out that 'there is no cogent reason to suppose that laughter erupts from, or is reducible to, a single type of feeling, mood, or psychic state'.[101] Whether a 'message' is intended to provoke a laugh of amusement, or of contempt or scorn or schadenfreude or anger, it would still fit Bremmer and Roodenburg's definition. For one thing, the laughter and emotional reactions of the target are likely to be very different from the laughter and emotional reactions of other audiences of the 'message'. For another, as we know, one person might feel amused by something that another finds only offensive or distateful or silly; that person might themselves feel different levels of amusement at any given time, depending on a host of other factors.

So what does all this mean for 'humour' as a conceptual category in early Scandinavia? I distinguish humour as a conceptual category here from humour as a phenomenon: clearly people joked, quipped, played with words, bantered, played pranks, engaged in whimsy and even self-deprecation, without animus towards others. Words for these activities are likely to be underrepresented in the extant written corpus, while mockery and insult, which tend to be more important to saga plotlines, are likely to be overrepresented. Ephemeral joking moments 'er [...] fátt hermt' [are little reported], as *Þorgils saga* puts it.[102]

Moreover, there are no theoretical treatises on 'humour' or laughter; much of what might be deemed 'humorous' is not explicitly labelled by authors and scribes.

From the evidence considered here we can envisage for Old Norse a category containing a spectrum with *glens* towards one end and *háðung* towards the other. *Níð, fullréttisorð*, and other forms of 'hate-speech' sit at the extreme, past *háðung*, noticeably different in degree but ultimately not fully separable or easily distinguished in form. Would puns and wordplay, say, be part of this category? Wordplay need not be funny, and so it is difficult to categorise even in the Anglophone concept of humour. It is a key feature of most Old Norse poetry and was clearly valued in its own right—but it could also be used in mockery, so intention and effect are as important to understand as they are in contemporary usage. The characteristic understatement of the sagas, often recognised as humorous by modern readers, could also find a place on the spectrum: there might not be a convenient Old Norse term for it, but in modern parlance, it often slides into 'throwing shade'.

It is difficult to think outside the tyranny of the umbrella term 'humour', but it is also difficult to propose an obviously different category or set of categories for early Scandinavia that would include or exclude items very differently to English. Perhaps it is easier to suggest a different 'focal point' for such a category. While we would perhaps think of 'funniness' and the 'emotion' or feeling of amusement at the centre of the Anglophone concept of 'humour' (and I acknowledge that not everyone will agree with me here), we could think of a form of 'mockery' and perhaps feelings of scorn at the centre of the early Scandinavian mental analogue. The Scandinavian concept might encompass more and more extreme forms of mockery, which might be pushed out of the Anglophone concept of 'humour' at a different point. A more comprehensive study than has been possible here would need to be undertaken to map such a category in full. However, this preliminary examination has suggested some of the methodological and conceptual complexities in considering 'humour' in non-Anglophone linguistic, cultural, and historical contexts and has begun to map the contours of the Old Norse 'sense of humour'.

## NOTES

1. See especially Condren, this volume. I am grateful to Ralph O'Connor for his helpful comments on a draft of this chapter.
2. See, for example Dixon, '"Emotion"'. See also Tierney-Hynes, this volume.
3. For example, Rosenwein, 'Emotion Words', 96–97.
4. Rosenwein, 'Emotion Words', 101; Wierzbicka, *Emotions.*
5. Halliwell, *Greek Laughter*, ix.
6. *ONP, User's Guide*, § I.D.i.
7. Ibid.
8. Items are presented with semantic considerations in mind, rather than in alphabetical order.

9. A revised edition, supplemented by W. A. Craigie, was produced in 1957, but I have been unable to access this work during the Covid-19 pandemic in 2020. In any case, since it is online, the older edition is the more widely accessible.

10. Such literary-critical studies for Old Norse specifically, which generally utilise modern terms for humour or subtypes of it, include: Abram, 'Trolling'; Anderson, 'Form'; Ashurst, 'Elements of Satire'; Ármann Jakobsson, 'Young Love'; Bartusik, 'Sarð'; Classen, 'Sarcasm'; Clover, 'Hárbarðsljóð'; van Dijk, 'Amused'; Durrenberger and Wilcox, 'Humor'; Grønlie, 'Preaching'; Jóhanna Katrín Friðriksdóttir, 'Gender'; Meulengracht Sørensen, 'On Humour'; McKinnell, 'Þórr as Comic Hero'; North, 'goð geyja'; Vésteinn Ólason, 'List og tvísæ'; Willson, 'Parody'.

11. See, for example Stewart, 'Laughter and the Greek Philosophers', 29.

12. Sif Rikhardsdottir, *Emotions*, 118.

13. Wolf, 'Laughter', 94.

14. Steblin-Kamenskij, 'On the History', 154. A division along similar lines is common; for other contexts cf. Burde, 'The *parodia*', 215; Halliwell, 'The Uses', 280.

15. Steblin-Kamenskij, 'On the History', 157, 160.

16. Magennis, 'Images of Laughter', 196.

17. Wolf, 'Laughter'.

18. Ibid., 98.

19. See, for example Burde, 'The *parodia*', 215.

20. Finsen, *Grágás: Islændernes Lovbog*, Ib, 182 (K §237).

21. Finnur Jónsson, ed. *Brennu-Njálssaga*, 264. All translations are my own unless explicitly stated otherwise in text.

22. Unger, *Heilagra*, II, 438.

23. Ranisch, *Die Gautrekssaga*, 26–27.

24. Bjarni Einarsson, *Ágrip-Fagrskinna*, 135.

25. Finlay, *Fagrskinna*, 107.

26. The story is told differently in *Jómsvíkinga saga*, where the narratorial comment is absent and the executioner is not amused, calling the Jomsviking 'manna armastr' [most wretched man] and putting him to death. Blake, *The Saga of the Jomsvikings*, 31.

27. Finlay, *Fagrskinna*, 107.

28. Guðbrandr Vigfússon and Unger, *Flateyjarbok*, 291.

29. Wolf, 'Laughter', 94; cf. Le Goff, 'Laughter', 162.

30. Low, 'The Mirthless'.

31. Loth, *Karlamagnús saga*, 288.

32. Page, *Gibbons saga*, 26.

33. Ibid. The late date of AM 585c 4to does not necessarily imply language change; modern Icelandic *glotta* means 'sneer, grin, smirk' (Sverrir Hólmarsson et al., *Íslensk-ensk orðabók: glotta*).

34. Low, 'The Mirthless', 102.

35. Bjarni Aðalbjarnarson, *Heimskringla III*, 154.

36. Ibid., 155.

37. Ibid.

38. Gering, *Islendzk æventyri*, 178.

39. Einar Ólafur Sveinsson, *Brennu-Njáls saga*, 61.

40. Normalised from af Petersens, *Jómsvíkinga saga*, 125.

41. Kålund, *Laxdæla saga*, 261.
42. See Meulengracht Sørensen, *The Unmanly Man*, especially 17–20.
43. Kålund, *Sturlunga*, II, 170–71.
44. Indrebø, *Gamal norsk Homiliebok*, 38.
45. Faulkes, *Prologue and Gylfaginning*, 34.
46. Ibid.
47. Kålund, *Sturlunga*, I, 23.
48. Ibid.
49. Jiriczek, *Die Bósa-Saga*, 7.
50. Guðbrandr Vigfússon, *Barðarsaga*, 28.
51. Anderson, 'Bard's Saga', 254.
52. Björn K. Þórólfsson, *Fóstbrœðra saga*, 93.
53. Regal, 'The Saga of the Sworn Brothers', 360.
54. Kålund, *Heiðarvíga saga*, 107.
55. Ólafur Halldórsson, *Óláfs saga*, 233.
56. Guðbrandr Vigfússon and Unger, *Flateyjarbók*, 397.
57. Kålund, *Sturlunga*, I, 355.
58. Guðrún Nordal, *Ethics*, 78.
59. Kålund, *Laxdæla saga*, 180.
60. Bjarni Aðalbjarnarson, *Heimskringla*, I, 5.
61. Ólsen, *Den tredje*, 113–14.
62. Finsen, *Grágás: Islændernes Lovbog*, Ib, 183 (K §238).
63. Sverrir Hólmarson et al., *Íslensk-ensk orðabók: háð*.
64. Finnur Jónsson, *Gunnlaugs saga*, 52.
65. On the borrowing of ON *gabb* into Old French and its development there, see Grigsby, *The Gab*, especially 7–29.
66. Finsen, *Grágás: Islændernes Lovbog*, Ib, 182 (K §237).
67. Finsen, *Grágás: Efter*, 380–81 (St §361).
68. Finsen, *Grágás: Islændernes Lovbog*, Ib, 183 (K §238).
69. Ibid.
70. Ibid.
71. On *nið* see especially Ström, *Nið*; Meulengracht Sørensen, *The Unmanly Man*.
72. Sverrir Hólmarson et al., *Íslensk-ensk orðabók: spott*.
73. Ólafur Halldórsson, *Óláfs saga*, I, 15.
74. Björn K. Þórólfsson, *Fóstbrœðra saga*, 169.
75. Ibid.
76. Kålund, *Sturlunga*, I, 51.
77. Ibid., 342.
78. Marold, '*Mansǫngr*'. On later Nordic comic ballads see Hansen, this volume.
79. Guðrún Nordal, *Ethics*, 172.
80. Sverrir Hólmarson et al., *Íslensk-ensk orðabók: skop*.
81. Finnur Jónsson, *Vatsdælasaga*, 100.
82. For discussion of the requirement of an element of humour in the definition of satire, see Marshall, *The Practice of Satire*, 2.
83. Cf. Derrin's introduction to this volume.
84. Einar Ólafur Sveinsson, *Brennu-Njáls saga*, 87.
85. Ibid., 89.
86. Ibid.

87. Jón Helgason, *Heiðreks saga*, 37.
88. Tolkien, *Saga Heiðreks konungs*, xvi.
89. Kålund, *Sturlunga*, I, 19–20.
90. Ibid., 20.
91. Ibid., 21.
92. Even if mockery (*brigzli*) were true it was subject to lesser outlawry in *Grágás*. See Finsen, *Grágás: Islændernes Lovbog*, Ib, 182 (K §237).
93. On the *senna* see, for example Abram, 'Trolling'; Swenson, 'Performing Definitions'; Harris, 'The *senna*'.
94. See, for example Krupnik and Müller-Wille, 'Franz Boas'.
95. See for instance Blake, 'Taboo Language'.
96. On the honour culture of early Scandinavia, see, for example Meulengracht Sørensen, *Fortælling og ære*.
97. Halliwell, *Greek Laughter*, 25.
98. Ólafur Halldórsson, *Óláfs saga*, 233.
99. Finsen, *Grágás: Islændernes Lovbog*, Ib, 182 (K §237).
100. Bremmer and Roodenburg, *A Cultural History*, 1.
101. Halliwell, *Greek Laughter*, 10–11.
102. Kålund, *Sturlunga*, I, 19.

## Bibliography

Abram, Christopher. 'Trolling in Old Norse: Ambiguity and Incitement in *Sneglu-Halla þáttr*'. In *Words that Tear the Flesh: Essays on Sarcasm in Medieval and Early Modern Literature and Cultures*, edited by Alan Baragona and Elizabeth L. Rambo, 41–62. Berlin: De Gruyter, 2018.

Anderson, Philip N. 'Form and Content in *Lokasenna*: A Re-evaluation'. In *The Poetic Edda: Essays on Old Norse Mythology*, edited by Paul Acker and Carolyne Larrington, 139–58. London: Routledge, 2002.

Anderson, Sarah M., trans. 'Bard's Saga'. In *The Complete Sagas of Icelanders Including 49 Tales*, edited by Viðar Hreinsson, 5 vols, II, 237–66. Reykjavík: Leifur Eiríksson, 1997.

Ashurst, David. 'Elements of Satire and Social Commentary in Heathen Praise Poems and Commemorative Odes'. In *Social Norms in Medieval Scandinavia*, edited by Jakub Morawiec, Aleksandra Jochymek and Grzegorz Bartusik, 75–90. Amsterdam: Amsterdam University Press/Arc Humanities Press, 2019.

Ármann Jakobsson. 'Young Love in Sagaland: Narrative Games and Gender Images in the Icelandic Tale of Floris and Blancheflour'. *Viking and Medieval Scandinavia* 10 (2014): 1–26.

Bartusik, Grzegorz. '*Sarð hann yðr þá eigi Agði?* Humour and Laughter in the *Sneglu-Halla þáttr*'. In *Histories of Laughter and Laughter in History: HistoRisus*, edited by Rafał Borysławski, Justyna Jajszczok, Jakub Wolff and Alicja Bemben, 119–38. Newcastle-upon-Tyne: Cambridge Scholars, 2016.

Bjarni Aðalbjarnarson, ed., *Heimskringla*. 3 vols. Íslenzk fornrit 26–28. Reykjavík: Hið íslenzka fornritafélag, 2002.

Bjarni Einarsson, ed., *Ágrip-Fagurskinna*. Íslenzk fornrit 29. Reykjavík: Hið íslenzka fornritafélag, 1985.

Björn K. Þórólfsson. *Fóstbrœðra saga*. STUAGNL 49. Copenhagen: Jørgensen, 1925–27.

68  H. BURROWS

Björn Magnússon Ólsen. *Den tredje og fjærde grammatiske afhandling i Snorres Edda tilligemed de grammatiske afhandlingers prolog og to andre tillæg.* STUAGNL 49. Copenhagen: Knudtzon, 1884.

Blake, Barry J. 'Taboo Language as Source of Comedy'. In *The Oxford Handbook of Taboo Words and Language*, edited by Keith Allen, 353–71. Oxford: Oxford University Press, 2019.

Bremmer, Jan and Herman Roodenburg, eds. *A Cultural History of Humour: From Antiquity to the Present Day.* Cambridge: Polity Press, 1997.

Burde, Mark. 'The *parodia sacra* Problem and Medieval Comic Studies'. In *Laughter in the Middle Ages and Early Modern Times Epistemology of a Fundamental Human Behavior, Its Meaning, and Consequences*, edited by Albrecht Classen, 215–42. Berlin: De Gruyter, 2010.

Classen, Albrecht. 'Sarcasm in Medieval German and Old Norse Literature: From the Hildebrandslied to Fortunatus: The Dark Side of Human Behavior'. In *Words that Tear the Flesh: Essays on Sarcasm in Medieval and Early Modern Literature and Cultures*, edited by Alan Baragona and Elizabeth L. Rambo, 249–69. Berlin: De Gruyter, 2018.

Clover, Carol. '*Hárbarðsljóð* as Generic Farce'. *Scandinavian Studies* 51, no. 2 (1979): 124–45.

*CV* = Cleasby, Richard and Gudbrand Vigfússon, eds. *An Icelandic-English Dictionary.* Oxford: Clarendon, 1874.

Dijk, Conrad van. 'Amused by Death? Humour in *Tristrams saga ok Ísoddar*'. *Saga-Book* 32 (2008): 69–84.

Dixon, Thomas. '"Emotion": The History of a Keyword in Crisis'. *Emotion Review* 4, no. 4 (2012): 338–44.

Durrenberger, E. Paul and Jonathan Wilcox. 'Humour as a Guide to Social Change: *Bandamanna saga* and Heroic Values'. In *From Sagas to Society: Comparative Approaches to Early Iceland*, edited by Gísli Pálsson, 111–24. Enfield Lock: Hisarlik, 1992.

Einar Ólafur Sveinsson, ed. *Brennu-Njáls saga.* Íslenzk fornrit 12. Reykjavík: Hið íslenzka fornritafélag, 1954.

Faulkes, Anthony, ed. *Snorri Sturluson: Edda. Prologue and Gylfaginning.* 2nd ed. London: Viking Society for Northern Research, 2005.

Finlay, Alison, trans. *Fagrskinna, A Catalogue of the Kings of Norway: A Translation with Introduction and Notes.* Leiden: Brill, 2004.

Finnur Jónsson, ed. *Brennu-Njálssaga (Njála).* Halle: Niemeyer, 1908.

Finnur Jónsson, ed. *Gunnlaugs saga ormstungu.* STUAGNL 42. Copenhagen: Møller, 1916.

Finnur Jónsson, ed. *Vatsdælasaga.* STUAGNL 58. Copenhagen: Jørgensen, 1934.

Finsen, Vilhjálmur, ed. *Grágás: Efter det Arnamagnæanske Haandskrift Nr. 334 fol., Staðarhólsbók.* Copenhagen: Gyldendal, 1879.

Finsen, Vilhjálmur, ed. *Grágás: Islændernes Lovbog i Fristatens Tid, udgivet efter det Kongelige Bibliotheks Haandskrift.* 2 parts (Ia, Ib). Copenhagen: Berling, 1852.

Gering, Hugo, ed. *Islendzk æventyri/Isländische Legenden Novellen und Märche.* 2 vols. Halle: Buchhandlung des Waisenhauses, 1882–83.

Grigsby, John. *The Gab as a Latent Genre in Medieval French Literature: Drinking and Boasting in the Middle Ages.* Cambridge, MA: Medieval Academy of America, 2000.

Grønlie, Siân. 'Preaching, Insult and Wordplay in the Old Icelandic *kristniboðsþættir*'. *Journal of English and Germanic Philology* 103, no. 4 (2004): 458–74.

Guðbrandur Vigfússon, ed. *Bárðarsaga Snæfellsáss, Víglundarsaga, Þórðarsaga, Draumavitranir, Völsaþáttr.* Copenhagen: Berling, 1860.

Guðbrandur Vigfússon and C. R. Unger, eds. *Flateyjarbok: En Samling af norske Konge-Sagaer med indskudte mindre Fortællinger om Begivenheder i og udenfor Norge samt Annaler.* 3 vols. Christiania, Oslo: Malling, 1868.

Guðrún Nordal. *Ethics and Action in Thirteenth-Century Iceland.* Odense: Odense University Press, 1998.

Halliwell, Stephen. *Greek Laughter: A Study of Cultural Psychology from Homer to Early Christianity.* Cambridge: Cambridge University Press, 2008.

Halliwell, Stephen. 'The Uses of Laughter in Greek Culture'. *The Classical Quarterly* 41, no. 2 (1991): 279–96.

Indrebø, Gustav, ed. *Gamal norsk Homiliebok: Cod. AM 619 4°.* Oslo: Dybwad, 1931.

Jiriczek, Otto Luitpold, ed. *Die Bósa-Saga in zwei Fassungen nebst Proben aus den Bósa-Rímur.* Strasboug: Trubner, 1893.

Jóhanna Katrín Friðriksdóttir. 'Gender, Humor, and Power in Old Norse-Icelandic Literature'. In *Laughter, Humor, and the Unmaking of Gender: Historical and Cultural Perspectives,* edited by Anna Foka and Jonas Liliequist, 211–28. New York: Palgrave Macmillan, 2015.

Jón Helgason, ed. *Heiðreks saga: Hervarar saga ok Heiðreks konungs.* STUAGNL 48. Copenhagen: Jørgensen, 1924.

Krupnik, Igor and Ludwig Müller-Wille. 'Franz Boas and Inuktitut Terminology for Ice and Snow: From the Emergence of the Field to the "Great Eskimo Vocabulary Hoax"'. In *SIKU: Knowing Our Ice: Documenting Inuit Sea-ice Knowledge and Use,* edited by Igor Krupnik, Claudio Aporta, Shari Gearheard, Gita J. Laidler and Lene Kielsen Holm, 377–400. Dordrecht: Springer, 2010.

Harris, Joseph. 'The *senna*: From Description to Literary Theory'. *Michigan Germanic Studies* 5 (1979): 65–74.

Kålund, Kristian, ed. *Heiðarvíga saga.* STUAGNL 31. Copenhagen: Møller, 1904.

Kålund, Kristian, ed. *Laxdæla saga.* STUAGNL 19. Copenhagen: Møller & Thomsen, 1889–91.

Kålund, Kristian, ed. *Sturlunga saga efter membranen Króksfjarðarbók udfyldt efter Reykjarfjarðarbók.* 2 vols. Copenhagen: Gyldendal, 1906–11.

Le Goff, Jacques. 'Laughter in *Brennu-Njals saga*'. In *From Sagas to Society: Comparative Approaches to Early Iceland,* edited by Gísli Pálsson, 161–66. Enfield Lock: Hisarlik, 1992.

Loth, Agnete, ed. *Karlamagnús saga: Branches I, III, VII et IX,* translated by Annette Patron-Godefroit with Povl Skårup. Copenhagen: Reitzel, 1980.

Low, Soon Ai. 'The Mirthless Content of Skarpheðinn's Grin'. *Medium Aevum* 65, no. 1 (1996): 101–08.

*ONP* = The Arnamagnæan Commission, eds. *Ordbog over det norrøne prosasprog/A Dictionary of Old Norse Prose.* Copenhagen: The Arnamagnæan Commission, 1989–. www.onp.ku.dk/onp/onp.php?

Magennis, Hugh. 'Images of Laughter in Old English Poetry, with Particular Reference to the "hleahtor wera" of *The Seafarer*'. *English Studies* 3 (1992): 193–204.

Marold, Edith. '*Mansǫngr* – A Phantom Genre?'. In *Learning and Understanding in the Old Norse World: Essays in Honour of Margaret Clunies Ross,* edited by Judy Quinn, Kate Heslop and Tarrin Wills, 239–62. Turnhout: Brepols, 2007.

Marshall, Ashley. *The Practice of Satire in England, 1658–1770.* Baltimore: The Johns Hopkins University Press, 2013.

McKinnell, John. 'Þórr as Comic Hero'. In *La Funzione dell'eroe Germanico: Storicita, Metafora, Paradigma. Atti del Congrevio Internazionale di Studio Roma, 6–8 Maggio 1993*, edited by Teresa Pàroli, 141–83. Rome: Il Calamo, 1995.

Meulengracht Sørensen, Preben. *Fortælling og ære. Studier i islændingesagaerne*. Oslo: Universitetsforlaget, 1995.

Meulengracht Sørensen, Preben. *The Unmanly Man: Concepts of Sexual Defamation in Early Northern Society*, translated by Joan Turville-Petre. Odense: Odense University Press, 1983.

Meulengracht Sørensen, Preben. 'On Humour, Heroes, Morality, and Anatomy in *Fóstbræðra Saga*'. *NOWELE: North-Western European Language Evolution* 21–22, no. 1 (1993): 395–418.

North, Richard. '*goð geyja*: The Limits of Humour in Old Norse-Icelandic Paganism'. *Quaestio* 1 (2000): 386–95.

Ólafur Halldórsson, ed. *Óláfs saga Tryggvasonar en mesta*. 2 vols. Editiones Arnamagnæanæ series A, 1–2. Copenhagen: Munksgaard, 1958–61.

Petersens, Carla F., ed. *Jómsvíkinga saga efter Arnamagnæanska handskriften N:o 291. 4:to*. STUAGNL 7. Copenhagen: Berling, 1882.

Ranisch, Wilhelm, ed. *Die Gautrekssaga in zwei Fassungen*. Berlin: Mayer & Müller, 1900.

Regal, Martin, trans. 'The Saga of the Sworn Brothers'. In *The Complete Sagas of Icelanders Including 49 Tales*, edited by Viðar Hreinsson, 5 vols, II, 329–402. Reykjavík: Leifur Eiríksson, 1997.

Rosenwein, Barbara. 'Emotion Words'. In *Le Sujet de l'émotion au Moyen Âge*, edited by Damien Boquet and Piroska Nagy, 93–106. Paris: Beauchesne, 2009.

Sif Rikhardsdottir. *Emotions in Old Norse Literature: Translations, Voices, Contexts*. Cambridge: D. S. Brewer, 2017.

Steblin-Kamenskij, M. I. 'On the History of Laughter'. *Mediaeval Scandinavia* 11 (1978–79): 154–62.

Stewart, Zeph. 1994. 'Laughter and the Greek Philosophers: A Sketch'. In *Laughter Down the Centuries*, edited by Siegfried Jakel and Asko Timonen, 3 vols, I, 29–36. Turku: Turun yliopisto, 1994–97.

Ström, Folke. *Níð, Ergi and Old Norse Moral Attitudes*. London: Viking Society for Northern Research, 1974.

Sverrir Hólmarsson, Christopher Sanders, and John Tucker. *Íslensk-ensk orðabók/Concise Icelandic-English Dictionary*. Reykjavík: Iðunn, 1989.

Swenson, Karen. *Performing Definitions: Two Genres of Insult in Old Norse Literature*. Columbia: Camden House, 1991.

Tolkien, Christopher, ed. and trans. *Saga Heiðreks konungs ins vitra/The Saga of King Heidrek the Wise*. London: Nelson, 1960.

Unger, C. R., ed. *Heilagra manna søgur: Fortællinger og legender om hellige mænd og kvinder*. 2 vols. Christiania, Oslo: Bentzen, 1877.

Vésteinn Ólason. 'List og tvísæ í Snorra Eddu'. *Gripla* 12 (2001): 41–65.

Wierzbicka, Anna. *Emotions across Languages and Cultures: Diversity and Universals*. Cambridge: Cambridge University Press, 1999.

Willson, Kendra. 'Parody and Genre in Sagas of Icelanders'. In *Á austrvega: Saga and East Scandinavia. Preprint Papers of the 14th International Saga Conference, Uppsala, 9th–15th August 2009*, ed. Agneta Ney, Henrik Williams and Frederik Charpentier Ljungqvist, 2 vols. Gävle: Gävle University Press, 2009, II, 1039–46.

Wolf, Kirsten. 'Laughter in Old Norse-Icelandic Literature'. *Scripta Islandica* 51 (2000): 93–117.

CHAPTER 4

# Rewriting Laughter in Early Modern Europe

*Lucy Rayfield*

In the 1534 letter prefacing his fantastical tales of the giant Gargantua, the great doctor, priest and comedian François Rabelais wrote: 'Rire est le propre de l'homme' [laughter is what makes us human].[1] Although this claim did not go undisputed, laughter was generally considered by early modern thinkers to be a marker of the human.[2] Far less, however, had been decided about what laughter could tell us *about* being human. This question was taken up by a wide range of humanists—including rhetoricians, physicians, philosophers and performers—with increasing urgency throughout the sixteenth century. As we shall see throughout this chapter, Renaissance thinkers made a significant and meaningful intervention to theories about humour, proposing innovative approaches to the subject and testing out their many ideas in a variety of literary forms. With a focus on sixteenth-century England, France and Italy, this chapter draws on a range of these forms—such as jestbooks, comic plays, short stories and medical treatises—to provide a broad survey of early modern theoretical approaches to humour and also to consider humour and laughter in practice. This work thus brings together a set of historically distant thinking about humour, evaluating the varied and complex engagement of early modern writers with laughter and the laughable.

In exploring the Renaissance engagement with humour and laughter, this chapter follows three main lines of enquiry. Firstly, it provides a paradigm case study of a history of humour 'theory', rather than focusing on humour itself. Secondly, it considers in turn the three best-known modern humour theories—of superiority, incongruity and relief—foregrounding the challenge of

L. Rayfield (✉)
University of Oxford, Oxford, UK
e-mail: lucy.rayfield@mod-langs.ox.ac.uk

© The Author(s), under exclusive license to Springer Nature
Switzerland AG 2020
D. Derrin, H. Burrows (eds.), *The Palgrave Handbook of Humour, History, and Methodology*, https://doi.org/10.1007/978-3-030-56646-3_4

surveying early modern laughter by showing that Renaissance humour theory exceeds the three modern categories in different ways. Finally, this chapter reveals the uniqueness of early modern thinking about humour. It brings to light, for example, the intense interest in the effects as well as the causes of laughter; it also focuses on the rhetorical culture that contextualises those interests, addressing the many mixed and conflicting notions about humour and the inescapable sense of rewriting the classical past. Scholars such as Daniel Ménager and Indira Ghose have demonstrated the importance of considering laughter in its sixteenth-century context, but many others have considered Renaissance laughter only from a modern perspective. This chapter shows that while there is contiguity between early modern thinking about laughter and the three modern categories, there is also distance. Historical humour theory can only be brought into sharper focus if we identify and engage with its historical and contextual distinctness.

## SUPERIORITY THEORY AND THE EARLY MODERN

In a well-known paradox, humanist thinkers sought to create new works by relying on their ancient counterparts, harking back to the past in order to look forward to new and innovative ideas and writings. Many scholars (John Morreall, Rod Martin and Joel Elias Spingarn, to name but a few) have thus jumped from Aristotle to Hobbes without considering any new thinking about laughter in between and concluding that early modern thinking about laughter can be summed up by 'the little that Aristotle says on the subject';[3] that is, that all early modern laughter theory falls under the category of superiority.[4] Certainly, in Renaissance humour theory we do find repeated a number of Aristotelian statements which could be labelled as such: for instance, the idea that it is natural for humans to laugh at 'any fault or mark of shame'.[5] However, it is likely that these ideas derived not from Aristotle but from his commentators, such as Donatus and Guido Juvenalis.[6] Other classical authorities, too, were more explicit than Aristotle when discussing superiority in laughter: Plato in the *Philebus* (c. 400 BCE) suggests that comedy is enjoyed through malicious gloating over the problems of others (we might term this today *schadenfreude*);[7] Cicero in his *De Oratore* (55 BCE) claims that the laughable (the *ridiculus*) is always caused by ugliness or immorality (*turpitudo*);[8] and Quintilian in the *Institutio Oratoria* (95 CE) underscores the fine line between laughter (*ridere*) and derision (*deridere*).[9] It would thus be wrong to suggest that Aristotle was the sole—or even the main—source of inspiration for early modern writers discussing superiority in laughter. As we shall see, many also expanded ancient thought to consider the nuances of this particular sense of superiority or even to promote it as a useful rhetorical device.

We can identify a range of early modern 'superiority theorists' across Europe. No doubt the most widely cited is Thomas Hobbes (1588–1679), who in his 1651 *Leviathan* describes how laughter always emanates from a perceived superiority over another person, action or object. Yet Hobbes's theories were pre-empted by a number of other English writers: Philip Sidney (1554–1586) in his *Defence of Poesie* (1580) promotes the idea of malicious laughter, provoked by ugliness (*deformitas*) and scorn;[10] in his 1621, *Anatomy of Melancholy* Robert Burton (1577–1640) also discusses in equal terms the laugh and the 'scoffe'.[11] Although Nietzsche famously despised Thomas Hobbes for his attempts to undermine laughter, judging his attitudes to be characteristically straight-laced and English,[12] the notion of laughter as an expression of superiority was prominent in numerous other cultures. In France, the physician Laurent Joubert (1529–1582) suggests in his groundbreaking 1579 *Traité du Ris* [Treatise on Laughter] that laughter is only ever evoked by the ugly or unseemly: 'Tout ce qui est ridicule […] est quelque chose laide ou messeante' [everything laughable … is ugly or immoral].[13] In Italy, Niccolò Machiavelli (1469–1527) equates laughter at one's own favourable situation with laughter at another's hardships: 'Ridi tu perché hai bene o perché un altro ha male?' [Are you laughing because you are doing well or because another is doing badly?].[14] Baldassare Castiglione (1478–1529) in *Il Cortegiano* [The Courtier], his ubiquitous 1528 guide to the principles of courtiership, advises the aspiring courtier on how often to use laughter as an expression of derision: 'Il termine e misura del far ridere mordendo bisogna ancor esser diligentemente considerate, e chi sia quello che si morde' [the bounds and limits of derisive laughter must be diligently considered, as must the object of this laughter].[15] In the '*Peroratio*' of the lengthy 1598 treatise *De risu, ac ridiculis* [On laughter, and the laughable] by Celso Mancini (1542–1612), the author is so specific as to identify miserliness as the vice worthiest of scorn and therefore laughter.[16] The potential of superiority to manifest itself as laughter was widely put into practice, in contexts such as the sixteenth-century stage. Elizabethan clowning culture, for instance, created a series of caricatures—for example the country bumpkin newly arrived in London—which provoked laughter through unconcealed scorn in many audiences of seasoned city-dwellers.[17]

There were many more antecedents to Hobbes's theory. Indeed, the sense of superiority that laughter could provoke was often deliberately exploited as a canny rhetorical tool; it was, for instance, thought to be a highly effective means of insulting or humiliating a rival. The jestbook of papal secretary Poggio Bracciolini (1380–1459) is an infamous example of such weaponised laughter in the early Renaissance, indiscreetly pointing out the vices and offenses of various adversaries, using supposedly secret stories that he had overheard in the antechambers of the secretariat.[18] Practical jokes were a popular means of humiliating rivals, and many had their emphasis on causing *turpitudo*, or ugliness, with the intention of inciting laughter among onlookers. Italian secretbooks, for example, included advice on how to make one's rival fall asleep when eating dinner at a banquet, or how to dye their hair an unsightly colour.[19] It was also common practice for servants to be instructed to turn on water fountains just as their master's enemy had reached the desired position, soaking them in front of the entire party; Montaigne, for example, was once humiliated by this particular joke.[20] Laughter as an expression of superiority could be used to ridicule entire nations, as well as individual rivals, thus communicating a sense of supremacy over the culture in question. More's satirical epigram on Lalus, the would-be French courtier who attempts to behave in the French style but is able only to speak French with an exaggerated English accent, is an example of laughter as an expression of English superiority over the French culture.[21] Similarly, the French mocked the Italianised courtier: Joachim Du Bellay (1522–1560), in his 1553 poem 'Contre les Pétrarquistes' (Against the Petrarchists), ridicules the artificial language used by the Italians at the French Court; Jacques Grévin's comedy *Les Esbahis* (1561) also depicts the boastful and duplicitous Italian soldier Pantaleoné as so unpopular with his fellow Frenchmen that they beat him and chase him from the stage. Laughter was tested as a means of expressing superiority in a wide range of cultural practices, from literature (Luigi Pulci's 1483 *Morgante*, to name but one example, derided the chivalric romance)[22] to architecture (see Inigo Jones's notorious comments about his Italian master Andrea Palladio).[23] Laughter had been recognised long before Hobbes as a deliberate mode of communicating a sense of superiority, particularly with the purpose of rivalling or belittling.

Yet laughter which expressed superiority could be highly dangerous, especially when it was directed against those of an elevated social position. Such jests were often taken in good faith: Heinrich Glaraen's *Dodecachordon* (1547) recounts a joke played on Louis XII, who loved music and had asked a composer to write him a part in a choral piece. The king had a famously dreadful singing voice, however, and so the composer wrote a four-part harmony in which the king had only to hold one note from beginning to end.[24] The laughter provoked by this jest—as well as the musical superiority expressed by its composer—were very well received by the king. Others were severely punished for their jibes. Charles VIII, for example, had arrested a number of law clerks who, in their morality plays, had painted humorous though highly unflattering portraits of himself and of France.[25] Consequently, many writers advised extreme caution when joking. The rhetorician Giambattista Giraldi Cinzio (1504–1573) urged the courtier to wait for a prince to jest before telling a joke himself, in case the prince took the boldness of the joker's laughter as an expression of superiority.[26] Castiglione appealed to the courtier to be particularly careful in his jokes about women: 'He must be respectful towards women [...] especially regarding their honour' ('sopra tutto aver rispetto e riverenzia [...] alle donne, e massimamente dove intervenga'offesa della onestà').[27] Given the power of laughter to cause emotional distress—Thomas Wilson (1524–1581), for example, observed that joking could put a man 'at his wittes ende'—it was often suppressed also outside of the Court.[28] Thomas More (1429–1535), a well-known wit, was for example denounced by other Christians for his humorous writings, and even scathingly dubbed 'Master Mock' by William Tyndale.[29] The Council of Trent was frequently occupied in deciding which comic literary works should be publicly available: the short stories of Giovanni Boccaccio (1313–1375), for instance, were censored, and Giovanni Francesco Straparola (c. 1485–1558) was invoked by the Venetian Inquisition to provide a defence of his own bawdy tales.[30] Giovanni Della Casa (1503–1556) addressed more general advice to 'chi si diletta di fare arrossire altrui' [those who enjoy making others blush], claiming that 'niuna differenza è da schernire a beffare: se non fosse il proponimento, e la intentione, che l'uno ha diverso dall'altro' [there is no difference between insulting and joking, except for the intention and purpose of the joker].[31]

Although the superiority expressed in laughter was considered to be effective in causing offence, it was also thought to have a number of alternate functions. For example, such a form of superiority could be employed as a powerful persuasive tool. Early modern thinkers considered Cicero's *De Oratore* to be a canonical text, and often reiterated the value he placed on persuasive and compelling discourse, which could 'induce [the minds of the listeners] to feel any emotion the case may demand'.[32] In compiling classical instructions on speaking and writing persuasively, it became clear to sixteenth-century rhetoricians that laughter could greatly assist in achieving this objective. Cicero advised that 'cheerfulness by itself wins goodwill for the one who has excited it';[33] Quintilian, too, explores how humour 'dispels [the judge's] gloomy emotions [and] frequently diverts his attention from the facts'.[34] Turning to the sixteenth century, humour was frequently used in the early modern sermon as a means of convincing hearers of the superiority of a religious faction; the Menippean satire was also experimented with as a persuasive literary practice. The collaborative 1594 pamphlet *Satyre menippée*, for instance, disparaged the French Catholic League and parodied the recent *États généraux* (Estates General) assembly meetings, using the sense of superiority in the laughter it provoked to persuade readers of the benefits of moderate Catholicism.[35] The superiority expressed in laughter was also employed as a useful means of self-promotion; Castiglione, for example, repeatedly underlines the social power of laughter at the Court. Harking back to Aristotle, who first proposed that laughter could impress others with the good taste it expressed,[36] Castiglione judged that laughter could be an excellent proof of one's erudition and quick wit. Providing examples of Cicero's witticisms, Castiglione advises that one should continually delight ('continuamente diletti')[37] with laughter, and that the superiority and refinement which this action expresses could help to elevate one's position at the Court. He advises caution, however, emphasising that some are more naturally gifted at inducing laughter than others. It is better, he states, to make your listeners laugh through wit than through trying and failing to be funny:

> Ad ognun non si convien ogni cosa, a trovarssi talor un omo, il qual di natura sarà tanta pronto alle facezie, che ciò che dirà porter seco il riso [...] e s'un altro che abbia manera di gravità [...] vorrà mettersi far il medesimo, sarà freddissimo e disgraziato.[38]

> We do not all have the same talents. Sometimes you find a man whose nature is so given to jokes that whatever he says will stir up a laugh [...] and then if a more serious man [...] tried the same thing, he would be shunned and given the cold shoulder.

Even the same material will be met with a diverse reaction, so caution must be exercised when seeking to use humour to impress or to persuade, especially if one is not naturally inclined to make others laugh.

The persuasive power of laughter also made it an excellent means of teaching morals. Horace's well-known precept that all art should both teach and delight was widely taken up by early modern rhetoricians, and so often cited in reference to laughter that it was eventually coined as *castigat ridendo mores* [one can correct customs by laughing at them].[39] The French writer Jacques Pelletier du Mans (1518–1582), the first translator of Horace's *Ars Poetica* into French, claimed in his own 1555 literary treatise that he admired Terence's comedies precisely because they were relatable ('accommodées à la vie'), showing spectators something of their own lives and subsequently teaching them a lesson.[40] In Italy, Antonio Minturno (1500–1574) argued in his *De poeta* (1559) that comedy was exceptionally placed for the correction of morals;[41] Gian Giorgio Trissino (1478–1550) also reflected that in opposition to tragedy, which teaches through inspiring pity and fear in the audience, comedy teaches a moral lesson through the ridicule of *turpitudo* (ugliness).[42] John Dryden (1631–1700) compares the rapport between the satirist and their reader to the doctor and patient relationship, claiming that although comedy may insult, it is highly beneficial in improving morals: 'the true end of Satyre, is the amendment of Vices by correction. And he who writes Honestly, is no more an Enemy to the Offendour than the Physician to the Patient when he prescribes harsh remedies to an inveterate disease'.[43]

There is of course a sense of superiority inherent to this correcting laughter since, in order to teach a lesson, the laughable characters must display to the spectator or reader the foolish behaviour to avoid.[44] In this way, Donatus noted in his fourth-century commentary on Terence's *Eunuchus* that seemingly ridiculous people are particularly well placed to communicate serious, edifying messages.[45] For instance, the anonymous French *Farce nouvelle et fort joyeuse du Pect* [*The new and delightful Farce of the Fart*]—in which a foolish husband, shocked that his new wife is able to pass wind, tries to sue her—reads as a lesson against prudishness. Other texts incite laughter at ugly or grotesque scenes; Conrad Badius's 1561 *Comédie du pape malade* (*Comedy of the Mad Pope*), for example, teaches its spectators or readers the principles of Huguenotism through a mock exorcism of the Pope. Vincenzo Maggi (1498–1564) in his 1550 treatise *De Ridiculis* outlines the rhetorical potential of false ignorance as opposed to true ignorance, both of which could provoke laughter, but only the first of which could teach a useful lesson.[46] A number of More's epigrams draw on a dual sense of superiority in laughter, which exploit these notions of true and false ignorance in order to teach two lessons. One such example is his anecdote of a peasant who does not recognise the king as he passes through the town, but mistakes him, in his finery, for a person in fancy dress.[47] According to a 1532 jestbook version of this anecdote, the superiority in the witnesses' laughter is directed against the peasant, for being so uneducated that he fails to recognise the king. However, this superiority could also be aimed against the king—with the peasant only pretending to be ignorant of the king's true status—thus expressing ridicule for his excessively elaborate dress and adornments.[48] Although, as we have seen, some Christians warned against laughter, its edifying function led others to deem it highly useful. While Paolo Cortesi (1471–1510), for example, accepts that humour might on occasion be unseemly for a Christian authority to display, he includes in his 'De Cardinalatu' (1510) a sub-division of jokes that are fitting for use by a cardinal, the grand majority teaching a moral lesson.[49] The superiority in laughter, then, could teach a wide range of lessons which may appear heretical (the *Comédie du pape malade*) or condescending (the *Farce nouvelle et fort joyeuse du Pect*) when communicated by literary practices other than comedy.

The superiority expressed in laughter might, according to sixteenth-century theorists, have the additional function of community building. It could be used to unite friends, family and romantic partners: a common response to the laughable was, for example, proposed by Erasmus in his *The Praise of Folly* (1511) as a crucial mode of forging a bond between husband and wife: 'What frequent divorces, or worse mischief, would oft sadly happen, except man and wife, were so discreet as to pass over light occasions of quarrel by laughing?'[50] Additionally, laughter was regarded as fundamental not only in solidifying existing relationships but also in uniting strangers. Members of an audience could, for instance, be brought together by the shared experience of laughter, and Castiglione advocated laughter as a means of building relationships at the Court, claiming that 'noi amiamo que che son causa di tal nostra recreazione' [we love those who can give us this kind of enjoyment].[51] Again, however, there is an element of superiority to this laughter, since to use it to build a community one must necessarily laugh at, and thus exclude, those who are unwelcome in that community. One such community might be religious. Elizabethan theatre, for instance, used laughter as a highly effective means of building a religious community, and this practice is reflected in a number of its characters: as Indira Ghose points out, Shakespeare's Puritanical Malvolio in *Twelfth Night* (1601) is an outsider precisely because he does not share in the laughter of others, declining to 'join in the game'.[52] Many sermons, too, were aimed at building a religious community through laughter: the sermons of John Donne invited their listeners to scorn and laugh at Catholicism, creating a community which was able to recognise and strengthen shared values at the expense of alternative views.[53]

Laughter could also be used to unite strangers belonging to shared social ranks. The festival, for example, was a means of channelling community spirit through laughter: the playwright Pierre Gringore (1475–1539) used many of his carnival *sotties*, the most famous being his 1511 *Le jeu du prince des sotz* [*The play of the Prince of the Crazy*], to unite his generally lower-class audience by pitting them against those of a higher social rank.[54] Additionally, the superiority in laughter was capable of bringing a nation or culture closer together, at the expense of other cultures. As Simon Critchley has noted, the distinctiveness of a culture has often been expressed through humour, the 'ostensive untranslatability' of which is able to heighten the culture's sense of its uniqueness.[55] In French comic theatre, we frequently find jokes written solely for the amusement of the inhabitants of the town in which the play is set. For instance, Odet de Turnèbe's *Les Contens* (1580) contains highly specific jokes aimed only at the writer's fellow Parisians, deliberately excluding any other spectators: the comedy's servant character, for example, is described as searching for someone in a series of churches, and only a Parisian would understand that he has taken a laughably convoluted and inconvenient route. The French dubbed syphilis the 'mal de Naples' [the Neapolitan disease], laughing at Italian hygiene and expressing the superiority of their own healthful living; at the same time, the Italian name for syphilis was the 'mal francioso' [the French disease], which functioned simultaneously as a source of laughter and scorn in a number of comedies.[56] Thus, while this effect of community building evidences the superiority which laughter communicates, it also establishes that this expression of superiority could be productively employed: it was not intended to cause mindless offence; rather, it could convey an important message and work to strengthen relationships and bring together factions or communities.

## Incongruity Theory and the Early Modern

As we have seen, early modern thinkers were not so preoccupied with the idea that laughter communicates a sense of superiority; rather, many were more concerned with how this unique expression could be employed, the forms it might take and the limits which might be placed upon it. Additionally, superiority was not considered by sixteenth-century writers to be the sole cause of laughter. Although Lodovico Castelvetro (c. 1505–1571) writes that laughter is often a malicious expression of superiority, usually provoked by the Ciceronian concept of ugliness, he does argue that laughter might also be produced through affection.[57] Similarly, Francisco Valleriola (c. 1505–1585) points out that though children are not grotesque or ugly, they still incite one to laugh.[58] Surprise—or the unanticipated—was also widely thought to provoke laughter. This is a notion that we might today categorise as 'incongruity theory'; that is, the idea that we laugh when something subverts our expectations. Incongruity theory rose to prominence in the eighteenth century, in the wake of arguments proposed by Blaise Pascal, Francis Hutcheson and Immanuel Kant. Throughout the Middle Ages, the element of incongruity or surprise was frequently employed to provoke laughter: the widespread appreciation of verbal incongruity, such as puns and innuendo, led Bruno Roy to even term the period 'la culture de l'équivoque' [culture of the equivocal].[59] In the sixteenth century, writers started to generate theories surrounding incongruity. Although Trissino, for example, outlined the importance of ugliness and the grotesque in laughter, he also claims that surprise is highly effective in making an onlooker or listener laugh.[60] In the same way, although Maggi reproduces the Ciceronian vision of *turpitudo* (ugliness) as provoking laughter, in his *De Ridiculis* he includes a sense of wonder or novelty (*admiratio*) in this notion of non-derisive laughter;[61] as evidence of this, he reminds us that even a very funny joke will induce contempt rather than joy if it is repeated or heard too frequently.[62] Castiglione proposes in his *Il Cortegiano* that 'il fonte onde nascono i ridiculi consiste in una certa deformità [...] si ride di quelle cose che hanno in sé disconvenienza e par che stian male' [the source of the laughable is a sort of incongruity ... we laugh when something sits oddly with us].[63] Girolamo Fracastoro (c. 1476–1553) also emphasises in his widely influential 1546 *De sympathia & antipathia rerum* [*On the sympathy and antipathy of things*] that laughter is most often induced when a situation 'has a certain novelty about it', and when it occurs 'suddenly and unexpectedly'.[64]

Early modern rhetorical treatises often advised writers to use surprise and incongruity as an effective means of inciting laughter. In his 1577 *The Garden of Eloquence*, Henry Peacham (1546–1634) acknowledged the usefulness of *asteismus* (facetious dialogue) in evoking pleasure, outlining the delightful effects of a situation in which 'a word having two significations is exprest in the one and understood in the other'.[65] Joubert, when listing the various uses of *verba* (words) when evoking laughter, cites puns as one of the most useful means of creating one's desired effect: 'Les propos ridicules sont petites subtilités, railleries, rancontres, equivoques' [Laughable sayings are little subtleties, railleries, puns, equivocal phrases].[66] Antonio Riccoboni (1541–1599) outlines in his 1587 essay *Ars Comica ex Aristotele* that a comedian should strive always to induce *admiratio*, or surprise, in their dramatic works. Perhaps the most memorable example of surprise in early modern Italian dramatic practice is in *Il marescalco*, a 1533 comedy by Pietro Aretino (1492–1556), where a stablemaster, who clearly has a preference for men, is aghast at the Duke of Mantua's plans to have him married. To the stablemaster's astonishment, it transpires when he is moments away from marrying his spouse-to-be that the duke has played an elaborate trick, since his bride is in fact a groom. John Manningham's 1602 anecdote about the attempted affair of actor Richard Burbage (1567–1619) with an adoring theatregoer is another remarkable example of laughter through surprise: upon arriving at the lady's house, Burbage is informed that Shakespeare is already there, and Shakespeare himself is alleged to have told Burbage: 'William the Conqueror was before Richard the Third'.[67] We laugh not only at the unexpected presence of Shakespeare at the lady's house, but also at the incongruity between the historical Williams and Richards and those competing for their lady's attention, which seem to be two incompatible and unexpected frames of reference.

Turning to the early modern preoccupation with the effects that laughter could provoke, we might observe that causing laughter through surprise appears to be more good-natured than using laughter to insult or to persuade. It is worth pointing out that laughter was also considered by some to be an expression of simple and altruistic pleasure, unrelated to malice or premeditation. As early as 1480, the humanist philosopher Marsilio Ficino (1433–1499) advises that *risus ille gratissimus* (gracious laughter) represents 'serene happiness in life and perfect joy'.[68] Similarly, Fracastoro claims that laughter originates from 'laetitia interna' [internal happiness]; like Valleriola, he provides as evidence the example of laughter when we see children and friends, which, he asserts, could never have its roots in malice.[69] In a number of languages, including Latin, French and Italian, the word for 'laughter' is an augmentative of 'smile', formed by removing its diminutive prefix ('subridere'/'ridere'; 'sourire'/'rire'; and 'sorridere'/'ridere'); even its etymology, then, indicates pure happiness.[70] In England, too, the theologian William Perkins (1558–1602) stresses the idea of laughter as a straightforward expression of pleasure, exploring how many jestbooks aimed only at delighting, rather than at teaching a lesson or fulfilling any ulterior objective.[71]

## RELIEF THEORY AND EARLY MODERN MEDICINE

The notion of laughter as connected to pure mirth, rather than as an expression solely of superiority or intent, gained impetus throughout the century, and was supported by a range of medical writings. Jacques le Goff is correct to assert that we must take into consideration the 'association between laughter and the body' when analysing laughter from a historical perspective, and it is important to remember that the joy inherent to laughter was—as it is today—widely promoted for its significant physiological benefits.[72] Just as humanists were keen to explore the literary and rhetorical effects, as well as the causes, of the superiority expressed through laughter, efforts were also made to uncover the health effects of the pleasure felt when we laugh. As early as 1444, a group of clerics promoted the beneficial health effects of laughter at the Feast of Fools: comparing themselves to old barrels, which burst open 'if the air hole is not opened from time to time', they explain that the opportunity to behave pleasurably once a year allowed them, like barrels, to purge themselves of pent-up energy.[73] Erasmus posits that the pleasure that laughter expressed was extremely useful for making cheerful day-to-day actions and, above all, refreshing the mind; Wilson also claims that laughter can help the mind to 'be refreshed, and find some swete delite'.[74] Nicholas Udall, in the 1538 *Ralph Roister Doister*, observes that 'mirth prolongeth life, and causeth health',[75] and Castiglione, too, advises on a number of occasions in his *Il Cortegiano* that laughter will invariably 'recrear gli animi degli auditori' (refresh the minds of its hearers).[76]

By the time Joubert put together his landmark *Traité du Ris* in 1579, which he spent over 25 years compiling, he was able to cite more than 60 previous writers on the subject of laughter, many of them promoting its physiological benefits.[77] When proposing one of the central and most influential theories of his own treatise—namely, that it is important to laugh often and worry seldom—he draws on Ficino:

> Parquoy ceus sont bien sages, et pourvoyent bien à leur santé, qui vivent joyeusemant, riet souvant, et ne s'accablent d'un fardeau de pansemans et affaires, se tuans pour les biens de ce monde, comme dit le vulgaire. Ils suivent prudammant le tressain conseil de Marsile Ficin, où il exhorte ses amis an cette sorte: Vivés

joyeusemant, dit-il. Le ciel vous ha crées de sa liesse, laquelle il ha declaré de sa fasson de rire [...] comme an s'ebaudissant.[78]

And thus those who are extremely wise, and who pay close attention to their health, are those who live joyously, laugh often, and do not weigh themselves down with thoughts and worries, working their fingers to the bone, so to speak. They prudently follow the very wise advice of Marsilio Ficino, who advised his friends thus: 'Live joyously', he said, 'The heavens have created you out of delight, which they have declared to be their way of laughing'.

As well as exhorting every reader to laugh often, he prescribes laughter as a particular remedy for patients, explaining that 'la dignité et excellence du Ris est fort grande, puis que il ranforce tellemant l'esprit, qu'il peut soudain changer l'etat d'un malade, et de mortel le randre guerissable' [the dignity and excellence of laughter is great indeed, since it so reinforces the soul that it can quickly invert the condition of a sick person, making even a deathly illness curable].[79] Even the full title of his treatise advertises the physiological benefits and effects of laughter, which Joubert claims to have personally identified: *Traité du Ris contenant son essance, ses causes, et mervelheus effais, curieusement recerchés, raisonnés et observés par Laurens Joubert* [*Treatise on laughter containing its nature, its causes, and marvellous effects, assiduously researched, reasoned and observed by Laurens Joubert*]. Perhaps owing to his status as *médecin ordinaire du roi*, the king's personal physician, and his overt elaboration on the theories of Fracastoro,[80] the celebrated doctor responsible for overseeing the health of the cardinals of the Council of Trent, Joubert's treatise swiftly gained impetus across Europe, inciting a far greater number of physicians to investigate laughter as a physiological phenomenon. Nicolas de Nancel, a doctor from Tracy-le-Mont, relies on Joubert's treatise when writing his 1587 *De risu*, though he adds a number of original arguments: Nancel posits for example that laughter starts in the brain and spreads to the head; this is why, he suggests that the head reddens, the mouth opens, the teeth appear and the eyes shine when we laugh.[81] Mancini's 1598 treatise again takes Joubert's work as an important starting point, though he argues that laughter has its source not in the brain but in the heart.[82]

While Joubert's treatise played a key role in the rising number of medical studies on the causes of laughter, it is his discussion of the physiological effects of laughter which we find most often reiterated. Riccoboni suggests in 1587 that laughter 'incites a purgation of the spirits';[83] Castiglione claims that by mocking the 'noiose molestie, della quale la vita è piena' [bothersome troubles, of which all our lives are full] it is possible to relieve the discontent and exasperation that these troubles instigate: he also describes laughter directly as a 'rimedio' [remedy] and as a 'medicina' [medicine].[84] The English court jester John Scogan, in his compilation of jests gathered in 1626 by Andrew Boord, praises the particular health benefits of laughing at dinnertime, suppertime and bedtime.[85] In the same way as Joubert had described the comic antics of monkeys as having a restorative effect on ill patients,[86] in 1639 Thomas Nash tells of a man dying from an intestinal obstruction. When this man's jester scorns that since God has withheld him 'so small matter as a fart', he will most certainly not be given passage to Heaven, the ill man laughs so much that his obstruction is cleared, and he recovers.[87]

The therapeutic effects of laughter outlined by Joubert and his imitators, who prescribed laughter literally as the best medicine, bear some resemblances to the 'relief theory' of humour more recently proposed by Freud and others. The 'relief theory' posits that laughter is a means of relieving pent-up tension, a response to a 'feeling passing a certain pitch [which] habitually vents itself in bodily action',[88] releasing itself in nervous energy and leaving us feel more relaxed. The arguments of early modern thinkers that laughter can 'purge the spirits', 'refresh the minds of its hearers' or relieve tension in the way that an old barrel releases air do indeed pre-empt some characteristics of relief theory. However, the physiological effects of laughter were still very much under discussion. Laughter was considered by many to be a highly delicate and complex mode of behaviour, which—if even slightly imbalanced or unrestrained—could detrimentally impact one's health. Many early modern thinkers identify the uncontrollable physical effects of laughing, most often pointing out the shaking of the body. Erasmus explores the danger of the *risus syncreusus* (shaking with laughter), which he describes as a sure indicator of 'a mind which has lost control';[89] he also advises against laughing so much that one bares one's teeth, since this is an unsightly behaviour.[90] The Italians even coined words for the immoderate and undignified body movements caused by laughter: *sganasciarsi* (roaring with laughter) and *smascellarsi* (breaking one's jaw through laughter).[91] Others advised against losing control of one's body through laughter not because it was socially unacceptable but because it was extremely dangerous: Gentile Sermini (c. 1400), for example, warns against the dangers of choking or contorting oneself into a strange position through laughter.[92] Taking inspiration from the classics, Jean-Antoine de Baïf, one of France's foremost rhetoricians, cautions in his *Les mimes, enseignements, et proverbes* (1581) that 'de rire on meurt' [you can die from laughter].[93] The aforementioned playwright Aretino was thought to have died from choking with laughter; the first translator of Rabelais's writings into English, Thomas Urquhart, was also fabled to have died in an uncontrollable fit of laughter. Even moderate laughter could at times be dangerous and was thought to pose a particular risk to certain people. Joubert, for example, advises that laughter could make one put on weight, including in his treatise an entire chapter entitled 'Pourquoy et-ce que les grans rieurs devienet aisemant gras' [Why hearty laughers easily become fat]; conversely, he claims that 'les gras [riet plus aisémant] que les maigres' [fat people laugh more easily than thin people].[94] He also includes chapters in his treatise entitled 'De la douleur qu'on sant au vantre par trop rire' [On the stomach pain one feels from laughing too much], 'D'où vient qu'on pisse, fiante, et suë à force de rire' [On the causes of pissing, shitting and sweating because of laughter] and 'Qu'on peut evanoüir de rire, et si on an pourroit mourir' [That one can faint from laughter, and whether or not one can die from it].[95] He concludes that though death from laughter is rare, it can happen, and occurs most often through tickling:

> Toutesfois nous ne voions guieres, qu'on meure d'une grand' risee, si ce n'et pour le chatoulher. J'ay ouy parler d'un jeune homme, que deus garses chatoulherent importunamant, jusqu'à tant qu'il ne dit plus mot. Elles pansoient qu'il fut evanouy, quand ebahies le connuret mort etouffé.[96]

> However, it is not often that we see anyone die from laughter, unless it is from tickling. I once heard of a young man, whom two girls were importunely tickling, until he could no longer say a word. They thought he had fainted when, shocked, they found him to have suffocated to death.

Tickling, then, was thought to be especially perilous, and could cause fainting, choking or suffocation in its recipient.

As well as being potentially dangerous, it was thought that laughter could induce sadness, or even be an ambiguous expression of misery. Maggi in his *De Ridiculis* states that laughter is caused by a melting pot of cheerful and miserable mental states, which can only resolve themselves through the physical effects which laughter produces.[97] Joubert determines that since we laugh at ugliness, such as a bare bottom—provided there is no pity for the object of laughter, such as when 'un fer rouge de feu' (a red-hot iron) might be placed on that bottom—laughter must invariably be interconnected with misery.[98] The London doctor Timothy Bright, another imitator of Joubert, also explores the melting pot of conflicting emotions in laughter, including in his 1586 *Treatise of Melancholie* a chapter entitled 'Why and how one weepeth for joy, and laugheth for grief'. Bright claims that the sadness arising from joy can be as powerful as the feeling of sorrow itself: 'the weeping caused of joy is as hartie, as that which riseth upon conceit of sorowe',[99] and his explanation for the simultaneity of these contradictory emotions is that in nature, diverse causes may produce the same effect:

> We do see in the works of nature contrary effects wrought by the same cause; so the same effect ensueth upon contrary causes [...] You see how the Sunne altereth the whitenesse of a mans skinne into blacknesse, and how it maketh cloth white, it softeneth waxe, and hardeneth clay.[100]

It is thus, Bright claims, that we laugh at a displeasing tickling or after we pick up a painfully hot object that we anticipated to be cold.[101] This notion of laughter as simultaneous joy and sadness manifested itself widely as a literary trope: Grévin's *La Gélodacrye* (1561)—which signifies literally 'laughter and tears'—at once mocks the proliferation of Italians at the French Courts, while lamenting and mourning the concomitant decline of French culture. Thus, while laughter was thought to have the unparalleled powers of what we might term today Freudian 'relief', as well as restoring one's energy or helping a patient to recover, it was also considered to cause tears, sorrow, a bodily or sensory loss of control or even death. Although debates on the physiological

84   L. RAYFIELD

complexity of laughter's effects were increasingly widespread, with Joubert at the forefront of these arguments, no network of doctors or humanists could fully agree on the relation of laughter to the body, and it remained for many a source of mystery, magic and fear.

## UNIVERSALISING HUMOUR, UNIVERSALISING HUMANITY

As this chapter has shown, it is possible to identify some correlation between modern, universalising humour theories and early modern thinking about laughter. It is true, for example, that we find numerous ideas in early modern texts which modern scholarship might categorise as belonging to 'superiority theory'. However, it is important to bear in mind the sixteenth-century preoccupation with the various effects, and not just the causes, of laughter. Many early modern rhetoricians point out that laughter is an expression of superiority; nonetheless, more attention is devoted to how this particular expression could be employed to useful ends, and what its limits might be. Laughter was thus thought to be useful for community building, bolstering rapports between strangers, friends, spouses or even religious factions: festival culture is an important example of this. The capacity of laughter to hurt or to humiliate was also exploited, through practical jokes or comic theatre for instance, and these modes of disgracing and degrading were so effective that they were often censored. Laughter could function as a means of rhetorical persuasion, convincing the hearer of a political or polemical viewpoint which may otherwise have been condemned; it could also function as a powerful edifying tool or as an assurance of one's erudition and good taste.

It is also possible to find in sixteenth-century texts a range of explorations which appear to pre-empt incongruity and relief theories. The laughable element of surprise, or the unexpected, was put to the test in a range of literary practices, such as comic drama. Many thus argued that laughter was simply an expression of mirth, and did not necessarily communicate malice, nor a hidden agenda. Leading on from this innocent and pleasurable element of laughter, we find wide-ranging arguments that laughter was physically beneficial and an excellent cure for a variety of illnesses. Others, however, advised caution and moderation in laughter, since excess or loss of control could be fatal, and arguments were also made that laughter was an expression of sadness, and not of mirth. Debates surrounding the true nature and functions of laughter—social, physical and mental—were by no means settled, and it is difficult to find many consistent methodologies surrounding laughter throughout the sixteenth century. Additionally, humanists were still experimenting with a wide variety of literary practices, and the power of laughter as a rhetorical device, as well as the limitations of laughter in poetics and performance, were largely unclear. Early modern thinking about laughter was speculative and constantly shifting, and we cannot clearly separate between treatments of the causes and effects of laughter nor delineate consistent approaches, even within one particular culture. When adopting a methodological approach to early modern laughter, then, it is often counterproductive to foist our modern conception of humour theory onto its sixteenth-century forms, or to perpetually consider laughter outside of its historical context. Indeed, the prioritisation of our current theoretical positions on humour over historical ones would—ironically—be an expression of superiority in itself.

Although we cannot identify clearly defined theories of humour in the sixteenth century, we do find extensive original thinking about it, and humour was widely considered to wield remarkable power. Across the three cultures in question—Italy, France and England—humour and laughter were recognised to be exceptional modes not only of proving ourselves to be human but also of revealing precisely what it *meant* to be human. Humour could expose our true selves and our aims; our rivalries and insecurities; our innate need for joy and our desire to belong. It could lift spirits, elevate morals, endear and impress; at the same time, it could outrage, offend or physically damage. Humour was—and still is—thought to provide a unique lens on the human condition, renewing our perspective on ourselves, on others and on the society in which we live.

## Notes

1. Rabelais, *Gargantua*, 53. All translations in this chapter are my own, unless otherwise indicated.
2. Erasmus (1466–1536), for example, wrote that words and not laughter were a marker of the human, since laughter was also common to dogs and apes: 'It is ridiculous that what is attributed to man as his own seems to be shared with dogs and apes'. Erasmus, *De ratione concionandi*, 5:922, 650. Translation by Butrica.
3. This particular statement is from Spingarn, *History of Literary Criticism*, 101.
4. In short, the notion that when we laugh, it is always because we experience a sense of superiority over something or someone else.
5. Aristotle, *Poetics*, 5:45. Translation by Halliwell.
6. Marvin Herrick discusses the influence of Aristotle's commentators throughout his *French Comic Theory*.
7. 'When we laugh at the ridiculous aspects of our friends, the admixture of pleasure in our malice produces a mixture of pleasure and distress'. Plato, *Philebus*, 51. Translation by Gosling.
8. 'The seat, the region, so to speak, of the humorous—for this is the next question—lies in a certain dishonorableness and ugliness'. Cicero, *De Oratore*, 2:187. Translation by May and Wisse.
9. 'Laughter is not far from derision'. Quintilian, *Institutio Oratoria*, 6:3, 67. Translation by Russell.
10. 'Wee laugh at deformed creatures, wherein certainly wee cannot delight'. Sidney, *Defence of Poesie*, in *Prose Works*, 40.
11. Burton, *Anatomy of Melancholy*, 4.
12. Nietzsche, *Beyond Good and Evil*, 218. Also cited in Skinner, 'Why Laughing Mattered', 418.
13. Joubert, *Traité du Ris*, 1:1, 16. In the sixteenth century, the various forms of 'ridicule' ('ridiculous', 'ridicolo') indicated 'laughable' in its etymological sense, rather than today's sense of the word as meaning foolish or outlandish.

14. Machiavelli, *La vita di Castruccio Castracani da Lucca*, in *Opere complete*, 175.
15. Castiglione, *Il Cortegiano*, 2:46, 153.
16. 'Any avaricious man is deformed, and turned into a monster'. Mancini, *De risu, ac ridiculis*, 145.
17. Wiles discusses this culture in his excellent chapter centring on Richard Tarlton. Cf. *Shakespeare's Clown*, 11–23.
18. Lotte Hellinga discusses the laughter caused by this jestbook in chapter six of her *Texts in Transit*, 168–200.
19. Cited in Burke, 'Frontiers of the Comic', 64. These, and many more examples, can also be found throughout Eamon, *Science and the Secrets of Nature*, especially 240, 243, 411.
20. This incident is recounted in full in Robertson, *Il Gran Cardinale*, 128. Cited in Burke, 'Frontiers of the Comic', 64.
21. More, *Epigrammata*, 'In anglum gallicae linguae affectatorem' (On an Englishman Affecting the French Language). 45–47. McCutcheon assesses this epigram in her 'Laughter and Humanism', 230.
22. Burke, 'Frontiers of the Comic', 63.
23. These comments are reproduced in Ann Marie Borys's *Vincenzo Scamozzi and the Chorography of Early Modern Architecture*, 2–4.
24. This anecdote is examined in further detail throughout Minamino, *Fabricated Laughter*.
25. Rousse, 'Le pouvoir royal et le théâtre des farces', 183–84.
26. Giraldi Cinzio, *Discorsi intorno*, 35r. Cited in Burke, 'Frontiers of the Comic', 69.
27. Castiglione, *Il Cortegiano*, 2:89, 201–2.
28. Wilson, *Arte of rhetorique*, 275. Wilson's treatise is discussed in further detail in Lake Prescott, 'Humour and satire in the Renaissance', 285.
29. More, *The Answer to a Poisoned Book*, 8. Cited in Lake Prescott, 'Humour and satire in the Renaissance', 287.
30. Burke, 'Frontiers of the Comic', 68.
31. Della Casa, *Galateo*, 31–32.
32. Cicero, *De Oratore*, 2:155. Translation by May and Wisse.
33. Ibid., 2:187.
34. Quintilian, *Institutio Oratoria*, 6:3, 65. Translation by Russell.
35. This satire was a collaborative effort by Nicolas Rapin, Florent Chrestien, Jean Passerat and Pierre Pithou. Martial Martin's 2010 edition of the *Satyre* is the most up to date.
36. As Indira Ghose has detailed, in the *Nicomachean Ethics* (4:8, 247) Aristotle points out that 'the jesting of a gentleman differs from that of a person of servile nature, as does that of an educated from that of an uneducated man'. Ghose, *Shakespeare and Laughter*, 60. Translation of Aristotle by Rackham.
37. Castiglione, *Il Cortegiano*, 2:41, 147.
38. Castiglione, *Il Cortegiano*, 2:20, 118–19.
39. The poet Jean-Baptiste de Santeuil (1630–1697) first used this term when describing the *commedia dell'arte* character Arlecchino.
40. Peletier, *L'Art poétique*, 70v.
41. Minturno, *De Poeta*, 280.
42. Trissino, *Della Poetica*, 2:30v. Cited in Herrick, *French Comic Theory*, 83–84.
43. Dryden, *Absalom and Achitophel* (1681), preface.

44. Henri Bergson, as John Parkin has neatly summarised, has more recently sought to show that 'laughter must be derisive and corrective in its function, scorning and punishing the aberrant comic figure'. Parkin, *French Humour*, Introduction, 6.
45. Terence, *Eunuchus*, 4:4, 87v.
46. Maggi, *De Ridiculis*, 304–5.
47. More, *Latin Poems*, 233.
48. This possibility is explored in McCutcheon, 'Laughter and Humanism', 229.
49. Cortesi, 'De cardinalatu', in his *Ad Episcopum*, 2:9. Cited in Bowen, 'Rire est le propre de l'homme', 186.
50. Erasmus, *The Praise of Folly*, 18. Translation by Wilson.
51. Castiglione, *Il Cortegiano*, 2:45, 152.
52. Ghose, *Shakespeare and Laughter*, 106.
53. This idea is assessed in detail in Derrin, 'Self-Referring Deformities', 265.
54. Hindley, 'Pierre Gringore, Satire and Carnival', 188. Mikhail Bakhtin has of course assessed the community-building function of the carnival in his *Rabelais and his World*, although a number of scholars have instead shown the early modern carnival to be a form of oppression, with lower classes exchanging temporary freedom for obedience at all other times. See for example Beard, *Laughter in Ancient Rome*, 39.
55. Critchley, *On Humour*, 67–68.
56. See for example Machiavelli's *La Mandragola*, 1:1.
57. Castelvetro, *Poetica d'Aristotele vulgarizzata*, 92–98. Cited in Herrick, *French Comic Theory*, 53.
58. Valleriola, *Enarrationum medicinalium libri sex*, 218. Cited in Ménager, *La Renaissance et le Rire*, 32.
59. Roy, *Une culture de l'équivoque*.
60. Trissino, *Della Poetica*, 2:39v. Cited in Herrick, *French Comic Theory*, 41.
61. Maggi, *De Ridiculis*, 306.
62. Ibid., 305. Cited in Herrick, *French Comic Theory*, 45.
63. Castiglione, *Il Cortegiano*, 2:47, 153.
64. Fracastoro, *De sympathia*, fol. 23v. Also cited in Skinner, 'Why Laughing Mattered', 442.
65. Peacham, *Garden of Eloquence*, 34. Also cited in Skinner, 'Why Laughing Mattered', 442.
66. Joubert, *Traité du Ris*, 1:3, 33. Joubert's examination of the pun is discussed at greater length in De Rocher, *Rabelais's Laughters and Joubert's Traité du Ris*, 13.
67. Manningham, *Diary*, 40.
68. Ficino, *Letters*, 4:66, 67. Translation by London School. Cited in O'Rourke Boyle, 'Gracious Laughter', 712.
69. Fracastoro, *De sympathia*, fol. 23v. Also cited in Skinner, 'Why Laughing Mattered', 421 and 435.
70. These etymologies are discussed in further detail in Critchley, *On Humour*, 108.
71. Perkins, *Foundation of Christian Religion*, A2. Also cited in Ghose, *Shakespeare and Laughter*, 109.
72. Le Goff, 'Laughter in the Middle Ages', 45.
73. Cited in Burke, 'Popular Culture', 202.
74. Wilson, *Arte of Rhetorique*, 75.

88   L. RAYFIELD

75. Cited in Chambers, *The Elizabethan Stage*, 188.
76. Castiglione, *Il Cortegiano*, 2:41, 147.
77. Ménager, *La Renaissance et le Rire*, 8.
78. Joubert. *Traité du Ris*, 3:14, 330.
79. Ibid., 3:14, 335.
80. Ménager, *La Renaissance et le Rire*, 8.
81. Nancel, *Analogia microcosmi ad macrocosmum*, III, 'De risu', 2220. Many of Nancel's theories were also inspired by Pierre de la Ramée, who had been principal of the Collège de Presles, where Nancel undertook his training.
82. Mancini, *De Risu*, 78v.
83. Riccoboni, *Poetica Aristotelis*, 157. Cited in Herrick, *French Comic Theory*, 52. Translation by Herrick.
84. Castiglione, *Il Cortegiano*, 2:45, 152.
85. Scogan, *Scoggin's Jests*, 46.
86. Joubert recounts the story of a patient being cured after laughing at a monkey jumping up on a table and drinking (and subsequently throwing away) the medicine that was originally intended for the patient. He describes the monkey as being an 'animal de soy ridicule' (a laughable animal in itself). Joubert, *Traité du Ris*, 3:14, 335.
87. See Nash, 'Philopolites', in *Miscellanea*, sig. nn 3. This anecdote is also cited in Prescott, 'Humour and Satire', 285.
88. Spencer, *Essays Scientific*, 200.
89. Erasmus, *The Collected Works of Erasmus*, 33:312. Translation by Mynors. Cited in O'Rourke Boyle, 'Gracious Laughter', 717.
90. Erasmus, *De ratione concionandi*, 5:964, 761.
91. Lacroix, 'Esquisse d'une signification', 208.
92. Cited in Ménager, *La Renaissance et le Rire*, 154.
93. Baïf, *Les mimes, enseignements, et proverbes*, 158.
94. Joubert, *Traité du Ris*, 2:4, 164.
95. Ibid., 1:25, 1:26, 1:27, 125–34.
96. Ibid., 1:27, 132.
97. Maggi, *De Ridiculis*, 304. Cited in De Rocher, *Rabelais's Laughters and Joubert's Traité du Ris*, 16.
98. Joubert, *Traité du Ris*, 1:2, 17. Many others, such as Maggi (*De Ridiculis*, 302) iterated that no pity must be felt for the object of laughter. Michael Screech discusses the role of pity in laughter at length in his *Laughter at the Foot of the Cross*, 56–60.
99. Bright, *Treatise of Melancholie*, 14.
100. Ibid., 14.
101. Ibid., 14.

## BIBLIOGRAPHY

Aristotle. *Nicomachean Ethics*. Translated by Harris Rackham. Cambridge, MA: Harvard University Press, 1994.
Aristotle. *Poetics*. Translated by Stephen Halliwell. Cambridge, MA: Harvard University Press, 1995.
Baïf, Jean-Antoine de. *Les mimes, enseignements, et proverbes*. Edited by Jean Vignes. Geneva: Droz, 1992.

Bakhtin, Mikhail. *Rabelais and his World*. Indiana: Indiana University Press, 2009.

Beard, Mary. *Laughter in Ancient Rome: On Joking, Tickling, and Cracking Up*. Berkeley and Los Angeles: University of California Press, 2014.

Borys, Ann Marie. *Vincenzo Scamozzi and the Chorography of Early Modern Architecture*. Farnham: Ashgate, 2014.

Bowen, Barbara. 'Rire est le propre de l'homme'. In *Études rabelaisiennes* 21, edited by Jean Céard and Jean-Claude Margolin, 184–203. Geneva: Droz, 1998.

Burke, Peter. 'Frontiers of the Comic in Early Modern Italy, c. 1350–1750'. In *A Cultural History of Humour*, edited by Jan Bremmer and Herman Roodenburg, 61–75. Cambridge: Polity Press, 1997.

Burton, Robert. *Anatomy of Melancholy*. Oxford: John Lichfield and James Short, 1621.

Castelvetro, Lodovico. *Poetica d'Aristotele vulgarizzata*. Vienna: Gaspar Steinhofer, 1570.

Castiglione, Baldassare. *II Cortegiano*. Turin: Einaudi, 1965.

Chambers, Edmund. *The Elizabethan Stage*. Vol. 4. Oxford: Clarendon, 1923.

Chrestien, Florent, Nicolas Rapin, Jean Passerat and Pierre Pithou. *Satyre menippée*. Edited by Martial Martin. Saint-Étienne: Presses Universitaires Saint-Étienne, 2010.

Cicero. *De Oratore*. Edited and translated by James May and Jakob Wisse. Oxford: Oxford University Press, 2016.

Cortesi, Paolo. *Ad Episcopum Ubris Romae Sanctiss*. Rome: Castro Cortesio, 1510.

Critchley, Simon. *On Humour: Thinking in Action*. London: Routledge, 2002.

Della Casa, Giovanni. *Galateo*. Piacenza: Iacopo and Bernardo Giunti, 1561.

De Rocher, Gregory. *Rabelais's Laughters and Joubert's Traité du Ris*. Alabama: University of Alabama Press, 1979.

Derrin, Daniel. 'Self-Referring Deformities: Humour in Early Modern Sermon Literature'. *Literature and Theology* 32, no. 3 (2018): 255–69.

Dryden, John. *Absalom and Achitophel*. Hamden: Archon Books, 1984.

Eamon, William. *Science and the Secrets of Nature: Books of Secrets in Medieval and Early Modern Culture*. Princeton: Princeton University Press, 1996.

Erasmus, Desiderius. *Erasmus, Spiritualia and Pastoralia: Exomologesis and Ecclesiastes: Ecclesiastes sive de ratione concionandi*. Edited by Frederick McGinness, Michael Heath, and James Butrica. Translated by James Butrica. Toronto: University of Toronoto Press, 2015.

Erasmus, Desiderius. *The Collected Works of Erasmus*. Vol. 33. Translated by Roger Aubrey Baskervile Mynors. Toronto: University of Toronto Press, 1991.

Erasmus, Desiderius. *The Praise of Folly*. Translated by John Wilson. New York: Barnes and Noble, 2004.

Ficino, Marsilio. *The Letters of Marsilio Ficino*. Vol. 1. Edited and translated by London School. London: Shepheard-Walwyn, 1975.

Fracastoro, Girolamo. *De sympathia & antipathia rerum*. Venice: Heirs of Lucantonio Giunta, 1546.

Ghose, Indira. *Shakespeare and Laughter: A Cultural History*. Manchester: Manchester University Press, 2011.

Giraldi Cinzio, Giovambattista. *Discorsi intorno a quello che si conviene a giovane mobile nel servire un gran principe*. Pavia: Bartoli, 1565.

Hellinga, Lotte. *Texts in Transit: Manuscript to Proof and Print in the Fifteenth Century*. Leiden: Brill, 2014.

Herrick, Marvin. *French Comic Theory in the Sixteenth Century*. Urbana: University of Illinois Press, 1964.

Hindley, Alan. 'Pierre Gringore, Satire and Carnival: *Le Jeu du Prince des Sotz et de Mère Sotte*'. In *Court and Humour in the French Renaissance: Essays in Honour of Professor Pauline Smith*, edited by Sarah Alyn Stacey, 193–98. Oxford: Peter Lang, 2009.

Joubert, Laurent. *Traité du Ris contenant son essance, ses causes, et mervelheus effais, curieusement recerchés, raisonnés et observés par Laurens Joubert*. Paris: Nicolas Cheseau, 1579.

Lacroix, Jacques. 'Esquisse d'une signification du rire chez les novellistes italiens des XVIIIᵉ, XIVᵉ et XVᵉ siècles'. In *Le rire au moyen âge dans la littérature et dans les arts: actes du colloque international des 17, 18, et 19 novembre 1988*, edited by Thérèse Bouché and Hélène Charpentier, 201–25. Bordeaux: Presses Universitaires de Bordeaux, 1990.

Lake Prescott, Anne. 'Humour and satire in the Renaissance'. In *The Cambridge History of Literary Criticism*, Vol. 3, *The Renaissance*, edited by Glyn Norton, 284–91. Cambridge: Cambridge University Press, 2001.

Le Goff, Jacques. 'Laughter in the Middle Ages'. In *A Cultural History of Humour*, edited by Jan Bremmer and Herman Roodenburg, 40–53. Cambridge: Polity Press, 1997.

Machiavelli, Niccolò. *Opere complete di Niccolò Machiavelli*. Florence: Borghi e Compagni, 1833.

Maggi, Vincenzo. *In Aristoteles librum de poetica communes explanationes*. Venice: Vincenzo Valgrisi, 1550.

Mancini, Celso. *De somniis, ac synesi per somnia De risu, ac ridiculis. De synaugia Platonica*. Ferrara: Victorium Baldinum, 1591.

Manningham, John. *John Manningham, of the Middle Temple, and of Bradbourne, Kent, Barrister-at-Law, 1602–1603*. London: J. B. Nicholls and Sons, 1868.

McCutcheon, Elizabeth. 'Laughter and Humanism: Unity and Diversity in Thomas More's *Epigrammata*'. *Moreana* 52, no. 201–2 (2015): 221–33.

Ménager, Daniel. *La Renaissance et le Rire*. Paris: Presses Universitaires de France, 1995.

Minamino, Hiroyuki. 'Fabricated Laughter: Wit and Humor in Renaissance Music'. *Discoveries: South-Central Renaissance Conference News and Notes* 18, no. 1 (Spring 2001), 1–12.

Minturno, Antonio. *De poeta*. Venice: Franceso Rampazzetto, 1559.

More, Thomas. *Epigrammata clarissimi dissertissimique viri Thomae Mori, pleraque e Graecis versa*. Basel: Johann Froben, 1520.

More, Thomas. *The Answer to a Poisoned Book*. Edited by Stephen Merriam Foley and Clarence Miller. New Haven: Yale University Press, 1985.

More, Thomas. *The Complete Works of St. Thomas More*. Vol. 3. Edited by Clarence Miller, Leicester Bradner, Charles A. Lynch, and Revilo P. Oliver. New Haven: Yale University Press, 1984.

Nancel, Nicolas de. *Analogia microcosmi ad macrocosmum*. Paris: Jacques de Nancel, 1611.

Nash, Thomas. *Miscellanea, or a fourefold way to a happie life*. London: J. Dawson, 1639.

Nietzsche, Friedrich. *Beyond Good and Evil*. Translated by Richard Hollingdale. Harmondsworth: Penguin, 1990.

O'Rourke Boyle, Marjorie. 'Gracious Laughter: Marsilio Ficino's Anthropology'. *Renaissance Quarterly* 52, no. 3 (1999): 712–41.

Parkin, John., ed. *French Humour: papers based on a Colloquium held in the French department of the Unievrsity of Bristol, November 30th 1996*. Amsterdam: Rodopi, 1999.

Peacham, Henry. *The Garden of Eloquence*. London: H. Jackson, 1577.

Pelletier du Mans, Jacques. *L'Art poétique*. Lyon: Jean de Tournes, 1555.

Perkins, William. *Foundation of Christian Religion Gathered into Six Principles*. London: Christopher Barker, 1591.

Plato. *Philebus*, Edited and translated by Justin Gosling. Oxford: Oxford University Press, 1975.

Quintilian. *Institutio Oratoria*, Vol. 6. Edited and translated by Donald Russell. Cambridge, MA: Harvard University Press, 2002.

Rabelais, François. *Gargantua*. Paris: Gallimard, 1969.

Riccoboni, Antonio. *Poetica Aristotelis ab Antonio Riccobono latine conversa*. Padua: Paolo Meietti, 1587.

Robertson, Clare. *Il Gran Cardinale: Alessandro Farnese, Great Patron of the Arts*. New Haven: Yale University Press, 1992.

Rousse, Michel. 'Le pouvoir royal et le théâtre des farces'. In *Le pouvoir monarchique et ses supports idéologiques*, edited by Jean Dufournet, Adeline Fiorato, and Augustin Redondo, 185–97. Paris: Sorbonne Nouvelle, 1990.

Roy, Bruno. *Une culture de l'équivoque*. Montreal: Presses de l'Université de Montréal, 1992.

Scogan, John. *Scoggin's Jests: Full of Witty Mirth, and Pleasant Shifts; Done by Him in France and Other Places, being a Preservative against Melancholy*. Edited by Andrew Boord and William Carew Hazlitt. London: Willis and Sotheran, 1864.

Screech, Michael. *Laughter at the Foot of the Cross*. Chicago: University of Chicago Press, 2015.

Skinner, Quentin. 'Why Laughing Mattered in the Renaissance: The Second Henry Tudor Memorial Lecture'. *History of Political Thought* 22, no. 3 (2001): 418–47.

Sidney, Philip. *The Prose works of Sir Philip Sidney*. Edited by Albert Feuillerat. Cambridge: Cambridge University Press, 1962.

Spencer, Herbert. *Essays Scientific, Political, and Speculative*. Vol. 1. London: Williams and Norgate, 1868.

Spingarn, Joel Elias. *A History of Literary Criticism in the Renaissance*. New York: The Macmillan Company, 1899.

Terence. *P. Terentii Afri Comoediae Sex, Accedunt Interpretes Vetustioresm Aelius Donatus, Eugraphius, Calphurnius*. Vol. 1. The Hague: Peter Gosse, 1726.

Trissino, Gian Giorgio. *La quinta e la sesta diuisione della poetica del Trissino*. Venice: Andrea Arrivabene, 1563.

Valleriola, Francisco. *Enarrationum medicinalium libri sex*. Venice: Baldassare Costantino, 1555.

Wiles, David. *Shakespeare's Clown: Actor and Text in the Elizabethan Playhouse*. Cambridge: Cambridge University Press, 1987.

Wiley, William. *The Early Public Theatre in France*. Cambridge, MA: Harvard University Press, 1995.

Wilson, Thomas. *Arte of rhetorique*. London: Richard Grafton, 1553.

CHAPTER 5

# The Humour of Humours: Comedy Theory and Eighteenth-Century Histories of Emotions

*Rebecca Tierney-Hynes*

The first thing I want to observe about tackling humour and emotions history is that there is nothing new under the sun. From George Farquhar, Corbyn Morris and James Beattie in the eighteenth century to Stuart Tave in the 1960s and Frank Ellis in the 1990s,[1] scholars of humour and comedy have consistently relied on the explanatory power of eighteenth-century emotions theory. Humour, as a disposition—psychic and bodily—and as a literary genre or mode remained, in both senses, central to eighteenth-century cultural self-assessments. The way humour conceptually bridges the discursive worlds of medicine, natural and moral philosophy and imaginative literature and literary criticism makes it a strong gauge of the degree to which our relationship to literature is imbricated with discourses of selfhood and embodiment. Patrick Coleman and Eugenia Zuroski summarise the particular significance of the eighteenth century to studies of humour, observing that this period saw 'the conversion of ancient medical humours into the cultural materials of a modern "sense" of humour', arguing that the transition 'generated vexed forms of embodiment' that, uniquely in the period, serve 'to formalize a pervasive sense of uneasiness'.[2] Zuroski and Coleman confirm that there is something about the shifting ground of eighteenth-century concepts of emotion, and particularly of humour, that names a new, characteristically modern social relationship to funniness.

Here, then, I will bring together two broad surveys, necessarily incomplete, that will serve as a kind of mutual commentary. The first, a survey of

R. Tierney-Hynes (✉)
Department of English, University of Edinburgh, Edinburgh, UK
e-mail: r.tierneyhynes@ed.ac.uk

© The Author(s), under exclusive license to Springer Nature
Switzerland AG 2020
D. Derrin, H. Burrows (eds.), *The Palgrave Handbook of Humour, History, and Methodology*, https://doi.org/10.1007/978-3-030-56646-3_5

methodological and theoretical approaches to emotion and to humour in particular, seeks to understand how studies of emotion have pressed us to find new critical methods and to upend critical norms. Examining the claims of emotions history in contrast to various strands of affect theory, I assess the convergences among these approaches. The second survey, of some key late seventeenth- and eighteenth-century discussions of humour, examines in particular the way theories of comedy in this period seize on humour as a critical method. In the eighteenth century, humour could be a critical term of art—as in 'humours comedy'—and an aspect of the self. Humour serves, in different contexts, as a prescription for playwrights, a description of comic characters, a national diagnosis and a fundamental perceptual capacity. This survey seeks to understand how humour bridges corporeality and cognition in ways that comment on critical axioms then and now. The tentative suggestion of this chapter is that studies of emotion, historical and theoretical, insistently refuse us methodological certainty.

The methods of emotions history were established in twentieth-century critical paradigms. From Norbert Elias, who effectively linked cultural revolutions to emotional dispositions in *The Civilizing Process* (1939, trans. 1969) to Raymond Williams, who argued in *Marxism and Literature* (1977) that 'structures of feeling' are the indices of the interpenetration of history and form, and Richard Sennett, who observed that eighteenth-century England was 'a society where intimate feeling is an all-purpose standard of reality',[3] critics across disciplines have agreed that the foundations of cultural materialism relied on a deep recognition of two important truths: that emotion is an essential (perhaps *the* essential) register of ideology; and correlatively that emotion is historically specific and culturally determined. With regard to studies of humour and comedy in particular, Stephen Halliwell sums up the contrast between the theory and the history of emotions this way: 'the "canonical" modern triad of laughter theories (or, perhaps preferably, theories of humour)—those of superiority, incongruity and release—all fail as monolithic explanations of the full gamut of data to be accounted for [...] They fail not only because of their unsustainably totalising ambition, but also because they isolate psychology from culture'.[4] This sharp dismissal of ahistorical or universalising approaches to emotion has come into play again more recently in response to an approach to emotion we have gathered under the rubric of 'affect theory'. In contrast to the history of emotions, affect theory has been characterised as resistant to the ideology-critique that is the stock-in-trade of historicist criticism, as regressively universalising and as biologically essentialist.

The movement that Ruth Leys has named the 'turn to affect'[5] can seem like nothing more than an extreme version of the ahistorical approach to emotion of which Halliwell is so critical. Leys' response is principally to the branch of affect theory—most influential about 10 or 15 years ago—that adopted and adapted the conclusions of some neuroscientific investigations to examine the expressions of emotion in the field of cultural production.[6] This particular neuroscientific study purged psychology of its more nuanced approach to cultural and historical specificity and forwarded a one-size-fits-all idea of emotion. Leys considers this kind of affect theory and its adoption by humanities disciplines blinkered partly because of its inattention to extant historical methods and partly because of its insistence on a kind of automaticity that disarms ideology-critique.[7] Leys' critique is typical of an approach to the intellectual history of emotions that has, somewhat polemically, set itself apart from affect theory and espoused a rigorous historicism. This practice has tended to reinforce a neo-Foucauldian method, in which isolated discursive constructions are sometimes represented as unproblematic mirrors of cultural formations.[8]

Both affect theorists and historians of emotion have been much exercised about the definition of emotion—is it cognitive or affective? To what extent does it participate in cognitive activities like judgement?[9] Can we isolate emotion either by insisting on a distinction between affect—which solely concerns the body—and feeling—the cognitive activities associated with affects[10]—or by refusing a sharp Cartesian distinction[11] and understanding emotions as a subset of mental states defined by their mutual participation in both cognition and affect? This last phenomenological schema emerges primarily out of Merleau-Ponty's argument for a phenomenology grounded in bodily experience and its attendant perceptual variability.[12] The variability of perception leaves room for the expansion of the perceptual field to include the pervasive social and historical influences that shape both the perceiving subject and their material environment, which are mutually determining.[13]

On the whole, cultural criticism in the field of emotions has turned back to (or has never entirely turned away from) the critical concerns that have long animated the study of cultural history. Lauren Berlant, for example, turns to Althusser and Williams to explore 'affective realism'[14] and Sianne Ngai takes Adorno for her starting-point.[15] A careful reading of even Eve Kosofsky Sedgwick's *Touching Feeling*, a particular target of Leys' critique, reveals Sedgwick's interest in affectivity, not as a retreat from social, cultural or political reading, but rather, as a methodology that might intensify, nuance and vary our approaches to cultural texts. Sedgwick understands affect as interpretation—really, as a kind of 'reading' that can be pre- or paralinguistic[16]—and in this, she embraces a radically non-binary approach in contrast to the binarism she argues inheres in constructionism's focus on discourse. And in fact, if we look to some of the seminal texts of emotions history—Gail Kern Paster's *Humoring the Body* or Susan James' *Passion and Action*, for example—we will see that the compulsion to examine emotion in particular emerges out of a drive to understand the ways in which the emotional structures of the past might unpick the binarism, not simply of the Cartesian mind/body split, but also of the reified split between discourse and materiality that has sometimes been seen to characterise contemporary post-structuralism.[17] Of the early modern system of emotions, Paster writes that in 'the dynamic reciprocities between self and environment imagined by the psychophysiology of bodily fluids, circumstance engenders humors in the body and humors in the body help to determine circumstance by predisposing the individual subject to a characteristic kind of evaluation and response'.[18] In other words, in early modern emotional schemas, cognitive elements of emotion—'evaluation and response' (i.e. judgement)—and affects—'psychophysiology'—are mutually constitutive. In examining the relevance of materiality to past interpretive systems, Paster hints at the integrative potentialities of our own. Laughter in particular, as Halliwell writes, 'exists at the interface, so to speak, between body and mind, between instinct and intention'.[19] For Norbert Elias, writing in the late 1950s, laughter provides a 'key-problem'[20]: it demands that we reconsider our understanding of the physiology of laughter as an outward expression of an internal state, and thus that we reconsider a sharp distinction between internal states and bodily mechanisms altogether. Affect theory and emotions history are not so readily separable; their mutual object of investigation seems to press for methods that occupy a variety of messy middle grounds. Venturing into the territory of emotion demands that we turn insides out, that we acknowledge the significance of the material to the discursive, the affective to the cognitive. And of course, humour in particular has a long-standing investment in upsetting orthodoxies, in turning upsides down.[21]

## HUMOUR AS METHOD

If we want to know whether we can look to humour as a way of unravelling the binaries that underpin our critical methods, we might best begin with a deeper understanding of its particular invocation in a particular place and time. What does the discussion of humour and comedy in the eighteenth century bring to the excavation of the techniques and cultural impacts of humour across time? This moment, characterised simultaneously by the conceptual reconfiguration of the material body and by clear lexical transitions, seems an ideal target for historians of emotion. Tracking the definition of 'humour' should show us how the historical shifts posited by emotions history are marked out by discursive change. But humour can do more: because humour is both a comic technique and a diagnosis, it is first and foremost a *method*. Humour is the commonly prescribed method for writing comedy in this period, especially at the end of the seventeenth century. But it is equally the property of audiences: it is an interpretive stance as much as it is a disposition. Humour is tied to critical interpretation and eighteenth-century cultural theory in strange and unprecedented ways.

Eighteenth-century humour theorists came late to the party—in the Western tradition, classical and early modern theorists were fascinated by laughter and its provocations[22]—but they did uniquely insist on the anatomisation of the literary techniques of humour.[23] They turned their attention away from the physiology of laughter and even, to some extent, its purpose (to establish superiority or, in contrast, ties of fellowship), to explore instead, in analytic detail guaranteed to evacuate its entertaining possibilities, the theory of comedy.[24] This is the period in which the object of laughter takes centre-stage: the object is increasingly protected and treated with a degree of compassion, at least in theory, and the target of ridicule might equally be the popular class clown.[25]

Joseph Addison observes that a man who finds himself routinely the butt of jokes has ordinarily 'a good deal of Wit and Vivacity, even in the ridiculous side of his Character'. He adds, 'A *Butt* with these Accomplishments frequently gets the Laugh of his side, and turns the Ridicule upon him that attacks him'.[26]

This is also the period in which the incongruity theory of laughter—still the dominant theory—comes to the fore. Alexander Gerard, in his *Essay on Taste* (1759), identifies a 'sense of ridicule', which is activated by incongruity: 'Objects, conceived to be [...] incongruous, always gratify the sense of ridicule'.[27] There are some suggestions of a classical precedent for incongruity theory in Aristotle's *On Rhetoric* and Cicero's *Orator*, but the incongruity here is held to reside principally in the jarring violation of audience expectation.[28] Gerard, followed by James Beattie in 1779, identifies the incongruities that trigger laughter as those observed among objects more generally. Beattie argues that '[l]aughter seems to arise from the view of things incongruous united in the same assemblage', concluding that 'the greater the number of incongruities that are blended in the same assemblage, the more ludicrous it will probably be'.[29] Typifying an empiricist approach to cognition, Gerard and Beattie understand the manipulation of mental objects—ideas—in the mind to be the source of abstract thought, making laughter dependent on the ordering (or disordering) of our ideas. Kant, the thinker now most commonly referred to in theoretical discussions of incongruity theory, returns in the *Critique of Judgement* (1790) to the classical version: the incongruity specific to deflated expectations: 'Laughter is an affect resulting from the sudden transformation of a heightened expectation into nothing'.[30] In Norbert Elias' reading, Kant's discussion of the funniness of naiveté adds a crucial element to the bursting of the 'bubble of our expectation'. The deflation of our expectations is also the revelation of nature, so that the incongruity consists both in the difference between our expectations and what the comedy delivers and in the difference between culture—'artificiality'—and raw nature.[31] Elias thus links Kant's theory of comedy to Bergson's central argument: that comedy is '[s]omething mechanical encrusted on the living'.[32] Eighteenth-century theories of comedy, laughter and humour track—or even help to inaugurate—the development of the modern self. Moreover, we can see that this investigation embeds a process of accounting for the 'raw nature', the materiality of humour.

In sum, the eighteenth century sees the development of a series of key concepts that still underpin our understanding of humour: it reduces the significance of superiority theory in favour of social bonding theories, develops an idealised notion of the 'humourist' (Addison's 'butt' or Kant's naif), and extends and nuances incongruity theory. Crucially, it works these concepts out through explications of the term 'humour'. The following traces discussions of humour in this period. Though an exhaustive survey is not possible here, I note some key moments in the shift in the dominant definition of 'humour' from temperament to a genre of literature and performance. According to the OED, by 1685, humour had almost entirely lost its relevance as a medical category.[33] It cites Thomas Willis' *The London Practice of Physick*:

> We do not allow of the Opinion of the Ancients, That the Mass of Blood consists of the four Humours, viz Blood, Flegm, Choler, and Melancholy; [...] nor has this Opinion been so generally used for solving the Phænomena of Diseases, since the Circulation of the Blood [...] came to light.[34]

Casual uses of the term to describe temperament persist—one can still be in a 'humour'—but Galenic medicine increasingly took a back seat to more mechanistic medical theories and then to vitalism.[35] In its place, literature (in the broad eighteenth-century sense) and its theorists and critics claimed the term for its own, and late seventeenth-century dramatists and literary critics had made 'humorous' an essential descriptor for the English nation as well as for English comedy.

Early on, it is clear that 'humour' is a much looser category than its theorists might wish. Ben Jonson's touchstone definition of humour, Asper's speech in *Every Man Out of His Humour* (1599), emerges as an irritable response to what he considers a problematically imprecise use of the term. Humour in its medical sense—defined by its liquid incontinence, its 'fluxure'—can also, he argues, be used appropriately in its transferred meaning ('by metaphor') to describe an imbalanced temperament: 'As when some one peculiar quality/ Doth so possess a man that it doth draw/All his affects, his spirits, and his powers/In their confluxions all to run one way'.[36] Asper's vow to 'scourge those apes' (l. 116) represents the central claim of satiric comedy. Humours should be scourged, not celebrated. This presents something of a difficulty for the moral function of comedy. As Corbyn Morris writes, Jonson's enthusiasm for the scourge means that he is 'in Justice oblig'd to *hunt down* and *demolish* his own Characters'.[37] Increasingly after the Restoration, the justification for comedy was correction and cure: impossible if a humour is an incurable natural temperament, as Jonson suggested.[38] Thus, when Shadwell revives that claim in an energetic embrace of Jonsonian humours at the Restoration, he adds a key classical disclaimer: setting aside Cicero's injunction not to ridicule 'outstanding wickedness' and focusing instead on his parallel interdiction against ridiculing 'outstanding wretchedness',[39] Shadwell argues that 'it were ill Nature, and below a Man, to fall upon the natural Imperfections of Men; as of Lunaticks, Ideots, or Men born Monstrous'. Comedy's targets should be corrigible, its goal the 'Reformation of Fops and Knaves', of artifice, not of nature.[40] Shadwell's emphasis on comedy's (theoretical) obligation not to 'punch down'[41] sets the tone for discussions of the humours in this period and establishes a specific link between the moral function of comedy and what he figures as its obligation to represent humours. In his preface to *The Humourists* (1670), he sets out his commitment to Jonsonian comedy and the utility of comedy in general. Tragedy, he observes, concerns only a few, but comedy deals with the 'the Cheats, Villainies, and troublesome Follies, in the Common Conversation of the World', and is thus 'of concernment to all the Body of Mankind'.[42] Humour is comedy's moral method: it identifies the comic target, but it also sets the allowable limits of our pleasure. We can be amused by the foolish, but not the pitiable.

Congreve, while following in his mentor Dryden's footsteps in embracing a general disdain for Shadwell's comic theory, nonetheless repeats in the strongest terms the comic obligation to compassion. He writes: 'Sure the Poet must both be very Ill-natur'd himself, and think his Audience so, when he proposes by shewing a Man deform'd, or deaf, or blind, to give them an agreeable Entertainment; and hopes to raise their Mirth, by what is truly an object of Compassion'.[43] Fielding echoes Congreve in *Joseph Andrews* (1742): 'Surely he hath a very ill-framed mind who can look on ugliness, infirmity, or poverty, as ridiculous in themselves'.[44] And toward the end of the century, even Sheridan, who, along with Goldsmith, professed his resistance to sentimental trends in comedy,[45] adheres to the same compassionate model in his *School for Scandal* (1777). Maria, the moral centre of the play, declares: 'If, to raise malicious smiles at the infirmities and misfortunes of those who have never injured us be the province of wit or humour, heaven grant me a double portion of dullness'.[46] Even playwrights who aggressively championed a satiric emphasis in comedy—from Shadwell to Sheridan—agreed that comic objects could not be objects of pity.

Here, too, is the clear emergence of the more common definition of 'humour' as a comic genre or practice rather than a disposition or foundation of comic character. In Maria's speech, we can see the conceptual yoking of wit and humour, often held to be distinct and even oppositional concepts at the end of the seventeenth century, in a single 'province'. A century earlier, wit was 'the faculty of imagination' and in poetry, consists of 'the delightful imaging of persons, actions, passions, or things',[47] while Locke's famous definition of wit in the 1690 *Essay Concerning Human Understanding* considers that its appeal lies in its characteristic 'assemblage of *Ideas*'.[48] Wit's relationship either to comedy or to humour was uneasy. Congreve, in his 1695 essay, 'Concerning Humour in Comedy', observes censoriously that '*Wit is often mistaken for Humour*':

> when a few things have been Wittily and Pleasantly spoken by any Character in a Comedy; it has been very usual for those, who make their Remarks on a Play, while it is acting, to say, *Such a thing is very Humorously spoken: There is a great Deal of Humour in that Part*. Thus the Character of the Person speaking, may be, Surprizingly and Pleasantly, is mistaken for a Character of *Humour*, which indeed is a Character of *Wit*. But there is a great Difference between a Comedy, wherein there are many things *Humorously*, as they call it, which is *Pleasantly* spoken; and one, where there are several Characters of *Humour*, distinguish'd by the Particular and Different Humours, appropriated to the several Persons represented, and which naturally arise, from the different Constitutions, Complexions, and Dispositions of Men.[49]

In 1744, Corbyn Morris repeats this firm distinction between wit and humour in his *Essay Towards Fixing the True Standards of Wit, Humour, Raillery, Satire, and Ridicule*. Returning to Locke's definition of wit as an 'Assemblage',[50] and to the Jonsonian tradition of humours comedy, Morris attacks the looser conception of humour that coexisted through the period with Congreve's strict definition. He critiques Addison's *Spectator* 35, which outlines a genealogy of humour. Addison's 'Humour' is the child of 'Wit' and 'Mirth' and the grandchild of 'Good Sense'. Morris rejects this filial alignment, insisting that 'HUMOUR is derived from the *Foibles*, and whimsical *Oddities* of *Persons* in real Life, which flow rather from their Inconsistencies, and Weakness, than from TRUTH and GOOD SENSE' (xxi). He also, however, considers that Congreve's definition of humour is faulty, as it confuses humour with 'disposition': 'At this Rate every *Weakness* of *Nerves*, or *Particularity* of *Constitution*, is HUMOUR' (xxiv). It is not enough to be different; to be comically humorous, one must be strange. Morris' emphasis on the 'inconsistencies' in temperament that define humour in opposition to truth is another nod to the Lockean subject: Morris' humours character suffers from a misassociation of ideas of exactly the type that shapes individual temperament and draws us away from truth and reason.[51] At mid-century, humour is still an expression of the fundamental shape of the self, but it has successfully absorbed the empiricist associationism that characterises the eighteenth-century picture of the psyche.

Congreve's censure also, however, makes it clear that the contemporary usages of 'humour' to mean 'comic entertainment' and 'humorous' to mean comical or droll were already commonplace 50 years earlier. Though the OED records the earliest use of 'sense of humour' in Richard Hurd's 1753 *Dissertation on the Provinces of Dramatic Poetry*, it records a similar definition of 'humour' as 'a sense of what is amusing or ludicrous' emerging much earlier in the seventeenth century.[52] In 1711, Shaftesbury, in 'Sensus Communis: An Essay on the Freedom of Wit and Humour', had already conflated the terms in arguing for a social practice of 'raillery' as a key ingredient in a liberal society. '[W]ithout wit and humour', Shaftesbury argued, 'reason can hardly have its proof or be distinguished'.[53] For Shaftesbury, comic practice of all kinds tests the rationality of our assumptions, exposing hypocrisy, but equally, validating beliefs and mores unassailable by ridicule. Wit and humour, for Shaftesbury, are intersubjective practices that enshrine the utility of conversational exchange, which can then provide a model for literature, broadly defined.

The splitting off of humour as it is defined by humours comedy from its popular definition as a generalised comic practice is a deliberate attempt to contain and preserve the idea of humour as part of a medicalised discourse of temperament, and to meld this discourse with comedy as a literary genre. Essentially, comedy theory self-consciously refused to countenance the exclusion of the body from aesthetic theories. Retaining the medicalised definition of the humours allows comedy its own particular affiliation with catharsis which, reworked as medicalised purgation, explained and justified tragedy's arousal of unpleasant emotion,[54] and which, along with the Longinian sublime, became the theoretical underpinning of the eighteenth-century sublime. John Dennis writes, 'as the Humors in some distemper'd Body are rais'd, in order to the evacuating that which is redundant or peccant in them; so Tragedy excites Compassion and Terrour to the same end'.[55] Here, the function of tragic catharsis is explicitly to purge the passions in a fashion precisely analogous to the medical purging of the humours. On this reading, the humours are physiological, the passions their intellectual echo. In 1668, Dryden had had the pro-French critic, Lysideus, of his *Essay of Dramatick Poesie*, make a similar claim in a diatribe against English tragicomedy: 'Would you not think that Physician mad', asks Lysideus, 'who having prescribed a Purge, should immediately order you to take restringents upon it?'[56] Here comedy acts to restrain effective catharsis, but the parallel to the physiological action of medicine remains. Dryden observed in 1671 that 'there is the same difference betwixt Farce and Comedy, as betwixt an Empirique and a true Physitian: both of them may attain their ends; but what the one performs by hazard, the other does by skill'.[57] By 1742, Fielding had declared, though somewhat tongue-in-cheek, that farce constituted a 'wholesome Physic for the Mind' and a 'purge' for 'ill Affections'.[58] Retaining the analogy between the physiology of the humours and their literary representation, between the poet and the physician, allows comic playwrights to insist on the key social function of comedy: to purge, like tragedy, the ill temper of the English body politic.[59] This allows comedy a method of direct social action.

In the late seventeenth century, humours comedy becomes a kind of national diagnosis. In 1690, William Temple was the first to insist that the 'variety of Humor' displayed in English comedy echoed 'a greater variety in the Life' produced by England's heterogeneous soil, climate and government.[60] In 1695, Congreve influentially reiterated these claims in his essay 'Concerning Humour in Comedy'. He writes that humour is 'almost of English Growth', and is produced by 'the great Freedom, Privilege, and Liberty which the Common People of *England* enjoy'.[61] George Farquhar adds, in 1701, in his 'Discourse Upon Comedy', that comedy's somewhat loose adherence to form is proof of 'its Charter for Liberty and Toleration' (377). He concludes that the purpose of an '*English* Play' is to address the 'new Distempers' of 'an English Audience', characterised by 'the most unaccountable Medley of Humours [...] of any People upon Earth' (378). This nationalistic fervour for linking English liberty, English heterogeneity—'we are a Mixture of many Nations' (378), observes Farquhar—and the English taste for humours comedy was short-lived, disappearing almost completely after the 1737 Licensing Act. Corbyn Morris drops the idea of humours belonging generally to the disorderly liberty of the nation as a whole, naming, instead, comic characters ideal in their capacity to induce feelings of good-fellowship: Falstaff, Sir Roger de Coverley and Don Quixote.[62] In this brief moment, between the Restoration and the Licensing Act, we can see that humour is associated with a constitutive heterogeneity. Humour serves to interpret the temper of a nation, and it does this work as a literary-critical methodology, showing us why and how the techniques of literature are tied to human states of being.

Even after the stubbornly retained idea of medicalised humour has been allowed to drift away from eighteenth-century ideas about funniness, sometime about the middle of the century, the idea of humour keeps its close relationship to ideas about human subjectivity. When Richard Hurd defines a 'sense of humour' in 1753, in fact he means something more closely affiliated with the moral sense theory that underpins Alexander Gerard's 'sense of ridicule' than with our modern understanding of the term. Moral sense theory is the eighteenth-century philosophical movement that argues from the proposition that the moral judgements of human beings are not distinct from perceptions: they are automatic and non-cognitive. A 'sense of humour', like a 'sense of ridicule', is, in this schema, a universal human capacity to perceive funniness. In Hurd's pseudo-Horatian dissertation, a 'sense of humour' comes up in the context of his resistance to double plots and his recommendation of the unity of action in comedy. The '*sense* of *humour*', he argues, is preserved by the simplicity of plot and undermined 'when the *attention* is split on so many interfering objects'.[63] Less a general disposition to appreciate or to create comedy than an evaluation of comic effect, Hurd's 'sense of humour' denotes a feeling of funniness that is occasional, triggered by an event or performance—a set of objects—rather than the property of an individual person. By the middle of the eighteenth century, though we have moved away from a densely embodied idea of humour towards a more free-floating perceptual ability, humour still carries with it a close association with the sensorium. Our current understanding of a 'sense of humour' emerges directly out of moral sense theory, the philosophical position that rejects a firm distinction between feeling and judgement, corporeal and cognitive 'senses'. From this perspective, moral sense theory begins to look very much like affect theory *avant la lettre*. In investigating eighteenth-century humour, we have slid almost imperceptibly from a history of emotion to a theory of affects, from a comic method to an interpretive methodology.

Eighteenth-century humour provides us with an ideal 'key-problem' for the study of emotion more broadly. Humour works simultaneously as a quality of art and as a quality of a person, as a method of production and a procedure of interpretation. In its defiance of a clear distinction between discourse and materiality, it demands that we consider the relevance of corporeality to our own critical methods.

## NOTES

1. See Farquhar, 'A Discourse Upon Comedy'; Morris, *An Essay Towards*; Beattie, 'On Laughter'; Tave, *The Amiable Humorist*; Ellis, *Sentimental Comedy*.
2. Jenkins and Coleman, 'Introduction', 509.
3. Sennett, *The Fall of Public Man*, 8.
4. Halliwell, *Greek Laughter*, 11.

5 THE HUMOUR OF HUMOURS: COMEDY THEORY AND EIGHTEENTH-CENTURY... 103

5. Leys, 'The Turn to Affect'.
6. As Frank and Wilson have pointed out in a critical response ('Like-Minded'), Leys problematically conflates distinct kinds of investigations of affect in different disciplines, gathering all affect theory under the umbrella of 'anti-intentionalism' (Leys, 'The Turn to Affect', 472).
7. Leys' is in some ways a belated summary of a broad resistance to the extreme end of these essentialist approaches to emotion, often associated with the blunt theoretical instruments used by such emotions researchers as Paul Ekman. Key interventions include Ahmed's *Cultural Politics of Emotion* and Brennan's *Transmission of Affect*, both of which emphatically politicise emotion and resist exclusively non-cognitive definitions of it. See also Dixon, *From Passions to Emotions*. Dixon espouses a strongly historicist view, refusing to countenance any real historical continuity between the experience and definition of emotion in the pre- and early modern world and the modern (post-Darwinian) moment.
8. See, for example, Freverte, et al., *Emotional Lexicons*, which collects and analyses dictionary definitions of terms having to do with emotion in order to track cultural and historical shifts across time and across European nations.
9. See, for example, Nussbaum's neo-Stoic *Upheavals of Thought*.
10. See, for example, Massumi, 'The Autonomy of Affect'. See also Reddy's *The Navigation of Feeling*. Reddy universalises emotion but finds in this essentialism a method of ideological intervention.
11. In *Passion and Action*, Susan James brilliantly assesses the way in which the passions collapse Descartes's distinction between sensory perception and cognition. James's argument underlines the ways in which emotion has always intervened in binarism.
12. See Kramnick's reading of Merleau-Ponty's phenomenology in *Paper Minds*.
13. See Scheer, 'Are Emotions a Kind of Practice?' Scheer uses Bourdieu's concept of *habitus* to reexamine the ways in which emotions history might be able to integrate the study of the human subject in history in ways that do not undermine the historical value of subjective emotional experience and individual perception. Scheer's illuminating use of Bourdieu reaches essentially the same conclusions as Kramnick's discussion of Merleau-Ponty, though Scheer is firmly in the history of emotions camp while Kramnick looks to an 'ecological' approach that would make a less rigid distinction between historicist and new materialist approaches.
14. Berlant, *Cruel Optimism*, 52, 64.
15. Ngai, *Ugly Feelings*.
16. She writes, for example, that 'the line between words and things or between linguistic and non-linguistic phenomena is endlessly changing, permeable, and entirely unsusceptible to any definitive articulation' (Sedgwick, *Touching Feeling*, 6).
17. New materialist challenges to this problem have principally emerged out of new readings of Deleuze, and especially of Deleuze and Guattari's *A Thousand Plateaus*.
18. Paster, *Humoring the Body*, 15.
19. Halliwell, *Greek Laughter*, 5.
20. Elias, 'Essay on Laughter', 304.
21. See Donaldson, *The World Upside Down*.

22. See, for example, Halliwell, *Greek Laughter* and Steggle, *Laughing and Weeping*. Key early modern primary sources include Goclenius, *Physiologia de Risu et Lacrumis* and Joubert, *Treatise on Laughter*.

23. For a text that simultaneously represents and undercuts the eighteenth-century tendency to taxonomise literary technique, see Pope's *Peri Bathous* (1727).

24. Though Greek and Roman thinkers listed comic techniques, they did not tend to be interested, as Alison Sharrock observes, in trying 'to find some overarching scheme into which all these causes of laughter may be fitted, [the] centralising drive being more towards the purposes of comedy (a reflection of the Aristotelian cathartic effect of tragedy) rather than its causes': Sharrock, 'Introduction: Roman Comedy', 2.

25. Again, there is some precedent for both of these theories of comedy in classical comedy theory, but they are not central concerns, neither is treated very extensively and they are balanced by a strong thread of agelasticism. For the first, see Halliwell, *Greek Laughter*, 317–318, and 327–328; for the second, see 21–22. For classical agelastic theory and its impact in the eighteenth century, see Heltzel, 'Chesterfield'.

26. Addison, *Spectator* 47, vol. 1, 182.

27. Gerard, *Essay on Taste*, 68.

28. Aristotle, *On Rhetoric*, Part 3, Sect. 11. Here, novelty works as a kind of incongruity, inducing surprise and thwarting audience expectations.

29. Beattie, 'On Laughter', 344, 349.

30. Kant, *Critique of the Power of Judgement*, 209.

31. Elias, 'Essay on Laughter', 295.

32. Bergson, *Laughter*, 84.

33. 'Humour' persisted in medical texts as a general term for fluid substances in the body, but no longer specifically connoted the humoral system, in which humoral imbalances were linked both to illness and to temperament.

34. Willis, in *The Oxford English Dictionary*, s.v. 'humour'.

35. See Brown, 'From Mechanism to Vitalism' and Broman, 'The Medical Sciences'.

36. Jonson, *Every Man Out*, Induction, 118, ll.101–106.

37. Morris, *An Essay Towards*, 34.

38. Corman, *Genre and Generic Change*, 16.

39. Cicero, *On the Ideal Orator*, quoted in Galbraith, 'Theories of Comedy', 7.

40. Shadwell, *The Humourists* (1670), preface.

41. Stuart Tave emphasised this progressive trend in comedy, arguing for a triumphant national progress towards enlightened compassion. Simon Dickie has more recently delivered a sharp riposte to this somewhat self-satisfied view, arguing that cruelty remained an essential component of comic practice through the century. See *Cruelty and Laughter*.

42. Shadwell, preface to *The Humourists*.

43. Congreve, 'Mr. Congreve, to Mr. Dennis', 64.

44. Fielding, *Joseph* Andrews, 7.

45. See Goldsmith, 'An Essay on the Theatre', and Ellis, *Sentimental Comedy*.

46. Sheridan, *The School for Scandal*, 2.2.185–88, 230.

47. Dryden, 'Dedication to *Annus Mirabilis*', 53.

48. Locke, *An Essay*, II.xi.2, 156.

49. Congreve, 'Mr. Congreve, to Mr. Dennis', 65.

50. Morris, *An Essay Towards*, xiv.

51. Locke, 'Of the Association of Ideas' (1704) in *An Essay*, II.xxxiii.
52. *OED*, s.v. 'humour', 9.a.
53. Shaftesbury (Cooper), *Characteristics*, 35.
54. This theory of Milton's is outlined in his preface to *Samson Agonistes*, and is taken up by Thomas Rymer, who calls tragedy a 'Physick of the mind' (75), and by John Dennis ('The Usefulness', vol. 2, 185). See Martha Nussbaum's objection to a medicalised reading of Aristotle's original text in *The Fragility of Goodness*. See also Elizabeth Belfiore's *Tragic Pleasures*.
55. Dennis, 'The Impartial Critick', vol. 1, 33.
56. Dryden, *An Essay of Dramatick Poesie*, 35.
57. Dryden, 'Preface to *An Evening's Love*'.
58. Fielding, *Joseph Andrews*, 6.
59. Satire was similarly analogised to medicine: see Gallagher, 'Satire as Medicine'.
60. Temple, 'Upon Poetry', 333. For summaries of this nationalist trend in discussions of English humours comedy, see Tave, 'Corbyn Morris' and Freeman, *Character's Theater*, 210–211.
61. Congreve, 'Mr. Congreve, to Mr. Dennis', 71.
62. Morris, *An Essay Towards*, 26, 32, 40.
63. Hurd, 'On the Provinces', 233.

## BIBLIOGRAPHY

Addison, Joseph. 'Spectator 47'. In *The Spectator*, 5 vols., edited by Donald F. Bond. Oxford: Clarendon, 1965.

Ahmed, Sara. *The Cultural Politics of Emotion*. New York: Routledge, 2004.

Aristotle, *On Rhetoric: A Theory of Civic Discourse*. Edited and translated by George A. Kennedy. Oxford: Oxford University Press, 2007.

Beattie, James. 'On Laughter and Ludicrous Composition'. In *Four Essays*, 320–486. Edinburgh, 1776.

Belfiore, Elizabeth S. *Tragic Pleasures: Aristotle on Plot and Emotion*. Princeton, NJ: Princeton University Press, 1992.

Bergson, Henri. 'Laughter'. In *Comedy*, edited by Wylie Sypher. Baltimore, MD: Johns Hopkins University Press, 1956.

Berlant, Lauren. *Cruel Optimism*. Durham, NC: Duke University Press, 2011.

Brennan, Teresa. *The Transmission of Affect*. Ithaca, NY: Cornell University Press, 2004.

Broman, Thomas H. 'The Medical Sciences'. In *The Cambridge History of Science, Volume 4: Eighteenth-Century Science*, edited by Roy Porter, 463–484. Cambridge: Cambridge University Press, 2003.

Brown, Theodore M. 'From Mechanism to Vitalism in Eighteenth-Century English Physiology'. *Journal of the History of Biology* 7, no. 2 (1974): 179–216.

Congreve, William. 'Mr. Congreve, to Mr. Dennis. Concerning Humour in Comedy'. In *The Works of William Congreve*, edited by D.F. McKenzie, vol. 3, 63–72. Oxford: Oxford University Press, 2011.

Cooper, Anthony Ashley, 3rd Earl of Shaftesbury. *Characteristics of Men, Manners, Opinions, Times*. Edited by Lawrence E. Klein. Cambridge: Cambridge University Press, 1999.

Corman, Brian. *Genre and Generic Change in English Comedy, 1660–1710*. Toronto: University of Toronto Press, 1993.

Deleuze, Gilles, and Félix Guattari. *A Thousand Plateaus: Capitalism and Schizophrenia*. Translated by Brian Massumi. Minneapolis, MN: University of Minnesota Press, 1987.

Dennis, John. 'The Impartial Critick'. In *The Critical Works of John Dennis*, 2 vols., edited by Edward Niles Hooker, vol. 1, 11–42. Baltimore: Johns Hopkins, 1939a.

Dennis, John. 'The Usefulness of the Stage'. In *The Critical Works of John Dennis*, 2 vols., edited by Edward Niles Hooker, vol. 1, 146–193. Baltimore: Johns Hopkins, 1939b.

Dickie, Simon. *Cruelty and Laughter: Forgotten Comic Literature and the Unsentimental Eighteenth Century*. Chicago, IL: University of Chicago Press, 2011.

Dixon, Thomas. *From Passions to Emotions: The Creation of a Secular Psychological Category*. Cambridge: Cambridge University Press, 2003.

Donaldson, Ian. *The World Upside Down: Comedy from Jonson to Fielding*. Oxford: Clarendon, 1970.

Dryden, John. 'Dedication to *Annus Mirabilis*' (1667). In *The Works of John Dryden*, vol. 1, edited by H.T. Swedenberg, Jr. and Vinton A. Dearing. Berkeley: University of California Press, 1956.

Dryden, John. *An Essay of Dramatick Poesie*. In *The Works of John Dryden*, vol. 17, edited by Samuel Holt Monk. Berkeley: University of California Press, 1971.

Dryden, John. 'Preface to *An Evening's Love*'. In *The Works of John Dryden*, vol. 10, edited by Maximillian E. Novak. Berkeley: University of California Press, 1970.

Elias, Norbert (edited by Anca Parvulescu). 'Essay on Laughter'. *Critical Inquiry* 43, no. 2 (2017): 281–304.

Ellis, Frank H. *Sentimental Comedy: Theory and Practice*. Cambridge: Cambridge University Press, 1991.

Farquhar, George. 'A Discourse Upon Comedy, In Reference to the English Stage'. In *Love and Business* (1701). In *The Works of George Farquhar*, 2 vols., edited by Shirley Strum Kenny, vol. 2, 364–386. Oxford: Clarendon, 1988.

Fielding, Henry. *Joseph Andrews and Shamela*. Edited by Douglas Brooks-Davies and Thomas Keymer. Oxford: Oxford University Press, 1999.

Frank, Adam, and Elizabeth A. Wilson. 'Like-Minded'. *Critical Inquiry* 38, no. 4 (2012): 870–877.

Freeman, Lisa. *Character's Theater: Genre and Identity on the Eighteenth-Century English Stage*. Philadelphia: University of Pennsylvania Press, 2002.

Freverte, Ute, et al., eds. *Emotional Lexicons: Continuity and Change in the Vocabulary of Feeling 1700–2000*. Oxford: Oxford University Press, 2014.

Galbraith, David. 'Theories of Comedy'. In *The Cambridge Companion to Shakespearean Comedy*, edited by Alexander Leggatt, 3–17. Cambridge: Cambridge University Press, 2001.

Gallagher, Noelle. 'Satire as Medicine in the Restoration and Early Eighteenth Century: The History of a Metaphor'. *Literature and Medicine* 31, no. 1 (2013): 17–39.

Gerard, Alexander. *An Essay on Taste*. London: Printed for A. Millar, in the Strand, 1759.

Goclenius, Rudolph. *Physiologia de Risu et Lacrumis*. Leyden, 1597.

Goldsmith, Oliver. 'An Essay on the Theatre; or, A Comparison Between Laughing and Sentimental Comedy' (1773). In *The Collected Works of Oliver Goldsmith*, 5 vols., edited by Arthur Friedman, vol. 3, 209–213. Oxford: Clarendon, 1966.

Halliwell, Stephen. *Greek Laughter: A Study of Cultural Psychology from Homer to Early Christianity*. Cambridge: Cambridge University Press, 2008.

Heltzel, Virgil B. 'Chesterfield and the Anti-Laughter Tradition'. *Modern Philology* 26, no. 1 (1928): 73–90.

Hurd, Richard. 'On the Provinces of the Several Species of Dramatic Poetry'. In *Q. Horatii Flacci epistolae ad Pisones, et Augustum*. 2 vols. London: W. Thurlbourne, 1753.

James, Susan. *Passion and Action: The Emotions in Seventeenth-Century Philosophy*. Oxford: Oxford University Press, 1997.

Jenkins, Eugenia Zuroski, and Patrick Coleman. 'Introduction'. *Eighteenth-Century Fiction* 26, no. 4 (2014): 505–514.

Jonson, Ben. *Every Man Out of His Humour*. Edited by Helen Ostovich. Manchester: Manchester University Press, 2001.

Joubert, Laurent. *Treatise on Laughter*. Translated by Gregory David de Rocher. Tuscaloosa, AL: University of Alabama Press, 1980.

Kant, Immanuel. *Critique of the Power of Judgement* (1790). Edited and translated by Paul Guyer. Cambridge: Cambridge University Press, 2013.

Kramnick, Jonathan. *Paper Minds: Literature and the Ecology of Consciousness*. Chicago, IL: University of Chicago Press, 2018.

Leys, Ruth. 'The Turn to Affect: A Critique'. *Critical Inquiry* 37, no. 3 (2011): 434–472.

Locke, John. *An Essay Concerning Human Understanding*. Edited by Peter H. Nidditch. Oxford: Oxford University Press, 1975 [1690].

Massumi, Brian. 'The Autonomy of Affect'. *Cultural Critique* 31 (1995): 83–109.

Morris, Corbyn. *An Essay Towards Fixing the True Standards of Wit, Humour, Raillery, Satire, and Ridicule*. London: J. Roberts; W. Bickerton, 1744.

Ngai, Sianne. *Ugly Feelings*. Cambridge, MA: Harvard University Press, 2007.

Nussbaum, Martha C. *The Fragility of Goodness: Luck and Ethics in Greek Tragedy and Philosophy*. Cambridge: Cambridge University Press, 1986.

Nussbaum, Martha C. *Upheavals of Thought: The Intelligence of Emotions*. Cambridge: Cambridge University Press, 2001.

Paster, Gail Kern. *Humoring the Body: Emotions and the Shakespearean Stage*. Chicago, IL: University of Chicago Press, 2004.

Pope, Alexander. 'Peri Bathous'. In *The Prose Works of Alexander Pope*, 2 vols., edited by Norman Ault and Rosemary Cowler, vol. 2, 171–276. Oxford: Blackwell, 1936–1986 [1727].

Reddy, William. *The Navigation of Feeling: A Framework for the History of Emotions*. Cambridge: Cambridge University Press, 2001.

Rymer, Thomas. 'Tragedies of the Last Age'. In *The Critical Works of Thomas Rymer*, edited by Curt A. Zimansky. New Haven: Yale University Press, 1956.

Scheer, Monique. 'Are Emotions a Kind of Practice (And Is That What Makes Them Have a History)? A Bourdieuian Approach to Understanding Emotion'. *History and Theory* 51, no. 2 (2012): 193–220.

Sedgwick, Eve Kosofsky. *Touching Feeling: Affect, Pedagogy, Performativity*. Durham, NC: Duke University Press, 2003.

Sennett, Richard. *The Fall of Public Man*. New York: Norton, 1974, reprinted by Knopf, 1977.

Shadwell, Thomas. *The Humourists* (1670). In *The Dramatic Works of Thomas Shadwell*, 132–203. London: J. Knapton and J. Tonson, 1720.

Sharrock, Alison. 'Introduction: Roman Comedy'. In *The Cambridge Companion to Roman Comedy*, edited by Martin T. Dinter, 1–14. Cambridge: Cambridge University Press, 2019.

Sheridan, Richard Brinsley. *The School for Scandal and Other Plays*. Edited by Michael Cordner. Oxford: Oxford University Press, 1998.

Steggle, Matthew. *Laughing and Weeping in Early Modern Theatres*. Farnham: Ashgate, 2007.

Tave, Stuart. *The Amiable Humorist: A Study in the Comic Theory and Criticism of the Eighteenth and Early Nineteenth Centuries*. Chicago, IL: University of Chicago Press, 1960.

Tave, Stuart. 'Corbyn Morris: Falstaff, Humour, and Comic Theory in the Eighteenth Century'. *Modern Philology* 50, no. 2 (1952): 102–115.

Temple, William. 'Upon Poetry'. In *Miscellanea*. The Second Part. 2nd edition, 279–341. London: R. and R. Simpson, 1690.

CHAPTER 6

# Bergson's Theory of the Comic and Its Applicability to Sixteenth-Century Japanese Comedy

*Jessica Milner Davis*

## BERGSON'S 'THEORY OF THE COMIC'

Henri Bergson (1859–1941) was the first modern theorist of humour and laughter to derive his ideas from contemporary observation of laughter in the theatre, the circus and children's games. Successful comedies on the 1890s Parisian stage together with their predecessors such as the plays of Molière provided him with data from which he identified a range of traditional comic devices. In his principal study relating to humour and the comic, *Le Rire* (*Laughter*, originally published in 1900),[1] he discussed these under three headings, 'the comedy of forms, gestures and movements', 'the comedy of situations and words' and 'the comedy of character'. In the first section, he dissects the comic actor's use of gesture rather than productive action and the nature of stage movement in comedy. In the second, he looks at plot-structures typical of comedy and how certain recurring phrases or bons mots elicit laughter. In the last section, he discusses the type of stock characters he so frequently encountered in these comedies, noting how in their fixed ideas and lack of adaptability they resemble children's toys such as puppets, jack-in-the-boxes or marionettes rather than human beings. He also observed the importance of tempo (pace of speech and action) in comedy performances and how frequently jokes turn on literal renderings of metaphor (i.e. mocking degradation or

J. Milner Davis (✉)
University of Sydney, Sydney, NSW, Australia
e-mail: jessica.davis@sydney.edu.au

© The Author(s), under exclusive license to Springer Nature
Switzerland AG 2020
D. Derrin, H. Burrows (eds.), *The Palgrave Handbook of Humour, History, and Methodology*, https://doi.org/10.1007/978-3-030-56646-3_6

reification of verbal tropes). Plot devices he considered include repetition and duplication, inversion and the trope of the robber robbed, the quiproquo (mistaking one thing or word for another), the reciprocal interference of series (or crossed wires effect, where two or more characters continually misinterpret the same signal—think of Abbott and Costello's classic 'Who's on first base?' routine[2]) and the snowball in which a plot sweeps all its characters into a comic maelstrom of sound and fury.

Bergson did not claim to invent these devices although he named some of them for the first time (e.g. quiproquo's and ironic plot twists are scarcely novel concepts, but '*la boule à neige*' [the snowball effect (83)] is Bergson's own). Nevertheless, he was the first theorist of humour to collect and list such techniques and concepts and to reflect on their collective nature. From them, he extracted his key idea: that laughter-provoking comedy stems from a rigidity (*raideur*, a lack of flexibility)[3] in the thoughts, words and actions of characters and in the formal patterning of typical comic plots.

### *Bergson and Humour Studies*

In humour studies, Bergson is often seen as a theorist of incongruity in general.[4] In fact, as we shall see below, he stressed one particular aspect of incongruity— the mismatch between the rigidly mechanical and the flexibility that characterises life's vitality. The first he saw as being the essence of humour or the comic (*le comique*) and the second as characterising the ever-evolving and dynamic life-force (*l'élan vital*) that drives us and our world. In his writings on time,[5] Bergson often imagined the mechanical as an actual machine, especially as that ubiquitous symbol of the modern urbanised world, the clock. He noted that when the mechanical dominates everyday life, it constructs a kind of phantom self in a human being so that a person thinks and behaves for all practical purposes in 'mechanical time' rather than being able to transcend circumstances and live their life freely in a more reflective form of time. When he came to write *Laughter*, he argued that at the centre of the comic is the image of a person acting not like a free-willed human but like a machine, with something *du mécanique plaqué sur du vivant*, or 'something mechanical encrusted on the living' (37). The comedian's art directs our attention to this image so that it functions as 'a cross[roads] at which we must halt, a central image from which the imagination branches off in different directions' (26). If a named theory of humour can be assigned to Bergson, it might properly be termed the theory of the mechanical.[6]

Another view of Bergson is to see him as an advocate for laughter as a mode of social correction. He argued that laughter is a response to what is too socially deviant and inconveniently inelastic: 'the comic is rigidity, and laughter is its punishment' (21). Stressing the element of mockery for social imperfections led Bergson to propose that condescension, perhaps even malice, is essential to the comic. At the very least, a lack of empathy is necessary if an audience is to laugh outright at the troubles afflicting a comic victim. Such a 'temporary anaesthesia of the heart' (3–4) prevents any sympathetic identification with the comic victims at whose mechanical traits they are laughing.

This is of course a narrow view of humour that ignores the case of sympathetic laughter combining pity and ridicule, but many humour scholars have accepted it as summing up Bergson's theoretical approach, classing him accordingly as a superiority theorist.[7] From this perhaps results his somewhat lowly profile in humour studies[8] since contemporary humour research prefers to focus upon what is benign in laughter and humour rather than its negatives.[9] However, one Bergson specialist has pointed out that, even when considered as a superiority theorist, Bergson is far from adopting a simple approach. Following Thomas Hobbes and others, that theory conventionally emphasises the dominance of one individual (the laugher or joke-maker) over another (the butt); to this, Bergson adds the notion of socially bonding through humour and corrective laughter.[10]

In general, the complexity of Bergson's ideas is largely disregarded in humour studies. *Le Rire* (*Laughter*) alone of his writings is well-recognised and is usually given either a slight acknowledgment or dismissed. Attardo for example thinks that '[h]umor research has advanced [...] well beyond Bergson'.[11] Amy Carrell adds, 'Bergson's view of humor is very narrow and puritanical'.[12] Both Martin and Provine mention him only as a simple superiority theorist, while more recent surveys such as Scheel's simply ignore him.[13]

### *Bergsonian Studies*

While most Bergson specialists pass over his theory of the comic to concentrate on his philosophy, evolutionary thought and ethics, a recent study by Mark Sinclair (2019) is a notable exception.[14] Surveying the whole of Bergson's work, he is able to place *Laughter* in the context of his other more philosophical writings. As I have argued elsewhere, this allows a more nuanced appreciation of Bergson's ideas.[15] Sinclair agrees that Bergson falls into the superiority theory camp (with the qualifications noted above), but sees him also an incongruity theorist. And importantly, he goes beyond these two rather simple classifications, linking the central formula of *Laughter* (the mechanical encrusted on the living) to Bergson's writings on life, time and freedom. Surveying the complete *œuvre*, Sinclair concludes that *Laughter* 'is not just an incidental contribution to a particular topic dear to its author, but a transitional, pivotal moment in Bergson's philosophy as a whole'.[16] It is in this light that we must search for Bergson's true contribution to humour theory, looking not just at his writing and thinking about laughter and the comic but also at those that are about time, freedom and the nature of human existence.

### *Bergson on Time and Freedom*

Bergson's thinking about time, relativity and human freedom were well ahead of their era. It is only recently that they have begun to be re-appraised in the light of recent scientific investigations of the nature of human consciousness.[17] Despite having been awarded the Nobel Prize (for literature) in 1927, Bergson came under increasing attack for his philosophical and scientific ideas which fell foul of Hegelianism and its belief that the rational alone is real. Across the channel, Bertrand Russell dismissed Bergson as a 'cosmic poet' who exalted irrationalism and wanted to displace rational intelligence with a 'heaving sea of intuition'. Intuition, he thundered in his review of *Laughter*, was at its best in 'bats, birds, bees and Bergson'.[18] However, starting with the study of Bergson made by Gilles Deleuze, the writer has come to be seen as a precursor of post-structuralism who recognises the relativity of human experience but who also offers 're-engagement with the concreteness of the real', that is, insight into the solidity of what we experience in daily life as well as the reality of imagination and creative inspiration.[19] Indeed, scientific advances in cognitive psychology and the nature of memory and consciousness, especially the advent of Theory of Mind, also favour Bergson's ideas. In his disagreement with Einstein over the workings of relativity, he has even been seen as a precursor of quantum physics.[20]

In his philosophical writings (and indeed in his Nobel acceptance speech), Bergson expressed the view that evolution does not merely apply to species and life-forms but also to the development of moral and empathetic rapprochement between peoples; this he considered an essential accompaniment to material and mechanical progress.[21] It was, he argued, illusory to believe that mechanical inventions would raise the moral as well as the material level of humankind's existence. He pointed out that advances like steam and electricity, while they might diminish distances, had done nothing to bring together people of different nations and cultures.[22] By 1927, that kind of simplistic belief had long been disproved by World War 1: indeed it had shown that antagonisms had been aggravated rather than diminished. History was of course to prove Bergson tragically right on this point.

The importance of these aspects of Bergson's thinking about time and personal freedom for his investigation of comic techniques is that they too centre on the concept of the mechanical. Time that is measured by the cyclical repetition of clocks suppresses human flexibility, creating a kind of phantom, mechanised form of human life. Time is thus a relative concept; or perhaps multiple concepts, one of which is subject to individual experiential variations so that what seems to one person to last a long time can pass in a flash to others.[23] To exercise free choice, one must aspire to escape the bonds of mechanical time and become aware of self as a free entity. Such an ability is however rare:

> But the moments where we tune into ourselves [*nous nous resaisissons*] in this way are extremely rare and this is why we are rarely free. Most of the time we live outside ourselves; we only perceive the colourless phantom of ourselves, the shadow that pure duration projects into homogenous space. Our existence unfolds in space rather than time. We live for the external world rather than for ourselves. We speak rather than think; we are acted upon rather than acting ourselves. To act freely is to retake possession of oneself [*le soi*]; it is to place oneself back in pure duration [of time].[24]

For Bergson, it is only during such moments that true creativity, true freedom, can be experienced. To make the link: comic victims are by definition not free and, more than we would wish, we the audience resemble such mechanical beings. Thus, experiencing what is comic and reacting with laughter towards it presents itself as a route of escape into a freer realm of existence.

### *The Role of Laughter*

Despite its title, *Laughter* is not really a study of this form of human behaviour, certainly not in its evolutionary context. Various types of laughter are simply omitted: tickling, hysteria, laughter induced by shock, politeness, nervousness, and so on.[25] Bergson's focus is exclusively on the laughter that is produced by what is comic, that is, the kind that demands his famous formula of a temporary anaesthesia of the heart. One can see this as a very French view, one that appertains better to laughter in response to pure wit or farcical humour rather than the gentler, more sympathetic (traditionally English) style of laughter and humour.[26] It would be easy from this to dismiss Bergson's view of the comic as cold-hearted.

In fact even in *Laughter*, let alone in his later works such as *Time and Free Will* and *Creative Evolution*, he makes it clear that he is not promoting a galvanic kind of laughter in response to a stimulus, like a dead frog kicking out in reaction to an electrical current. Rather he is drawing attention to the moral dimension that underlies much laughter, whether sympathetic or corrective. The source of the laughter may be a mechanical device, repetition, puppet-like behaviour or physical rigidities. But the fact that laughter is our response draws him into a deeper speculation about its significance and effects.

Prefiguring Bakhtin's study of carnivalesque laughter,[27] Bergson outlines at some length the comedy that is created by situations in which the physical body dominates the spiritual soul, drawing a parallel with the letter of the law being elevated over its intention. He cites a case from Moliere's comedy, *L'Amour medecin* [*Love Doctor*, 1665] when the foolish Dr Bahys advises his patient, 'It is better to die through following the rules than to recover through violating them'. Ridicule of the professions (medical or legal), Bergson concludes, illustrates the principle of 'THE BODY TAKING PRECEDENCE OF THE SOUL' or 'THE MANNER SEEKING TO OUTDO THE MATTER, THE LETTER AIMING AT OUSTING THE SPIRIT' (capitals in the original):

> Constant attention to form and the mechanical application of rules here bring about a kind of professional automatism analogous to that imposed upon the soul by the habits of the body, and equally laughable. Numerous are the examples of this on the stage. ([1910] 2005: x)

It follows that laughing at this behaviour is essentially a redemptive act: protesting against rigidities and absurdities, it can help restore a free-living self to those trapped in a mechanised life. This redemptive aspect applies not only to the laugher—and potentially their targets if they could but see the comic in their own situations—but above all to those who can laugh at themselves. *Laughter* dissects the nature of the comic character or stereotype, imprisoned in vanity, lacking in self-awareness, expressing its will more through gesture than constructive action; Bergson's conclusion is that '[t]he chief cause of rigidity is the neglect to look around—and more especially within oneself' (147). If comedy, both in real life and as constructed on the stage, has a serious social significance, that is not merely corrective in the conformist sense, it also brings us more into touch with humanity, our own as well as that of others.

Guerlac points out that Bergson 'argues against the application of mechanistic modes of thinking to living beings'.[28] It was the flexibility of life, not the galvanic, that he valued. At the outset of his book, he rejects the idea of 'imprisoning the comic within a definition' because it is 'a living thing [...] however trivial [...] we shall treat it with a respect due to life' (11). Viewed in this light, laughter that results from the mechanical in comedy can be seen not just as laughter at others being held captive by the clock and their own internal mechanisms, but also as part of a human(e) and humanising reaction by individuals to their own personal domination by time. Laughter presents itself as a way to regain lost sensibilities. In laughing at the very human tendency for life to be driven by the mechanical, audiences can gain a momentary freedom. We may speculate that perhaps, in the euphoria that is enjoyed post-laughter, they may even reflect on a deeper, freer way of life for themselves to avoid mechanical capture. In the context of his other philosophical work, then, Bergson's approach offers not merely a theory of laughter as social corrective but also a theory of humour as personal insight and potential liberation.[29]

Bergson's ideas about the purposes of laughter and its connection with human freedom are complex and thought-provoking but relevant, whether the humour under consideration belongs to a modern or an older text or image. Further, the comic devices he found in comedies and games of his time quite reliably occur in many forms of humour, not just performative comedy, and are likely universal, relating to many if not all cultures and times. They deserve close inspection since they may well serve as useful markers of humour in any work in which they can be identified. Independent of the interesting question of the purpose and philosophical meaning of humour, Bergson's analysis of how comedy construes the mechanical can offer us useful tools for understanding characters, situations, plots, imagery and dialogue with humorous connotations. The idea that the humour that we identify—and hopefully enjoy—may help us overcome our personal subjection to mechanical dominance and regain a degree of human freedom and agility is certainly worth considering in such cases, even if his theory of liberation through laughing at the mechanical may not explicate all aspects of what we find. As I will show, it can add to our understanding of a text.

## Applying Bergson in a Different Comic Tradition— Japanese Kyōgen

Given the importance of French comedy for Bergson's work on laughter, it seems likely that his ideas and tools would apply much more straightforwardly to stage comedies in the European tradition than to ones from remote cultures and times. Testing this assumption, this chapter will focus on a comic piece that dates from the Muromachi period (1336–1573) in Japan. During this period, the aristocratic nō drama took a set shape which has persisted to this day. Along with these serious (often tragic, even religious in theme) dramas, short pieces called kyōgen (literally, 'crazy words') were played as comic relief.[30] These texts are far less well known and studied than the serious drama, although they remain popular.

While the two genres are performed by differently trained actors, they frequently share the same stage and programme and some aspects of performance, for example, traditional costume and a degree of 'stage voice' that is differentiated from normal speech. The texts of kyōgen plays were handed down in an oral tradition and first committed to writing in the early Edo period (seventeenth century). They are now preserved and interpreted by several different actor training schools including two possessing an unbroken tradition, the Ōkura and the Izumi Schools. In recent years, some modern English translations of kyōgen have been published.[31] Apart from the scripts (which do vary slightly from one school to another), their characters, costumes, settings and acting style have also been handed down with little alteration.[32] A full nō programme used to be longer, but today typically includes three nō plays interspersed with two kyōgen plays. While nō is chanted throughout with musical accompaniment, kyōgen is not usually accompanied; although festive song and dance may appear, along with other scenes of lively physical action that make a distinct contrast to the more stately, static nō. Similarly, the actions of kyōgen actors are more natural and somewhat less stylised than in nō; and, while nō is played with masks, most kyōgen characters are unmasked (exceptions are demons and women, since, as in nō, all the actors are male).

Because kyōgen are short plays (from 20 to 45 minutes long), there is not sufficient time to develop elaborate plots such as the five-act pieces of the nineteenth-century European stage familiar to Bergson. Despite this, kyōgen are far from simple in their construction. They achieve considerable complexity, even within the restrictions of time and the use of stock characters and themes that are often well-known to Japanese audiences because they derive from folk-lore or classical texts. Whether they employ the same comic devices that Bergson identified remains to be seen.

## Summary of Busu (Poison)

The text from the kyōgen repertoire selected for discussion is *Busu* (*Poison*), a well-known and popular piece even today.[33] It was probably adapted from a story in the late-thirteenth century *Shasekishū* (*Collection of Sand and Pebbles*) by Mujū Ichien (1226–1312), which tells a tale of how some Buddhist disciples trick their abbot who is refusing to share the temple's sugar.[34] The play-script is found in Koyama; and the English translation used here is by Sakanishi.[35] Given its verbal simplicity (which nonetheless offers a rich basis for an actor's dramatic interpretation), it seems justifiable to study the play here in translation.

For any scholar approaching an unfamiliar kyōgen text, the first thing that must command attention is the plot or story line; summarising that will provide a good initial basis for judging whether Bergson's toolkit is relevant. The plot of *Busu* turns on a common kyōgen theme in which a master (a small-holding rural landlord or *daimyō*) is leaving his home and telling his two selfish but wily servants that, during his absence, they are in charge of the house and its contents—which include a pot of a terribly dangerous poison called 'busu'. The two servants, traditionally named Tarō Kaja and Jirō Kaja (*kaja* means boy or servant), are wary but irresistibly curious. As with many other kyōgen plots, they disobey orders and approach the pot to investigate (see Fig. 6.1). Eventually, they realise that the poison is actually sugar—a rare and precious substance in days when the only common sweetener was honey—and they taste it. Very rapidly, they eat the lot (see Fig. 6.2). Terrified at what they have done, they try to work out how to escape their master's wrath. Tarō Kaja (the smarter of the two) has an idea and tells the other to tear up the master's scroll painting and smash his valuable display bowl. His partner is bemused and asks how on earth it can be helpful to make things worse; nevertheless, he carries out the plan. When the master returns, he finds them sitting and pretending to cry over the wreckage. Tarō Kaja explains that, to occupy the time, they were trying out their sumō wrestling and in the process, accidentally tore the priceless scroll and smashed the bowl—after which naturally they tried to commit suicide by eating what the master had told them was a deadly poison. Between sobs, he explains that when this did not work, they simply ate more and more. By accepting the original lie as fact and then telling their own, the servants hilariously turn the tables on their less-than-honest master.

## Locating Bergson's Comic Devices in Busu—Types of Farce Plots

Even this simple plot summary reveals many of Bergson's comic devices and techniques being put to work. At a different level, closer examination of the internal structure of individual scenes or episodes will reveal others. Starting here with the skeleton outline I have just given, this can be compared with four basic categories of comedy plot-structure which derive from Bergson's ideas of predictable mechanical patterning and are typical of short farces. The four are listed below as follows:[36]

**Fig. 6.1** Shigeyama Shigeru (b. 1975, left) as Tarō Kaja and Shigeyama Dōji (now Sennojō, b. 1983, right) as Jirō Kaja in a 13 January 2013 performance of *Busu* at the Kongō Nō Theatre, Kyoto. (Photo by Uesugi Haruka, reproduced courtesy of Shigeyama Kyōgenkai Jimukyoku)

1. **Humiliation or deception plots** in which an unpleasant victim is exposed to a predictable fate, without opportunity for retaliation. These unidirectional comedies are usually short and require justifications to be given for the pleasure they take in the victim's suffering.
2. **Reversal plots** in which the tables are turned on the original trickster, allowing the victim/s to retaliate. Further switches of direction may occur to prolong the mirth and perhaps to ensure a 'proper' conventional outcome.

**Fig. 6.2** Shigeyama Dōji (now Sennojō, b. 1983, left) as Jirō Kaja and Shigeyama Shigeru (b. 1975, right) as Tarō Kaja in a 13 January 2013 performance of *Busu* at the Kongō Nō Theatre, Kyoto. (Photo by Uesugi Haruka, reproduced courtesy of Shigeyama Kyōgenkai Jimukyoku)

3. **Equilibrium or quarrel plots** that focus upon a perpetual-motion kind of movement between two opposing forces wrestling each other, either literally or metaphorically, in a tug-of-war that has no resolution, so that the two remain in semi-permanent balance; and
4. **Snowball plots** in which all characters are equally caught up as victims in a maelstrom of escalating sound and fury. Such plots are often driven by an elaborate series of misunderstandings and errors, giving rise to many 'crossed lines' or quiproquos between the different parties. They also reflect the power of nature and inanimate objects, tools and machines to dominate mere humans.

All of these structures turn on reversals, repetition and duplication, inversion and the trope of the robber robbed, but place them within different patterns of how the overall dramatic narrative progresses, as illustrated in Fig. 6.3. Contained within these outlines are Bergson's jack-in-the-boxes and marionettes and the kind of type or stock characters who are not fully rounded as in real life, who are easily recognisable as a caricature and whose fixed ideas and lack of adaptability feed into the lines of direction of the plot. Also located within the larger structures in individual scenes and episodes are the devices and techniques that Bergson found in his own comic examples: literal

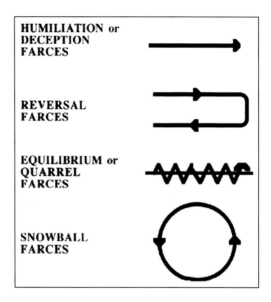

Fig. 6.3 Graphic representation of four basic comic plots types, showing the directions taken by the dramatic narrative in each. (Milner Davis, *Farce*, 7)

renderings of metaphor or speech taken at its face value, crossed wires (mutual misunderstandings) and verbal humour that is marked by mechanical patterns such as repetition of stock phrases or word-play with dual meanings. When the texts with these patterns are performed, they will likely feature several alterations of pace or tempo in both speech and action with sudden speeding up of events or slowing them down and dragging things out in order to emphasise a smaller detail in the scene, the dilemma of a particular character or a symmetrical pattern created by the actors in their actions and reactions.

### *Plot-Types and* Busu

Applied to *Busu*, these four types show that its basic structure belongs to the second category, a revenge plot in which lied-to servants themselves lie to their master in return and by disobeying orders manage to defeat their master's wish to keep his precious edible treasure all to himself. This version of comic revenge embodies a social inversion which in normal circumstances might evoke disapproval rather than comic indulgence by the audience: in any culture, but particularly in medieval Japan, servants are not supposed to outwit their master and certainly not to get away with it scot-free. The Japanese term for this inversion is *gekokujō* or 'the tail wagging the dog'[37] and Japanese culture strongly prefers that it take place—if at all—within a highly circumscribed time and place, effectively a safe comic frame. That is certainly the case here, where the whole play is contained within a traditional time and place for comedy and an established theatre programme structure.[38]

While social inversion and tit-for-tat are not patterns that are funny in and of themselves, their recognisable shape as they unfold in a performance moulds an audience's expectations about what will happen next and creates a degree of satisfaction when the pattern is fulfilled. The overarching structure of the plot-type that contains them reassures the audience that only a controlled and limited challenge to conventional authority will be made. The rebellious characters intent on getting their own way, or indulging themselves or revenging themselves on their betters thus manage to achieve their aim of overturning the social order but fail to have it all their own way. Each of the plot-types in one way or another delimits the rebellion and contains its threat to authority. I shall discuss below the way in which the two rebellious servants of *Busu* are paid out in the end.

The basic reversal plot of *Busu* is however deceptively simple: on closer inspection, it is combined with elements from several of the other types, some, like the snowball, located in smaller episodes. For example, the revenge taken by the two servants is not commensurate with their master's original deceit but goes far beyond that simple lie. After the 'poison' is completely consumed, things turn violent as his precious art objects are also destroyed one by one. Inside the revenge/reversal structure, there is a gathering snowball of activity as Tarō Kaja directs his fellow-servant in a whirlwind of ripping, tearing and smashing that involves escalating speed of action and accompanying noises, with a satisfying crash of pottery as the vase finally goes.[39] As we shall see, this upping of the original ante is far from being merely decorative and is essential to ensuring that the revenge remains comic in the overall logic of the robber robbed plot.

### *Locating Bergson's Mechanical Devices in* Busu

In addition to the tropes of inversion, repetition and snowball, individual scenes also turn upon the use of misunderstandings and crossed wires in communication. Before the master's return, neither Jirō Kaja nor the audience can understand why Tarō should think the proposed destruction is a good idea. Jirō says repeatedly, 'What a reckless fellow you are! Tear the scroll on top of eating the *busu*? I can't!'. But Tarō merely laughs and directs him to smash the bowl as well. Jirō responds, 'You must be out of your mind. They are Master's pet treasures. I can't'. Despite his inability to understand and his trembling fear, he does what he is told most effectively, enjoying the destruction, it would seem. It is only when their master returns and listens to Tarō's invented explanation of what has been going on that Jirō and the audience grasp his cunning scheme: he saw that to account convincingly for why in all innocence the poison was eaten up when it was so dangerous, truly extravagant sins would be needed. When the audience is finally enlightened, their laughter will be all the greater for their former puzzlement and the delayed moment of understanding.

But the master himself cannot laugh. Despite his anger, he is trapped in a device of his own making which holds him fast in its machine-like grip. He must listen in silent amazement as the two outline their story, only gradually coming to realise that his own words have in fact been accepted as the truth and that the lie has been believed—at least in the servants' story. At the opposite end of these crossed wires are the audience and the servants who share a very different interpretation of what is being said. Bergson's image of something mechanical encrusted on the living aptly describes the frozen figure of the master who should be wreaking active vengeance of his faithless servants. The moment is drawn out by lengthy narration of events, focussing attention upon the hapless victim and the empty pot embodying the reification of the verbal lie.

The dramatic moment is a familiar one to any kyōgen audience, creating a pleasurable kind of 'here we go again' moment in which they expect some tarradiddle of excuses from the mischievous servants. Being stock characters, driven by their own predictable natures and known from previous plays, Tarō and Jirō are always up to their tricks. Nevertheless, there is an element of surprise built into this repetition of the familiar, since no-one—not even Jirō Kaja—knows in advance what web of lies will be spun by his partner. Thus, predictability and surprise combine to create a further incongruity in addition to those of inversion, repetition, exaggeration, implausibility and reification of the verbal involved in this scene.

Delving a little further into this comic scene, the master's dilemma is evidently a moral one: should he explode the myth and acknowledge his own lie, or accept their story at face value and put up with his losses? It is also a battle of the body and the mind: his anger is palpable, yet he fears to lose face if he admits his lie. He remains locked in silence as the two servants take over the dialogue. The tell-tale comic pattern of verbal repetition is noteworthy here, as is its culmination in a jointly delivered chant improbably invoking the religious themes of fate and destiny:

| Tarō: | We were so mortified that we decided to kill ourselves at once, and since you told us that the *busu* in the box would kill us instantly, we opened the box and ate it. But unfortunately we are not dead yet. |
|---|---|
| Jirō: | Alas, not yet. |
| Tarō: | As death came not with a mouthful, I took another mouthful. Yet no death. |
| Jirō: | Three mouthfuls and four mouthfuls! Alas, I could not die. |
| Tarō: | Even five and six! Alas no! |
| **Tarō and Jirō:** | Though we have taken ten mouthfuls, nay all that there was of the *busu*, yet we are alive. Our lives are charmed. They have not come to their appointed close. |

As they embroider their story, Tarō's and Jirō's voices alternate with each other; in physical terms, they are presumably jigging about with excitement and nervousness. By contrast, their silent master remains still. While that is a standard convention for characters who are not speaking in kyōgen, a skilled actor would exploit stillness here to good dramatic effect using facial expression and projected emotion. This would reflect his internal turmoil as, despite his stillness, the man oscillates between two alternatives about what to say or do and does neither. In Bergson's terms, the conflicting emotions impose rigidity on the body. This occurs within a larger comic pattern: that of an equilibrium plot in which two equal but opposing parties, servants and master, are locked in battle and unable to break the tie. The battle of wits comes to its climax when the two servants comically chant as one to deliver their final blow, a claim that divine fate must be on their side since it has protected them from the poison. The outrageousness of this assertion effectively breaks their master free from his frozen silence and thus precipitates the conclusion of the play. Driven by his own type-character and its unalterable instincts, he becomes the angry master expected by the audience and reaches for a tried and true comic conclusion for any farce: beating the culprits off stage.

It turns out however, as in many other kyōgen, that the beating-off is more of a gesture than an effective act. Despite the master's stock cry of '*Yarumai zo, yarumai zo!*' [I won't let you get away with this!], the text makes it very clear that these two scoundrels run off to live and misbehave another day in another play (repetition again):

**Lord:**          You confounded scoundrels!
**Tarō and Jirō:**  Pardon us! Pardon us!
**Lord:**          Never, never! Running away? Catch them, catch them!

Focussing on the pair of comic servants, one smarter than the other, both ruled by their appetites despite their obligation to serve their master loyally, it is significant to note that this play shares its traditional straight man and his stooge with many others in Western comedy from Plautus onwards to Abbott and Costello. As in Plautus' *Mostellaria* (*Ghost House*, ?139 BCE), Shakespeare's *The Comedy of Errors* and *The Taming of the Shrew* (both probably from the 1590s), Molière's *Bourgeois Gentilhomme* (1670) and many others, they are assigned the social role of servant. This stereotypical pair reappears in play after kyōgen play with the same names and characteristics. Although the social roles are different, they have much in common with contemporary Japanese manzai or stand-up comedy which also features a straight (clever) man and his (rather dim) partner, but evidently the tradition is home-grown rather than a modern import from the West.[40] In kyōgen, their behaviour is predictable: Tarō is the clever leader who initiates the mischief and Jirō the follower, the slower sidekick. The audience expects them to disobey their orders, make a mess of things and generally to try their master's patience to the limit, in a word, to be the tail wagging the dog (*gekokujo* is the Japanese word, a form of behaviour normally frowned upon).[41]

Stereotypes like these embody the principles of repetition (from play to play and within the play) and rigidity (predictability of behaviour). In *Busu* however predictability and rigidity alternate with an important inverse, the servants' ability to be more flexible in thinking and decision-making than their stolid, countrified lord and master which gives them the chance not just to wag the tail but to get away with it. This is, as Bergson noted, 'inversion of *roles*, and a situation which recoils on the head of its author' (95). The master is like his servants a stock type who reappears from play to play, always serving as the comic butt unable to anticipate his servants' entirely predictable trickery—unlike the audience who do precisely that. Bergson's description of comic characters as like *pantins a la ficelle* or 'puppets on a string' (69) is well illustrated in this comic array of opposing minds and bodies where instinct not reflection seems to drive behaviour, without insight into their own motivation. They exemplify Bergson's remark that 'the chief cause of rigidity is the neglect to look around—and more especially within oneself' (147).

In terms of verbal humour, *Busu* does not contain the clever wit and punning typical of high comedy of manners: as a short play, it depends more on plot and physical action. Accordingly, the brief text features rich opportunities for extended passages of mime, conveying such emotions as trepidation in approaching the poison, delighted gusto in savouring the forbidden sugar and trembling with fear at the return of the master. This privileging of visual humour over verbal accords with the use of stock characters who produce dialogue that is more instrumental than self-aware.[42] There is however some quick fire repartee involving crossed wires and misunderstandings, an example of which is discussed below, and also important instances of dialogue being comically speeded up or conversely slowed down to await another's delayed reaction. Finally, as noted above, the comic pair sometimes speak separately and sometimes in unison, calling attention to their nature as duplicates rather than individuals. These aspects of verbal humour accord with Bergson's stress on control of timing as part of the mechanical patterning found in comedy.

One comic exploitation of a key word turns on 'wind' or the imaginary breeze blowing on stage which is repeatedly referred to by the servants in the early part of the play. As he leaves, their master instructs them that even the wind blowing across the supposed poison they are guarding will carry a deadly taint. Left alone with the *busu*, the over-imaginative Tarō thinks he feels a fatal gust and reacts suitably. Jirō who points out his mistake:

**Tarō:** Oh mercy!
**Jirō:** What is the matter?
**Tarō:** A gust of wind came from the direction of the *busu*, and I thought that was the last of me.
**Jirō:** That was not wind.
**Tarō:** Lucky it wasn't.

Cue laughter at exaggeratedly comic panic—in this instance by the smarter of the pair which adds to the funniness—which, as later in the piece, proves to be unnecessary.[43]

This comic scene is repeated with variations when the pair overcome their trembling fear enough to decide to approach the mysterious box in which the poison is being kept. Jirō speaks first, highlighting 'the wind problem' to which Tarō proposes a solution, use a fan to create a wind in the opposite direction. Since the slower Jiro does not quite get the proposal correct, Tarō has to take the matter out of his hands (literally):[44]

**Jirō:** What you say is reasonable enough but if the wind kills us, what will happen if we just have a peek. Let it alone.
**Tarō:** That is the point. If the wind from that direction kills us, we must not get in the wind. You fan while I take a look
**Jirō:** Take a look while fanning? That is a good idea.
**Tarō:** Then I will fan while you untie the cord.
**Jirō:** All right. Fan hard, please, while I am about it.
**Tarō:** All right.
**Jirō:** Fan hard, hard!
**Tarō:** I am. I am fanning.
**Jirō:** Coming! Coming!
**Tarō:** Go on! Go on!

And so on, until Jirō has the cord off and hands over to Tarō to remove the box's cover and duly reveal the futility of all these elaborate precautions, much to their relief.

Use of the fan gives the actor an opportunity to create a whirlwind of increasing speed with his skilled mastery of the prop accompanying the quick fire exchange of dialogue. This mini-snowball serves as an effective physical correlate to the carefully drawn-out suspense on stage as to what the jar will contain. It would naturally be accompanied by appropriate comic side-play—grimaces, fumbling and bumbling and straining with the corded lid and so on (see Fig. 6.1 for both the fan and the delayed opening, where fear contends with attraction). As soon as the contents are revealed, the focus of dramatic action shifts away from the wind and the fan and the portrayal of physical terror contending with curiosity to another level of bodily domination: the act of tasting, then slurping and gobbling the sugar (see Fig. 6.2). Fear is in abeyance now as greed dominates and is satisfied.

As noted above, Bergson correctly identified this trope of the body taking precedence of the soul but half a century later it was amplified by Bakhtin in his study of the carnivalesque.[45] While Bergson helps us identify the mechanical control exerted by the physical body and its appetites, it is to Bakhtin that we must look for the concept of the playframe or *warai-no-ba* that allows their explicit portrayal on stage. In *Busu*, there is a complex progression in the servants' bodily strata from the domain of the stomach to a higher physical level. The comic clash between animal instinct and human cunning migrates upwards and outwards and finally wreaks havoc with what appears to be simple delight in destruction. As we have seen, Jirō, despite having no understanding of why he should do so and indeed fearing the consequences of the act, blindly proceeds to carry out Tarō's orders, first destroying the hanging scroll and then the porcelain jar.[46] Again, a fine opportunity for the actor to portray a mixture of fear and glee to accompany the gathering snowball of sound and disorder. Finally, the comedy moves fully into the mental domain with the comic battle of wits, the clash between anger and fake remorse as excuses are put forward. Inability to match the flexible inventiveness of his servants casts the master as a rigid impotent comic victim whose selfish lies have rebounded on him and whose slowness of wit allows the sinners to escape.

## Bergson's Insights and Their Limitations

At both the macro and the micro level, Bergson's principles and devices assist in approaching the humour to be found in this historical text. Searching for mechanical patterning identifies repetition and duplication of characters, acts and words, the inversion of moral and social roles and presentation of characters as comic stereotypes who lack self-awareness and behave with a comic combination of rigidity and flexibility. The fact that the servants prove to be smarter than their master adds a further layer of irony to the play, confirming Bergson's observation that inversion is funniest when it results in 'a situation which recoils on the head of its author' (95). The play is a perfect exemplar of the trope of the robber robbed and almost getting away with it.[47] The centrality to the text and dramatic action of misunderstandings (deliberate and accidental) and reification of the imaginary highlights the deliberate mechanical patterning of dialogue, action and character as outlined in *Laughter* and serves as a reliable indication of the text's comic nature.

To fully grasp the nature of the comedy and laughter in this play however, additional theoretical perspectives need to be marshalled. Consider the key question: whom do we laugh at in this play? As in many of the comedies that Bergson observed at the turn of the nineteenth century in Paris, the central drama is a series of clashes between self-absorbed stock comic characters where both sides are dominated by self-interest and lack of personal insight and where we have no real empathy invested in either side. Accordingly, both are suitable targets for laughter and they duly receive it. However, the original audience for *Busu* would have been an aristocratic one since the play forms part of a full nō performance, a genre patronised by the Shogunate.[48] Would not its sympathies have been enlisted on behalf of the master rather than the cheeky servants? Significantly, the rustic landowner would probably have ranked lower than— and is certainly portrayed as aping the sophistication of—samurai members of the audience. What makes him truly ripe for ridicule is his lack of capacity to control his own servants. Thus, when the plotters manage to carry off their daring plan, the laughter of amazement that they should pull it off turns very easily into laughter at their slow-witted master. The laughter of superiority and social correction that Bergson identified requires that masters too slow-witted to manage their own servants should be ridiculed as comic exceptions to the social norm, at least until they reassert their authority.

The play's conclusion however does not present a simple restoration of authority. The master is obliged to swallow his losses and, as we have seen, it remains moot whether he will catch the tricksters or not. Bakhtin's concept of the carnival playframe that permits such disorder as part of the process of maintaining order assists us in understanding this conundrum and his careful appraisal of the conditions and effects of traditional carnival celebrations has been extended to humour more broadly in the Benign Violation Theory of Humour by McGraw and Warren. This 'suggests that anything that is threatening to one's sense of how the world "ought to be" will be humorous, as long as the threatening situation also seems benign'.[49]

Ceremonies of inversion like carnival have been found in many cultures around the world and still exist to some degree today.[50] They are traditionally delimited by a dedicated time and place (*warai-no-ba*) and are usually carefully signaled. Perhaps the customary performance of kyōgen within the larger context of a full bill of nō plays satisfied these conditions, especially in the past, and despite the high value Japanese culture even today sets on propriety. The *gekokujō* elements of kyōgen and of *Busu* in particular need to be seen in this light as well as that of Bergson's theories. Their violations of propriety are real but somehow perceived as non-threatening,[51] due not only to the mechanical patterning of the play's action and characters but also to the fact that it takes place within a restricted playframe.

### *The Functions of Laughter in* Busu

Notwithstanding the emphasis on topsyturvydom in *Busu*, the audience laughs throughout the main body of the play not indirectly at the absent landowner but directly at the pranks of the two lower status characters. This is not simply the laughter of social correction and superiority. It also involves the recognition of incongruity and, beyond that, acknowledgement by the audience of a common humanity with the actors on stage. Taken as a pair, the servants embody two different combinations of rigidity with its opposite. Mentally, their simplistic stupidity combines with a dexterity that allows them to exploit their master with seeming effortlessness. And physically, their weaknesses of greed and fear are combined with the acrobatic strength of giftedly flexible bodies.

As the representation of the human, they are thus both like and unlike their audiences. We all share the same corporeal state in which mind (and morality) is imprisoned in matter and to that extent we secretly share the desire to satisfy our appetites and escape punishment, but know that we would most likely not get away with it ourselves. Similarly, these stage-players transcend human norms in their ability to master challenges of dexterity such as fan-play, mimicry and weeping crocodile tears of contrition. In laughing at this, an audience's socially corrective laughter ridiculing (if empathising with) their bad behaviour is allied to a laughter of surprise and amazement at their physical ability. Laughter is also a recognition of our common human condition, of the fact that none of us is able to control our bodily weaknesses and desires as we should, that we all give in to temptation. The plot shows that some of us can get away with it, sometimes. Thus, beneath the servants' superhuman performance ability lies a shared bond of human frailty with the audience whose laughter recognises self on both sides of the struggle on stage, a desire that hierarchy be maintained, as is proper, combined with a sneaking delight that clever flexibility should win out.

This ironic and eternal truth seems to support Bergson's view that laughing at the mechanical in others is tantamount to an instinctive recognition of our own limitations and fallibilities. In this play's carefully delimited play-space, we observe rigidity and flexibility at play in the clash between human nature on the one hand and social norms and moral conventions on the other. We observe the age-old competition for scarce goods and scarcer pleasures. We observe authority being defied when it uses unfair means like lying and, in watching and laughing, we escape, if only for a moment, the unsmiling mechanical dominance in our own lives of rules and propriety. The spoils here go to the quick-witted and the speedy and the adaptable escape punishment—at least for today. In laughing at these puppets, perhaps we do feel ourselves to be wiser and freer than they are, possessing a greater flexibility to make choices in our own lives. Certainly we can draw the moral that if you lie, you cannot complain if you are then lied to, and if we reflect upon that, we can plan our lives accordingly.

But we can do more than that. Even without reflection, we can celebrate in laughter our most human strivings: the impulse to rebel against convention and morality and our continual efforts to master our own bodies and our physical environment. When as here the joke set out before us entails the characters' failed attempts to do this, their failure touches the audience because the joke is on all of us as members of the human race.

## Conclusion

Bergson provides in *Laughter* a checklist of comic devices and a larger interpretation of his theory of the mechanical in humour that sees human creativity and freewill as being fostered through laughter. Both of these offer highly relevant tools for approaching humour in a performative text such as *Busu*, despite its provenance in a time and culture of the past. Bergson's stress on the comic domination of the mind by the body can usefully be linked, firstly to Bakhtin's study of carnival comedy, and also to McGraw and Bennett's theory of the benign violation of norms in humour. The functions of a playframe turn out to be of considerable importance in this and other kyōgen plays, especially when considering original audience reaction and the context of Japan's cultural preference for containing humour in a clearly marked *warai-no-ba*. This suggests the relevance of what has been called the Play Theory of Humour which links not only to to Bakhtin's study but also to the concept of benign violation in

128    J. MILNER DAVIS

general. Deriving from anthropological and evolutionary studies of humour and laughter, play theory stresses the importance of context and framing in eliciting humour's accompanying emotions of non-seriousness and playfulness.[52] The longlived popularity of *Busu* and other short kyōgen interludes suggests that these aspects of the play have indeed succeeded in resonating with audiences down the ages. They continue to do so in revival today, giving the pleasures of humour and laughter to many who watch and appreciate them.

## NOTES

1. Bergson's work, originally appearing as three essays in the *Revue de Paris* in 1899, was first published in French as a book in 1900 and in an authorised English translation in 1910. Of the many subsequent editions, the twenty-third of 1924 is significant since it contains a new preface and appendix in which the author explains and updates his thinking. That edition is available online at Project Gutenberg (2003) but without pagination. The text cited here is a modern edition of the authorised English translation. References to page numbers are given in brackets after quotations. I do not aim to provide a complete summary of *Laughter* but to focus on the comic devices and techniques that Bergson observed at work in comic entertainment of his time.
2. 'The Actors Home' 1953 version (copyright Koch Entertainment) is at: https://www.youtube.com/watch?v=kTcRRaXV-fg (accessed 14 October 2019).
3. Translated as 'lack of sprightliness', 26.
4. See Latta, *The Basic Humor Process*, 109. The term humour is used in this chapter in its modern broad umbrella sense to embrace any and all instances of the laughable. Bergson himself did not use the term, which had then (and still does) in French a distinctly English connotation of gentle, benign humour—see note 26.
5. Particularly *Time and Free Will* (originally published in French in 1889) and *Creative Evolution* (1907).
6. For example, Oring, *Engaging Humor*, 11; Milner Davis, 'Bergson and the Theory of the Comic'.
7. For example, Morreall, *The Philosophy of Laughter*, 15.
8. Examples of how he is usually dismissed appear below. Other more recent advocates of laughter as a reflection of the superiority of the laugher over a victim such as Charles Gruner usually receive equally dismissive treatment.
9. Recent psychological studies on personality traits and humour by Willibald Ruch and colleagues examining the use of benevolent and corrective humour (e.g. Ruch et al., 'Broadening humor') are a significant exception to this preference for rose-coloured glasses about the nature and effects of humour.
10. See the careful discussion of Bergson as a superiority theorist in Sinclair, *Bergson*, 145.
11. Attardo, *Linguistic Theories*, 59.
12. Carrell, 'Historical Views', 375.
13. Attardo, *Linguistic Theories*, 59; Carrell, 'Historical Views', 375; Martin, *The Psychology of Humor*, 44; Provine, *Laughter*, 16–17; Scheel, 'Definitions, Theories, and Measurement'.

14. I am indebted to Alexander Lefebvre for drawing this study to my attention and also for expert advice on contemporary Bergsonian studies, in particular for information about his own studies of Bergson and human rights.
15. Milner Davis, 'Bergson and the Theory of the Comic'.
16. Sinclair, *Bergson*, 145.
17. Guerlac, *Thinking in Time*, sums up the movement for reappraisal that began with Gilles Deleuze's study of him in 1966.
18. Russell, [Untitled] review of Henri Bergson's *Laughter*.
19. Guerlac, *Thinking in Time*, 4.
20. On Bergson and the Theory of Mind, see Robbins, 'Bergson and the Holographic Theory of Mind'; on relativity, Dolbeault, 'From Mind to Matter'. Bergson and Albert Einstein were caught up in the Franco-German tension between the Wars at a time when Bergson chaired the League of Nations' Scientific Co-ordinating Committee and Commission for Intellectual Cooperation (1921–1926). However, it seems likely that, much to Bergson's disappointment, it was their personal intellectual dispute that frustrated his efforts to retain Einstein as the sole German member of the Commission. Einstein had denounced the way in which Bergson's *Durée et simultanéité* (*Duration and Simultaneity*), published in 1922, dealt with relativity.
21. For relevant works, see note 5.
22. See Bergson's Laureate speech, delivered for him by the Committee's President owing to his own inability to travel, which can be found at: http://nobelprize. org/nobel_prizes/literature/laureates/1927/bergson-speech.html (accessed 13 April 2020).
23. See Worms, 'Time Thinking'. The relevant Bergson work is *Time and Free Will*, significantly first published in 1889, the year that Bergson began his essay series resulting in the 1900 publication of *Le Rire*.
24. Bergson, *Time and Free Will*, 99.
25. Parkin, 'The Power of Laughter', 120–121. For the evolutionary study of laughter, see Ross et al., 'Reconstructing the Evolution'.
26. Howarth, 'Bergson revisited'; Noonan, 'Reflecting Back'.
27. Bakhtin, *Rabelais and His World*.
28. Guerlac, *Thinking in Time*, 8.
29. Milner Davis, 'Bergson's Theory of the Comic', 79–80.
30. I am indebted to M. W. Shores for his expert advice, particularly on the history and background of kyōgen as an art-form and on details of interpretation of the text of *Busu*.
31. Eleven English translations since 1917 are listed in Iezzi, '"Kyōgen" in English', 216.
32. For a concise overview of kyōgen, its history and nature, see Kominz, 'Kyōgen'. For a bilingual Japanese-English performance that illustrates the traditional stage-setting, performance style and costumes of kyōgen, with Shigeyama Dōji playing Jirō Kaja, Shigeyama Ippei as Tarō Kaja and Hiromi Shimada as their master, see: https://www.youtube.com/watch?v=DWxZhtPG0Nw (accessed 14 October 2019).
33. Kominz, 'Kyōgen', 349.
34. Ibid.
35. Koyama, *Kyōgenshū*, vol. 1, 315–323; Sakanishi, *Japanese Folk-Plays*, 84–89. All *Busu* quotations are from this English edition which, oddly, is not included in

Iezzi's list published in 2007. English kyōgen translations vary, reflecting a translator's view of how much elaboration should be provided and also the tradition and text of the acting school being followed. Sakanishi's text is succinct and restrained, not adding much in the way of stage directions and 'business' compared to others such as that by Don Kenny, 'The Delicious Poison'.

36. This summary follows Milner Davis, *Farce*, 7–8. Longer comedies usually possess a wider range than these four categories, although they are likely to include one or more of them within a larger structure that might for example be a festive romantic comedy, an extended satirical parody or a bleak absurdist comedy.

37. Discussed in Wells and Milner Davis, 'Farce and Satire in Kyōgen', 145–147.

38. Oda has termed such containers, *warai-no-ba*, times and spaces for laughter ('Laughter and the Traditional Japanese Smile', 18). The idea of a playframe was not something considered by Bergson, but its importance in the transformation of rebellion and violence into comedy is undeniable and it certainly applies to *Busu* and kyōgen generally.

39. One of the triumphs of kyōgen, as in Japanese traditional comedy more generally, is the skilled mimicry with which such actions are carried out, depending greatly upon the imaginative consent of the audience, as in the fanning to create imaginary wind.

40. For a succinct account of manzai, see Katayama.

41. In this particular play, prior knowledge of the stereotypes is reinforced by the fact that the play's source is a well-known Buddhist tale (see note 33) so that the general outline of the story and its rebellion is already known to the audience.

42. Soliloquies by comic stock characters such as Shakespeare's Falstaff or the learned Doctor of the *commedia dell'arte* tend to be bombastic rather than insightful.

43. While contemporary schools of performance do not make any reference to a possible fart joke here, it is always possible that before the scripts were standardised and sanitised in the early Edo period, such bodily stratum jokes were one of their highlights. For contemporary references to their vulgarity, see Wells and Milner Davis, 'Farce and Satire in Kyōgen', 146.

44. In Kenny's version of the play, the servants take turns in fanning as they repeatedly approach and then run away from the container.

45. Bakhtin, *Rabelais and His World*, 21–23.

46. The trained kyōgen actor's ability to convey this destruction through mime rather than actual smashing of jars and so on contributes an additional layer of comic incongruity, since portraying rigidity and clumsiness convincingly requires astounding flexibility and bodily control.

47. For other farces with this overall structure, see Milner Davis, *Farce*, 105–119.

48. Kominz, 'Kyōgen', 348–349.

49. McGraw and Warren, 'Benign Violations', 1142.

50. Milner Davis, 'The Fool and the Path', 235.

51. For historical exceptions when a kyōgen piece was considered a threat and earned suppression, see Kominz, 'Kyōgen', 348.

52. See Chafe, *The Importance of Not Being Earnest*, and Moreall, 'The Philosophy of Humor'. Another link is to the 'non-bona fide' (not in good faith) mode of communication as opposed to bona fide identified as essential in the communication and comprehension of verbal humour (Raskin, *Semantic Mechanisms*).

## BIBLIOGRAPHY

Attardo, Salvatore. *Linguistic Theories of Humor*. Berlin: Mouton de Gruyter, 1994.

Bakhtin, Mikhail. *Rabelais and His World*. Translated by Hélène Iswolsky. Cambridge MA: MIT Press, 1968.

Bergson, Henri. *Creative Evolution*. Translated by Arthur Mitchell. New York: Barnes and Noble, (1907) 2005.

Bergson, Henri. *Laughter: An Essay on the Meaning of the Comic*. Translated by Cloudesley Brereton and Fred Rothwell. Mineola, NY: Dover, (1910) 2005.

Bergson, Henri. *Time and Free Will: An Essay on the Immediate Data of Consciousness*. Translated by F. L. Pogson. Minneola, NY: Dover, (1889) 2001.

Carrell, Amy. 'Historical Views of Humor'. In *Primer of Humor Research*, edited by Victor Raskin, 361–398. Berlin: Mouton de Gruyter, 2008.

Chafe, Wallace. *The Importance of Not Being Earnest: The Feeling Behind Laughter and Humor*. Amsterdam and New York: John Benjamins, 2007.

Davila Ross, Marina, Michael Owren, and Elke Zimmermann. 'Reconstructing the Evolution of Laughter in Great Apes and Humans'. *Current Biology* 19, no. 11 (2009): 1106–1111.

Deleuze, Gilles. *Bergsonism*. Translated by Hugh Tomlinson and Barbara Habberjam. New York, NY: Zone Books, (1966) 2004.

Dolbeault, Joel. 'From Mind to Matter: How Bergson Anticipated Quantum Ideas'. *Mind and Matter* 10, no. 1 (2012): 25–45.

Guerlac, Suzanne. *Thinking in Time: An Introduction to Henri Bergson*. Ithaca, NY: Cornell University Press, 2006.

Howarth, William D. 'Bergson Revisited: *Le Rire* a Hundred Years On'. In *French Humour*, edited by John Parkin, 139–156. Amsterdam: Rodopi, 1999.

Iezzi, Julie A. 'Kyōgen' in English: A Bibliography'. *Asian Theatre Journal* 24, no. 1 (2007): 211–234.

Katayama, Hanae. 'Humor in Manzai Stand-Up Comedy: A Historical and Comparative Analysis'. *International Journal of the Humanities* 6, no. 1 (2008): 213–224.

Kenny, Don. 'The Delicious Poison'. In *An Anthology of Traditional Japanese Theatre*, edited by Karen Brazell, 235–244. New York: Columbia University Press, 1998.

Kominz, Laurence. 'Kyōgen: Comic Plays That Turn Medieval Society Upside Down'. In *Cambridge History of Japanese Literature*, edited by Haruo Shirane, Tomi Suzuki and David Lurie, 347–354. Cambridge and New York: Cambridge University Press, 2015.

Koyama, Hiroshi, ed. *Kyōgenshū*. 2 vols. Tokyo: Iwanami Shoten, 1960; 1961.

Latta, Robert. *The Basic Humor Process: A Cognitive-Shift Theory and the Case against Incongruity*. Berlin: Mouton de Gruyter, 1999.

Martin, Rod A. *The Psychology of Humor: An Integrative Approach*. Burlington, MA: Elsevier, 2007.

McGraw, A. Peter and Caleb Warren. 'Benign Violations: Making Immoral Behavior Funny'. *Psychological Science* 21, no. 8 (2010): 1141–1149.

Milner Davis, Jessica. 'Bergson's Theory of the Comic'. In *Encyclopedia of Humor Studies*, edited by Salvatore Attardo, 1: 77–80. Thousand Oaks, CA: Sage, 2014.

Milner Davis, Jessica. *Farce*. Piscataway, NJ: Transaction, 2003.

Milner Davis, Jessica. 'The Fool and the Path to Spiritual Insight'. In *Humour and Religion*, edited by Hans Geybels and Walter van Herck, 218–247. London: Continuum, 2011.

Morreall, John, ed. *The Philosophy of Laughter and Humor*. Albany, NY: State University of New York Press, 1987.

Moreall, John. 'The Philosophy of Humor', *Stanford Encyclopedia of Philosophy*, 2012. https://plato.stanford.edu/entries/humor/#HumPlaLauPlaSig (accessed April 13, 2020).

Noonan, Will. 'Reflecting Back; or What Can the French Tell the English About Humour?'. *Sydney Studies in English*, 37 (2011): 92–115.

Oda, Shōkichi. 'Laughter and the Traditional Japanese Smile'. In *Understanding Humor in Japan*, edited by Jessica Milner Davis, 15–26. Detroit, MI: Wayne State University Press, 2006.

Oring, Elliott. *Engaging Humor*. Urbana, IL and Chicago: University of Illinois Press, 2003.

Parkin, John. 'The Power of Laughter: Koestler on Bergson and Freud'. In *Laughter and Power*, edited by John Phillips and John Parkin, 113–143. Bern: Peter Lang, 2006.

Provine, Robert R. *Laughter: A Scientific Investigation*. New York: Penguin Books, 2000.

Raskin, Victor. *Semantic Mechanisms of Humor*. Dordrecht, Netherlands: D. Reidel, 1985.

Robbins, Stephen E. 'Bergson and the Holographic Theory of Mind'. *Phenomenology and the Cognitive Sciences* 5, no. 3 (2006): 365–394.

Ruch, Willibald, Sonja Heintz, Tracey Platt, Lisa Wagner, and René T. Proyer. 'Broadening Humor: Comic Styles Differentially Tap Into Temperament, Character, and Ability'. *Frontiers in Psychology* 9 (2018): 6.

Russell, Bertrand. [Untitled] Review of Henri Bergson's *Laughter: An Essay on the Meaning of the Comic. Cambridge Review* 33 (1912): 193–194.

Sakanashi, Shio. *Japanese Folk-Plays: 'The Ink-Smeared Lady' and Other Kyōgen*. Tokyo: Tuttle, 1960.

Scheel, Tabea. 'Definitions, Theories, and Measurement of Humor'. In *Humor at Work in Teams, Leadership, Negotiations, Learning and Health*, edited by Tabea Scheel and Christine Gockel, 9–31. Cham: Springer Nature, 2017.

Sinclair, Mark. *Bergson*. Abingdon, UK and New York: Routledge, 2019.

Wells, Marguerite and Jessica Milner Davis. 'Farce and Satire in *Kyōgen*'. In *Understanding Humor in Japan*, edited by Jessica Milner Davis, 127–153. Detroit: Wayne State University Press, 2006.

Worms, Frédéric. 'Time Thinking: Bergson's Double Philosophy of Mind'. *Modern Language Notes* 120, no. 5 (2005): 1226–1234.

CHAPTER 7

# Comic Character and Counter-Violation: Critiquing Benign Violation Theory

## Daniel Derrin

Why is it partly funny when Falstaff stands on the battlefield in Shakespeare's *1 Henry IV* and famously proclaims that 'honour' is just a word made of air, a 'mere scutcheon', thus ending his 'catechism'?[1] I say *partly* funny because of course the scene can be played with pathos, not with humour. Nevertheless, the fact that it can and has been funny raises questions about identifying 'humour'. If there is a pattern of amusement for audiences, across time, even when the scene is not *inherently* funny, one must still ask why it can be and has been amusing. Benign violation theory (BVT) is one way of addressing that question.

This chapter presents a critique of the use of BVT in historically-distant humour contexts. BVT is a universalising theoretical view of 'humour' associated in particular with Thomas C. Veatch, and, more recently, with Peter McGraw and Caleb Warren.[2] I focus here on the theory's uses and limits with respect to two comic characters from Renaissance plays: Shakespeare's Falstaff and Machiavelli's Frate Timoteo (Brother Timothy) from his play *Mandragola* (*The Mandrake*). The argument will be that while BVT is useful for identifying humour produced through such characters, and for drawing attention to the political and/or ethical structure of humour, the theory is nevertheless insufficient for dealing with other aspects of those historically-distant comic characterisations.

---

D. Derrin (✉)
Department of English Studies, Durham University, Durham, UK
e-mail: daniel.derrin@durham.ac.uk

© The Author(s), under exclusive license to Springer Nature
Switzerland AG 2020
D. Derrin, H. Burrows (eds.), *The Palgrave Handbook of Humour, History, and Methodology*, https://doi.org/10.1007/978-3-030-56646-3_7

133

134   D. DERRIN

First of all, it captures only one part of the comic structure. To put it very concisely, with more elaboration to follow, BVT claims that humour exists in situations where two conditions obtain simultaneously: (1) salient 'norms' are violated and (2) those violations are in some sense benign. This means that humour, so understood, is the enjoyment of situations that violate in a benign or safe manner the 'norms' we live by (culturally speaking). Thus, humour does not really bring its structuring norms into question. It reinforces them because what we are laughing at is the *safe* violation of them. Falstaff can be said to be funny, for an audience who believes in the importance of norms around military honour, because he violates them (benignly), just as Timoteo, likewise, violates the norms of priestly vocation. At one level then, Falstaff and Timoteo reinforce those norms through the safe way in which they violate them. That, at least, is what BVT suggests. However, at another level, Shakespeare and Machiavelli produce Falstaff and Timoteo so as to make the violated norms themselves partly laughable. Shakespeare famously makes Falstaff call the military norm of 'honour' into question; Machiavelli, in his own way, uses Timoteo to call into question the assumption that Christian virtue is reconcilable with political action. Shakespeare and Machiavelli do this covertly, I would suggest, by making the characters primarily laughable in a conventional sense, and it is only that conventional sense that is describable through BVT. Shakespeare and Machiavelli do not just benignly violate the moral norms—military honour and priestly honour—through their comic characters but make the norms out to be, in themselves, violations of something else. I shall call the other side of that two-sided process here 'counter-violation'. BVT cannot (quite) handle such duality, as helpful as the theory is. Laughable violations might be structured by 'norms', but counter-violations make 'norms' themselves laughable, that is, abnormal, and from an alternative perspective. What then structures counter-violations? Perhaps, it is some kind of ethical-political structure that is *normative*, in the philosophical sense, but cannot really be called a 'norm'. The terminological problems arising here, I believe, are instructive for an understanding of the limits of BVT (and other) universalising modern theories of 'humour'.

For that reason, I shall explore at the end of this chapter the possibilities afforded by the use of an ethical discourse that was widely understood in the early modern period in which Shakespeare and Machiavelli were writing: the ancient discourse of prudence (*prudentia*). I want to show that while BVT does help to coordinate a sense of the 'humour' generated by comic characters such as Falstaff and Timoteo, a more historically-relevant ethical discourse is needed for explicating the duality I have identified.

First, the benign violation theory should be addressed in a little more detail. It is an attempt to correlate—structurally and psychologically—several phenomena under the banner of 'humour': amusing jokes, tickling, and punning. The basic ideas are fairly simple to elaborate. McGraw and Warren can be quoted directly: 'the benign violation hypothesis suggests that three conditions are jointly necessary and sufficient for eliciting humor: A situation must be appraised as a violation, a situation must be appraised as benign, and these two appraisals must occur together'.[3] But a violation of what? The examples identified include the following norms: physical security (violated in playfighting and tickling), personal dignity (violated in slapstick and physical deformity), linguistic norms (violated in puns and malapropisms), social norms (violated, for instance, in fish-out-of-water humour), and moral norms (violated, for instance in disrespectful behaviours). For humour to occur, McGraw and Warren say, there must be some such violation of a principle or norm that the amused person has a psychological stake in.

However, none of those violations can be amusing, the theory claims, if they are not at the same time also benign in some sense. 'Anything that is threatening to one's sense of how the world "ought to be" will be humorous, as long as the threatening situation also seems benign'.[4] Thus, puns can be funny because they 'violate language convention' but are 'technically correct according to an alternative interpretation'.[5] One might add to that the humour of malapropisms: they violate linguistic norms but are simultaneously benign because when recognised as such (as humorous) they do not entail actual confusion. In the same way, tickling can be understood within BVT's terms as a violation because it invades personal space but is benign because it is (usually) only 'a mock attack'.[6]

McGraw and Warren account for three ways in which a situation can be benign or relatively benign. Their choice of language is significant. 'A violation can seem benign if (a) a salient norm suggests that something is wrong but another salient norm suggests that it is acceptable, (b) one is only weakly committed to the violated norm, or (c) the violation is psychologically distant'.[7] Further on in their article, several forms of 'psychological distance' are specified: temporal, social, spatial, and that of 'likelihood'.[8] One of their core (and, in fact, symptomatic) examples of a 'humorous' situation they describe thus: 'a man goes to the supermarket once a week and buys a dead chicken. But before cooking the chicken, he has sexual intercourse with it. Then he cooks the chicken and eats it'.[9] The example actually forms part of McGraw and Warren's experiments; they report that it did elicit humour. Abstractly, they describe the benignity-conditions of that scenario thus: (a) it is harmless because the chicken is dead; (b) sexual norms making it 'immoral' are not universal; and (c) it is hypothetical and thus psychologically distant.

It may be pointed out that benignity is in the eye of the beholder, that what is benign for one person is malign for another. That certainly seems to be the case for the chicken joke. But this does not unsettle their point, which is that if an individual finds the situation funny it is because *they* have experienced the two conditions simultaneously. The implication here seems to be that the violation and the benignity must be in a kind of balanced tension for humour to occur as a response. If there is not enough of a sense of violation, for a given individual, the situation will likely be boring. Jokes that make us merely groan or attempts at self-tickling are comparable to that response. On the other side, if there is not enough of a sense of benignity, the violating situation will likely be offensive or merely disgusting. Jokes about religion or paedophilia can easily fall into that second category. BVT describes a structure for the individual, psychological, and subjective conditions that accompany the experience of humour, though none of those, of course, are completely unconnected with culture.

'BVT' has been developed in other contexts than the article just cited. Peter McGraw runs a research group called the Humor Research Lab to test out the theory of BVT.[10] He has also popularised some of this research in a book called *The Humor Code*, co-written with the journalist Joel Warner.[11]

Furthermore, and as mentioned before, something like BVT was advanced by Thomas C. Veatch in 1998, 12 years before McGraw and Warren's paper. Both papers agree that 'violations' are one necessary condition; but what McGraw and Warren identify as 'benignity', Veatch calls 'normal'. Veatch, too, believes that both conditions must be simultaneous for 'humour perception' to occur (to someone). He formulates the whole conditionality thus, where V equals violation and N equals normal: 'humor occurs when it seems that things are normal (N) while at the same time something seems wrong (V). Or, in an only apparent paradox, Humor is (emotional) pain (V) that does not hurt (N)'.[12] The caveat about paradox is perhaps symptomatic. However, to identify the second necessary condition as 'normal' only compounds the problems identified here in the discussion of Falstaff and Timoteo: one can say that their cowardice and avarice, respectively, are understandable, or common, but 'normal'? They are certainly not *normative*, though I will argue later that the way they embody those vices comically has a normative element. In any case, while I think the language of 'benignity' instead is more descriptive, McGraw and Warren are very close to Veatch. They are surely saying almost the same thing as Veatch does with 'normal (N)' where they suggest that one form of benignity is when a further 'salient norm' makes the basic violation benign—that is, category (a) above.

It should be noted in passing that BVT, in a sense, has a history unacknowledged by McGraw and Warren (and Veatch). While they note that many past thinkers about 'humour' identify the two significant conditions—violation and benignity—they claim that a third (the simultaneity) has been missed: 'with the exception of Veatch (1998), researchers have not considered these three conditions together'.[13] But in Aristotle's *Poetics* an implicit connection between the two jointly sufficient conditions is, at the very least, discernable in his comment that: 'the laughable comprises any fault or mark of shame which involves no pain or destruction'.[14] Furthermore, Aristotle's comments and the idea of the two conditions they give rise to have a very long history.[15] For instance, the Aristotelian idea that comic distortions of ordinary expectations and behaviour have the further condition of being 'without pain' found its way into the discussions of Latin-speaking intellectuals in the Renaissance period in the phrase *sine dolore*.[16]

BVT has been critiqued on other grounds too. Elliott Oring has identified a number of interesting limitations. First, as an 'emotional theory' of humour

(Oring's phrase), BVT acknowledges the 'subjective moral order'; but, he suggests, it is possible that the subjective is 'so variable and contingent as to be unascertainable'.[17] For Oring, BVT struggles to explain why some jokes are funnier than others, and this relates to the difficult question of what makes a violation more or less benign.[18] As an 'emotional theory', it must always resort to psychological factors to explain such variables. However, when Oring claims that BVT needs to show that all humorous violations 'arouse negative emotions', something seems unfair: after all, BVT's claim is that humour constitutes a psychological reaction that is not quite negative emotion but a particular (benign) version of it—humour is pleasurable because it is safe.[19] Oring prefers his own version of incongruity theory—'appropriate incongruity'—because instead of making emotion central it simply makes space for it: 'humor is not at root an emotional process'.[20] The perception of appropriate incongruity by contrast 'is not emotional but intellectual'.[21] But is it really possible to separate 'emotions' and 'intellect' so readily? And if 'emotion' can enhance or restrain humour, as Oring goes on to claim, why is it *not* somehow centrally connected even if minimally in some instances? Oring's objection to BVT here seems to turn on the assumption that emotion and cognition are separable.

For Oring, there are many benign violations that are not funny and which might be considered counter examples—accidental linguistic slips for instance. If BVT were right, we should be constantly laughing at them. But BVT suggests that what makes the difference between banal accidents and amusing linguistic slips is deeply individual. In each case, we might ask: for whom are accidental slips *not* funny? Oring puts small social violations in the same basket:

> If someone knocks a knife from a dinner table while dining in a restaurant, it is a small violation. One is supposed to keep the tableware on the table [...] it is not usually a matter of amusement unless one of the parties at dinner says something like 'Good thing you don't work at the plutonium-processing facility at Oak Ridge' to make it funny. The possible counter examples to BVT seem endless.[22]

This is presented as if its status as a counter example were self-evident. But the example itself confirms BVT's interest in emotional stakes. I agree that the plutonium reference suddenly makes it funny, but one might easily argue that that reference is precisely how the emotional stakes (and the humour) enter the picture. That is to say, until the plutonium reference, the knife knocked on the floor was just an unmeaningful accident, not a benign violation. But suddenly there is an implied violation in the hypothetical scenario in which accidents of the hand might have huge emotional stakes. Yet these are benign because (obviously) the violation is imaginary, and also because, as Oring's own footnote says, it seems that Oak Ridge stopped processing plutonium after World War II.

Oring's interesting objections notwithstanding, historians have found BVT useful.[23] Aside from providing a helpful way of modelling humour from the past as a meaningful psychological experience, fitting at different points across

138   D. DERRIN

a cultural spectrum from the outrageous to the mundane, I would suggest BVT has two further useful strengths. First, it offers a way of helping to confirm the intuition that something humorous is happening in an historical example far removed in time. And second, it pays attention to the ethical and ideological substance of humour that moves us. There is an obvious sense in which BVT and its conditions of humour perception for individuals cannot work on historical examples because we cannot do psychological tests on people long dead. But if we use their basic structuring ideas (violation/benignity) and apply it to what we know of cultural, rather than individual conditions, it is one way of approaching examples we intuit as historical humour.

Applying this to the first example, Falstaff, I will focus primarily on the famous honour speech (5.1.127–140). Near the end of Shakespeare's *1 Henry IV*, Falstaff is called upon to enter the fray at the battlefield of Shrewsbury. As his fear mounts, he tells the prince: 'I would'twere bedtime, Hal, and all well'. At the prince's reply, 'Why, thou owest God a death', he begins his comic soliloquy thus: ''Tis not due yet. I would be loath to pay him before his day. What need I be so forward with him that calls not on me?' (127–129). Stopping to reflect on the 'honour' that is driving everybody into battle he now promptly talks himself out of any need to bother fighting!

'Honour pricks me on', he continues:

> Yea, but how if honour prick me off when I come on? How then? Can honour set to a leg? No. Or an arm? No. Or take away the grief of a wound? No. Honour hath no skill in surgery, then? No. What is honour? A word. What is in that word 'honour'? What is that 'honour'? Air. A trim reckoning. Who hath it? He that died o'Wednesday. Doth he feel it? No. Doth he hear it? No. 'Tis insensible then? Yea, to the dead. But will it not live with the living? No. Why? Detraction will not suffer it. Therefore I'll none of it. Honour is a mere scutcheon. And so ends my catechism. (130–140)

The scene can be performed either with humour or with pathos, perhaps both. Nevertheless, could BVT help confirm the intuition that Shakespeare has created something humorous in this speech for his early modern audience?

The first question, obviously, needs to be: what is 'violated'? An answer might be given at two levels. First, the speech and Falstaff's wider characterisation violate norms of language, reason, and rhetoric. He violates the meaning of 'catechism' by using that word to gloss the kind of self-addressed rhetoric he has just engaged in: what in early modern rhetorical theory would be called *rogatio* (or, using the Greek term, *antipophora*), the act of asking and answering one's own questions.[24] Rather than using this rhetorical structure to affirm the doctrine of 'honour' catechistically, he uses it to gnaw the heart out of honour's assumed substance. Even more characteristically, Falstaff engages here as elsewhere in the comedy of equivocation. Violating the functional use of the term 'honour', he redefines it so that it is something he can ignore. In just the same way, a little later on in the play, having saved his skin by playing dead, he says to himself:

> 'twas time to counterfeit [...] Counterfeit? I lie; I am no counterfeit. To die is to be a counterfeit, for he is but the counterfeit of a man who hath not the life of a man. But to counterfeit dying when a man thereby liveth is to be no counterfeit but the true and perfect image of life indeed. (5.4.111–118)

As Brian Vickers put it: 'whereas in earlier plays equivocation was essentially a clown's trick to provide simple jokes, for Falstaff it is a way of life'.[25] A further layer to equivocation-as-violation here is the context of anti-Catholic, anti-Jesuit antipathy by the Protestant establishment of Shakespeare's time. For instance, it is a common manoeuvre to link Shakespeare's interest in equivocation in *Macbeth* to the context of the Gunpowder Plot and the trials of the hated conspirators. In *Macbeth*, the Porter (imagining himself at the doors of hell) speaks of 'an equivocator [...] who committed treason enough for God's sake, yet could not equivocate to heaven'.[26] Critics have linked that scene and the focus on equivocation to the trial of Jesuits involved in the Gunpowder Plot; 'equivocation' became closely associated in Protestant minds with Jesuits and their forms of defence.[27]

But at another level than language, Falstaff has long been identified as a kind of military 'defect' because he dissolves 'honour' in order to rationalise his own cowardice. Thus, he embodies dishonour in a militarised culture.[28] It has been suggested that Falstaff's speech parodies a passage in the *Iliad* where Odysseus more successfully persuades himself to fight against the impulse to run.[29] Furthermore, the 'mere scutcheon' has been read as a reference to a shield, making Falstaff here an ancient type of shameful soldier: *rhipsaspis*, 'shield-tosser', one who gives in to his primal instinct for self-preservation and drops his shield so that he can run away more quickly.[30] So, at a further level, Falstaff is laughable in early modern culture because he violates military values or, as McGraw might say, the 'norms' of militarised culture: bravery and self-sacrifice.

But for BVT to work, the violations must be construable as simultaneously benign. Does Falstaff here fulfil those further conditions? Yes, to the extent that Shakespeare does not represent the battle of Shrewsbury and its emotional stakes as depending on Falstaff's active involvement. First of all, he is an old fat drunkard, not a powerful young soldier.[31] Second, all his operations in this battle have a kind of superfluity (from the perspective of the king's war effort). For instance, the poor and weak members of the press gang he has assembled—'ragamuffins' he calls them (5.3.36), having acknowledged earlier that he 'misused the King's press damnably' in gathering them (4.2.12–13)—have all been 'peppered' (5.3.36), likely without having achieved much towards the victory of the king and prince. In addition, Falstaff can do what he does with Hotspur's body, obviously, only because Hotspur has already been killed, by Hal. Again, his actions are not really integral to the restitution of political order and the

140    D. DERRIN

rapprochement between father and son, king and prince. This *rhipsaspis* does not really threaten the king's aim of defeating the rebels, as shameful as he is: as a violation of military honour, he is benign. Both conditions obtain at once: Falstaff embodies a sufficiently significant violation of cultural norms around military bravery, in a context that emphasises its importance, to be amusing to an early modern audience, but his questioning of 'honour' does little more than protect the life of a useless solider. The balance here can therefore be read reasonably in terms of BVT because a level of benignity and a level of violation are held in tension. Furthermore, it seems plausible that, for many early modern audience members, neither one of those two conditions would entirely cancel out the other. Of course, a sense of the balance might also hang on how an audience member reads Falstaff's appalling treatment of the 'ragamuffins': his treatment of them (and of the king's press) is certainly in itself an ethical violation but in what sense is it benign, in the aesthetic and political context of the play?[32]

Nevertheless, such a simple explanation gives us merely one layer of Falstaff's comic power and laughability—even in this brief scene. BVT helps describe momentary aberrations from cultural norms but it is insufficient to deal with characterisations that produce subtler comic criticisms of cultural 'norms'. In Falstaff's case, what must be considered is that which is emotionally attractive and intellectually engaging about who he is and what he says. To some extent, one might say that such attractiveness is just a function of modern taste and interest—the sort of history that Conal Condren, in chapter one, terms 'genealogy'. For instance, Falstaff has been read as the spirit of holiday or of freedom from war.[33] But aside from the obvious fact that Falstaff—ever popular from the beginning—always represented the pleasures of the body, there are other levels of comic attractiveness more pertinent to his specifically early modern context. Some, for instance, have read the honour speech as expressing Shakespeare's 'disillusionment with chivalry'.[34] Others, A. D. Nuttall especially, have argued that Falstaff's honour speech enacts a nominalist scepticism about 'universals' (such as 'honour' or 'beauty'): a nominalism that was a part of the early modern development of *philosophia naturalis*, of what we now call science.[35] In medieval philosophy, 'nominalists' debated with 'realists' about whether things like 'beauty' and 'honour' had a real existence separate from the concrete particulars of life that people describe as beautiful or honourable, or whether such terms were just empty signifiers. Nuttall sees Falstaff's reference to 'air' as a tell-tale sign of his nominalism.[36] So while Condren is right to draw attention to the potential for anachronism when seeing Falstaff as an attractive comic character, it is certainly possible to overstate the case that his comic attractiveness is exclusively modern.[37] In any case, the problem for BVT is that it can only register such attractiveness (modern or early modern) as 'benignity', even if it effectively describes, at one level, the humour Falstaff produces.

BVT, then, seems limited in its capacity to account for humour's pleasure, and its attraction. If we laugh heartily with real amusement at things that benignly violate our principles, why are we so attracted to those violating things and why do we get pleasure from them? BVT's implicit answer to that question is that the violations are, in effect, safe. But can that be all? There is perhaps an irreducible duality here: an attraction and a repulsion. And in the case of some comic characters, the attraction and repulsion seem connected. The two sides of Falstaff's comic power are *simultaneous*. In other words, it is perhaps only within his benign violation of military norms—amusing from one point of view—that Falstaff is able to get audiences on side in his attempt to point out what is empty about the honour code: that its central value is less substantial than we want it to be (especially in times of war). I want to explore that duality further now with the notion of 'counter-violation'.

First, by way of counterpoint, I will introduce the second comic character in this discussion, who instantiates a similar kind of duality. This is the figure of Frate Timoteo in Machiavelli's comedy *Mandragola* (*The Mandrake*).[38] The basic situation of this play is as follows: a rich but silly old man, Messer Nicia, is trying to have a child by his young wife, Lucrezia, whom he cannot get pregnant. Meanwhile, a younger man, Callimaco, having heard of Lucrezia's beauty in France, returns to Florence to see for himself. He quickly becomes enamoured and plans to seduce her. In order to get access to her, Callimaco (pretending to be a doctor) and his friend Ligurio convince Messer Nicia and Lucrezia that she will be fertile if she drinks a potion made from mandrake root. Unfortunately, so their swindling story goes, the potion will have a deadly effect for the first man that sleeps with her afterwards. Nicia can resolve the problem this poses for him if he agrees to coerce (with them) an unsuspecting random captive who will draw off the poison in his stead. Unbeknown to Nicia, the random captive will, of course, be Callimaco. Nicia needs to go along with this because the respectability that comes from having a son and heir is the most important thing to him. Lucrezia, on the other hand, requires more convincing to carry out a plan that, notionally, will involve adultery, deception, and complicity in murder! The allusions to the ancient Roman story of Tarquin's rape of the chaste Lucretia are significant, for Machiavelli's Lucrezia is a moral person and the plot involves inflicting on that morality a kind of rape. To convince her to go through with this, her avaricious confessor, Frate Timoteo, is paid handsomely to convince Lucrezia of the plan's 'wisdom' in the bigger picture. Timoteo feels a little lost himself but his general sentiment is signified in what seems to be an aside: 'I think I'm getting into an awful mess. I'm dealing with a crazy man [Ligurio] on one side and a deaf man [Nicia] on the other [...] But unless these coins are counterfeit, I can use them better than they can!' (3.5).

The amusing scene in which he persuades Lucrezia is central to the play's politics. As he awaits her and her mother, Sostrata (who has been asked to bring Lucrezia to the confessor), Timoteo confronts some obstacles. Speaking in soliloquy, and having resolved himself concerning the problem of secrecy, the unholy priest now confronts a further problem: 'It is true, of course, that I may still have some trouble, because, unfortunately, Madonna Lucrezia is a good and virtuous woman' (3.9). This sets the tone of the encounter to follow. Having consulted his books for 'two whole hours' he is now replete with (dubious) arguments. The first is this: 'where there is a certain good and an uncertain evil, one must never abandon that good for fear of the evil' (3.11). On this basis, he tells Lucrezia that getting pregnant is the certain good and the uncertain evil the captive's death. But, of course, the pregnancy is *not* certain and the death *is*, at least according to the swindlers' tale. His next point is, as sin resides in the will and not in the body, Lucrezia can be sure that in following her husband's will she is doing no wrong. This may be cogent for loyal Lucrezia but it completely dissolves her will into her husband's when *her* moral will was the issue in question. Finally, Timoteo points to the story of Lot's daughters told in Genesis 19, who slept with their own father to preserve their family line, and he constructs for her the analogous half-truth that 'because their intentions were pure, they did not commit a sin' (3.11).

Just as with Falstaff, the comic foibles of avaricious Timoteo include not only his willingness to distort reason itself for personal gain but also to violate the principles of the very identity that serves him. Thus, we might understand Timoteo's humorous presence here in part with BVT. Machiavelli makes Timoteo's unpriestly actions and rhetoric comical because they facilitate his avarice, they violate Lucrezia's trust, and work against her better moral judgement. Yet it is relatively benign because we/the audience know that the 'random captive' will not die, as does Timoteo who seems to have been apprised of the plan, across 3.6-9, to make Callimaco the 'captive'. At one level, then, Machiavelli mobilises a conventional laughter at avaricious priests here, just as Shakespeare does at cowardly fat knights who ought to be more honourable when called upon. Such conventional humour can easily be described as arising, respectively, from benign violations of the expected normative behaviour of priests (who *ought* not to be greedy and deceitful) and of soldiers (who *ought* not to be cowards). We might call this the primary (benign) violation.

Yet, as with Falstaff, there is another side to Timoteo. In part, this is achieved through the voice of Lucrezia's mother, Sostrata, who is present as Timoteo counsels the shocked and horrified Lucrezia. Sostrata pleads with her daughter: 'Listen to him, my dear. Don't you see that a woman without children is a woman without a home? If her husband dies, she is left like an animal, abandoned by everybody'. Sostrata makes us see Timoteo in another light—not that that simply redeems him from being an agent in a patriarchal rape of Lucrezia's innocence. Yet his arguments, self-serving though they are, are also agents in a process through which he comes to take a level of 'appropriate' (to use Oring's term) care for Lucrezia—for she will follow his and her mother's advice, go through with the plan, and be rewarded, in an unexpected way.

The conflict at this point in the play between Lucrezia, on the one hand, and Timoteo and Sostrata (and Nicia) on the other, turns on the relationship between morality and socially mediated desire, in this case the desire for a child and the social validation that comes with it. As Harvey C. Mansfield puts it, the conflict is between 'morality' and 'respectability'.[39] Lucrezia desires, in fact *requires* that both be maintained together; everyone else sees that as impossible and asks her to sacrifice morality to respectability. But Machiavelli in a sense asks us to sympathise with them, for morality itself is being called into question: as Mansfield, again, puts it, 'Lucrezia is a moral person, and her failings are the failings of morality, not particular to her'.[40] Machiavelli has constructed a scenario in which morality is killing Lucrezia's ability to thrive as a social being. Thus, Timoteo's morally flexible, pragmatic rhetoric functions in a much larger context than just the facilitation of his avarice.

The play, as a whole, bears this out, as Timoteo's pragmatism comes to have a positive fulfilment. Precisely because they have gone along with an immoral scheme, Machiavelli makes everyone get what they (supposedly) need: Messer Nicia gets his child, Callimaco the woman he wants, and Lucrezia a satisfied husband and a handsome young lover. When Nicia eventually invites 'Doctor' Callimaco into his house and gives him 'a key to the downstairs guest room' since he and his friend 'don't have women at home to take care of their needs' (5.6), adultery is in effect domesticated; immorality is 'made respectable'.[41] This capacity to exhibit 'the incommensurability of ultimate values' is precisely what Machiavelli has been admired for in the round: Eugene Garver suggests that Machiavelli's originality consisted in confronting the fact that often 'to achieve one good is to fail to achieve another'.[42]

The ordinary assumption (or 'norm') that respectability and morality are commensurable and reconcilable underlies Timoteo's comic failure as a priest but it is this norm which is called into question. Lucrezia, as has been said, more than anyone else in the play demands that respectability does not entail failing to maintain morality. That demand of hers underlies her expectation that Timoteo, her priestly confessor, ought to be acting differently. But if the harmonious outcomes of the plot validate Timoteo's pragmatism and other characters' ability to separate morality and respectability, then we can see that what Machiavelli is doing is using the convention of laughable priest to critique the very norm that assumes the connection between morality and respectability. He makes that assumption laughable in itself by suggesting it is itself a violation of how things really are. Benign violation is an opportunity for counter-violation. In just the same way, Shakespeare makes the primary benign violation of Falstaff-as-shameful-soldier into an opportunity for counter-violation: Falstaff is able to make the very thing he is benignly violating—'honour'—into something laughable itself, a violation of how things really are from a different material (?) perspective. In other words, humour as a species of violation is operating in two directions at once.

A counter argument here might be that the two-sided comic power I have been talking about—primary benign violation and counter-violation—is entirely conceivable simply within the terms of BVT, if, that is, what I am calling 'counter-violation' is just the case of one 'salient norm' making the violation of another benign, or, to use Oring's key term, 'appropriate'. It will be recalled that McGraw and Warren's benignity type (a) was when 'a salient norm suggests that something is wrong but another salient norm suggests that it is acceptable'. Thus, it might be argued that the violation of military bravery is funny because the will to self-preservation makes it acceptable/appropriate, and likewise, that the violation of morality (and priestly duty) is funny because the need for respectability makes it acceptable/appropriate. But even if that is a good description, it is not all that is going on.

The counter-violation exceeds such descriptions because it turns the norms that structure the primary violations into laughable violations in their own right, violations of something else, and it is that something else which is hard to name. I have already suggested above that it might be called a 'material perspective' of 'how things really are'. In Falstaff's case, what structures the counter-violation is the belief that categories like 'honour' are empty, and in Timoteo's, the belief that the need for union between morality and respectability is disabling. While those beliefs have a normative critical force, they are not really 'norms'. They cannot be glossed as just other 'salient norms' or dismissed as the benignity condition for the humour of the primary violation. Furthermore, the counter-violations seem indissolubly linked to the primary violations. To put that in other words, one can ask, for example: how could Falstaff so engagingly call the norms of bravery into question with his deflation of 'honour' other than by being a ludicrous soldier? How could Timoteo implicitly call into question the assumption that Christian morality and social respectability are always reconcilable so effectively but as laughable priest?

We can now address some problems of terminology more generally. An obvious problem with the term 'norm' in this case is that Falstaff's cowardice and Timoteo's avarice were probably seen by Shakespeare and Machiavelli themselves as more normal—in the sense of common—than the moral 'norms' that BVT suggests they are violating. But more than that, what are the further implications of the 'counter-violations' I have been talking about for the use of BVT and its terminology? I have identified the way Falstaff as laughable soldier and Timoteo as laughable priest might be seen as benign violations of what McGraw and Warren call 'norms': 'moral' principles with ethical-political-ideological substance. The violated moral norms give their laughability a kind of structure. But I have also identified the counter-violations emerging within their conventional laughability, which make those structuring norms themselves laughable from the perspective of some kind of external 'value system'. The alternative value systems analogously give structure to the counter-violations but they cannot be called 'norms', even if they are, in the philosophical sense *normative*, because they are the perspectives from which norms are questioned. What terms, then, could we use for the different kinds of ethical and political meaning being negotiated in complex comic situations from the past like those of Falstaff and Timoteo? 'Norm' is multiply insufficient and is as anachronistic as 'value'. 'Virtue' would be less anachronistic in these cases but Falstaff's and Timoteo's counter-violating agencies can hardly be described as virtuous. Thus, one of BVT's major limits in this historical context is its terminology.

My final point will be that this problem of terms and the comic duality could be addressed in part, and in this case, by utilising an ethical-political discourse that was specifically meaningful in Machiavelli's and Shakespeare's times. I am referring to the discourse of practical wisdom, or prudence.

Prudence (in Latin, *prudentia*, in Machiavelli's Italian *prudenzia*) signified more than just a cardinal virtue. It was an ancient category of practical wisdom that meant using ethically meaningful knowledge from experience to deliberate well about the future. It was not a set of rules for behaviour but an ability to negotiate the problems of particular deliberative situations as well as can be expected within the constraints of limited knowledge. In the classical discourse of prudence, its results were the formation of character rather than of technique, and its determination tended to defer to past examples of its embodiment: thus it was, in a sense, always 'nested into the nooks and crannies of an individual personality', as Robert Hariman puts it, and, we might add, those of an individual context.[43] Some of the key discussions in its intellectual history before the modern period were those of: Aristotle, Cicero, Thomas Aquinas, Giovanni Pontano (1429–1503), and Machiavelli himself.

Of course, nowadays, the general idea of prudence is 'a shadow of its former self', something more closely associated with economic rationalism, political realism and the calculations of power.[44] Nevertheless, some of the features that would have been recognisable to Machiavelli and Shakespeare about the discourse of prudence they inherited can be identified. What was 'prudent' turned on: knowledge of patterns in the world based on experience; accurate knowledge of oneself and others (desires, capabilities, and temperaments); the capacity to distinguish the relative value of different possible good outcomes; the capacity to distinguish real from mere notional possibilities; the attempt to balance (or bring back into balance) considerations of expediency against considerations of honour, or to balance private expediency against public honour; and the practice of seeking good ends for oneself and others by the best available means.

Each of those things is a feature that differentiates prudence from *im*prudence: to act in those ways is prudence, to fail is the opposite. We can now see the way both sides of the duality addressed above are intimately linked, since Falstaff and Timoteo *violate* prudence in part but in so doing *embody* it too. Viewed from one angle, they benignly violate the norms of prudence, and so they are comically imprudent from the perspective of those norms, yet certain aspects of their comic 'imprudence' reveal a different kind of prudence if viewed from another. What looks foolish on one side of the coin looks wiser on the other.

Consider Falstaff's case first. He puts personal safety above the needs of the realm, pursuing his own expediency at the expense of public honour. From everybody else's point of view, the inexpediency of a short life is balanced by the gravity and public honour of protecting the realm. But Falstaff forges a fresh rift between expediency and honour, deemphasising the sort of 'honour' possessed by 'He that died o'Wednesday' and making the expediency of preserving physical life's value almost into a kind of honour itself. Thus, his comic rhetoric destabilises but then renews the balance of honour and expediency on his own (alternative) terms, through his benign violation of the view of prudence (in this situation) taken by everybody else around him. In a way, his rhetoric is a kind of comical prudence in its own right since it is based on a knowledge of patterns in the world (one's 'honour' is quickly forgotten), as well as a distinct idea of what constitutes a valuable life, and it certainly distinguishes (if on his own terms) both real goods and real likelihoods. It is plausible then that Shakespeare gives us in Falstaff a comically mangled prudence—failing at one level (benign violation) and working at another (counter-violation)—in order to think out loud, so to speak, about prudence in this particular context.

And so with Machiavelli. Though a partially repellent priest, Timoteo articulates nevertheless a kind of prudential wisdom. He seeks a version of 'good' ends, if by questionable means, and not just for himself. His persuasion turns on the genuinely plausible consequences of Lucrezia's not going through with the plan (i.e. the plight of women who cannot bear children). Timoteo's moral flexibility in favour of the social 'good' of having a child is, from the play-world's perspective (since the implication is that Nicia is impotent), the best available means of balancing out honour and expediency for the whole family. This prudential rhetoric, in so far as it is that, has the counter-violating force of showing how a complete alignment of honour (Christian morality) and expediency (the social good of having a child) is impossible. In both cases, Timoteo's and Falstaff's, the benign violations and the counter-violations can be seen as different perspectives on what is truly prudent in the respective situation. This gives us a much more powerful and historically-relevant description of how the humour of these comic characters works though, at the same time, of course, it is built on or framed by BVT.

What can be concluded from the discussion above? Benign violation theory is useful because it draws attention to the ethical and emotional significance of 'humour', whether old or new. In one sense, Oring is right to call BVT an 'emotional theory' since it asks us to consider what values the enjoyment of humour reflects. This is often precisely what cultural historians are interested in: the cultural meanings of Lear's fool's jests, for instance, or of comic characters like Falstaff and Timoteo, are closely bound up with the valuations that they instantiate.

Nevertheless, this case study has shown that, when applied to Shakespeare's and Machiavelli's comic characters, BVT comes up against two main problems:

1. The problem of duality: each of the characters is both repellent *and* attractive, they violate and validate; that duality cannot (quite) be captured by BVT.
2. The problem of terminology: the notion of structuring 'norms' is anachronistic and thus insufficient for capturing the way that each character instantiates a 'norm' through benign violation but at the same time ques-

tions that norm's norm-alcy and its moral value through counter-violation, which comes from a different perspective entirely; the different perspective in each case has its own ethical and emotional substance, or significance, but is not itself a 'norm'.

The problem of duality (1) is a problem that BVT might face when being used to investigate humour in any time period, including our own. Even just in the context of verbal humour (i.e. joke texts), BVT has trouble accounting for its pleasure except by means of the category of benignity. A theory like Freud's provides a much more powerful—if not particularly compelling—explanation of why humour gives us so much pleasure: the saving of psychic energy. The pleasures generated by watching Falstaff or Timoteo were not, and are not, circumscribed by the fact that they seem to violate the things that matter benignly, and the same thing might be said of any number of comic characters from contemporary TV programmes and films.

The problem of terminology (2), however, comes to the fore more prominently when applying BVT to a historically-distant context like Renaissance comic characters in plays. BVT's terminology is symptomatic of a modern context for moral thought, in which reified cultural forces like 'norms' and 'values' exert their power over and are resisted by human subjects. By contrast, Falstaff and Timoteo were created in and for a context in which moral philosophy proceeded primarily in terms of the way in which the individual human character could instantiate or deform the larger divine order, or *natura*, by embodying virtue (as, for instance, prudence) or its opposite. Falstaff and Timoteo, as comic characters, are agents in a cultural negotiation of what virtue or vice really is in their particular dramatic contexts, even if it can be said that Machiavelli's thought is moving in a modern direction. The same thing could hardly be said, for instance, about a comic character like Sheldon Cooper in the TV sit-com *The Big Bang Theory*, who does 'benignly' violate the 'norms' of social behaviour and assert his freedom from them. Falstaff has certainly been read in a similar way—as in the spirit of 'holiday', mentioned above—but that twentieth-century reading is, in my view, itself symptomatic of modern thought. There is more to Falstaff than freedom from the tyranny of 'norms'.

I have argued that if in the case of Renaissance comic characters like Falstaff and Timoteo we are to make the most of BVT's capacity to point up the ethical significance of humour, then we need less anachronistic terms. Relatedly, I have suggested that the discourse of prudence is particularly relevant in this historical context. Such 'Conceptual grafting', as we might call it, then, is one way to get around some of the specific problems that arise when trying to exploit, in specific historical contexts, the benefits of a wide-angle view offered by universalising modern theories of 'humour'.

# Notes

1. Reference here and throughout is to the edition of Shakespeare's *King Henry IV, Part 1* edited by Kastan; the scene occurs at the end of 5.1.
2. The two seminal papers are: Veatch, 'A Theory of Humor', and McGraw and Warren, 'Benign Violations'.
3. McGraw and Warren, 'Benign Violations', 1142.
4. Ibid., 1142.
5. Ibid., 1147.
6. Ibid., 1147.
7. Ibid., 1142.
8. Ibid., 1146.
9. Ibid., 1142.
10. See http://humorresearchlab.org/.
11. McGraw and Warner, *The Humor Code*.
12. Veatch, 'A Theory of Humor', 164.
13. McGraw and Warren, 'Benign Violations', 1142.
14. See Aristotle, *Poetics*, Chap. 5 (1449b). The key example, famously, is a comic mask, which is: 'ugly and twisted, but not painfully'.
15. For further discussion of Aristotle, see Derrin, 'The humorous unseemly', 427–428.
16. For more comment, see Derrin, '*Sine Dolore*', 84. See also Lucy Rayfield's chapter in this volume.
17. See Oring, *Joking Asides*, 60.
18. Ibid., 63–64.
19. Ibid., 60.
20. Ibid., 61.
21. Ibid., 60.
22. Ibid., 66–67.
23. For one example, see Janse, '"Anti Societies Are Now All the Rage"', 254.
24. See Sonnino, *A Handbook*, 165.
25. Vickers, *The Artistry*, 94.
26. Reference is to the edition of Shakespeare's *Macbeth* edited by Kenneth Muir, 2.3.9–11.
27. Ibid., xv–xxxii.
28. See for instance, Tillyard, *Shakespeare's History Plays*, 265.
29. Doloff, 'Falstaff's "Honour"'.
30. McDonough, '"A Mere Scutcheon"'.
31. For further discussion of the way such structures of emotional distance from the seriousness of the battle—what BVT terms benignity—are built into the representation of Falstaff and other Shakespearean characterisations, see Derrin, '*Sine Dolore*'.
32. I thank the anonymous peer-reviewer who helpfully made this important point.
33. A. C. Bradley thought of Falstaff as 'the bliss of freedom gained in humour': see Bradley, *Oxford Lectures*, 262. C. L. Barber focused on Falstaff and Hal as embodying 'holiday' and 'everyday', respectively, but emphasised Falstaff's comic power as a capacity to disrupt the expected balance between them: see Barber, *Shakespeare's Festive Comedy*, 192–221.

34. See Shapiro, *1599*, in addition to Merriam, 'Shakespeare's Supposed Disillusionment'.
35. See Nuttall, *Shakespeare* the *Thinker*, 157–158.
36. Ibid., 157.
37. See Condren's chapter in this volume.
38. Reference here and throughout is to the edition of Machiavelli's *The Mandrake* edited by Sices and Atkinson. Act and scene numbers are given in text. There are no line numbers.
39. Mansfield, 'The Cuckold in *Mandragola*', 6.
40. Ibid., 22.
41. Ibid., 6.
42. Garver, 'After *Virtù*', 67.
43. See Hariman, 'Theory without Modernity', 4–14.
44. Ibid., 15.

## Bibliography

Aristotle. *Poetics*. Translated by Stephen Halliwell. *Loeb Classical Library*. Cambridge, MA: Harvard University Press, 1995.

Barber, C.L. *Shakespeare's Festive Comedy*. Princeton: Princeton University Press, 1959.

Bradley, A.C. *Oxford Lectures on Poetry*. London: Macmillan, 1909.

Derrin, Daniel. 'The Humorous Unseemly: Value, Contradiction, and Consistency in the Comic Politics of Shakespeare's *A Midsummer Night's Dream*'. *Shakespeare* 11, no. 4 (2015): 425–445.

Derrin, Daniel. '*Sine Dolore*: Relative Painlessness in Shakespeare's Laughter'. *Critical Survey* 30, no. 1 (2018): 81–97.

Doloff, Steven. 'Falstaff's "Honour": Homeric Burlesque in *1 Henry IV* (1597–1598)'. *Notes and Queries* 55, no. 2 (2008): 177–181.

Garver, Eugene. 'After *Virtù*: Rhetoric, Prudence, and Moral Pluralism in Machiavelli'. In *Prudence: Classical Virtue, Postmodern Practice*, edited by Robert Hariman, 67–97. University Park: Pennsylvania State University Press, 2003.

Hariman, Robert. 'Theory Without Modernity'. In *Prudence: Classical Virtue, Postmodern Practice*, edited by Robert Hariman, 1–32. University Park: Pennsylvania State University Press, 2003.

Janse, Maartje. '"Anti Societies Are Now All the Rage": Jokes, Criticism, and Violence in Response to the Transformation of American Reform, 1825–1835'. *Journal of the Early Republic* 36, no. 2 (2016): 247–282.

Machiavelli, Nicolò. *The Comedies of Machiavelli: The Woman from Andros, The Mandrake, Clizia*. Edited and translated by David Sices and James B. Atkinson. Indianapolis: Hackett Publishing Company, 2007.

Mansfield, Harvey C. 'The Cuckold in *Mandragola*'. In *The Comedy and Tragedy of Machiavelli: Essays on the Literary Works*, edited by Vickie B. Sullivan, 1–29. New Haven: Yale, 2000.

McDonough, Christopher M. '"A Mere Scutcheon": Falstaff as *Rhipsaspis*'. *Notes and Queries* 55, no. 2 (2008): 181–183.

McGraw, Peter and Joel Warner. *The Humor Code: A Global Search for What Makes Things Funny*. New York: Simon & Schuster, 2014.

McGraw, Peter and Caleb Warren. 'Benign Violations: Making Immoral Behavior Funny'. *Psychological Science* 21, no. 8 (2010): 1141–149.

150  D. DERRIN

Merriam, Thomas. 'Shakespeare's Supposed Disillusionment with Chivalry in 1599'. *Notes and Queries* 54, no. 252 (2007): 285–287.

Nuttall, A.D. *Shakespeare the Thinker*. New Haven: Yale University Press, 2007.

Oring, Elliott. *Joking Asides: The Theory, Analysis, and Aesthetics of Humor*. Logan: Utah State University Press, 2016.

Shakespeare, William. *Macbeth*. Edited by Kenneth Muir. *The Arden Shakespeare*. 2nd ed. London: Bloomsbury, 1951.

Shakespeare, William. *King Henry IV, Part 1*. Edited by David Scott Kastan. *The Arden Shakespeare*. 3rd ed. London: Bloomsbury, 2002.

Shapiro, James. *1599: A Year in the Life of William Shakespeare*. London: Faber and Faber, 2006.

Sonnino, Lee. *A Handbook to Sixteenth-Century Rhetoric*. London: Routledge & Kegan Paul, 1968.

Tillyard, E.M.W. *Shakespeare's History Plays*. London: Chatto and Windus, 1948.

Veatch, Thomas C. 'A Theory of Humor'. *Humor: International Journal of Humor Research* 11, no. 2 (1998): 161–215.

Vickers, Brian. *The Artistry of Shakespeare's Prose*. London: Methuen, 1968.

CHAPTER 8

# Humour and Religion: New Directions?

*Richard A. Gardner*

The relation of humour and religion poses a bit of a puzzle. Both have commonly been regarded as universals to be found in all cultures and periods of history. Even if not granted the status of universals, both do seem to be found most everywhere. With a few notable exceptions, however, the relation of the two has received little attention. Classical and contemporary theories of religion make virtually no mention of humour; textbooks on religion, aside from occasional references to topics such as trickster figures, pass over the issue; and encyclopaedias and reference works on religion more often than not contain no entry on humour. Either humour and religion have little connection or the relation of the two has been overlooked.[1]

The latter of these options is, I think, closer to the truth. Elsewhere I proposed some simple strategies and questions for mapping the relations of humour to what Joachim Wach termed the theoretical (myth, sacred texts, folklore, etc.), practical (ritual, ethical action, etc.), and social (definitions of community, leadership, gender issues, etc.) dimensions of religion. Included was a consideration of the various ways humour has been directed against religions. More boldly, I proposed that conceiving of religion as involving a complex interplay of congruity and incongruity might provide a basis for more fully exploring the relation of humour and religion.[2]

The terms 'religion' and 'humour' are, of course, English language terms of fairly recent origin that have received extensive theoretical discussion over the last couple of hundred years and been raised to the status of theoretical terms. Within religious studies, the concept of religion has recently been subject to

R. A. Gardner (✉)
Sophia University, Tokyo, Japan
e-mail: r-gardne@sophia.ac.jp

© The Author(s), under exclusive license to Springer Nature
Switzerland AG 2020
D. Derrin, H. Burrows (eds.), *The Palgrave Handbook of Humour, History, and Methodology*, https://doi.org/10.1007/978-3-030-56646-3_8

151

intense critical reflection, with some questioning its universal status and even arguing that the term be abandoned.[3] As the introduction to this volume indicates, many historians have similarly questioned the concept of humour. In both fields, scholars have often made their critiques by suggesting that concepts such as 'humour' and 'religion' are historically constructed.

Given this situation, I should at least briefly suggest my understanding of these two terms at the outset. Paraphrasing a definition approved, if not authored, by Jonathan Z. Smith, I understand religion as referring to a system of beliefs and practices relative to superhuman beings and powers.[4] This leaves aside, at least for the moment, equally problematic terms such as 'myth' and 'ritual'. For my understanding of humour, I follow those who understand it as involving a perception of comic incongruity and who include within the category notions such as wit, mockery, satire, and derision.[5] Our theoretical terms always exist in tension with the phenomena we apply them to; theoretical reflection thus requires recognizing the limits of our categories and making continual adjustments.

One of the purposes of the present volume is to explore and critique the 'universalising' tendencies present in theories of humour with the aim of exploring how our theories can obscure the meanings of phenomena we perceive as related to humour in different cultures and periods of history. The scant attention given to humour and religion can be related, I think, to a universalizing tendency in our understanding of the relation of religion and humour. Put simply, religion has been conceived in such a way, primarily by implicitly or explicitly identifying it with the 'serious', that its various entanglements with humour have been obscured. A greater appreciation of the various ways in which humour and religion have been 'entangled' might well enrich our understanding of both terms.

The purpose of this chapter is to provide a critical overview of works in English that have, in the last 50 years or so, explicitly addressed, or seem particularly relevant to, the question of the relation of humour and religion and which have developed, if not a full-bodied theory, at least an approach to the topic. While I have no doubt overlooked some key works, the paucity of works to review should testify to the neglect of the topic. The works reviewed here also make little if any reference to one another; a sustained theoretical debate about the topic is yet to emerge.

A range of works that might be read as making important contributions to the discussion of the relation of humour and religion have nevertheless been excluded from this review. Included here are works taking a predominantly theological approach and books focusing primarily on the relation of Christianity and humour.[6] Also excluded are the many works on topics such as tricksters, jesters, ritual clowns, and fools that demonstrate ways in which humour and religion have been ineluctably related at times. There does seem to have been a growing interest in the relation of humour and religion in recent years, as illustrated by a number of edited books on the topic.[7] There are also a number of significant works by historians in recent years that have illustrated how intimately humour and religion have been intertwined in different periods of history.[8] I have passed over these works because they do not offer much in the way of articulating a general approach to the topic of humour and religion.

As I review these works, I will attempt, along the way, to indicate ideas and paths that might be fruitfully pursued further as well as raise questions and problems concerning some of the ways in which the relation of humour and religion has been approached. I would emphasize, however, that all of the works reviewed here deserve serious consideration; they contain a wealth of suggestive ideas and insights that I have not been able to present in full. By way of conclusion, I will offer some suggestions for further exploring the various relations of humour and religion.

## Humour and Myth

One of the more provocative efforts to relate humour and religion has been offered by Kees W. Bolle, a noted scholar of religion and myth as well as a distinguished Indologist. In *The Freedom of Man in Myth*, Bolle attempts to provide a new understanding of myth by relating it to humour and thus also to explain the continued interest in myth throughout the modern period.[9] In addition to illustrating the difficulties sometimes encountered in determining whether phenomena in different cultures and periods of history were considered humorous, Bolle's argument represents an effort to significantly, if not radically, alter our understandings of humour, myth, and religion.[10]

Bolle begins with a critical review of efforts to define and explain myth and rejects evolutionary theories treating myth as a primitive form of philosophy, science, or religious doctrine as well as social-scientific theories that treat myth in functional terms as merely supporting the status quo of either culture or society.[11] Bolle rejects such theories not simply because of their reductive tendencies but also because they do not give proper attention to the 'looseness' that characterizes the form of mythic narratives: myth is not concerned with facts, logic, and consistency; it is a form of thought that presents experiences more concretely than philosophy and rationalized religious doctrine and thought; and it deals with extraordinary events and states at odds with the categories and experiences of everyday life. While not irrational, myth speaks to the imagination more than reason as defined during the western Enlightenment.[12]

For Bolle, the 'looseness' of the form of mythic narratives gives myth a humorous dimension. Bolle draws his understanding of humour from the writings of the German romantic Jean Paul (Johann Paul Friedrich Richter, 1763–1825) and is careful to note that the notion of humour used by romantic writers such as Jean Paul was not so much concerned with humour in the sense of the funny or the hilarious (perhaps the 'amusing' would be more accurate) as with humour that deals with matters of ultimate importance and gives rise to 'the smile which liberates'.[13] This is a type of humour, in other words, that frees one from the constraints of the sorts of dualities that tend to dominate daily life and common sense.[14]

Writing in part concerning the comic novel, Jean Paul identified four forms of humour (all of which might be understood as types of incongruity): (1) the dimming of opposites, as seen in some cosmogonies that describe a time when heaven and earth were not yet separated; (2) the inverse effect, as when a disastrous event leads unexpectedly to something good; (3) subjective reservedness, as when some myths highlight that it is, ironically, a limited human voice that narrates a sacred, more than human reality; and (4) the grotesque (the fantastic, the ludicrous, and the comically distorted or exaggerated), as might be seen in myths of tricksters.[15] While these four types are not inevitably found in all myths, Bolle argues that they are present in one combination or another. Bolle does acknowledge, however, that not all have necessarily found their myths to be humorous; this is particularly the case where there is a tendency (especially prominent in Jewish, Christian, and Islamic traditions) to rationalize and explain away the incongruities and contradictions to be found in myths once they are put into written form.[16] This suggests one way in which history and changes in religious sensibilities have impacted our understanding of the relation of humour and religion.

Among the examples Bolle presents of the dimming of opposites are the account of creation in *Genesis*, the myth of the churning of the ocean in the *Râmâyana*, and an account of creation in *Rig Veda* (X 129), a passage from which he translates as follows.

> The nonexistent then existed not, nor the existent.
> There was no air nor sky that is beyond it.
> Death then existed not, nor life immortal.
> Of neither night nor day was any sign.[17]

I must assume that most readers do not find this passage very 'humorous'. I can only recommend reading Bolle's explanation as well as Wendy Doniger O'Flaherty's reading of this and other texts from *Rig Veda*.[18]

In a fashion reminiscent of Bolle, Johan Huizinga treats this same myth in his discussion of myth, cosmogonies, riddles, and sacred play in *Homo Ludens*.[19] While Huizinga focuses on play, he does note its close relation with laughter and the comic.[20] At one point, he even characterizes myth as 'playing on the borderline between jest and earnest'.[21] The liberating power Bolle attributes to mythic humour parallels the power Huizinga attributes to the sacred play of mythic speculation. Though there is not room here to argue the point, I think that almost everything Huizinga has to say about myth, even without appealing to his concept of play, could be used to illustrate Bolle's argument about the inherently humorous nature of mythic narrative.[22]

While I have not been able to locate the work of any scholars who have explicitly cited Bolle on the theme of humour and pursued his insights, I think the work of Wendy Doniger (O'Flagherty), perhaps the most prolific and creative of writers on myth in recent decades, might be read as illustrating and developing many of Bolle's ideas. Though she makes little reference to the notion of humour, Doniger's writings are marked by a whimsical sense of humour that is directed towards myths, scholars of myth, and the human condition itself. In addition, many of the myths Doniger is drawn to do seem to be humorous in the sense that it is hard to imagine at least some tellers and hearers of the myths as not regarding them as 'amusing', as well as humorous in other senses.

Many of Doniger's works might be read as illustrating some of Richter's forms of humour. Drawing on Levi-Strauss at points, Doniger treats, without using the same words, the theme of 'subjective reservedness' (form 3 above) in her effort to define myth: in telling myths, narrators often acknowledge the stories come from somewhere else.[23] Though at times defining myth as stories believed to be true, she acknowledges at other times that there is a fundamental ambiguity about whether myths are regard as true stories or not.[24] She notes, for instance, that the Malagasy end the recitation of any myth with the following statement: 'It is not I that lie; this lie comes from olden times'.[25] As can be seen through her commentaries on this theme, the point is that myths often signal, quite incongruously, that they are to be believed and yet also maybe not quite to be believed. This does seem to suggest a view of myth as 'playing on the borderline between jest and earnest'.

Doniger might also be read as introducing new 'forms', analogous to Jean Paul's, that render myth humorous. In *The Implied Spider*, Doniger introduces the metaphors of telescopic and microscopic to describe two themes or perspectives that many myths present us with; they show us the details of our everyday sense life while at the same time contrasting it with a suddenly cosmic vision of the whole, as seen in one story of Krishna and Yashoda, his mother. In the microscopic view, Krishna's mother heard from other children that he had eaten dirt. His mother asked him about it and he denied it. She did not believe it and so he asked her to look in his mouth. She did so and saw, in telescopic fashion, the whole cosmos, including her own insignificance, as well as that of her family. But, as the text says, God intervened and she lost her memory of this vision and was once again content.[26] Is this humorous? It is a question worth taking seriously.

Even if in need of some clarification and qualification, Bolle's analysis of what might be termed the at least potentially humorous incongruities marking mythic narratives is, I think, compelling and convincing and deserves further exploration. While Bolle is equivocal at times about whether the tellers and hearers of myth found the tales amusing, there is at least some ethnographic evidence that some peoples have looked upon their own myths, as well as the myths of others, with a sense of amusement.[27] Though it might entail broadening his understanding of humour beyond 'the smile that liberates', Bolle's argument might also find further support in three topics he gives only passing attention to: the humorous treatment given myths in some rituals; the parodic versions of myths that often exist side by side with, but do not reject, more 'serious' versions of myths; and laughter and humour as explicit themes in myth.[28]

## The Comic Vision and Religion

In 1969, perhaps the most exuberant and prolific of writers on humour and religion, Conrad Hyers, published an edited volume on the topic entitled *Holy Laughter*. The introduction and two essays by Hyers included in this volume might be characterized as ground-breaking, though Hyers never quite brought his initial vision to fruition and other scholars have made only passing reference to his writings. For Hyers, humour is closely identified with the comic, the comic spirit, and the comic vision.[29]

Much of Hyers' concerns are theological and normative; he argues that Christian theologians have given insufficient attention to humour and the comic and that Christianity, properly understood, represents a comic vision. He also implies throughout a number of his works that neglect of the relation of humour and religion has to do with the influence of Christianity and particularly Protestantism, on our notions of religion.[30] In addition, Hyers argues for the superiority of the comic vision over the tragic vision but does grant that comic and tragic perspectives are in a constant interplay or dialectical relationship.

At times, however, Hyers writes as a historian of religion. He draws on materials from a range of religions and argues that a proper understanding of all religious traditions requires a greater appreciation of the role of humour and the comic within them. Hyers' most provocative and significant argument is that theorists of religion (including Emile Durkheim, Rudolf Otto, Mircea Eliade, etc.) have failed 'to treat, as an integral movement within the experience of and response to the sacred, the dialectical interrelation of the sacred and the comic'.[31]

Whether one agrees with his formulation of this dialectic or not, Hyers has identified one important way in which our understanding of the relation of humour and religion has been universalized: religion is concerned with the serious and humour with the non-serious and thus, with a few exceptions, they have been treated as having little to do with one another. According to Hyers, humour and religion are inevitably and intrinsically related. Hyers might also be read here as making a crucial point that deserves to be stressed. Humour and religion are deeply related even when there seems to be no relation. The sense of the sacred, as seen in many solemn rituals, is often created, either explicitly or implicitly, by excluding humour.

In his early essays, Hyers describes three movements of the dialectic of the sacred and the comic in terms of 'the laughter of Paradise, of Paradise-lost, and of Paradise-regained'.[32] Though acknowledging these terms derive from the Christian tradition, he argues that they are applicable to all religious traditions and draws on anthropological studies and studies in the history of religions to illustrate his point. His argument is difficult to follow in places, the typology he presents does seem more suited to Christianity than some other religious traditions, and Hyers abandons the notion of a 'dialectic' in his later works.

Hyers would go on to write two books on Buddhism and humour,[33] a book on the comic vision and Christianity,[34] and a book on humour and comedy in the Bible.[35] The books on Buddhism and humour might also be characterized as ground-breaking; they clearly illustrate how our understanding of a religious tradition might be altered by giving due attention to humour. In part a reworking of his book on the comic vision and Christianity, his fullest treatment of humour and religion is *The Spirituality of Comedy*, which draws on many examples of myths and rituals from outside the Christian tradition.[36] Hyers sees this volume as being a companion piece to Joseph Campbell's *The Hero with a Thousand Faces* and subtitles the introduction as 'The Comic Hero with a Thousand Faces'.

A slight digression might be in order here. Campbell's *The Hero with a Thousand Faces* was, despite not getting a lot of positive acknowledgement from scholars (except perhaps in the field of literature), one of the most widely read books on myth in the second half of the twentieth century. At one point, Campbell describes myth as breaking 'the whole world into a vast, horrendous Divine Comedy', as embodying an 'Olympian laugh', and as expressing a comic rather than tragic vision.[37] While this may not tell us much about myth, it, as well as the works of Hyers', might be used to illustrate a topic to be discussed below: a turn to the celebration of the spiritual value of humour in the west during the twentieth century.

As in his prior works, Hyers argues in *The Spirituality of Comedy* for the superiority of the comic vision to the tragic vision. His outline of the comic hero's journey is somewhat simpler than Campbell's. At the level of the individual, it moves from childhood to adolescence and then on to maturity (marked by a joyful sense of humour); at the mythic level, the journey roughly corresponds to the typology of paradise, paradise-lost, and paradise-regained. He fills in the journey by examining the rogue, the humourist, the comedian, the fool, the clown, the underdog, the trickster, and the simpleton. These categories are, at best, loosely defined and most of the examples are drawn from the modern, secular world; Charlie Chaplain, for better or worse, seems to be the central hero in Hyers' vision.

Much like Peter Berger (who will be discussed below), Hyers seems to be more concerned here with arguing for the redemptive, salvific, and liberating value of the comic in the here and now of modernity rather than exploring the relation of humour and religion throughout the range of human experience across time and space or history and culture. Like all theorists who privilege the comic over the tragic, Hyers also struggles with dealing with those aspects of humour—such as derision, mockery, and satire—that do not seem to contribute to a happy ending when all is redeemed.[38]

## COMEDY, TRAGEDY, AND RELIGION

While Hyers has been the most prolific writer on humour and religion, John Morreall has perhaps been the most prolific writer on the philosophy of humour in recent decades.[39] Morreall addresses the relation of humour and religion in *Comedy, Tragedy, and Religion* where he identifies the core of comedy as humour.[40] In Morreall's view, comedy, tragedy, and religion are linked by dealing with the varieties of incongruity posed by the disparities between the way things are and the way one might hope them to be. They are linked, in short, by dealing with issues such as death, evil, and suffering along with less pressing or ultimate sorts of incongruities.[41] This is, I think, a suggestive formulation.

Morreall proceeds by first examining Greek comedy and tragedy as dramatic genres and contrasts the two in terms of their understanding of the hero, of the conflict or incongruities they encounter, of what attitude should be taken toward suffering, and of the response to suffering.[42] Based on this analysis, Morreall then proceeds to present what he terms the differences between 'the comic vision' and 'the tragic vision'. He compares the two visions in terms of 20 different themes or topics: simple versus complex conceptual schemes, idealism versus pragmatism, vengeance versus forgiveness, and heroism versus anti-heroism, and so on.[43] Many of these oppositions, such as the opposition between simple and complex intellectual schemes, do seem a bit overly simple and reductive.

Morreall then turns to examining how the tragic and comic visions have been expressed in religions, though it should be noted that the religions examined here are those religions, aside from a brief and very limited discussion of new religions, that have often been termed 'world religions'. Included here are discussions of Buddhism, Christianity, Daoism, Confucianism, Hinduism, Islam, and Judaism. He does this by looking at how the 20 comic and tragic themes and values noted above relate to these religious traditions.[44]

Morreall analyses Buddhism, for example, as having more pro-comic than pro-tragic features as seen in the value it attaches to: (1) emotional detachment, (2) mental flexibility, and (3) the hope that all might be eventually saved. Islam, on the other hand, comes out as decidedly pro-tragic in terms of the features it embodies: (1) militarism, (2) general lack of mental flexibility, and (3) no sense of playfulness. Morreall concludes the book in normative fashion by offering friendly advice to religions that they should emphasize their pro-comic features and downplay their pro-tragic features.[45]

While this is a valuable book, I have of number of reservations but will offer only a few here. Being a philosopher, it is understandable that Morreall spends most of his time examining what might be termed the central 'sacred' texts that most resemble philosophy, though some of them, such as the Bible and the *Qur'an* are clearly not philosophical texts. Little attention, except perhaps in the treatment of Christianity, is given to how these central 'sacred' texts have been interpreted throughout the course of history in folklore, ritual, legend, and subsequent interpretations of sacred texts. The assumption here seems to be that we can deduce a religion's attitude to humour, comedy, and tragedy from an examination of its central sacred texts. As I have suggested elsewhere, this is an assumption that should be questioned.[46]

While this is a relatively brief book, the engagement with the literature on the religions treated is still rather thin and quite questionable at places. Based on a reading of a few Zen texts, Morreall concludes that Buddhism tells its practitioners not to take rituals too seriously.[47] This is a statement difficult to reconcile with any history of Buddhism in general or Zen in particular. The treatment of Islam is particularly thin and perhaps even unfortunate in that it supports the view that Muslims are lacking in, among other things, humour. He argues, for instance, that there are no comic role models in Islam, no emphasis on the love of God, and no sense of playfulness.[48] One source of the problems here, I think, is again an overreliance on the analysis of a few central 'sacred' texts. There is also a tendency to overgeneralize the orientation or outlook of different religious traditions that most present-day scholars of religion would be uncomfortable with.

Additional questions might also be raised about 'the comic vision'. Both Hyers and Morreall celebrate the comic vision and seem to assume at points, despite a recognition of variety, that there are views of the world that correspond to the comic vision and the tragic vision. These notions derive, of course, from western reflection on Greek dramatic genres. As genre theorists have recognized for some time, the tragic genre of drama seems to be primarily a western phenomena. Perhaps we are, to a degree at least, reading western preoccupations into our treatment of other cultural and religious traditions? Perhaps what we need is an exploration of how what might be termed 'comic and tragic perceptions' interact to produce a variety of visions, even within a single religious tradition, that cannot be reduced to either a comic or tragic vision.[49]

## An Anthropological Perspective

In *Humor and Laughter*, Mahadev Apte presents what he describes as the first cross-cultural study of humour. Apte understands humour as provoking laughter, amusement, and smiling. At one point, he suggests that: 'Humor is primarily the result of cultural perceptions, both individual and collective, of incongruity, exaggeration, distortion, and any unusual combination of cultural elements in external events'.[50] While the term 'comic' is used at times, there is no reference made to comedy and tragedy as genres or as generalized 'visions'. Taking primarily a structural-functionalist approach, he notes that he will not deal with the 'symbolic and metaphorical aspects of humour', though he inevitably does at many points.[51]

Aside from providing a very valuable review of the anthropological literature on humour, Apte presents a very methodical and sensible way of approaching the relation of humour and religion. To understand humour (as well as the relation of humour and religion), he suggests, we should explore how humour is related to: (1) dimensions of social organization such as kinship, sex role, age, gender, class, and political structures and (2) the expressive dimensions of culture such as ritual, myth, folklore, religion, and language. While this suggestion may seem obvious, few of the works reviewed here have so clearly expressed this approach. Of particular value for readers interested in how our notions concerning humour might have been universalized is Apte's extensive discussion of how our theoretical terms exist in tension with the concepts related to 'humour' to be found in different historical and cultural contexts.[52]

In the first four chapters of the book, Apte explores the relation between humour and social structure and examines joking relationships, gender and humour, children's humour, and humour as it relates to ethnicity and the relations of one group of people to another. The topic of religion arises at a number of points. Apte has made an important contribution here, in particular, by exploring the relation of humour to children and women. Though it is obviously a topic of importance, there is yet to appear much in the way of research concerning how children and women relate to humour and religion.[53]

Apte devotes two chapters of his book to the question of the relation of humour and religion. In one, he provides a review of the literature on humour and ritual; in another, a review of humour in myth and folklore. Religion is defined as a belief in and interaction with supernatural beings and powers.[54] Apte also notes that anthropological studies have shown that humour and religion have been intimately related in many cultures and that anthropologists have, in terms of some topics such as clowns and tricksters, given extensive treatment to the topic.[55] This raises a question I will not attempt to answer here: why then has so little attention been given to humour by, among others, historians of religion?

In his chapter on humour and ritual, Apte primarily explores the roles humour plays in calendrical rituals and life cycle rituals, with an emphasis placed on the phenomena of ritual clowning. Based on his review of the literature, Apte lists a number of features commonly involved in ritual humour: behaviour contrary to social norms, a seeming breakdown in social control, sexual and scatological elements, and a comic treatment of sacred rituals, authority figures, and foreigners.[56] He also provides a valuable critical, and basically sceptical, examination of theoretical explanations of ritual humour.[57] He concludes by offering what he terms 'theoretical propositions'. Included among them is the following: 'The degree to which humour is integrated in rituals seems to vary not only across cultures but from ritual to ritual within individual cultures'.[58] Apte underlines, in other words, the difficulty of formulating broad, cross-cultural generalizations.

Apte also explores how humour is expressed in religious myth and folklore. He focuses on the figure of the trickster, a theoretical construct developed by reflection on mythic figures first encountered, by scholars anyway, in the study of indigenous religions in North America. As Apte's survey of the literature illustrates, the concept has since been extended to identify tricksters, or at least trickster-like figures, in many religions throughout the world. While I have doubts about the validity of the notion of the trickster as a universal category, I would agree with one of Apte's concluding theoretical propositions: 'Trickster tales demonstrate that humour is indeed an integral part of religious ideology in many parts of the world'.[59] This would seem to add some support to Bolle's argument about the relation of humour and myth. Apte also cites O'Flaherty as arguing that myth bridges the gap between the psychological and cognitive aspects of religion by the use of humour.[60]

Despite this book's value, there seems to have been very little follow-up theoretical reflection on the topic of humour and religion in anthropology, as Apte notes in a relatively recent reflection on his career.[61] Henk Driessen has provided a critique of the book and indicated how anthropological approaches to humour have moved beyond Apte's largely structural-functional approach.[62] Being an effort to review and synthesize a vast literature on anthropology and humour, Apte inevitably presents examples of religion and humour removed from the intricacies and complexities of their cultural contexts. As historians have suggested, perhaps what we need now is more detailed explorations of the meaning of humour in different cultural, religious, and historical contexts.[63]

## HUMOUR, LAUGHTER, AND RELIGION

In an important article published in 1991, Ingvild Gilhus argued that historians of religion have paid scant attention to the relation of the ludicrous and religion and should draw more fully on what she saw then as the fast-growing interest in humour studies. For Gilhus, the ludicrous is closely related to, if not identified with, the comic and the humorous; laughter is one of the primary, though not inevitable, responses to the ludicrous.[64] Though not as clearly stated as by Bolle and Hyers, Gilhus at least suggests that we cannot fully understand religion without taking into account its relation with humour. She also introduces what I would describe as a valuable methodological point: any instance of the ludicrous or humorous within a religion must be interpreted in terms of the totality of the religious system and, indeed, effects the meaning of all elements of the religious system.[65]

In *Laughing Gods and Weeping Virgins*, Gilhus develops many of the themes presented in her article and makes, I think, an important contribution to the study of humour and religion. This last point requires some explanation. Though acknowledging that humour, the ludicrous, and religion have often been linked in meaningful ways, she chooses to focus on the meaning of laughter and explicitly states that she is not concerned with 'religious humour in general'.[66] The reasons given are that: (1) laughter is not always a result of humour, (2) laughter that involves mocking does not have much to do with humour, (3) ritual joking is better explained by its relation to cult rather than humour, and (4) the spheres of laughter and humour do not overlap completely.[67] As the reference to 'mocking' suggests, Gilhus seems to have excluded humour, at least partially, because it does not relate to phenomena such as mocking, ridicule, and satire, topics that are given extensive treatment in this book. If humour is defined more broadly to include what I have referred to elsewhere as 'the dark side of humour', [68] then Gilhus' book can be read I think as a valuable study of humour and religion. The same could be said about Stephen Halliwell's *Greek Laughter*. While Halliwell also rejects the category of humour, the book can be read, I think, as one of the more sophisticated treatments of the topic in recent years.

Rather than humour, Gilhus has decided to focus on laughter, its relation to the body, and the sorts of religious meanings attached to it in different cultural and historical contexts. Drawing on Levi-Strauss, she describes laughter as an opening up of the human body that brings into play the wide range of symbolic meanings of 'opening' when related to other elements of religious and cultural systems.[69] Though the meanings attributed to laughter vary widely, laughter tends to be perceived as either 'destructive or life-giving' and thus symbolically connected to a range of meanings that can be grouped into themes related to (1) creation and birth and (2) destruction and death.[70]

Readers of this book might be particularly interested in Gilhus' understanding of the superiority, incongruity, and relief theories of laughter or humour. While noting that these theories can be of great use and arguing that they are not mutually exclusive, she does suggest that they have tended, partially because of their focus on explaining the causes of laughter, to overlook the variety of meanings attributed to laughter in different historical and cultural contexts.[71]

Gilhus explores three major historical periods: (1) the ancient near east and classical Greek culture, (2) Hellenistic cultures and western Christianity, and (3) the modern period. Her basic strategy is to explore how laughter has been related to myths, rituals, and communal life in different historical contexts as well as to examine texts where laughter became an explicit topic of reflection and debate.[72] This is not the place to explore in detail the shifts in the meanings attributed to laughter in different historical contexts. I would note, however, that her exploration of the negative attitudes towards humour and laughter in Enlightenment philosophy and Christianity, especially Protestantism, are suggestive as to why the relation of humour and religion has been overlooked in theories of religion.[73] Also included here is a valuable discussion of a rediscovery of the positive values of humour and laughter that can help explain the increased interest on the part of some Christians (such as Hyers) and others, such as Morreall, in the redemptive value of humour and laughter.[74]

Gilhus' work illustrates, I think, a number of important points. She clearly demonstrates that the different meanings attributed to laughter can be explained in terms of the different understandings attributed to the cosmos, the gods, and the human body in varying historical contexts. Just as importantly, Gilhus shows that understanding the meaning of laughter can provide a key to understanding the religious system in its totality. Gilhus' work also provides a valuable corrective to the work of scholars, such as Hyers, who wish to celebrate the value of the 'comic vision' and thus have some ambivalence dealing with what I have termed 'the dark side of humour'. Gilhus demonstrates some of the key roles played by derision, ridicule, and mockery in different religions.

## Finite Provinces of Meaning

Though better known for his works on the sociology of knowledge, religion, modernization, and development, Peter Berger made a number of significant forays into what he termed 'lay theology' and often used these occasions to address the relation of religion to humour and the comic.[75] Berger's work clearly illustrates Gilhus' discussion of the renewed interest in humour among Christian theologians in the last 50 years or so. While his at times theological approach to humour might be grounds for excluding him from this review, his work also contains valuable suggestions about how the relation of religion and humour might be approached.[76]

One of the major influences on Berger's efforts to develop a sociology of knowledge was Alfred Schutz. At key points in his writings both on religion and humour, Berger drew on Schutz's notion of multiple realities that contrasted the paramount common sense of everyday reality with other realms that he characterized as finite provinces of meaning; included here are realms of experience such as dreams, aesthetic experience, play, religion, and science. While Schutz himself does not comment much on the comic, Berger develops an understanding of the comic as a finite province of meaning and on this basis, particularly in his latter work, offers an explanation of the relation of religion and the comic.[77]

Though grounding all of his 'theological' writings in the sociology of religion, Berger was usually careful to note at what point he moved from sociological analysis to a theological perspective. One of Berger's first books, *The Precarious Vision*, begins with a sociological analysis of the precariousness of the social fictions on which societies are built and then moves on, following the neo-orthodox writings of Karl Barth (a position he later abandoned), to argue that Christianity is not to be counted as a religion but as a critique of religion that 'embodies a specific type of comic perspective' that both provides a critique of society and offers hope for some form of final redemption.[78]

In 1969, Berger published *A Rumor of Angels* in order to develop what he thought were the theological implications of *The Sacred Canopy* (1967), perhaps his most influential work in the sociology of religion. Breaking with the neo-orthodox tradition, Berger returns to the tradition of liberal Protestant theology in order to sketch out a theological programme described as an inductive approach 'that examines ordinary human experience' to discover what he terms 'signals of transcendence'.[79] Humour is analysed here as one of the important signals of transcendence.[80] Berger's subsequent effort in *The Heretical Imperative* (1979) to outline his inductive approach to theology makes only passing reference to humour but is much more 'ecumenical' than his earlier efforts in that it is intended to serve as a guide to theological reflection for any religious tradition.[81] His final effort at clarifying his theological understanding of Christianity, *Questions of Faith* (2003), also makes scant reference to humour.

Berger's fullest treatment of humour and religion is found in *Redeeming Laughter*. For Berger, humour and the comic, like religion, are universals, though they take on different meanings in different historical and cultural contexts. Humour is the capacity to perceive the comic and is grounded in an experience of incongruity.[82] As finite provinces of meaning, both religion and humour are experienced as intrusions upon the assumptions of everyday life. Both of these intrusions indicate, if only temporarily, that there is a world of experience, if not literally another world, that differs from that of everyday life.[83] The intellectual labour of this book consists of explaining how these two finite provinces of meaning converge, at points anyway, to suggest, but not prove, that there is an order beyond the empirically given world that is 'ultimately God-given and salvific'.[84]

Berger proceeds to offer an extended overview of philosophical, psychological, sociological, and theological understandings of humour. Despite long lists of the psychological and sociological functions of humour, the main point here seems to be that both humour and religions are responses to the fundamentally incongruous situation of human existence, which includes oppositions between finitude and infinitude, life and death, order and disorder, and so on.[85]

By way of illustration, Berger explores a range of comic forms of expression (including benign humour, tragicomedy, wit, satire, folly, etc.) and gives due attention to what I have termed 'the dark side of humour'. Many of these comic forms of expression are, it should be noted, not redemptive. As in the case of Hyers' *The Comic Hero*, most of the examples are drawn from modern literature, though some reference is made to Buddhism, Judaism, and indigenous cultures. In his conclusion, Berger suggests that some forms of the comic, if they are accompanied by an act of faith, deliver one into a realm where there is no more pain and suffering but only redemption.[86] While some readers will no doubt have reservations about Berger's theological concerns, all readers will find much of interest here, particularly in Berger's survey of the variety of forms of comic expression.

Given its basic question and title, *Religion and Humor as Emancipating Provinces of Meaning*, it would be inappropriate not to give attention to this book here. Like Berger, Michael Barber takes as his starting point Schutz's notion of finite provinces of meaning and then attempts to refine Schutz's understanding of religion and humour as different but related provinces of meaning that have the potential of transcending the limits of everyday life. There are lengthy discussions of both humour and religion as finite provinces of meaning but neither discussion refers much to the other. The sources drawn on for his theory of religion are quite thin and dated and little reference is made to the vast ethnographic and historical treatments of religion and humour. The two topics are finally brought together in a very brief conclusion that focuses for the most part on Flannery O'Connor. For readers initiated into the intricacies of phenomenology, this book will be of great interest.

I will close this review of the notion of finite provinces of meaning and humour with a somewhat wistful 'what might have been' reflection on the work of Clifford Geertz. In his very influential 'Religion as a Cultural System', Geertz relies on Schutz's notion of finite provinces of meaning to define the religious perspective by contrasting it with the perspectives of common sense, science, and aesthetics.[87] Geertz makes no reference here to humour or the comic perhaps because, as Berger notes, Scuhtz himself gives little attention to the comic as a finite province of meaning. The major example Geertz presents to illustrate his understanding of the religious perspective, however, is a cultural performance from Bali in which 'a terrible witch called Ranga engages in a ritual combat with an endearing monster called Barong'.[88] In his brief analysis of the performance, Geertz notes how it involves humour, hilarity, and low comedy throughout.[89] While the example clearly points to an intimate relation between religion and humour, Geertz does not, as some say now, 'theorise' the relation of the two. If he had done so, where might we be now in thinking about the relation of humour and religion?

## CONCLUDING REFLECTIONS

In addressing the question of the relation of humour and religion, Berger, Hyers, and Morreall all relied heavily on the opposition of comic and tragic visions and, indeed, took normative positions in regarding the comic as superior to the tragic. I assume that some historians have reservations about highly generalized formulations of comic and tragic visions that tend to obscure the variety and complexities to be found in particular cultural, historical, and religious contexts.

There is a subtheme, however, running throughout the work of these three authors that is at times perhaps at odds with their overall arguments: the ways in which the perception of comic and tragic incongruities are continually interacting to produce a variety of views not reducible to a simple opposition of the comic and tragic or of comic and tragic visions. This is a theme worth further exploration.

The work of Jonathan Z. Smith, one of the most influential scholars of religion in the last 50 years, might provide a new framework for exploring the relation of religion and humour.[90] Smith's work is marked by a relentless critique of many of our received theoretical categories in the study of religion often with an eye to revealing how our theoretical constructs hide the variety to be found under general labels such as 'early Christianity' or 'primitives'. It should be noted that much of Smith's work is devoted to refining our categories rather than simply abandoning them.[91]

One of Smith's key insights was to question what he saw as a preoccupation with congruity in our understanding of religion (such as in theories of ritual that view ritual as merely a repetition of mythic events or theories of religion assuming that all ends in 'salvation'). In contrast, Smith emphasized the element of incongruity to be found in religious materials and viewed religious thought, as expressed in myth and ritual for example, as involving a complex interplay between perceptions of congruity and incongruity that at times at least involve humour.[92] In Smith's view, the ideals, models, and patterns to be found in myths and other religious texts are always confronted with incongruities arising from an encounter with the ever-changing vicissitudes and contingencies of daily life as well as what might be termed built-in contradictions in cultural, social, and religious systems.

An example of Smith's approach can be found in his 'Response' to the chapters in an edited volume entitled *Sacred Play: Ritual Levity and Humor in South Asian Religions*.[93] While applauding the authors' rejection of broad theories such as Mikhail Bakhtin's notion of carnival or 'safety valve' explanations of ritual humour, Smith does express doubts about whether *Sacred Play* has established ritual levity as a clear 'second-order term or theory'. He does acknowledge that the chapters illustrate that levity provides an occasion for 'critical reflexivity' concerning a variety of types of incongruity. He hesitates to recognize ritual levity as a coherent theoretical construct precisely because of the different types of incongruity confronted and reflected on in the rituals.

Influenced by Smith, I have suggested elsewhere that religion might be characterized as involving a complex interplay of perceptions of congruity and incongruity, some of which might be characterized as 'comic' or 'tragic'.[94] I also have argued this point in an analysis of medieval Japanese plays raising questions about the power of ritual to bring human life into some form of redeeming conformity with religious ideals and mythic models.[95] The plays reveal no agreed response to the questions raised but just ongoing reflections on congruity and incongruity (that often involve humour) and cannot be reduced to a simple opposition of comic and tragic visions.

In closing, it might be appropriate to echo Smith's concluding comments in 'Response'. Smith praises the book for raising important issues for ritual studies and indicating the need to clarify terms such as 'play', 'parody', and 'joke' in relation to ritual. The study of humour and religion might be similarly characterized. While we should not eschew comparison or the effort to formulate clearer theoretical formulations, we are in need of further reflection on how our theoretical terms often obscure the variety to be found throughout culture and history.

## NOTES

1. Gardner, 'Humor and Religion', 4194. Compare here Saroglou, 'Religion' and Cooper, 'Humor', 1007–1038.
2. Gardner, 'Humor and Religion', 4194.
3. Useful guides to some of the key issues here are Segal, 'Classification and Comparison', 1175–1188 and Smith, 'Religion, Religions, Religious', 179–196.
4. *HarperCollins Dictionary*, 'Religion, definition of', 893–894.
5. Unless we are in search of an essence, I do not think incongruity theory rules out the insights of superiority and relief theories that also involve, I think, the recognition of incongruity.

6. See, for instance, Lippitt, *Humour and Irony in Kierkegaard's Thought;* Götz, *Faith, Humor, and Paradox;* Arbuckle, *Laughing with God;* and Martin, *Between Heaven and Mirth.*
7. See here, for example, Tamer, *Humour in Arabic Culture;* Raj, *Sacred Play;* and Geybels, *Humour and Religion.*
8. See, for example, Screech, *Laughter;* Siebeck, *Rabbinic Parodies;* and Lindvall, *God Mocks.*
9. Bolle, *Freedom,* 7. Bolle also treats the relation of humour and myth in Bolle, *Enticement,* 54–59 and Bolle, 'Myth', 6362–6365.
10. For a discussion of the difficulties involved in understanding the humour of the past, even when only a few years have passed, see Gardner, 'The Blessing', 35–75.
11. Bolle, *Freedom,* xii–xiii, 5–7.
12. Ibid., 36.
13. Ibid.
14. Ibid., 48–49; Bolle, 'Myth', 6363–6364; Bolle, *Enticement,* 55.
15. Ibid., 41–70; Bolle, *Enticement,* 54–59; and Bolle, 'Myth', 6362–6365.
16. Bolle, *Freedom,* 63.
17. Ibid., 44.
18. O'Flagherty, *Implied Spider,* 12–14. Patton, 'The Frogs', also discusses one humorous hymn and provides references to discussions of the possible roles of humour in *Rig Veda.*
19. Huizinga, *Homo Ludens,* 106–107.
20. Ibid., 5–6.
21. Ibid., 5.
22. See here Huizinga, *Homo Ludens,* 5–6, 105–118, and 136–145.
23. O'Flagherty, *Other People's Myths,* 28–29.
24. Ibid., 33.
25. Ibid., 25. For a similar ethnographic example, see Doniger, *Implied Spider,* 2.
26. O'Flaherty, 'Inside and Outside', 95.
27. See, for instance, Colin Trumbull's discussion of how the Mbuti of Central Africa often listen to many of their myths with a sense of 'amusement'. Trumbull, *Wayward Servants,* 247.
28. See Gardner, 'Humor and Religion', 4194–4199; Gilhus, *Laughing Gods,* 14–42.
29. Hyers, 'Introduction', 3.
30. For related discussions, see, Morreall, 'The Rejection of Humor', 243–265 and Gilhus, *Laughing Gods,* 99–101.
31. Hyers, 'The Comic Profanation of the Sacred', 9–10. Anton Zijderveld has made a similar point in *Reality in a Looking-Glass,* 1, 40. Zijderveld, however, does not elaborate on his suggestion at length.
32. Hyers, 'Dialectic', 209–210.
33. Hyers, *Zen and the Comic Spirit;* Hyers, *The Laughing Buddha.*
34. Hyers, *Comic Vision and the Christian Faith.*
35. Hyers, *And God Created Laughter.*
36. Hyers, *Spirituality of Comedy.*
37. Campbell, *The Hero,* 45.
38. See here Hyers, 'Comic Profanation', 24–25.
39. Among his many works, see Morreall, *Taking Laughter Seriously, Philosophy of Laughter,* and *Comic Relief.*

40. Morreall, *Comedy, Tragedy, and Religion*, 13. See here also Morreall, 'Philosophy and Religion', 211–242.
41. Morreall, *Comedy, Tragedy, and Religion*, 4.
42. Ibid., 7–20.
43. Ibid., 21–40.
44. Ibid., 42.
45. Ibid., 147–154.
46. Gardner, 'Humor and Religion', 4197.
47. Ibid., 48.
48. Ibid., 128–129. For accounts of Islam that supply many examples to counter Morreall's generalizations, see Weber, 'Humor and Islam', 4210–4217 as well as the chapters in Tamer, *Humor in Arabic Culture*.
49. Though he does not make this point, Morreall's book can certainly be read as suggesting this strategy.
50. Apte, *Humor and Laughter*, 16.
51. Ibid., 25.
52. Ibid., 177–211.
53. See here also Gardner, 'Humor and Religion', 4198–4199 and Weber, 'Humor and Islam', 4211–4212.
54. Apte, *Humor and Laughter*, 151.
55. Ibid., 151–152.
56. Ibid., 155.
57. Ibid., 169–175.
58. Ibid., 176.
59. Ibid., 236.
60. Ibid., 233. Unfortunately, for my concerns at least, O'Flaherty does not use the term 'humour' in the passage he cites. But like me, he seems to have sensed some connection with humour in O'Flaherty's approach to myth.
61. Apte, 'My Research'.
62. Driessen, 'Humour, Laughter, and the Field', 222–237. For more recent overviews, see Drissen, 'Anthropology of Humor', 416–419 and Morton, 'Anthropology', 43–47.
63. Bremmer and Roodenburg, 'Introduction', 1–10.
64. Gilhus, 'Religion, Laughter, and the Ludicrous', 257–259.
65. Ibid., 273.
66. Gilhus, *Laughing Gods*, 1.
67. Ibid., 5.
68. See here, Gardner, 'Humor and Religion', 4199–4201.
69. Gilhus, *Laughing Gods*, 3.
70. Ibid., 4.
71. Ibid., 5–6.
72. Ibid., 1.
73. Ibid., 99–101.
74. Ibid., 109–115.
75. Berger's autobiographical *Adventures of an Accidental Sociologist* provides an informative overview of his intellectual career.
76. For suggestions along these lines, see Felmate, 'The Sacred Comedy', 531–550.
77. See Berger's discussion of Schutz in *Redeeming Laughter*, 7–13.
78. Berger, *Precarious Vision*, 217.

79. Berger, *Rumor of Angels*, x. This reference is to the new introduction included in the enlarged 1990 edition of the book.
80. Berger, *Rumor of Angels*, 77–81.
81. Berger, *Heretical Imperative*, x–xi.
82. Berger, *Redeeming Laughter*, x.
83. Ibid., 6.
84. Ibid., xi.
85. Ibid., 33–34.
86. Ibid., 205.
87. Gerrtz, 'Religion as a Cultural System', 111.
88. Ibid., 114. Gilhus draws upon this passage to illustrate her understanding of the relation of religion and the ludicrous. Gilhus, 'Religion, Laughter and the Ludicrous', 271.
89. Ibid., 115.
90. For overviews of Smith's work, see Gill, 'No Place' and Segal, 'Classification'. For an overview of his work by Smith himself, see Smith, "When the Chips are Down', 1–60.
91. See here, for example, Smith's influential essay on ritual, 'Bare Facts', 53–65.
92. Smith, 'Map', 293–297. For further suggestions along these lines, see Chidester, 'Incongruity', 58–72.
93. Raj, *Sacred Play*.
94. Gardner, 'Humor and Religion', 4194.
95. Gardner, 'Reflections', 209–228.

## BIBLIOGRAPHY

Apte, Mahadev L. *Humor and Laughter: An Anthropological Approach*. Ithaca, NY: Cornell University Press, 1985.

Apte, Mahadev. 'My Research on Humor: An Anthropologist's Reflections'. *Studies in American Humor*, n.s. 3, no. 13 (2005–2006): 149–154.

Arbuckle, Gerald A. *Laughing with God: Humor, Culture, and Transformation*. Collegeville, MN: Liturgical Press, 2008.

Barber, Michael. *Religion and Humor as Emancipating Provinces of Meaning*. Cham, Switzerland: Springer, 2017.

Berger, Peter L. *Adventures of an Accidental Sociologist: How to Explain the World without Becoming a Bore*. Amherst, NY: Prometheus Books, 2011.

Berger, Peter L. *The Heretical Imperative: Contemporary Possibilities of Religious Affirmation*. Garden City, NY: Anchor Press, 1979.

Berger, Peter L. *The Precarious Vision: A Sociologist Looks at Social Fictions and Christian Faith*. Garden City, NY: Doubleday & Company, 1961.

Berger, Peter L. *Redeeming Laughter: The Comic Dimension of Human Experience*. New York: Walter de Gruyter, 1997.

Berger, Peter L. *A Rumor of Angels: Modern Society and the Rediscovery of the Supernatural*. New York: Anchor Press, 1969.

Berger, Peter L. *A Rumor of Angels: Modern Society and the Rediscovery of the Supernatural*. Expanded with a New Introduction. New York: Anchor Press, 1990.

Berger, Peter L. *Questions of Faith: A Skeptical Affirmation of Christianity*. Chichester, UK: Wiley-Blackwell, 2003.

Berger, Peter L. *The Sacred Canopy: Elements of a Sociological Theory of Religion.* New York: Doubleday, 1967.

Bolle, Kees W. *The Enticement of Religion.* Notre Dame, IN: University of Notre Dame Press, 2002.

Bolle, Kees W. *The Freedom of Man in Myth.* Nashville, TN: Vanderbilt University Press, 1968.

Bolle, Kees W. *Encyclopedia of Religion*, 2nd ed., sv. 'Myth: An Overview'. New York: Palgrave Macmillan, 2005.

Bremmer, Jan, and Herman Roodenburg. 'Introduction'. In *A Cultural History of Humour: From Antiquity to the Present Day*, edited by Jan Bremmer and Herman Roodenburg, 1–10. Cambridge, UK: Polity Press, 1997.

Campbell, Joseph. *The Hero with a Thousand Faces.* New York: Bollingen Foundation, 1949.

Chidester, David. 'Incongruity'. In *Religion: Material Dynamics*, David Chidester, 58–72. Oakland, CA: University of California Press, 2018.

Cooper, David J. 'Humor'. In *Religion in the Practice of Everyday Life and Culture*, edited by Richard D. Hecht and Vincent F. Biondo, 1007–1038. Vol. 3. Santa Barbara, CA: Praeger, 2010.

Davis, Scott, and Richard A. Gardner. *Encyclopedia of Religion*, 2nd ed., s.v. 'Humor and Religion in East Asian Contexts'. New York: Palgrave Macmillan, 2005.

Doniger, Wendy. *The Implied Spider: Politics and Theology in Myth.* New York: Columbia University Press, 1998.

Drissen, Henk. *International Encyclopedia of the Social & Behavioral Sciences*, 2nd ed., sv. 'Humor, Anthropology of'. Oxford, UK: Elsevier Science, 2015.

Drissen, Henk. 'Humour, Laughter and the Field: Reflections from Anthropology'. In *A Cultural History of Humour: From Antiquity to the Present Day*, edited by Jan Bremmer and Herman Roodenburg, 222–241. Cambridge, UK: Polity Press, 1997.

Feltmate, David. 'The Sacred Comedy: The Problems and Possibilities of Peter Berger's Theory of Humor'. *Humor: International Journal of Humor Research* 26, no. 4 (2013): 531–549.

Gardner, Richard A. *Encyclopedia of Religion*, 2nd ed., s.v. 'Humor and Religion: An Overview'. New York: Palgrave Macmillan, 2005.

Gardner, Richard A. 'Reflections on Ritual in Noh and Kyôgen'. In *Teaching Ritual*, edited by Catherine Bell, 209–228. Oxford: Oxford University Press, 2007.

Gardner, Richard A. 'The Blessing of Living in a Country Where There are *Senryû*!: Humor in the Response to Aum Shinrikyô'. *Asian Folklore Studies* 61, no. 1 (2002): 35–75.

Geertz, Clifford. 'Religion as a Cultural System'. In *The Interpretation of Cultures*, Clifford Geertz, 87–125. New York: Basic Books, 1963.

Geybels, Hans and Walter Van Herck, eds. *Humor and Religion: Challenges and Ambiguities.* London: Continuum International Publishing Group, 2011.

Gilhus, Ingvild Sælid. *Laughing Gods, Weeping Virgins: Laughter in the History of Religions.* London and New York: Routledge, 1997.

Gilhus, Ingvild Sælid. 'Religion, Laughter, and the Ludicrous'. *Religion* 21, no. 3 (1991): 257–277.

Gill, Sam. 'No Place to Stand: Jonathan Z. Smith as *Homo Ludens*, The Academic Study of Religion as *Sub Specie Ludi*'. *Journal of the American Academy of Religion* 66, no. 2 (1998): 283–312.

Götz, Ignacio L. *Faith, Humor, and Paradox.* Westport, CT: Praeger, 2002.

*The HarperCollins Dictionary of Religion*, ed. Jonathan Z. Smith, s.v. 'Religion, Definition Of'. San Francisco: HarperCollins, 1995.

Halliwell, Stephen. *Greek Laughter: A Study or Cultural Psychology from Homer to Early Christianity*. Cambridge: Cambridge University Press, 2008.

Huizinga, Johan. *Homo Ludens: A Study of the Play Element in Culture*. Boston, MA: Beacon Press, 1955.

Hyers, Conrad. *And God Created Laughter: The Bible as Divine Comedy*. Atlanta, GA: John Knox Press, 1987.

Hyers, Conrad M. 'Comic Profanation of the Sacred'. In *Holy Laughter: Essays on Religion in the Comic Perspective*, edited by M. Conrad Hyers, 9–27. New York: Seabury Press, 1969.

Hyers, Conrad. *The Comic Vision and the Christian Faith: A Celebration of Life and Laughter*. Eugene, OR: Wipf and Stock, 1981.

Hyers, Conrad M. 'The Dialectic of the Sacred and the Comic'. In *Holy Laughter: Essays on Religion in the Comic Perspective*, edited by Conrad Hyers, 208–240. New York: Seabury Press, 1969.

Hyers, M. Conrad, ed. *Holy Laughter: Essays on Religion in the Comic Perspective*. New York: Seabury Press, 1969.

Hyers, Conrad M. 'Introduction'. In *Holy Laughter: Essays on Religion in the Comic Perspective*, edited by Conrad Hyers, 1–8. New York: Seabury Press, 1969.

Hyers, Conrad. *The Laughing Buddha: Zen and the Comic Spirit*. Eugene, OR: Wipf and Stock, 1989.

Hyers, Conrad. *The Spirituality of Comedy: Comic Heroism in a Tragic World*. New Brunswick, Canada: Transaction Publishers, 1995.

Lindvall, Terry. *God Mocks: A History of Religious Satire from the Hebrew Prophets to Stephen Colbert*. New York: New York University Press, 2015.

Lippit, John. *Humour and Irony in Kierkegaard's Thought*. New York: St. Martin's Press, 2000.

Martin, James. *Between Heaven and Mirth: Why Joy, Humor, and Laughter Are at the Heart of the Spiritual Life*. New York: HarperCollins, 2011.

Morton, John. *Encyclopedia of Humor Studies*, s.v. 'Anthropolgy'. Los Angeles: Sage Publications, 2014.

Morreall, John. *Comic Relief: A Comprehensive Philosophy of Humor*. Chichester, UK: Wiley-Blackwell, 2009.

Morreall, John. *Encyclopedia of Humor Studies*, sv. 'Comic Versus Tragic Worldldviews'. Los Angeles: Sage Publications, 2014.

Morreall, John. *Comedy, Tragedy, and Religion*. Albany: State University of New York, 1999.

Morreal, John. 'The Rejection of Humor in Western Thought'. *Philosophy East and West* 39, no. 3 (1989): 243–265.

O'Flaherty, Wendy Doniger. 'Inside and Outside the Mouth of God: The Boundary between Myth and Reality'. *Daedalus* 109, no. 2 (1980): 93–125.

O'Flaherty, Wendy Doniger. *Other People's Myths: The Cave of Echoes*. New York: Macmillan Publishing, 1988.

Patton, Laurie. 'The Frogs Have Raised Their Voice: Rg Veda 7.103 as a Poetic Contemplation of Dialogue'. In *Dialogue in Early South Asian Religions*, edited by Brian Block and Laurie Patton, 25–36. London and New York: Routledge, 2015.

Raj, Selva J. and Corrine G. Dempsey, eds. *Sacred Play: Ritual Levity and Humor in South Asian Religions*. Albany: State University of New York Press, 2010.

Saroglou, Vassilis. *Encyclopedia of Humor Studies*, s.v. 'Religion'. Los Angeles: Sage Publications, 2014.

Screech, Michael A. *Laughter at the Foot of the Cross*. Chicago: University of Chicago Press, 1998.

Segal, Robert A. 'Classification and Comparison in the Study of Religion: The Work of Jonathan Z. Smith'. *Journal of the American Academy of Religion* 73, no. 4 (2005): 1175–1188.

Smith, Jonathan Z. 'The Bare Facts of Ritual'. In *Imagining Religion: From Babylon to Jonestown*, edited by Jonathan Z. Smith, 53–65. Chicago: University of Chicago Press, 1982.

Smith, Jonathan Z. 'Map is Not Territory'. In *Map is Not Territory: Studies in the History of Religions*, edited by Jonathan Z. Smith, 289–309. Leiden: E. J. Brill, 1978.

Smith, Jonathan Z. 'Religion, Religions, Religious'. In *Relating Religion: Essays in the Study of Religion*, edited by Jonathan Z. Smith, 179–196. Chicago: University of Chicago Press, 2004.

Smith, Jonathan Z. 'Response'. In *Sacred Play: Ritual Levity and Humor in South Asian Religions*, edited by Selva J. Raj and Corrine G. Dempsey, 205–216. Albany: State University of New York Press, 2010.

Smith, Jonathan Z. 'When the Chips are Down'. In *Relating Religion: Essays in the Study of Religion*, Jonathan Z. Smith, 1–60. Chicago: University of Chicago Press, 2004.

Tamer, Georges, ed. *Humor in der arabischen Kultur, Humor in Arabic Culture*. Berlin and New York: Walter de Gruyter, 2009.

Trumbull, Colin M. *Wayward Servants: The Two Worlds of the African Pygmies*. Garden City, NJ: Natural History Press, 1965.

Weber, Sabra J. *Encyclopedia of Religion*, 2nd ed., s.v. 'Humor and Religion: Humor and Islam'. New York: Palgrave Macmillan, 2005.

Zellentin, Holger Michael. *Rabbinic Parodies of Jewish and Christian Literature*. Tübingen: Mohr Siebeck, 2011.

Zijderveld, Anton C. *Reality in a Looking-Glass: Rationality through an Analysis of Traditional Folly*. London: Routledge & Kegan Paul, 1982.

PART II

# Case Studies

CHAPTER 9

# Visual Humour on Greek Vases (550–350 BC): Three Approaches to the Ambivalence of Ugliness in Popular Culture

*Alexandre G. Mitchell*

## INTRODUCTION

The importance of ugliness in ancient Greece, be it in literature, philosophical thought or the pictorial arts, is difficult to assess but is key to understanding ancient visual humour. According to most of our ancient literary, philosophical and visual sources, Athenian society from the sixth to the fourth centuries BC aspired to a certain esthetic ideal.[1] When Plato distinguished the different steps that lead to beauty, from objects in the sensible world to the idea of Beauty itself in the intelligible world, he was developing philosophically ideas that had already been in vogue for nearly a century. Indeed, the treatise entitled *Kanon* by the sculptor Polykleitos, which he expressed in his statuary (the *Diadumenos*, the *Doryphoros*), already substantiated a Greek vision of beauty linked to the notions of balance and mathematical harmony between the whole and its parts. The word *kosmos* expressed these ideas more accurately than the word *kalos* ('beautiful') for it referred not only to the concept of 'ornament' but also to 'universe' and 'order'.

In a society where the world was seen as beautiful and ordered or beautiful because it was ordered, was there any room for disruption, errors, humour and ugliness? Aristotle defined the laughable as 'a mistake or a kind of ugliness

A. G. Mitchell (✉)
Department of Art History and Archaeology, University of Fribourg, Fribourg, Switzerland
e-mail: am@expressum.eu

© The Author(s), under exclusive license to Springer Nature Switzerland AG 2020
D. Derrin, H. Burrows (eds.), *The Palgrave Handbook of Humour, History, and Methodology*, https://doi.org/10.1007/978-3-030-56646-3_9

175

(*aischos*) that causes no pain or destruction: so for example the comic mask is something ugly and distorted but causes no pain'.[2] *Aischos*, ugly, the base, the deformed, was opposed to *kalos*, the beautiful, the noble. Both adjectives applied to moral character, to actions, as well as to appearance and things.[3] To understand ancient Greek humour, we must focus on ugliness. Obviously, it is not ugliness per se that causes laughter, it is ugliness in context or instrumentalised or the presence of surprise as a laughing catalyst. Already in the Renaissance, Madius (Vincenzo Maggi), in his treatise *On the Ridiculous* (1550), comments on Aristotle's poetics. He writes 'If ugliness alone were the cause of laughter, while it continues to exist, laughter should also continue. But, without ceasing the cause of ugliness, we nevertheless cease laughing; also those things that are ugly but are familiar to us, do not cause laughter. Therefore it is clear enough that the cause of laughter does not reside only in ugliness, but it is also the work of surprise'.[4]

It is obvious from a strictly logical point of view that ugliness is the inalienable companion of beauty: without a relevant visual comparison—except in a Platonic context—*beauty* does not mean anything. But why show visual ugliness (as opposed to moral ugliness) rather than hide it? The Greek approach was to expose in order to demonstrate. Even in Sparta, deformed children were not hidden, but left to die in full view of the public. There was no place in classical Greece for the kind of ultra-realistic stone portraiture that appeared four hundred years later at the end of the Roman republic, of fifty-year-old men with shrivelled faces, their features almost caricatured either because of an acute sense of morality, or because the busts were based on death wax masks. Greek artists would certainly have been able to produce similar portraits had they wished to but when having to choose between the two poles of *mimesis* (faithful imitation of nature) and aesthetic ideal, Greek artists leant towards their idealistic aspirations and yet drew on physical reality, including ugliness.

We need to distinguish between different kinds of ugliness when considering visual humour on Greek vases. At least three forms were displayed on vases: (1) caricature, an *intentional* form of ugliness, a popular and democratic egalitarian tool. (2) Then came the *inherent* ugliness of deformity, foreigners with non-Caucasian facial traits, the decrepitude of the elderly, all of which reveal deep anxieties about disease, the 'other' and the inevitability of death. (3) And, finally, the *construction* of ugliness both physical and moral through the intrusion of a ubiquitous and humorous mythological creature called the satyr in a 'civilised' society presents a third pathway to ugliness, that of the ambivalence of the (*Eliasian*) *civilising process*.

## Intentional Ugliness: Caricature, a Popular and Democratic Egalitarian Tool

One of the major changes that accompanied the advent of democracy was when democratic egalitarianism finally took precedence over an aristocratic society built on honour and shame. It was in this context that ugliness finally gained the right to be heard. This process is only visible over a long period of time. We observe the first fledgling signs with Thersites, the tremendously ugly crowd-pleaser in the *Iliad*: 'He is the ugliest man ever to come to Ilion, bandy-legged and stooped. His head is covered with only a small amount of thin downy hair. Achilles and Ulysses really abhor him for he quarrels with them constantly'.[5] As Halliwell writes, 'It is no accident that Thersites, a symbolic figure of ridicule incarnate from Homer onwards, receives an exceptionally full physical description in the Iliad that seems to match up his ugliness with the subversive unruliness of his bent for mockery'.[6] Thersites was not allowed to speak, as he was excluded from any deliberative participation in the aristocratic context of the Achaean camp. When he pushes too far his criticism of Agamemnon, 'king of men', he is violently beaten up by Odysseus amongst a laughing and jeering crowd, heroes and common sailors included. Thersites' speech is not unreasonable as such but he is too far ahead of his time. He is prevented from speaking out loud because he does not show enough *aidos* ('respect') towards aristocratic authority. It will only be in the context of democracy that *parrhesia*, the right to express oneself freely, would become law. The intentional visual ugliness of caricature, this visceral need to express one's opinion through ugliness in a movement of egalitarian democratic par-rhesia, by belittling the values of beauty and harmony, was a way of levelling the aristocratic ideal and all its values to the ground. It is a necessary form of burlesque. Caricature was an egalitarian tool in a society that was seeking to emancipate itself from ancient kingly feats of arms, to promote the power of the people, of the Demos. The ugliness of caricature, exaggerated and inten-tional, had a political function.

Athenian black- and red-figure vases were the perfect expression of this emi-nently popular culture, as they cost almost nothing to produce, being made from clay and involved almost negligible labour costs. They were therefore accessible to everyone, rich and poor.[7] As most vases were produced for the market and not on commission, craftsmen had to comply with the rules of market economy: they followed fashion or went against it, to sell more vases. Since they had to be appreciated by as many buyers as possible in order to be sold, their figurative scenes represent what most Athenians believed at the time. In this sense it truly was a popular artform. The concept of 'popular' culture has a convoluted and controversial history. It was traditionally opposed to a dominant 'high' culture which controlled it by imposing its values and cultural norms. In this view, popular culture developed on the reception of these values, through the imitation of the 'high' culture. But this dichotomy was completely revised by Pierre Bourdieu,[8] moving to different perceptions altogether, on different modes of cultural appropriation.[9] In terms of fashion and the culture that is reflected through the images depicted on the vases it is evident that some representations aspire to aristocratic and elite values that trickle down to the entire *demos* (population).

Caricature is a transformation, a grotesque or ridiculous representation of people or things by exaggerating their most characteristic features. To ensure their caricatures were understood by their contemporaries, ancient painters were in possession of a veritable comic arsenal.[10]

Some ancient caricatures still surprise the modern observer, such as a small wine container in the Louvre Museum (Fig. 9.1).[11] On one side of this *askos*, we see a man, naked, leaning over his cane from which hangs his only garment, a folded tunic. This male character is almost entirely bald and wears a goatee. The most surprising aspect of this scene is the disproportionate size of his head, which is simply gigantic compared to his stunted body, a large head that reminds us of press cartoons or Punch and Judy shows. Who was the butt of the joke? His attitude is a very common one in Greek vase-painting, that of the passer-by or onlooker (Fig. 9.2),[12] one of many thousand images of idle citizens found on vases, often in the context of the palaestra. The excessive size of his head and his thoughtful attitude also recall the caricature of a sophist, the intellectual whose head was larger than his body and who spent his time talking.

He was sketched by a simple craftsman from the potters' district who had little reason to respect these smooth talkers who travelled from city to city to offer their services, as described by Aristophanes: 'a crowd of sophists, diviners [...] with long hair [...] horoscope makers, lazy-bones'.[13] It may be the same kind of intellectual who was mocked in the *Philogelos*, a collection of jokes in ancient Greek.

> People tell a young egg-head that his beard is coming in, so he goes to the front door to welcome it. When his friend realises what he's doing, he says 'No wonder

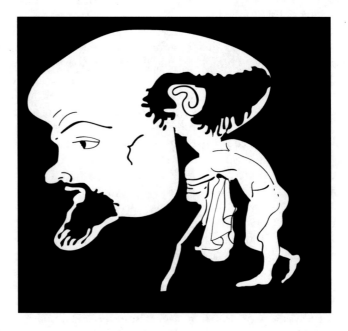

Fig. 9.1

**Fig. 9.2**

people think we're idiots—how do you know your beard isn't coming through the back door?'[14]

Mythology was not immune to caricature. Most Greek heroes were either the result of the union of a god and a mortal like Herakles, or the offspring of kings, like Odysseus, son of Laertius, king of Ithaca. Painters often present Odysseus at his best, highlighting his famous *metis*, or craftiness, a quality the Greeks were particularly fond of, being great negotiators in politics and trade.[15] But some vases deliberately caricature the hero. Among the most famous, those of the Kabirion sanctuary, ten miles from Thebes (Greece) caricature him in a completely grotesque way on several occasions, either when he escapes from the island of Calypso on two amphorae, running on the waves, or in the company of the magician Circe.[16] But one of the most interesting vases is in London. This oinochoe (or jug) (Fig. 9.3)[17] shows a highly caricatured Odysseus, wearing his sailor's *polos* hat and carrying off the *Palladion*—the small statue of Athena which, according to tradition, was the guarantor of Troy's safety. The scene is easily understood if we compare it to its 'serious' version, an oinochoe from the Louvre for example (Fig. 9.4).[18]

**Fig. 9.3**

In the caricature, Odysseus has stolen the sacred image of Athena from the city of Troy. The painter has given him a pot belly and a bloated scrotum, a head that is not proportionate to his body and a particularly hairy face. His sailor's hat is worn very low on his forehead, which increases the hero's inelegant appearance, just like his ruffled hair sprouting from either side of the *polos*. If Diomedes is the other caricatured character, with his gigantic nose, we have an additional source of amusement here, because of Odysseus' trickery. According to tradition it was Diomedes who returned to the Greek camp with the *Palladion*, not Odysseus. For those who might want to interpret this scene as a visual representation of a theatrical stage scene, it should be noted that their entire bodies are caricatured, not just the face, which eliminates the possibility that they are wearing comedy masks. There are no hints to the *realia* of stagecraft. The painting even escapes Oliver Taplin's list of 'visual theatre signals'.[19] We must adjust our perspective to that of the ancient customer and insist on the fact that on the one hand we are dealing here with playfulness between images and on the other hand that the burlesque of the scene is due

9 VISUAL HUMOUR ON GREEK VASES (550–350 BC): THREE APPROACHES... 181

**Fig. 9.4**

to a social need to belittle even the great eponymous hero of the *Odyssey*. With these figures, we are now in the fifth and fourth centuries BC, a time in which society had become far more egalitarian and where, unlike Thersites, the unfortunate dishevelled hunchback of the Homeric era, one could make fun of the powerful kings of old with impunity. The fact that the vase was designed in Apulia and not in Athens does not hurt our interpretation of the vase, since a city like Taranto, even if founded by Sparta, also became a democracy from the fifth century onwards.

This burlesque humour and the need to humble a king is particularly clear in the many representations of Herakles bringing the Erymanthean boar *alive* to King Eurystheus. Here, burlesque and comic inversion serve to satisfy a need for democratic justice. The ugliness here is moral (the king's cowardice) and not physical.

The burlesque was often linked to situations of comic inversion where gods, heroes or kings were ridiculed as we have seen with Odysseus. Among Herakles' twelve labours imposed on him by King Eurystheus, only the capture of the Erymanthean boar contains a touch of humour for not only did Herakles survive the ordeal, but he brought the monstrous beast alive back to the palace. Eurystheus, terrified both by the hero and by the boar, hid in a *pithos*, a kind of

Fig. 9.5

huge grain container. It seems that vase-painters particularly enjoyed showing the last stage of the story. On numerous vases in the fifth and fourth centuries BC, Eurystheus is found hiding in a pithos. In these scenes, Herakles is carrying the wild boar, either on his back or over his shoulder, placing his foot on the edge of the pithos and preparing to throw the beast inside the container. Painters often show Eurystheus gesticulating in despair, begging Herakles to spare his life. The position of the boar like Damocles' sword above the king's head begging from the bottom of his pithos expresses Herakles' genuine superiority as a popular and Panhellenic hero. Our vase (Fig. 9.5) shows him fleeing as Herakles approaches, one foot already in the pithos.[20] Eurystheus was king of Mycenae. To see a man of superior status flee in a cowardly manner to hide in his own palace is burlesque. It is the ridicule, the degradation of the king, that makes the masses laugh, especially at a time when there were no more kings. But this scene was so often reproduced in Greek art that one might wonder if, stripped of any surprise effect, it made viewers laugh at all. The repetitiveness of the representations suggests something else: it was not so much the surprise that made the viewers laugh, but a ridiculed false king and the comical reversal of the situation. Indeed, the humour of this scene owes something to the tricked trickster, the fact that the king gets a taste of his own medicine. As Henri Bergson writes: 'Not infrequently comedy sets before us a character who lays a trap in which he is the first to be caught. The plot of the villain, who is the victim of his own villainy, or the cheat cheated, forms the stock-in-trade of a good many plays'.[21] Despite the fact that Herakles was faithful to the king throughout all his labours, the king abused his monarchical powers to impose impossible ordeals in the hope of getting rid of him. The situation is ironic because it turned out to be to his disadvantage. This often-reproduced burlesque scene reveals a kind of visceral need for justice. Eurystheus gets what he deserves because he never behaves as a true king.

## Inherent Ugliness Hinting at Deep Anxieties in Greek Society: The Dwarf, the Foreigner and the Elderly

Regardless of the technique of caricature, some figures differed from the classical ideal body type and were considered ugly per se: the dwarf, the foreigner with African traits, the decrepit elderly man. Each of those is addressed separately.

### *The Dwarf and Social Cohesion*

Achondroplasia was the most common form of dwarfism among the representations of short-legged dwarfs on Greek vases. Why were the latter mocked in ancient Greece beyond the obvious contrast between their physical appearance and a 'normal' or idealised body type?[22] This phenomenon is easily explained by Henri Bergson's 'social laughter'.[23] This kind of laughter is linked to the fear of difference, and all the more so in a democratic and egalitarian society where no head should surpass any other. People mock and laugh at each other within a group because laughter is a social tool that forces each person to remain in his or her place, to conform to rules and customs, not to break out of the ranks, to ensure the group remains a harmonious entity. In doing so, social laughter emphasises the rules, values and elements that bind a society together and imposes a form of social cohesion.

Giving birth to certain congenital deformities must have caused, like it often does today, a feeling of guilt coupled with divine injustice, which may explain the presence of representations that hoped to counter fate or the evil eye. Why a feeling of injustice?[24] One might have grown used to the loss of a limb due to sudden illness or combat, but how could one reconcile one's faith in the wisdom and justice of the almighty gods when children were born mentally or physically diminished? To escape this feeling of powerlessness, artists ensured that their approach to art based on experience and mimesis remained constrained by an idealism that tried to show what one should look like rather than what one really did. In such a society, artists and citizens in general tried to control the world around them by striving for order and balance. Dwarves played the same role as various representations of the *Other*. The origin of *ethnic jokes*, or jokes on other cultures,[25] is often linked to the fear of the *Other*, to the perception of differences. Dwarves lent their distinctive features to caricature to amuse the general public, reassure them and reaffirm the Polyclitean canon - a tribute to normalised imagery.

A black-figure kantharos from the Kabirion of Thebes (Fig. 9.6) shows five grotesque athletes exercising.[26] Two figures are wrestling, their penises dangling instead of being tied like most ancient Greek athletes, who practised in the nude. The athlete on the left is prognathic, with a snub nose and scruffy hair. The second pair of wrestlers are caricatured dwarfs. Their legs amount to a quarter of the total length of the body, and the dwarf on the right's head is particularly disproportionate. To the far right, another dwarf is performing a

Fig. 9.6

war dance, the *pyrrhike*, his hand almost touching the ground as he leans to the ground, weighed down by his large and heavy shield (*oplon*) and helmet. The humour in this scene is particularly apt: the athlete and the warrior embodied superior moral and physical values in Greek society. Only the wealthiest citizens had the idle time to exercise at the palaestra or arm themselves. They were perfect targets for potters.

African pygmies were no longer represented in the fifth century as they had been in the previous century. The foot of the famous François vase (570 BC) showed pygmies fighting cranes: they were abnormally small men but whose body parts were well proportioned. Most red-figure vases in the fifth century that depict pygmies, however, present them as if they were dwarfs,[27] like a rhyton in the Saint-Petersbourg museum (Fig. 9.7), attributed to the Brygos painter.[28] These warriors are grotesquely misshapen. They are small, have stocky legs, fat bellies and large buttocks; their scrotum bag hangs so far down it is almost being dragged on the ground. They both wear pointed Scythian soft hats, more suitable for oriental warriors than dwarfs even claiming to be pygmies. The reference to Scythians, oriental foreigners per se, alienates them even more from Greek figures. The first pygmy grabs the crane by the neck and is about to strike it with a club, while the second pokes the hindquarters of the beast with the tip of his sword. In doing so, his left arm is shown dangling like a monkey's arm. The physician Galen tells us that painters or sculptors could not make a better parody of a human hand than by drawing a monkey's paw.[29] And, according to Athenaeus: 'The Scythian sage Anacharsis said that when human jesters were introduced at a banquet, he did not smile, but burst out laughing when an ape was brought in. This animal, so he said, was laughable by nature, but human jesters only by practice'.[30] Our pygmy-dwarfs' attitude—despite their beards—also resembles that of the babies or toddlers represented on the hundreds of miniature choes sold at the Anthesteria, with painted images of toddlers up to all kinds of mischief and very often teasing animals. Evidently, toddlers acting as battle-hardened warriors are ridiculous. In short, the two figures on this vase encapsulated a wide range of what vase-painters thought were inherently ugly or ridiculous traits: African miniature men, dwarfs, Orientals, apes and toddlers.

Fig. 9.7

### *The Foreigner and the Fear of the 'Other'*

The fear of the outsider is the fear of the 'other' and of course of the dissolution of the group by *barbaric* pollution. Difference was not seen as an enrichment but as social impoverishment, a weakness. The Greek defines himself in opposition to the 'other'. Greece's city-states discovered their quasi-national identity as a so-called free and civilised Greece built in opposition to a so-called totalitarian Persian empire during and after the Persian wars. In this context, the need to make fun of the 'barbaric' foreigner (from *barbaros*, who does not speak Greek), whether they are Persian or African, is both linked to the fear of losing what the Greeks had gained, civilisation, and to forging a coherent and social identity that was distinct from other cultures.

Just as the unsightly physical appearance of dwarfs was used to ridicule certain characters, so were African physical characteristics because of their stark contrast with (idealised) Caucasian features. The destruction of the group or social fabric by its pollution with foreigners most certainly explains the marked fear of the other and the fear of difference. Among the many representations of African slaves or servants, there is, for example, a comic image on a fragmentary black-figure Boeotian kantharos (Fig. 9.8).[31]

A naked slave, caricatured, with typical African traits, prominent lips, snub nose, curly hair, ithyphallic (with a sexual erection), desperately tries to keep a dog from gobbling up the meat that was placed on a *trapeza*, or small two-tray banquet table, by pulling with all his might on the dog's leash. Frank Snowden could not understand why Greek artists represented so many Africans and pygmies with African traits.[32] It seems that Greek artists actually chose to borrow African traits as a caricature device. Their appearance was so different from the 'average Greek', their skin colour, their curly hair, their prognathism, their fleshy lips, their flat or snub nose, made them to be 'natural caricatures'. If we add dwarfism, these traits become even more caricatured and grotesque than they already were to the Greek eye.[33]

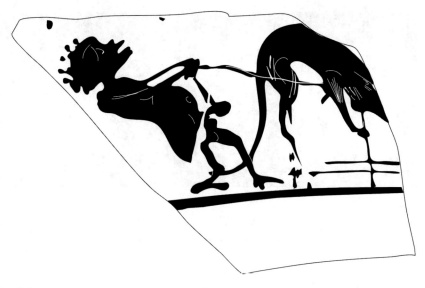

**Fig. 9.8**

All these elements are integrated in the caricature of Kephalos, a well-known Boeotian hero, on a kantharos preserved in the Athens Museum (Fig. 9.9).[34] This caricatured figure, with its round skull, prognathic lower jaw, thick lips and a snub nose, wears a ridiculous, stunted and twisted petasos. The petasos was a hat often worn by hunters and travellers because its wide edges protected its wearer from the rain. The personage is naked, except for his stick and the hunter's chlamys wrapped around his left arm, which reveals his huge belly and swaying genitals. His name is inscribed, *KEPHALOS*. The ugliness of his caricatured face is all the more amusing given that usually in Greek vases, the handsome version of this hunter is the one chased by the lovesick goddess Eos ('Dawn'). The hound, whose appearance is as grotesque as his master's, is chasing a fox with a bushy tail. Thanks to Apollodoros and other ancient authors,[35] we know the story of Kephalos' magic hunting dog who caught every prey it set its sights on, including the famous Teumessian fox, which ravaged the region of Cadmeia. However, it is very difficult to imagine that our pot-bellied dog or his master on the Athens vase will catch or catch up to anything.

### *The Old Man*

Old age was feared for it was a reminder of the inevitability of death and the eventual annihilation of the social group. Caricature is sometimes only present to exaggerate pre-existing physical ugliness. When a painter insists on the ugliness and decrepitude of old age rather than its nobility, like that of the venerable and wise Nestor, this reveals something other than the egalitarian and

Fig. 9.9

democratic need that we have previously analysed. We are dealing with an anxiety linked to the coming of death, because of the Greeks' gloomy vision of the afterlife, where souls, good and bad, live like shadows (*eidola*) in the underground world of Hades.[36] Even the great hero Achilles told Odysseus—who had come to the underworld to ask Tiresias to help him find his way home to Ithaca—that he would rather be a cow herder, the servant of a poor peasant than roam the glorious Elysian fields.[37] The grey kingdom of Ploutos, an epithet of Hades meaning 'wealthy' (in souls), was not seen as a sort of peacefulness that followed the turmoil of life. One understands better the Greek obsession with youth which was seen as a value in itself. The contrast between youth and old age was far more pronounced then than it is today. The arrival of old age was a threat to be mocked or mourned. Theognis writes that old age was destructive, lethal and 'the most evil of all things among mortals; more grievous than death and all diseases'.[38] Other authors make fun of it, like Aesop in 'The Old Man and Death': an exhausted old man, tired of carrying wood, invokes Death. When it appears and inquires as to why it was invoked, the old man replies: 'to help me carry my burden'; and Aesop adds: 'the fable shows that every man, even in misfortune, is fond of life'.[39] Demetrius writes 'Lysias is said to have remarked to an old woman's lover that it was easier to count her teeth than her fingers'.[40] In vase-painting, the fear of death and its closest physical state, old age, was expressed differently. The emphasis is placed on youth, beauty and virile strength. There are few representations of old age. A number of black- and red-figure vases depict the encounter between the paragon of youth, Herakles, and the personification of old age, the vile Geras. The interpretation of these scenes is not easy because it is not mentioned in any ancient text.

A red-figure pelike (Fig. 9.10) depicts Herakles, tall and athletic, the paws of his lion skin nicely tied across his chest, leaning over his club, elongated like a cane.[41] His right hand nonchalantly placed to his hip he converses with the old man. The name of the latter is inscribed on the other vases that show the same meeting.[42] He is a stunted character, a hunchback, crooked, bent over a cane just as twisted as he is. He is macrophallic (with a very large penis), bald, with an unusually curved nose. The macrophallia of Geras is a sign of social inelegance, even debauchery.[43] There are other mythological characters considered to be inherently ugly: Charon, the Underworld's ferryman, often found on white-ground *lekythoi*, wearing his old hat, an emaciated face with high cheekbones or Boreas, the North Wind, with his scruffy beard and shaggy hair. According to mythographers, the latter only managed to lay with a Fury and a harpy. The God Hephaestus himself was ridiculed by his peers because the ugliness of his malformed foot contrasted with his divinity and the beauty of his wife, the goddess of beauty and love, Aphrodite. All these characters are ugly, but Geras' ugliness is exaggerated to the point of being grotesque.

Bergson explains it very well: 'For exaggeration to be comic, it must not appear as an aim, but rather as a means that the artist is using in order to make manifest to our eyes the distortions which he sees in embryo'.[44] The comedy in the image also comes from the obvious parallel with the numerous representations of citizens conversing, leaning over their cane (Fig. 9.2). Herakles' club looks more like a cane than a weapon. The superiority of youth over the

Fig. 9.10

Fig. 9.11

decrepitude of old age is tragic-comic, all the more so if we compare this scene to the other four scenes of the meeting. Indeed, in those the old man is violently knocked out. We better understand the inscription, which comes out of Herakles' mouth, *KLAUSEI*, 'you will cry!' The painter is referring to the next stage of the encounter, that is the caning. According to Shapiro, this episode has been interpreted as the symbolic victory of Herakles against death and his apotheosis.[45] But he is not only mocking death here, it is also old age and the fact that he is striking old age reveals an anxiety rather than a victory. Finally, if Herakles' apotheosis is a great moment in the cycle of his adventures, his death itself—poisoned by a scorned wife—is not heroic, to say the least.

The next scene (Fig. 9.11) shows, like so many other vases of the Theban Kabirion, a comic world upside down.[46] We are shown an unusual race between an old white-bearded man making broad and measured arm movements while a young athlete follows him closely, out of breath, with his elbows thrown backwards as if to give himself more momentum. Clearly in this scene, age comes before beauty, hence its comedy.

### Constructed Ugliness Both Physical and Moral: The Ambivalence of the Satyr's Presence in a 'Civilised' Society

The satyr, mythological servant of Dionysos, is the epitome of physical and moral ugliness. He is half man, half beast, has the donkey's tail and ears; has shaggy hair, a scruffy beard and a snub nose.[47] He is also a coward who cares only for wine. In addition to this, he is in perpetual erection, because his immense sexual desire is almost always frustrated. What does this living symbol of physical and moral ugliness have to do with a polite society? As I will elaborate further, inspired by Norbert Elias' *Civilizing Process*, we are now in the fifth century BC at the height of what Elias would have called the *monopolisation of violence*, an era obsessed with culture and civilisation, and a political regime that forced the former nobility to adapt. They moved from a time when violence was inflicted with impunity by the aristocracy and from gargantuan feasts to the contests and games of the symposium, the democratic *Court*

## 190 A. G. MITCHELL

*culture* par excellence, organised with meticulousness, with rules, an *archos* (head of the banquet), values, customs, the way to behave and acceptable topics of discussions. Norbert Elias speaks of the *civilising process*, a dual movement of aristocratic values trickling down and people aspiring to these same values. What is the function of the satyr in this context?

### The Civilising Process Applied to Greek Antiquity

Elias' brilliant theory of the civilising process, the monopolisation of violence by the state, the adaptation of nobility and the creation of a curial culture, as well as the aspiration to imitate the mores and values of this Court by the people, has been of benefit to many researchers in very different fields.[48] Elias demonstrated all these phenomena based on the evidence of an increased public demand for etiquette manuals from the Renaissance to the nineteenth century with hundreds of rules of propriety, explaining how to properly eat, drink, blow one's nose, spit or defecate. These manuals of good manners were Elias' best source to investigate the civilising process. This theory has been criticised for its ethnocentrism and its penchant for evolutionism, given the specific European and chronological nature of this phenomenon, from the ninth century AD to the nineteenth century, but even the most vociferous detractors like H. P. Dürr have not offered any alternative models. A recent article by Jon P. Jørgensen shows however that Elias' theory can apply with some adjustments to ancient Greece, to the transition from the archaic (aristocratic) to the classical (democratic) period.[49] Besides what can be gleaned from this article as an antiquarian, it has the potential to open the *civilising process* to areas other than Western Europe from the medieval period to the nineteenth century.

The Greek classical period is characterised by an increasingly firm social control of violence and aggression and corresponds to Elias' civilising process. This process is possible in the civic space and political structures of the city-state. It is for instance the passage from a civilisation where one was armed before stepping out the door to an Athenian city where it was unthinkable to walk in arms in the streets of the city, even at the height of the Peloponnesian war. So much so that Aristotle wrote in the fourth century BC that 'the Greeks bore arms and bought wives from each other. In general, the remnants of these old customs that have persisted are completely ridiculous'.[50] The comparison does not end there. The way the tyrant Pisistrates seized power in 561 is comparable to Elias' principle of 'monopolisation of violence by the State'. In this case, the monopolisation of violence is reflected in the transition from an aristocratic to a tyrannical government. The tyrants came from the ranks of the nobility and therefore won a fierce competition with other aristocrats. What is fascinating here is the build-up to the tyrannical coup. Despite its violence, it took place with the help of clubs and not deadly spears.[51] Symbolically and in a very pragmatic way, the baton puts things in order. It is a punitive and reformist instrument. Athenian society had already had to develop a certain restraint due to the 'monarchical' mechanism which had transformed the behaviour of the aristocrats from an unrestrained violent group to a form of agonistic competition with a more curial character. Just as Elias associates *curial society* with the control of violence and explains how the aristocracy restructured its war customs into civilities, so can change in Athens be associated with the dynamics of the symposium culture. There is an excellent passage from Aristophanes' *Wasps* performed in 422 BC where we witness a real culture clash between the peasant Philocleon and his young son Bdelycleon as they are heading to a symposium.[52] The son explains to his father how to behave appropriately at the symposium, from clothing to behaviour, even humour (especially to avoid dirty jokes), and keep to certain conversation topics (politics, sports). In short, he must learn to behave in an elegant, civil and social manner. We understand how the 'good' behaviour at the symposium means that the aristocracy had totally changed its way of being, from violent and externalised behaviour to a refined and civilised style where it was necessary to avoid offending others.[53] Clearly these aristocratic court manners had trickled down to the point of embracing the entire population. One would really have to live far from the city not to be aware of it, like Philocleon. As Jørgensen explains it, the aristocracy naturally preserved an important role in democracy, since its members were orators and generals and therefore had considerable influence in the laws that had been adopted. But we can see that the aristocrats had adapted to the new political system and that they were now behaving like good little democrats.

Let us return now to the satyr and his incongruous presence in a society where civility has become a value in itself. Literature is not of much help, but Greek vases can provide an answer to this enigma. For different reasons, commercial ones, especially the vases, reproduced all these various movements, values and counter-values, elite culture trickling down and popular culture aspiring to imitate, as suggested by Elias.

### *The Right Way to Use a Wine Jug: Symposium Etiquette*

Fifth century sympotic culture was the equivalent to Elias' *curial culture*. The vases show us very clearly how to behave at the banquet, if only the way to use wine from the krater where the pure wine was mixed with water in very precise proportions decided by the banquet *archon*.

A skyphos in the Oxford Museum (Fig. 9.12), shows two young men on either side of a column krater.[54] One of them carries a skyphos in one hand and holds a cup at arm's length that he presents to his companion. The latter fills an oinochoe directly from the krater and then pours the mixture into the drinking cup. Sometimes painters also added ladles to serve wine or wine filtering cups to purify the liquid. The scene presents the quintessential symposium, the democratic, collective and regulated domestication of the liquid, the absorption of which could make one lose their control and their rational mind.

The satyr follows a very different etiquette because he is not subject to the rules and laws that govern the City. He is a forest creature, uncivilised and individualistic. A series of cups and *lekythoi* show satyrs fornicating with

**Fig. 9.12**

amphorae or jumping out of craters and pithoi. A satyr shown on the inside of a cup in Geneva (Fig. 9.13) has already plunged headfirst into a krater.[55] Only the lower body, legs, tail and genitals are visible hanging out of the krater. He is shown upside down, as if he were doing a headstand in the container. His grotesque attitude reveals the satyr's immense gluttony. The presence of a wine cup (*kylix*) drawn in black figure like an emblem, in the foreground, on the body of the crater indicates that it is a krater filled with wine and what the satyr hopes to find there.

Hundreds of vases are livened up by visual puns based on the transgression of stylistic rules, much like some comic book characters who emerge from the frame of their vignette. These puns were visual games without narrative elements, which caused comic shifts between container and content, blurring the formal differences between the decorative frame and the characters painted within it. Painters transformed small conventional details into series of images that were often repeated and known to the public to create a comic effect, stand out from the competition, surprise viewers and attract potential buyers. Parodies were similar to visual puns, except that the transgression was not stylistic but narrative in nature. Parodies made fun of well-known aspects of everyday life or mythology. The codes of imagery were obvious to the people of Athens who saw them every day, but the painters who wanted to make sure that the viewers would recognise a visual parody at first glance always made sure to leave enough details in the scene to recognise the serious model and enough quirky details to understand how the image had been distorted. Let us take an example.

Satyrs, with their frenetic sexuality, drinkers of unmixed wine, and frenzied servants of Dionysos living in the mountains and forests, are at the opposite end of the spectrum from athletes, living incarnations of *arete* (virtue). However, a column krater in Munich (Fig. 9.14), shows us precisely the impossible, satyrs at the heart of the Polis, trying to participate in agonistic events.[56] To show satyrs acting (or pretending to act) as citizens is absurd and highly amusing. Our satyrs are all ithyphallic and training for the pentathlon: the disc,

**Fig. 9.13**

**Fig. 9.14**

the javelin, the long jump, boxing. Two others, covered in long clothes, carry large objects resembling the forked sticks typical of palaestra's trainers. A double-pipes player stands at the centre of the composition. On the other side of the same vase, human athletes are also training for the pentathlon. From left to right, we recognise the coach (identified by his forked stick), two boxers, a javelin thrower, a double flute-player, another javelin thrower, a discus thrower, a second double-pipes player and a runner. Because the satyrs on this krater are placed in a 'role' that is not theirs, pretending to be citizens of the city, this vase has been considered by a number of researchers to be inspired by a satyric drama. Two dramas are mentioned: Aristias is said to have staged a satyric drama by his father Pratinas in 467, entitled *Palaistrai*, which included boxer satyrs,[57] and Aeschylus' *Isthmiastai*, in which satyrs prepare the Corinthian Games.[58] As I have demonstrated elsewhere there are numerous scenes in which satyrs pretend to be citizens.[59] In fact, our scene is simply a parody and not a scene of satyric drama. All it takes is looking on the other side of the vessel to find 'real' athletes. In addition to the parody, there are two additional sexual jokes in the scene: first, the non-forked sticks of our satyr trainers are actually giant dildos, and second the satyrs' usual erection in an athletic context.[60] Athletes could not be in erection because the foreskin of their penis was always tied with a *kynodesme*, which made it impossible to have an erection or unwanted movements during sportive workouts.

Parody is a two-way process. By means of satyrs, real athletes with physical prowess and aristocratic values are belittled, degraded to the level of alcoholic braggarts, which was certainly comforting on some level for average Athenians. But, the latter also laughed at the satyr, this mythological prankster and his all-too-human shortcomings, at the opposite of good manners, of the City and of 'well-behaved' citizens. This figure of the in-between, as fascinating as the king's buffoon, made it possible to make fun of what citizens sometimes thought quietly to themselves. What was the function of the satyr in a society where the *civilising process* was almost finalised, where *sophrosyne* (civility and restraint) was seen as a virtue, a society where everyone spoke of *kalos kagathos* (handsome and upstanding) as an almost universal principle? The satyr served as a safety valve, an agent of carnival that disrupted this self-righteous world by acting as a clown. He represented the secret desires, the animal impulses that slumbered within the 'civilised' being, the Dionysian primordial forces and the 'shivers of intoxication' Nietzsche wrote about.[61] The satyr functions like an Athenian fantasy caught in a social entanglement. It allows him to make fun of good manners, while highlighting them, to breathe a little, in an increasingly hierarchical, claustrophobic world of citizens who 'must' behave well in all circumstances.

Norbert Elias' ideas have been particularly useful for understanding the purpose of the satyr and its humorous function in ancient Greek visual culture. The animality described by Elias, which had to be overcome by society in order to be able to move forward, is reflected in Athens by the comic and ugly satyr who symbolises the transition from a world of Dionysian ecstasy and mysteries, wild rites that included tearing animals alive and eating them raw (*diasparagmos* and *omophagy*), to the theatrical world in a new civilisation of the 'cooked' with its 'acceptable' sacrifices.[62] What is left of the ancient violence and unruliness in the beautiful and orderly world of the symposium? The ambivalence of the satyr, a curious and comical figure because of its moral and physical ugliness.

# NOTES

1. Abbreviations of reference works in vase-painting: *ABV*: Beazley, J. D., *Attic Black-figure Vase-painters*, Oxford: Oxford University Press, 1956; *ARV²*: Beazley, J. D., *Attic Red-figure Vase-painters*, 2nd ed., Oxford: Oxford University Press, 1963; *Add*: Burn, L, Glynn, R., *Beazley Addenda*, Oxford: Oxford University Press, 1982; *Add²*: Carpenter, T. H., Mannack, T., Mendonca, M., *Beazley Addenda*, 2nd ed., Oxford: Oxford University Press, 1989; *(BA#)*: Oxford: Beazley Archive (BA) Database number; *CVA*: *Corpus Vasorum Antiquorum*; *KH 1*: Wolters, P. and Bruns, G., *Das Kabirenheiligtum bei Theben*, vol. 1, Berlin, 1940; *KH 4*: Braun K. and Haevernick, T. E., *Bemalte Keramik und Glas aus den Kabirenheiligtum bei Theben*, Berlin, 1981; *LIMC*: *Lexicon Iconographicum Mythologiae Classicae*; *Para*: Beazley, J. D., *Paralipomena; Additions to Attic Black-figure Vase-painters and to Attic Red-figure Vase-Painters*, Oxford: Oxford University Press, 1971; *PV²*: Trendall, A. D., *Phlyax Vases*, 2nd ed. (*BICS*, Suppl. 19, 1967); *RVAp*: Cambitoglou, A., Trendall, A. D., *The Red-figured Vases of Apulia*, vol. 1–2, Oxford: Oxford University Press, 1979, 1982; *RVP*: Trendall, A. D., *The Red-figured Vases of Paestum*, British School at Rome, 1987.
2. Aristotle, *Poetics*, 1449a34–35. Common editions of ancient texts are cited in the bibliography; however, all translations of the Greek are my own.
3. See also Sidwell, *From Old to Middle*, 252–253.
4. Quoted and discussed further by S. Attardo, *Linguistic Theories of Humor*, 37–39.
5. Homer, *Iliad*, 2: 212–277.
6. Halliwell, *Greek Laughter*, 10.
7. A red-figure pelike in the Ashmolean Museum in Oxford, LOAN399 (BA 44463) attributed by Lezzi-Hafter to the Achilles painter, has a graffito under its foot '4 for 3.5 obols', that is 0.15 ancient drachma or 1.05 euros for four vases. See Vickers and Gill, *Artful Crafts*, 85–87, Figs. 4.3–4.4.
8. Bourdieu, *La distinction*.
9. In recent years, studies of 'popular' cultural practices in the classical world have tried to redefine the ancient sociological landscape. See especially the works of Grig, *Popular culture*, and Forsdyke, *Slaves Tell Tales*.
10. On ways of distinguishing representations of masks worn by painted characters from *caricatured* faces on Greek vases, see Mitchel, *Origins*, 254–257.
11. Athenian red-figure askos, Paris, Louvre Museum, G610; (BA 2720). Provenance: Italy. 460–440 BC. Vectorised drawing © Alexandre G. Mitchell.
12. Athenian red-figure skyphos, Laon, Municipal museum, 37.1034; (BA 212122), *ARV²* 832.32, *Add²* 295. Provenance: Eretria (Greece); Amphitrite painter; 450–430 BC. Vectorised drawing © Alexandre G. Mitchell.
13. Aristophanes, *Clouds*, 102–103.
14. Baldwin, *Philogelos*, 43.
15. See Detienne, *La mètis*.
16. Boeotian black-figure skyphos from the Theban Kabirion sanctuary, Oxford, Ashmolean Museum, G249; *KH* 4.67.409, pl. 23. 450–375 BC; Boeotian black-figure kantharos from the Theban Kabirion sanctuary, London, British Museum, 1893.3–3.1. 450–375 BC; Boeotian black-figure kantharos from the Theban Kabirion sanctuary, Nauplion, archaeological museum, 144; *KH* 4.67.405. 450–375 BC; Boeotian black-figure kantharos from the Theban

Kabirion sanctuary, Mississippi, Mississippi University, P 116; *KH*1.100K20=*KH* 4.67.402. 450–375 BC.

17. Apulian red-figure oinochoe, London, British Museum, F366, close to the style of the Felton painter, 350 BC; *PV²* 85, no. 194, *RVAp* 177, no. 94. Photograph © Alexandre G. Mitchell.

18. Apulian red-figure oinochoe, Paris, Louvre museum, K36, 360–350 BC, Circle of the Ilioupersis painter. (https://commons.wikimedia.org/wiki/File:Diomedes_Odysseus_Palladion_Louvre_K36.jpg).

19. Taplin, *Pots and Plays*, 37.

20. Athenian black-figure amphora, Syracuse, Regional Archaeological museum Paolo Orsi, 21965; Leagros Group; 520–500 BC. Digitised drawing after Perrot, *Histoire de l'Art*, 10, 210–211, figs. 136–137.

21. Bergson, *Laughter*, 2.2.

22. Dasen, *Dwarfs*; Dasen, 'Infirmitas'.

23. See the chapter by Jessica Milner Davies in this handbook.

24. Mitchell, 'Disparate bodies'; Mitchell, 'The Hellenistic turn'; Mitchell, 'Les handicaps à l'époque de Galien'.

25. Davies, *Ethnic Humor*.

26. Black-figure Boeotian kantharos from the Theban Kabirion sanctuary, Berlin, Staatliche Museen, 3179; *KH* 1.99K16, pl. 29.1–2, 50.11=*KH* 4.64.355. 450–375 BC. Vectorised drawing © Alexandre G. Mitchell. As explained above in the context of Taranto in Apulia, Greek democracy was no longer the monopoly of Athens: from the end of the fifth century and early fourth, Thebes had also moved from an oligarchic government to a democratic one. Statements based on Greek vases from different regions of the Mediterranean are therefore not invalidated because of their dispersion.

27. Mitchell, *Greek Vase Painting*, 208–209.

28. Athenian red-figure rhyton, St Petersbourg, Hermitage museum, 679; (BA 204087), *ARV²* 382.188 (1649), *Para* 512, *Add* 113, *Add²* 228; Brygos painter; 480–470 BC. Vectorised drawing © Alexandre G. Mitchell.

29. Galen, *On the Natural faculties*, I, 22.

30. Athenaeus, *The Learned Banqueters*, 14.613d.

31. Fragment of a black-figure Boeotian kantharos from the Theban Kabirion sanctuary, Athens, National archaeological museum 10530; *KH* 1.103K44, pl. 15.4 = *KH* 4.63.320. 450–375 BC. Vectorised drawing © Alexandre G. Mitchell.

32. Snowden, *Blacks*, 161.

33. See the (non-exhaustive) bibliography on the representations of Africans in classical antiquity in Mitchell, *Greek Vase Painting*, fn. 90.

34. Boeotian black-figure kantharos from the Theban Kabirion sanctuary, Athens, National Archaeological Museum, 10429; *KH* 1.98K9, pl. 10.11, 44.4=*KH* 4.63.303. 450–375 BC. Vectorised drawing © Alexandre G. Mitchell.

35. Apollodorus, *The Library*, 2.4.6–7; Pausanias, *Description of Greece*, 9.19.1; Suidas, *s.v.* 'Teumēsia'; Ovid, *Metamorphoses*, 7.762.

36. On humour as a revealing catalyst of hidden anxieties, see Mitchell, 'Humor, women, and male anxieties'.

37. Homer, *Odyssey*, 11: 489–491.

38. Theognis II, 1021. See *Greek Elegiac Poetry*.

39. Babrius, Phaedrus. *Fables*, 60.

40. Demetrius of Phalerum, 262.

41. Athenian red-figure pelike, Rome, National Etruscan museum of Villa Giulia, 48238; (BA 202567), *ARV*² 284.1, *Add* 104, *Add²* 208. Provenance: Ceveteri (Italy). Matsch painter; 480–460 BC. Vectorised drawing © Alexandre G. Mitchell.
42. Athenian black-figure lekythos, Adolphseck, Schloss Fasanerie, 12; (BA 303575), *ABV* 491.60, *Add²* 122, *Para* 223. Provenance: Greece; Class of Athens 581; 510–500 BC. Athenian red-figure skyphos, Oxford, Ashmolean Museum, 1943.79; (BA 211723), *ARV*² 889.160, *Add²* 302, *Para* 428. Provenance: Spina (Italy). Penthesilea painter; 460–440 BC. Athenian red-figure neck-amphora, London, British Museum, E290; (BA 207611), *ARV*² 1571, 653.1, *Add²* 276. Charmides painter; 460–440 BC. Athenian red-figure pelike, Paris, Louvre museum, G234; (BA 202622), *ARV*² 286.16, 1642, *Add* 104, *Add²* 209. Provenance: Capua (Italy). Geras painter; 510–490 BC.
43. Aristophanes, *Clouds*, 1011–1020.
44. Bergson, *Laughter*, 1.3.
45. Shapiro, *Personifications*, 94.
46. Boeotian black-figure kantharos from the Theban Kabirion sanctuary, Bonn, Akademisches Kunstmuseum, 301. 450–375 BC. Vectorised drawing © Alexandre G. Mitchell. See also Mitchell, *Greek Vase Painting*, 248–279.
47. On the ambivalence of the satyr, see Lissarrague, 'l'ambivalence'; Lissarrague, 'sexualité'; Lissarrague, 'satyres bons à montrer'.
48. Elias, *Civilising Process*.
49. Jørgensen, 'taming'.
50. Aristotle, *Politics*, II, 1268b.
51. On the bearing of arms in ancient Greece, see Wees, 'Bearing Arms'.
52. Aristophanes, *Wasps*, 1212–1217.
53. Herman, *Morality*.
54. Athenian red-figure skyphos, Oxford, Ashmolean Museum, 520; (BA 200611), *ARV*² 76.84, *Add* 83, *Add²* 168, *Para* 328. Epiktetos; 520–490 BC. Vectorised drawing © Alexandre G. Mitchell.
55. Athenian red-figure cup, Geneva, Museum of Art and History, 16908; (BA 11019), *Add* 88, *Add²* 178. 510–490 BC. Vectorised drawing © Alexandre G. Mitchell.
56. Athenian red-figure column krater, Munich, Antikensammlungen, 2381; (BA 202099), *ARV*² 221.14, *Add* 98, *Add²* 198. Provenance: southern Italy; Nikoxenos painter; 525–490 BC. Vectorised drawing © Alexandre G. Mitchell.
57. Simon, 'Satyr-plays', 130.
58. Brommer, *Satyrspiele*, 60.
59. Mitchell, *Greek Vase Painting*, 156–206. On the innocuous presence of the double-pipes player in the scene as well as on hundreds of other black- and red-figure vases featuring athletes and without the presence of satyrs or actors, see Mitchell, *Greek Vase Painting*. 188.
60. Compare to the giant dildo on the Athenian red-figure amphora, Boston, Museum of Fine Arts, 98.882; (BA 202711), *ARV*² 279.7, *Add* 102, *Add²* 208, *Para* 354. Provenance: Capua (Italy); Flying-angel painter; 500–490 BC.
61. Nietzsche, *Birth of Tragedy*, 18.
62. See Lévi-Strauss, *Raw*.

# BIBLIOGRAPHY

Apollodorus. *The Library. Volume I: Books 1-3.9*. Edited by James G. Frazer. *Loeb Classical Library*. Cambridge, MA: Harvard University Press, 1921.

Aristophanes. *Clouds. Wasps. Peace*. Edited and Translated by Jeffery Henderson. *Loeb Classical Library*. Cambridge, MA: Harvard University Press, 1998.

Aristotle. *Poetics*. Translated by Stephen Halliwell. *Loeb Classical Library*. Cambridge, MA: Harvard University Press, 1995.

Aristotle. *Politics*. Translated by H. Rackham. *Loeb Classical Library*. Cambridge, MA: Harvard University Press, 1932.

Athenaeus. *The Learned Banqueters, Volume I: Books 1-3.106e*. Edited and Translated by S. Douglas Olson. *Loeb Classical Library*. Cambridge, MA: Harvard University Press, 2007.

Attardo, S. *Linguistic Theories of Humor*. Berlin: Walter de Gruyter, 2010.

Babrius and Phaedrus. *Fables*. Translated by Ben Edwin Perry. *Loeb Classical Library*. Cambridge, MA: Harvard University Press, 1965.

Baldwin, Barry, ed. *The Philogelos or Laughter-Lover*. Amsterdam: J. C. Gieben, 1983.

Bergson, Henri. *Laughter: An Essay on the Meaning of the Comic*. London: The Macmillan Company, 1921.

Bourdieu, Pierre. *La Distinction. Critique sociale du jugement*. Paris, 1979.

Brommer, Frank. *Satyrspiele. Bilder griechischer vasen*. Berlin: Walter de Gruyter, 1959.

Dasen, Véronique. *Dwarfs in Ancient Egypt and Greece*. Oxford: Oxford University Press, 1993.

Dasen, Véronique. 'Infirmitas or Not? Short-statured Persons in Ancient Greece'. In *Infirmity in Antiquity and the Middle Ages: Social and Cultural Approaches to Health, Weakness and Care*, edited by Christian Krötzl, Katariina Mustakallio, and Jenni Kuuliala, 29–49. Dorchester: Ashgate, 2015.

Davies, Christie. *Ethnic Humor Around the World: A Comparative Analysis*. Bloomington: Indiana University Press, 1990.

Demetrius. *Demetrius of Phalerum: Text, Translation, and Discussion*. Edited by William W. Fortenbaugh and Eckart Schütrumpf. *Rutgers University Studies in Classical Humanities*, 9. New Brunswick and London: Transaction Publishers, 1999.

Detienne, Marcel, and Jean-Pierre Vernant, eds. *Les ruses de l'intelligence: La mètis des Grecs*. Paris: Flammarion, 1974.

Elias, Norbert. *The Civilizing Process: Sociogenetic and Psychogenetic Investigations*. Revised edition. Oxford: Blackwell, 2000.

Forsdyke, Sara. *Slaves Tell Tales: And Other Episodes in the Politics of Popular Culture in Ancient Greece*. Princeton: University Press, 2012.

Galen. *On the Natural Faculties*. Translated by A.J. Brock. *Loeb Classical Library*. Cambridge, MA: Harvard University Press, 1916.

*Greek Elegiac Poetry: From the Seventh to the Fifth Centuries BC*. Edited and Translated by Douglas E. Gerber. *Loeb Classical Library*. Cambridge, MA: Harvard University Press, 1999.

Grig, Lucy, ed. *Popular Culture in the Ancient World*. Cambridge: Cambridge University Press, 2016.

Halliwell, Stephen. *Greek Laughter: A study of Cultural Psychology from Homer to Early Christianity*. Cambridge: Cambridge University Press, 2008.

Herman, Gabriel. *Morality and Behaviour in Democratic Athens: A Social History*. Cambridge: Cambridge University Press, 2006.

Homer. *Iliad, Volume I: Books 1-12*. Translated by A.T. Murray. *Loeb Classical Library*. Cambridge, MA: Harvard University Press, 1924.

Homer. *Odyssey, Volume I: Books 1-12*. Translated by A.T. Murray. *Loeb Classical Library*. Cambridge, MA: Harvard University Press, 1919.

Jørgensen, Jon Ploug. 'The Taming of the Aristoi—An Ancient Greek Civilizing Process?'. *History of the Human Sciences* 27, no. 3 (2014): 38–54.

Lévi-Strauss, Claude. *The Raw and the Cooked. Introduction to a Science of Mythology*. London: Penguin, 1966.

Lissarrague, F., and F. Frontisi-Ducroux. 'De l'ambiguïté à l'ambivalence: un parcours dionysiaque'. *AION Arch St V* (1983): 11–32.

Lissarrague, F. 'De la sexualité des satyres'. *Métis* 2, no. 1 (1987a): 63–90.

Lissarrague, F. 'Pourquoi les satyres sont-ils bons à montrer ?'. *Anthropologie et Théâtre antique, Cahiers du GITA* 3 (1987b): 93–106.

Mitchell, Alexandre G. *Greek Vase Painting and the Origins of Visual Humour*. Cambridge: Cambridge University Press, 2009.

Mitchell, Alexandre G. 'Disparate Bodies in Ancient Artefacts: The Function of Caricature and Pathological Grotesques Among Roman Terracotta Figurines'. In *Disabilities in Roman Antiquity: Disparate Bodies: A Capite ad Calcem*, edited by Christian Laes, Chris Goodey, and M. Lynn Rose, 275–297. Leiden: Brill, 2013.

Mitchell, Alexandre G. 'Humor, Women, and Male Anxieties in Ancient Greek Visual Culture'. In *Laughter, Humor, and the (Un)making of Gender, Historical and Cultural Perspectives*, edited by Anna Foka and Jon Liliequist, 163–189. Palgrave Macmillan, 2015.

Mitchell, Alexandre G. 'The Hellenistic Turn in Bodily Representations: Venting Anxiety in Terracotta Figurines'. In *Disability in Antiquity*, edited by Christian Laes, 182–196. Oxford: Routledge, 2016.

Mitchell, Alexandre G. 'Les handicaps et malformations à l'époque de Galien'. In *Catalogue de Exposition Galien, Musée de Mariemont*, edited by A. Verbanck-Pierard, V. Boudon-Millot, and D. Gourevitch, 175–180. Musée royal de Mariemont, 2018.

Nietzsche, Friedrich. *The Birth of Tragedy and Other Writings*. Edited by Raymond Geuss. Translated by Ronald Speirs. Cambridge: Cambridge University Press, 1999.

Ovid. *Metamorphoses, Volume I: Books 1-8*. Translated by Frank Justus Miller. *Loeb Classical Library*. Cambridge, MA: Harvard University Press, 1916.

Pausanias. *Description of Greece, Volume IV: Books 8.22-10 (Arcadia, Boeotia, Phocis and Ozolian Locri)*. Translated by W.H.S. Jones. *Loeb Classical Library*. Cambridge, MA: Harvard University Press, 1935.

Perrot, G., and Chipiez, C. *Histoire de l'Art dans l'Antiquité*. Paris: Hachette, 1882.

Shapiro, H. A. *Personifications in Greek Art, The Representation of Abstract Concepts 600–400 BC*. Zurich: Akanthus, 1993.

Sidwell, Keith. 'From Old to Middle to New? Aristotle's *Poetics* and the History of Athenian Comedy'. In *The Rivals of Aristophanes: Studies in Athenian Old Comedy*, edited by David Harvey and John Wilkins, 247–258. London: Duckworth and the Classical Press of Wales, 2000.

Simon, E., 'Satyr-Plays on Vases in the Time of Aeschylus'. In *The Eye of Greece: Studies in the Art of Athens*, edited by Dona Kurtz and Brian Sparkes, 123–148. Cambridge: Cambridge University Press, 1982.

Snowden, Frank M., Jr. Blacks in Antiquity: Ethiopians in the Greco-Roman Experience. Cambridge, MA: Bellnap Press of Harvard University Press, 1970.

*Suidae Lexicon*. Pars I. p. xxxii 6 549. Edited by Ada Adler. Leipzig: Teubner, 1928.

Taplin, Oliver. *Pots and Plays: Interactions between Tragedy and Greek Vase-Painting of the Fourth Century B.C.* Los Angeles: Getty Publications, 2007.

Vickers, Michael, and David Gill. *Artful Crafts: Ancient Greek Silverware and Pottery.* Oxford: Clarendon Press, 1994.

Wees, Hans van. 'Greeks Bearing Arms: The State, the Leisure Class and the Display of Weapons in Archaic Greece'. In *Archaic Greece: New Approaches and New Evidence,* edited by Nick Fischer and Hans van Wees, 333–378. London: Duckworth and the Classical Press of Wales, 1998.

CHAPTER 10

# Approaching Jokes and Jestbooks in Premodern China

*Giulia Baccini*

This chapter considers premodern Chinese jokes and jestbooks. It seeks to clarify certain issues that arise when trying to understand them and their humour: the problem of textual history and textual classification as well as the problem of contextual knowledge. In order to do this, the chapter first considers debates about humour and literature at the beginning of the twentieth century, before addressing more precisely the premodern period in order to clarify terminology, highlight methodological problems, and identify the primary sources in which to look for premodern Chinese jokes and jestbooks. The chapter will then provide, as useful case studies, an overview of the two oldest jestbooks to have been transmitted, presenting their humorous content in relation to their cultural backgrounds.

In China, the early twentieth century saw the rise of a new wave of intellectuals who, following the ideals of the May Fourth Movement (also known as the New Culture Movement), sought to describe the historical development and transformation of the Chinese literary tradition.[1] In pursuing such a goal, these authors were heavily influenced by Western books about literary theory and Western histories of national literatures. Up until that time, the Chinese literary landscape had lacked comprehensive accounts of the history of Chinese literature, as in premodern times it was not the literary habit to analyse a literary tradition as a comprehensive object of discourse in a fully fledged analytical way.[2] Accordingly, scholars like Zhen Zhenduo 鄭振鐸 (1898–1958), Hu Shi

G. Baccini (✉)
Ca'Foscari University of Venice, Venice, Italy
e-mail: giuliabaccini@unive.it

© The Author(s), under exclusive license to Springer Nature Switzerland AG 2020
D. Derrin, H. Burrows (eds.), *The Palgrave Handbook of Humour, History, and Methodology*, https://doi.org/10.1007/978-3-030-56646-3_10

胡適 (1891–1962), Lu Xun 魯迅 (1881–1936), Wang Guowei 王國維 (1877–1927), and several others took Western literary histories as a model and were therefore heavily influenced by Western categories in their histories of Chinese literary genres and classifications.[3] One of the most critical consequences of this process, not least because of its impact on later scholarship, was the choice to use the term 'xiaoshuo' 小説. Despite this term already having a long history in the Chinese literary tradition as a classificatory category for prose (meaning 'lesser sayings'), it was reapplied as a category to identify the Western literary genre of 'fiction'. This step created an ambiguous overlap between the two different meanings that produced anachronistic readings of ancient literary material. The confusing legacy of this is still detectable in the studies of some scholars today.

The beginning of the twentieth century was a period of heavy social and political changes for China, since it bore witness to the end of the political institution of the Empire (1911), with all the social consequences this entailed. The same *literati* who were engaged in writing Chinese literary histories were also active in discussing and imagining what the new China should look like, and what features of the old China should be set aside in order to make China really 'modern'. Great figures in the intellectual debate like Lu Xun, Hu Shi, and their peers were actively anti-traditionalist in their call for change. For example, they identified orthodox Confucian thought as one of the core ideologies of the recently deceased feudal society. Humour and discourses about it became part of the themes debated in the public arena; in particular, thanks to Lin Yutang 林語堂 (1895–1976), who adopted humour as the main theme of his particular cultural agenda, and Confucian decorum was seen as responsible for the lack of attention to humour in the Chinese tradition.[4] Lin Yutang introduced the Western concept of humour (*youmo* 幽默 in Chinese), translating the word phonetically into Chinese in deliberate opposition to the native term *huaji* 滑稽 (funny, comic), and advocating the right to a literature of leisure.[5] In one of his famous articles, originally published in 1924, he stated that, in Chinese tradition, humour was never considered an appropriate topic for literary texts, so he coined the word *youmo* to identify a dignified kind of humour which could serve as a tool for modernisation.[6] Lu Xun, for his part, harshly criticised Lin Yutang's view, calling for an engaged literary production which could help build a modern China. In a direct refutation of Lin's 'humor' he forwarded the concept of 'satire' (*fengci* 諷刺), which, according to him, was the only tool that could fruitfully be employed to criticise social distortions and hence to provide the basis for change.[7] As a result of the public debate on the topic of humour, scholars identified different Chinese terms to qualify humorous phenomena, always trying to provide an English translation or bearing the English terminology in mind as a counter-model.[8] This process generated an all-too-easy connection between Chinese and English terminologies. The limits of the translation of terms which already have a particular cultural history should be seriously taken into consideration when comparing similar phenomena or concepts across different cultures.

In this same period, two features of the new literature identified by the May Fourth Movement, vernacular language and mass literature, fostered a new interest in folk literature (*minjian wenxue* 民間文學). Zhen Zhenduo was one of the first exponents of the new movement, in which Zhou Zuoren 周作人 (1885–1967),[9] Lu Xun's brother, and Gu Jiegang 顧頡剛 (1893–1980) also had prominent roles. The folk literature movement, which emerged from Peking University in 1918 and endured until the end of the 1930s,[10] made folk literature—jokes, fairy-tales, nursery-rhymes, folk songs, and so on—the central focus of its investigation.[11] Since it was understood as coming from the common people, this literature represented for these intellectuals the authentic expression of the people. Therefore, it was considered suitable for inclusion as part of the new literature of modern China.

The literary view of the Chinese scholars of the early twentieth century has greatly influenced later scholarship with the result that jokes and jestbooks are still classified as folk literature in a number of modern works.[12] However, the place of these texts in literary history has to be assigned taking into consideration the language, the authors, the contents, and the particular social and cultural features of the various ages in which jokes and jestbooks have been shaped and circulated.

## CHINESE PREMODERN JOKES AND THE LITERARY CANON: A PROBLEM OF CLASSIFICATION

One of the problems connected with accessing and understanding these humorous texts in their original context is dealing with the history of their classification. In the study of Chinese literature, to study a genre or a type of text, in the absence of a conspicuous number of ancient texts discussing literary theory in an analytical way, the literary historian must turn to the bibliographical chapters contained in official histories in order to grasp how a text was classified and hence judged by the dominant ideology of a given time.[13] These bibliographical chapters were not designed to provide an exhaustive list of all the texts gathered in imperial collections, nor were they an objective presentation of the literary material. Rather, since the compilers arranged the textual material not only according to its content but also according to its 'value', these chapters reflect 'a selective and prescriptive vision of the textual heritage'.[14] The texts were classified according to different categories, the most important being 'Classics' (*jing* 經), which was considered the fountainhead of all knowledge—a position that remained undisputed across the ages until the end of the empire. Those texts which are today defined as jestbooks were originally classified under the 'xiaoshuo' 小説 (lesser sayings) category, which was the least important section of the 'Zi' 子 (Masters of Thought) macro-category.[15] *Xiaoshuo*, since its first appearance in the bibliographical chapter of the *Hanshu* 漢書 (Book of Han, c. 92 CE), referred to records derived from petty talks and gossip. The main characteristic of this kind of texts was that 'it was recorded information of lesser significance rather than it was a narrative form, and that it was collected rather than invented'.[16] These texts were considered superficial, or morally ambiguous; their didactic aims were not so evident, or they were difficult to ascribe to other better-defined categories (such as the Confucian tradition and Daoist tradition) for several reasons. In their narratives, they could contain fictional elements, but the events they recorded were simply understood as having a low level of historical reliability. Differently from the new usage given to the term *xiaoshuo* by modern literary scholars, as identifying the literary genre of 'fiction', in premodern times it did not identify works belonging to this genre. 'Fiction' was a genre alien to the Chinese literary tradition.[17] In fact, in the earliest bibliographical chapters, works categorised as *xiaoshuo* are quite similar in their content to works classified under the 'zashi' 雜史 (miscellaneous histories) category. The two groups of texts are distinguished because of the different degree of plausibility and historical accuracy perceived by the compilers; however, the border between them is quite blurred. The bibliographical chapter of the *Suishu* 隋書 (Book of Sui, 656) followed the *Hanshu* model and listed under the category *xiaoshuo* twenty texts mainly centred on speeches and anecdotes related to historical figures, among which we find the titles of what are in all likelihood the first collections of humorous anecdotes to have been recorded. Since *xiaoshuo* had a marginal cultural status and writing them was not considered a cultural accomplishment, they were not carefully preserved over the centuries, so most of the texts listed in these bibliographies are known only by their title. Since they were not considered important, the official biographies of their putative authors mostly remain silent regarding their existence, and even when they record the title of a text, they do not provide any information about its content or how it was circulated. In addition, most of the texts compiled before the widespread use of woodblock printing technology during the Song era (960–1279) are lost in their integrity, and this is particularly true for texts which did not hold a prestigious position; we lack, then, a clear picture of the original shapes and arrangements of the textual material in these works.

Despite this situation, several lost texts can still be objects of scholarly investigation since fragments of them have been preserved in *leishu* 類書 (encyclopaedias, lit. 'classified books') and *congshu* 叢書 (collectanea).[18] Traditional encyclopaedias were conceived as an aid for writing. They do not catalogue texts; rather, they use texts to explain categories of knowledge by arranging textual passages according to topics such as geography, food, and celestial objects. More importantly, they always cite their sources. Nonetheless, these encyclopaedias must be used with caution since their compilers often quoted not from the original texts but from other encyclopaedias, sometimes correcting passages or updating the language.[19] Even so, they do still provide valuable information about texts that, otherwise, would have vanished from the history of Chinese literature. The *Yiwen leiju* 藝文類聚 (Anthology of Literary Excerpts Arranged by Categories, 624), *Taiping yulan* 太平御覽 (Imperial Reading of the Taiping Era, submitted to the throne in 984) and *Taiping guangji* 太平廣記 (The Extensive Records Assembled in the Taiping Era, 978) are encyclopaedias which constitute some of the most important repositories of ancient humorous tales (in particular pre-tenth century).

Last but not least, other sources in which to look for humorous anecdotes are the so-called *biji* 筆記 or *biji xiaoshuo* 筆記小説, a term that is variously translated as notebooks or miscellaneous notes.[20] Starting in the Song dynasty, *biji* has mostly been used to identify works which provide a collection of texts on different subjects (ancient tales, anecdotes, geographical notes, and curious facts) put together according to the author's taste. Most of these texts were written during retirement or during leisure time and were not considered a prestigious form of writing. Still, they are a valuable reservoir of information on social history independent of official sources. An interesting example available in English translation is the *Zuiweng tanlu* 醉翁談錄 (Tales of an Old Drunkard) ascribed to Luo Ye 羅燁 (thirteenth century), in which the author brings together different kinds of stories that he has heard or read in various texts, including several jokes.[21]

The current Chinese word for jestbook, *xiaohua ji* 笑話集, is a modern term used to identify a collection (*ji*) of humorous stories or jokes (*xiaohua*). Sometimes they are called *wenyan xiaohua ji*, to specify the language in which they were written, the literary language (*wenyan* 文言), a common feature of premodern jestbooks. Literary language (sometimes called classical Chinese), employed from the Han (206 BC–220 AD) to the early twentieth century, was the only written medium used by the educated elite for the documents or other official purposes of the imperial administration as well as the only legitimate one for literary production.[22] Starting from the Han dynasty, this language had been standardised and had lost its connection with the spoken language. No evidence has been found of the word *xiaohua* being used as a term identifying humorous stories before the seventeenth century.[23] The prolific Ming author Feng Menglong 馮夢龍 (1574–1645) defined his work as a collection of *xiaohua* in the preface to his collection of jokes, *Xiaofu* 笑府 (Treasury of Jokes). However, this term was far from identifying a precise genre, as can be judged by the fact that the later Qing dynasty catalogue *Siku quanshu zongmu tiyao* 四庫全書總目提要 (Catalogue of the Complete Library of the Four Branches, 1794), still placed collections of humorous anecdotes not in a *xiaohua* category, which have never been created, but in the traditional *xiaoshuo* category, without providing a formal description of their features. This catalogue plays an important role as a source for investigating texts written in the literary language because, unlike those that preceded it, it provides a detailed bibliographical abstract for every text listed. The abstracts evaluate the text, offering information about its contents and possible affiliations. The *xiaoshuo* are placed from chapter (*juan*) 140 to 144. In chapters 140–142 we find a list of works included in the *Siku quanshu* collection (they are defined as *cunshu* 存書, 'stored books'), but the more significant part for our investigation are the works listed in chapters 143–144 (*cunmu* 存目, 'stored titles'), of which only the titles and the abstracts are provided. In particular, in the sub-section *suoyu* 瑣語 (accounts of trivia) of chapter 144 we find the titles and abstracts of several collections which gather humorous material (albeit not exclusively, as they also contain other kinds of prose or poetry). The words used to describe the contents provide a typology for the stories, although the various types are not formalised. For example, the *Kaiyan ji* 開顏集 (Collection of stories to smile), ascribed to Zhou Wenji 周文玘 (Song dynasty), is defined as collecting 'humorous facts from the past' 皆古來詼諧事; the *Tanxie* 談諧 (Humorous talks) by Chen Rihua 陳日華 (Song dynasty) is made up of 'records of jester-like and playful speeches' 所記皆俳優嘲弄之語; the *Xieshi* 諧史 (Humorous history) by Shen Chu 沈俶 (fl. 1247) gathers 'records of old anecdotes about Bianjing (modern Kaifeng) retold in a funny way' 所錄皆汴京舊聞，以多詼嘲之語 and so on. Overall, the abstracts often provide a textual affiliation by linking a text to a previous work, employing the following formulas: 'this text is like text X' 此《X》之流; 'of a similar type as text X' 如《X》之類; 'modeled on the example of the X-text' 仿《X》例, and so on. According to Chen Pingyuan,[24] it is only in the preface of Wu Jianren's 吳趼人 (1866–1910) *Xin Xiaolin guangji* 新笑林廣記 (New extensive records from the forest of laughter) that the expression *xiaohua xiaoshuo* 笑話小説 (used by Wu Jianren to define his text) shows some kind of genre awareness. However, Wu Jianren lived at the dawn of the modern era, and *literati* at that time, as mentioned in the introduction to this chapter, were already discussing and giving new meanings to the term *xiaoshuo*.

Even if an analytical discourse about genres was absent and the identification of different types of text was the result of a classification (which varied across the centuries), compilers across the ages sometimes reused similar or the same titles (in particular the title of the earliest collection of humorous anecdotes that has been verified, *Xiaolin*) in creating their collections, as though acknowledging the existence of a literary tradition. The titles of the collections might guide the readers in the identification of the content. They often employ terms related to the humorous sphere; in particular, the character *xiao* 笑 'to smile, to laugh' (which can be both a verb or a noun), or words related to laughter such as *jieyi* 解頤, 'to smile, to laugh'; *xiexue* 諧噱, 'so humorous as to cause laughter'; *qiyan* 啓顏, 'to laugh, to smile'; *kaiyan* 開顏, 'to smile'; and *xuanqu* 軒渠, 'heartily laughing'.[25]

On the whole, the various surviving collections of jokes—reconstructed on the basis of fragments or transmitted as manuscripts and printed versions—represent a derivative genre, produced by gathering and cataloguing previous material. Their authors were compilers, sometimes known only by their pen names, or were associated with given texts by later compilers merely because of their reputation. Joke collections are texts that defy attribution of authorship, as jokes and humorous tales are orally transmitted and can be reshaped according to the situation and performance; however, despite being considered a type of folk literature (and with good reason, since their motifs and stories can be an interesting source for comparative approaches in folk studies), the jokebooks transmitted from premodern China are written in a literary language and were produced by *literati*, and they should be considered accordingly.[26] These stories, once recorded as written texts, albeit ones not original in their content, inform us about the process of selection and reshaping of the material, and provide useful information about the compiler and the society in which the text was produced.

## THE FIRST TWO COLLECTIONS OF JOKES: HUMOUR AND LAUGHTER FROM EARLY MEDIEVAL CHINA

Culture affects the forms which humour takes in a society and the perception of what it is appropriate or inappropriate to laugh at in a given situation—that is, the type of targets and sources of humour (objects, roles, etc.). As far as Chinese jestbooks are concerned, readers need a certain amount of knowledge of premodern Chinese culture to appreciate most of the anecdotes recorded in these texts. However, there are also examples in which jokes can be immediately understood without a deep knowledge of the source culture, because they concern general targets found in other societies too, or because they play on simple situations of incongruity which are easy to understand. In the following sections, I will provide two examples of jestbooks that are representative of the tastes and cultures of their particular times.

### THE *XIAOLIN* (FOREST OF LAUGHTER)

A text entitled *Xiaolin* is mentioned for the first time in the 'xiaoshuo' category of the bibliographical chapter of the *Book of Sui*, where it is also ascribed to Handan Chun 邯鄲淳 (*fl.* 220), a talented official. In the official histories, the few biographical details included inform us about his service at the court of prince Cao Zhi 曹植 (192–232),[27] with whom he exchanged literary compositions and probably humorous stories.[28] These accounts never mention the *Xiaolin*, but—if he ever was the author—considering the low status attributed to writings of this kind, this is not an unusual occurrence. The place of the *Xiaolin* in literary history is important because, even if collections of anecdotes were already an established textual type, the *Xiaolin* is the first ever collection of stories exclusively designed for entertainment, as its title suggests. It was only with its appearance that collections of this kind started receiving a literary treatment. Accordingly, it was possible for a text like the *Xiaolin* to be created at this time because by the third to fourth century to be able to joke or compose humorous literature had become an appreciated ability. In his *Wenxin diaolong* 文心雕龍 (The literary mind and the carving of dragons) (chapter 45) Liu Xie 劉勰 (ca. 465–ca. 521) described the period as follows:

[Cao Cao, Cao Pi and Cao Zhi], important as their positions were, all showed great respect for others who had outstanding literary talent. Hence many talented writers gathered around them like vapours and clouds. [...] Goblets in hand, they proudly showed their elegant style and, moving with leisurely grace while they feasted, composed songs with a swing of the brush, and out of the well-ground ink created witty pieces that served as subjects of talk and laughter.[29]

The collection is not listed in bibliographical chapters written after the Song period, the period in which it probably also disappeared as a complete text; however, twenty-nine stories[30] have been retrieved from traditional encyclopaedias, in particular, the *Taiping yulan* and the *Taiping guangji*. Given the fragmentary nature of the text, it is not easy either to make assumptions about its internal organisation or to get a clear picture of the author's selection criteria. Nevertheless, *Xiaolin* narratives can still provide some insight as to what themes and subjects were considered humorous in the early medieval period (third to sixth century CE). Most of the transmitted stories are numskull tales, but historical anecdotes or look-like-historical stories are also present.

Numskull tales are stories based on the foolish behaviour of the protagonist, who acts or says things that go against normal logic, or ignores basic common-sense notions. These tales are often enjoyable independently of the cultural differences of their source culture, since their narratives are simple and the cultural elements, if present, often do not overshadow the storylines of the anecdotes. They can be humorous tales, or retold as a didactic aid, and they are found across a wide range of traditions and cultures around the world.[31] *Xiaolin* numskull tales feature anonymous protagonists, sometimes only identified by their place of origin ('a man of Chu', 'a man of Qi', etc.), in a way that makes them closely resemble stories of foolish behaviour used allegorically in the works of the masters of thought of pre-imperial China.[32] Others are identified by their city of residence ('a man of Taiyuan', 'a man of Pingyuan', etc.) or even more generically by their provenance from the North or the South (a southern simpleton goes north or vice versa). Tales of the last type are more representative of the early medieval period, since they betray a social tension that reflects the political and cultural situation of these centuries, which witnessed first the appearance of three different political entities (Wei in the North, Shu in the south-west, and Wu in the south-east, in the third century) out of the ashes of the Han Empire, and then a division between Northern[33] and Southern dynasties (fourth to sixth century). As Christie Davis has pointed out, jokes of this kind cannot be considered true ethnic jokes, as these are more a product of modern societies.[34] Rather, they target 'a group who lives on the edge of the joke-tellers' social universe'[35] and 'the relationship between the joke-tellers and the butts of their jokes is one of centre and periphery within a common culture'.[36] The different regional political entities perceived themselves, in turn, as the legitimate successors of the former imperial legacy, so the centre-periphery point of view changed according to the position of the one who was speaking or writing, but—even at a later date—the tension was not a sign of ethnic conflict or hostility.[37]

Some stories are brief and end with a punch-line, a feature which makes them appear similar to the stories collected in the *Philogelos* (The

Laughter-Lover, fourth to fifth century), the first collection of jokes transmitted by the Mediterranean tradition.[38] Take the following story, for example:

> A man was going to pay a condolence visit and wanted to give something to contribute to the sacrificial rites. He asked: 'What kind of thing should I give?' One man answered: 'Money, clothes, cereal, and silk, whatever you have!' So he gave one bushel of beans in support to the mourner, and put it before the mourning son, saying: 'I have nothing, but I will help with one bushel of big beans in your support'. The mourning son cried aloud: 'What will I do!?' The man said: 'You can make fermented soy beans!' The son in mourning again cried: 'Poor me!!' and that fellow said: 'If I knew you were so poor, I would have given you another bushel!'[39]

The anecdote involves a misunderstanding generated by a wordplay. Its anonymous protagonist is a stupid man who is unable to decode linguistic information in a specific situation, mourning. This inability leads him to understand expressions of grief (like 'what will I do!?', *naihe* 奈何, and 'Poor me', *guqiong* 孤窮) in a literal way, providing a source of laughter. Even if jokes which play with language can sometimes be difficult to translate, this one does not present any obstacle in English and can be understood without the aid of any notes. Some numskull stories are instead more literarily refined, as they play with quotations from canonical texts or present more narrative details. Consider the following story:

> A man of Chu (*churen* 楚人) was very poor. He read the following sentence in the *Huainan fang* 淮南方 (Methods of Huainan): 'Once one obtains the leaf that the mantis, waiting for the cicada, uses to cover itself, it is possible to make oneself invisible.' Therefore, he stood under a tree and faced upward to pick a leaf. He saw a mantis holding a leaf and waiting for the cicada and as he was picking it the leaf fell from the tree. There were already some fallen leaves under the tree, so it was not possible to distinguish which was the one that had just fallen; so he gathered several pecks of leaves and went back home. One by one he used the leaves to cover himself, [each time] asking his wife: 'Can you see me?' In the beginning, the wife was constantly answering, 'Yes I do', but after an entire day she got extremely tired of it and deceived [him], saying: 'I don't see you'. He then gasped in delight and, holding the leaf, he entered the city market and snatched goods away right under people's eyes. Therefore, the county's officer tied him up and brought him to the county government office. The county magistrate listened to the confession, and the accused told the story from beginning to end. The magistrate laughed out loud and released him without any punishment.[40]

This story of a simpleton, who is deceived by the belief that an object can make him invisible, is based on the same motif that appears in the more famous story, in the West, of Calandrino and the heliotrope,[41] which Stith Thompson's index lists as a sub-category of the motif 'gullible fools': J2337 'dupe persuaded that he is invisible'. In this Chinese story, there are no friends who tease the protagonist but his wife is the one who lies about the invisibility, only to stop the husband from annoying her.[42] The popularity of this story is attested by its presence in later compilations, in particular[43] the *Xiaozan* 笑贊 (Appraisals of laughter) by Zhao Nanxing 趙南星 (1550–1627), where it is abridged but provided with a commentary explaining the story's didactic value, a convention of this anthology.[44]

*Xiaolin* numskull tales present a variety of narrative elements which can also be verified in later collections. For example, we find the motif of the 'stupid son-in-law' (*dainüxi* 呆女婿),[45] which will appear as a sub-type of numskull tales in several later collections.[46]

Six *Xiaolin* stories show, instead, features typical of Wei–Jin historical anecdotes, in particular ones found in the *Shishuo xinyu* 世説新語 (New account of tales of the world) by Liu Yiqing 劉義慶 (403–444), a collection of historical anecdotes that embodies early medieval Chinese *elite* lifestyle and culture. These stories present historical or quasi-historical characters. Three stories target the stinginess of the protagonist, and their narrative style is comparable to that of the stories gathered in the 'Jian se' 劍嗇 (Frugality and Stinginess) chapter of the *Shishuo xinyu*.[47] In the *Shishuo xinyu* as well as in the *Xiaolin*, stinginess can be seen as an inborn personality trait and hence as a natural impulse.[48] Accordingly, the description of a trait that would be considered a flaw today is probably designed to bring a benign smile to the reader's lips. One story is centred on the excessive affection that a man felt for his wife, and implies a Confucian view of the theme; like those about stinginess, it is better understood if the reader is acquainted with early medieval Chinese culture. The other two are about the fatness of their protagonists, a brother and his sister. These stories inform us about a type of humour which targeted physical features. The more famous story of the two reads as follows:

> Zhao Boweng 趙伯翁 was very fat (*fei da* 肥大). On a summer day, he was lying asleep drunk, when his grandson, who was only a few years old, climbed up on his stomach to play; so he put eight or nine plums inside the man's navel. The day after, the plums were very rotten and the juice came out. Crying, he said to his family: 'My intestine is rotten, I'm going to die'. The day after, the plum–stones rolled out from his belly, so he realized that it was his grandson who had put them inside his navel.[49]

The practice of pointing at one's physical features to bring laughter is evidenced also in the historical writings of the early medieval period as a form of entertainment performed by jesters for their lord. The biography of Wu Zhi 吳 質 (d. 230), a high official of the Wei court, records[50] that during a banquet held at his house he instructed the jester to 'speak about fatness and thinness' (*shuo feishou* 説肥瘦),[51] pointing at some important guests, thinking that everyone would enjoy it. Witty remarks about one's appearance were exchanged during social conversations among the elite, as is recorded in the 'Paitiao' 排調 (Taunting and Teasing) chapter of the *Shishuo xinyu*, in which the exchanging of mockery is instrumental in showing the ability of the conversationalists to respond promptly and outwit their rival.[52] Sometimes these comical comments are even reworked into humorous literary pieces.[53] The *Xiaolin* story about Zhao Boweng presents a mild variant of this kind of humour as no one explicitly targets Zhao Boweng's fatness to elicit laughter, yet his fatness is certainly what sets the story in motion. His big belly is large enough to transform his navel into a casket of fruits, without him even noticing. This story, as well as the one about his sister, is later found in the 'Fei shou' 肥瘦 (Fat and thin) chapter of the *Leilin zashuo* 類林雜說 (Fragmentary writings from the forest of categories, 1189), a collection of biographical anecdotes arranged by subject.[54] In this text the two *Xiaolin* stories are grouped with those about actual historical figures, such as Han dynasty official Chen Ping 陳平 (d. 178 BCE), Southern scholar Shen Yue 沈約 (441–513), and Han dynasty general Dong Zhuo 董卓 (d. 192). Even if the protagonists of these *Xiaolin* stories are not found elsewhere, their narratives show them as plausible historical characters; at least they appeared to be such to the twelfth-century compiler, who saw these stories as similar to historical biographical narratives. The Zhao Boweng story, like other stories of the same kind, gained a renewed popularity during the folk literature movement. Zhou Zuoren, who had also translated Grimm Brothers' s fairytales and those of Andersen, and who had a strong interest in children's literature,[55] reworked this *Xiaolin* story into a nursery rhyme and published it along with several others in his *Ertong zashi shi* 兒童雜事詩 (Poems on random subjects for children),[56] later republished with Feng Zikai's cartoon(s) as a commentary (1950).[57]

## THE *QIYAN LU* (RECORDS OF BRIGHT SMILES)

The *Qiyan lu* is listed along with the *Xiaolin* in the 'xiaoshuo' section of the bibliographical chapters of both the *Jiu* 舊 and the *Xin Tang shu* 新唐書 (Old and New book of Tang), and it is normally considered the second oldest collection of jokes after the *Xiaolin*. The bibliographical chapters attribute the work to the early Sui official Hou Bai 侯白 (*fl.* 581), but the text was probably an anonymous stratified text which was connected to Hou Bai because he was famous for his wittiness. He is also the protagonist of several anecdotes ascribed to this text. Around the Yuan dynasty (1279–1368), the *Qiyan lu* disappeared from official catalogues and so probably from the imperial archives, but its anecdotes were preserved in several encyclopaedias and collectanea (such as the *Taiping guangji*).[58] A manuscript version of it (Stein no. 610), dated 723, was discovered and retrieved from the caves of Dunhuang (Gansu province). As such, this is the only specimen that survives intact among the collections of humorous stories of pre-Song times. Even if it is not possible to say if it is a complete edition or a section of it, this Dunhuang edition is also the only specimen that comes closer to what is commonly perceived as a book in format.[59] It is, therefore, an invaluable source to investigate the typology of jestbooks. The manuscript is neatly written and does not present any changes or corrections. The body of the texts, with its division into chapters and anecdotes, is clearly shown. According to Zhu Yao, this means that the scroll was written formally; it was not a draft copy, written down for practical use.[60] The manuscript is divided into four titled chapters—'Lun nan' 論難 (To argue and rebut), 'Bian jie' 辯捷 (Quick to argue), 'Hun wang' 昏忘 (Confused and forgetful), and 'Chao qiao' 嘲誚 (Mockery and blame)—with a total of forty stories.

The first chapter is centred on rhetorical performances; in particular, five out of seven stories feature the jester Shi Dongtong 石動筩—who presumably lived at the court of Emperor Gaozu of the Northern Qi 北齊高祖 (496–547)—confronting Buddhist monks and experts in traditional learning (*ru* 儒). Invariably the jester, twisting and reworking passages from the texts of both traditions, leaves his opponents speechless and unable to reply, greatly delighting the ruler.[61] The recorded dialogues are reminiscent of medieval inter-religious court debates and in line with the tradition of 'pure conversations' (*qingtan* 清談),[62] a type of social conversation among the cultured elite, which promoted rhetorical displays and clever argumentation. The second chapter better represents this kind of social activity, recording witty remarks by historical personalities, of both the Northern and the Southern dynasties. In the following story, Xu Ling 徐陵 (507–583), a famous poet and official who served two Southern dynasties (the Liang and then the Chen), is sent on a diplomatic mission to the North and mocked by his northern host. However, like his opponent, he has the *bian jie* quality suggested by the title of the chapter; he is quick witted, he has a sharp mind and great eloquence, which helps him to win over his opponent:

> While he was in office as Senior Recorder, Xu Ling of Chen was sent as an envoy to the Sui. At that time Emperor Wen of Sui 隋文帝 (r. 581–604) was in Luoyang, and, among the officials selected to be at court, there was one who had sharp eloquence (*bian jie*) and whom was ordered to confront the southern envoy. At that time, it was the beginning of summer and it was mildly hot and Xu was a Southerner, [so] the Sui official made fun of Xu Ling saying: 'Today's heat is all brought by officer Xu'. Xu Ling answered back: 'In the past, when Wang Su 王肅 (464–501; an official of a Southern dynasty) entered Luoyang, he helped the northern Wei (386–535, a northern dynasty) to establish their bureaucratic system and rituals; today I came here to show you the difference between hot and cold'. No one had anything to reply.[63]

The twenty-sixth chapter of the *Chenshu* 陳書 (Book of Chen), a Tang dynasty historical text, records this event but places it a little bit earlier (548), when Xu was still serving the Liang (502–557) and in the North there was the Eastern Wei dynasty (534–550). This evidence indicates a blurred distinction between historical and fictional records. The fourth chapter still features mostly historical characters and testifies to a medieval form of entertainment among peers. The following story features Xu Zhicai 徐之才 (d. 572), a famous early medieval physician, and Wang Yuanjing 王元景, a literary man, both from the

# 10 APPROACHING JOKES AND JESTBOOKS IN PREMODERN CHINA    213

northern dynasties, making fun of each other by playing on the characters compounding their names:

> Xu Zhicai of the Northern Qi was later enfeoffed as Prince of Xiyang (east of today's Huanggang prefecture in the Hubei), and the Imperial Secretary Wang Yuanjing joked with Zhicai saying: 'Why are you named Zhicai 之才 (talented)? As far as I can see, it should be Feicai 乏才 (without talent)'. Zhicai immediately answered back and, making fun of Yuanjing's surname, said: 'As far as the character "wang" 王 of your name is concerned, if you put the "word" (*yan* 言) character next to it, it becomes "to deceive" (*kuang* 誆); if you combine it with "dog" (*chuan* 犬), it is "fool" (*kuang* 狂), if you add a neck and feet, it becomes "horse" (*ma* 馬); and if you apply horns and a tail, it becomes "goat" (*yang* 羊)'. Yuanjing thereupon had nothing to reply.[64]

The story, which appears *verbatim* as part of the biography of Xu Zhicai in the *Beiqishu* 北齊書 (Book of Northern Qi),[65] bears witness to a word play based on Chinese script called 'chaizi' 拆字 (dissecting characters). As Andrew Plaks has noted, these kinds of games can be considered 'visual puns',[66] because they consist in dissecting or combining characters in order to imply a diverse meaning (e.g., here 'dog' 犬 as a radical assumes the form of 犭 and combined with the character 王 makes 狂, 'fool', an insult directed at Wang Yuanjing). In early imperial times, and in particular during the Later Han period, the practice of dissecting characters was employed as a way to interpret and reveal political prophecies forged by officials in order to justify and legitimise the rise to power of a person or a dynasty.[67] But, as the anecdotes recorded in the *Shishuo xinyu* show,[68] already by the end of the third century this practice had come to be used playfully among the educated elite. The word *chao* 嘲, 'to mock, to ridicule', in the title of the fourth chapter alludes, instead, to a codified form of entertainment, which consisted in 'mocking' (*chao*) someone or something, by playing with characters or composing derisory couplets. This chapter records an anecdote about the Tang poet Pei Lüe 裴略 (late sixth century), who, having failed the examination and lost the chance to obtain an official position, informs high official Wen Yanbo 溫彥博 (573–636) about this. Wen Yanbo is busy talking to his friend Du Ruhui 杜如晦 (585–630) and does not pay attention to Pei, but when Pei introduces himself boasting his skills in writing and ridicule (*chao*), he gets Wen Yanbo's attention. Yanbo then asks him to ridicule the bamboo out in the courtyard, and Pei says:

> 'Bamboo, whose greenery the wind blows swiftly, makes it through the winter without its leaves being withered, it passes through spring without ripen sprouts, and its empty heart cannot serve literati and officials of the state. What use are the knots growing on its surface?' Yanbo was greatly pleased.[69]

The story goes on with Pei inventing phrases on another object, a wall, leaving his audience so pleased that, in the end, he gets a position. His performance displays a skilful use of language and erudition, as he describes the bamboo through features which allegorically allude to the scholar—this being an already established allegorical *topos*—and ultimately to himself. The sound of the wind which blows 'swiftly' (*susu* 蕭蕭) allegorically alludes to a dignified and solemn appearance; the empty heart of the bamboo represents the ability of a scholar to store knowledge, and bamboo knots, which make the plant firm, his moral integrity. The story shows how the Tang dynasty's educated society appreciated those who combined literary ability and playfulness. Pei Lüe's story later appears in the *Da Tang xinyu* 大唐新語 (New Accounts of the Great Tang), 807, a text written by Liu Su 劉肅 (*fl.* 806–820) as an imitation of the *Shishuo xinyu*. Liu Su's work changed 'the original genre from the character writing of the gentry into didactic writing for the gentry'[70] in order to provide models of self-cultivation and behaviour, and expanded the categories which referred to the moral qualities of a character. Nevertheless, it preserved the category dedicated to jokes among the educated elite, here called 'Xie xue' 諧謔 (Humour and jests), testifying to the iconic social import of these humorous conversations.

The *Qiyan lu* stories presented above are linked to the cultural elite and represent a highly refined form of humour, which requires familiarity with rhetoric, erudite allusions, wordplay, and literary artistry in order to be fully appreciated. Since most of the *Xiaolin* stories transmitted are numskull tales, this could create the wrong impression that the *Xiaolin* and the *Qiyan lu* are directed to two different kinds of audience. However, the Dunhuang *Qiyan lu* has a third chapter dedicated to 'forgetful' people, forgetfulness being a quality of several numskull protagonists of the stories collected in it. The chapter presents a varied set of fools, from people who forget their own wife or the actions they just performed to ones who do not recognise their own reflection in mirrors or water; from a man who mistakes tadpoles for his beans, or a vase for a hat, to a scholar who fails to distinguish a monkey from a goat. The presence of this chapter in what is otherwise an extremely literary collection disproves the simplistic division between elite and popular taste. Moreover, the variety of the anecdotes collected in this edition would suggest an affinity in terms of formal features between the *Qiyan lu* and the *Xiaolin*. While, from what we know today, the latter collection mostly features numskull tales, it may well have originally included a larger number of *literati* stories than the few which have been transmitted.

## Concluding Remarks

Collections of humorous anecdotes still represent an understudied field of research in sinological studies. Their marginal cultural status within their own source tradition has also affected their history as research objects. However, their value as a repository of information on material culture, social practices, tastes, stereotypes, and, in particular, with regard to humour qualifies them as a literary source that demands more attention, as this chapter has shown. The amusing tales of ancient Chinese numskulls provide themes and topics of universal humour, which can contribute to cross-cultural comparisons. On the other hand, anecdotes about *literati* and officials clearly show how humour is a culturally determined phenomenon, since culture affects humorous taste and narrative features. The humour historian must be able to decode the explicit and implicit cultural signs in the texts and to identify possible allusions, revisions, reinterpretations, and even distortions of specific themes and cultural features that can create humour. A side of the story remains in the shadows, that is, how the collections were circulated and received. As I have pointed out, these texts remained at the margins of the discourse on literary tradition and were seldom discussed or quoted in the transmitted texts. This is especially true for those collections that were created before the Song dynasty, those on which the analysis in this chapter is focused. Once we assume that the jestbooks were a literary product of the educated elite, a number of further questions arise: in which occasions were these texts read, and how? Were they silently read or used as a handbook in social conversations? Were they kept with care or quickly copied on cheap supports? The transmitted texts do not offer valuable information about the extra-textual environment that surrounded jestbooks, or maybe clues are scattered in the florilegia of texts, still waiting to be discovered.

## Notes

1. For a critical approach to this period, see Dolezelova-Velingerova and Wang, 'Introduction'.
2. The earliest History of Chinese literature, *Zhongguo wenxue shi* 中國文學史 (History of Chinese literature), by Lin Chuanjia 林傳甲 (1877–1922), dates to 1904 (printed in 1910).
3. See Owen, 'The End of the Past'.
4. Lin, 'Introduction', xxxi. See also Hu, 'The Confucian Politics of Appearance'.
5. For a detailed account of Lin Yutang's enterprise, see Qian, *Lin Yutang and China's Search for Modern Rebirth*, 96–125. See also Rea, *The Age of Irreverence*, 132–58.
6. Chey, 'Youmo and the Chinese Sense of Humour', 3; Qian, *Lin Yutang and China's Search for Modern Rebirth*, 103.
7. Laughlin, *The literature of leisure*, 103–38.
8. Qian Suoqiao (*Lin Yutang and China's Search for Modern Rebirth*, 96) affirms that: 'the discourse of humor in modern Chinese literature and culture was very much a bilingual practice of cross-cultural translation'.
9. Zhou Zuoren published his first collection of jokes, the *Kucha'an xiaohua xuan* 苦茶庵笑話選 (A selection of jokes from the bitter tea studio), in 1933.
10. A second wave occurred between the 1950s and the mid-60s.
11. For a seminal account of this movement see Hung, *Going to the People*.
12. Collections of jokes are defined as such in both Nienhauser, *The Indiana Companion*, 78, and in Wilkinson, *Chinese History*, 414.
13. On the bibliographical chapters see Wilkinson, *Chinese History*, 940–44.
14. Kern, 'The Han construction of Warring States textual lineages', 61.

15. The 'Zi' 子 category encompassed texts divided according to different intellectual lineages such as the 'Ru jia' 儒家 (Confucian tradition) and 'Dao jia' 道家 (Daoist tradition).
16. Allen, 'Narrative Genre', 283.
17. Wu, 'From Xiaoshuo to Fiction'.
18. For an overview of Chinese traditional encyclopaedia and collectanea see Wilkinson, *Chinese History*, 955–64; Tian, 'Literary Learning'.
19. See Kurz, 'The Compilation and Publication', 46.
20. Wilkinson, *Chinese History*, 650.
21. See Luo, *The Drunken Man's Talk*, xvi, 53–57.
22. See Harbsmeier, *Language and Logic*, 26–29, 44–46.
23. See Lévy, 'Notes bibliographiques', 85, n. 46.
24. Chen, *Zhongguo xiaoshuo xushi moshi de zhuanbian*, 169. Wu's preface is translated and discussed in Rea, *The Age of Irreverence*, 19.
25. For a description of other titles, see Rea, *The Age of Irreverence*, 22. For an overview of premodern jestbooks, see Baccini, 'Forest of Laughter and Traditional Chinese Jestbooks'.
26. This is especially true for collections created before the Ming dynasty (1368–1644). During the Ming merchants were also readers of *xiaoshuo*, see Wang, 'Lun Ming Qing shiqi', 35.
27. *Sanguo zhi*, 21. 603, n. 1.
28. A well-known anecdote records that in order to impress Handan Chun, Cao Zhi recited 'thousands of words from humorous works'; see Qian, *Spirit and Self*, 35.
29. Wu, *Written at Imperial Command*, 24.
30. Lu Xun provided the most extensive collection of fragments in his *Gu xiaoshuo gouchen* 古小説鉤沉 (Ancient anecdotes retrieved, 1912).
31. For a description of the main features of numskull tales, see Luomala, 'Numskull Clan and Tales', 160–61.
32. On these allegorical tales, see Els and Queen, *Between History and Philosophy*.
33. The ruling elite of the Norther dynasties were of Tabgach (Tuoba) ethnicity.
34. Davies, 'Fooltowns', 11–14.
35. Davies, 'Fooltowns', 12.
36. Davies, 'Ethnic humor, hostility, and aggression', 418.
37. For a presentation of the sociopolitical situation, see Holcombe, 'Was Medieval China Medieval? (Post Han – Mid Tang)'.
38. On the *Philogelos* see Hansen, *Anthology*, 272–76.
39. *Taiping guangji*, 262. 2052.
40. *Taiping yulan*, 946. 4201.
41. The story is recorded in the *Decameron*, VIII.3.
42. For an example of a study in folklore which involves Chinese tradition see Ding Naitong, 'A Comparative Study of the Three Chinese and North-American Indian Folktale Types'.
43. Wang, *Lidai xiaohua ji*, 288.
44. On this collection see Lutz Bieg, 'Laughter in China' and Zhao Jingshen, 'Zhongguo xiaohua tiyao', 52–54.
45. Gu, 'Zhongguo zuizao de xiaoshuo jia: Handan Chun', 79.

46. See for example the stories: 'The stupid son in law' 呆婿 or 'Ice drink' 凍水, in Feng Menglong's *Xiaofu*; Hsu, *Feng Menglong's Treasury of Laughs*, 175–76.
47. One of these stories may be found in Baccini, 'Forest of Laughter and Traditional Chinese Jestbooks', 247.
48. Qian, *Spirit and Self*, 135.
49. *Taiping yulan* 371. 1713; a variant is recorded in *Taiping yulan* 968. 4294.
50. This story is recorded in the 'Unofficial biography of Wu Zhi' 吳質別傳, recorded in Pei Songzhi's 裴松之 (372–451) commentary on the *Sanguo zhi* 三國志 (Records of the Three Kingdoms), 21. 609. See Qiao Xiaodong, 'Handan Chun *Xiaolin* yu "Xiaolinti" wenti duli de shifan yiyi', 158.
51. Hu Shiying, *Huaben xiaoshuo gailun*, 11.
52. See, for example, anecdote no. 18 and no. 21 in this *Shishuo xinyu* chapter; Liu, *Shih-shuohsin-yü*, 441–42.
53. In the *Shishuo xinyu*, chapter 25, story no. 7, we find the poem 'Touze Qin Ziyu' 頭責秦子羽 (Qin Ziyu's head reproaches him), in which the head of Zheng Xu is compared to a pestle; Liu, *Shih-shuohsin-yü*, 435.
54. The text was compiled during the Jin 金 dynasty (1115–1234) by Wang Pengshou 王朋壽.
55. On this topic see Hung, *Going to the people*, 107–34.
56. The nursery rhyme reads as follows: 'It is usual to find naughty children, but the one of the Zhao family is the most extraordinary, he has put plums into his grandfather's navel, the old man was so worried that he was almost about to die' 小孩淘氣平常有，惟獨趙家最出奇，祖父肚臍種李子，幾乎急殺老頭兒. See Zhong, *Zhong Shuhe sanwen*, 381.
57. See Barmé, *An Artistic Exile*, 286–87.
58. Wang Liqi in his *Lidai xiaohua ji* collected six different editions of the *Qiyan lu* from different encyclopaedia and collectanea.
59. Dong, *Qiyan lu jianzhu*, 7.
60. Zhu, *Qiyan lu chengshu kao*, 140.
61. These stories, along with others from the *Taiping guangji*, are translated in Otto, *Fools are Everywere*, 18, 86, 147, 162–63, 182–83; Shi Dongtong's name is translated literally as 'Moving Bucket' (*dongtong*). The anecdote about Shi Dongtong confronting traditional scholars is analysed in He, 'Talking Back to the Master', 246–47.
62. See Assandri, 'Inter-religious Debate', 18–19.
63. Dong, *Qiyan lu jianzhu*, 20.
64. Dong, *Qiyan lu jianzhu*, 58.
65. *Beiqi shu*, 33. 447.
66. Plaks, 'Riddle and Enigma', 232.
67. For more on this topic, see Lü, *Power of the Words*.
68. Liu, *Shih-shuohsin-yü*, 313–14 (story no. 1, 2, 3), 425 (story no. 24).
69. Dong, *Qiyan lu jianzhu*, 68.
70. Qian, *Spirit and Self*, 211.

# BIBLIOGRAPHY

Allen, Sarah. 'Narrative Genre'. In *The Oxford Handbook of Classical Chinese Literature*, edited by Wiebke Denecke, Wai-Yee Li, and Xiaofei Tian, 273–87. New York: Oxford University Press, 2017.

Assandri, Friederike. 'Inter-religious Debate at the Court of the Early Tang: An Introduction to Daoxuan's Ji gujin Fo Dao lunheng'. In *From Early Tang Court Debates to China's Peaceful Rise*, edited by Friederike Assandri and Dora Martins, 15–32. Amsterdam: Amsterdam University Press, 2009.

Baccini, Giulia. 'Forest of Laughter and Traditional Chinese Jestbooks'. In *Encyclopedia of Humor Studies*, edited by Salvatore Attardo, 246–48. Los Angeles: SAGE Publications, 2014.

Barmé, Geremie. *An Artist Exile: A Life of Feng Zikai (1898–1975)*. Berkeley: University of California Press, 2002.

*Beiqi shu* 北齊書. Li Baiyao 李百藥 (564–647). Beijing: Zhonghua shuju, 1972.

Bieg, Lutz. 'Laughter in China during the Ming and Qing Era: Preliminary Comments on Zhao Nanxing's *Xiao Zan*, Kubin'. In *Symbols of Anguish: In Search of Melancholy in China*, edited by Wolfgang Kubin and Helmut Martin, 55–75. Bern: Peter Lang, 2001.

Chen, Pingyuan 陳平原. *Zhongguo xiaoshuo xushi moshi de zhuanbian* 中國小說敘事模式的轉變. Shanghai: Shanghai renmin chubanshe, 1988.

Chey, Jocelyn. 'Youmo and the Chinese Sense of Humour'. In *Humour in Chinese Life and Letters: Classical and Traditional Approaches*, edited by Jocelyn Chey and Jessica Milner Davies, 1–29. Hong Kong: Hong Kong University Press, 2011.

Davies, Christie. 'Ethnic Humor, Hostility, and Aggression: a Reply to Elliott Oring'. *Humor: International Journal of Humor Research* 4, no. 3/4 (1991): 415–22.

Davies, Christie. 'Fooltowns: Traditional and Modern Local, Regional and Ethnic Jokes about Stupidity'. In *Jokes and their Relations to Society*, edited by Christie Davies, 11–26. Berlin, Boston: De Gruyter Mouton, 1998.

Ding Naitong 丁乃通. 'A Comparative Study of the Three Chinese and North-American Indian Folktale Types'. *Asian Folklore Studies* 44, no. 1 (1985): 39–50.

Dolezelova-Velingerova, Milena and David Der-wei Wang. 'Introduction'. In *The Appropriation of Cultural Capital: China's May Fourth Project*, edited by Milena Dolezelova-Velingerova and Oldrich Kral, 1–30. Cambridge, MA and London: Harvard University Press, 2001.

Dong Zhixiao 董志. *Qiyan lu jianzhu* 啓顏錄淺注. Beijing: Zhonghua shuju, 2014.

Els, Paul van, and Sarah A. Queen, eds. *Between History and Philosophy: Anecdotes in Early China*. Albany: State University of New York Press, 2017.

Gu, Nong 顧農. 'Zhongguo zuizao de xiaoshuojia: Handan Chun' 中國最早的小說家: 邯鄲淳. *Gudian wenxue zhishi*, no. 4 (2000): 77–80.

Hansen, William F. *Anthology of Ancient Greek Popular Literature*. Bloomington: Indiana University Press, 1998.

Harbsmeier, Christoph. *Language and Logic*. Part 1, vol. 7 of *Science and Civilization in China*, edited by Joseph Needham. Cambridge: Cambridge University Press, 1998.

He, Yuming. 'Talking Back to the Master: Play and Subversion in Entertainment Uses of the Analects'. In *The Analects. Norton Critical Editions*, translated by Simon Leys, edited by Michael Nylan, 243–57. New York: W. W. Norton, 2014.

Holcombe, Charles. 'Was Medieval China Medieval? (Post Han – Mid Tang)'. In *A Companion to Chinese History*, edited by Michael Szonyi, 106–17. Chichester, West Sussex, UK: Wiley-Blackwell, 2017.

Hsu Pi-Ching. *Feng Menglong's Treasury of Laughs: A Seventeenth-Century Anthology of Traditional Chinese Humour*. Boston: Brill, 2015.

Hu, Weihe. 'The Confucian Politics of Appearance: And Its Impact on Chinese Humor'. *Philosophy East and West* 54, no. 4 (2004): 514–32.

Hu Shiying 胡士瑩. *Huaben xiaoshuo gailun* 話本小說概論. Beijing: Zhonghua, 1980.

Hung, Chang-tai. *Going to the People: Chinese Intellectuals and Folk Literature, 1918–1937*. Cambridge, MA: Council on East Asian Studies, Harvard University, 1985.

Kern, Martin. 'The Han Construction of Warring States Textual Lineages'. In *The Cambridge History of Chinese Literature*, edited by Kang-i Sun Chang and Stephen Owen, 60–66. Cambridge: Cambridge University Press, 2010.

Kurz, Johannes L. 'The Compilation and Publication of the *Taiping Yulan* and the *Cefu Yuangui*'. *Extrême-Orient Extrême-Occident* (2007): 39–76.

Laughlin, Charles A. *The literature of leisure and Chinese modernity*. Honolulu: University of Hawaii press, 2008.

Lévy, André. 'Notes bibliographiques pour une histoire des 'histoires pour rire' en Chine'. *Études sur le conte et le roman chinois*, 67–95. Paris: École Française d'Extrême-Orient, 1971.

Lin Yutang. 'Introduction'. In *Chinese Wit and Humour*, edited by George Kao, xxix–xxxv. New York: Coward-McCann, 1946.

Liu, Yiqing, Liu Xiaobiao. *Shih-shuo hsin-yü: A New Account of Tales of the World*. Translated by Richard B. Mather. Ann Arbor: Center for Chinese Studies, The University of Michigan, 2017.

Lü, Zongli. *Power of the Words: Chen Prophecy in Chinese Politics, AD 265–618*. Peter Lang: Oxford, 2003.

Luo, Ye. *The Drunken Man's Talk: Tales from Medieval China*. Translated by Alister D. Inglis. Seattle: University of Washington Press, 2015.

Luomala, Katharine. 'Numskull Clans and Tales: Their Structure and Function in Asymmetrical Joking Relationships'. *The Journal of American Folklore* 79, no. 311 (1966): 157–94.

Nienhauser, William H. *The Indiana Companion to Traditional Chinese Literature*. Taipei: SMC Publishing, 2003.

Otto, Beatrice K. *Fools Are Everywhere: The Court Jester Around the World*. Chicago: University of Chicago Press, 2000.

Owen, Stephen. 'The End of the Past: Rewriting Chinese Literary History in the Early Republic'. In *The Appropriation of Cultural Capital: China's May Fourth Project*, edited by Milena Dolezelova-Velingerova and Oldrich Kral, 167–92. Cambridge, MA and London: Harvard University Press, 2001.

Plaks, Andrew. 'Riddle and Enigma in Chinese Civilisation'. In *Untying the Knot: On Riddles and Other Enigmatic Modes*, edited by Gālīt Ḥazzān-Ròqēm, 227–36. New York: Oxford University Press, 1996.

Qian, Nanxiu. *Spirit and Self in Medieval China: the Shih-shuo hsin-yü and its legacy*. Honolulu: University of Hawai'i Press, 2001.

Qian, Suoqiao. *Lin Yutang and China's Search for Modern Rebirth*. Singapore: Palgrave Macmillan, 2017.

Qiao, Xiaodong 橋孝冬. 'Handan Chun *Xiaolin* yu "Xiaolin ti" wenti duli de shifan yiyi' 邯鄲淳《笑林》與'笑林體'文體獨立的示範意義. *Pu Songling yanjiu*, no. 2 (2017): 150–60.

Rea, Christopher. *The Age of Irreverence: a New History of Laughter in China*. Oakland, CA: University of California Press, 2016.

*Sanguo zhi* 三國志. Chen Shou 陳壽 (233–97). Beijing: Zhonghua shuju, 1971.

*Taiping guangji* 太平廣記. Li Fang 李昉 (925–96) et al. Beijing: Zhonghua shuju, 1961.

*Taiping yulan* 太平禦覽. Li Fang 李昉 (925–96) et al. Beijing: Zhonghua shuju, 1960.

Tian, Xiaofei. 'Literary Learning: Encyclopedias and Epitomes'. In *The Oxford Handbook of Classical Chinese Literature*, edited by Wiebke Denecke, Wai-Yee Li and Xiaofei Tian, 132–46. New York: Oxford University Press, 2017.

Wang, Liqi 王利器. *Lidai xiaohua ji* 歷代笑話集. Shanghai: Shanghai guji, (1956) 1981.

Wang, Ping 王平. 'Lun Ming Qing shiqi xiaoshuo zhuanbo de jiben tezheng' 論明清時期小説轉播的基本特徵 (On the Basic Characteristics of the Spreading of Ming Qing xiaoshuo). *Wenshizhe* 6 (2003): 33–37.

Wilkinson, Endymion. *Chinese History: A New Manual*. Cambridge, MA: Harvard University Asia Center, 2012.

Wu, Fusheng. *Written at Imperial Command: Panegyric Poetry in Early Medieval China*. Albany: State University of New York Press, 2008.

Wu, Laura Hua. 'From Xiaoshuo to Fiction: Hu Yinglin's Genre Study of Xiaoshuo'. *Harvard Journal of Asiatic Studies* 55, no. 2 (1995): 339–71.

Zhao Jingshen 趙景深. 'Zhongguo xiaohua tiyao'. 中國笑話提要 In *Zhongguo xiaoshuo congkao* 中國小説叢考, edited by Zhao Jingshen, 22–60. Jinan: Qi Lu shushe, (1938) 1980.

Zhong Shuhe 種叔河. *Zhong Shuhe sanwen* 種叔河散文. Hangzhou: Zhejiang wen yi chu ban she, 1999.

Zhu, Yao 朱瑤. '*Qiyan lu* chengshu kao' 《啓顏錄》成書考. *Sichuan daxue xuebao*, no. 2 (2011): 139–42.

CHAPTER 11

# Testing the Limits of Pirandello's *Umorismo*: A Case Study Based on *Xiaolin Guangji*

*Antonio Leggieri*

### Pirandello and *L'Umorismo*

In 1908, Italian writer and playwright Luigi Pirandello (1867–1936) published an essay entitled simply *L'Umorismo* (*Humour*, rendered elsewhere as *On Humour*), in which he offered a long and intricate introduction about the various kinds of humour of the past. His starting point was that the concept of 'humour' had long been misunderstood by the Italian readers, who often confused it with 'the laughable', much as they had long been misunderstanding and misusing 'romantic' as a mere synonym for 'sentimental'. Humour, Pirandello affirms, is by nature hard to grasp and to define, a rather *slippery* concept, and as evidence of this he quotes such authors as Manzoni, Heine, and Cervantes, among others, pointing out each writer's own distinctive style, and arguing that they are all *bona-fide* humourists. In 1920, Pirandello revised his essay, and formulated in more detail his famous view about humour as the *feeling of the opposite*, as opposed to the comic or laughable, which is a simple *perception of the opposite*. The most famous example of this definition does not come from any previous literary work, but it is an imaginary situation created by Pirandello himself, and added to the 1920 edition, for the purpose of proving his point. The author imagines this:

> *I see an old lady, whose hair is dyed and completely smeared with some kind of horrible ointment: she is all make-up in a clumsy and awkward fashion and is dolled-up like a young girl. I begin to laugh. I perceive that she is the opposite of what a respect-*

A. Leggieri (✉)
University of Salento, Lecce, Italy
e-mail: antonio.leggieri@studenti.unisalento.it

© The Author(s), under exclusive license to Springer Nature
Switzerland AG 2020
D. Derrin, H. Burrows (eds.), *The Palgrave Handbook of Humour, History, and Methodology*, https://doi.org/10.1007/978-3-030-56646-3_11

*able old lady should be. Now I could stop here at this initial and superficial comic reaction: the comic consists precisely of this perception of the opposite. But if, at this point, reflection interferes in me to suggest that perhaps this old lady finds no pleasure in dressing up like an exotic parrot, and that perhaps she is distressed by it and does it only because she pitifully deceives herself into believing that, by making herself up like that and by concealing her wrinkles and grey hair, she may be able to hold the love of her much younger husband—if reflection comes to suggest all this, then I can no longer laugh at her as I did at first, exactly because the inner work of reflection has made me go beyond, or rather enter deeper into, the initial stage of awareness... herein lies the precise difference between the comic and humour.*[1]

We can identify at least two pivotal texts from which Pirandello drew inspiration: one is Giovanni Marchesini's pedagogical essay *Le finzioni dell'anima* (*The fictions of the soul*, 1905), and one is Alfred Binet's 1892 psychological essay *Les altérations de la personnalité* [*The alterations of personality*]; Franz Rauhut (but he is not the only one) speculates that Pirandello may have developed an interest in psychology because of first wife's mental illness.[2] From these two texts, Pirandello allegedly learned about fiction and illusion as necessities of the soul, and about the fragmentary quality of the human personality, respectively. Such notions are instrumental in understanding where he is coming from, and what kind of reasoning lies behind this theory; what Pirandello shows us in the example quoted above is Binet's 'juxtaposition de plusieurs existences psychologiques qui ne se confondent pas' [A juxtaposition of manifold psychological existences which do not mix up][3] set in motion: the first psychological existence in the author/observer is the laughing one, the one which acts upon perception, and which in seeing the old lady all dolled-up, laughs instinctively. Then reflection acts upon him, and triggers, possibly within a split second, the change into his new personality: this new status brings about a muffled and bitter kind of laughter.

For Pirandello, reflection is the key factor to understanding how humour operates; in conceiving an 'ordinary' work of art, he argues, the artist's reflection goes into hiding, assists passively to the act of creation, looks at it from a distance; when instead a humorous work of art is created, reflection takes on a more active role, analyses the work as if it were a device, and actively deconstructs it.[4] I suspect that the Sicilian writer is describing something akin to the suspension of disbelief, but from the author's, not the reader's, point of view. Pirandello then goes through a series of literary configurations of *Umorismo*, which readers of European literature may be more or less familiar with, such as Giuseppe Giusti's poem *Saint Ambrogio's Church*, Alessandro Manzoni's novel *The Betrothed*, but also Cervantes's *Don Quixote*. I will limit my quoting to *Don Quixote*, about which Pirandello affirms:

> We would like to laugh about all the comic features in the representation of this poor estranged man, who uses his madness as a mask on himself, on others, and on all things. We would like to laugh, but laughter does not come easy on our

lips. We feel that something hinders it, it is a sense of commiseration, of pity, and admiration, too [...] Our laughter is therefore made bitter by this feeling.[5]

It is intriguing to see how this theory of humour fares when compared to superiority, incongruity, and tension. Is superiority a considerable element in the equation? If so, only unconsciously, as we will see later; Pirandello is not interested, at least not visibly, in ridiculing the old lady for being all clumsy and awkward. Nor does he look interested in releasing his pent-up energy at her expenses. If we solely accept Pirandello's view, his theory can be ascribed as a variation, a different stage, of the incongruity theory, where the observer laughs upon perceiving the inequality between what the woman is and what she ought to be, and Pirandello may also have been inspired by what James Russell Lowell had written in 1870: 'Humour in its first analysis is a perception of the opposite'.[6] Pirandello is indeed interested in going beyond this first analysis! If he is right, we should assume that all incongruously laughable matters, if filtered through human reflection and inquiry, can turn into something tragic. When reflection intervenes, we are brought to ask the reason why something happens, and ultimately sympathise with the person we were laughing at one second ago. If by laughing we perceive the other person's behaviour as *fiction*, by reflecting upon it we can feel the reasons behind this fiction.

Even though he himself is not willing to admit it, Pirandello's theory is at least informed by another kind of superiority. This is pretty evident when we realise that in order for anyone to understand his *Umorismo*, we have to put ourselves into a privileged position, a pedestal, as if were, from which it is possible to observe better the incongruities of the world surrounding us. This position is of course inaccessible for the people that we are observing, and for this we are able to see the incongruities in a clearer way. However, Pirandello mitigates this superiority by bringing into play the factors of human reflection and empathy, thus removing the pedestal where he positioned his ideal observer. We can see how Pirandello's theory harmonises and complements the two approaches and in so doing manages to overcome the limits of the one-sided superiority or incongruity.

For this reason, Pirandello's reflection on humour as a double herm resonates well with the Daoist-inspired view on humour as a carrier of empathy that we will analyse in a moment. We can notice how this sudden change in the state of things is described within the Daoist classics; here I will quote two sentences, one recorded in *Zhuangzi* 莊子, the Daoist text that will recur later, in which we can imagine *it* as *laughter* and *other* as *humour*, forming Pirandello's double herm: '*Other*' comes out from '*it*', '*it*' likewise goes by '*other*'.[7] Likewise, in the Daoist text *Liezi* 列子, this maxim is recorded:

*The eye is about to grow dim when it can discern the tip of a hair; the ear is about to go deaf when it can hear the wings of a gnat; the palate is about to deteriorate when it can discriminate between the waters of the Zi and the Sheng; the nostrils are about to clog when they can distinguish scorched and rotten smells; the body is about to stiffen when it delights in sprinting; the mind is about to go astray when it can recognise right and wrong. Therefore, if a thing does not reach its limit it will not revert.*[8]

A considerable difference has to be pointed out between Pirandello and the Daoist masters: in *Liezi*, what urges to be transmitted is a sense of impermanence and volubility, which happens *outside* of the human mind, whereas the sudden change is triggered by human reflection *inside* the human mind. In fact, we can affirm that humour, for Pirandello, starts 'with man's unique ability to see himself in the very act of living'.[9]

Pirandello's essay is not particularly easy to read, and some critics have advised interpreting it in various ways, in order to justify his apparent lack of cohesiveness. One should not start a critical discussion on the topic without mentioning Benedetto Croce, who, in reviewing the first edition of the essay, pointed out some illogical flaws in the author's reasoning, but more importantly he sharply denied Pirandello the ability to express himself, by affirming that 'his concepts lose their shape when he tries to offer them to his readers'.[10] Croce himself had previously declared humour as indefinable, in the same way as all psychological states, and successively ascribed it to the multiple concepts of an *Aesthetics of Sympathy*, to which Pirandello replied with his view of humour as something which gives life to concepts, but is itself a non-concept.[11] In addition, Croce reprimanded Pirandello for contraposing art and humour, to which Pirandello, who had never intended to do so, harshly replied: 'Either I cannot write, or Croce cannot read!'. Now, without trying for the nth time to settle this age-old dispute, Croce's starting point was that of a man who, deprived of religious and positivistic beliefs, found new support by devoting himself to the religion of logic, of dialectics, and of critical thinking; this informed his optimistic view on art (and life in general) as a continuing progress.[12] Pirandello, on the contrary, saw these as obstacles to the unrestrained flowing of life. Croce wanted to use primarily logic and dialectics as critical tools to dissect and arrange systematically and unequivocally Pirandello's notion,[13] but *L'Umorismo* is not, by admission of his author, a logical work, since Pirandello uses reflection (and humour) as 'a small devil who disassembles the device' of any work of art.[14] His essay is an asymmetrical and largely intuitive work, rich in metaphors and in poetic images, with which the Sicilian writer attempts to pry not only on the reader's intelligence, but also on his/her intuition and perception.[15] This gave life to one of the longest feuds in the history of Italian literature, however many years after Pirandello's death, this work was rediscovered and analysed copiously.

Linda Armao, while identifying Pirandello's humour as an evolution of the incongruity theory, argues that 'since the humourist's job is to go one step beyond the comedian to reach the feeling of the opposite, it is no wonder that Pirandello's humour is more elusive than comedy'.[16] Jonathan Druker proposes to read this essay with 'a healthy scepticism', since it presents the incoherence of two essays in one, often working 'at cross purposes', and puts Pirandello's view in relation to his contemporaries Bakhtin, Bergson, Freud.[17]

Umberto Eco shows us how *L'Umorismo*, after promising to enlighten us about humour becomes a metaphysical treatise which fails to define his author's primary purpose; Eco even proposes to read this essay as if it were one of Pirandello's plays, merely disguised as an academic work, and links the origin of his *feeling of the opposite* to the superiority theory.[18] Nevertheless, I would like to argue that, for all its incoherence, Pirandello's essay, especially in the passages about the old lady and *Don Quixote*, proves that humour is characterised by an ever-changing state of the mind, which brings us to consider laughable what appeared to be tragic one moment before, and vice-versa: a point which is at the same time fascinating in its quirkiness and extremely lifelike. Eco tells us that the theoretical basis for Pirandello's fictional writing is not his own *Umorismo*, but rather Bertold Brecht's *Verfremdung* (alienation/estrangement).[19]

What happens, then, when we attempt to give his theory an occasion to prove itself? What happens if we take Pirandello's notion of humour and put it in relation to a Chinese jestbook from more than two-hundred years ago (with much older jokes)? What is the reason to compare the two works in the first place? One of the main factors which characterise *Umorismo* is the existing *contradiction* between real life and human ideals, brought about by the activity of pondering and reflection. Moreover, Pirandello implicitly pointed out that humour can serve as consolation for mankind. In 1924 he wrote in a letter:

> *I think that life is a very sad piece of buffoonery; because we have in ourselves, without being able to know why, wherefore or whence, the need to deceive ourselves constantly by creating a reality (one for each and never the same for all), which from time to time is discovered to be vain and illusory[...] My art is full of bitter compassion for all those who deceive themselves; but this compassion cannot fail to be followed by the ferocious derision of destiny which condemns man to deception.[20]*

In the following paragraphs I will introduce the second object of this research, a premodern Chinese jestbook which lends itself to being analysed through the lens of *Umorismo*, together with a number of theories on laughter which appeared in China, in order to contextualise it in a more cohesive way.

## On *Xiaolin Guangji* 笑林廣記

'[...] The Master knows how to compose unusual poems in an unrestricted style; he disdains to assume the pose of a pedantic Confucian frowning in disdain. When one is young, his aspiration reaches all four directions, and his footprints are visible in the whole world; therefore, his knowledge expands day after day, together with his skills. When one tries to write, although his brush has lost all its hairs, his path has become arduous and his clothes raggedy, one understands that everything can change in a second; who could then have clear eyes prone to smile? In these circumstances we often rehearse Dongfang Shuo's jocoseness or imitate Zhuangzi's parables; we offer clear words to all the people in the room, not only to follow the style of the Jin dynasty, but also to stimulate everyone's interest; we do not take anything seriously! Xiaolin Guangji does not refrain from vulgar language, because it is the result of various sources collected and put together, and this is its most visible trait.

These are the opening words to *Xiaolin Guangji* 笑林廣記 (*Extended records from the Forest of Laughter*, henceforth *XLGJ*), one of the most appreciated jestbooks in premodern China. Its earliest edition available today dates back from the fifty-sixth year of the *Qianlong*乾隆era (1791) in the Qing 清 dynasty (1644–1911).[21] Its compiler names himself *Youxi Zhuren* 游戲主人 (*The Master of Games*), and its editor adopts an equally extravagant pen name, *Canran Jushi* 粲然居士 (*The smiling Scholar*), while the preface that I just quoted is signed *Xianran Sou* 掀髯叟 (*The old Man lifting his Beard*, where 'to lift one's beard', is a synonym of 'to laugh'); it is not implausible, however, that all three personas are in fact a single author hiding behind different pen names. The book is also known as *Xinjuan Xiaolin Guangji* 新雋笑林廣記 (*Newly carved Extended Records from the Forest of Laughter*), because it was not the first book to be called by this name, nor would it be the last, for that matter: there are at least two latter homonym works, one signed by Cheng Shijue 程世爵 (*Nobleman Cheng*, pseudonym of an unknown compiler) published in 1899, and one by writer Wu Jianren 吳趼人 (1866–1910). If things were not complicated enough, the book draws heavily from Feng Menglong's 馮夢龍 (1574–1646) collection called *Xiaofu* 笑府 (Literally *Mansion of Laughter*, but mostly rendered as *Treasury of Laughs*, circa 1610), reprising its structure and most jokes.[22] However, a couple of differences should be pointed out: *Xiaofu* contains thirteen chapters, arranged thematically, while *XLGJ* has only twelve, and in different order. In addition, the narrating voice of *Xiaofu* appears in the introduction to every paragraph and after almost every single joke, to comment caustically on it, or to inform the reader that in another province they tell a punchline differently; this trait is completely absent in *XLGJ*, where an external voice partakes in the simulated storytelling setting only in the introduction. Even though *Xiaofu* has long been considered as the most famous jestbook in the Chinese literary tradition, after the fall of the Ming 明 dynasty (1368–1644) it survived in Japan, while *XLGJ* was mostly read and admired within the Chinese borders.[23]

One should not commit the mistake of neglecting the historical context and considering these jestbooks as single instances in the history of Chinese literary tradition; Karin Myhre informs us that, with popular and oral literary forms becoming more socially acceptable during the Ming and Qing eras, and thanks to economical methods of printing being developed, various compilers collected and published jokes in a more organised way than in the past. Myhre points out that 'there are twice as many joke books extant from the five hundred odd years between the beginning of the Ming dynasty and the end of the Qing as there are from the period of more than one thousand years from Handan Chun's 邯鄲淳 volume to the beginning of the Ming dynasty'.[24]

Myhre is obviously referring to *Xiaolin* 笑林, the *Forest of Laughs*, see Baccini's chapter in this book.

Such an overabundance of titles, possibly reliant on the same source materials, led to many jokes appearing in different versions in more than one text. In his *Zhongguo Xiaoshuo Shilüe* 中國小説史略 (*A brief History of Chinese Fiction*, 1924) Lu Xun 魯迅 (1881–1936) argues that *Aizi Zashuo* 艾子雜説 (*Miscellaneous facts about Master Mugwort*), conventionally attributed to Song 宋 dynasty (960–1279) poet Su Shi 蘇軾 (1037–1101) makes for a slightly better reading, with its benign and rather harmless anecdotes, than most Ming and Qing works, which unlike what had been done before are mainly preoccupied with reflecting and satirising the abuses of their times.[25] *Aizi Zashuo* is also believed to have influenced a certain number of Ming jestbooks, first and foremost Lu Zhuo's 陸灼 (?–?) *Aizi Houyu* 艾子后語 (*Later stories about Master Mugwort*) and Tu Benjun's 屠本君 (?–1622) *Aizi Waiyu* 艾子外語 (*Apocryphal stories about Master Mugwort*).[26] It is worth noting that, apart from a couple of recurring tropes (talking statues of Immortals, debates on diets, contrast between the rich and the poor, which can be seen as a commonality in themes rather than a direct influence of one text on the other), no trace or remnant of the thirty-nine stories in *Aizi Zashuo* is detected in *XLGJ*, with its more mature and sourer jokes. Together with a huge quantity of jestbooks, the early stage of what can be considered a critical *discourse* on jokes took form in the Ming epoch.[27]

No doubt humour was touched upon in other critical writings, and it is almost obligatory to mention Chap. XV of Liu Xie's 劉協 (465–522) *Wenxin Diaolong* 文心雕龍 (*The literary mind and the carving of dragons*), titled *Xie Yin* 諧隱 (*Humour and Riddles*), with its ambivalent view of laughter as both a socially acceptable instrument of criticism and a dangerous tool for hiding one's own true intentions. However, the compilers themselves encouraged a more open and conscious discourse on the theme of laughter, since in their attached prefaces they often discussed and highlighted the literary legitimacy of jokes, together with the necessity of collecting them. Guo Zizhang 郭子章 (1543–1618) explains in the preface to his *Xieyu* 諧語 (*Humorous words*) that since humorous traits are perceivable in many works from the past, laughter should not be cast away from culture.[28] Sometimes compilers asked for an external voice to intervene and explain the importance of jokes; that is the case of Mei Zhiyun 梅之熉 (?-?), who wrote a preface for Feng Menglong's alleged third collection, *Gujin Tangai* 古今譚概 (*Accounts of Old and New Conversations*), in which he declared that satire and ridicule should be elements of an open discussion, in the same way as beauty and praise were openly discussed.[29]

Xianran Sou's preface, while apologetically acknowledging the vulgarity of many a joke, at the same time attempts to legitimise the content of the jestbook by referring to Zhuangzi's 莊子 (fourth century BC) parables and court jester Dongfang Shuo's 東方朔 (second century BC) playfulness, as antidotes to our sense of hopelessness facing the world's volubility.[30] Apart from this veiled allusion to the past, jokes are thus praised and justified for their *sentimental*, rather than *intellectual* or *didactic* appeal; they serve as a momentary consolation in front of the world's apparent entropy.

*XLGJ* is formed by twelve chapters arranged thematically, each chapter has its own name, and touches upon a different subject. The twelve themes are divided as follows: magistrates, scholars, trades, body parts, mental illnesses, married life, age-old taboos, priests and monks, stingy people, poor people, general satire, mistakes. However, we should notice that this is not an absolute categorisation, since one can find a few independent and detached jokes in almost each chapter. The text is written in Classical Chinese (*wenyan* 文言),[31] a language that, with its standardised usage through the whole Empire, together with its conservatism, was probably more accessible to a wider audience than the vernacular (*baihua* 白話).[32]

Despite its intelligibility, and despite being very widely read and appreciated, *XLGJ* lacks a proper critical apparatus; no authoritative edition with commentary (be it premodern, modern, or contemporary) exists, and no exhaustive book-length study focusing exclusively on this text can be found to this day (not counting some unpublished MA and PhD theses). Nonetheless, one can find a few sparse opinions which can help cement a critical view of the text. Late-Qing writer Wu Jianren 吳趼人 (1866–1910), in the preface to his own reworking of *XLGJ* (1902), stated that most ancient Chinese jokes followed a set of routine without any fresh knowledge or new flavour, and that even though '*XLGJ* is a text which can be understood by anyone, it is a shame that its content is so vulgar and unrefined, completely made out of lewd jokes, mostly coming from the lower classes; not only does it have no benefit for the reader, but it can also lead progressively to obscene behaviour'.[33] Wu is not alone in condemning the text; in 1949 scholar Wu Xiaoru 吳小如 (1922–2014) wrote that he did not consider it to be a bad book, even though it was not particularly good either.[34] More recently (2001), the scholar of folk and popular literature Wang Xuetai 王學泰 (1942–2018), while acknowledging the historical value of the text, advised potential readers to handle with care the ideological degeneration and lowly interests permeating the text.[35] These comments are all pointing towards the same direction and the same problem: every chapter presents a significant number of jokes on sex and the human body in general, with an obvious gravity surrounding the male and female genitalia. Among the recent comments on the text, Mario Liong affirms that '*Xiaolin Guangji* is considered of low status because it not only targets at commoners but it also contains a lot of sexual jokes that explicitly describe sex organs and deviant sexual activities. It implies the *literati*'s view that commoners are morally lower. [...] Excessive sexuality is thought to be dangerous to the morality as well as the physical health in Confucian and Taoist notions, respectively'.[36] In this regard, the paper by Huang Kewu 黃克武 and Li Xinyi 李心怡 relates *XLGJ* to Bakhtin's concept of grotesque body, eventually remarking that the text 'goes beyond the categories of rude and refined, public and private, male and female, to represent some rather popular ideas within the people of the Ming and Qing dynasties'.[37]

Questions and doubts about how intelligible *XLGJ* can be for a Western audience should, in theory, be laid to rest by the already existing translated versions. However, translators have time and again either resorted to copious footnotes (Hsu's 2015 rendition of *Xiaofu*), interpolated their own explanations (Herbert Giles's 1925 abridged translation of an unidentified jestbook, which is probably *XLGJ*), or bowdlerised heavily the source material (Giles, again); this leads me to conclude that, in their original forms, some jokes can be baffling for someone not knowing the thick layer of rituality, social conventions, and contextual events behind them, and that we should not blame the translators for trying to convey the gist of the original text one way or another. In addition, apart from the cultural gap surrounding some tales, the only unintelligible and therefore untranslatable puns are those which rely heavily on wordplay and homophony, whose puns need to be replaced rather than reproduced. As for their laughability and liveliness, we must remember that *wenyan* had become the standardised written medium for official texts and thus detached itself from the spoken language already in the early stages of the Chinese empire;[38] for this reason, it is implausible to assume that these jokes were told in the same way (i.e. with the same words) as they are recorded, and I would suggest that *XLGJ* and similar jestbooks could have been used as promptbooks, whose content was then modified into the local language for the actual telling. Its laughability 'in real life' depends on a series of extratextual factors (tellers, audience, occasion, and so forth) that for the moment should not preoccupy us.

## On the Concept of *Youmo* 幽默 in Relation with *Xiaolin Guangji*

The thematic link between *XLGJ* and Pirandello's take on *Umorismo* that I promised to highlight early on is better explained if I first expound the way in which the concept of humour was reintroduced and interpreted in Early Republican China. Pirandello's theory, when compared to both *XLGJ* and the rediscovery of humour that I will explain here, can lead to a deeper reflection on the very nature of humour. It is undoubtedly worth noticing how Pirandello came to reprise and elaborate his views on humour roughly in the same period (the 1920s) in which a discourse on humour developed in China.

Xianran Sou's preface, quoted earlier, presents, albeit in a rather rough way, all the traits of Chinese humour, as successively promoted in a more organised way by Chinese writer and linguist Lin Yutang 林語堂 (1895–1976). In 1924, Lin invented (or reinvented) the word *youmo* 幽默, as a phonetic translation of the English *humour*.[39] He drew inspiration from a poem written by Chinese poet Qu Yuan 屈原 (340–278 BC), in which the characters *you* 幽 and *mo* 默 appeared together for the first time. These two characters were originally used to indicate a dark (*you*) and silent (*mo*) landscape, and Lin managed to reinforce his concept by bringing into play their original meaning, thus attempting to attach a philological sense to his otherwise purely phonetic translation of *humour*:

> *Everyone who is good at humour will enjoy its fun taste primarily in a hidden place* [*youyin*], *and everyone who is good at appreciating humour will appreciate it in a state of understanding inspired by a silence of his inner mind* [*jingmo*].[40]

In another related article (*Lun Youmo* 論幽默, or *On Humour*, 1932), Lin proceeded to give out his own personal vision of the humorous Chinese spirit, which, in his view, originates from none other than Laozi 老子 and Zhuangzi themselves, the alleged founders of Daoism. Humour, Lin continues, is a view of life, which at the same time is detached (*chaotuo* 超脫), gentle and soft (*wenrou* 溫柔), and bemoaning the state of things (*beitian minren* 悲天憫 人).[41] It is a flavour, a way of living that, even though much present and encouraged in the classical texts, had, for Lin, been cast aside and eventually forgotten by the 'long-faced' Confucianists as well as many of his contemporaries. Surprisingly, in his copious writings on the subject, Lin did not touch upon the long-standing tradition of jestbooks running through all Chinese literary history. This would supposedly prove that for him, the Chinese jestbooks were not a representative of this 'detached, gentle, soft, and bemoaning the state of things' quality which characterises the Chinese sense of humour. On the contrary, he argued that humour possesses a flavour which is 'not easy to communicate to others, and much different than those visibly contemptible jokes. The more secluded (*you*) and the more silent (*mo*) humour is, the better'.[42]

Nonetheless, serendipities can occur: the most visible link between *XLGJ* and Lin Yutang's writings is obviously the mentioning of Zhuangzi, whom Lin considered a master of humour, and of court jester Dongfang Shuo (Xianran Sou calls him by his courtesy name *Manqian* 曼倩), who was, in Lin's view, the pioneer of the Chinese *huaji* 滑稽 (jocose, laughable) but not of what he characterised as humour.[43] Apart from that, the conceptualisation of Lin's *youmo* is a way to detach oneself from the worries of the world and find the long-lost joy of living reverberates in *XLGJ's* preface. Even though Lin rehearses the overused trope of humour as a tradition, he too appears as more sentimental than didactic in his purpose; he appeals to humour in order to restore a certain feeling of empathy between people. It is visible that humour, for him, consists of something much deeper than laughter for the sake of laughter.

Bitter compassion is what *XLGJ* evokes in its preface, and ferocious derision is largely present in many a joke; these two traits can be harmonised and analysed once we decide to deliberately misread the text, trying to behave as that same 'small devil' who enjoys disassembling devices. As readers, we do not find ourselves reading a single joke, but a whole book of jokes, in which each chapter contains a variable number of variations on a single theme. My hypothesis is that by way of this obstinacy, this insistence on a single theme, the punchlines become feeble, and this activates reflection and empathy for the protagonists of the joke, which, in turn, triggers the feeling of the opposite that Pirandello advocates.

## THE LIMITS OF THE JOKE AND THE LIMITS OF *UMORISMO*

As briefly mentioned before, the sixth chapter of *XLGJ*, *Guifeng Bu* 閨風部 (*The lady's chamber*), deals primarily with a married couple's problems in bed, especially with women's dissatisfaction. I chose this particular chapter because its theme is easily relatable and present in most cultures of the world. What do we obtain if we try to read it one joke after another, as if it were a single story? We can rearrange all the jokes into one macro-narrative and divide it into five phases.

*Phase 1*: A woman is about to get married and discover sexual pleasure: this part deals mostly with the change of feelings in such woman, from her grief upon abandoning her parents' house to her newfound happiness in bed. Here are two jokes, which show how *XLGJ* presents variations on the same theme:

> *A woman has not married yet, and she privately asks her sister in law: 'Is that thing rather pleasant or not?' To which her sister in law replies: 'How could it be pleasant? It is merely a rite which Zhou Gong*[44] *prescribed for married couples'. When the woman comes back to visit her parents after marriage, upon seeing her sister in law, scorns her laughing: 'What an incurable liar you are!'. (I.I)*

> *During the initial stages of her marriage, a woman breaks into tears and asks her sister in law: 'Where does this rite come from?', her sister in law replies: 'Zhou Gong', and the woman starts cursing this name. Upon going back to see her parents after the first month of marriage, she asks her sister in law: 'Who is this Zhou Gong anyway?', 'He was a personality of the past, what business would you have with him?' 'I want to make a pair of shoes to thank him!'. (I.II)*

These two jokes are rather benign and harmless; their comic factor comes from a visible incongruity, the change of state in the woman's attitude before and after marriage, combined with the veiled allusion to sex. It is a bit early for the feeling of the opposite to manifest itself, especially because we are laughing *with* the woman, not *at* her.

*Phase 2*: The same bride enjoys her new life to the fullest. This part shows how forgiving she can be with anything else, provided that she has a satisfactory night with her husband.

> *A poor man and his wife are in bed, when she says: 'We don't even have rice, what are you so happy about?' A moment after the husband's penis shrinks. The wife then says: 'Well, that is the way things are, however I am sure that if we put together what we have in our jars, it should be enough for at least two more days!'. (II.I)*

Voluntary empathy may or may not arise, depending on the reader/listener's sensitivity.

*Phase 3*: The bride gives birth to a child, and she obviously goes through a different state of mind. This part highlights the contrast between her sexual life and the bearing of a child.

> *A woman has great difficulties in giving birth to a child, therefore she blames her husband: 'It is all because of you that I am suffering so much!' Her husband, feeling so sorry for her, proposes to refrain from having sex: 'Starting from today we will sleep in separate beds, and will not even touch each other', to which the woman agrees. One month after giving birth, he hears a door opening in the night, 'Who is there?' he asks, 'The one who does not fear death is here again!'. (III.I)*

The punchline is benign, once again playing on incongruity and change of attitude on the woman's part.

*Phase 4*: Various kinds of incest happen in the family:

> *An old man wants to get intimate with his daughter-in-law, who does not agree, and denounces him to her mother-in-law. She replies: 'This old tortoise behaves just like his old man. It just runs in the family'. (IV.I)*

> *An old man gets intimate with his daughter-in-law. Once they finish, he bows to her, saying: 'Thank you, dear daughter-in-law, for being so generous.' She replies: 'Dear father, where does all this politeness come from? Nobody else does that in our family'. (IV.II)*

Or alternatively, the husband takes a concubine with him:

> *After taking a concubine, a man goes to bed with his wife, who reprimands him: 'I can see that your body is here with me, but your mind is there with her'. The man replies: 'Then what would you think if my body went there, and my mind came here?'. (IV.III)*

*Phase 5*: The man grows old, to the point where he can no longer satisfy his wife:

> *An old man forces himself to have sex with his wife, but his penis cannot enter. He brandishes it for a long time, and without noticing, mucus starts flowing from his nose; he sighs: 'That is why I was so weak: it all needed to come out from above!'. (V.I)*

Alternatively, the husband passes away, and his widow wants to remarry:

> *A widow who plans to remarry tells her matchmaker that she wants her new husband to pay an exorbitant sum in betrothal gifts, the matchmaker asks: 'Getting married a second time is different than getting married the first time, who would be willing to pay such a high price?', the woman replies: 'I am still chaste, I never lost my virginity!', the matchmaker asks, doubtfully: 'Obviously, you were married before, and now*

*you are a widow, who could believe you?', to which the woman suddenly confesses: 'I should not hide this from you, my previous husband's penis was too small, he could only put it halfway through; that is why even though I will marry a second time, I am still chaste!'.* (V.II)

These five phases result in the story of a woman's marriage, going from the first period of pleasure and joy to the last phase in which continuous embarrassment is mixed with absurdity. Does this situation provide an ideal hotbed for *Umorismo*? It is plausible, on the one hand, that the obstinate repetition of a theme tears laughter away and makes the variations on single macro-themes less 'fresh' and more predictable. On the other hand, is it enough for the feeling of the opposite to thrive on in the unimpressionable reader? I think otherwise; if I had to set a golden rule (implicit in Pirandello) for the feeling of the opposite, first I would have to acknowledge that jokes cannot become the object of *Umorismo* at the reader/listener's will. The audience's reflection needs some objective conditions on which it will embroider and develop towards the feeling of the opposite. The first essential condition for *Umorismo* to appear is a punchline not involving us laughing *with* the characters, but rather laughing *at* them. For this exact reason, the jokes ranging from (I.I) to (IV.III) can be ascribed to the category of *comico*, but not of *umoristico*. The reason for this is mostly visible in (I.I), (I.II), and (IV.III); in all three stories there is a character who laughs, or who makes a witty remark *inside* the story, which causes the readers (and in case of (I.I) and (I.II) the other character as well, if we want to imagine it this way), to laugh together with the protagonist of the story, in a harmless way. No feeling of the opposite can bloom, because there is no opposite, there is no tragedy behind the comic.

Considering jokes (V.I) and (V.II), the tragic element is there for everyone to see: the man in the first one cannot have a proper erection, and the woman in the second one tries to attract a wealthy second husband by trying to disguise herself as something she is clearly not. Reflection can intervene and deconstruct their fabrications, their 'devices', showing how their amusing excuses are in fact hiding personal tragedies.

It becomes clear that one can do away with at least one factor that I took for granted in my hypothesis about how much feebler a joke becomes when its theme is repeated; here we do not need any repetition, a single joke is enough for reflection to intervene and for the feeling of the opposite to manifest itself. In addition, laughter may come from *inside* the jokes (i.e. from the characters looking at themselves in the act of living); we can consider for example the following joke:

*A blind man, a dwarf, and a hunchback are discussing over who should sit at the place of honour while they drink some wine, so they set this simple rule: the one who brags the most obtains the seat of honour. The blind man begins: 'I do not see anyone better than me, I should take the seat', the dwarf replies: 'I am no ordinary person ('chang' 常 'ordinary', homonym of 'chang' 长 'long-legged'), the seat should be*

> *mine!', the hunchback declares: 'There is no need for quarrelling! At the end of the day you are both my nephews ('zhibei'* 侄背, *'nephew', homonym of 'zhibei'* 直背, *'straight back'): it has to be me!'*

Provided that it has some potentially uneasy element, a single joke is enough for us to ponder and to feel compassion for these three characters. As briefly mentioned before, laughter can come from *inside* of a text, because the three protagonists laugh about themselves and each other's misfortune in a self-depreciating way.

## CONCLUSION: *UMORISMO* AS A 'RECTIFIED' SUPERIORITY THEORY?

For this conclusion, let me go back to the concept of superiority: not all laughter deriving from the so-called sudden glory has be contemptuous; on the contrary, empathy and congeniality can be combined with one's perceived superiority.[45] Pirandello himself tried to disguise his concept of *Umorismo* as an example of incongruity, since his mechanism of humour is triggered merely by inequality, which is at first perceived, and subsequently felt and reflected upon, between what is and what should be; his very words point towards incongruity. However, I hope this study made clear that, when *Umorismo* becomes the lens through which we observe humorous anecdotes, we understand that incongruity is not the sole factor at play in the humourist's mind, and the jokes in *XLGJ* have made clear that benign superiority is necessary for Pirandello's formula to work. Through Pirandello's ideas, I explored the limit that a joke can reach before turning into its opposite, as well as how one single humorous anecdote can be pushed to the aforementioned limit, under a number of conditions.

On the other hand, the chapter has reflected largely upon Chinese jestbooks, with the intent of proving that, despite Lin Yutang's contempt, a compassionate and amiable sense of humour can also be found in jestbooks from the premodern period.

## NOTES

1. Italian version in Pirandello *Umorismo*, 122–123. English version in Pirandello, *On Humour*, 113.
2. Rauhut, 'Wissenschaftliche Quellen', 185–205.
3. Ibid., 136.
4. Pirandello, *Umorismo*, 120–121.
5. Ibid., 124–125.
6. Quoted in Critchley, *On Humour*, 3.
7. Graham, Chuang-Tzu, 52.
8. Graham, *Lieh-tzu*, 84.
9. Armao, 'From Il Fu Mattia Pascal to Liolà', 55.

10. Ragusa, 'Nota', 140.
11. Quoted in Pirandello, *Umorismo*, 196.
12. Caserta, 'Croce, Pirandello', 21–22, and Iliano, 'Momenti', 139.
13. Iliano, 'Momenti', 138.
14. Quoted in Ragusa, 'Nota', 139.
15. Iliano, 'Momenti', 138.
16. Armao, 'From Il Fu Mattia Pascal to Liolà', 63.
17. Druker, 'Self-estrangement', 57.
18. Eco, *The Limits of Interpretation*, 167: 'Reflection (artistic consciousness) undergoes here a new development: it attempts to understand the reason why the old woman masks herself under the delusion of regaining her lost youth. The character is no longer separate from me; in fact, I try to get inside the character. In so doing, *I lose my own sense of superiority* because I think that I could be she (sic). My laughter is mixed with pity; it becomes a smile. I have moved from the Comic to Humor' (Italics are mine).
19. This, however, can be disputed, see Mariani, *Living Masks*, 61, where a character from the play *Each in his own Way* 'evolves into a pure instance of Pirandellian *Umorismo*'.
20. Quoted in Chandler, *Modern Continental Playwrights*, 573.
21. Some sources (e.g. Qi Lianxiu, *Minjian gushi*, 361) assume that *XLGJ* was first printed in 1781.
22. It has to be noted, however, that *Xiaofu* was itself an anthology of jokes which had appeared in other collections, both contemporary to Feng Menglong and from previous dynasties. For an extensive list of texts that Feng may have consulted, see Hsu, *Treasury*, 5–6.
23. See Mair and Weinstein.
24. Myhre, 2001, 135. However, notice that in the same chapter, Myhre erroneously identifies 1899's homonym *XLGJ*, edited by Cheng Shijue, as the object of this study. The homonymy of such works is indeed confusing more often than not!
25. Lu Xun, *Xiaoshuo Shilüe*, 61. It is intriguing to notice how Lu Xun, arguably the sharpest novelist of his time, favoured the benign and harmless *Aizi Zashuo* over more overtly satirical jestbooks.
26. Wang Yunxi, and Gu Yisheng, *Wenxue Piping*, 867.
27. Wang Liqi (*Lidai xiaohua*, index) includes a total of forty-nine Ming and Qing collections in his anthology.
28. Quoted in Wang Yunxi, and Gu Yisheng, *Wenxue Piping*, 866.
29. Wang Yunxi, and Gu Yisheng, *Wenxue Piping*, 864. For a discussion on the prefaces and postfaces of Ming jestbooks, see Wu Shaoping, *Xiaohua Pingdian*, 194–204. A block printed version of *Gujin Tangai* which circulated during the Kangxi 康熙 (1661–1722) era had its preface penned by famous writer and playwright Li Yu 李漁 (1610–1680), as noted in Chen Pingyuan, *Yanbian*, 148.
30. The inclusion of *Zhuangzi* as a text which justifies mean language may be informed by the following passage: 'Four Men, Masters Si, Yu, Li, and Lai, were talking together. 'Which of us is able to think of nothingness as the head, of life as the spine, of death as the rump? Which of us knows that the living and the dead, the surviving and the lost, are all one body? He shall be my friend'. The four men looked at each other and smiled, and none was reluctant in his heart. So they became friends' (Graham, *Chuang-tzu*, 87–88). As for Dongfang Shuo,

236    A. LEGGIERI

see his biography, where some of his jests and tricks are reported in Minford and Lau, *Classical Chinese Literature*, 352–356 (a translation of his biography in *Guji Liezhuan* 滑稽列傳, *Biographies of Court Wits*).

31. I stand with Hanan (*Vernacular Story*, 3–4) in preferring *Classical Chinese* over *Literary Language* as a translation for *wenyan*.
32. This hypothesis is pointed out in Hsu Pi-Ching, *Treasury*, 17. For a discussion on the differences between Classical and Vernacular Chinese as written languages in Late-Imperial China, see Hanan, *Vernacular Story*, 1–27.
33. Quoted in Wang Jingmin, 'Cong Ming Qing Xiaohua', 14.
34. Wu Xiaoru, *Du XLGJ*.
35. Wang Xuetai, 'Xiaolin Guangji Qianyan', 50.
36. Liong, 'Hegemony and Humour', 194.
37. Huang Kewu and Li Xinyi, 'Ming Qing Xiaohua', 370.
38. Hanan, *Vernacular Story*, 3 and following; for an introduction to *wenyan*, see also Pulleyblank, *Classical Chinese*, 4–11.
39. Some sources say 1923 (Chey, 'Youmo', 1–5, but also Kao, *Wit and Humor*, XXII), other sources say 1924 (Yan Guanglin and Xu Tong, *Guanjianci*, 120).
40. Lin Yutang, *Youmo Zahua*, 249, my translation.
41. Lin Yutang, *Lun Youmo*, 260. The whole essay appeared translated in English by Joseph C. Sample, in the volume *Humour in Chinese Life and Letters*. Sample has chosen as his translation 'gentle and sincere, unbiased, and at the same time concerned with the destiny of humankind'. See Sample, *On Humour*, 175.
42. Lin Yutang, *Youmo Zahua*, 249, my translation.
43. For a discussion on the differences between *Huaji* and *Youmo*, see Chey, 'Youmo', 1–5.
44. Zhou Gong, or The Duke of Zhou, is said to have instituted marriage as a rite.
45. Keith-Spiegel, 'Early Conceptions', 7.

## Bibliography

Armao, Linda. 'From Il Fu Mattia Pascal to Liolà: An Analysis of Pirandello's Humor'. *Carte Italiane* 1, no. 3 (1982): 51–65.

Bassanese, Fiora A. *Understanding Luigi Pirandello*. Columbia: University of South Carolina Press, 1997.

Bassnett-McGuire, Susan. *Luigi Pirandello*. London and Basingstoke: The Macmillan Press, 1983.

Bloom, Harold, ed. *Bloom's Major Dramatists: Luigi Pirandello*. Broomall: Chelsea House Publishers, 2003.

Caserta, Ernesto G. 'Croce, Pirandello e il problema estetico'. *Italica* 51, no. 1 (1974): 20–42.

Chandler, Frank W. *Modern Continental Playwrights*. New York: Harper & Brothers, 1931.

Chen Pingyuan 陳平原. *Zhongguo Xiaoshuo Xushi Moshi de Yanbian* 中國小説敘事模式的演變 (The Changing of the Narrative Techniques in Chinese Fiction). Beijing: Beijing University Press, 2003.

Chey, Jocelyn. 'Youmo and the Chinese sense of Humour'. In *Humour in Chinese Life and Letters: Classical and Traditional Approaches*, edited by Jocelyn Chey and Jessica Milner Davis, 1–30. Hong Kong: Hong Kong University Press, 2011.

Critchley, Simon. *On Humour: Thinking in Action*. New York: Routledge, 2004.

Druker, Jonathan. 'Self-Estrangement and the Poetics of Self-Representation in Pirandello's "L'Umorismo"'. *South Atlantic Review* 63, no. 1 (1998): 56–71.

Eco, Umberto. *The Limits of Interpretation*. Bloomington and Indianapolis: Indiana University Press, 1994.

Graham, A.C., trans. *The Book of Lieh-tzu: A Classic of the Tao*. New York: Columbia University Press, 1990.

Graham, A.C. *Chuang-Tzu: The Inner Chapters*. London: Unwin Hyman Limited, 1989.

Hanan, Patrick. *The Chinese Vernacular Story*. Cambridge, MA and London: Harvard University Press, 1981.

Hsu, Pi-Ching, trans. *Feng Menglong's Treasury of Laughs: A Seventeenth-Century Anthology of Traditional Chinese Humour*. Leiden: Brill, 2015.

Huang Kewu 黃剋武 and Li Xinyi 李心怡. 'Ming Qing Xiaohua Zhong de Shenti yu Qingyu: Yi 'Xiaolin Guangji' wei zhongxin zhi fenxi'. 明清笑話中的身體與情慾:以'笑林廣記'為中心之分析. (Joking About Sex and the Body in Late Imperial China: An Analysis Based on the Jest Book Xiaolin Guangji). *Hanxue Yanjiu* 漢學研究 (Research on Sinology) 19, no. 2 (2001): 343–374.

Iliano, Antonio. 'Momenti e Problemi di critica pirandelliana: 'L'Umorismo', Pirandello e Croce, Pirandello e Tilgher'. *PMLA* 83, no. 1 (1968): 135–143.

Kao, George. *Chinese Wit and Humor*. New York: Coward-McCann, 1946.

Keith-Spiegel, Patricia. 'Early Conceptions of Humor: Varieties and Issues'. In *The Psychology of Humor: Theoretical Perspectives and Empirical Issues*, edited by Jeffrey H. Goldstein and Paul E. McGhee, 1–34. New York and London: Academic Press, 1972.

Lin Yutang 林語堂. *Lun Youmo* 論幽默 (On Humour). In *Lin Yutang Zizhuan* 林語堂自傳 (Lin Yutang's autobiography), 257–275. Xi'an: Shaanxi Shifan Daxue Chubanshe, 2002.

Lin Yutang 林語堂. *Youmo Zahua* 幽默雜話 (Miscellaneous Words on Humour). In Lin Yutang Zizhuan 林語堂自傳 (Lin Yutang's Autobiography), 247–254. Xi'an: Shaanxi Shifan Daxue Chubanshe, 2002.

Liong, Mario. 'Hegemony and Humor: Class and Hegemonic Masculinities in Three Premodern Chinese Humorous Texts'. In *Laughter, Humor, and the UnMaking of Gender: Historical and Cultural Perspectives*, edited by Anna Foka and Jonas Liliequist, 191–210. New York: Palgrave Macmillan, 2015.

Lu Xun 魯迅. *Zhongguo Xiaoshuo Shilüe: Wai Yi Zhong* 中國小說史略:外一種 (A Brief History of Chinese Fiction: With Another Essay). Beijing: Commercial Press, 2011.

Mair, Victor, and Maxine Belmont Weinstein. 'Popular Literature. Part I: Folk Literature'. In *The Indiana companion to Chinese literature* (Taiwan edition), edited by William Nienhauser, Jr., 75–81. Taipei: Southern Material Center, Inc., 2006.

Mariani, Umberto. *Living Masks: The Achievement of Pirandello*. Toronto: University of Toronto Press, 2008.

Minford, John, and Joseph S.M. Lau, eds. *Classical Chinese Literature: An Anthology of Translations, Volume I: From Antiquity to the Tang Dynasty*. New York: Columbia University Press, 2002.

Myhre, Karin. 'Wit and Humor'. In *The Columbia History of Chinese Literature*, edited by Victor Mair, 132–148. New York: Columbia University Press, 2001.

Pirandello, Luigi. *L'Umorismo (On Humour)*. Milan: Mondadori, 1986.

Pirandello, Luigi. *On Humor*. Translated by Antonio Illiano and Daniel P. Testa. Chapel Hill: University of North Carolina Press, 1974.

Pulleyblank, Edwin G. *Outline of Classical Chinese Grammar*. Vancouver: UBC Press, 1995.

Qi Lianxiu 祁連休. *Zhongguo Minjian Gushi Shi: Qingdai Juan* 中國民間故事史:清代卷 (History of Popular Chinese Tales; Qing Dynasty). Taipei: Xiuwei Chuban, 2012.

Ragusa, Olga. 'Nota su 'L'Umorismo' di Luigi Pirandello' *Italianistica: Rivista di letteratura italiana* 17, no. 1 (1988): 139–144.

Rauhut, Franz. 'Wissenschaftliche Quellen von Gedanken Luigi Pirandellos'. *Romanische Forschungen* 53, Bd., 2.H. (1939): 185–205.

Sample, Joseph C. 'Contextualizing Lin Yutang's essay 'On Humour': Introduction and Translation'. In *Humour in Chinese Life and Letters: Classical and Traditional Approaches*, edited by Jocelyn Chey and Jessica Milner Davis, 169–190. Hong Kong: Hong Kong University Press, 2011.

Wang Jingmin 王敬敏. 'Cong Ming Qing Xiaohua Kan Xiaohua de Wenti he Gongneng' 從明清笑話看笑話的文體和功能 (An Analysis of the Literary Format and Function of Jokes from the Point of View of Ming and Qing Jestbooks). *Zhongguo Gudai Wenxue Yanjiu* 中國古代文學研究 (Research on Classical Chinese Literature) 2 (2007): 13–15.

Wang Liqi 王利器. *Lidai Xiaohua Ji* 歷代笑話集 (A Collection of Jokes Through the Ages). Shanghai: Gudian Wenxue Chubanshe, 1956.

Wang Xuetai 王學泰. 'Xiaolin Guangji Qianyan' 笑林廣記前言 (A Preface to XLGJ). *Xu yu Ba* 序與跋 (Prefaces and Postscripts) 9 (2001): 49–50.

Wang Yunxi 王運熙 and Gu Yisheng 雇易生, eds. *Zhongguo Wenxue Piping Tongshi: Mingdai Juan* 中國文學批評通史: 明代卷 (A Comprehensive History of Chinese Literary Criticism: Ming Dynasty). Shanghai: Guji Chubanshe, 2007.

Wu Shaoping 吳少平. 'Ming Qing Xiaohua Pingdian Chutan' 明清笑話評點初探 (A Preliminary Analysis on Commentaries in Ming and Qing Jestbooks). *Ming Qing Xiaoshuo Yanjiu* 明清小説研究 (Research on Ming and Qing Dynasties Novels) 4 (2005): 194–204.

Wu Xiaoru 吳小如. *Du Xiaolin Guangji* 讀笑林廣記 *(On Reading XLGJ)*, in *Jiushiyuese: Wu Xiaoru Zaonian Shuping*. 舊時月色:吳小如早年書評 (The Appearance of the Moon in the Old Times: Book Reviews written by Wu Xiaoru in his Early Years). Beijing: Beijing University Press, 2012.

Yan Guanglin 閆廣林 and Xu Tong 徐侗. *Youmo Lilun Guanjianci Yanjiu* 幽默理論關鍵詞研究 (Study on Keywords in Humour Theory). Shanghai: Xuelin Chubanshe, 2010.

Youxi Zhuren 遊戲主人 (compiler), Research Center of Classical Literature at National Cheng Chi University 國立政治大學古典小説研究中心, ed. *Xinjuan Xiaolin Guangji* 新鐫笑林廣記 (Newly Carved Extended Collection of the Forest of Laughter). Taipei: Tianyi Chubanshe, 1985.

CHAPTER 12

# The Monsters That Laugh Back: Humour as a Rhetorical Apophasis in Medieval Monstrology

*Rafał Borysławski*

### INTRODUCTION: FROM FEAR AND LAUGHTER TO WISDOM

Monsters and humorousness, although contradictory at first glance, are often both complementary and similar in their roles under closer scrutiny: after all, images of monstrosities may elicit laughter and ridicule, while instances of humour may be frightening and threatening. Both are effectuated by the element of surprise and by juxtapositions of opposing elements and values. Both rely on the element of indeterminacy, and, functioning as cultural markers in critical circumstances, both may simultaneously carry serious and yet entertaining admonitions. Perhaps the most conspicuous example of this correlation in contemporary popular culture is the figure of the evil or monstrous clown, such as the terrifying and yet amusingly alluring Pennywise from Stephen King's *It*. Similar representations may be found in medieval iconography: the frequently reproduced marginalia from the fourteenth-century Luttrell Psalter are a good case in point: the grotesque anthropo- and zoomorphic hybrids featuring on the manuscript's margin are at once ludicrous and hideous.[1] The aim of this chapter is to consider the parallels between the way monstrosities and humorousness have been theorised in order to discuss how early medieval discourses of monstrology appear to be encompassing reactions that are only seemingly far apart: those of laughter and dread. The chief question to be

R. Borysławski (✉)
Institute of Literary Studies, University of Silesia, Katowice, Poland
e-mail: rafal.boryslawski@us.edu.pl

© The Author(s), under exclusive license to Springer Nature
Switzerland AG 2020
D. Derrin, H. Burrows (eds.), *The Palgrave Handbook of Humour, History, and Methodology*, https://doi.org/10.1007/978-3-030-56646-3_12

239

addressed here is whether we can speak of the mechanisms of humour (and laughter) and those of fear (and dread) as ways of exploring cognitive and social limits in the early Middle Ages. In this chapter, I will refer to instances of geographically and textually marginal monstrosities that appear in several medieval texts known to the Anglo-Saxons, notably the Prologue to the *Liber monstrorum de diversis generibus* [The Book of Monsters of Various Kinds], the Exeter Book's poem *The Whale* and one of the Exeter Book poetic riddles. In illustrating and concluding my point, however, I also intend to venture out of the broadly understood Middle Ages towards contemporary medievalism and refer to Umberto Eco's *Baudolino*. In this novel, originally published in 2000, Eco composes what may be called an attempt at recreating the mentality behind medieval storytelling and behind conceptualising the apparently monstrous alterity, also through humour. I will consider all of this against the critical background of humour studies and approaches to medieval monstrology. By comparing the anthropology of the monstrous proposed by Jeffrey Jerome Cohen with four traditional humour theories—the superiority and disparagement theory, the release and relief theory, the incongruity theory and a script-based semantic theory of humour—I will argue for essential similarities between the mechanics of humour and terror and for the way in which they could be both accommodated within early medieval Neoplatonic thought.

Clearly, both laughter and dread may and do form psychologically understandable emotional reactions to human social and perceptive limits, that is to whatever is unknown, unfamiliar, marginal and vague. However, they also belong to the forms of expression and representation that are constructed upon negations of whatever may be called an existing emotional and intellectual descriptive model of and prescriptive model for perceivable reality. The interaction between the monstrous, the humorous and that which is neither may be understood as, so to speak, a teasing gaze of the monster from the margins towards the anthropic centre, and, vice versa, an ironic and playful human gaze towards the margins. The geographic location of both monstrosities and the Biblical Paradise in the east may be granting this interaction a potentially serious, perhaps even gnomic angle.[2] And insofar as both the humorous and the monstrous are founded on the sense of surprise, laughter and dread, they replicate the reactions of reaching out towards what has either previously been unimaginable, or unimagined or unexpressed. In both cases, they are attempts at probing into, and then transcending and transgressing the cultural, social and religious limitations. Consequently, the debate on approaching monstrosity through humour and humour through monstrosity may display a rhetorical effect that is parallel to the one postulated by the Neoplatonic apophatic necessity of transcending whatever is known in order to approach the truth not from its centre—which, in Christian sense, is oriented around the divinely inspired Logos—but from its edges. These edges are marked by the presence of the theologically restricted extremes, that is monstrosities and humour, which represent the boundaries of what is known and what is permitted respectively. Humorous, ironic, terrifying and monstrous subversions of the truth are then the very margins which are strongly present in early medieval culture as indeed they are in any culture. It is the Neoplatonic Christian outlook which allows for seeing their sense and making their presence meaningful and, as a matter of fact, also practical for Christian cognitive models. In his discussion of apophasis and pseudonymity in Pseudo-Dionysian thought, Charles Stang coins the phrase of 'apophatic anthropology', an anthropology of negating one's intellectual faculties in order to approach the divine truth in a previously uninhibited way. In more senses than one this approach could be used to describe the discourse of monstrosity and humour, both, at least to some extent, based on the ideas of reversing what is familiar and known: 'These "uninitiated" provide the foil to his [Pseudo-Dionysius's] apophatic anthropology: they cling to the efficacy of their own intellectual faculties and their knowledge of beings. Sight, intellect, and knowledge in fact become obstacles to our union with the invisible, unknown God'.[3]

*Liber monstrorum* can be an example of what Stang described as 'apophatic anthropology'. Its survival in five different manuscripts from the ninth and tenth centuries attests to its considerable popularity in the early Middle Ages.[4] It is divided into three parts, the first of which concerns monstrous human races, the second, monstrous beasts, and the third, monstrous serpents. It is particularly its first part that shows the elements of 'apophatic' or 'negated' anthropology as it speaks of numerous, more or less fantastic races, in terms of how they reflect differences between the human and the beyond-human, more-than-human or not-so-human races. However, the didacticism, pansemiotism (meaningfulness of everything) and the polysemy (multiple layers of meaning) of medieval Christian thought mean that the reception of this text was obviously directed from the 'monstrous' margin to the 'human' centre. By probing into the alterities of humanity, it naturally spoke of humanity and, what must be added, of its place in the divinely ordained scheme of things.

The emotional attitudes and reactions related to terror and humour that the *Liber monstrorum* may have been envisioned to elicit were evidently directed not at the monstrosities described, but at those intending to read about them. The difficult issue is ascertaining the degree to which we can specify the experience of terror or humour by the *Liber monstrorum*'s audiences. Both humour and terror need to be understood in their relations to the social order in which they exist. What are then the criteria with which we are to judge whether what we might see as irony in the Prologue to the book of monsters resounded with such tones for its eleventh-century audience? In his critical edition of the text, Andy Orchard emphasises how abundant the text is in wordplay and punning.[5] The punning begins already in the text's fifth word, *situs*, which may mean both 'region' as well as 'filth', 'decay'.[6] Thus, depending on the disposition of the reader, the first part of the initial sentence:

> *De occulto orbis terrarum situ* interrogasti, et si tanta monstrorum essent genera credenda quanta in abditis mundi partibus

> You have asked about the secret arrangement [or 'filthiness'] of the lands of the earth, and if as many kinds of monsters are to be credited as demonstrated in the hidden parts [or 'births'] of the world[7]

reads either as a matter-of-fact statement of intention in response to a curiosity-driven enquiry, or as a justification of having to take up such an improper subject matter which, at the same time, condemns the vulgar interests of whoever supposedly put the question forward. While not precisely playing on the double entendre, the Prologue's exposition is not very far from it. The Prologue thus allows for humour to seep into the text treating predominantly fearsome creatures. Similarly, the Prologue's authorial comment—that all that is unknown is not necessarily monstrous and that the readers must be prepared for some disillusionment with the lack of monsters in the world they inhabit—may have been originally received at its face value, as a statement of a certain truth. At the same time, in the ears of a differently educated or differently predisposed original recipient of the treatise, it may have reverberated with a wry message of certain mockery directed at those who were susceptible to believe in what they wanted to hear and read about:

> Quaedam tantum in ipsis mirabilibus uera esse creduntur, et sunt innumerabilia quae si quis ad exploranda pennis uolare potuisset, et ita rumoroso sermone tamen ficta probaret, ubi nunc urbs aurea et gemmis aspersa litora dicuntur, ibi lapideam aut nullam urbem et scopulosa cerneret.

> Only some things in the marvels themselves are believed to be true, and there are countless things which if anyone could take winged flight to explore, they would prove that, although they should be concocted in speech and rumour, where now there is said to lie a golden city and gem-strewn shores, one would see there rocks and a stony city, if at all.[8]

Finally, reading the comment a couple of sentences later about how the increase of mankind led to the decrease in the number of monsters, are we allowed to imagine the readers in the past as smiling, laughing or maybe smirking?

> [Q]uia nunc humano genere multiplicator et terrarium orbe replete, sub astris minus producuntur monstra, quae ab ipsis per plurimos terrae angulos eradicate funditus et subuersa legimus et nunc reuulsa [...]

> Now, when humankind has multiplied and the lands of the earth have been filled, fewer monsters are produced under the stars, and we read that in most of the corners of the world they have been utterly eradicated and overthrown by them.[9]

In a comparable manner, equally vexing is the question about the way of judging and setting the criteria with which we may specify the degree of terror or its lack incited in the audiences of the past by the descriptions of the fantastic races contained within the *Liber monstrorum*. Did the description of the race apparently populating the area east of the Brixontis River inspire terror or did it also carry a potential for a sense of grotesqueness felt by the Anglo-Saxon readers of the text?

> I.33 Hominum quoque genus inmensis corporibus Brixontis fluminis ab Oriente nascitur, corpore nigri, et .XVIII. pedes altitudinis accipiunt; et, ut ferunt, homines cum comprehendant, crudos manducant.

> I.33 Also a race of people with huge bodies is born in the east of the river Brixontis black in body, and who reach eighteen feet in height; and, so they say, when they catch folk, they eat them raw.[10]

Meanwhile, the description of the monstrous race which immediately follows the account of the cannibalistic giants seems to invite both: fear or, perhaps, rather repulsion, combined with a sense of disbelief or grotesqueness at what even the narrator sees as outlandish:

> I.34 Et dicunt monstra esse in paludibus cum tribus humanis capitibus et sub profundissimis stagnis sicut nimphas habitare fabulantur. Quod credere profanum est: ut non illuc fluant gurgites quo inmane monstrum ingreditur.

> I.34 And they say there are monsters in swamps with three human heads and they are alleged to live like nymphs under the deepest pools. It is a profanity to believe this, since floods do not flow there, where a huge monster enters.[11]

The authorial comment added to the description does not only imply incredulity, but it may read both as a warning against transgression and a remark with a touch of ridicule directed at the naivety of readers. This instance of a monstrous race, the narrator seems to be saying, is a contradiction in terms and as such it may be both grotesque and enigmatic, leaving us with more questions than answers about judging the degrees of terror and humour in the reception of monsters.

## RIDDLES INTO MONSTERS, MONSTERS INTO RIDDLES

In partial answer to the problem of ascertaining the levels of humorousness and terror in early medieval descriptions of monstrosities, I shall now consider more closely two examples which, even more than the cases cited above, rely on the idea of enigmaticity. In both of them the confluence between terror, laughter and wisdom is their formative essence. Although only the first of the two comes from a collection of Old English poetic riddles, they are both examples of enigmas, as indeed, monstrosities may or, perhaps, should be treated. Riddles are monstrous and monsters are enigmatic since the assumptions upon which they are constructed are analogous: they both are emanations of a fascination with whatever is strange, secretive and mysterious; they both are among the oldest textual and visual forms;[12] both monsters and riddles are universally present in folklore and both have been studied as its important emanations;[13] and, by their unusual, bizarre and unexpected relations to reality, they both challenge their audiences and demand confrontations from them. Riddles, by their nature, are to be tackled in the act of guessing, while monsters are either to be tackled as threats or to be made sense of as elements of new knowledge. In what is arguably the best-known early Christian piece of guidance on approaching the idea of monstrosity, St Augustine, speaking in his *De civitate Dei* on the accounts of monstrous births, made a very clear point that whatever may seem abnormal should not so much draw attention to itself, but to the limitation of human knowledge and cognition.

> Sed si homines sunt, de quibus illa mira conscripta sunt: quid, si propterea Deus uoluit etiam nonnullas gentes ita creare, ne in his monstris, quae apud nos oportet ex hominibus nasci, eius sapientiam, qua naturam fingit humanam, uelut artem cuiuspiam minus perfecti opificis, putaremus errasse?[14]

> But if we assume that the subjects of those remarkable accounts are in fact men, it may be suggested that God decided to create some races in this way, so that we should not suppose that the wisdom with which he fashions the physical being of men has gone astray in the case of the monsters which are bound to be born among us of physical parents; for that would be to regard the works of God's wisdom as the products of an imperfectly skilled craftsman.[15]

Monsters, like riddles, therefore offer wisdom which is yet to be disclosed and determined. St Augustine states the obvious that the focus should not be on them, but on how they serve as vehicles expanding human awareness, also of human divinely ordained limitations. In a similar manner, we could say that riddles are not merely centred on their solutions, but also on the process of mental grappling with the ways they textually distort elements of reality. Both riddles and monsters function inasmuch as we confront ourselves with them.

Understandably, any confrontation with both monsters and riddles on the most immediate level demands answers. As much as the moment a riddle is solved, it ceases to be enigmatic; the moment a monster is made sense of, it ceases to be terrifying and monstrous. In this sense dispensing with a monster is akin to solving a riddle, and, conversely, solving a riddle is turning its defamiliarised, strange and 'textually monstrous' description into something ordinary and familiar. The element of playfulness, of teasing and of tricking their audiences is present in both monsters and riddles which, only when decrypted, are deprived of their unexpected aspects and qualities.[16] These points are central to the two monster figures featuring in Old English poetry that shall serve here as examples.

The first of the two depictions is a one-eyed and yet, mysteriously, twelve-hundred-headed creature that enters the company of the wise sitting at a council in Riddle 85 of the Exeter Book. I cite it here in full:

> Wiht cwom gongan       þær weras sæton
> monige on mæðle,       mode snottre;
> hæfde an eage       ond earan twa,

ond II fet,      XII hund heafda,
hrycg ond wombe      ond honda twa,
earmas ond eaxle,      anne sweoran
ond sidan twa.      Saga hwæt ic hatte.[17]

A weird creature came to a meeting of men,
Hauled itself into the high commerce
Of the wise. It lurched with one eye,
Two feet, twelve hundred heads,
A back and belly—two hands, arms,
Shoulders—one neck, two sides.
Untwist your mind and say what I mean.[18]

It has widely been accepted that the solution to this riddle may have been inspired by one of the *Aenigmata* by Symphosius, a little-known late Roman author from the turn of the fourth century.[19] The crux of the riddle is constructed on the idea of a sudden recognition, similar to the Aristotelian idea of *anagnorisis*, centred on the double meaning of *heafod* 'head' as both a head of an animate creature and as a head of garlic. Etymologically, the Old English word *gar-leac* 'garlic' is a compound connecting *gar* 'spear' and *leac* 'leek', creating thus a sense of a piercingly sharp vegetable. In this vein then, the riddle 'bites' and 'pierces' with its simultaneous humour and terror, although the latter seems to be largely overlooked:[20] the answer to it is assumed to be the one-eyed garlic seller, although it is only assumed to be so because of its notable relation to Symphosius's jocular enigma XCIV under this very title. The Latin original, or at least inspiration for Riddle 85 is nevertheless written in a relatively lighter and more humorous tone:

XCIV. Luscus alium vendens.
Cernere iam fas est quod vix tibi credere fas est:
unus inest oculus, capitum sed milia multa;
qui quod habet vendit, quod non habet unde parabit?

XCIV. One-Eyed Garlic Vendor
Now you may see what you scarcely may believe: one eye within, but many thousand heads. Whence shall he, who sells what he has, procure what he has not?[21]

The Old English version of the riddle (if, indeed, it can be called a version and not an altogether different poem) does seem much darker, however, and perhaps even ominous. It is so mainly because of the sharper sense of confrontation with someone or something that, like the evil clowns mentioned at the beginning, possesses the marks of the uncanny, the familiar unfamiliar. Furthermore, the confrontation takes place within the riddle, as the creature clearly interrupts a council of wise men sitting together pensively who are suddenly challenged by an eerie visitor. Perhaps, for the audiences of the turn of the first millennium AD, the one-eyed guest who makes a sudden, confrontative appearance among those who consider themselves wise would be an echo of the one-eyed god of confusion, Odin, and not so much a disguised reference to an otherwise obscure late Latin author. When in 1999 Enitharmon Press published a collection of one hundred riddle poems in commemoration of the millennium from the creation of the Exeter Book, it featured a short haiku-like poem by the acclaimed Peter Reading which seems to bear some semblance to Riddle 85:

> Soon and silently, in a dark suit […]
> men at the mead-bench, meditate, name him.[22]

The solution provided by Reading in the collection is 'death'. Provided then that the echo of Riddle 85 indeed is present in Reading's poem, it may indicate that he too may have sensed that the Old English riddle is not only humorous because of its traditionally accepted solution, but it is also tinged with some ominousness.

Nonetheless, although the Exeter Book riddle clearly lacks the joviality of the Latin source which involves playing on words and assonances, the humour of the Old English version results not from what is present in the Symphosian riddle, but from a sudden release of the tension between what may seem dark, serious, uncanny and even apocalyptic confronted with the realisation of the pun on the word *heafod* 'head'. It is more cryptic than its Latin source since it lacks the reference to selling a commodity present in the title-cum-solution of its Symphosian precedent and it defamiliarises the solution by enumerating the body parts whereby the audience is challenged by two surprising elements: the *XII hund heafda* 'twelve hundred heads' and the incongruous with them *an eage* 'one eye'. It seems that at least two of the main three theories of humour, that is those of relief and incongruity, are at play here. How obvious the solution would be to the original audiences, however, is not clear. Equally unclear is whether the riddle would initially strike them as funny or as sinister—perhaps an answer to this issue would depend on whether the riddle's audience were familiar with its Symphosian precedent or not.

The second example of an Old English poetic monster that bears within itself the aspect of enigmaticity emerges from the sea in the deceptive likeness of an island. It is the fabled Fastitocalon, the whale whose name is derived from garbled Greek and Roman names for 'asp turtle'.[23] The account is located in another Exeter Book poem, *The Whale*, which belongs to the Old English version of the didactic tradition of the Latin *Physiologus* presenting lessons and homiletic teachings which are to be drawn from the figures of animals.[24] The substance of the poem, although not a riddle proper, is largely centred on the idea of pansemiotism of reality and on the necessity to be able to decipher the messages encoded into it, or, perhaps particularly, into its monstrous deformations. Given the etymological explanation of the term *monstrum* as related to signs and portents articulated in Isidore of Seville's *Etymologiae* (Book XI, chapter 3),[25] the pansemiotic perspective on the monstrous creature is hardly surprising as the function of monsters was to serve as significant omens for those confronted with them. The poem and its monstrous whale is therefore a frightening lesson in inadequate understanding and falling into the temptation of superficial judgements. The terror wrought by the whale lies in its apparent duplicity, first in its luring weary sailors to land on what they think is an island; second in the way it seduces sailors to enter its gaping mouth. The failure in deciphering the true nature of the monster is thus life-threatening, both in terms of earthly existence and of spiritual afterlife, as the poem clearly is a warning about being misled by the forces of evil. The whale's first manner of deception is described as follows:

> Is þæs hiw gelic       hreofum stane,
> swylce worie       bi wædes ofre,
> sondbeorgum ymbseald,       særyrica mæst,
> swa þæt wenaþ       wægliþende
> þæt hy on ealond sum       eagum wliten,
> ond þonne gehydað       heahstefn scipu
> to þam unlonde       oncyrrapum,
> setlaþ sæmearas       sundes æt ende,
> ond þonne in þæt eglond       up gewitað
> collenferþe       [ll. 8–17][26]

> His form is like rough stone
> Like sea-weed floating near sandbanks,
> Drifting up and down at the water's edge.
> Sailors think his a lovely island,
> When they see him, so they can safely fasten
> Their high-prowed ships to that un-land
> With anchor-ropes, moor their sea-steeds,
> At the dark edge of this dissembling strand[27]

*The Whale* is an example of how a monster resembles a riddle which must be adequately solved in order to vouchsafe literal and spiritual survival. Failure to identify it correctly is equivalent to the intellectual failure of solving a riddle. The confrontation with the monster is therefore a confrontation with an enigma.

Yet this confrontation with the whale's monstrous duplicity is precisely also the point where the menacing meaning of the monster gains a humorous aspect. Misinterpreting it is, after all, also humiliating to those who do so and, as such may elicit contemptuous laughter. It may be an example of humour understood as an instance of incongruity in the juxtaposition between the whale and the island. It may also be an instance of relief, or its lack, as, ultimately, the poem is set to provide a lesson on what should not be done and laughter may appear here as relieving the tension of the terror associated with the enormous animal. Thus, although the ominous and admonitory tones undoubtedly prevail in *The Whale*, it may also be relatively easily turned into its ridiculing reversal, being similar in this to the parallel reversal of the humorous tone of Riddle 85 into a darker, brooding and terrifying dimension. In the world of the North Atlantic where whalebone was often used, whale sightings and beachings were not infrequent.[28] Mistaking a whale, however barnacled, for an island is not very likely. It is equally unlikely that the animal would release any smell which may be described as sweetly scented. In the literal sense of the poem, it would thus indeed take a foolish person to be deceived in the way suggested by it. If we agree about a degree of humorousness in *The Whale*, the joke is being played not on it as a monster, but on the gullible and unintelligent people.

## HUMOUR INTO TERROR, TERROR INTO HUMOUR

The riddlic and poetic monsters of the Anglo-Saxon literary imagination are, depending on the vantage point, both enigmatic and humorous. In all likelihood then, the combination between these two features is also applicable to other monstrosities since both humorous and terrifying experiences are largely founded upon semantic indeterminacies. In other words, terror is frequently felt in the situations involving unfamiliar, uncanny and surprising experience. Likewise humour is often based on similar mechanisms of unfamiliarity, surprise, bewilderment and, sometimes even, uncanniness. Alison Ross in the *Language of Humour* reiterates what is indisputable and what might as well be applied to monstrosities: 'this is the essence of humour: surprise, innovation and rule-breaking'.[29] The similarities in the theoretical stances which attempt to encompass the past and present understandings of monstrosity and humour are located in the importance of inconclusiveness common to them both.

Indeterminacy is notably present throughout the seven theses of the monster culture proposed by Jeffrey Jerome Cohen in his opening chapter to *The Monster Theory* (1996). To recapitulate it briefly here, monstrosity, according to Cohen's proposition, (1) is always effectuated by cultural constructs; (2) 'always escapes' and thus, in a literal and figurative sense, is always elusive; (3) marks or foreshadows a crisis of categories; (4) is, by principle, engendered by and as a cultural, political, sexual and racial difference; (5) protects and yet also explores 'the borders of the possible'; (6) is an expression of repressed desires; and (7), in the words of Cohen, 'stands at the threshold of becoming', posing questions about how we perceive the familiar categories and about how we misrepresent what we tried to represent and categorise.[30] Interestingly, in several of these points we can observe how akin monstrosity is to enigmaticity and how, again, dealing with the monster resembles resolving it as a form of a riddle. We can however also see that precisely all of the seven points are equally applicable to the discussion of humour and playfulness on the one hand and terror and dread on the other. After all, the sensations of humour and terror clearly are (1) cultural constructs; (2) whose very point may also be either cleverly elusive or relying on indeterminacy. Comparably (3) both humour and terror foreshadow or accompany crises of categories (for instance in the political and propagandist applications of humour and of fear); (4) whose effects often result from cultural, political, sexual and racial differences. Furthermore (5) both humour and terror explore and express the limits of what is possible and what is permissible; (6) simultaneously disclosing repressed desires; and (7) offering new ways of reconfiguring, through humour and terror, familiar categories and (mis)interpretations.

Clearly then, the theories of humour stressing the importance of the role of indeterminacy in connection with laughter may also be implemented in the discussion of monstrosities and the terror of the unfamiliar. In *Laughter and Ridicule. Towards the Social Critique of Humour*, Michael Billig stresses that no single theory can explain the complexity of humour and that the traditional approaches represented by the theories of superiority, incongruity and relief overlook not only the social, but also the paradoxical aspects of laughter.[31] Billig identifies what he sees as three fundamental paradoxes of laughter and humour, all of which are equally germane to monstrological studies and to the studies of terror as well. The first paradox lies in the universality and yet also particularity of humour, which is found everywhere, but not everyone laughs at the same things. The second paradox is the social and simultaneously anti-social aspects of humour, which offers bonds and which, at the same time, excludes. The third paradox listed by Billig is the duality between the mysteriousness and transparency of humour, which eludes analysis and which is yet also analysable.[32] It is immediately clear how much of this corresponds to the universality and particularity of what is deemed monstrous, which is evident from the theses proposed by Cohen. Correspondingly, the social, anti-social and cultural aspects of humour connect it with monstrosity. And, finally, the mysteriousness and transparency of humour appears proportionate to the elements of concealment and disclosure present in the construction and discussion of monstrosity, bringing into focus the element of emotional and semantic discharge offered by jokes, monsters and riddles alike. Perhaps it is in this discharge that we may find an answer to the fact that the moment a monster is revealed in its form or structure, it ceases to be monstrous and, often, begins to elicit laughter.

Despite their shortcomings pointed out by Billig, the traditionally established humour theories of superiority and disparagement, release and relief, and incongruity are nonetheless not necessarily entirely dismissible. Let us consider them briefly here, not in order to claim any of them as more suitable than others in the ways of approaching the issues of humour, but to illustrate how comparably applicable they are to the discourses of monstrosity. In doing so, I will be largely relying on Cristina Larkin-Galiñanes's 2017 overview of humour theory.[33]

The superiority and disparagement theory views humour and its manifestation of laughter though the perspectives of social allegiance and social identification, often expressed through irony, derision and deriding laughter. Humour and laughter construct and express a sense of belonging to a community. Frequently, this sense of belonging is realised through derision of the elements outside the communal sphere. Thus the focus of studying laughter through the prism of this theory is predominantly on the issues of the moral acceptability of comedy and laughter. The interest lies also in the object of humour or derision, with the fundamental question of what can be socially and culturally deduced from realising what and who is laughed at. The nature of laughter and derision is central: whether they are perceived as good or evil, what their social or class orientation is, and to what extent they are disruptive.[34] Now, it is, perhaps, immediately visible that similar areas are explorable and are applicable to the study of monstrous representations and the study of terror. Cohen's theses outlined above present monstrosities as social and cultural emanations and the 'us vs. them' principle behind singling out whatever may be considered monstrous has been practiced, with all of its enormously negative consequences, to this day. Like humour and laughter, fear and monstrosities are therefore used (and are 'useful') in constructing a sense of negative social allegiance and negative identification. The 'show me your fears and monsters and I will tell you who you are' idea and the senses of superiority and disparagement are very much operative towards monstrosities. In other words, the study of fear and monstrosities is frequently centred on what can be socially deduced from whoever or whatever is branded fearsome and monstrous.

The psycho-physiological approaches of the release and relief theory discuss and are concerned with individually and socially positive psychological and physiological effects of laughter. From the times of Aristotle, laughter and what we now call humour have been understood to bring social release and relief. Through the unexpectedness of a positive emotional discharge, they assist in restoring internal equilibrium. Larkin-Galiñanes observes that the release and relief approach has been argued to be the theory of laughter rather than of humour in general, but it may be understood as providing perspectives of the psychosomatic experience of humour.[35] Psychosomatic experience is directly related to the presence and levels of neurotransmitters in the human brain: in the case of humour, it is dopamine, responsible for reward-motivated behaviour; in the case of fear, it is noradrenaline, present in the fight-or-flight experiences. It is, therefore, equally possible to discuss the fear-motivated behaviour, and in particular the experience associated with cultural representations of monstrosities through the psycho-physiological perspectives of release and relief. In terms of monstrosities, it involves a sense of release or relief connected with channelling, practising, taming and domesticating fear in the act of confronting a representation of a monstrous figure. It is reflected in Cohen's monster culture theses as forms of expression of repressed desires and the way monstrosities explore 'the borders of the possible', allowing the release of tension arising from confrontations with unfamiliar categories.

The cognitive-perceptual orientation of the incongruity theory is, perhaps, one of the most popularly applied approaches explaining the nature of humour-related and humour-inducing phenomena. Again, as was the case with the two previous perspectives, this broad theory is equally well applicable to the discussion of fear and monstrosity. The cognitive focus on humour of the incongruity theory leads to the study of the mechanisms (aside from ridicule and derision) used to cause a sense of amusement and laughter. The most important among them are, naturally, the idea of discrepancy and/or of surprising, seemingly inappropriate linguistic, social and contextual contrasts. The study of humour and laughter is, in this perspective, focused also on the rhetorical effect of incongruity (understood as wit) leading to laughter.[36] Monstrosities likewise, as emanations of fear, are, by their very nature, incongruous considering that they are based on the idea of radical difference and radical incompatibility with whatever is not considered monstrous. As I have already stated, monstrosities and fear are found and experienced in surprising contexts and the notion of cultural, political, sexual and racial difference is their obvious *sine qua non*. At the same time, like humour and laughter, they have been understood to display important functionality as rhetorical devices—from Isidorian omens and portents, to what Cohen indicates as their relation to category crises, and to the way in which they reflect probing into the borders of the possible again.

Finally, among numerous, relatively recently arising theories of humour, Cristina Larkin-Galiñanes singles out one which is based on the semantic reformulation of the incongruity theory. Proposed by Victor Raskin in 1985 and founded on script-based semantics,[37] it attempts to provide a formula for what he calls 'a single-joke-carrying text'. He convincingly claims that it is so when a given text is compatible fully or in part with two different scripts—semantic fields, and when these two semantic fields are opposed to one another.[38] Again, as with all the above approaches and theories, this too encompasses the world of monstrosities which, as such, are constructed across different and opposing scripts. Their physical figures are founded on the principles of hybridity, superfluity and absence of elements, and as much as such amalgams are terrifying, they are also humorous. It is so because of the incongruity which occurs when different semantic fields, be it related to humour or related to monstrosity and fear, collide. Such collisions take place, as it were, on the margins of scripts and discourses—the marginality of humour and laughter as well as the marginality of fear and monstrosities is evidently analogous.

## Conclusions: The Sense of the Humour of Medieval Monsters

Published in the year 2000, Umberto Eco's *Baudolino* is a novel which provides an anthropological commentary on the perennial allure and importance of monstrosities in their terrifying and humorous dimensions. Its eponymous protagonist and narrator is a twelfth-century incurable liar whose stories gain lives of their own and are impossible to be distinguished from the truth. After other earlier adventures, Baudolino reflects on his journey to find the legendary Prester John, the alleged author of an epistolary tale of wonders addressed to the pope and circulating in Western Europe around 1165.[39] Eco's Baudolino takes us to the domains of medieval legends and fantastic races, and travels to the world of the fabled East, meeting many of the creatures and representatives of the races recognisable from the *Liber monstrorum*. As may be expected, it is Baudolino who is fantastic, terrifying and amusing to them and it is him who is expected by Deacon Johannes, their leader, to share with him the tales of what

252    R. BORYSŁAWSKI

is marginal to their world, that is the tales of the Wonders of the West. In so doing, Baudolino reverses the world familiar to us into a vision which is true, yet which is also as grotesque, as full of bafflement, mystery, but also of terror and humour, as the *Liber monstrorum* and other similar medieval narratives.[40] It is also as imaginative as the inventiveness of a storyteller allows:

> I tried to make him [Deacon Johannes] live through my tales. And I may also have invented: [...] I told him of the wonders of the lands where the sun dies [...] [of] a fish the size of a mountain, capable of swallowing a whole ship, but I had to explain to him what ships were, fish made of wood that cleave the waves, while moving white wings; I listed for him the wondrous animals of my country [...] the ladybug, which is like a small mushroom, red and dotted with milk-colored spots [...] the oyster, a living jewel box that sometimes produces a dead beauty but of inestimable value, the nightingale that keeps vigil singing and lives worshiping the rose, the lobster, a loricate monster of a flame-red color, who flees backwards to escape the hunters who dote on its flesh, the eel, frightful aquatic serpent with a fatty, exquisite flavor, the seagull, that flies over the waters as if it were an angel of the Lord.[41]

Eco, through Baudolino's words, asks us to reverse perspectives and to imagine un-thinking what is well familiar. It is a mental exercise of reimagining what is common into what may be conceptualised into both terror- and humour-inducing ideas and beings. Like medieval monster narratives, *Baudolino*'s land of monsters is both humorous and also terrifying in how it invites and enforces a reconfiguration of seemingly recognisable concepts.

The conclusion that can be reached after the discussion of the confluences between the terror of the monster and the humour kindled by it is that these two forms of marginalities adhere to and bolster epistemological applications in the early and later medieval visions of the world. It is the marginality and pointing to boundaries that connects the terror and humour of the monster. At the same time, because of its inherent indeterminacy, the boundaries pointed to are indeterminate too. It is so since what both monstrous humour and monstrous terror evoke is a reaction of negation—in the case of terror, the negation of whatever is unfamiliar, in the case of humour, the negation of whatever is an established hierarchy. Both the terror and the humour of the monster serve the purposes of rhetorical negation and are then a form of rhetorical apophasis. The monstrous races are not so much or not only objects of wonder, but rather rhetorical tools resorting to the combination of terror and humour to address the limits of human cognition and humanity itself. The interplay of the serious and the humorous, of the terrible and the comical which is to be found in them is parallel to what is familiar from early Christian mystical theology, that is, it is an apophasis of reality applied in order to enhance its perception.

The search for the possibility of expressing the ineffable through the extremities of humour and terror continues. In contemporary cultural discourse, for instance, it is frequently proposed by modern conceptual art, which often seeks to elicit the reaction of laughter and dread.[42] In medieval hermeneutics, and, more precisely, in early medieval Neoplatonic mysticism, it is evident in how Pseudo-Dionysius the Areopagite demands imagining thinking beyond what is known and unknown to the extent of overstepping language itself. In the poetic incipit to Chapter One of *The Mystical Theology* he pleads with the heavenly wisdom to:

ἴθυνον ἡμᾶς ἐπὶ τὴν τῶν
μυστικῶν λογίων ὑπεράγνωστον
καὶ ὑπερφαῆ καὶ ἀκροτάτην κορυφήν·
ἔνθα τὰ ἁπλᾶ καὶ ἀπόλυτα καὶ
ἄτρεπτα τῆς θεολογίας μυστήρια
κατὰ τὸν ὑπέρφωτον
ἐγκεκάλυπται τῆς κρυφιομύστου
σιγῆς γνόφον,
ἐν τῶι σκοτεινοτάτωι τὸ ὑπερφανέστα.[43]

Lead us up beyond unknowing and light,
up to the farthest, highest peak
of mystic scripture,
where the mysteries of God's Word
lie simple, absolute and unchangeable
in the brilliant darkness of a hidden silence.
Amid the deepest shadow
they pour overwhelming light
on what is most manifest.[44]

Pseudo-Dionysius speaks of, as it were, unseeing, of looking for the enlightenment in the darkness of shadows, and of seeking illumination not in what is central, but in what is marginal. As Charles Stang stresses in the passage cited above in the introductory part of this chapter, it is the quest for moving beyond rationality. Similarly, if the characters of *Baudolino* or the narrator of *Liber monstrorum* reach the land of monsters that is impenetrable to their reason, they do so perhaps partly because, as Pseudo-Dionysius asserts, it is somewhere beyond thinking that the hope of making sense lies. It is then also in the misunderstanding of the monster—whose terror may be disarmed by the laughter it elicits—that the epistemological senses of monstrous humour and humorous monstrosity lie. In order to make more sense of the corporeal, early medieval imagination proliferated monsters and then in order to understand the workings of the real, it questioned and doubted them with humour.

## NOTES

1. A comprehensive discussion of medieval manuscript marginalia is provided by Sandler, 'The Study of Marginal Imagery', 1–49.
2. For a discussion of the locations of medieval monstrosities see Friedman, *The Monstrous Races*, 37–58. Maja Kominko has recently presented a review of medieval locations of Paradise: Kominko, 'New Perspectives on Paradise', 139–54.
3. Stang, *Apophasis and Pseudonymity*, 159. See also 158–69.

4. Orchard, *Pride and Prodigies*, 86.
5. Ibid., 87–90.
6. Ibid., 89.
7. Orchard, *Liber monstrorum*, 254–55.
8. Ibid., 256–57.
9. Ibid., 256–57.
10. Ibid., 276–77.
11. Ibid., 276–77.
12. On the presence of riddles among the earliest preserved written Egyptian and Sumerian texts see Hansen, *The Solomon Complex*, 12–41.
13. On the folkloristic aspects and appearances of riddles see the fundamental essays by Taylor, 'The Riddle', 129–47; Georges and Dundes, 'Toward a Structural Definition of the Riddle', 111–18; and Frye, 'Charms and Riddles', 123–47.
14. Augustine, *De civitate Dei*.
15. Augustine, *City of God*, 663–64.
16. In folk- and fairy tales, shapeshifters are rendered powerless or brought back to their primeval shape once a key to their transformations is identified, such as when the animal skin or bird feathers of heroes turned to animals or birds are destroyed or stolen in European fairy tales. See, for instance: 'The Swan Maiden' in Tatar, *The Classic Fairy Tales*, 72–73; 'The Twelve Brothers' and 'Bearskin' in Pullman, *Grimm Tales*, 39–46 and 289–95 respectively.
17. Riddle 85 (82) in Muir, *The Exeter Anthology*, 376.
18. Riddle 85 (82) in Williamson, *The Complete Old English Poems*, 592.
19. See for example Wilcox, 'Mock-Riddles in Old English', 180–87; Borysławski, *The Old English Riddles*, 34–37; Bitterli, *Say What I Am Called*, 14–15.
20. See Fry, 'Exeter Book Riddle Solutions', 22–33; and Bitterli, *Say What I Am Called*, 215–16.
21. Ohl, *The Enigmas of Symphosius*, 129.
22. Reading, 'Riddle 69', unpaginated.
23. DeAngelo, '*Discretio spirituum*', 284.
24. Discussions of the poems belonging to the Old English *Physiologus* are offered by Letson, 'The Old English Physiologus', 15–41, Rossi-Reder, 'Beasts and Baptism', 461–76 and specifically of *The Whale* by DeAngelo, '*Discretio spirituum*', 271–89.
25. Isidore, *Etymologies*, 243: 'Portents are also called signs, omens, and prodigies, because they are seen to portend and display, indicate and predict future events. The term "portent" (*portentum*) is said to be derived from foreshadowing (*portendere*), that is, from "showing beforehand" (*praeostendere*). "Signs" (*ostentum*), because they seem to show (*ostendere*) a future event. Prodigies (*prodigium*) are so called, because they "speak hereafter" (*porro dicere*), that is, they predict the future. But omens (*monstrum*) derive their name from admonition (*monitus*), because in giving a sign they indicate (*demonstrare*) something, or else because they instantly show (*monstrare*) what may appear; and this is its proper meaning, even though it has frequently been corrupted by the improper use of writers'.
26. *The Whale* in Muir, *The Exeter Anthology*, 272.
27. *The Whale* in Williamson, *The Complete Old English Poems*, 509.
28. Mark Gardiner provides a detailed overview of the exploitation of whales and other sea mammals and of its social context in Anglo-Saxon and later England. Gardiner, 'The Exploitation of Sea-Mammals in Medieval England', 173–95.

12 THE MONSTERS THAT LAUGH BACK: HUMOUR AS A RHETORICAL APOPHASIS... 255

29. Ross, *The Language of Humour*, xii.
30. Cohen, 'Monster Culture (Seven Theses)', 3–25.
31. Billig, *Laughter and Ridicule*, 175–76.
32. Ibid., 176.
33. Larkin-Galiñanes, 'An Overview of Humour Theory', 4–16.
34. Ibid., 5–9.
35. Ibid., 9–12.
36. Ibid., 12–15.
37. Raskin, 'Linguistic Heuristics of Humor', 11–25.
38. Cited in Larkin-Galiñanes, 'An Overview of Humour Theory', 15.
39. Editions and translations of the twelfth-century versions of the letter are provided by Brewer, *Prester John*, 29–96.
40. Among those familiar to literate audiences of the late Anglo-Saxon England are also the Old English *The Wonders of the East* and *The Letter of Alexander to Aristotle*. Both are edited and translated in Orchard, *Pride and Prodigies*.
41. Eco, *Baudolino*, 405–6.
42. For an analysis of the uses of laughter and dread in contemporary conceptual and visual arts see Klein, *Art and Laughter*, 93–109.
43. Pseudo-Dionysius Areopagite, *De Mystica Theologia*, 142.
44. Pseudo-Dionysius, *The Complete Works*, 135.

## Bibliography

Augustine, Saint. *City of God*. Translated by Henry Bettenson. London: Penguin Books, (1972) 2003.

Augustine, Saint. *De civitate Dei*, Book XVI, Chapter 8. *The Latin Library*. Accessed 5 June 2019. http://www.thelatinlibrary.com/augustine/civ16.shtml

Billig, Michael. *Laughter and Ridicule: Towards the Social Critique of Humour*. London: Sage Publications, 2005.

Bitterli, Dieter. *Say What I Am Called. The Old English Riddles of the Exeter Book and the Anglo-Latin Riddle Tradition*. Toronto: University of Toronto Press, 2009.

Borysławski, Rafał. *The Old English Riddles and the Riddlic Elements of Old English Poetry*. New York: Peter Lang, 2004.

Brewer, Keagan. *Prester John: The Legend and Its Sources*. Farnham: Ashgate, 2015.

Cohen, Jeffrey Jerome. 'Monster Culture (Seven Theses)'. In *Monster Theory. Reading Culture*, edited by Jeffrey Jerome Cohen, 3–25. Minneapolis, London: University of Minnesota Press, 1996.

DeAngelo, Jeremy. '*Discretio spirituum* and *The Whale*'. *Anglo-Saxon England* 42 (2013): 271–89.

Eco, Umberto. *Baudolino*. Translated by William Weaver. London: Secker and Warburg, 2000.

Friedman, John Block. *The Monstrous Races in Medieval Art and Thought*. Syracuse, New York: Syracuse University Press, 2000.

Fry, Donald K. 'Exeter Book Riddle Solutions'. *Old English Newsletter* 15, no. 1 (1981): 22–33.

Frye, Northrop. 'Charms and Riddles'. In Northrop Frye. *Spiritus Mundi. Essays on Literature, Myth, and Society*, 123–47. Bloomington: Indiana University Press, 1976.

Gardiner, Mark. 'The Exploitation of Sea-Mammals in Medieval England: Bones and Their Social Context'. *Archaeological Journal* 154, no. 1 (1997): 173–95.

Georges, Robert A. and Alan Dundes. 'Toward a Structural Definition of the Riddle'. *Journal of American Folklore* 76, no. 300 (1963): 111–18.

Hansen, Elaine Tuttle. *The Solomon Complex. Reading Wisdom in Old English Poetry*. Toronto: University of Toronto Press, 1988.

Isidore of Seville. *Etymologies*. Translated by Stephen A. Barney, W. J. Lewis, J. A. Beach and Oliver Berghof. Cambridge: Cambridge University Press, 2006.

Klein, Sheri R. *Art and Laughter*. London: I.B. Tauris, 2007.

Kominko, Maja. 'New Perspectives on Paradise – the Levels of Reality in Byzantine and Latin Medieval Maps'. In *Cartography in Antiquity and the Middle Ages*, edited by Richard J. A. Talbert and Richard W. Unger, 139–54. Leiden: Brill, 2008.

Larkin-Galiñanes, Cristina. 'An Overview of Humour Theory'. In *The Routledge Handbook of Language and Humour*, edited by Salvatore Attardo, 4–16. New York: Routledge, 2017.

Letson, D. R. 'The Old English *Physiologus* and the Homiletic Tradition'. *Florilegium* 1 (1979): 15–41.

Muir, Bernard J., ed. *The Exeter Anthology of Old English Poetry. Volume I: Texts*. Exeter: University of Exeter Press, 1994.

Orchard, Andy, ed. and trans. *Liber monstrorum de diversis generibus*. In Andy Orchard, *Pride and Prodigies. Studies in the Monsters of the* Beowulf-*Manuscript*, 254–317. Toronto: University of Toronto Press, 2003.

Orchard, Andy. *Pride and Prodigies. Studies in the Monsters of the* Beowulf-*Manuscript*. Toronto: University of Toronto Press, 2003.

Ohl, Theordore, ed. and trans. *The Enigmas of Symphosius*. Philadelphia: University of Pennsylvania Press, 1928.

Pullman, Philip, trans. *Grimm Tales*. London: Penguin Classics, 2013.

Pseudo-Dionysius the Areopagite. *De Mystica Theologia*. Edited by G. Heim and A. M. Ritter, 142–50. Patristische Texte und Studien 36. Berlin: De Gruyter, 1991.

Pseudo-Dionysius. *The Complete Works*. Translated by Colm Luibheid. London: SPCK, 1987.

Raskin, Victor. 'Linguistic Heuristics of Humor: A Script-based Semantic Approach'. *International Journal of the Sociology of Language* 65 (1987): 11–25.

Reading, Peter. 'Riddle 69'. In *The New Exeter Book of Riddles*, edited by Kevin Crossley-Holland and Lawrence Sail, unpaginated. London: Enitharmon Press, 1999.

Ross, Alison. *The Language of Humour*. London: Routledge, 2005.

Rossi-Reder, Andrea. 'Beast and Baptism: A New Perspective on the Old English *Physiologus*'. *Neophilologus* 83 (1999): 461–77.

Sandler, Lucy Freeman. 'The Study of Marginal Imagery: Past, Present, and Future'. *Studies in Iconography* 18 (1997): 1–49.

Stang, Charles, *Apophasis and Pseudonymity in Dionysius the Areopagite*. Oxford: Oxford University Press, 2012.

Taylor, Archer. 'The Riddle'. *California Folklore Quarterly* 2, 2 (1943): 129–47.

Tatar, Maria, ed. *The Classic Fairy Tales*. New York, London: W. W. Norton & Company, 1999.

Wilcox, Jonathan. 'Mock-Riddles in Old English: Exeter Riddles 85 and 19'. *Studies in Philology* 93, no. 2 (1996): 180–87.

Williamson, Craig, trans. *The Complete Old English Poems*. Philadelphia: University of Pennsylvania Press, 2017.

CHAPTER 13

# Medieval Jokes in Serious Contexts: Speaking Humour to Power

*Martha Bayless*

### SUDDEN ERUPTIONS OF TRUTH

In his collection of stories about twelfth-century events and beliefs, the courtier Walter Map recalled a conversation he had witnessed about the death of a young boy and the response of the renowned Bernard (later St Bernard), abbot of Clairvaux. The group, including Map, two monks, and Gilbert Foliot, bishop of London, had heard many of Bernard's miracles recounted, when one of the monks added his first-hand observation. Map reports:

> Euolutis autem multis, ait alter: 'Cum uera sint que de Barnardo dicuntur, uidi tamen aliquando quod ipsi gracia miraculorum defuit. Vir quidam marchio Burgundie rogauit eum ut ueniret et sanaret filium eius. Venimus et inuenimus mortuum. Iussit igitur corpus deferri dompnus Barnardus in talamum secretum, et eiectis omnibus incubuit super puerum, et oratione facta surrexit; puer autem non surrexit, iacebat enim mortuus.' Tum ego: 'Monachorum infelicissimus hic fuit. Nunquam enim audiui quod aliquis monachus super puerum incubuisset, quin statim post ipsum surrexisset puer.' Erubuit abbas, et egressi sunt ut riderent plurimi.[1]

> After recounting many [stories], one of them said, 'Although the things they say of Bernard may be true, nevertheless I saw an occasion when that power to work miracles was lacking. A certain man from the borders of Burgundy asked him to come and heal his son. We came and found him dead. So the lord Bernard ordered the body to be taken into a private chamber, and having dismissed every-

---

M. Bayless (✉)
University of Oregon, Eugene, OR, USA
e-mail: mjbayles@uoregon.edu

© The Author(s), under exclusive license to Springer Nature Switzerland AG 2020
D. Derrin, H. Burrows (eds.), *The Palgrave Handbook of Humour, History, and Methodology*, https://doi.org/10.1007/978-3-030-56646-3_13

257

one, he lay on the boy, and having made his prayers, rose again; the boy however did not rise, but lay dead'. Then I said: 'That was the most unlucky of monks. For I never heard that any monk lay on a boy without the boy getting up again right after him'. The abbot blushed, and many went out so they could laugh.

What are we to make of Map's satirical quip, interjected in the middle of a sombre narrative about the death of a boy and the limitations of earthly sanctity? One school of literary criticism might address the fact that the story takes a turn towards the carnivalesque, puncturing an earnest religious narrative with a transgressive ending and a deflating allusion to the things of the unruly lower body.[2] A cognitive turn of mind might view the story as a test case in a consideration of incongruity theory, in which the two meanings of 'lying on' a person are contrasted and reconciled; or reversal theory might be applied, in which the listener flips between contrasting states of mind: between one meaning of 'lay on' and the other, and between sorrow and merriment.[3] Others might make use of Terror Management Theory, in which an acute awareness of death, exacerbated by the demise of the boy and the inadequacy of religious response, provokes a defensive turn of thought towards humour and towards the possibilities rather than the failure of the body.[4] My own work has involved looking at the social dimension of laughter in the presence of death, and the ways in which laughter functions as a social signal.[5] The fact that Map mentions the laughter of the bystanders after his jibe would, in this view, serve to underline the tension caused by the death and the failure of the holy cleric, and the way in which laughter serves to allay that distress.

All of these models, and a good many others, might usefully be applied to this story. By and large, however, scholars of medieval humour have taken literary or historical approaches, examining issues such as narrative structures or power relations as they develop in an extended scenario, and thus have concentrated on pieces or instances of extended humour such as the fabliaux or carnival.[6] The fabliaux, humorous stories of trickery and bodily excess, have alone generated a voluminous literature of commentary and analysis.[7] Similarly, modern sociology and psychology have often studied humour by using the joke, a discrete and self-contained form of humour, as the typical test object. As an example, this joke, of lukewarm funniness, has been used to analyse incongruity theory:

> O'Riley was on trial for armed robbery. The jury came out and announced, 'Not guilty'. 'Wonderful', said O'Riley, 'does that mean I can keep the money?'[8]

In the 'world' of this example, the trial is serious and the jury's verdict is in earnest, and the robber's innocent question is the only blatantly humorous line in the scenario. But since the entire joke is a fiction, and the trial and the verdict merely a prelude to a punchline, in fact the entire work is in a non-serious mode. The crime, the trial, and the verdict are fantasies, carefully pitched so that the punchline will work; for instance, if the joke involved the death of a boy during the course of armed robbery—an analogue to the death of the boy in Map's story—the punchline would likely appear too callous to be funny. The lack of visible victims helps keep sympathy from leaking in; it keeps the crime effectively inconsequential and the robber's response trivial, and therefore allows the joke to be funny.

This set-up differs from the situation described by Walter Map, in which a serious scenario is interrupted, indeed disrupted, by a sudden change of tone. In this study I want to address the type of humour represented by Map's example: humour in serious medieval contexts. In these the serious situation prefacing the quip is not merely a set-up but is genuinely in earnest. This occurs most frequently in accounts from real life, such as Map's, but also appears in largely serious imaginative works. In particular, I want to analyse and highlight one feature of this less usual form of humour: not the more predictable elements such as its capacity to disrupt or subvert, but its capacity to tell the truth. This truth, in turn, may alter the dynamics of power, and so both humour and truth-telling may serve as means of asserting authority and transfiguring hierarchies.

## Humour That Tells the Truth

In this function of telling the truth, such humour fulfils the description of the classical poet Horace, who wrote in his first *Satire*:

> praeterea ne sic ut qui iocularia ridens
> percurram: quamquam ridentem dicere verum
> quid vetat? Ut pueris olim dant crustula blandi
> doctores, elementa velint ut discere prima
> sed tamen amoto quaeramus seria ludo. (*Sat.* 1.1.23-27)

> In addition, lest I rush through these things laughing, like a joker—what prevents me from telling the truth while laughing, just as beguiling teachers used to give tidbits to boys so that they would learn the basics?—but nevertheless, putting play aside, let us seek after serious matters.

Despite Horace's ostensible turn to serious things after the question, it was the possibility of combining truth and laughter that fired the imagination of later authors. Medieval writers took to heart the possibility of *ridentem dicere verum*—telling the truth while laughing. The phrase itself turned up in the work of a number of authors. In his *Policraticus*, John of Salisbury refers to the concept in his accounts of faithless women, arguing that neither laughter nor falsehood was antithetical to a deeper truth:

> In muliebrem leuitatem ab auctoribus passim multa scribuntur. Fortasse falso interdum figuntur plurima; nichil tamen impedit ridentem dicere uerum et fabulosis narrationibus [...].[9]

About the shallowness of women, many things are written in various places by the authors. Perhaps a great many things are depicted falsely; but nothing keeps laughter from telling the truth, and likewise by means of fantastic stories [...].

The eleventh-century cleric Anselm of Besate, who served in the household of the Holy Roman emperor Henry III and wrote a tome on rhetoric, similarly championed the idea of *ridendo dicere verum*, and his own treatise, the *Rhetorimachia*, served as what he called a *iocosus sermo*, a 'joking discourse', combining the serious exposition of rhetoric with playful jokes and insults.[10] Works such as these promoted the idea of amusements that told the truth, a form that gained favour in the genre of sermon *exempla*, humorous stories that conveyed a moral point, embedded in sermons. These became such an important form in the later centuries of the Middle Ages that some humorous stories, such as the trickster tale *Dame Sirith*, survive principally as parts of sermons.[11] But other authorities were more suspicious of humour, and even noted that humour might be an unwitting betrayer of truths. Such was the twelfth-century French bishop Peter of Celle, who reproved a fellow cleric for enjoying Paris too greatly, saying 'Ridendo tamen uerum dixisti' [But you have spoken the truth while laughing], in praising Paris for its earthly pleasures, which, admonished Peter, he ought to regard with more serious reprehension.[12]

The potential of humour was also expressed in other phrasing. William of Malmesbury noted the skill of Lanfranc in managing the temperamental moods of William the Conqueror:

Porro Willelmus rex eius solius contuitu superbiam contundebat suam; quem et ille sancta tractabat arte, quod perperam fecisset non seuere obiurgando, sed seria iocis condiendo. Itaque eum plerumque ad sanitatem reuocabat, sententiae suae conformando.

What is more, King William needed only a glance from Lanfranc to quell his haughty manner. For his part, Lanfranc managed the king with a holy skill, not sternly upbraiding what he did wrong, but spicing serious language with jokes. In this way, he could usually bring him back to a right mind, and mould him to his own opinions.[13]

Lanfranc, then, was speaking humour to power. This use of humour is in a way surprising, as much humour, such as the punchlines of jokes, is typically focused on effect rather than on truth. A late medieval question-and-answer joke from France may serve to illustrate this:

Lesquelles brebis menguent le plus: ou les blanches, ou les noires?
 —Ce doibt estre des blanches, quant il en y a plus grant nombre.[14]

Which sheep eat the most: the white ones, or the black ones?
 —It has to be the white ones, because there are a greater number of them.

It is a true statement that the white sheep eat more than black ones, but this fact is entirely inconsequential. The point of the joke, of course, is that the question posed by the first part is misinterpreted in the second part: the question refers to the amount eaten per individual sheep, but the ambiguous wording allows for an answer relating to the collective amount eaten by all sheep in each category. So in an absolute sense the answer is true, but it is not true of the question asked, and therefore in this instance the truth is beside the point, or rather there are two truths, the truth required by the question and the divergent truth supplied by the answer. In that sense the joke calls the stability of truth into question, and so if any truth is articulated by the joke, it is the instability of language. But the instability of language has to be configured in a very particular way to be funny, and the humour, rather than the philosophy, is the real point of the joke.

## THE CONTEXT OF HUMOROUS TRUTH

This example is one of many that might be given to demonstrate the fact that, despite Horace's assertion, truth is not regarded as a central feature of most types of humour. Rather than depicting the world accurately, humorous narrative is better known for its exaggeration, extending even to fantasy. In the fabliaux, for instance, peasants are always bumpkins, old men are outwitted by their wives, young wives are frisky, clerics are lecherous, and all the characters are in avid pursuit of their own interests. The things of the body are foremost, to the extent that genitalia may be handily detachable or have their own agency. Perhaps most unrealistically, everything ends tidily, with all plot threads sewn up. In the words of Oscar Wilde, 'The good ended happily, and the bad unhappily. That is what Fiction means'.[15]

This unrealistic convention of tidy endings, whether happy or melancholy or of mixed tone, also is shared by serious medieval fiction. The difference between comic and serious fiction is more in where exactly the ending comes: in the words of the famous quotation, 'Tragedy plus time equals comedy'.[16] So the long term, in which individual events are put into divine perspective, is a comedy. The medieval theologian would certainly have agreed with this perspective, as would Dante, whose *Divina Commedia* focused on the afterlife, at the end of a person's toil in the earthly realm. It was also the perspective achieved by Troilus at the end of Chaucer's *Troilus and Criseyde*, when he is carried high above the earth and laughs at the small passions of earthly grief and lust below, comparing them to the joy of heaven.[17]

But it is also clear from the fabliaux and other comic texts that people need not wait for the afterlife to experience certain kinds of pleasures. The competing quotation in this area would be that of the theme song of the musical *A Funny Thing Happened on the Way to the Forum*: 'Tragedy tomorrow, comedy tonight'.[18] Short-term pleasures allow one to ignore the tragedy of the larger earthly narrative. In the words of the nineteenth-century critic William Hazlitt, 'We weep at what thwarts or exceeds our desires in serious matters: we laugh at

262 M. BAYLESS

what only disappoints our expectations in trifles'.[19] In other words, for a thing to have comic appeal, it must be non-threatening, and restricting the view to the short term helps retain this air of triviality. For this reason, it is easiest if a comic joke or narrative is self-contained, detached from any immediate historical reality. A fictional joke, self-contained and detached from any particular social context, can focus on the *raison d'être* of such a joke: to be funny. Reality makes comedy harder.

The challenge of presenting the truth in comic guise is what makes the truth-tellers in serious contexts so skilful. They dismantle the fantasies of genre and formality, and reveal the wizard behind the curtain. Walter Map's story of Bernard is a case in point: those who hear of Bernard's attempt to induce a miracle may wonder whether they have entered the realm of the miraculous, the realm in which resurrection is a possibility. But in the everyday world monks lie on boys for much more sordid purposes, and Map recalls that world to mind. If the story had ended with the boy rising from the dead, the joke would have been pointless and even offensive. But one of the truths the joke tells is that boys do not rise from the dead. The everyday truths of the body are much more tawdry.

An instance from another elite conversation operates similarly. Liudprand of Cremona's *Relatio de Legatione Constantinopolitana* is a withering account of the time that Liudprand, a tenth-century Italian bishop and diplomat, spent at the court of Byzantium, where the Byzantine emperor had ambitions of extending his conquests. At one point in his visit Liudprand attempted to persuade one of the emperor's chamberlains that the emperor might usefully follow the example of Liudprand's own lord, Berengar II, king of Italy, who had piously restored to the church all its lands and properties. Liudprand recounts his conversation as he lectured the defiant chamberlain, Basil, on the point:

> 'Cur imperator vero non itidem facit, ut ea quae suis insunt regnis apostolorum ecclesiae reddat et per laborem atque munificentiam domini mei ditem et liberam ditiorem ipse ac liberiorem reddat?'

> 'Sed hoc,' ait Basilius parakimomenos, 'faciet, cum ad nutum suum Roma et Romana ecclesia ordinabitur.' Tum 'Homo,' inquam, 'quidam multam ab alio passus iniuriam his Deum aggressus est verbis: "Domine, vindica me de adversario meo!" Cui Dominus "Faciam," inquit, "in die cum reddam unicuique secundum opera sua". At ille "Quam tarde!" infit'.[20]

> 'Why truly does the emperor not do this same thing, so that he gives back those things that are in his kingdom to the church of the apostles, and thereby himself increases the wealth and freedom of that which is already wealthy and free, through the labour and generosity of my lord?'

> 'And that,' said Basil the chamberlain, 'he will bring about, when he puts Rome and the Roman church in order at his command.' Then I said, 'A man, having suffered great injury from another man, approached God with these words: "Lord, avenge me on my enemy!" To which the Lord replied, "I will do that, on the day when I repay each one according to his deeds". "That late!" said the man'.

Here the grandiosity of the emperor is punctured by an acknowledgement of the impossibly long timescale of ambitious desires. Justice will be levied on wrongdoers—at the end of time. Liudprand acknowledges that the emperor may indeed be generous to his churches—no sooner than the Lord levies justice on wrongdoers. And at the same time, he sets the emperor's grandiose plans of conquest, relayed by his boastful chamberlain, in a realistic timescale— no sooner than any of the other improbable events. Where Map used humour to puncture the pretensions of those who sought to import the divine into everyday life, Liudprand uses the divine to show the gap between everyday life and the unreachable.

The deflation of political grandiosity is also on show in an anecdote related by John of Salisbury and Gerald of Wales. In John of Salisbury's version, from the *Policraticus* (*a.* 1159):

> Pirrus percunctatus est eos qui in conuiuio Tarentinorum parum honoratum sermonem de se habuerunt, an quae audierat uera essent. Tum ex his unus: Nisi, inquit, uinum nobis deficisset, ista quae tibi relata sunt prae his quae dicturi eramus ludus ac iocus fuissent.[21]

> Pirrus asked, from some people at a feast in Tarentum who had had a conversation about him in which he was held in minimal respect, whether the reports he had heard were true. One of them replied: 'If our wine hadn't run out, those things reported to you would have been mere fun and games compared to what we were going to say!'

John of Salisbury goes on to remark, 'Tam urbana crapulae excusatio tamque simplex confessio ueritatis iram tiranni conuertit in risum' [So the witty excuse of drunkenness, together with the simple confession of truth, converted the wrath of the tyrant into laughter].

The version by Gerald of Wales, in an addendum to the *Vita S. Remigii* (*c.* 1198), localises the joke to England, where he gives the starring role to Roger, bishop of Worcester:

> Item, accusatis quibusdam in praesentia domini regis, quod indecentia de ipso et inhonesta dixisset, ad suggestionem episcopi ejusdem unus eorum facete subintulit; 'Ea forsan diximus, et illa quidem minima respectu illorum erant, quae nisi vinum defecisset dicturi eramus'. Ad quae conversis in risum omnibus, et rege cum aliis in gaudium resoluto, imputatis ebrietati cunctis, immunes relicti sunt illi tam ab accusatione quam suspicione.[22]

> Likewise, when certain men were accused in the presence of the lord king, because they had said disgraceful and shameful things about him, at the suggestion of the bishop one of them offered wittily: 'We might have said those things, but they were very minimal compared to what we were going to say if the wine hadn't run out'. At this everyone was moved to laughter, and the king softened into merriment with the others, with everyone charging drunkenness, they were left as free from accusation as from suspicion.

This follows a previous anecdote about a dispute about the primacy of the archibishopric, a dispute which had involved physical blows, in which 'ob elegantium verborum urbanitatem, rege in riso converso' [by the elegant wittiness of words, the king was turned to laughter].[23] It may seem extraordinary that a bishop was shoehorned into a popular joke, but it is clear that the ability to handle powerful people through humour was a skill to be praised. It is distinctive that in each of these stories, whether from Map, Liudprand, John, or Gerald, the narrator follows the tale by emphasising the laughter of the spectators or the wit of the joke, underscoring the success of the joker's boldness, which might otherwise be in question. The success of the joke depends on the response of the audience, and so the approval of the audience must be registered.

A further example, also in John of Salisbury's *Policraticus*, involves a situation in which a subordinate takes it upon himself to give advice to his superior, in this case to Alexander the Great. John of Salisbury relates the anecdote as part of his discussion of different forms of taunts, in which he concludes that skilful humour used to correct faults—to tell truth—is permissible.[24] In this instance the senior figure wields humour to lampoon the fallible pomposity of the inferior party, and thereby to assert his own superiority:

> Vnum tantum de scomatibus Alexandri quasi in calce libelli huius superioribus adnectam. Cum ei rex Darius, uno et altero praelio uirtutem eius expertus, partem regni Tauro monte tenus et filiam in matrimonium, cum decies centum milibis talentis polliceretur, eique Parmenion uir magnus inter Alexandrinos dixisset se, si Alexander esset, usurum hac conditione, respondit: Et ego, si Parmenion essem, eadem uterer...[25]

> I will add one more about the taunts of Alexander, like an extra to this little book, in addition to those above. When the king Darius, having tested his power in first the one and then the other battle, offered him a section of his kingdom up to Mount Taurus, and his daughter in marriage, along with a million talents; and when Parmenion, a great man amongst the followers of Alexander, said to him that, if he were Alexander, he would agree to these arrangements, he replied: 'And I, if I were Parmenion, I would agree to them too'.

Here Alexander pointedly distinguishes between an authority and inferiority by speaking the truth that asserts his identity.

## Sociology and the Power Relations of Humour

These interactions are far removed from modern culture, and yet the dynamics depicted are consistent with the findings of modern sociology. Just as fabliaux and comic narratives alone do not account for all the humour of the medieval period, in recent years sociological and psychological humour research has expanded from analysis of the ready-made joke to the humour of interpersonal dynamics, with substantial attention paid to conversations and conflict. These accord remarkably with medieval practices of interpersonal humour such as those described above, and thus it is worth outlining some of the findings of modern research and so providing a larger context for medieval examples.

Scholarship on modern interaction has identified a great many possible social functions of humour. These include softening or preserving deniability in delivering criticism or compliments, particularly when aimed at preserving dominance; self-disclosure and face-saving in difficult interpersonal manoeuvring such as sexual approaches or admitting failure; tentative violation of taboos; fostering group cohesion; keeping conversations on track and non-threatening ('discourse management'); and social play.[26] Of course several of these may overlap; for instance, Walter Map's quip levies criticism on both Bernard and monastic corruption, while softening it under the guise of humour, at the same time as it carefully violates the taboos of criticising pious figures and church practices; in addition it certainly serves as social play, and in all of these things it establishes Map as a dominant figure.

Three functions in particular are most pertinent to informal interpersonal interaction. One academic model suggests that humour is used to assert power, to foster interpersonal intimacy and self-expression, and to build group solidarity.[27] A similar method of categorising interpersonal humour divides it into negative humour (used to express criticism), expressive humour (fostering intimacy and self-expression), and positive humour (used to 'make light of a situation').[28] But, as researchers note, humour can be risky:

> the intrusion of humor into ongoing topical talk may itself be interactionally aggressive [...]. A humorous remark during serious conversation or during goal-directed talk like a debate, lesson or business meeting could be perceived as aggressive, in that it constitutes an intrusion, an interruption, a waste of time. This interactional aggression jeopardizes the progress of the transaction in progress and threatened to trivialize its goal. In such cases, the joker risks being regarded as abrasive, insolent, or stupid.[29]

In changing the tone of the conversation, and potentially derailing its subject, the joker risks threatening the authority of those of higher status. At the same time, if humour is wielded skilfully, its rewards can be significant. Humour may disarm disagreement, and in some circumstances it was found that laughter alone is sufficient to end a conflict.[30] Sustained use of humour can also foster closeness. Anthropologists have described the phenomenon of joking relationships, in which two people of unequal status, such as grandparent and grandchild or uncle and nephew, nevertheless have 'joking rights' with each other, or a relationship characterised by joking interaction.[31] The participants in these relationships are often of distinct status, and so the use of humour is not threatening. In less close relationships, humour is more often used to perpetuate or challenge status.

In this regard, researchers have found that negative or critical humour is the hallmark of higher status, and particularly the hallmark of men:

[...] men and women have somewhat different conversational goals: for women, the primary goal of friendly conversation is intimacy, whereas for men the goal is positive self-presentation. These different goals are also reflected in the ways men and women use humor. Women more often use humor to enhance group solidarity and intimacy through self-disclosure and mild self-deprecation, whereas men more often use humor for the purpose of impressing others, appearing funny, and creating a positive personal identity. Thus, humor is a mode of communication that, along with more serious communication, is used to achieve gender-relevant goals.[32]

A study of interactions between managers and subordinates found that those with a dominant communication style used more negative humour, and men used it more than women, even when the men were in a subordinate position to other men. As one sociologist has noted, 'humour is a control resource operating both in formal and informal contexts to the advantage of power groups and role-players'.[33] Another study of group interactions found that men were eight times less likely than women to use humour to foster group solidarity; instead they were more likely to use humour to establish power.[34] In a study of groups working on appointed tasks, researchers found that higher-status participants used more humour, and men used more humour than women.[35] In a classic study of staff meetings at a psychiatric hospital, senior staff were much more likely to use humour than junior staff, and the humour used by those senior in the hierarchy was frequently critical.[36] The correlation of humour to status and gender is striking; to cite one summary of the findings:

The average witticisms per staff member were 7.5 for senior staff, 5.5 for junior staff, and only 0.7 for the lowly paramedicals. These values are especially striking because junior staff did most of the talking at meetings. Also notable was the male contribution of 96 percent (!) of witticisms, despite substantial female representation in all staff ranks.[37] (Exclamation in original.)

Further, subordinates were more likely to be the target of humour. Even though women may be in a higher-status position in some instances, as a group women are in the designated 'subordinate' position in culture, and accordingly dominate with humour less, and are more often the target of humour. As Diane Martin observes, 'Taken together this research suggests that men initiate more humor, designate women as the brunt of jokes, and are often spared from being joke victims themselves'.[38] In the words of Lizbeth Goodman, 'There is a lingering perception that women are not best suited to telling jokes but rather to being the punchlines'.[39]

The power function in particular is in clear evidence in these scenarios from Map, Liudprand, John, and Gerald. The scenarios described by these medieval authors are informal interactions, but they are not merely 'friendly conversation'; they involve elite dignitaries involved in questions of power. In each, the joke-teller assumes power, both over his interlocutor and over the tone of the conversation. In each of these cases, the jokester, in speaking humour to power, is simultaneously speaking truth to power. And in each case the jokester is a man.

## 13 MEDIEVAL JOKES IN SERIOUS CONTEXTS: SPEAKING HUMOUR TO POWER   267

### WOMEN IN COMMAND OF HUMOUR

The number of medieval accounts of women who used humour in real life are vanishingly few, just as women appear in disproportionately small numbers in medieval chronicles and histories altogether. Yet there is one area of medieval life in which women can be seen to deploy humour: in fiction. Most of these instances are in narrative, particularly in the fabliaux, where women's humour has often been understood as a force counteracting male domination.[40]

Yet there are also fictional instances in which women use humour to assert power, by speaking truth, in more serious contexts. Several of these occur in the corpus of medieval Welsh literature. The character of Rhiannon, for instance, is known for her dry wit. A characteristic instance occurs in the tale *Pwyll Pendeuic Dyuet* [*Pwyll, Prince of Dyfed*]. There the main character, Pwyll, has heard of a mound with a magical peculiarity: the person who sits atop it will either receive a blow or see a wonder. He goes out with his companions to sit atop the mound, and sees a woman on a white horse, proceeding past the mound at an amble. He sends one of his companions after the woman on a swift horse, but no matter how fast the horse gallops, it cannot catch up with the woman. The same thing happens on the second night. On the third night, Pwyll himself mounts his horse, this time adding spurs, but again no matter how fast he drives the horse, it cannot catch up with the lady. Finally he addresses her:

> Yna y dywot Pwyll, 'A uorwyn', heb ef, 'yr mwyn y gwr mwyhaf a gery, arho ui!' 'Arhoaf yn llawen', heb hi, 'ac oed llessach y'r march pei ass archut yr meityn'.[41]
>
> Then Pwyll said: 'O maiden,' he said, 'in the name of the man you love most, wait for me!' 'I will wait gladly', she said, 'and it would have been better for your horse if you had asked a while ago'.

The maiden, Rhiannon, in fact has come for Pwyll: it is he whom she loves most. But she is not blinded by the romance of their meeting; she retains a sharp-eyed perspective on the realities of the situation. It is she who maintains a down-to-earth appraisal of Pwyll's failings.

A wry outlook is not an unusual characteristic of elite women in Middle Welsh literature. A further example comes from *Breudwyt Maxen Wledic* [*The Dream of the Emperor Maxen*], another tale in which a high-born man pursues an out-of-reach woman. In this case the Roman emperor Maxen has a dream about a beautiful maiden in an unknown but impressive location, becomes desperate to find her, and sends messengers to seek her out. Eventually the messengers come to Britain, locate the court of the maiden, whose name is Elen, and inform her that the Roman emperor has seen her in a dream and is lovesick for her. They conclude by asking whether she would prefer to go to Rome and become empress, or whether she would prefer Maxen to come to Britain and marry her there. Her dry response is free from the grandiosity that marks the announcements of the emperor and his messengers:

'A wyrda', hep e vorwyn, 'amheu er hyn a dywedwch chwi nys gwnaf vi na'e gredu heuyt en ormod. Namen os mivi a gar er amperauder, deuet hyt eman e'm ol'.[42]

'Ah, gentlemen', said the maiden, 'I do not doubt what you say, nor do I believe it overmuch. But if the emperor loves me, let him come here and get me'.

Once again the effusive romanticism of the high-status man is deflated by the wry and sceptical pragmatism of the woman.

It should be no surprise that the same dynamic operates in the cases of Rhiannon and Elen, as these episodes are very similar. Rhiannon clearly comes from the Otherworld, as evidenced by her appearance when Pwyll sits on the wonder-working mound and by the inability of a galloping horse to catch up with her own ambling mount. She also resembles a sovereignty goddess, both in attributes and in her role in the story.[43] Elen, the maiden in *Maxen*, is also presented as if her habitation is Otherworldly, and even though Maxen begins as emperor of Rome, the plot requires him to lose his station, and Elen's marriage to Maxen is presented as though he cannot regain and expand the full glory of his imperial station without her. In this way she too represents sovereignty. As exalted, Otherworldly women, it is no wonder that they possess the power of humour to speak truth.

But high status is not the only position from which women's power can operate: another character in the Welsh tradition does the same from a lowlier position. This is Luned, a subordinate woman in the household of a countess, in the Middle Welsh *Owein*. Owein, a knight from King Arthur's court, comes upon a mysterious knight at a mysterious fountain and slays the knight in combat. Hiding out from the consequences of the conflict, he is sheltered by a woman, Luned, from the knight's compound. Looking out of the window from his hiding place in Luned's quarters, Owein observes a mournful procession headed by a sorrowful woman, and proceeds to fall desperately in love with the woman. His exchange with Luned exposes his overblown and almost laughably unrealistic romanticism:

A gofyn a oruc Owein y'r uorwyn pwy oed y wreic. 'Duw a wyr,' heb y uorwyn, 'gwreic y gellir dywedut idi y bot yn deckaf o'r gwraged, ac yn diweiraf, ac yn haelaf, ac yn doethaf, ac yn vonheckidaf. Vy arglwydes i yw gonn racko, a Iarlles y Ffynnawn y gelwir, gwreic y gwr a ledeist di doe.' 'Duw a wyr,' heb yr Owein, 'arnaf, mae mwyhaf gwreic a garaf i yw hi.' 'Duw a wyr,' heb y uorwyn, 'na char hi dydi na bychydic na dim!'[44]

Owein asked the maiden who the woman was. 'God knows', said the maiden, 'a woman who could be said to be the most beautiful of women, and the most chaste, and the most generous, and the wisest and the noblest. She is my lady, called the Lady of the Fountain, the wife of the man you killed yesterday'. 'God knows', said Owein, 'as for me, she is the woman I love best'. 'God knows', said the maiden, 'she does not love you, not a small amount, not even one little bit'.

Later Luned acts as a go-between and manages to win the countess for Owein, again by speaking plain truths, although not so humorously. These examples affirm the power of combining truth and humour, and the power of such scenes in narrative, where the hierarchy of personages is either underlined or undermined, not only to those present in the conversation, but to the reader who is a silent witness to the power of the joke.

## THE POWER OF HUMOUR

From these examples it is clear that women can also take advantage of the power of humour to influence serious situations. The fact that fewer instances of such womanly wit are recorded in historical sources may reflect an official unease with the situation when it does happen, as well as the fact that fewer women make it into the medieval historical record at all. Whichever gender wields the humour, however, the sources show that skill at humour is a way of commandeering power in an interaction, and that that power is often used to speak the truth. As the truth is often a deflation from the grandiose posturings of official power, truth lends itself to humour. These observations accord with the findings of modern sociology and psychology, and point to constants in the uses and effects of humour over time. Where humour makes use of surprise, sometimes that surprise, both amusing and influential, is the telling of the truth.

## NOTES

1. Map, *De Nugis Curialium*, 80 (dist. I cap. 24). The edition includes an English translation, but for copyright reasons this and all translations below are my own unless otherwise specified.
2. The foundational text of the theory of the carnivalesque is Bakhtin's *Rabelais and His World*. The literature on the carnivalesque is voluminous. A few works indicating the scope of the field are Stallybrass and White, *The Politics and Poetics of Transgression*; Hoy, 'Bakhtin and Popular Culture'; Burke, 'Bakhtin for Historians'; and Humphrey, 'Bakhtin and the Study of Popular Culture'.
3. On incongruity theory see for instance Suls, 'Cognitive Processes'; for reversal theory see for instance Apter, *The Experience of Motivation*; Wyer and Collins, 'A Theory of Humor Elicitation'; and Apter and Desselles, 'Disclosure Humor and Distortion Humor'. On options for humour analysis see Attardo, *Humorous Texts*.
4. Greenberg et al., 'Causes and Consequences'; Solomon et al., *The Worm at the Core*; Becker, *The Denial of Death*.
5. Bayless, 'Laughter in a Deadly Context'.
6. On studies of particular carnivals, see also Humphrey, *The Politics of Carnival* and Le Roy Ladurie, *Carnival in Romans*.
7. A very few of the landmark studies include Muscatine, *The Old French Fabliaux*; Schenk, *The Fabliaux*; and Levy, *The Comic Text*.
8. Suls, 'A Two-Stage Mode', 90.

9. John of Salisbury, *Policraticus*, ed. Webb, 2.301 (Book VIII cap. XI). For more on the humour of John of Salisbury see Jaeger, 'Irony and Role-Playing in John of Salisbury' and Jaeger, *The Origins of Courtliness*.
10. Anselm, *Rhetorimachia*, ed. Manitius, 107 (Book I cap. 1).
11. Wenzel, 'The Joyous Art', 318.
12. Peter of Celle, *Letters*, ed. Heseldine, 656 (Letter 170).
13. William of Malmesbury, *Gesta Pontificum* 90–91 (I.42.6, version β). This passage was originally discovered by Winterbottom, 'A New Passage'.
14. Roy, *Devinettes*, no. 279.
15. Wilde, *The Importance of Being Earnest*, in *Complete Works*, 376.
16. The origins of this quotation are disputed, but the online Quote Inspector has traced it to an interview with Steve Allen in a 1957 *Cosmopolitan*. The larger context reads: 'When I explained to a friend recently that the subject matter of most comedy is tragic (drunkenness, overweight, financial problems, accidents, etc.) he said, "Do you mean to tell me that the dreadful events of the day are a fit subject for humorous comment?" The answer is "No, but they will be pretty soon". Man jokes about the things that depress him, but he usually waits till a certain amount of time has passed. It must have been a tragedy when Judge Crater disappeared, but everybody jokes about it now. I guess you can make a mathematical formula out of it. Tragedy plus time equals comedy.' https://quoteinvestigator.com/2013/06/25/comedy-plus/. Accessed 19 August 2019.
17. Chaucer, *Troilus and Criseyde*, ed. Windeatt, V.1814–1825.
18. Stephen Sondheim, 'Comedy Tonight', 1962.
19. Hazlitt, 'On Wit and Humour', 1.
20. Liutprand, *Relatio*, 7 (cap. 17–18).
21. John of Salisbury, *Policraticus*, ed. Webb, 2.222 (Book VII cap. XXV).
22. Gerald of Wales, *Vita S. Remigii*, ed. Dimock, 63 (cap. XXVIII).
23. Gerald of Wales, *Vita S. Remigii*, ed. Dimock, 63 (cap. XXVIII).
24. John of Salisbury, *Policraticus*, ed. Webb, 2.217 (Book VII, Cap. XXV).
25. John of Salisbury, *Policraticus*, ed. Webb, 2.224 (Book VII, cap XXV).
26. For a survey of scholarship on these functions see Martin, *The Psychology of Humor*, 113–52.
27. For example Hay, 'Functions of Humor'.
28. Graham *et al.* 'Functions of Humor'; Martin *et al.*, 'Humor Works', 213.
29. Norrick *et al.*, 'Humor as a Resource', 1663, citing Sherzer, 'Puns and Jokes' and Sherzer, 'Oh! That's a Pun'.
30. Norrick *et al.*, 'Humor as a Resource', 1679.
31. Radcliffe Brown, *Structure and Function in Primitive Society*, Apte, *Humor and Laughter*.
32. Martin, *The Psychology of Humor*, 149.
33. Powell, 'A Phenomenological Analysis', 100.
34. Hay, 'Functions of Humor'; see also Crawford, 'Gender and Humor'.
35. Robinson and Smith-Lovin, 'Getting a Laugh'.
36. Coser, 'Laughter Among Colleagues'.
37. Provine, *Laughter*, 30.
38. Martin *et al.* 'Humor Works', 210.
39. Goodman, 'Gender and Humour', 286.
40. Perfetti, *Women and Laughter*, Burns, 'This Prick Which is Not One'; and Burns, *Bodytalk*.

41. *Pwyll*, ed. Thomson, 10.271–73. It is translated by Davies, *Mabinogion*, although this translation is my own.
42. *Breudwyt Maxen*, ed. Roberts, 7.194–96. It is translated by Davies, *Mabinogion*, although this translation is my own.
43. McKenna, 'The Theme of Sovereignty'.
44. *Owein*, ed. Thomson, 14.362–69. It is translated by Davies, *Mabinogion*, although this translation is my own.

## BIBLIOGRAPHY

Anselm of Besate. *Gunzo: Epistola ad Augienses und Anselm von Besate: Rhetorimachia*. Edited by Karl Manitius. Monumenta Germaniae Historica, Quellen zur Geistesgeschichte des Mittelalters, vol. 2, 95–183. Weimar: Hermann Böhlaus Nachfolger, 1958.

Apte, Mahadev. *Humor and Laughter: An Anthropological Approach*. Ithaca: Cornell University Press, 1985.

Apter, Michael J. and Mitzi Desselles. 'Disclosure Humor and Distortion Humor: A Reversal Theory Analysis'. *Humor: International Journal of Humor Research* 25, no. 4 (2012): 417–35.

Apter, Michael J. *The Experience of Motivation: The Theory of Psychological Reversals*. London: Academic Press, 1982.

Attardo, Salvatore. *Humorous Texts: A Semantic and Pragmatic Analysis*. Berlin: Mouton De Gruyter, 2001.

Bakhtin, Mikhail. *Rabelais and His World*. Translated by Hélène Iswolsky. Bloomington: Indiana University Press, 1984.

Bayless, Martha. 'Laughter in a Deadly Context: *Le Sacristain, Maldon*, Merlin, Troilus'. In *Tears, Sighs and Laughter: Expressions of Emotion in the Middle Ages*, edited by Per Förnegård, Erika Kihlman, and Mia Åkestam, 153–65. Stockholm: Kungl. Vitterhetsakademien (KVHAA) / Royal Swedish Academy of Letters, History, and Antiquities, 2017.

Becker, Ernest. *The Denial of Death*. New York: Free Press, 1973.

*Breudwyt Maxen Wledic*. Edited by Brynley F. Roberts. Dublin: Dublin Institute for Advanced Studies, 2005.

Burke, Peter. 'Bakhtin for Historians'. *Social History* 13, no. 1 (1988): 85–90.

Burns, E. Jane. *Bodytalk: When Women Speak in Old French Literature*. Philadelphia: University of Pennsylvania Press, 1993a.

Burns, E. Jane. 'This Prick Which is Not One: How Women Talk Back in Old French Fabliaux'. In *Feminist Approaches to the Body in Medieval Literature*, edited by Linda Lomperis and Sarah Stanbury, 188–212. Philadelphia: University of Pennsylvania Press, 1993b.

Chaucer, Geoffrey. *Troilus and Criseyde*. Edited by B. A. Windeatt. London: Longman, 1984.

Coser, Rose Laub. 'Laughter Among Colleagues: A Study of the Functions of Humor among the Staff of a Mental Hospital'. *Psychiatry* 23 (1960): 229–48.

Crawford, Mary. 'Gender and Humor in Social Context'. *Journal of Pragmatics* 35, no. 9 (2003): 1413–30.

Davies, Sioned, trans. *The Mabinogion*. Oxford: Oxford University Press, 2008.

Francis, Linda E. 'Laughter, the Best Mediation: Humor as Emotion Management in Interaction'. *Symbolic Interaction* 17, no. 2 (1994): 147–63.

Gerald of Wales. *Vita S. Remigii et Vita S. Hugonis*. Vol. 7 of *Giraldi Cambrensis Opera*. Edited by James F. Dimock. London: Longman and Co., 1877.

Goodman, Lizbeth. 'Gender and Humour'. In *Imagining Women: Cultural Representations and Gender*, edited by Frances Bonner, 296–300. Cambridge: Polity Press, 1992.

Graham, E. E., M. J. Papa and G. P. Brooks. 'Functions of Humor in Conversation: Conceptualization and Measurement'. *Western Journal of Communications* 56 (1992): 161–83.

Greenberg, J., T. Pyszczynski and S. Solomon. 'The Causes and Consequences of a Need for Self-Esteem: A Terror Management Theory'. In *Public Self and Private Self*, edited by R. F. Baumeister, 189–212. New York: Springer-Verlag, 1986.

Hay, Jennifer. 'Functions of Humor in the Conversations of Men and Women'. *Journal of Pragmatics* 32, no. 6 (2000): 709–42.

Hazlitt, William. 'On Wit and Humour'. In *Lectures on the English Comic Writers*, by William Hazlitt, 3rd edition. London: John Templeman, 1841.

Hoy, Mikita. 'Bakhtin and Popular Culture'. *New Literary History* 23, no. 3 (1992): 765–82.

Humphrey, Chris. 'Bakhtin and the Study of Popular Culture: Re-thinking Carnival as a Historical and Analytical Concept'. In *Materializing Bakhtin: The Bakhtin Circle and Social Theory*, edited by C. Brandist and G. Tihanov. London: Macmillan, 2000.

Humphrey, Chris. *The Politics of Carnival: Festive Misrule in Medieval England*. Manchester: Manchester University Press, 2001.

Jaeger, C. Stephen. 'Irony and Role-Playing in John of Salisbury and the Becket Circle'. In *Culture politique des Plantagenêt (1154-1224): Actes du Colloque tenu à Poitiers du 2 au 5 mai 2002*, edited by Martin Aurell, 319–31. Poitiers: Civilisation Médiévale, 2003.

Jaeger, C. Stephen. *The Origins of Courtliness: Civilizing Trends and the Formation of Courtly Ideals, 939-1210*. Philadelphia: University of Pennsylvania Press, 1985.

John of Salisbury. *Policraticus, sive de nugis curialium et vestigis philosophorum*. Edited by Clement C. J. Webb. 2 vols. Oxford: Clarendon Press, 1909.

Le Roy Ladurie, Emmanuel. *Carnival in Romans: A People's Uprising in Romans 1579-1580*, translated by Mary Feeney. New York: G. Braziller, 1979.

Levy, Brian J. *The Comic Text: Patterns and Images in the Old French Fabliaux*. Amsterdam: Rodopi, 2000.

Liudprand of Cremona. *Liudprand of Cremona, Relatio de Legatione Constantinopolitana*. Edited and translated by Brian Scott. London: Bristol Classical Press, 1993.

Map, Walter. *De Nugis Curialium: Courtiers' Trifles*. Edited and translated by M. R. James, revised by C. N. L. Brooke and R. A. B. Mynors. Oxford: Oxford University Press, 1983.

Martin, Diane M., Craig O. Rich and Barbara Mae Gayle. 'Humor Works: Communication Style and Humor Functions in Manager/Subordinate Relationships'. *Southern Communication Journal* 69 (2004): 206–22.

Martin, Rod A. *The Psychology of Humor: An Integrative Approach*. Amsterdam: Elsevier, 2007.

McKenna, Catherine A. 'The Theme of Sovereignty in *Pwyll*'. *Bulletin of the Board of Celtic Studies* 29 (1980–81): 35–52.

Muscatine, Charles. *The Old French Fabliaux*. New Haven: Yale University Press, 1986.

Norrick, Neal R. and Alice Spitz. 'Humor as a Resource for Mitigating Conflict in Interaction'. *Journal of Pragmatics* 40, no. 10 (October 2008): 1661–86.

*Owein, or Chwedyl Iarlles Ffynnaun*. Edited by R. M. Thomson. Dublin: Dublin Institute for Advanced Studies, 1968.

Perfetti, Lisa. *Women and Laughter in Medieval Comic Literature*. Ann Arbor, MI: University of Michigan Press, 2003.

Peter of Celle, *The Letters of Peter of Celle*. Edited and translated by Julian Haseldine. Oxford: Clarendon Press, 2001.

Powell, Chris. 'A Phenomenological Analysis of Humour in Society'. In *Humour in Society: Resistance and Control*, edited by Chris Powell and George. E. C. Paton. Basingstoke: Macmillan Press, 1988.

Provine, Robert R. *Laughter: A Scientific Investigation*. New York: Viking, 2000.

*Pwyll Pendeuic Dyuet*. Edited by R. L. Thomson. Dublin: Dublin Institute for Advanced Studies, 1957.

Radcliffe-Brown, A. R. *Structure and Function in Primitive Society*. New York: Free Press, 1982.

Robinson, Dawn and Lynn Smith-Lovin. 'Getting a Laugh: Gender, Status, and Humor in Task Discussions'. *Social Forces* 80, no. 1 (2001): 123–58.

Roy, Bruno. *Devinettes françaises du Moyen Age*. Paris: Vrin, 1977.

Schenk, Mary Jane Stearns. *The Fabliaux: Tales of Wit and Deception*. Amsterdam: John Benjamins, 1987.

Sherzer, Joel. 'Oh! That's a Pun and I Didn't Mean It'. *Semiotica* 22 (1978): 335–50.

Sherzer, Joel. 'Puns and Jokes'. In *Handbook of Discourse Analysis*, vol. 3: *Discourse and Dialogue*, edited by T. A. van Dijk, 213–21. London: Academic Press, 1985.

Solomon, Sheldon, Jeff Greenberg, and Tom Pyszczynski. *The Worm at the Core: On the Role of Death in Life*. London: Allen Lane, 2015.

Stallybrass, Peter and Allon White. *The Politics and Poetics of Transgression*. Ithaca: Cornell University Press, 1986.

Suls, J. M. 'Cognitive Processes in Humor Appreciation'. In *Handbook of Humor Research, Vol. 1: Basic Issues*, edited by Paul E. McGhee and Jeffrey H. Goldstein, 39–57. New York: Springer-Verlag, 1983.

Suls, J. M. 'A Two-Stage Model for the Appreciation of Jokes and Cartoons: An Information-Processing Analysis'. In *The Psychology of Humor: Theoretical Perspectives and Empirical Issues*, edited by Jeffrey H. Goldstein and Paul E. McGhee, 81–100. New York: Academic Press, 1972.

Wenzel, Siegfried. 'The Joyous Art of Preaching; Or, The Preacher and the Fabliau'. *Anglia* 97 (1979): 304–25.

Wilde, Oscar. *Complete Works*. 3rd ed. Glasgow: HarperCollins, 1994

William of Malmesbury. *Gesta pontificum anglorum. The History of the English Bishops, I: Text and Translation*. Edited and translated by M. Winterbottom with R. M. Thomson. Oxford: Clarendon, 2007.

Winterbottom, Michael. 'A New Passage of William of Malmesbury's *Gesta Pontificum*'. *Journal of Medieval Latin* 11 (2001): 50-59.

Wyer, R. S. and J. E. Collins. 'A Theory of Humor Elicitation'. *Psychological Review* 99, no. 4 (1992): 663–88.

CHAPTER 14

# 'Lightness and Maistrye': Herod, Humour, and Temptation in Early English Drama

*Jamie Beckett*

Medieval 'mystery plays' make up a broad and somewhat anachronistic genre of early performance, most easily understood as medieval drama which enacted episodes of the biblical (or apocryphal) history of the world. Performed throughout Europe from the medieval period, and in England until at least the Reformation, this early drama is often comprised of sophisticated renderings of the biblical story, usually produced by the laity. It was a form of devotional theatre whose surviving scripts still challenge our expectations of the period, through the questions they raised and the ways they used humour to raise them. From the evidence which remains, comic moments played a prominent role in these plays. Humour was wielded as a devotional tool, both to draw spectators into the biblical narrative, and to prompt them to think about how the grand arc of spiritual history (from Creation to the Last Judgement) related to their own lives.

The way humour was written into performances of the biblical narrative might surprise us as modern readers: comic elements are woven into episodes including the Great Flood, the Nativity, and even the Crucifixion. The mere existence of comic elements within this biblical performance tradition, which ran alongside and even complemented the 'official sphere of high ideology and literature', challenges Bakhtin's notion that the 'comic folk aspect' of contemporary culture was incontrovertibly at odds with the established Church.[1] Widespread across medieval Europe, this type of drama was often performed in public places to diverse audiences, to mark festivals or other such events. The

J. Beckett (✉)
Durham University, Durham, UK

© The Author(s), under exclusive license to Springer Nature
Switzerland AG 2020
D. Derrin, H. Burrows (eds.), *The Palgrave Handbook of Humour, History, and Methodology*, https://doi.org/10.1007/978-3-030-56646-3_14

275

plays were produced for a demographic who largely could not access a written 'Bible', making them vital pieces of media—they offered the stories of God and Christ in the vernacular to eager spectators.

The plays did not stick to the kind of dourly pious scripts we might initially expect. But approaching the humour within these texts still raises certain challenges. Although plays of this kind were common across Europe from the late medieval period onwards, scripts have rarely survived, and those which have should only ever be considered the bare textual remnants of living performances: once fleshed-out, adapted, or staged in ways now difficult for us to fully comprehend. Added to this, we approach comic performance of this period with certain expectations. Medieval humour is all too often defined by easy jokes on the body, corpulence, or scatology—earthy forms which may be derided as far from the sophistication of playwrights composing works in the post-medieval period. But in these biblical plays we often find something at odds with this crude stereotype: the development of comic ideas which entertain but also challenge their intended spectators, and prompt them to explore the depths of their devotional understanding.

When approaching this form of drama there is still a tendency to generalise and hold low expectations of the cognitive abilities of late medieval spectators. Recent work on spectatorship and audience response prompts us to reconsider this assumption, especially when we consider that the plays were intended for diverse groups of spectators, who brought a complicated and varied range of experiences and knowledge to productions.[2] Medieval people, like people today, thought about things in many different ways. Humorous aspects of biblical plays had to be flexible enough to satisfy those coming to the performances with a broad range of expectations, prejudices, and knowledge.

Whilst a number of short scholarly works have previously considered comic aspects of these dramas, they have tended to view them either as aesthetic embellishments to serious performances—the frivolous icing on pious cakes— or else within a Bakhtinian framework which does not hold up to contextual scrutiny.[3] The shadow of Mikhail Bakhtin still looms large in the field of humour studies, but his central idea that any humour in these plays came at the expense of devotional edification should be challenged as unnecessarily reductive. In the 'mystery plays' humour—present in varying forms—could work in sophisticated ways. Rather than raising or reflecting ructions with the established Church, humour could drive audiences towards a deeper understanding of Christ, and a richer sense of devotion.

The following chapter focuses on one character present in a number of 'mystery plays'—Herod—whose reputation as both an evil and a comic figure raises certain questions about how humour could be utilised in the period. A number of scholars have used superiority theory as a way to understand audience appreciation of Herod, suggesting that their laughter was prompted exclusively by the figure's comic inferiority—a tyrant and child-killer, played as a fool with no understanding of Christ. This chapter seeks to complicate that view, questioning the limits of superiority theory by considering how the humour surrounding Herod actually functioned.

In England, two of the most prominent collections of 'mystery plays' come from the York Register and the Towneley MS collections which survive from the region of York and West Yorkshire in the late-fifteenth and mid-sixteenth centuries respectively. These collections well demonstrate the ways biblical stories were adapted to fit their particular audiences, sometimes far from the narratives offered in official versions of the Old or New Testaments today. Although characters and broad plots remain largely familiar to us, the way certain figures are portrayed, and the sense in which aspects of narratives are exploited for clear entertainment purposes, reveals new ways to view how contemporary people would have considered them.

One such character is Herod. In England at least, during the late medieval period the character of Herod often represented a conflation of three historical rulers of Judea, each known for their rage and cruelty: Herod the Great, Herod Antipas, and Herod Agrippa.[4] Although some contemporary works distinguished between the figures, the three generations of the Herod dynasty were regularly conflated to establish a unitary character type, suffused with malevolent dynamism and wickedness. Other figures in the York and Towneley plays are characterised in similar ways, associated with Herod through the way they wield temporal power at odds with the divine authority of Christ. This group includes the pagan emperor Caesar Augustus, the nefarious pseudo-prelates Annas and Caiaphas, and Pontius Pilate, each portrayed as vainglorious tyrants. Within the play-scripts they threaten spectators, posturing wildly and attempting to express a sense of their own fearsome potency on stage. Bombastic and angry, the pomp of these characters—whether expressed through words, or in the elaborate gestures, costume, or staging that records allude to—was consciously antithetical to the humble figure of Christ.

Importantly Herod and his fellow tyrants were portrayed as comic figures. Heather Mitchell-Buck has referred to Herod, or the 'ranting tyrant', as 'the superstar of the early English stage', wearing lavish costumes, giving 'the longest and most elaborate speeches', and bringing actors 'a substantial wage'.[5] As today, there is evidence to suggest that the baddies got the best lines. The tyrants in both York and Towneley always begin with grandiose orations which establish their claims to power, using impressively alliterative phrases and barking commands at their retainers in a way that was easy for spectators to mock. They were figures of false authority whose trumped-up self-importance was made all the more laughable by the dramatic irony that all spectators knew clearly that they were destined to fall.[6]

Moreover, it is clear that as comic characters, they were appreciated. Surviving records indicate that in certain productions the actor playing Herod gained a particularly high wage; in Coventry in 1478 the performer was paid double that of the man playing Christ.[7] References to the renown and reputation of such performances in broader media attest to this: in 'The Miller's Tale' Chaucer tells us that the weaselly Absolon sometimes performed as Herod 'to shewe his lightness and maistrye'.[8] Wherever the irony lies here, it is clear that this particular characterisation of Herod was well-known, and influential for future generations. Writing some two centuries after Chaucer, in Shakespeare's *Hamlet* the eponymous prince complains that the intemperate volume of some players 'out-Herods Herod', and it has been suggested that the comic performance of these biblical tyrants informed other works by the playwright.[9]

In an article considering the nature of medieval audience response, Sarah Carpenter has suggested the possible similarities of experiencing contemporary biblical drama with attending modern-day pantomime performances, with spectators expected to emphatically—and noisily—engage with the narrative being enacted, cheering for the good and remonstrating with the evil onstage.[10] It is easy to imagine how—as in modern pantomimes—an evil character such as Herod might goad his audience, rebuke them, and whip them into a frenzy though the comically knowing performance of nefariousness. Yet unlike the comical villains presented in pantomimes or in children's films today, those presented in early drama were not fictional entities, created for the enjoyment of their audiences. Staged for devotional edification as much as entertainment, the plays were a form of history-telling, and spectators would have considered Herod and other tyrants as real-life figures, from the not-so-distant past.

But if this is true, how could it have been justifiable to treat such evil characters as figures of entertainment? If audiences were supposed to be edified by these performances, how could the comic presentation of Herod and other tyrannical characters—responsible between them for slaughtering innocents, torturing Christ, and ultimately condemning Him to execution—possibly be justified? In the past, scholars have generally approached this problem in a way which draws on the concept known in humour studies as superiority theory. In his influential work *Shakespeare and the Popular Tradition in Theater*, Robert Weimann argued that within the 'mystery plays' Herod is depicted as a 'burlesque' imitation of tyranny, blending horror and humour to produce 'a liberating effect' where 'exaggerated authority becomes laughable'.[11] Ingvild S. Gilhus has similarly noted that Herod's wickedness and the terror he could arouse was undermined by his comic portrayals, laughter taking 'the sting' out of evil. As the tyrant was reduced to a fool, an audience could judge him and his bombastic outbursts from a position of 'superior knowledge'.[12]

Scholars have tended to consider the humour associated with Herod to be driven by mockery and scorn, which to some extent it clearly was: Herod is shown to be a ridiculous figure, at odds with the Christian truth. But they largely ignore the sense in which the Herod was as much a figure of temptation as of revulsion onstage, whose comic attributes contributed to his desirable appeal. Considering this paradox—that Herod is balanced at a point between attractiveness and loathsomeness—I argue that within performances laughter functioned in a complex way, doing more than merely undermining the character's tyrannical authority. The humour surrounding tyrants such as Herod is ambiguous: it expresses the enjoyment of a character, but this should not be understood throughout as a straightforward condemnation. Whereas some spectators may have regarded these figures only as objects of mockery, the attractive aspect of their comic positions should not be ignored. It allows us to better understand the complexity which humour could hold in this early period, wielded to tempt, teach, and entertain, sometimes simultaneously.

To properly consider the intended relationship between audience and performed tyrant in these plays, it is useful to look at the way portrayals of the character developed. Central to this development is Herod's shift from a character presented in a discrete performance space alongside a handful of his disreputable retainers, to a tyrant inhabiting a broader and more overarching place at the centre of a large court of people. David Staines outlines a development of Herod's representation from the High Medieval period to the later fifteenth century, whereby in textual sources (including the writings of Church fathers, and popular written works such as the *Legenda Aurea*) the tyrant remains 'a figure solely of evil', whilst in performance his folly is emphasised, and his character is fleshed out for the stage.[13]

Staines argues that it is through the presence of the court on stage, and the 'servants, courtiers, knights, counsellors and messengers' who inhabit it, that Herod's character was developed, essentially through 'the external circumstances' surrounding him.[14] As Miriam Skey points out, within the vernacular biblical drama of continental Europe Herod is generally presented as a tragic figure, ruling over a sophisticated and sumptuous court, who ultimately commits suicide following the failure of his plans.[15] At some odds with this, in England the folly of his character was emphasised, leading to a comic portrayal—certainly present in surviving scripts from York, Coventry, and the Towneley MS. The court, used in continental drama to emphasise Herod's sophistication, is here made into an arena where the tyrant's evil is rendered comic, his booming voice couched farcically in a nest of supporters and sycophants.

As other scholars have noted, during performance the court extends well beyond the handful of other actors gathered on the stage; in their position as bystanders, real-life spectators of the drama became members of it, their noisy responses to the figure pulling them imaginatively into the performed narrative.[16] Staines even suggests that Herod's comic development in England was driven by audience expectation, reflecting 'the delight' which the character gave to them, and 'the dramatists' ability to cater to this delight'.[17] Within these English performances, Herod's character can be discounted as a comic braggart, performing for a court which was mocking him. But this perhaps ignores the power balance established in performances through the court, of which spectators become members.

Spectators are likely to have cheered the character on in the same breath they used to rail against him, taking delight in Herod's performance of ridiculous evil. But as a tyrant whose words are designed to dominate audience members, and draw them into his court, Herod's comic nature allows him to accomplish his aims, and make the cheering crowd surrounding him somewhat complicit in his actions. This complicity challenges the idea that humour here is roused through the audience's feelings of superiority towards Herod: whilst spectators would have understood he was a figure to be reviled, paradoxically it is his comic nature which attracts those around him. Peter Ramey supports such a view when he notes that Herod is 'more than […] a send-up of the political class or an occasion for mocking'; he is also 'an enactment of real power over the crowd', exhibiting the 'coercive realities of temporal power'.[18] Following Ramey, bringing together humour and coercion, the laughter raised within this court—derisive or otherwise—does not necessarily result in spectators challenging Herod: instead, the tyrant's words may represent his powers of temptation.

Within English performances it is likely that Herod's performance space was characterised by its decadence: he is a villainous sinner, who luxuriates in a court whose authority will wane with Christ's coming. Records from Coventry note that up to twenty shillings were spent on maintaining Herod's costume and props every year, whilst in York the Goldsmiths complained about the expense of staging both Herod's court and the finery of the Magi.[19] Even after the Goldsmiths had successfully detached themselves from producing the pageant, they appear to have retained the expensive costumes needed, and the city's memorandum book records that 'neither the Corones nor gownes' should be lent out for under 8d a piece.[20] Fantastical costumes, sets, and props afforded Herod a sense of pomp and grandeur in performance. Whilst these were necessary to demonstrate his despotic power, and the tangible evil he represented in the face of Christ, such wealth and glamour associated with the figure might also have been considered attractive.

To compound this, evidence survives to suggest that the regal dress Herod performed in was also ostensibly foreign—something visible in contemporary depictions of the figure.[21] It has been established that actors playing Herod were sometimes dressed in turbans rather than crowns, and acted with faces painted black, or covered with dark masks. [22] These portrayals framed the character with tropes associated with 'Orientalized' bodies, presented as 'overemotional, irrational, and given to lascivious behaviour'.[23] Herod rants and raves at the news of Christ's coming and denies the reality of the Christian God, whilst his 'lasciviousness' may be read through his consistent representation a figure of decadence, and interest in his male retainers. He describes himself as 'fairer of face' and in 'riche array' (York, *Herod Questioning the Three Kings*, ll. 17, 147), indeed 'fairere be ferre' (York *The Trial Before Herod*, l. 240) than all others, 'Clenly shapen, hyde and hare' (Towneley *The Offering of the Magi*, l. 35).[24] After directing his abuse at spectators, in the Towneley MS he even nominates himself 'youre lovely lorde' to his courtiers (York *The Massacre of the Innocents*, l. 8).

Kathleen Ashley has observed that such figures as Herod were monstrously evil, but could also be considered pleasurably 'exotic' in spectacle or display; in this sense Herod could offer 'an alternative, pleasurable experience of otherness' to spectators.[25] Certainly in late medieval England there was considerable interest in the lands of the East over which Herod and the other tyrants allegedly ruled. The sites of the Holy Land—associated with the crusades, but also of great interest in spiritual and historical terms to many—were eagerly written about as travel destinations in a wealth of literature.[26] Added to this there was a keen appetite for accounts of the 'wonders' of the East, circulated in texts such as *The Travels of John Mandeville* and other works.[27] Herod is present on stage to shock and terrify, to act as a representation of alterity and Christian enmity, but he is also a figure from the other side of the world like those in these fanciful travel narratives, present to rouse laughter, to fascinate and entertain.

In the opening of the York *Questioning* Herod claims authority over 'Jubiter and Jovis, Martis and Mercurii' (l. 2) as well as 'Saturne' (l. 5) and 'Venus' (l. 10). His words are clearly absurd as he cannot have any such powers, and they express his identity as an eastern despot whose reputation for potency should be brought into question. But in calling himself 'prince of planetis' (l. 12), and naming these celestial bodies, his speech also rouses excitement, evoking contemporary 'astro-meteorological' ideas on the one hand and the pagan grandeur of the classical deities on the other, fanciful objects of interest to many late medieval people.[28]

As in all of these plays, in the York *Trial* Herod is a verbose and intimidating figure: carrying a 'bright' 'brande' Herod threatens to 'brest' the 'brayne' of spectators who deny his authority (l. 4); he will 'dress you to drede / with dasshis' (ll. 6–7); he will 'brittyn all youre bones' and lusshe all your lymmis with lasschis' (ll. 10, 11). Akin to the 'fee fi fo fum' of the fairytale giant, Herod's alliterative frenzy establishes the potency of his anger, and expresses his semicomic claims of strength and authority. After the comic verbosity of his threats the tyrant goes on to evoke genuine marvels, claiming for himself the role of explorer, or at least expounder of the mysterious beings at the edges of the world:

> Herod: Dragons that are dredfull schall derk in ther denne
> In wrathe when we writhe or in wrathenesse ar wapped
> Agaynste jeauntis ongentill have we joined with ingendis,
> And swannys that are swymmyng to oure swetnes schall be snapped (ll. 12–15)

Herod summons up these marvels in order to impress his audience, emphasising both the authority he has over these creatures, and the similarities which they bear to him. The 'jeauntis ongentill' and 'dredfull' dragons are fearsome but also exotic, the beings of bestiaries or fanciful travel narratives. They are terrifying, fantastical, and otherworldly. The tyrant presents himself as having subdued these marvellous creatures as a means to threaten others into subservience, calling out 'ye that luffis youre liffis, listen to me' (l. 21). But Herod's words suggest that he is as much of a marvel as the creatures he can tame; having defeated them (a least in his imagination) he claims the powers of the giant and the dragon.

A character of apparently marvellous powers (or, at the very least, one who offers descriptions of marvels which spectators could enjoy), the authority which Herod holds onstage is not necessarily undermined by the comic verbosity and bombast which erupts from his mouth. Taken alongside his splendid robes, despotic manner, and the array of courtiers surrounding him, Herod is presented at least in part as a tempting figure: certainly a tyrant, but a character designed to be enjoyed by the audiences experiencing his presence. The idea that spectators were enabled to mock Herod through a sense of Christian superiority is complicated by the sheer power of his performance. This comic characterisation was entertaining and endearing in the broadest sense, attractive to those gathered to watch him on his platform.

If we consider Herod as a figure of temptation as much as a character to be deplored, humorous elements of his characterisation can be read differently. Performances such as this drew on humour to better embody biblical performances, to entertain and to teach the story of Christ's life. But a balance had to be drawn between creating engaging drama and the risk of making sinful characters more palatable or popularly attractive onstage. Deanne Williams notes that as early as the twelfth century the German theologian Gerhoh of Reichersberg criticised the embodied performance of Herod, claiming that dramatic entertainment which focused on the character often held little didactic purpose, and drove both actors and spectators to imaginatively indulge in 'manifold sins and fleshly pleasures' instead.[29] Similar concerns are raised in the early fifteenth-century work the *Treatise of Miraculis Pleying*, a piece which comments on aspects of early drama in performance. Here the writer criticises those spectators who mistake the 'worschipyng of [th]eire maumetrie'—the false images presented on stage—for true devotion.[30]

Comparing the dynamic to modern laws on obscene images, John McGavin has commented that in the medieval period there was a critical consciousness over the 'ethical implications' of spectatorship, and the responsibilities tied up with it.

> Recent legislation in the area of child pornography has reversed traditional notions of the spectator as passive recipient of images, and has argued that the spectator's desire to watch encourages the production of the abuse on which it is based. In this respect, modern law is beginning to approach the more sophisticated view of causation held in the Middle Ages: while the image may be the *formal* cause of the spectator's experience, that experience is the *efficient* cause of the image.[31]

In performances involving Herod we find a character not only observed by the court surrounding him, but enabled and emboldened by it. Spectators, as members of the court and as audiences of the dramatic figure, were the 'efficient cause' of Herod's actions—both the comic, and the evil.

As an evil figure both prompting humour and feeding off it, Herod can be considered threatening even whilst he is laughable. We can see that this dynamic was consciously utilised throughout these plays if we look to figures associated with Herod such as the other tyrants or temporal leaders acting against Christ. Embodied by their presence on stage, but also to some extent sanitised by the playful nature of performances, these tyrants are threatening not so much for their evil acts, but more for their powers of temptation: a powerful force with the capacity to lead Christian worshippers astray.

In calling for attention and bringing contemporary spectators into his court, Herod gains a platform on which to speak, and to use his deviant voice. We have discussed the possibility that within performances Herod was a somewhat 'Orientalised' figure, associated with both contemporary and biblical ideas of the East. Interestingly, in the plays of York and Towneley Herod and the other tyrants regularly make invocations to 'Mahounde', denoting their relationship with an ambiguous entity closely aligned at this time in England with followers of the Islamic faith. These references to Islam by a historical figure supposedly living during the life of Christ are of course firmly anachronistic, but so were many other elements of this drama, which tied together the lives of spectators with the early Christian past. Conceptions of Islam in late medieval England were predictably at some distance from the true tenets of the faith, with 'Mahounde' or 'Machamet' usually identified either as some kind of painted idol, or—perhaps more intriguingly—a trickster who had led his followers astray, presenting himself as a false version of Christ.[32]

Both influencing and necessarily reflecting this perception of Islam were a variety of texts which circulated in the high-to-late medieval period in England, concerned with the origins of the religion. Various Latin, French, and Middle English texts of the eleventh to fifteenth centuries circulated in Western Europe giving a somewhat warped history of the Prophet's life, from works such as the *Vita Mahumeti*, the *Otia Machomete*, and the *Roman de Mahomet*, to the narratives set out in John Lydgate's *Fall of Princes* and William Langland's *Piers Plowman*. All portray him as 'a deceptive magician, controlling his followers by means of false miracles', and a 'false messiah-figure who looks and seems like Christ [...] but proves to be an imposter'.[33] In York and Towneley, Herod and the other tyrants refer repeatedly to their association with, relation to, or power over 'Mahounde', demonstrating their status as eastern potentates, but also hinting at the false nature of their powers, and the heretical intentions associated with them.

Herod was portrayed as an exotic and attractive entity, superficially entertaining and popular as a figure of the East. Yet through fanciful speeches and spectacular courts, performances also displayed the intention to lure spectators away from Christ. Scholars of early drama have considered Herod as a typological expression of the Antichrist, a 'parodic and false approximation' of the incoming saviour, leading Christians to sin.[34] References to 'Mahounde' are part of this, and also tap into a tradition which emerged in fourteenth-century England where portrayals of Islam and Islamic practices were used to address anxieties about forms of Christian worship, and criticise malpractice amongst spiritual leaders such as clergy.

Islam was popularly categorised as a Christian heresy rather than a pagan religion in this period, and it was also used more widely in religious discourses surrounding proper devotional practices, throughout both the fifteenth and

284    J. BECKETT

sixteenth centuries.[35] In the fourteenth-century work *Piers Plowman*, Langland asserts that 'English clerks feed a dove called covetousness, and behave like Muhammad so that no man holds the truth', using Islam to express anticlerical criticisms, and call for Church reform.[36] Similarly, during the long period of the English Reformation adherents of both traditionalist Catholicism and reformist Protestantism compared their respective doctrinal opponents to followers of Islam, representing it as 'a standard of false belief' or heresy.[37]

Whether heretical tricksters, leaders of heterodox sects, or clergy abusing their authority, those who misled Christian worshippers might all be considered in the same light as Herod: voices attempting to establish a warped spiritual authority, expropriating existing models of devotion for their own nefarious ends. In this light, we might consider the entertaining nature of Herod as something more complicated than a means to enable spectators to laugh at him. Like a populist orator, the tyrant's words and comical manner are attractive, leading the audience to follow him even whilst rousing their laughter. In this way, playing on a bombastic rhetoric and a wilful self-knowledge of his own evil, Herod is characterised as a complex source of comic temptation.

Whilst spectators would have known that Herod was a villainous figure in these biblical plays, the direct results of this evil are really only staged alongside the character in those featuring the so-called Massacre of the Innocents—the episode where, warned of the birth of Christ, the tyrant orders mass infanticide in an attempt to kill the new-born Messiah. [38] Herod's court is one of temptation, and it is interesting to look to the only episode staged which actually features the tangible evil of the tyrant being performed on stage. Arguably it is only in this episode that his true nature is exposed.

In the York *Massacre of the Innocents*, the nature of Herod as a slightly comic trickster, as developed in the *Questioning*, gives way to the presentation of a more serious and desperate tyrant. Herod begins, as in the other plays, with a twenty-four-line speech enticing people to worship him: 'lere you lowe to lowte [...] youre lovely lord' (ll. 7–8). But on being informed that his plan to fool the Magi into giving him the location of Christ has failed, the boisterous and scheming tyrant becomes 'lorne' (l. 114) and full of 'sorowe' (l. 136): as his messenger Nuncius states, 'that daunce is done' (l. 96). The use of 'daunce' here evokes the previous entertainment of Herod's court, as the tyrant had treated fooling the Magi as a kind of game, in which the audience were very much complicit. This is now dispelled—for the tyrant and his courtiers of both stage and audience—through the news of failure. Although there are moments of angry bluster in the York *Massacre*, Herod's speech becomes markedly less comic than in the *Questioning* pageant. This movement from entertainment to sorrow in the court prefigures the main event of the pageant, when the babes in arms are slaughtered by Herod's soldiers.

The York *Massacre* is characterised by the failure of Herod, and the brutality resulting from his desperation. The pageant ends with Herod's realisation of further failure, that the boy Christ 'be fledde' (l. 270). Bob Godfrey has argued that due to the comic nature of Herod, the audience can experience a sense of superiority over him 'even while being startled and possibly horrified by the matter of the slaughter itself'.[39] Although this view is in some ways convincing, it tends to ignore the complexity of the relationship Herod has established with the spectators gathered around him. Within this performance the court is shifted from a space of entertainment to one of horrifying death. This swift change in atmosphere, pleasure to pain, or attractiveness to revulsion, allows the scene of the *Massacre* a greater emotional impact, with those formerly laughing at Herod, sucked in by his comic nature, now reeling from the tragic outcome of his rhetoric.

Raging and raving in an increasingly uncontrolled way, in marked contrast the Towneley *Herod the Great* enthuses over the suggestion that he kill all 'knaue-chyldren of two yerys brede' (l. 371). Unlike the York Herod's muted promises to his knights that 'Ye schall fynde me youre frende, / And ye this tyme be trewe' after they have committed the killings (York *Massacre*, ll. 165–66), the Towneley Herod makes wild offers of lands, money, and the papal crown to the retainer who advises that his knights should carry out the gruesome task (*Herod the Great*, ll. 380–90). Unlike the sorrowful tyrant of the York *Massacre*, here Herod is unhinged and dangerous, his lengthy speeches asserting that the slaughter be a suitable act for the 'flowre of knyghthede' (l. 393), expressing a parodic take on the knightly ideal of chivalric culture.[40]

The fairly extensive length of the scene given over to the actual slaughter suggests that it was intended to prompt a strong emotional impact amongst spectators. Playing on the emotions of the audience, this scene stages prolonged disputes between Herod's knights and the mothers of those babes they have been ordered to kill (ll. 480–572). Whilst in some English plays this scene is given a comic touch, drawing on the incongruity of nursing women armed only with domestic tools chasing away armoured knights, in Towneley their actions are entirely pathetic.[41] The eloquence of the lengthy speaking parts afforded to the mothers in this scene contrasts with Herod's raving:

> II Mulier: Outt! mordor-man, I say, strand tratoure and thefe!
> Out, alas, and waloway! my child that was me lefe!
> My luf, my blood, my play, that neuer dyd man grefe!
> [...] Veniance I cry and call
> On Herode and his knyghtys all:
> Veniance, Lord, apon thaym fall,
> And mekyll warldys wonder! (ll. 521–26, 532–33.)

Accusations that Herod is a 'tratoure and thefe', and appeals made to the Christian 'Lord' against the tyrant and his men, contrast with Herod's invocations to 'Mahowne', and his claims of worthy rule. Indeed, the pathetic resistance made by these mothers to the knights, driving them to cry 'Peasse now, no more!' (l. 557) is set in contrast with Herod's claim following the slaughter, 'Now in peasse may I stand / I thank the, Mahowne!' (ll. 664–65).

*Herod the Great* ends with a speech by Herod directly to the audience, returning to the flamboyance of his opening monologue. As it follows the scene of the slaughter, Herod's words have now become more tangibly threatening—they are no longer designed to delight or amuse. Just as the spectators have previously been drawn in to laugh at him, so Herod consciously calls for them to join in the court again, to be entertained. Yet the consequences of their complicity in this are now revealed:

> Herod: Draw therfor nerehande,
>   Both of burgh and of towne:
>   Markys, ilkon, a thowsande,
>   When I am bowne,
>   Shall ye haue.
>   I shall be full fayn
>   To gyf that I sayn;
>   Wate when I com agayn,
>   And then may ye craue.
>   (ll. 668 676)

Directly summoning spectators to draw nearer to him as he previously called on his murderous knights, in this closing speech Herod implores those who have witnessed his massacre of the children to come into his court again, and revel in the rewards he can offer them. But the superficial attractiveness of Herod's domain is now tainted by the blood of those children massacred on his orders. Tipping the balance from comic attractiveness to a clear demonstration of evil, it becomes apparent that even the laughter of this particular scene cannot be of superiority, when faced with the revolting and dull truth of infanticide. Highlighting this, Herod cynically comments that the spectators will 'crave' him to 'com agayn', prompting discomfort amongst those who laughed either in attraction or in revulsion at him, sucked into a state of complicity which the murders enacted on the stage.

In his final speech Herod draws attention explicitly to the laughter of the spectators, and how this response should be evaluated. Despite his responsibility for the slaughter, Herod asserts that the horrifying act 'Mefys nothyng my mode / I lagh that I whese!' (l. 683–84). His laughter turns to wheezing, excessive, and shocking in its profligacy. Invoking 'Mahowne', he claims 'So light is my saull / That all of sugar is my gall' (ll. 686–87), suggesting that he regards the atrocities committed as superficial and unimportant. Through his words Herod makes known that the laughter of these spectators has not undermined his tyrannical power. Quite the opposite is true: instead it has authorised and allowed his reprehensible character to thrive. Herod's speech represents a metatheatrical confrontation where spectators are faced with the grim consequences of failing to truly challenge the performance of evil authority: their laughter, encouraging the entertainment before them, has made them complicit.

The popularity of characters such as Herod was determined by the spectacle which they offered in performance. Laughter at such characters cannot have merely represented a means to undermine the authority which this popularity feeds, tied up with the idea of the audience as part of the court. Instead, the mixture of comic entertainment and brutal action drove spectators to better engage with the narrative being enacted. Comic forms were utilised to encourage a nuanced understanding of tyrants such as Herod, who through their superficial attractiveness pose the greatest threat to good Christians, of driving their followers to sin. Not only entertaining villains, Herod and other similar figures also represent the threat of temptation, or of being seduced away from Christ.

Believing that he has killed Jesus and silenced 'many a tong' (l. 715), Herod's voice ends this play with the same claims of authority, and no recognition of reproof. By ending on this defiant, troublesome note, this play raises questions over the function of laughter, and the complicity of spectators in it. Rather than a means to demonstrate the Christian superiority audiences would have felt over Herod, humour is wielded in performances to complicate the dynamic of the scene. Although the audiences would have been aware from the start that the tyrant was a villainous figure, their initial enjoyment of the comic character would only deepen the significance of the ultimate consequences of his evil. Only when the laughter stops is Herod shown to be a tyrant whose temptingly comic nature veils his horrifying potential.

In C. S. Lewis' comic epistolary work *The Screwtape Letters,* the eponymous demon educates his nephew—fresh to the devil's work—on the many ways humans could be manipulated to sin. The character teaches that whereas humour held the power to banish evil, it also held the potential to obscure and thus enable it. 'A thousand bawdy, or even blasphemous, jokes do not help towards a man's damnation so much as his discovery that almost anything he wants to do can be done, not only without the disapproval but with the admiration of his fellows, if only it can get itself treated as a joke'.[42] Comic portrayals of Herod in early drama played on this dynamic in performances in a more sophisticated way than has previously been assumed—Herod could play the fool, but consciously so.

Jokes are powerful things, and complex too. Scholars have assumed that superiority is implicit in the humour sustained by and, apparently directed, at figures such as Herod—sinful grotesques, ripe for mockery. Yet thinking about the use of humour in performance specifically, as in this case study, can allow us to broaden our ideas on response, and consider the limits of superiority theory. Functioning as sometimes uneasy collectives, audiences offer an inherent plurality of responses (whether expressed outwardly or inwardly), which scholarly readings can sometimes limit or ignore.[43] The attraction in laughter can complicate things. Perhaps paradoxically, the enjoyment associated with such characters can allow the object of derision to become for some a plausible or even tempting figure—something which those producing the plays discussed were all too aware of.

The laughter directed at Herod cannot simply be read as mockery or scorn: a successful retaliatory measure against evil. Laughter at the audacity of such figures can also help mask the seriousness of their malice; comic derision—however righteous it feels—can act as a useful tool for those being derided. Within an audience, the negative impetus of derisory laughter is sustained unevenly. Late medieval play producers understood that humour could be utilised for evil as much as good, and saw the value in making spectators understand that too. Reviled by some, for others the laughable figure can sometimes be identified as the most attractive option—however evil or grotesque. A comic persona can mask the darkest intentions, and derision does little to banish the threats behind it. At a time when populists and populism are at the fore of political systems worldwide, raising laughter amongst their detractors as well as their supporters, the humour wielded by tyrants is something which we ignore at our peril.

## NOTES

1. Bakhtin, *Rabelais and His World*, 6, 72, 82. Indeed, within this dichotomy 'folk culture' is an ambiguous and—in the context of early biblical drama especially—a misleading label.
2. McGavin and Walker, *Imagining Spectatorship*, 8–16; Richardson, 'The Other Readers' Response', 31–33, 44–46; see also Lopez, *Theatrical Convention and Audience Response,* 13–34.
3. See for example Williams, 'The Comic in the Cycles', 109–23; Wickham, 'Medieval Comic Traditions and the Beginnings of English Comedy', 40–62; Tricomi, 'Re–Envisioning England's Medieval Cycle Comedy', 11–26; Diller, 'Laughter in Medieval English Drama', 1–19.
4. Staines, 'To Out–Herod Herod', 31–32; Wright, 'Acoustic Tyranny', 4–7.
5. Mitchell-Buck, 'Tyrants, Tudors, and the Digby *Mary Magdalen*', 241.
6. See Epp, 'Passion, Pomp, and Parody', 157; Wright, 'Acoustic Tyranny', esp. 10–14.
7. Mitchell-Buck, 'Tyrants, Tudors, and the Digby *Mary Magdalen*', 256 n.1: she cites *Records of Early English Drama: Coventry*, 61.
8. Chaucer, 'The Miller's Tale', in *The Riverside Chaucer*, 70–71, ll.3383–86; Shakespeare, *Hamlet*, 3.2. ll.13–14.
9. Gray, 'Caesar as Comic Antichrist', 1–31; Harris, *Untimely Matter in the Time of Shakespeare*, 80–84.
10. Carpenter, 'New Evidence: Vives and Audience Response',10.
11. Weimann, *Shakespeare and the Popular Tradition in the Theater,* 70–71.
12. Gilhus, *Laughing Gods, Weeping Virgins,* 97; see also Godfrey, 'Herod's Reputation and the Killing of the Children', 271.
13. Staines, 'To Out–Herod Herod', 31–2.
14. Ibid., 36.
15. Skey, 'Herod the Great in Medieval European Drama', 332–33.
16. See Wright, 'Acoustic Tyranny', 18, 21.
17. Staines, 'To Out–Herod Herod', 50–51.
18. Ramey, 'The Audience-Interactive Games', 60.

19. See Mitchell-Buck, 'Maintaining the Realm', 184; *Records of Early English Drama Coventry,* 71; *Records of Early English Drama: York,* I, 47–48. The proto-Christian nature of the Magi sets them in stark contrast to Herod, although all of them were probably portrayed as visually interesting 'Oriental' figures. See Ashley, 'Strange and Exotic', 84–85.
20. *Records of Early English Drama: York,* I, 334.
21. See Smith, *Images of Islam,* 94–5; also Hourihane, *Pontius Pilate, Anti-Semitism, and the Passion in Medieval Art,* 148, 153, 271–2.
22. Leach, 'Some English Plays and Players', 205–34, 213–34; Woolf, *The English Mystery* Plays, 391–92, ft. 64. Twycross and Carpenter, *Masks and Unmasking in Medieval and Early Tudor England,* 216.
23. Akbari, 'Placing the Jews in Late Medieval English Literature', 33; Harris, *Untimely Matter in the Time of Shakespeare,* 80–84.
24. All quotations are taken from Epp, *The Towneley Plays* and Davidson, *The York Corpus Christi Plays.*
25. Ashley, 'Strange and Exotic', 77.
26. See Lilley, *City and Cosmos,* 20–25, 78.; Morris, 'Pilgrimage to Jerusalem in the Middle Ages', 141–63, esp. 143–44; Norako, 'Crusades in Literature', 575–83.
27. Lomperis, 'Medieval Travel Writing and the Question of Race', 147–56, esp. 153–54; Mittman, *Maps and Monsters in Medieval England;* also Wittkower, 'Marvels of the East. A Study in the History of Monsters', 159–97.
28. Herod's feigned control of the skies is set up in contrast with the learned astronomical practices of the Magi. See Beadle, *The York Plays,* II, 131. On contemporary interest in classical deities see Phillips, 'Medieval Classical Romances', 3–25; Fumo, *The Legacy of Apollo,* esp. 76–123.
29. Williams, *The French Fetish from Chaucer to Shakespeare,* 58–59.
30. *Medieval Drama,* ed. Walker, 200, l.115.
31. McGavin, 'Medieval Theatricality and Spectatorship', 194–95.
32. See Akbari, *Idols in the East,* 200–203.
33. Akbari, 'The Rhetoric of Antichrist in Western Lives of Muhammad', 297–307. See also *The Prophet of Islam in Old French,* trans. and ed. Hyatte, 2–12; Paull, 'The Figure of Mahomet in the Towneley Cycle', 192, 197, 201.
34. Parker, *The Aesthetics of Antichrist,* 95–96; see also Taylor, 'The Once and Future Herod', 126–27.
35. See Tolan, 'European accounts of Muhammad's life', 226–250, esp. 232; Meserve, *Empires of Islam in Renaissance Historical,* 9–14.
36. Akbari, 'Rhetoric of the Antichrist', 298, 302–3.
37. Eppley, 'A New Perspective on Islam in Henrician England', 593.
38. Whilst the Crucifixion is of course another result of Herod's evil, in neither York nor Towneley is the tyrant actually a witness to this event.
39. Godfrey, 'Herod's Reputation and the Killing of the Children', 271.
40. Edminster, *The Preaching Fox,* 165–67.
41. On the comic character Watkyn in this episode in the N–Town Plays see McMurray Gibson, *The Theater of Devotion,* 42.
42. Lewis, *Screwtape Letters,* 55.
43. McGavin and Walker, *Imagining Spectatorship,* 8–16

# Bibliography

Akbari, Suzanne Conklin. 'Placing the Jews in Late Medieval English Literature'. In *Orientalism and the Jews*, edited by Ivan Davidson Kalmar and Derek J. Penslar, 32–50. London: University Press of New England, 2005.

Akbari, Suzanne Conklin. 'The Rhetoric of Antichrist in Western Lives of Muhammad'. *Islam and Christian–Muslim Relations* 8, no. 3 (1997): 297–307.

Akbari, Suzanne Conklin. *Idols in the East: European Representations of Islam and the Orient 1100–1450*. London: Cornell University Press, 2009.

Ashley, Kathleen M. '"Strange and Exotic: Representing the Other in Medieval and Renaissance Performance'. In *East of West: Cross–Cultural Performance and the Staging of Difference*, edited by Claire Sponsler and Xiomei Chen, 77–92. Basingstoke: Palgrave, 2000.

Bakhtin, Mikhail. *Rabelais and His World*. Translated by Helene Iswolsky. Bloomington, Indiana: Indiana University Press, 1984.

Beadle, Richard. *The York Plays: A Critical Edition of the York Corpus Christi Play as recorded in British Library Additional MS 35290*. 2 Vols. Oxford: Oxford University Press, 2013.

Carpenter, Sarah. 'New Evidence: Vives and Audience Response to Biblical Drama'. *Medieval English Theatre* 31 (2009): 3–12.

Chaucer, Geoffrey. *The Riverside Chaucer*. Edited by Larry D. Benson, 3rd edition. Oxford: Oxford University Press, 2008.

Colding Smith, Charlotte. *Images of Islam, 1453–1600: Turks in Germany and Central Europe*. London: Pickering and Chatto, 2014.

Diller, Hans–Jürgen. 'Laughter in Medieval English Drama: A Critique of Modernizing and Historical Analyses'. *Comparative Drama* 36, no.1 (2002): 1–19.

Edminster, Warren. *The Preaching Fox: Elements of Festive Subversion in the Plays of the Wakefield Master*. London: Routledge, 2005.

Epp, Garrett. 'Passion, Pomp, and Parody: Alliteration in the York Plays'. *Medieval English Theatre* 11 (1992): 150–16.

Eppley, Daniel. 'A New Perspective on Islam in Henrician England: The Polemics of Christopher St. German'. *Sixteenth Century Journal* 46, no. 3 (2015): 587–606.

Fumo, Jamie Claire. *The Legacy of Apollo: Antiquity, Authority and Chaucerian Poetics*. London: University of Toronto Press, 2010.

Gilhus, Ingvild S. *Laughing Gods, Weeping Virgins: Laughter in the History of Religion*. London: Routledge, 1997.

Godfrey, Bob. 'Herod's Reputation and the Killing of the Children: Some Theatrical Consequences'. In *Staging Scripture: Biblical Drama, 1350–1600*, edited by Peter Happé and Wim Hüsken, 253–78. Leiden: Brill, 2016.

Gray, Patrick. 'Caesar as Comic Antichrist: Shakespeare's Julius Caesar and the Medieval English Stage Tyrant'. *Comparative Drama* 50 (2016): 1–31.

Harris, Jonathan Gil. *Untimely Matter in the Time of Shakespeare*. Philadelphia: University of Pennsylvania Press, 2009.

Hourihane, Colum. *Pontius Pilate, Anti–Semitism, and the Passion in Medieval Art*. Princeton: Princeton University Press, 2009.

Leach, A. F. 'Some English Plays and Players'. In *An English Miscellany: Presented to Dr. Furnivall in Honour of his Seventy–Fifth Birthday*, edited by William Paton Ker, Arthur S. Napier and Walter W. Skeat, 205–34. Oxford: Clarendon Press, 1901.

Lewis, C.S. *The Screwtape Letters: with Screwtape Proposes a Toast* (Sixtieth Anniversary Edition). London: Harper Collins, 2002.

Lilley, Keith D. *City and Cosmos: The Medieval World in Urban Form*. London: Reaktion Books, 2009.

Lomperis, Linda. 'Medieval Travel Writing and the Question of Race'. *Journal of Medieval and Early Modern Studies* 31, no.1 (2001):147–56.

Lopez, Jeremy. *Theatrical Convention and Audience Response in Early Modern Drama*. Cambridge: Cambridge University Press, 2002.

McGavin, John J. 'Medieval Theatricality and Spectatorship'. *Theta: Théâtre Tudor* 8 (2009): 183–200.

McGavin, John J., and Greg Walker. *Imagining Spectatorship: From the Mysteries to the Shakespearean Stage*. Oxford: Oxford University Press, 2016.

McMurray Gibson, Gail. *The Theater of Devotion: East Anglian Drama and Society in the Late Middle Ages*. Chicago: University of Chicago Press, 1989.

*Medieval Drama: An Anthology*. Edited by Greg Walker. Oxford: Blackwell, 2000.

Meserve, Margaret. *Empires of Islam in Renaissance Historical Thought*. Cambridge, Massachusetts: Harvard University Press, 2008.

Mitchell–Buck, Heather S. 'Tyrants, Tudors, and the Digby *Mary Magdalen*'. *Comparative Drama* 48, no. 3 (2014): 241–59.

Mitchell–Buck, Heather S. 'Maintaining the Realm: City, Commonwealth, and Crown in Chester's Midsummer Plays'. In *The Chester Cycle in Context, 1555–1575: Religion, Drama, and the Impact of Change*, edited by Jessica Dell and David Klausner, 179–92. Farnham: Ashgate, 2012.

Mittman, Asa. *Maps and Monsters in Medieval England*. Abingdon: Routledge, 2006.

Morris, Colin. 'Pilgrimage to Jerusalem in the Middle Ages. In *Pilgrimage: The English Experience from Becket to Bunyan*, edited by Colin Morris and Peter Roberts, 141–63. Cambridge: Cambridge University Press, 2002.

Norako, Leila K. 'Crusades in Literature'. In *The Encyclopedia of Medieval Literature in Britain*, Vol. 1 (4 Vols.), edited by Siân Echard and Robert Rouse, 575–83. Oxford: Wiley–Blackwell, 2017.

Parker, John. *The Aesthetics of Antichrist: From Christian Drama to Christopher Marlowe*. London: Cornell University Press, 2007.

Paull, Michael. 'The Figure of Mahomet in the Towneley Cycle'. *Comparative Drama* 6, no. 3 (1972): 187–204.

Phillips, Helen. 'Medieval Classical Romances: The Perils of Inheritance'. In *Christianity and Romance in Medieval England,* edited by Rosalind Field, Philippa Hardman, and Michelle Sweeney, 3–25. Cambridge: Brewer, 2010.

Ramey, Peter. 'The Audience–Interactive Games of Middle English Religious Drama'. *Comparative Drama* 47, no. 1 (2013): 55–83.

*Records of Early English Drama: Coventry*. Edited by R. W. Ingram. Toronto: University of Toronto Press, 1981.

*Records of Early English Drama: York*. 2 Volumes. Translated and edited by Alexandra F. Johnston and Margaret Rogerson. Manchester: University of Manchester Press, 1979.

Richardson, Brian. 'The Other Readers' Response: On Multiple, Divided and Oppositional Audiences'. *Criticism* 39, no. 1 (1997): 31–53.

Shakespeare, William. *Hamlet*. Edited by Ann Thompson and Neil Taylor. London: Thomson Learning for the Arden Shakespeare, 2006.

Skey, Miriam. 'Herod the Great in Medieval European Drama'. *Comparative Drama*, 13, no. 4 (1979): 33–64.

Staines, David. 'To Out–Herod Herod: The Development of a Dramatic Character'. *Comparative Drama* 10, no.1 (1976): 29–53.

Taylor, Christopher. 'The Once and Future Herod: Vernacular Typology and the Unfolding of Middle English Cycle Drama'. *New Medieval Literatures* 15 (2013): 119–48.

*The Prophet of Islam in Old French: The Romance of Muhammad (1258) and the Book of Muhammad's Ladder (1264)*. Translated and edited by Reginald Hyatte. Leiden: Brill, 1997.

*The Towneley Plays*. Edited by Garrett Epp. Kalamazoo, Michigan: Medieval Institute Publications, 2018.

*The York Corpus Christi Plays*. Edited by Clifford Davidson. Kalamazoo, Michigan: Medieval Institute Publications, 2011.

Tolan, John V. 'European accounts of Muhammad's life'. In *The Cambridge Companion to Muhammad*, edited by Jonathan E. Brockopp, 226–250. Cambridge: Cambridge University Press, 2010.

Tricomi, Albert H. 'Re–Envisioning England's Medieval Cycle Comedy'. *Medieval and Renaissance Drama in England* 5 (1991): 11–26.

Twycross, Meg, and Sarah Carpenter. *Masks and Unmasking in Medieval and Early Tudor England*. Aldershot: Ashgate, 2002.

Weimann, Robert. *Shakespeare and the Popular Tradition in the Theater: Studies in the Social Dimension of Dramatic Form and Function*. Edited by Robert Schwartz. London: John Hopkins University Press, 1978.

Wickham, Glynne. 'Medieval Comic Traditions and the Beginnings of English Comedy'. In *Comic Drama: The European Heritage*, edited by W.D. Howarth, 40–62. London: Methuen, 1978.

Williams, Arnold. 'The Comic in the Cycles'. In *Medieval Drama,* edited by Neville Denny, 109–23. London: Arnold, 1973.

Williams, Deanne. *The French Fetish from Chaucer to Shakespeare*. Cambridge: Cambridge University Press, 2004.

Wittkower, Rudolf. 'Marvels of the East. A Study in the History of Monsters' *Journal of the Warburg and Courtauld Institutes* 5 (1942): 159–97.

Woolf, Rosemary. *The English Mystery* Plays. Berkeley: University of California Press, 1972.

Wright, Clare. 'Acoustic Tyranny: Metre, Alliteration, and Voice in *Christ before Herod*'. *Medieval English Theatre* 34 (2012): 3–29.

CHAPTER 15

# Embodied Laughter: Rabelais and the Medical Humanities

*Alison Williams*

The fictional works of François Rabelais (1483/94?–1553),[1] which narrate the epic adventures of the giants Gargantua and Pantagruel and their diverse brotherhood of advisors, supporters, and rogues, resist categorisation.[2] They blend influences from Classical literature and medieval romance, engage with the key intellectual debates of Renaissance Europe in domains such as law, theology, and, most importantly for this chapter, medicine. They demand much of the reader, in terms of contextual knowledge and a willingness to participate in the linguistic exuberance which characterises much of Rabelais's narrative. It is no surprise then that reactions to Rabelais's works have been mixed, and that the humour of his works elicits an even greater variety of responses, due in no small degree to the high level of subjectivity involved in reactions to humour. Two appraisals of Rabelais's work by Voltaire and William Hazlitt may stand as examples of opposing responses and of the poles of moral indignation and joyful participation that may be experienced by readers. In Letter 22 of his *Letters on England* (1733) Voltaire describes Rabelais's work in the following way:

> Rabelais in his extravagant and incomprehensible book, manifested extreme gaiety and even greater impertinence; he was lavish with erudition, obscenities and boredom—a good story in two pages at the expense of volumes of rubbish. Only a few people of peculiar taste fancy themselves able to understand and appreciate the whole of this work; the rest of the nation laughs at Rabelais' jokes and despises the book [...] people are sorry that a man with so much intelligence put it to such miserable use.[3]

A. Williams (✉)
Swansea University, Swansea, UK
e-mail: a.j.williams@swansea.ac.uk

© The Author(s), under exclusive license to Springer Nature
Switzerland AG 2020
D. Derrin, H. Burrows (eds.), *The Palgrave Handbook of Humour, History, and Methodology*, https://doi.org/10.1007/978-3-030-56646-3_15

Although Voltaire acknowledges that there is some potential for laughter, it is done grudgingly, and at the expense of any other value the works may hold. In 1818, in his lecture, 'On Gay, Swift, Young, Collins &c', the sixth in his series on the English poets, Hazlitt took a much more favourable view, directly linking Rabelais's extravagance with laughter and with health:

> He dwelt on the absurd and ridiculous for the pleasure they gave him, not for the pain. He lived upon laughter, and died laughing. He indulged his vein, and took his full swing of folly. He did not baulk his fancy or his readers. His wit was to him 'as riches fineless'; he saw no end of his wealth in that way, and set no limits to his extravagance: he was communicative, prodigal, boundless, and inexhaustible. His were the Saturnalia of wit, the riches and the royalty, the health and long life.[4]

The modern reader is similarly required to be ready to engage with intellectual learned knowledge, often relying on the detailed notes which accompany modern editions and translations, in order fully to understand the allusions and the characters and events inspiring the narrative. This is a challenge which itself may function to delay and disperse the immediacy and intensity of the pleasure created by the jokes, for, as Sigmund Freud argued, too much intellectual labour may have the effect of hindering spontaneous laughter.[5] Rabelais's humour does not just present sequential challenges to the reader, by which I mean that each new humorous scenario they encounter draws forth a different reaction, but frequently it elicits conflicting responses to the same episode. We may find ourselves both suspending emotional engagement in a show of Bergsonian indifference to the comic victim,[6] whilst simultaneously expressing an emotional connection to the heroes and their companions by aligning ourselves with them. Over and again when reading Rabelais and when sharing our reactions to his humour with others we are made aware of our individual thresholds of tolerance in humour.

There are clearly ways in which established theories of humour may be applied to aspects of Rabelais's work, although no one theory could adequately account for all the mechanisms at play in the various comic episodes or for the reactions they elicit in the reader. Laughter at the downfall of authority figures, such as the Paris watch and university lecturers (*Pantagruel*, 16), or any other number of victims of Panurge's tricks, may be explained with reference to Laurent Joubert's description in his *Treatise on Laughter* (1579) of how laughter intensifies when the victim of the joke is usually imbued with dignity and authority:

> but we will laugh incomparably more if a great and important personage who walks affectedly with a grave and formal step, stumbling clumsily on a heavy stone, falls suddenly in a quagmire.[7]

In such cases, we may pause to consider whether the violence of Rabelais's humour is at odds with Aristotle's definition of the laughable as being 'an error or disgrace that does not involve pain or destruction'.[8] We may experience the 'momentary anaesthesia of the heart' which Henri Bergson considered necessary for the operation of the comic,[9] when we fail to care about the deaths of the 659 knights in *Pantagruel*, 25 or the deaths of Frère Jean's guards in *Gargantua*, 44. When we read about the humiliation of the *haute dame de Paris* (*Pantagruel*, 21–22) or the drowning of Dindenault, the sheep trader (*Quart Livre*, 5–8), do we play the role of the third person in the operation of the obscene or hostile tendentious joke, defined by Freud as being the person in whom 'the joke's intention of producing pleasure is fulfilled'?[10] Do we share in Bakhtin's interpretation of the generative capacities of the material bodily lower stratum and the carnivalesque drive to 'overcome by laughter [...] all the central ideas, images, and symbols of official cultures'?[11] Yes, certainly, all of the above function as methodologies to account for different ways of explaining the comic episodes in Rabelais's work, but there are others, and some of these are most particularly suited to investigating laughter at and in the human body.

With the exception perhaps of Bakhtin's focus on the collective experience of folk humour, all of the above-mentioned theories pit the reader, often in alliance with the team of the giants and their companions, against a comic victim. I wish to propose here that there is a different approach, one which sees humour as being tied to the shared physical and emotional realities of being human. In doing so, Rabelais's work will be brought into dialogue with the medical (or health) humanities. Although the precise name of this field would have been unknown to him, Rabelais is a particularly apt partner for conversation with this discipline, given the importance of the study and practice of medicine in his own life, which I discuss in greater detail below. In addition to the references to medical knowledge which resonate throughout his fictional works, Rabelais's writing on the human condition and the role he attributes to laughter within it share in some of the central tenets of the modern medical humanities. Furthermore, I will seek to establish how Maurice Merleau-Ponty's conception of phenomenology may direct an interpretation of Rabelais's humour which emphasises the place of humour in the bodily experience of the world. While neither the medical humanities nor phenomenology would immediately be considered as natural methodologies for interpreting humour, I hope to demonstrate how they help us to understand the embodied laughter which is just one of the manifestations of the comic in Rabelais's works.

After first examining how embodied laughter and the medical humanities may provide a framework for understanding Rabelais's humour, the discussion of Rabelais's fictional work will be divided into three sections, each representing a different but complementary aspect of the medical humanities: the application of medical knowledge, the relationships between doctor and patient and between patients, and the text as therapeutic artefact. For each section a key representative example from Rabelais's works will be used to investigate the role of humour in this context. It will be seen that the potential for abjection binds together all of the examples of embodied suffering we will examine, but that Rabelais guides us towards seeing laughter at the abject body as one possible response. Furthermore, it will be argued that one interpretation of this laughter is to see it not as an excluding rejection of the target of humour, but as a more affiliative recognition of our own and of others' embodiment.

It is at this point that phenomenology can help us to understand such humour. Phenomenology may be described as a philosophical approach which seeks to explore how phenomena are perceived and experienced.[12] Maurice Merleau-Ponty put particular emphasis on how the body and the world interact, a dialectic whereby the body is 'our anchorage in a world [...] the mediator of a world [...] our general means of having a world'.[13] Although the individual's perceptions of the world are key to phenomenology, these perceptions do not remain in an individualised vacuum. Rather, Merleau-Ponty asserts:

> The phenomenological world is [...] the sense that shines forth at the intersection of my experiences and at the intersection of my experiences with those of others through a sort of gearing into each other. The phenomenological world is thus inseparable from subjectivity and intersubjectivity.[14]

Phenomenology is well established as an approach to investigating culture, embodiment, and illness and its effects on perceptions of the body.[15] Havi Carel describes illness as 'an abrupt, violent way of revealing the intimately bodily nature of our being',[16] and explains how illness makes the individual aware of his or her physical body and changes their experience of the world, both in the physical body and in their sense of identity.[17] Merleau-Ponty describes how we may come to recognise through our bodily perception that others perform the same encounters with the world as we experience ourselves:

> I experience my body as the power for certain behaviours and for a certain world, and I am only given to myself as a certain hold upon the world. Now, it is precisely my body that perceives the other's body and finds there something of a miraculous extension of its own intentions, a familiar handling of the world. Henceforth, just as the parts of my body together form a system, the other's body and my own are a single whole, two sides of a single phenomenon.[18]

In this chapter, phenomenology will be used to explain how laughter at the abject body of another is intertwined with laughter at a realisation of one's own potential for abjection, and recognition that the same interactions with the world occur in oneself as in others.

It is worth establishing the particular relevance of the medical humanities to Rabelais's own life and professional practice and considering some definitions of the field, as well as the role of laughter in health, both in Rabelais's time and in modern medicine. Invaluable resources for information on Rabelais's life and medical practice are Mireille Huchon's biography and Roland Antonioli's *Rabelais et la médecine*. Briefly, Rabelais's medical career in the 1530s is defined by his studies at the University of Montpellier, and possibly also in Paris; his work at the Hôtel-Dieu hospital in Lyon; his appointment as personal physician to the Bishop of Paris, Jean du Bellay, and his accompaniment of the bishop on diplomatic voyages to Italy in the 1530s and 1540s. The 1530s also saw the publication of his edition of the second volume of the medical letters of the Italian doctor Giovanni Manardo and of his commentaries on Hippocrates's *Aphorisms* and Galen's *Art of Medicine*.[19] It will be seen later in the sections on the application of medical knowledge and on the doctor-patient relationship how his study of Latin, Greek, and Arabic medical authorities and his empirical knowledge of interactions with the sick are used for comic purposes in his fictional works.

What would Rabelais think of the term 'medical humanities'? Today, scholars seeking to define 'medical humanities' or 'health humanities' face the challenge of bringing together the many different fields of study and practice which are involved. Indeed, the terms are generous and elastic, stretching to include history, literature, the expressive arts, arts therapy, and medical education. In the opening chapter of *Medicine, Health and the Arts: Approaches to the Medical Humanities* Victoria Bates and Sam Goodman emphasise the 'critical conversations' and the ambition for fruitful exchange and multidisciplinarity inherent in the name.[20] Paul Crawford et al. argue for the wider and more democratic nomenclature provided by the '*health* humanities', involving all those with an interest in health and wellbeing, including patients.[21] These terms developed from the mid-twentieth century, but Rabelais's writing shows that he was familiar with the enriching dialogue and enquiry into the education, practice, and care of practitioner and patient which they seek to encapsulate. One wonders whether Rabelais would not have been puzzled as to why we require a special term for an approach to healthcare, to the lived experience of the body, and to the expressive possibilities for articulating both of them which appears to have been embedded in his own medical training and his professional practice as a doctor. When Gargantua writes to his son, Pantagruel, in *Pantagruel*, 8, detailing the educational expectations he has of him, the study of the human body has its place in the manifesto, alongside languages, civil law, the liberal arts, natural sciences, and many others. The human body is a microcosm of the wider world and a literal insight into human anatomy places the student in dialogue with other disciplines:

> Puis songneusement revisite les livres des medicins Grecz, Arabes, et Latins, sans contemner les Thalmudistes, et Cabalistes, et par frequentes anatomies acquiers toy parfaicte congnoissance de l'autre monde, qui est l'homme. (*Pantagruel*, 8, 245)

> Then frequent the books of the ancient medical writers, Greek, Arabic and Latin, without despising the Talmudists or the Cabbalists; and by frequent dissections acquire a perfect knowledge of that other world which is Man. (49)

Gargantua's ambition is that he will see in his son 'un abysme de science' (245) [an abyss of erudition (49)], not one single knowledge set, bounded by disciplinary barriers, but a person embodying the types of critical conversations seen as providing the dynamic for the modern medical humanities. Indeed, Martyn

Evans and Ilora Finlay describe how the modern medical humanities 'recapture [...] a tradition in which arts and sciences are intertwined'.[22] Acknowledging how Rabelais anticipated the modern medical humanities, for the purposes of this chapter I should like to propose a sub-definition of the medical humanities apposite to Rabelais's life and practice: a playfully knowledgeable approach to being human, bearing witness to suffering and healing, and investigating the role of words and laughter in wellbeing.

If this definition sounds knowingly performative, then this is deliberate. In the dedicatory epistle which opens *Le Quart Livre*, Rabelais writes at length about how the appearance and demeanour of the doctor have an effect on the patient's prognosis. He cites numerous Greek, Roman, and Arabic sources on the effect of the doctor's physical appearance, an influence also noted in modern writing on the doctor's responsibility to model health for his or her patients.[23] Rabelais concludes with overt references to the theatricality of the interaction between doctor, patient, and, importantly, the disease:

> comme sil [le medicin] deust jouer le rolle de quelque Amoureux ou Poursuyvant en quelque insigne comœdie [...] Defaict la practique de Medicine bien proprement est par Hippocrates comparée à un combat, et farce jouée à trois personnages: le malade, le medicin, la maladie. (517–18)

> as though the physician were about to play the role of lover or suitor in some famous comedy [...] Indeed, practising medicine is compared by Hippocrates to a combat and to a farce with three characters: the patient, the physician and the malady. (640)

The connection between health, healthcare, and laughter is one that was familiar to students and practitioners of medicine in early modern France.[24] In his *Treatise on Laughter*, Joubert who, like Rabelais, studied medicine at Montpellier and later became the chancellor of the university, twice explicitly links laughter with psychological benefits. Quoting Quintilian, Joubert asserts that:

> It restores the mind overworked by cares, turning it away from dismal thoughts, satiating and renewing it after a great and tormenting burden, as it chases out all melancholy. Sick people have been cured by this sole remedy.[25]

Later, he considers the restorative and balancing functions of laughter:

> God has ordained, among man's enjoyments, laughter for his recreation in order to conveniently loosen the reins of his mind, just as he has given wine to men in order to temper and lighten the severity and austerity of old age. [...] Laughter, too, is very pleasant because it keeps a certain mediocrity between all the passions.[26]

Modern medicine concurs with Joubert's view of the effects of laughter on individuals and in the dynamics of interpersonal relationships within healthcare environments. Numerous studies attest to the positive physiological effects of laughter, noting benefits for the immune system and the cardiovascular system, its role in pain relief, and in promoting general physical and mental wellbeing.[27] Neurologists have studied how different parts of the brain such as the right frontal lobe and the hypothalamus are involved in the appreciation of humour and the production of laughter.[28] Arthur Frank cites the case from the 1960s of Norman Cousins, who claimed to have cured himself of an inflammatory disease of the connective tissue by watching slapstick films and reading joke books.[29] We will return to the restorative intent of cultural outputs in general and of Rabelais's works in particular in the final section below on the text as therapeutic artefact.

The role of laughter in the delivery and experience of healthcare (rather than the physical experience of illness) is equally one which attracts attention today and which has particular resonance for affiliative theories of humour in the healthcare environment and, as I will argue, within the community established between the reader, the text, and the fictional sick. Studies on the role of humour in modern healthcare environments list the numerous functions it fulfils, which include dealing with 'taboo subjects such as serious illness or death',[30] promoting 'bonding [...] and demonstrating camaraderie in the face of a common foe',[31] and allowing hospitalised patients to adapt to a new identity and a new space.[32] Athena du Pré acknowledges the apparent incompatibility of humour and medical settings,[33] but explains how the two may interact to generate new synergies:

> People commonly use humor to manage face-threatening situations. In doing so, they downplay the solemnity that might accompany a loss of dignity, reframing the episodes as affiliative and unserious instead.[34]

In their analysis of affiliative humour in Rabelais's works Ronald Hallett and Peter Derks argue that primarily affiliative jokes are more playful than aggressive jokes, and that the aggression usually directed at the butt of the joke is downplayed or absent, with more emphasis on communication than on exclusion.[35] I propose that within the context of the interaction between the reader and Rabelais's text there is a further form of affiliation, the type of intersubjectivity described by Merleau-Ponty, specifically with the sick described by the narrator. Rather than seeing the sick simply as comic victims, there is a sense of shared experience between the reader and these fictional patients, which is born of the recognition that to be human is to have the potential to be both sick and well. Whether we like it or not, we are forced into being part of a community of suffering by the narrator of *Gargantua*, who in the Prologue directly addresses the readers as 'vous Verolez tresprecieux' (5) [you, most becarbuncled of syphilitics (205)]. As Susan Sontag wrote: 'everyone who is born holds dual citizenship, in the kingdom of the well and in the kingdom of the sick'.[36] In the case of the reader of Rabelais, laughter at the sick—and there will be some, however uncharitable and even unethical that may seem—is an affiliative, inclusive laughter rather than an exclusive one. This laughter is multidirectional: we laugh as much at ourselves, in the knowledge that we may pass into the realm of the sick and share their bodily experience of illness, as at the sick in the text.

This introductory section has sought to establish a toolkit for analysing how humour operates in three aspects of Rabelais's representation of medical relationships in his fictional works. It has demonstrated how the critical interactions of the modern medical humanities, which promote the generative possibilities and mutual therapeutic benefits of permeable disciplinary boundaries, were familiar to Rabelais and his contemporaries, as were beliefs about the physiological and social functions of laughter. It has also explored how phenomenology's focus on embodiment and (inter)subjectivity may provide one approach to understanding laughter at the sick body.

## Humour and the Application of Medical Knowledge

Two of the issues which the medical humanities seek to address are the development of the medical curriculum and how medical knowledge may be applied successfully in interactions with users of healthcare, both in terms of prognosis and in terms of the establishment of interpersonal relationships. Alan Bleakley describes the aim of the medical humanities in medical education as being 'a redistribution of the sensible to create a common wealth'.[37] By 'sensible' here, Bleakley means sensitivity and empathy, qualities which are frequently absent from the humorous applications of medical knowledge found in Rabelais's works. Both John Parkin and Barbara Bowen have noted how many references to medical knowledge in Rabelais's works are exaggerated, comic misapplications, or spoofs.[38] This section will consider how humour is created from the deliberate misapplication of pharmacological knowledge with the intent simultaneously to cause harm and to provoke laughter.

There is ample evidence in Rabelais's works of strong medicines being used for unethical ends, certainly as far as the patient's comfort is concerned, and it is often Panurge, the trickster, thief, charlatan, jack-of-all trades, beloved companion, and, arguably, alter ego of Pantagruel who plays the role of doctor or apothecary on such occasions. Soon after Panurge makes his entrance into the text in *Pantagruel*, 9 we are made aware of his detailed knowledge of pharmaceuticals. He is a human drugs trolley, carrying with him a myriad of powders and potions, and he is said to have previously sold theriac, a wonder drug combining tens of simples which could supposedly cure all ills, and versions of which were often sold by charlatans.[39] Panurge's prescriptions are not designed with the wellbeing of the patient in mind, but are sometimes based on Panurge's own subjective opinion of the patient, and at others are directed at causing harm and humiliation.

The *tarte borbonnaise* [Bourbonese marmalade (87)] which he concocts in *Pantagruel*, 16 and spreads on the streets of Paris contains galbanum, asafoetida, and castoreum. These substances had a variety of medical applications, in gynaecology, as abortive agents, for toothache, and as anti-spasmodics, but they share a common characteristic: they all have very pungent and unpleasant odours.[40] It is this practical application which Panurge exploits to make a very powerful emetic for the Paris watch, which causes not only the expected vomiting, but also leprosy, syphilis, scabies, and death from plague.[41] His use of euphorbia is more conventional. It had several uses, both internally as a purgative and topically to remove hair and warts, but caution was required because of its ulcerative properties.[42] Panurge uses its pungent smell to make sneezing powder in *Pantagruel*, 16, and more vindictively mixes it with grains of Cnidos[43] to make caustic pastilles which are used as a type of biological warfare against Anarche, the enemy king in *Pantagruel*, 28:

> Mais tout soubdain qu'il en eut avallé une cueillerée, luy vint tel eschauffement de gorge avecque ulceration de la luette, que la langue luy pela. (313)

> But the very moment that he swallowed one spoonful of it he suffered such an inflammation of the throat with an ulceration of his uvula that his tongue peeled off. (135)

These episodes are evidently a deliberate misuse of Panurge's, and Rabelais's, medical knowledge. All these substances were used for genuine therapeutic reasons. But here they are used to provoke public abjection and misery, which for some lasts long after the prank is forgotten and may even be fatal. But do we care and do we laugh? Do these victims deserve their punishment? And what conclusions may we draw about the ethics of laughing here? In terms of the role of the medical profession we do have some licence to laugh, for these are of course not actually patients; they have not consulted Panurge about a medical complaint. We are not dealing with a breach of trust in the doctor-patient relationship, but we are dealing with the wilful use of medical knowledge for harm. As I have argued elsewhere, such episodes may be interpreted as invitations to participate in sick humour.[44] Our affiliative relationship with Pantagruel means that we are opposed to his enemy and we are not emotionally invested with the Paris watch who fleetingly disrupt Panurge's streetlife. Over and above these reactions is the fact that this harm takes place in a fictional joke space lacking in sensitivity and empathy, and that by being participants in this space we recognise that Rabelais is presenting us with a comically ironic inversion of medical practice. It is the very fact that we know that these medicines are prescribed vindictively rather than therapeutically, and that we appreciate that this is outrageously unethical, that allows us to laugh. But in addition to making us laugh, these episodes act as a form of reverse psychology: the wrongness of this model of practice also emphasises the rightness of its inverse. In this way we arrive at the sensibility which Bleakley identified as being necessary to the application of medical knowledge.[45]

## Humour and the Doctor-Patient and Patient-Patient Relationship

In the previous section, we saw how the misapplication of medical education caused deliberate harm and created abjection, outcomes which played out within the space of a comically conscious flouting of how medical knowledge should be used. The portrayal of abjection and the role of laughter in steering our reactions to it are also key themes of the relationship between doctor and patient and between patients in Rabelais's works. This section will take as a key example the depiction of pox-sufferers. No other illness is such a source of affectionate laughter and no other patients are accorded such prominence, a distinction reflected in them having prime position in the galleries where the sick wait to be cured in the kingdom of the Quinte Essence (*Cinquiesme Livre*, 18, 767). In *The Birth of the Clinic*, Michel Foucault attributes a 'loquacious gaze' to the doctor.[46] The medical gaze directed at Rabelais's pet patients certainly brims with words. I would argue, however, that this does not result in the impersonal abstraction of the patient which Foucault suggests and which we may have experienced in our attitudes to the unfortunate recipients of Panurge's prescriptions above. Instead of eliminating the patient's voice, they and we (for this includes us as readers) are drawn into a fellowship of shared, embodied experience.

It was in the 1490s that Europeans first became aware of the pox or the French Disease, to be known in later centuries as syphilis.[47] First descriptions of the disease come from observations of French troops at the battle of Fornovo on 6 July 1495,[48] and a variety of theories have been proposed for its apparently sudden arrival and its virulence, which meant it quickly became epidemic.[49] These include it having been brought back from Hispaniola by Columbus and his companions; it being a result of the mutation of a disease already present in Europe; it being a conjunction of different diseases.[50] Whatever its origins, it was a disease which Rabelais would have encountered in his medical practice and quite possibly amongst his acquaintances in early modern France.[51]

From the many references to the pox in Rabelais's works, three have been chosen here to investigate laughter at abjection, the use of symptoms of disease as entertainment, and the inclusivity of illness. In the Prologue to *Pantagruel* the narrator describes three typical treatments for pox: the topical application of mercury, which has side effects of loosening the teeth and causing excess salivation,[52] ointments leading to shiny skin,[53] and the use of sweatboxes:[54]

> Mais que diray je des pauvres verolez et goutteux? O quantesfoys nous les avons veu, à l'heure que ilz estoyent bien oingtz et engressez à poinct et le visaige leur reluysoit comme la claveure d'un charnier, et les dentz leur tressailloyent comme font les marchettes d'un clavier d'orgues ou d'espinette, quand on joue dessus, et que le gosier leur escumoit comme à un verrat que les vaultres ont aculé entre les toilles: que faisoyent ilz alors? toute leur consolation n'estoit que de ouyr lire quelque page dudict livre. (214)

But what shall I say about the wretches who suffer from the gout and the pox? O how often have we seen them after they had been well basted and duly daubed with unguents, their faces burnished like the clasp of a pork-barrel and their teeth clattering like the manual of an organ (or a set of virginals when the keys are struck) while they are foaming at the gullet like a wild boar which hound and whippet have hunted for seven hours and cornered in the nets. Then what did they do? Their only consolation lay in listening to a page read from that book. (12)

We will return in the final section to how suffering may be alleviated through engagement with a text. Here we should note how the medical gaze directs us into a detailed focus on physical humiliation, the patients' lack of control, and the dehumanising effect of their being likened to animals and inanimate objects. It could be argued that laughter at these patients is hostile or indifferent, that we observe them not with a dispassionate clinical eye, but perhaps with a condemnatory gaze, or a belief that their bodily experience of the world is nothing to do with us.

In chapter 23 of *Pantagruel*, Pantagruel receives news both of his father's death and of the invasion of his home territory of Utopie by the Dipsodes, led by their king Anarche. The climax of the ensuing conflict sees Pantagruel engaged in single combat with the monstrous Loup Garou, leader of the troop of giants who make up part of Anarche's army. While the two champions fight, the opposing sides retire together and partake in a tense banquet. In a clear reversal of the clichéd injunction not to mock the afflicted, Panurge turns the symptoms of pox, here the retracted limbs typical of *tabes dorsalis* in late-stage syphilis[55] and a hoarse voice, into a form of entertainment:

> Panurge […] contrefaisoit ceulx qui ont eu la verolle, car il tordoit la gueule et retiroit les doigts, et en parole enrouée leur dist…. (*Pantagruel*, 29, 317)

> Panurge […] mimicking men who have caught the pox, for he twisted his gullet, crooked his fingers, and croaked in a husky voice…. (139)

Despite the apparent reification of the pox-sufferer in these two examples, it is beyond doubt that in Rabelais's fictional works pox is a truly inclusive disease. First, with reference to the characters within the text: Gargantua's tutor, Thubal Holoferne, dies of it (*Gargantua*, 14, 43), Panurge views it as an occupational hazard of his womanising (*Tiers Livre*, 10, 378), and claims to have a particularly severe case (*Pantagruel*, 30, 324). He shares this last piece of information following the resurrection of Epistémon, who has visited the underworld after being decapitated and temporarily dead. He relates to his companions how fortunes are turned upside down in the afterlife, a reversal which sees Pope Sixtus being a greaser of pox sufferers. This elicits questions about the presence of the disease after death:

—Comment? dist Pantagruel, il y a des verollez de par delà?

—Certes, dist Epistémon. Je n'en veiz oncques tant, il en y a plus de cent milions. Car croyez que ceulx qui n'ont eu la verolle en ce monde cy, l'ont en l'aultre.' (*Pantagruel*, 30, 324)

'What!' said Pantagruel. 'Are there syphilitics in that other world?'

'Indeed there are,' said Epistémon. 'I never saw so many. Over a hundred million. For you should believe that those who don't catch the pox in this world will do so in the next.' (149–50)

Second, and drawing on the ubiquity of the disease explained by Epistémon, the reader is implicated too. We have already seen how the reader is addressed in the Prologue to *Gargantua* as belonging to a community of the sick, so in both texts pox is presented as an inevitability, as a contagion with the ability to reach out beyond the confines of the fictional space and to infect the reader. What is the purpose of this inclusivity and how are we to react? Despite the acknowledgement of the indignities of treatment and the bodily consequences of the pox, abjection and misery, rejection and fear are not part of the response which Rabelais advocates. In *Powers of Horror*, Julia Kristeva asserts that 'laughing is a way of placing or displacing abjection',[56] and it can be argued that both by laughing at pox sufferers and by directing an unflinching gaze at their symptoms and treatments, the potential for misery is lessened or removed and the potential for laughter is increased. Sontag also addresses how not facing disease head on can have negative consequences. Writing about cancer and tuberculosis she states: 'Any disease that is treated as a mystery and acutely enough feared will be felt to be morally, if not literally, contagious'.[57] In a similar vein, Bakhtin argues that laughter and the close inspection of a phenomenon are both liberating and brave:

Laughter demolishes fear and piety before an object, before a world, making of it an object of familiar contact and thus clearing the ground for an absolutely free investigation of it [...]. One can disrespectfully walk around whole objects; therefore the back and rear portion of an object (and also its innards, not normally accessible for viewing) assume a special importance.[58]

When Rabelais describes the sick, the doctor forces us to look closely at his patients' bodies and at their suffering, and in so doing the doctor also makes us reflect on ourselves as past, present, or future patients. This dual function finds parallels in phenomenology. Taylor Carman explains how Merleau-Ponty was driven to examine the fact that 'we are *open onto* the world and that we are *embedded in* it',[59] just as we may here perceive the sick and recognise our own fragile embodiment. The co-existence of direct personal experience and intuited awareness of others' experience is an inescapable part of social relationships. Merleau-Ponty describes the necessity and inevitability of this connection in the following way: 'I can certainly turn away from the social world, but I cannot cease to be situated in relation to it. [...] We must return to the social world with which we are in contact through the simple fact of our existence'.[60]

So who is laughing at whom here? The doctor at his patient? The reader at the pox sufferer? The reader at themselves? As it is clear that everyone has or will have pox, we are not just laughing at some abject sick person; we must also be laughing at ourselves and the potential within us to be the abject patient. This is not to say that the pox sufferer or the reader becomes some type of heroic patient, stoically greeting illness. Instead of turning away from illness in fear and denial, Rabelais's approach asks us to turn towards the realities of the physical body, and to use laughter as a way to acknowledge how knowing the body means knowing the world and vice versa. Merleau-Ponty writes: 'I have no other means of knowing the human body than by living it, that is, by taking up for myself the drama that moves through it and by merging with it'.[61] The drama of the pox draws fictional patient and reader into an affiliative bond and creates infectious laughter. There is another form of consolation in the image of the pox-sufferer: they are comforted by being read to; our final section will see how readers too can receive textual therapy through a therapeutic comic narrative.

## The Text as Therapeutic Artefact

This final section connects with the way the medical humanities engage with artworks of all kinds. Although I concentrate here on the therapeutic potential of the comic text (either read or listened to), the medical humanities' engagement is more broad, both in terms of the cultural outputs appreciated or produced (e.g. film, visual arts, dance), and in the perspective of this engagement: encompassing art *about* illness, narrative medicine,[62] and the production of art by patients and practitioners. Regarding the latter, creative writing and bibliotherapy have been the focus of particular interest.[63] Reading, not *about* illness or wellbeing, but as an embodied practice which brings therapeutic benefits, has received less attention in contemporary work on the medical humanities. Paul Crawford et al. describe its place within the health humanities in the following way:

> Reading in a therapeutic sense is an area of only newly developing research [...] There is enormous scope here for applied practice within a health humanities ethos, in terms of the health and well-being benefits for people experiencing ill health, their informal carers, and those professionals allied to medicine such as care workers—all could benefit from the act of reading as in itself therapeutic and also as a tool for broadening empathy, knowledge and understanding.[64]

As we saw above in the context of multidisciplinarity, this is another element of the modern medical humanities which appears to be rediscovering something familiar to Rabelais. Although Bowen rightly notes that there is no episode in Rabelais's works where the sick are cured by laughter, despite Joubert's conviction that this was possible, she recognises that the book itself functions as a *pharmakon*.[65]

306    A. WILLIAMS

The therapeutic force of the written or spoken word is made evident in the Prologue to *Pantagruel*. As this was the first book in the series to be written, if not the first in its internal chronology, this means that the message about therapeutic narratives is given particular prominence. Referring to the popularity of the '*grandes et inestimables Chronicques de l'enorme geant Gargantua*' (213) [*Great and Inestimable Chronicles of the Enormous Giant Gargantua* (11)], the narrator gives two examples of the physical and emotional healing potential of this work. First, he describes how topical application of the text may alleviate the pain experienced by those afflicted with toothache:

> Aultres sont par le monde [...] qui estans grandement affligez du mal des dentz, après avoir tous leurs biens despenduz en medicins sans en rien profiter, ne ont trouvé remede plus expedient que de mettre lesdictes chronicques entre deux beaulx linges bien chaulx, et les appliquer au lieu de la douleur, les sinapizand avecques un peu de pouldre d'oribus. (214)

> There are folk in this world [...] who, being plagued with the tooth-ache and having spent their all on the physicians [to no avail], have found no remedy more expedient than to place the aforesaid *Chronicles* between two very hot strips of fine linen and apply them to the seat of the pain, sprinkling a little powdered dung over them. (12)

This description offers visual comedy, as the reader imagines the careful binding of the book to the patient's face, with a touch of scatology for good measure. It offers a satirical glance at the incompetence, and perhaps venality, of doctors. Although farfetched claims are made for the remedy's physical capacities to heal, it actually draws more on the potential of a well-loved tale to distract from suffering and the healing benefits of laughter. The portrait of the abject pox sufferer which follows immediately afterwards showcases further the significant therapeutic force of narrative in Rabelais's work. We have already examined this passage for what it can tell us about the relationship between doctors and patients, and how laughter at abjection may rob it of its humiliating force. Here we will just emphasise the form of consolation offered to those undergoing treatment: 'toute leur consolation n'estoit que de ouyr lire quelque page dudict livre' (214) [Their only consolation lay in listening to a page read from that book (12)]. If we accept, as argued above, that we share in the experience of illness, do we not also share in the comfort of the therapeutic narrative?

This is certainly the idea put forward in a much more serious and moving way in the dedicatory epistle to the *Quart Livre*. Here Rabelais speaks as a writer, rather than through the intermediary narrator, the anagrammatic Alcofribas Nasier. Reflecting on the success of his previous works and on how people have reported that reading them has lightened their mood, Rabelais writes the following:

> Es quelz je suis coustumier de respondre, que icelles par esbat composant ne pretendois gloire ne louange aulcune: seulement avois esguard et intention par

escript donner ce peu de soulaigement que povois es affligez et malades absens, lequel voluntiers, quand besoing est, je fays es presens qui soy aident de mon art et service. (517)

To whom I normally reply that, as I wrote them for fun, I sought neither glory nor praise of any kind: my concern and intention were simply to provide such little relief as I could to those who are absent sick-and-suffering as I willingly provide to those who are present with me, seeking help from my Art and my care. (639–40)

The textual work of fiction therefore works as a proxy for the medical doctor, tending to the sad and the sick. The affiliative experience of illness is transformed by reading into an affiliative form of remote healing through laughter. Merleau-Ponty saw shared embodiment as the way in which we experience others,[66] and also argued that it is the body which 'gives a sense […] to cultural objects such as words'.[67] Engagement with Rabelais's comic text gives us infectious laughter to combat contagious abjection.

## Conclusion

Rabelais bases his address to readers at the start of *Gargantua* on how laughter generated by reading can cheer the downhearted, and on how laughter is part of what it means to be human:

> Vray est qu'icy peu de perfection
> Vous apprendrez, si non en cas de rire:
> Aultre argument ne peut mon cueur elire.
> Voyant le dueil, qui vous mine et consomme,
> Mieulx est de ris que de larmes escripre.
> Pource que rire est le propre de l'homme. (3)

> Little perfection here may hide
> Save laughter: little else you'll find.
> No other theme comes to my mind
> Seeing such gloom your joy doth ban.
> My pen's to laughs not tears assigned.
> Laughter's the property of Man. (203)

This chapter has sought to establish how the medical humanities and phenomenology can be used as one approach to interpret the humour derived from the human body in Rabelais's works.

Phenomenology has been used to acknowledge the primacy of the body in the experience of the world, particularly here in relation to illness and laughter. Even if each individual has their own unique perception of the world, the role of the body as the medium through which the world is lived and the positioning of the individual in a social world support the affiliative communities of abjection, laughter, and reading. We have seen how the modern medical humanities are rediscovering approaches to medicine and wellbeing which were parts of Rabelais's professional practice as both a doctor and a writer: multidisciplinarity and therapeutic reading.

By considering three aspects of the medical humanities in Rabelais's humour we have investigated how shared embodiment, in abjection, in laughter, and in reading, furnishes us with a way to respond to Rabelais's comic text. Our path through these examples has brought us progressively closer to affiliative embodiment. When considering the misapplication of medical knowledge, we were much nearer to the hostility and indifference to the butt of the joke typical of many theories of humour. But even here, we could see ourselves as belonging to a community of shared knowledge, aware of the ironic use of the pharmacopoeia, and of a playful approach to the human body. When laughing at the pox sufferers, we saw how exclusive laughter at the sick patient was mediated by the medical gaze to become an affiliative laughter, and that the perspective of doctor-patient became one of patient-patient. In taking this approach as readers of Rabelais, we witnessed through his texts the suffering of others and of ourselves, and saw how laughter functions as a weapon against fear and despair. Finally, shared laughter at the therapeutic text has created a further affiliative relationship between author and reader and between readers, as words and wellbeing are brought into a fruitful alliance.

## NOTES

1. For discussion on the contested date of Rabelais's birth, see Huchon, *Rabelais*, 31–33.
2. References to Rabelais's works: *Pantagruel* (1532?), *Gargantua* (1534/35?), *Le Tiers Livre* (1546), *Le Quart Livre* (1548 (incomplete), 1552), and *Le Cinquiesme Livre* (1564) are taken from Rabelais, *Œuvres complètes*. Translations are from Rabelais, *Gargantua and Pantagruel*. For a summary of the various opinions about the authorship of *Le Cinquiesme Livre* see Huchon's notes to the above edition, 1595–1607 and Cooper, 'L'Authenticité du *Cinquiesme Livre*'.
3. Voltaire, *Letters on England*, 108.
4. Hazlitt, *Lectures on the English Poets*, 150.
5. Freud, *The Joke and its Relation to the Unconscious*, 146.
6. Bergson, *Laughter*, 4.
7. Joubert, *Treatise on Laughter*, 20.
8. Aristotle, *Poetics*, 9.
9. Bergson, *Laughter*, 5.
10. Freud, *The Joke and its Relation to the Unconscious*, 97.
11. Bakhtin, *Rabelais and his World*, 394.
12. Moran, *Introduction to Phenomenology*, 4.
13. Merleau-Ponty, *Phenomenology of Perception*, 146–47.
14. Merleau-Ponty, *Phenomenology of Perception*, lxxxiv.
15. Saunders et al., 'Introduction', 4.
16. Carel, *Illness*, 27.
17. Carel, *Phenomenology of Illness*, 27.

18. Merleau-Ponty, *Phenomenology of Perception*, 370.
19. For more detail on all of these aspects of Rabelais's professional medical life, see Antonioli, *Rabelais et la médecine*, chapters 3 and 4; Huchon, *Rabelais*, chapter 4.
20. Bates and Goodman, 'Critical Conversations', 3–13.
21. Crawford et al., *Health Humanities*, 2.
22. Evans and Finlay, eds., *Medical Humanities*, 8.
23. Frank, *The Wounded Storyteller*, 87.
24. Antonioli, *Rabelais et la médecine*, 159; Screech and Calder, 'Some Renaissance Attitudes to Laughter', 216; Ménager, *La Renaissance et le rire*.
25. Joubert, *Treatise on Laughter*, 16.
26. Joubert, *Treatise on Laughter*, 94–95.
27. du Pré, *Humor and the Healing Arts*, 19; Dubb, 'Humour and Laughter in Medicine', 2–3; Calman, *A Study of Story Telling*, 40; Keith-Spiegel, 'Early Conceptions of Humor', 5.
28. Dubb, 'Humour and Laughter in Medicine', 1–3.
29. Frank, *The Wounded Storyteller*, 124–25.
30. Calman, *A Study of Story Telling*, 41.
31. Finlay and Ballard, 'Spirituality as an Integral Part of Healthcare', 141.
32. Martineau, 'A Model of the Social Functions of Humor', 110.
33. du Pré, *Humor and the Healing* Arts, 183.
34. du Pré, *Humor and the Healing Arts*, 4.
35. Hallett and Derks, 'Humour Theory and Rabelais', 137–40.
36. Sontag, *Illness as Metaphor*, 3.
37. Bleakley, *Medical Humanities and Medical Education*, 5.
38. Parkin, *Interpretations of Rabelais*, 17; Bowen, *Enter Rabelais, Laughing*, 140.
39. For theriac see: Palmer, 'Pharmacy in the Republic of Venice', 108, and Szczeklik, *Catharsis*, 22–23.
40. On galbanum see: Avicenna, *Canon*, 2.472; Dioscorides, *De Materia Medica*, 3.83; Gerard, *The Herball*, 1056, 1058; Pliny, *Natural History*, 24.13. On asafoetida see: Avicenna, *Canon*, 2.58. On castoreum see: Avicenna, *Canon*, 2.207; Dioscorides, *De Materia Medica*, 2.24; Pliny, *Natural History*, 8.47.
41. Rabelais, *Pantagruel*, 273; Screech translation, *Gargantua and Pantagruel*, 88.
42. On euphorbia (or spurge) see: Avicenna, *Canon*, 2.425; Dioscorides, *De Materia Medica*, 4.164, Gerard, *The Herball*, 1180; Theophrastus, *Enquiry into Plants*, 9.9.5.
43. Pliny, *Natural History*, 27.46, 13.35; Theophrastus, *Enquiry into Plants*, 9.20.2.
44. Williams, 'Sick Humour'.
45. For more on Rabelais's criticisms of the harm done by ill-educated doctors in sixteenth-century Europe, see my forthcoming article 'Rabelais, the History of Medicine, and Medical Humanism'.
46. Foucault, *Birth of the Clinic*, xii.
47. Brown, *The Pox*, 9.
48. Arrizabalaga et al., *The Great Pox*, 24; Brown, *The Pox*, 1; Quétel, *History of Syphilis*, 10.
49. Quétel, *History of Syphilis*, 15.
50. Hayden, *Pox*, 5.
51. Losse, *Syphilis*, 11.
52. Brown, *The Pox*, 24–25.

53. Losse, *Syphilis*, 13.
54. Brown, *The Pox*, 20.
55. Brown, *The Pox*, 4; Hayden, *Pox*, 58.
56. Kristeva, *Powers of Horror*, 8.
57. Sontag, *Illness as Metaphor*, 6.
58. Bakhtin, *The Dialogic Imagination*, 23.
59. Carman, *Merleau-Ponty*, 10.
60. Merleau-Ponty, *Phenomenology of Perception*, 379.
61. Merleau-Ponty, *Phenomenology of Perception*, 205.
62. Notable works on narrative medicine include: Charon, *Narrative Medicine*; Frank, *The Wounded Storyteller*; Greenhaigh and Hurwitz, *Narrative Based Medicine*; Kleinman, *The Illness Narratives*.
63. See for example works by Bolton, Lepore and Smyth, and Pennebaker.
64. Crawford et al., *Health Humanities*, 56.
65. Bowen, *Enter Rabelais, Laughing*, 145–46.
66. Carman, *Merleau-Ponty*, 188.
67. Merleau-Ponty, *Phenomenology of Perception*, 244.

## Bibliography

Antonioli, Roland. *Rabelais et la médecine*. Geneva: Droz, 1976.

Aristotle. *Poetics*. Translated by Malcolm Heath. London: Penguin, 1996.

Arrizabalaga, Jon, John Henderson, and Roger French. *The Great Pox: The French Disease in Renaissance Europe*. New Haven: Yale University Press, 1997.

Avicenna. *The Canon of Medicine*. Vol 2: *Natural Pharmaceuticals*. Translated by Laleh Bakhtiar. Chicago: Great Books of the Islamic World, 2012.

Bakhtin, Mikhail. *The Dialogic Imagination: Four Essays*. Edited by Michael Holquist. Translated by Caryl Emerson and Michael Holquist. Austin: University of Texas, 1981.

Bakhtin, Mikhail. *Rabelais and his World*. Translated by Hélène Iswolsky. Bloomington: Indiana University Press, 1984.

Bates Victoria, and Sam Goodman. 'Critical Conversations: Establishing Dialogue in the Medical Humanities'. In *Medicine, Health and the Arts: Approaches to the Medical Humanities*, edited by Victoria Bates, Alan Bleakley, and Sam Goodman, 3–13. London: Routledge, 2013.

Bergson, Henri. *Laughter: An Essay on the Meaning of the Comic*. Translated by Cloudesley Brereton and Fred Rothwell. London: Macmillan, 1911.

Bleakley, Alan. *Medical Humanities and Medical Education: How the Medical Humanities can Shape Better Doctors*. Abingdon: Routledge, 2015.

Bolton, Gillie. *The Therapeutic Potential of Creative Writing: Writing Myself*. London: Jessica Kingsley, 1999.

Bowen, Barbara C. *Enter Rabelais, Laughing*. Nashville: Vanderbilt University Press, 1998.

Brown, Kevin. *The Pox: The Life and Near Death of a Very Social Disease*. Stroud: Sutton, 2006.

Calman, Kenneth C. *A Study of Story Telling, Humour and Learning in Medicine*. London: Nuffield Trust, 2000.

Carel, Havi. *Illness: The Cry of the Flesh*. Stocksfield: Acumen, 2008.

Carel, Havi. *Phenomenology of Illness.* Oxford: Oxford University Press, 2016.

Carman, Taylor. *Merleau-Ponty.* Abingdon: Routledge, 2008.

Charon, Rita. *Narrative Medicine: Honoring the Stories of Illness.* Oxford: Oxford University Press, 2006.

Cooper, Richard. 'L'Authenticité du *Cinquiesme Livre*: État présent de la question'. In *'Le Cinquiesme Livre': Actes du colloque international de Rome (16–19 octobre 1998),* edited by Franco Giacone, 9–22. Geneva: Droz, 2001.

Crawford, Paul, Brian Brown, Charley Baker, Victoria Tischler, and Brian Abrams, eds. *Health Humanities.* London: Palgrave Macmillan, 2015.

Dioscorides, Pedanius. *De Materia Medica.* Translated by Lily Y. Beck. Hildesheim: Olms-Weidmann, 2011.

Dubb, Asher. 'Humour and Laughter in Medicine', *Adler Museum Bulletin* 26, no. 3 (2000): 1–3.

du Pré, Athena. *Humor and the Healing Arts: A Multimethod Analysis of Humor Use in Health Care.* Mahwah: Lawrence Erlbaum Associates, 1998.

Evans, Martyn, and Ilora G. Finlay, eds. *Medical Humanities.* London: BMJ Books, 2001.

Finlay, Ilora G., and Paul Ballard. 'Spirituality as an Integral Part of Healthcare'. In *Medical Humanities,* edited by Martyn Evans and Ilora G. Finlay, 136–47. London: BMJ Books, 2001.

Foucault, Michel. *The Birth of the Clinic: An Archaeology of Medical Perception.* Translated by A. M. Sheridan. London: Routledge, 1986.

Frank, Arthur W. *The Wounded Storyteller: Body, Illness, and Ethics.* Chicago: Chicago University Press, 1995.

Freud, Sigmund. *The Joke and its Relation to the Unconscious.* Translated by Joyce Crick. London: Penguin, 2002.

Gerard, John. *The Herball, or Generall Historie of Plantes.* London: Islip, Norton, and Whitakers, 1636, https://archive.org/details/herballorgeneral00gera/page/n1683

Greenhaigh, Trisha, and Brian Hurwitz, eds. *Narrative Based Medicine: Dialogue and Discourse in Clinical Practice.* London: BMJ Books, 1998.

Hallett, Ronald A., and Peter Derks. 'Humour Theory and Rabelais'. *Humor: International Journal of Humor Research* 11, no. 2 (1998): 135–60.

Hayden, Deborah. *Pox: Genius, Madness, and the Mysteries of Syphilis.* New York: Basic, 2003.

Hazlitt, William. *Lectures on the English Poets and the English Comic Writers.* London: Bell, 1884.

Huchon, Mireille. *Rabelais.* Paris: Gallimard, 2011.

Joubert, Laurent. *Treatise on Laughter.* Translated by Gregory David de Rocher. Tuscaloosa: University of Alabama Press, 1980.

Keith-Spiegel, Patricia. 'Early Conceptions of Humor: Varieties and Issues'. In *The Psychology of Humor: Theoretical Perspectives and Empirical Issues,* edited by Jeffrey H. Goldstein and Paul E. McGhee, 4–39. New York: Academic Press, 1972.

Kleinman, Arthur. *The Illness Narratives: Suffering, Healing and the Human Condition.* New York: Basic, 1998.

Kristeva, Julia. *Powers of Horror: An Essay on Abjection.* Translated by Leon S. Roudiez. New York: Columbia University Press, 1982.

Lepore, Stephen J., and Joshua M. Smyth. *The Writing Cure: How Expressive Writing Promotes Health and Emotional Well-Being.* Washington, DC: American Psychological Association, 2002.

Losse, Deborah N. *Syphilis: Medicine, Metaphor, and Religious Conflict in Early Modern Europe.* Columbus: The Ohio State University Press, 2015.

Martineau, William H. 'A Model of the Social Functions of Humor'. In *The Psychology of Humor: Theoretical Perspectives and Empirical Issues,* edited by Jeffrey H. Goldstein and Paul E. McGhee, 101–25. New York: Academic Press, 1972.

Ménager, Daniel. *La Renaissance et le rire.* Paris: Presses universitaires de France, 1995.

Merleau-Ponty, Maurice. *Phenomenology of Perception.* Translated by Donald A. Landes. London: Routledge, 2012.

Moran, Dermot. *Introduction to Phenomenology.* London: Routledge, 2002.

Palmer, Richard. 'Pharmacy in the Republic of Venice in the Sixteenth Century'. In *The Medical Renaissance of the Sixteenth Century,* edited by A. Wear, R. K. French, and I. M. Lonie, 100–17. Cambridge: Cambridge University Press, 1985.

Parkin, John. *Interpretations of Rabelais.* Lewiston: Mellen, 2002.

Pennebaker, James W. 'Writing about Emotional Experiences as a Therapeutic Process', *Psychological Science* 8, no. 3 (1997): 162–66.

Pennebaker, James W., and Cindy K. Chung. 'Expressive Writing and its Links to Physical and Mental Health'. In *Oxford Handbook of Health Psychology,* edited by Howard S. Friedman, 417–37. New York: Oxford University Press, 2011.

Pennebaker, James W., and Janel D. Seagal. 'Forming a Story: The Health Benefits of Narrative', *Journal of Clinical Psychology* 55, no. 10 (1999): 1243–54.

Pliny the Elder. *The Natural History.* Translated by John Bostock and H. T. Riley. http://www.perseus.tufts.edu/hopper/text?doc=Perseus%3atext%3a1999.02.0137

Quétel, Claude. *History of Syphilis.* Translated by Judith Braddock and Brian Pike. Cambridge: Polity Press, 1990.

Rabelais, François. *Gargantua and Pantagruel.* Translated by M. A. Screech. London: Penguin, 2006.

Rabelais, François. *Œuvres complètes,* edited by Mireille Huchon with François Moreau. Paris: Gallimard, 1994.

Saunders, Corinne, Ulrike Maude, and Jane Mcnaughton. 'Introduction'. In *The Body and the Arts,* edited by Corinne Saunders, Ulrike Maude, and Jane Mcnaughton, 1–7. Basingstoke: Palgrave Macmillan, 2009.

Screech, M. A., and Ruth Calder. 'Some Renaissance Attitudes to Laughter'. In *Humanism in France at the End of the Middle Ages and in the Early Renaissance,* edited by A. H. T. Levi, 216–28. Manchester: Manchester University Press, 1970.

Sontag, Susan. *Illness as Metaphor and AIDS and its Metaphors.* London: Penguin, 1991.

Szczeklik, Andrzej. *Catharsis: On the Art of Medicine.* Translated by Antonia Lloyd-Jones. Chicago: University of Chicago Press, 2005.

Theophrastus. *Enquiry into Plants.* Translated by Arthur Hort. London: Heinemann, 1916.

Voltaire. *Letters on England.* Translated by Leonard Tancock. London: Penguin, 2005.

Williams, Alison. '"Acquiers toy parfaicte cognoissance de l'autre monde, qui est l'homme": Rabelais, the History of Medicine, and Medical Humanism'. *Essays in French Literature and Culture.* Forthcoming 2021.

Williams, Alison. 'Sick Humour, Healthy Laughter: The Use of Medicine in Rabelais's Jokes'. *Modern Language Review* 101, no. 3 (2006): 671–81.

CHAPTER 16

# Naïve Parody in Rabelais

## *John Parkin*

Naïve parody I define as that brand of humour generated by a figure unable to function within the parameters of normal, responsible or respectable living. Examples would be a child tottering about in failed imitation of its elders, a drunk rambling inarticulately to whoever has the patience to listen, a foreigner who hasn't mastered the grammar or vocabulary of another language or much of the behaviour of animals insofar as they might be compared unfavourably with humans. I am reminded of Flaubert's nicknaming his two comic clowns Bouvard et Pécuchet 'mes deux cloportes' [my two woodlice] or Baudelaire comparing the poet's inability to cope with life to the stumbling of a beached albatross.[1]

As such, naïve parody in its purest form refutes aggression theory, and to that extent Baudelaire's albatross is a bad example. The bird in his poem is mocked by the sailors who have captured him and now scapegoat him for their own amusement, while naïve parody obviates a hostile response, as when we smile at a child's first attempts to walk, swim or play adult games. Now one could laugh derisively at a bumbling child, especially if that same child was getting above himself, but the humour then becomes satiric as empowered by an emotional charge at the victim's expense. Similarly the drunk whose verbiage deviates from the norms of coherent conversation cannot in his state of

---

A version of this chapter has already appeared in *Humor, Education and Art*, edited by Jaqueline Benavides, published by Ediciones Universidad Cooperativa de Colombia in 2019. A modified version is here published by kind permission of Ediciones UCC.

---

J. Parkin (✉)
University of Bristol, Bristol, UK
e-mail: j.parkin@bristol.ac.uk

© The Author(s), under exclusive license to Springer Nature
Switzerland AG 2020
D. Derrin, H. Burrows (eds.), *The Palgrave Handbook of Humour, History, and Methodology*, https://doi.org/10.1007/978-3-030-56646-3_16

advanced inebriation be expected to make clear sense, though again, if we for some reason do not like the person concerned, we may opt to desert the mode of naïve parody in order to vent our spleen.

Such of course is our legitimate choice, for no humourist can demand that his material be exploited in a particular way. The audience, and in Rabelais's case the readership, cannot and perhaps must not be coerced into one predetermined response, otherwise they risk becoming the victims of propaganda and prejudice, but fortunately for his readers and indeed for his own reputation his comic genius spreads far wider than the mere targeting of enemies, he being hugely varied in his comic modality. Much if not all satire depends on the prosecution of serious values, which in Rabelais's case are abundant, though nowadays less clear than to his contemporaries, and while they underpin his many campaigns and outcries, they scarcely exhaust his comic repertoire or one's approach to it. By contrast the spirit of naïve parody involves a response that is far more sympathetic than mocking, hence, cutting across the targets of these campaigns one also encounters a whole variety of naïve figures to whom mockery is a less appropriate response.

Where for instance? Well, to summarise, his four attested volumes describe the adventures of the giant heroes Gargantua and Pantagruel in a reflective adaptation of the hero legends of the Middle Ages, these involving a miraculous birth, an education in the use of arms which facilitates the eventual defeat of a hostile army followed by a pious act that acknowledges God's grace in supporting the victory, and then the establishment of a new generation: Pantagruel is Gargantua's son. Where Rabelais enhances this adopted tradition is by overlaying the pattern with a vast amount of satire, much of it derived from his mentor Erasmus, and in which he attacks sometimes without mercy the political, religious and cultural enemies that they share, and decades of research have gone into the analysis of this trend. One key figure to be mentioned is Michael Screech, whose monumental *Rabelais* summed up his many years of study of the author, providing a key to one's understanding of the abundant intellectual and spiritual themes that Rabelais's work developed.

However his key comic hero is neither the giant Gargantua nor the giant Pantagruel, but rather Panurge, the latter's companion, 'lequel il ayma toute sa vie' [whom he loved throughout his life],[2] and who belongs more centrally to the tradition of comic anti-heroes and lovable rogues again frequently encountered in medieval literature and folklore. Unlike the generators of naïve parody, who fail artlessly to embody the standards by which we live, knaves such as Panurge, Til Eulenspiegel or Reynard the Fox consciously defy those norms, so allowing us, however guiltily, to admire their insolence and rascality: the tradition is very ancient, dating back at least to Homer's Ulysses, and it is sanctified by the figure of the trickster endemic within so many cultures.

Thus identified, Panurge is not a figure of naïve parody, though in some scenes and moods he can embody that role. More particularly in this connection one is looking to Rabelais's portrayals of childhood, and therefore to the chapters describing the giant figures' early years, for Panurge comes to us in full adulthood at the significant age of 35, that is halfway through the threescore years and ten indicated in Psalm 90. By contrast we witness in somewhat grotesque detail the births of both Gargantua and his son, following which Rabelais parodies the traditional motifs of the education and training of an epic hero. What do we learn? That Gargantua spent his early days as a farmyard urchin, since:

> depuis les troys jusques à cinq ans feut nourry et institué en toute discipline convenente par le commandement de son pere. Et celluy temps passa comme les petitz enfans du pays, c'est assavoir à boyre, manger, et dormir: à manger, dormir, et boyre: à dormir, boyre et manger.
> Tousjours se vaultroit par les fanges, se mascaroyt le nez, se chauffouroit le visaige. [...] Il pissoit sus se souliers, il chyoit en sa chemise, il se mouschoyt à ses manches. (33–34)

> From three years upwards unto five, he was brought up and instructed in all convenient discipline by the commandment of his father; and spent that time like the other little children of the country, that is, in drinking, eating, and sleeping, in eating, sleeping, and drinking, and in sleeping, drinking, and eating. Still he wallowed and rolled up and down in the mire and dirt, he filthied his nose [...] He pissed in his shoes, shat in his shirt, and wiped his nose on his sleeve.

And how do we respond? With horror, yes, if we are demanding that convenient discipline be imposed on a child of three, but not if we are prepared to let nature rule in these early years. After all, medical science now teaches us that moderate contact with dirt has a determinable prophylactic effect, so may we not indulge the harmless behaviour of such peasant offspring as Rabelais, a man close to the earth, had no doubt witnessed often enough within the village folk of his Chinonais? A fastidious reader might condemn the child's guardians for neglecting proper norms of hygiene, but as a figure of naïve parody the child himself surely avoids any punitive response and will amuse an indulgent reader prepared, however temporarily, to suppress those norms.

That temporary indulgence must of course have its limits, otherwise the dirty behaviour simply becomes tiresome as one revives one's awareness of proper behavioural modes, and Rabelais is not unaware of that risk. Hence, though one cannot expect his three-year-old to be spick and span, the author tells us that by the age of five Gargantua was the cleanest boy in all the country and that owing to his invention, after long and curious experiment, of the ideal arse-wipe. This item, selected from a huge variety of materials applied during his research and which range from a page's bonnet to bunches of sage, fennel and lettuce, and include a lawyer's satchel and a falconer's lure, comprises the neck of a live goose held between the legs, which beatific experience must surely, the boy adds, be one of the key splendours of the Elysian Fields.

Naïve parody here features within the child's unconcern with any disgust that his performance may stimulate, and it also figures in the juvenile fixation with excrement that features in so much of children's humour, a fixation here represented in the mock syllogism that Gargantua has just announced to his father Grandgousier: 'il n'est [...] poinct besoing torcher cul, sinon qu'il y ayt ordure. Ordure n'y peut estre, si on n'a chié: chier doncques nous fault davant que le cul torcher' (41) [There is no need to wipe one's arse but when it is foul; foul it cannot be, unless one has had a shit; shit then we must before we wipe our arse.] The speech is met with exclamations of delight from his parent, who foretells (with exaggerated naïveté) that within days the boy will surely earn a Sorbonne doctorate.

That particular shaft of humanist satire Rabelais felt the need to blunt in later editions,[3] but the naïve pattern is evident not only in the child's fascination with filth, but also in his father's readiness to flatter and spoil him—and what father has not rendered himself ridiculous by pandering to his offsprings' tastes and pastimes? To this extent naïve parody makes fools of us all as we deliberately induce what one might call a humour of nostalgia whereby 'on tente de renouer avec l'enfant qu'on n'est plus' [one tries to reconnect with the child one no longer is],[4] as well as a humour of recognition whereby we realise that we are encountering an image of ourselves at our weaker moments. To this extent in our teeterings, our senescent memory lapses and our infantile enthusiasms we are all examples of naïve parody and might as well just get on with it.

At the same time the incongruous naïveté of Gargantua's anal fascination does contrast with his ingenuity in performing all these experiments, and that creates a kind of double contrast whereby the limitations of his infantile perspective are ruptured by his talent for enquiry and self-expression—what five-year-old is aware of such pleasures of the Elysian Fields as eating asphodel and drinking nectar?—and again we adults have surely all marvelled at the shafts of mental power that even the smallest kid can occasionally reveal, and which are sufficient here to redeem any displeasure that his father might have expressed over Gargantua's behaviour. In his investigation into children's taste for obscenity Claude Gaignebet notes that we customarily respond with 'la réprobation et la répression',[5] reactions shunned at this point by Rabelais, though within a couple of chapters he has us re-enter the satiric mode by presenting the boy as a product of the worst kind of scholastic, rather than humanist education. In a confrontation with the model humanist pupil Eudémon, his candidate hero, earlier so admirably inventive, is completely put to shame as the sympathy to be engendered by the naïve parodist is drowned out by the antagonism on which the successful satirist depends.

Concerning Gargantua's own son Pantagruel, whose early years Rabelais had described in his first book published two years previously, I shall pass to the university education to which Rabelais exposes him in a tour of the intellectual hotspots that his hero undertakes in *Pantagruel* chapter 5, and which take him from Poitiers (whose facilities afforded him great profit), to Bordeaux, Toulouse, Montpellier (Rabelais's own university), Avignon, Angers, Bourges (where again he swotted long and well), Orléans and finally Paris, centre of medieval learning, yes, but again a town where he studied to great effect. The tour is a mish-mash of elements, combining material drawn from local folklore with the usual anti-scholastic satire (Rabelais has in mind the humanist advances in law studies being achieved at Bourges), plus a shaft of self-mockery, given that the doctors at Montpellier smelt too strongly of enemas for Pantagruel to be tempted to study there as had Rabelais himself.

But the case of Orléans is more relevant to my theme, as here he was seduced by his fellow-students into abandoning the books in favour of tennis: 'Car les estudians dudict lieu en font bel exercice et le menoyent aulcunesfois es isles pour s'esbatre au jeu du poussavant' (232) [For the students there get thoroughly into it; and sometimes carried him off to the islands to enjoy the sport of nookie]. Now a stickler who demands that his pupils work all the time might well take issue with this passage, Orléans being, moreover, a faculty whose low standards allowed for easy passes in Civil Law (a subject not traditionally taught in Paris),[6] hence Rabelais's conclusion to the chapter whereby 'quelque jour que l'on passa Licentié en loix quelcun des escholliers de sa congnoissance, qui de science ne avoit gueres plus que sa portée' (232) [On a certain day one of his scholar mates was given a law degree when he barely knew more of it than his weight]. However, boys will be boys, and a bit of easy living and self-indulgence remains a part of student practice through to our own periods and lifetimes: so again we may respond here with nostalgia or even envy, noting those attractions of the spirit of Brideshead that may have passed us by, and we might note in passing that Rabelais was a mature man during his own period of medical study.

Once more one responds as one chooses, but the rebellious student, a knavish figure who defies his responsibilities, stands alongside the insouciant student, a naïve figure who is untouched by those responsibilities. Adult duties and even adult realities remain to a degree suspended during adolescence, which pattern grants the carefree undergraduate a comic glamour analogous to that of the mucky urchin. So the naïve scholar sails through his sojourn in Orléans, fortunately uncorrupted by the temptations of bad company, but the need to work hard and plan his future remains latent within his role, and Pantagruel will find those factors decisively reasserted in the letter that his father transmits to him during the Parisian period. I read that text, contained in *Pantagruel* chapter 8, as a somewhat idealised paean of Renaissance learning, and one both elegantly expressed and sincerely composed, though opinions do differ on the latter points.[7] However what is significant in terms of comic modality is the way in which the said missive closes off the period of Pantagruel's intellectual and perhaps even spiritual formation, prior to the immediate appearance of his own antithesis, the scoundrelly and disreputable Panurge, Falstaff to his Prince Hal, and of whom more anon.

In the meantime it is noteworthy how the naïve comic hero can figure as much in second childhood as in early childhood, an example being James Thurber's grandfather, celebrated in the short story collection *My Life and Hard Times* and who believed, among other eccentricities, that the American Civil War was still taking place in November 1915, date of 'The Night the Ghost Got In'. A victim of some form of dementia, he is protected by both the family that indulge him and the readers whom he surely amuses, and he has equivalents in various Rabelaisian episodes.

One example would be that scene in *Pantagruel* chapter 3 where the ancient Gargantua, though well into his fifth century, still managed to father a child.

Unfortunately, however, the baby proved so big and heavy that he suffocated his mother during parturition, the widower being thus faced with the dilemma of whether to mourn the death of his spouse or celebrate the birth of his son. Scholastic logic—'argumens sophisticques [...] *in modo et figura*': 225 [sophistical arguments logically framed]—is no help, but human optimism soon dissolves his despair as he determines to weep less and drink more, his wife being now happy in heaven. So, shunning even the chance to attend her funeral, he prefers to dandle the newborn Pantagruel on his knee, having offered the midwives a round of drinks before sending them off to the graveside in his place.

Do we condemn him as a bad husband, a misguided scholar and even a contemptible misogynist? Only if we choose to do so, ignoring the possibility that we forgive him his weaknesses in the name of the greater good of a new life. With the values of marital duty and respect for the dead laid firmly on one side, what therefore predominates, at least for me, is the image of a jovial and positive-thinking rather than confused, perplexed or shameful individual, and one whose 'affection naturelle' (229) can only be to promote the interests of the next generation. Nevertheless, the scholastic cast of mind (*argumens sophisticques*) plus his confusion and perplexity do remain significant, and are echoed in another famous scene where Gargantua (in *Gargantua* chapter 19) meets the epitome of medieval obscurantism, namely the Sorbonne doctor Janotus de Bragmardo.

This character has been deputed by his faculty to secure the return of the bells of Notre Dame cathedral, stolen earlier by the giant Gargantua in order to decorate his mare, but the speech he makes is a laughably incompetent mixture of confused argumentation, coughs and sneezes, bad Latin, nonsense words and misquotes from the Bible, and its satiric import could scarcely be clearer. Janotus is not only an example of degenerate scholarship, but also of religious intolerance: he and his fellow ecclesiastics invent (and then surely persecute) heretics ad lib. So where is the naïve parody? It is discernible both in his drunkenness (in part incited by Gargantua himself), plus the effects of advancing age—'Par mon ame, j'ay veu le temps que je faisois diables de arguer. Mais de present je ne fais plus que resver' (52) [By my soul, I have seen the time that I could play the devil in arguing, but now all I do is dream]—while the satire, though genuine, is blunted by the character's self-awareness: 'ne me fault plus dorenavant, que bon vin, bon lict, le dos au feu, le ventre à table, et escuelle bien profonde' (52) [Henceforth all I need is good wine, a good bed, my back to the fire, my belly to the table and a deep trencher].

For Barbara Bowen he is a basically despicable figure redeemed by his 'dazzlingly inventive' comic skills,[8] a point perhaps easier to accept were those comic skills more consciously deployed. However to see him as 'an old dodderer' (236) is to apply the mode of naïve parody more clearly. In this case the value systems embedded in his vocation are laid aside, even if he remains aware of them, but, as in the case of Thurber's grandfather, and given the scholar's age and condition, one might not indeed expect much more from him than the bumblings and rantings that he so abundantly supplies. Moreover those patterns also earn a degree of support from his fellow characters and therefore, one feels, from their author. When Gargantua and his friends burst into laughter at the man's performance, he joins them, whereupon they reward him for having amused them so much.

A further element that one could raise is the humour of recognition, though in this case it is less nostalgic than anticipatory. One cannot, after all, exclude the possibility of becoming a dodderer oneself, though hopefully to a less exaggerated degree, and Rabelaisian self-parody may in fact stretch this far. An example could reside in the somewhat tedious *Gargantua* chapters 9 and 10, where the narrator expatiates at length on the symbolic meaning of the colours white and blue, before closing off discussion—'icy doncques calleray mes voilles' (33) [So at this point I shall strike sail]—with a promise (fortunately unfulfilled?) that all will be explained in a future book. For Clark such 'endless digressions [...] have much about them which recalls the learned fool',[9] and a similar pose is struck, in my view, at the very end of Rabelais's *Tiers livre* where he expands, again at considerable if not excessive length, on the qualities of the herb Pantagruelion, intended at least initially as an image of the giant whose name it bears. He rambles, perhaps drunkenly (the scene is set with a bottle to hand, if not in fact in a tavern), and his irritated discourse—'Croyez la ou non. Ce m'est tout un. My suffist vous avoir dict verité' (509) [Believe it or don't believe it. I don't care. It's enough for me that I've told you the truth]—so resembles that of an inebriate that one is tempted to feel that little of ultimate importance is being expressed. If that is the strategy, it is certainly a dangerous one, Rabelais neglecting his avowed intention to communicate a 'sustantificque mouelle' (7) [significant marrow], but perhaps he is gambling, naïvely or daringly, on the tolerance of a readership now fully won over to his methods.[10]

As for Panurge, hero of the *Tiers livre*, but absent from its final chapters, vast amounts have been composed in his honour (witness Marrache-Gouraud's *Hors toute intimidation* to name but one) as a character whose roles vary massively, but who belongs centrally though not exclusively to the tradition of comic anti-heroes whose archetype is supplied by the disgraceful and indeed sacrilegious Reynard the Fox. Little more need therefore be said by me of this role, particularly as it in any case stands outside the pattern of naïve parody. More relevant here is the way Panurge develops from being a trickster and a prankster, swindling money out of the Church and discomfiting Parisian figures like the town's watch or the noble ladies, and becoming, in Rabelais's later volumes, an obsessive and a coward.

The obsession is most apparent in Rabelais's *Tiers livre*, published some 14 years after *Pantagruel*, and which revolves around his intention or rather desire to marry, for in fact he never puts that intention to the test. Instead he seeks advice from a vast range of oracles, including a mute, a madman, a witch, a dying poet and, to be sure, Pantagruel himself, none of whom allay his perpetual fears of cuckoldry and physical mistreatment by an eventual spouse.

Now he deserves no less, given the way he has in the past treated both women and their husbands, and it is very easy for one to convert Panurge into a satiric target: were he to take the plunge, the biter will, he fears, and perhaps we hope, be bit. However to me he retains a measure of naïve appeal in that this compulsive preoccupation has rendered his existence so straightforward. If only life were as uncomplicated as it is for Panurge who fruitlessly pursues his quest for knowledge of an unknowable future, protected in point of fact by Pantagruel's wealth and indulgence, even if the giant has early given him the soundest advice possible: that once he has made his mind up, he should go ahead and face the consequences. But Panurge remains in a state of existential suspense right through that book and beyond, a superannuated adolescent warned by his companion Frère Jean that he should not delay his decision, as his life is now well past its midpoint. So how do we react?

Well, that, and fortunately no doubt, is our own affair. We can condemn him as an irresolute weakling; we can condemn him as deserving no less than the fate that so worries him. However, in a reaction perhaps more motherly than aggressive and contemptuous, we can also comfort him, setting him mentally on our knee as we so often did our own plangent offspring, telling them to calm down, given that all will soon be well. Getting problems out of proportion is again one of children's lovable charms and if we smile about them behind their backs, there is surely no malice involved in that reaction. Nor does the reaction connote any constraint, for no-one can tell us how to laugh at a figure, nor indeed what figure we must laugh at. If we respond to Panurge as to a scapegoat (witness Shakespeare's portrayal of Malvolio), that is our legitimate choice. If we respond to him as an ageing lowlife who should be raising his perspectives (witness the bard's portrayal of Falstaff), so be it: again we can freely do so. Moreover, is he not also mad, 'genuinely and disturbingly mad',[11] Pantagruel certainly averring at one point that 'L'esprit maling vous seduyt' (408) [The spirit of evil is deceiving you]? Perhaps so, though not totally, given his admission later to Frère Jean that, 'Je crains que [...] ma femme me face coqu. Voy là le mot peremptoire. Car tous ceulx à qui j'en ay parlé, me en menassent. Et afferment qu'il me est ainsi prædestiné des cieulx' (439) [I fear that my wife will be unfaithful. That's the compelling word. For all those I have spoken to threaten me with it and assert that such is my fatal predestiny] which claim is in fact exaggerated, though still revealing a measure of self-awareness.

In addition, moreover, may his guileless inability to face life not also stimulate our sympathy, while his marital obsession has its own perverse glamour, one emulated by Molière in figures such as his Malade Imaginaire, his Avare, or even his Misanthrope, whom be it said, he never cures of, respectively, their hypochondria, avarice or unsociability? Like the monomaniac Panurge, their lives are so simple that the amusement they afford can even be tinged with a degree of admiration: insofar as a child cannot cope with life, so his incompetence, like that of Wilkins Micawber, is endearing; insofar as a fanatic reduces life to one compelling purpose (not unlike Micawber's obsessional faith that something will turn up), so his mania is a trait by which we can both recognise and even welcome him, and it is noteworthy in this connexion that Panurge's companions never shun the man, any more than Micawber's family ever reject him, however adversely a reader may regard his feckless behaviour.

Why this anomaly? Because, once more, of clan allegiance. Just as Thurber's grandfather belongs in the family home that surrounds and protects him, so Panurge belongs for better or for worse with the group of comrades who accompany him through various adventures, particularly in fact in the *Quart livre*, published probably incomplete in 1552 and not long before the author's death. These associates (exclusively male) are a very loosely associated group, comprising an erstwhile tutor, Epistémon, the apostate priest Frère Jean, their lord Pantagruel himself, plus a congeries of figures who bear little to identify them other than their names. But even when at his most pathetic, as at the end of the *Quart livre*, Panurge is still welcome in their midst as the resident fool whose antics are amusing in their comforting predictability.[12]

What Rabelais does in his final volume is to project the marriage theme into a search for ultimate truth, discoverable, perhaps, at the shrine of the Holy Bottle, though in fact their journey's end is never described. Instead we experience a series of weird landings and encounters where naïve parody again emerges to the extent that some of the figures represented are animal-like and/or subhuman, though, like all naïve heroes, ultimately harmless: one island is inhabited by a people who live not on food but on wind, another by a race of chitterlings who mistakenly attack Pantagruel and his followers in a battle that turns more into a feast, a further one where the people discovered have noses shaped like an ace of clubs and so on. Are these signs that the author's inspiration was beginning to flag, since, though the various episodes are dosed with significant elements of allegory and satire, they at face value amount to little more than children's adventures and fairy tales? Terence Cave asks relevant questions such as 'why Ruach, why the Physetère [a sea-monster killed by Pantagruel during the voyage], why these particular episodes in this particular sequence?',[13] and if we are amused at such points, and to claim as much begs the question, we may well be adopting a naïve role ourselves, demanding no more of the text than a series of grotesques with accompanying obscenity: the wind-eaters of the island of Ruach (Hebrew for wind) 'meurent tous Hydropicques tympanites. Et meurent les hommes en pedent, les femmes en vesnent. Ainsi leur sort l'ame par le cul' (639) [They all die of oedema and tympanites, the men farting and the women fizzling; hence their souls quit their bodies via the arse.]

At such points the narratee is being cajoled into being a parody of the sophisticated Erasmian satirist that Rabelais elsewhere seeks to encourage, so thwarting the expectation that the author will reward him with something of value or even something more genuinely entertaining. Of course the reader may baulk at the prospect of being so rewarded, for this puerile brand of humour, anal once more, has its limits, just as one may tire of the ramblings of a drunk or the babblings of a child. Fortunately, however, the whole volume is not composed on this level, given in particular that it contains what is for me the finest comic sequence that Rabelais ever composed, namely the storm at sea, made up of five whole chapters plus an intriguing aftermath whose in fact tragic overtones serve as a majestic climax to the episode, if not to the entire book.

## 322    J. PARKIN

Rabelais is clearly doing many things in this section, not least pursuing his Gallican satire of the Church of Rome, since the tempest is preceded by the sight of a ship of monks who are heading to the Council of Chesil (Hebrew for folly), a patent reference to the Council of Trent. Delighted at this vision, which in fact is a very bad omen, Panurge falls into total paralysis when the storm breaks, blubbering, gabbling, weeping and howling on deck in an almost incoherent prattle of terror:

> Frere Jan mon amy, mon bon pere, je naye, je naye mon amy, je naye. C'est faict de moy, mon pere spirituel, mon amy c'en est faict. Vostre bragmart ne m'en sçauroit saulver. Zalas, Zalas, nous sommes au dessus de Ela, hors toute la gamme. Bebe be bous. [...] Ha mon pere, mon oncle, mon tout. L'eau est entrée en mes souliers par le collet. Bous, bous, bous, paisch, hu, hu, hu, ha, ha, ha, ha, ha. Je naye. (584)

> Friar John, my friend, my good father, I am drowning, I'm drowning my friend, I'm drowning. I am a dead man, my dear father in God, I am a dead man, my friend. Your sabre cannot save me from this. Alas! alas! We are above the pitch, off the stave. Bu, bu, boo, boo. [...] Ha, my father, my uncle, my all. The water's got into my shoes by the collars; boo, boo, boo, paish, hoo, hoo, hoo, ha, ha, ha, ha, ha, I'm drowning.

Frère Jean meanwhile is swearing and yelling at him to at least do something to help, while Pantagruel struggles to hold the mainmast in place, while praying straightforwardly to God.

Obviously the sententious reaction is there for all to experience, annoyance being the kindest word one could use to describe it. However, though scholars have so often castigated Panurge's pusillanimous behaviour, he is never punished for it by the clan of which he is a member. Moreover his lengthy outpourings amount to one of the richest comic monologues that Rabelais ever created, denoting, in terms of naïve parody, a pathetically human reaction of terror set on an epic scale. One is almost forced by the power of his jabbering and blubbering to forget the dangers of their predicament (which we surely know will in due course be nullified), to set the values of cooperation and endeavour in abeyance, and perhaps to recall Milan Kundera's comment on the character, 'it is at the peak of his braggadocio that we love him most'.[14] Can one not adapt this by saying that it is at the nadir of Panurge's distress that we love him most? For surely it is not despite our fellow humans' weaknesses that we should love them, but rather because of those very weaknesses, hence the unremitting and uncompromising love that Pantagruel bore Panurge throughout his life.

Such at least is, for me, the spirit of the type of humour that I have been keen to delineate. Panurge's ravings are here like the sobbings of a child, and his rantings like the gibberish of a drunken man. Incongruous with such needs of the occasion as he cannot meet, they still remain the fulcrum of the comedy within that occasion, even if, once again, Rabelais cues in serious ideas via his religious allusions and the thoroughly self-serving and superstitious prayers and vows (never of course fulfilled) that he puts into Panurge's mouth. Yet for

Guy Demerson such reactions are a mere symptom of Rabelais's 'tendresse et curiosité pour la faiblesse' [tenderness and curiosity towards weakness] so may we not accordingly respond to the man in part as a gruesome caricature of a reaction we might all have felt, or feared we might have felt in similar circumstances?

Various conclusions can be drawn, all of which both enhance the study of humour and reveal the richness of Rabelais's comic texts. Firstly his naïve figures come in several forms (animal, infant, youngster, dotard, sot, weakling, fanatic, etc.), all of them acting in a manner incongruous with the behaviour of mature and capable human beings, which behaviour they therefore parody, however unwittingly. What saves them from an unrelentingly hostile response, if not from any degree of reader hostility, is the naïveté which they meanwhile embody. One cannot fairly expect a monomaniac to abandon his compulsion, or a drunk to talk clearly, or a child to reason like an adult; moreover it is a moot point whether, as readers of comic fiction or indeed as observers of human life, one would want them to. A child's malapropisms, like the blunderings of any neophyte, possess an endearing quality that links with our own erstwhile inadequacies, and at the same time summons up an image of a world that is simpler than the one that our mature identities force us to acknowledge. So just as black humour enables us to invert our sense of values, converting dead babies or Helen Keller into figures of fun, so naïve parody allows us temporarily to regress from sobriety, sanity, adulthood, competence, detachment and other such values into a mentality where they are not required. Meanwhile that shift of attitudes, however temporary, is if not secured then at least enhanced by an empathy with whichever simpleton whose naïve behaviour has cued it in.

Satire is a punitive mode, aiming to reassert the values one respects and to censure those who fail, incongruously, to exhibit or respect them. Naïve parody, by contrast, is a celebratory mode whose basis is a tolerant appreciation of a character who, again incongruously, cannot for whatever reason display or embody the patterns of behaviour that our own self-respect would forever impose upon us. Our pet animals, our little children, our aged relatives and our eccentric neighbours all have their weaknesses and their inadequacies, some of them tiresome. By shunning them, however, we may well be denying an important element of our own humanity.

## Notes

1. Q.v. 'L'Albatros' in the 'Spleen et Idéal' section of *Les Fleurs du Mal*.
2. Rabelais, *Œuvres complètes*, 246. All other quotations from Rabelais's works are from the Pléiade edition and will be cited in the text by page numbers in brackets.
3. 'Docteur en Sorbonne' became 'docteur en gaie science' (q.v. Rabelais, 1100).
4. Feuerhahn, *Le Comique et l'enfance*, 135.
5. Gaignebet, *Le Folklore obscène des enfants*, 12.

324    J. PARKIN

6. See Frijhoff, 'Graduation and Careers', 370.
7. See Gray, 'Reading the works of Rabelais', 23.
8. Bowen, 'Janotus de Bragmardo in the Limelight', 234.
9. Clark, *The Vulgar Rabelais*, 90.
10. In various places (e.g. pp. 340, 523, 951) Rabelais either addresses or refers to his 'lecteurs benevoles' directly, a clear hint that they comprise a kindred clan of 'bons pantagruelistes' (337).
11. Cf. Screech, *Rabelais*, 260.
12. Hence Dickow, «Remede contre fascherie?», 96 on the 'rire de la bonne compagnie' addressed to him at that point as a remedy for his distress.
13. Cave, *The Cornucopian Text*, 204.
14. 'The Day Panurge No Longer Makes People Laugh', 7.

## BIBLIOGRAPHY

Bowen, Barbara C. 'Janotus de Bragmardo in the Limelight (*Gargantua*, ch. 19)'. *French Review* 72 (1998): 229–37.

Cave, Terence. *The Cornucopian Text*. Oxford: The Clarendon Press, 1979.

Clark, Carol. *The Vulgar Rabelais*. Glasgow: Pressgang, 1983.

Feuerhahn, Nelly. *Le Comique et l'enfance*. Paris: PUF, 1993.

Demerson, Guy. *Humanisme et facétie. Quinze études sur Rabelais*. Orléans: Paradigme, 1994.

Dickow, Alexandre. '«Remede contre fascherie?» Critique de l'*apatheia* dans le *Tiers Livre de Pantagruel*'. *Etudes rabelaisiennes* 46 (2008): 77–99.

Frijhoff, Willem. 'Graduation and Careers'. In *A History of the University in Europe*, vol. 2, edited by Hilda de Ridder-Symoens, 355–415. Cambridge: Cambridge University Press, 1996.

Gaignebet, Claude. *Le Folklore obscène des enfants*. Paris: Maisonneuve et Larose, 1980.

Gray, Floyd. 'Reading the works of Rabelais'. In *The Cambridge Companion to Rabelais*, edited by John O'Brien, 15–30. Cambridge: Cambridge University Press, 2011.

Kundera, Milan. 'The Day Panurge No Longer Makes People Laugh'. In *Testaments Betrayed*, 3–33. Translated by Linda Asher. London: Faber, 1993.

Marrache-Gouraud, Myriam. *Hors toute intimidation. Panurge ou la parole singulière*. Geneva: Droz, 2003.

Rabelais, François. *Œuvres complètes*. Edited by M. Huchon. Paris: Pléiade, 1994.

Screech, Michael A. *Rabelais*. London: Duckworth, 1979.

CHAPTER 17

# 'By God's Arse': Genre, Humour and Religion in William Wager's Moral Interludes

*Lieke Stelling*

In the Wakefield *Second Shepherds' Pageant*, a mid- to late fifteenth-century English mystery drama, the most profound aspect of Christian faith, the celebration of the sacrificial death of Jesus Christ in the Eucharist is expressed in humorous terms. In a farcical subplot, Mak, a thief, steals a sheep from three shepherds, and, when the suspecting shepherds search his house, hides it in a cradle, pretending it is his and his wife Gill's newborn baby. Mak and Gill are exposed but let off with a merciful punishment, after which the brief main plot continues with the shepherds visiting the Christ child in Bethlehem. In the play's comical climax, Gill attempts to convince the searching shepherds of her honesty, drawing an analogy between the actual lamb and the *Agnus Dei*: 'I pray to God so milde / If ever I you beg[u]ild, / That I ete this childe / That ligys in this credyll'.[1] If the joke is funny, it is so because it is true on several levels, including a theological one: Gill is actually guilty of beguiling the shepherds, the disguised lamb is actually edible, and, according to late medieval Christian doctrine, Christ's flesh and blood are literally consumed as part of the Eucharist. Ostensibly a somewhat crude and simplistic farce, the play has been recognised for its complex portrayal of its characters, notably Mak, and its crafty combination of comedy and spirituality.[2] Rather than used as a

---

I would like to thank Jillian Snyder and Robert Pierce for their helpful comments on an earlier draft of this chapter. Of course, all mistakes and inadequacies are my own.

---

L. Stelling (✉)
Utrecht University, Utrecht, Netherlands
e-mail: L.J.Stelling@uu.nl

© The Author(s), under exclusive license to Springer Nature
Switzerland AG 2020
D. Derrin, H. Burrows (eds.), *The Palgrave Handbook of Humour, History, and Methodology*, https://doi.org/10.1007/978-3-030-56646-3_17

325

sugar-coat for a serious religious message, humour here is juxtaposed with a religious principle, with a mutually beneficial effect: the humour not only helps the audience to recognise an important Christian tenet, but the same tenet also informs and enhances the joke. Indeed, there is (ironic) humour in the idea that Christians consume the body of Christ and that, if we consider the play at large, it is precisely Mak, a thieving clown, who by means of his vice liberates what Rick Bowers calls the 'comic truth of salvation'.[3]

In combining humour with religion on such a serious level, offering a 'daring comical exploitation of divine flesh', the *Second Shepherds' Pageant* is not untypical of the English drama of the late Middle Ages, a period in which the Church (albeit not without discussion) occupied a key role in permitting, sometimes even promoting laughter for the spiritual benefit of the people.[4] This changed in the course of the Protestant Reformation when Church authorities became increasingly dismissive of festive and carnivalesque celebrations of Christian theology, imposing strictures on joyful religious culture, such as the representation of the Eucharist and other sacraments in theatre and the inclusion of jokes in sermons.[5] What is more, the Protestant Reformation triggered new questions of soteriology, emphasising the absence of personal agency in obtaining salvation and, more disturbingly, in avoiding the eternal hellfire of damnation: issues that seem to preclude any form of humorous treatment. It is therefore not surprising that modern scholars are inclined to argue that the period witnessed a separation between humour and religion.[6] As a consequence, interpretations of humour in Reformation drama are sometimes reductive, this humour being regarded as having a secondary and exclusively didactic function to convey a serious religious message.

In this chapter, I will discuss two early Protestant plays, that, like the *Second Shepherds' Pageant*, complicate the relationship between humour and religion. I will show how humour in these works could also have been appreciated for its own sake and in profound connection with religion, rather than solely as an instructive tool to help teach (Reformed) theology. While humour theory is relevant here, notably that of incongruity, I show that humour theory alone does not suffice to understand the plays' humour. To do this, we also need knowledge of medieval and Reformation theological history. Offering this information, this case-study is able to speak to the more general issue of how to interpret historical cases of religious humour, as well as of humour in early modern theatrical history.

The two plays in question are William Wager's *The Longer Thou Livest the More Fool Thou Art* (written between 1559 and 1568) and *Enough Is as Good as a Feast* (1560–1570). *The Longer Thou Livest* relates the life of Moros, from the time he is a silly young boy to his downfall as an impious old man. The plot is chiefly devoted to the virtues' attempts at reforming his character and to the vices' achievements in keeping him in a state of depravity. *Enough* depicts the conversion of Worldly Man, who, soon afterwards, relapses—much to the delight of the vices—and is eventually carried off to Hell on the back of Satan. Throughout the play, Worldly Man is contrasted with his virtuous foil, Heavenly Man.

Both works have been recognised as precursors to Christopher Marlowe's *Doctor Faustus* (1589–1592) in the sense that they feature foolish protagonists who are tempted by vices, fail to repent and are eventually taken to their infernal destinations by the devil. Indeed, the two interludes are exceptional in presenting a protagonist who is unregenerate and not offered salvation.[7] As such, they seem to be predicated on one of the most crippling questions that arose from Calvinist thought and one that famously agonises Marlowe's Faustus at the end of the tragedy: how to mend your ways if God has already decided on your fate? Yet surprisingly, and unlike Marlowe's work, Wager's interludes present themselves not as tragedies but as inherently humorous comedies. That is to say, they emphasise their 'quality of being amusing' and 'capacity to elicit laughter or amusement'.[8] Although I use the term 'humour' here in a modern sense, and thus not one familiar to Wager's audiences, the title pages of the plays leave no mistake about this purpose. *The Longer Thou Livest* is a 'very mery and pythie commedie', and *Enough*, a 'comedy or enterlude [...] ful of pleasant mirth'.[9] In that sense, they differ from, for instance, Nathaniel Woodes's *Conflict of Conscience* (c. 1570), which explores a similar theme, also ending with the damnation of the main character and also calling itself a 'commedie' on the title page, but without the addition that it is pleasant, merry or mirthful.[10] *Enough*'s Prologue, furthermore, stresses that the play strives to be 'pleasant in every part / That those which come for recreation / May not be void of their expectation', and reiterates, moments later, that 'now and then we will dally merrily. / So we shall please them that of mirth be desirous'.[11]

Wager wrote his plays when a fundamental principle of drama was shaken by the Protestant Reformation. Pre-Reformation theatre stimulated audiences to follow the path of godliness, a task that corresponded with the late-medieval view that people are able to contribute to their own salvation by means of repentance. As Robert Potter has it, to the spectators of the medieval morality play, 'and to their consciences, the plays reveal that the fall out of innocence into experience is unavoidable, theologically necessary, and solvable, through the forgiveness of sins'.[12] This solution through divine forgiveness, however, was significantly problematised when, as part of the Protestant Reformation, the Calvinistic doctrine of double predestination became increasingly accepted in England.[13] This teaching stressed that God, from the beginning of time, had not only chosen the elect, or those who were predestined to go to heaven, but also the reprobate, who were damned. The didactic function of drama, in the form of the positive example of the repenting and eventually redeemed protagonist, was largely precluded by double predestination in the sense that it denied free will in conversion. Martha Tuck Rozett has shown that the unconditional dualism of people's predestined fate had a major impact on drama and must be seen as an important shaping force of the Elizabethan tragedy.[14]

There is a critical consensus that *Longer* and *Enough* might most usefully be understood as early tragedies, an idea that is supported by Potter and Rozett, who discuss the plays under the headings of tragedy.[15] By the same token, Francis Guinle notes: 'The Catholic moral interludes offered a comic happy ending with the redemption and salvation of their protagonists [...]. W. Wager's plays present a tragic vision of the same story with protagonists who cannot or will not see their error and therefore are damned for it'.[16] The editor of the modern edition of the plays, R. Mark Benbow, draws a similar conclusion, noting that 'If the basic metaphor of [*The Longer Thou Livest*] is the traditional spiritual pilgrimage, there is no salvation for the fool and the play is tragic'.[17] Later, he qualifies this point somewhat by acknowledging that the 'tragic and comic implications' are both 'present', with the 'grotesque humour [...] look[ing] ahead to the fortunes of Faustus'.[18] As such, Benbow echoes Bernard Spivack and David Bevington who recognise the comedic parts in the plays, but lean towards a tragic interpretation.[19] Indeed, it is difficult to find scholars who make serious attempts to read Wager's works on their own comedic terms and do not dismiss their humour as external or secondary to what these scholars intimate is the superior theme of religion.

As a matter of fact, the mutual relationship between humour and religion in the two plays is rich. In one of the rare studies that offers an in-depth analysis of Wager's humour, Elisabetta Tarantino draws attention to the religious importance of humorous language abuse, notably in the form of nonsense, as an 'indication of moral depravity', that finds its ground in Matthew 12.33–37.[20] Examples abound in both *Longer* and *Enough* and seem to have been included by Wager, as Tarantino notes, with 'obvious relish'.[21] Thus, in *Longer*, the incorrigible fool who literally lives up to his Latin-derived name Moros, gives new nonsense names to the Virtues who are trying to correct his behaviour: Exercitation becomes 'Arse-out-of-Fashion', Discipline: 'Diricke Quintine' and Piety: 'Pine-nut-tee'.[22] Perhaps more tellingly, when Moros is given an instructive school book containing the ABC of the catechism, he, recognising it, enthusiastically relates which terms and concepts he has already covered, but in so doing ironically and unwittingly exposes his lack of understanding of the terms as well as the reality of his depraved condition:

> I may tell you I am past all my crossrows,
> I have learned beyond the ten commandments.
> Two years ago, doubtless, I was past grace;
> I am in the midst of God's judgments.
> I trust to be as wise as he within short space.[23]

Likewise, when Moros mocks the Virtues, he cannot help but betray his sinfulness. When instructed by them to repeat after them the lines of a confession of faith, appealing to God to give Moros 'sapience' and 'open [his] intelligence', Moros seems to comply with this at first, but he turns out to be ridiculing them when he continues to parrot the virtues after the last line, repeating phrases like 'well said' and 'You may say no more as he did say'.[24] In a second attempt, Moros gives his own nonsense interpretation of the lines; 'I will love and fear God above all' thus becomes 'I will love porridge, when they be sod, beef and all'.[25] In *Enough* it is not so much the protagonist, Worldly

Man, as the Vice characters who provide most of the humour. Their jokes are coarse and blasphemous and emphasise their wickedness, such as when they swear 'by God's arse' and 'God's mother'.[26] At times, they are satirical and nonsensical, for instance when Ignorance pretends to 'expound a piece of scripture' like a 'bishop' in an untranslateable and comical mishmash of Latin and English: '*Magistorum clericium inkepe miorum / Totus perus altus, yongus et oldus / Multus knavoribus et quoque fasorum / Pickpursus omnius argentus shavus et polus*'.[27] Indeed, as Tarantino argues, both plays are deeply concerned with language—and, more specifically, its abuse in the form of nonsense—which she sees as the 'outward sign of the state of a soul, and an indication of what the ultimate fate of that soul will be'.[28]

Yet I part ways with Tarantino in interpreting the plays' humour in exclusively negative terms, that is, in recognising the 'fun' as 'unwholesome', as concomitant with reprobation, and as counterproductive to didacticism.[29] As such, Tarantino recognises in the plays the ground for the development of Protestant, especially Puritan antitheatricalism; that is to say, Wager's plays'

> strict religious doctrine and relish for the comic and the dramatic were soon to become irreconcilable. Above and beyond the denunciation of the theatre on the part of Puritan writers and city and church authorities, what may have begun to emerge was a contradiction, not simply of a moral but of a theological nature, between the time-honoured comical representation of evil characters, and the fundamental tenets of Protestantism.[30]

This view privileges a post-Reformation point of view, one that arguably still informs the perception of the relationship between humour and religion today, and that renders the two phenomena as mutually exclusive. That is to say, today, the term 'puritan' has become a byword for a member of any religion or organisation who strives after purity of practice or doctrine, and present-day denotations of puritans as humourless killjoys are rooted notably in late sixteenth- and early seventeenth-century satirical depictions of puritans, an idea that manifests itself in, and is perpetuated by, for instance, Shakespeare's portrayal of the puritan character Malvolio in *Twelfth Night*, one of his most often performed works today. Yet Tarantino's claim does not help us understand how, for William Wager and his contemporaries (including the bookseller who may have come up with the title) the plays make sense *as comedies* while featuring a protagonist who is damned. To come to grips with this paradox, we need to pay more heed to the play's root tradition, that of late medieval drama, and to the endings of the plays themselves.

While Wager's plays push a reformist and anti-Catholic agenda, its comedy is still firmly rooted in the late medieval appreciation of comedy as a weapon against evil. It is precisely its coarse, boisterous humour that we also find in, for instance, the Corpus Christi drama, which sought, in the words of A. A. Kolve, 'the vulgar, guffaw, the laugh from the belly rather than the smile'.[31] It is worth noting that this drama was an 'institution of central importance to the English

330    L. STELLING

Middle Ages precisely because it triumphantly united man's need for festival and mirth with instruction in the story that most seriously concerned his immortal soul'.[32] It was not uncommon for drama to provoke mocking laughter at the expense of evil or vice characters and to present their exit to hell in humorous terms. In fact, in the plays of York and Wakefield, the very crucifixion of Christ was probably performed with comical effect, for instance in the form of clumsy craftsmen who were in charge of the crucifixion.[33] This laughter 'took the sting out of evil and reduced the champions of wickedness into raving and raging fools'.[34] This attitude similarly appears in the works of late-medieval humanists, notably the Catholics Desiderius Erasmus and Thomas More. The latter was famous for his explicit and dark religious jokes and his understanding of humour as offering solace and comfort in times of religious tribulation. Yet it also appears on the other side of the religious divide, in Martin Luther, who joked about farting to expel the devil and recognised in this type of humour a 'freeing response to the terrors of earthly life' and a way to 'highlight the paradoxes of a Christian's simultaneously saintly and sinful existence'.[35]

It is worth considering in closer detail the late-medieval bawdy sense of humour, because it is so far removed from modern ideas of what is appropriate in humour and religion, and because it can also be found in Wager. Not based on scriptural narratives and not featuring Christ as a character, Wager's plays certainly belong to a dramatic tradition that started with the Reformation, but its scurrilous humour is still part of the grotesque, physical comedy of medieval drama. Examples are the fart jokes in *Longer*, Moros's mutilation of Exercitation's name into 'arse out of fashion', the later part meaning 'out of shape'; his frequently used expletive 'by God's body' when he receives physical punishments; and, perhaps most interestingly, the oath 'by' and 'for' 'God's arse', articulated by the vice characters in *Enough*. While the latter utterance seems to be a prime example of a profanity, alert members of the play's audiences would have been reminded of what can be appreciated as a humorous passage in the Bible, in which it is none other than God himself who conjures up this image: in *Exodus* 33:18–23 the Lord promises a curious Moses to reveal himself, but, refusing to show his face, only offers Moses a glimpse of his 'back parts'.[36] I will return to this issue below.

Equally important to our understanding of Wager's works as religious comedies is their ending, specifically their depiction of the deaths of the main characters Moros in *Longer* and Worldly Man in *Enough*. While they eventually meet with their expected demise, like Marlowe's Faustus, there is reason to believe that Wager's audiences would have appreciated these as both funny and comedic, rather than tragic endings. When the middle-aged Moros, in *Longer*, is nearing his end and the character of God's Judgment has struck him with his 'sword of vengeance', God's Judgment appears to give Moros a final opportunity to reform himself, telling him to 'call' if he has 'grace for mercy'.[37] Moros does not make the least effort, which leads God's Judgment to the conclusion that 'indurate wretches cannot convert / But die in their filthiness like swine'.[38] Moments later, Confusion tells Moros that he will carry him to the devil to which Moros, strikingly and comically unfazed, responds: 'A due to the devil? God send us good speed. / Another while with the devil I must go to school'.[39] By contrast, Worldly Man's death in *Enough* is preceded by his suffering from sickness and pain as a result of his being struck by God's Plague. Yet the potential pathos of this moment is lost by the humorous quality of the scene. When attempting to dictate his will to the vices Covetous and Ignorance in order to arrange the repayment of all of his creditors, Ignorance first comically struggles to spell out the words. Then, when Worldly Man has finally dictated the first four words of the will, a 'common opening formula [...]: *in the name of God. Amen*', Worldly Man suddenly collapses, never to wake up again.[40] As Ignorance suggests, 'God would not suffer him to name Him in his will', possibly, and, considering the name of this Vice unwittingly, punning on the word 'will' as the omnipotent will of the Calvinistic God.[41] The play's ending thus has a serious message, warning against trust in deathbed conversion, but the abruptness of Worldly Man's demise, and Ignorance's clumsy execution of his task, simultaneously lend it a comical edge.

Yet how should we interpret these comical twists in relation to the seriousness of Moros's and Worldly Man's damnations? One way of looking at it is through the lens of ridicule, a concept mentioned above in relation to the medieval tradition of pious laughter at evil. Deeply rooted in Christian tradition, ridicule was one of the most common forms of laughter found in the Bible, especially on God's part. In Psalm 2.4, for instance, we find the notion of God and others 'that dwelleth in the heaven [who] shall laugh': the Lord having those who oppose him 'in derision'. Christopher Marlowe offers a chilling manifestation of this image in *Doctor Faustus*, when the Old Man, having given up on Faustus and menaced by devils, reminds them of his own election and of God's utter and sardonic contempt for them: 'Ambitious fiends, see how the heavens smiles / At your repulse and laughs your state to scorn! Hence, hell, for hence I fly unto my God'.[42] In *Enough*, Wager's version of Marlowe's Old Man is Heavenly Man, who represents the elect and serves a minor, choric role by commenting on the foolish decisions of Worldly man, highlighting his own moral superiority and blessed status, yet this is not with reference to divine sardonic mockery or with a sense of smugness. What is more, Marlowe, as opposed to Wager, cultivates a sense of godly sarcasm throughout the play by presenting the remark of the Old Man in a series of moments in which the pitiless indifference of God is highlighted, such as when Faustus asks Christ to 'save' his 'distressèd [...] soul', upon which it is not Christ, but Lucifer who appears, telling him that Christ's righteousness prevents him from saving Faustus.[43] This moment foreshadows what is probably the most unsettling moment of the A-text: Faustus's last outcry of anguish: 'My God, my God, look not so fierce on me!', which is evocative of Christ's own anguished outcry on the cross: 'My God, my God, why hast thou forsaken me?'[44] This moment of mental torment finds a physical equivalent in the last scene of the B-text, where the scholars contemplate the uniquely 'fearful shrieks and cries' that were produced by Faustus and discover his 'limbs / All torn asunder by the hand of death'.[45]

Indeed, a crucial difference in the ways in which Faustus on the one hand, and Moros and Worldly Man on the other, are ridiculed lies in the cultivation of pity for the former. The notion that pity and laughter were mutually exclusive goes back to classical antiquity and was maintained by Renaissance thinkers including Laurent Joubert, who wrote an elaborate study on laughter.[46] As Michael Screech notes, 'Fictional human beings can be laughed at as we witness their destruction, but the slightest feeling of sympathy or pity must first be eliminated. That calls for the well-established tricks and art of the comic writer'.[47] Dr Faustus might arguably be even more deserving of his damnation, as he willingly sells his soul to the devil, yet it is much easier to stomach Moros and Worldly Man's divine punishments. Whereas Faustus, a power-mad scholar turned pitiful clown, gains in humanity, both Moros and Worldly Man lose their sympathy as unregenerate stock figures. Worldly Man, a wealthy landlord, does undergo a genuine but temporary conversion, but his relapse, renewed avarice and callous rejection of cries for help by his impoverished hireling, tenant and servant just before he dies erode the audience's sympathy for him, or what is left of it. Moros is a funny child but undeserving of our compassion when showing himself utterly incapable *and* unwilling of change as a foolish old man. Indeed, Moros is not the relatable Mankind-figure we know from medieval drama, but, in the words of Spivack, 'a special example of the depravity that afflicts only a fraction of the human race. His name, at the same time that it condemns him from the start, separates him from humanity at large'.[48] The audience is thus invited to sunder themselves from Wager's protagonist, and, more importantly, distance themselves from his fate, just as their laughing at Moros's puns on the catechism implies that they would have grasped the basic theological essence of the ideas that Moros himself fails to understand.

Yet the comic essence of Wager's moralities lies not so much in their jokes themselves, their grotesque portrayal of vice, or lack of true suffering at the end, but in a more profound Christian conception of the human condition. An explanatory glimpse into this conception is offered by another term that *Enough* uses to classify itself on the title page: in addition to a comedy, it is also an 'enterlude' or interlude. The term is illuminating because it does not only re-emphasise the 'light or humorous character' of the play, but includes the notion of in-betweenness, or, more specifically, its playful positioning between the 'serious, mundane activities of everyday life'.[49] According to Peter Berger, what this term shares with the comic is that it enables 'the perception of an otherwise disclosed dimension of reality—not just of its own reality (as a player perceives the reality of a game), but of reality as such'.[50] In a Christian context, this is the reality of 'a world without pain', a world that is experienced during the fleeting moment of laughter.[51] Much of this laughter is generated through surprise. In an appropriately funny illustration, Berger shows how the notions of in-betweenness, comic surprise and religious faith are connected: he argues that humanity is subject to God's 'cosmic game of hide-and-seek', or of a 'soteriological [...] jack-in-the-box'.[52] The latter in particular is a helpful reminder of Christ's resurrection: 'In this imagery, Christ was the first little man who stood up and, as the Apostle Paul explained, this is the basis of our own hope to put the primal pratfall behind us forever'.[53] Religious faith is thus a 'childish faith [which] trusts that the clown will always jump up again [...] and that therefore one is free to laugh' in a world outside the game that is lethal and 'not at all trustworthy'.[54] Wager's interludes serve this role as comic diversions from a world afflicted by religious conflict and doubt. It is perhaps precisely the least appropriate joke, certainly from a current-day perspective, that captures this idea most profoundly: the expletive 'by God's arse' uttered by some of the vice characters in *Enough* and the Biblical passage it refers to, Exodus 33:18–23, in which Moses asks God to show him his 'glory'. God responds by saying:

> I will make all my good go before thee, and I will proclaim the Name of the Lord before thee: for I will show mercy to whom I will show mercy, and will have compassion on whom I will have compassion. 20 Furthermore he said, Thou canst not see my face, for there shall no man see me, and live. 21 Also the Lord said, Behold, there is a place by me, and thou shalt stand upon the rock: 22 And while my glory passeth by, I will put thee in a cleft of the rock, and will cover thee with mine hand while I pass by. 23 After I will take away mine hand, and thou shalt see my back parts: but my face shall not be seen.

God is playing an 'adult version' of peekaboo with Moses, not showing his face, but his buttocks.

In this context, even the damnation of Wager's protagonists can become comically comforting. We have already established that their deaths have comical overtones, especially that of Worldly Man and that a humorous perspective is enabled by a lack of pathos in these scenes. As a matter of fact, there is something deeply reassuring about their punishments, as they are entirely predictable and in line with the sinful behaviour of the characters. Indeed, both Moros and Worldly Man may theoretically and according to Calvinistic doctrine be doomed from the start, but the plays still present the divine retributions as logical consequences of their self-chosen behaviour. Robert Potter makes an important point about this when he claims about *Enough* that 'it would be premature to see darkness and doubt in the tragedy of Worldly Man. *Enough Is as Good as a Feast* may best be imagined as the photographic negative of a medieval morality play, a definition of the light by means of its shadows'.[55] I would argue that this is not only true for *Enough*, but also for *Longer*. The play's point is that if one avoids being like Moros (or Worldly Man), the opposite fate awaits in the form of heaven. This view is confirmed by the last speakers in *Enough*, Rest, Heavenly Man and Enough, who underscore the rewards for the 'heavenly'.

This emphasis on the positive side of predestination can also be found in the very text that defined the Church's conception of predestination. Article 17 of the *Thirty Nine Articles* (1563), which concerns the doctrine of predestination and election, emphasises its essentially joyful principle:

> predestination, and our election in Christ, is full of sweet, pleasant, and unspeakable comfort to godly persons, and such as feel in themselves the working of the spirit of Christ, mortifying the works of the flesh, and their earthly members, and drawing up their mind to high and heavenly things, as well because it doth greatly establish and confirm their faith of eternal salvation to be enjoyed through Christ, as because it doth fervently kindle their love towards God.[56]

Conversely, 'for curious and carnal persons, lacking the spirit of Christ, to have continually before their eyes the sentence of God's predestination, is a most dangerous downfall, whereby the Devil doth thrust them either into desperation, or into wretchlessness of most unclean living, no less perilous than desperation'.[57] It is telling that the article uses the first person plural in 'our election in Christ' and does not refer to the reprobate as such but as those who are 'curious and carnal', accentuating their behaviour deserving of divine retribution rather than their status as inherently damned. This is not to deny or mitigate the great spiritual anxiety that the doctrine of election would cause among early modern English men and women. As John Stachniewski has observed, this may even have led to a sharp rise in suicide rates in early seventeenth-century England.[58] Critics including Martha Rozett, Huston Diehl and more recently Adrian Streete, Jennifer Waldron and Steven Mullaney have, moreover, shown the profound impact Reformed theology had on the drama of the period.[59] Their focus, however, is on drama that succeeded Wager's, suggesting that the very early days of Elizabeth's reign were not marked by the perception of Calvinism as gloomy and uncompromising to the same degree as later.

By eschewing the genre of comedy virtually altogether, scholars who have concerned themselves with the correlation between early modern drama and the English Reformation have suggested that the genre does not take Reformed doctrine seriously, or is not concerned with it. By the same token, those who do consider Wager's comedies have shown great reluctance to treat them as such, either, as mentioned above, by classifying them as tragedies or by suggesting that they are not fully fledged or flawed comedies; Potter, for instance, maintains that they are 'hybrid', 'awkward' and, approvingly quoting Philip Sidney, 'mungrel tragy-comedy'.[60] I argue that the plays should be taken seriously as comedies and products of their own specific period, which allowed them to be experienced as fully comedic.

That is not to say that Wager's works are diametrically opposed to tragedy. Rather, and especially as *Christian* comedies, they are kin to it, a paradox famously explored by Søren Kierkegaard who regarded Christianity as both essentially tragic and comic.[61] According to the philosopher's speaker Johannes Climacus:

The difference between the tragic and the comic rests in the relation of the contradiction to the idea. The comic grasp brings out the contradiction, or lets it
become manifest, by having the way out in mind; that is why the contradiction is
painless. The tragic grasp sees the contradiction and despairs over the way out.[62]

Kierkegaard's understanding of the comic as based on contradiction tallies with
the incongruity theory of humour, which holds that humour involves a pleasant experience of a cognitive shift as part of a perception of an incongruity. The
painlessness of the contradiction is also a condition for making it pleasant. John
Lippitt reminds us, however, that we should be careful not to take this quotation too literally.[63] Suffering is an inherent part of religion and the '"true
comic" must *combine* the comic and pathos, the comic and the tragic. Thus we
need to ask: in what *sense* must a contradiction be "painless" if it is to be
comic?'[64] The answer, according to Lippitt, lies in the 'way out', which 'certainly does not deny the reality of suffering. But it does diminish the danger of
being utterly *overwhelmed* by it. […] So the Christian can have a certain "legitimate" lightness, because of his belief that despite life's suffering, God (and
good) will ultimately prevail'.[65] The 'way out' thus takes shape in the form of
one of the main virtues of Christianity: hope, a theme that Harvey Cox recognises as the essence of Christian comedy:

The comic sensibility can laugh at those who ferment war and perpetuate hunger,
at the same time it struggles to dethrone them. It foresees their down fall even
when their power seems secure. The comic, more than the tragic, because it ignites
hope, leads to more, not less, participation in the struggle for a just world.[66]

If the modern (lack of) appreciation of Wager's plays as comedies teaches us
one thing, it is that sense of humour and the understanding of comedy are still
taken for granted as universal, and, as such, in opposition to religion, a subject
that has, moreover, received far more scholarly attention for historical specificity. Wager's interludes have been dismissed as failed interludes and as tragedies
in essence, which have been misunderstood by his own audiences as comedies.
This is not entirely surprising as the indicators of humour are notoriously difficult to trace. While the theological content of the play remains largely intact
in script, its comedy requires more effort to be recognised when not experienced in performance. Yet even so, newer sensibilities that inform our current-
day appreciation of humour, and make us see it as clashing with religiosity,
prevent us from recognising earlier forms of understanding. In cases when
humour is recognised, it is often understood in instrumental or simplistic
terms, such as a tool to deride religious enemies or a didactic device to teach
religious doctrine. While these interpretations are not necessarily incorrect—
the latter was even part of the humanist tradition of employing humour to
disseminate ideals of reason, as well as by many plays themselves, as they take
pains to underline their instructive duties throughout the text—they offer only
a partial understanding of Wager's humour and prevent us from seeing how it

is precisely in humour that we gain a better understanding of the way in which religion was experienced by Wager and his audiences. In this chapter, I have tried to show that their understanding of faith was not only informed by Protestant doctrine, but also by late medieval theatrical culture that understood humour as an essential element of the religious experience of hope. It would not be long before this hope made its exit, and, as such, fostered the flourishing of Elizabethan tragedy, but that does not imply that Wager's drama was mistaken about the meaning of its comedy.

## Notes

1. Anonymous, 'The Second Shepherds' Pageant from Wakefield', ll. 535–38.
2. See, for instance, the second chapter of Bowers, *Radical Comedy*.
3. Bowers, *Radical Comedy*, 15.
4. Gilhus, *Laughing Gods*, 84, 94.
5. Thomas, 'The Place of Laughter', 79.
6. See, for instance, Ghose, *Shakespeare and Laughter*, 133; Burke, *Popular Culture*, 295.
7. Grantley, *English Dramatic Interludes*, 91.
8. 'humour', *Oxford English Dictionary*, 9b.
9. Wager, *The Longer Thou Liuest*, sig A1r; Wager, *Inough Is as Good as a Feast*, sig A1r. All further references to these works are to R. Mark Benbow's modern edition. One of the few scholars who have noted the contrast between the plays' endings and descriptions as comedies is Spivack, *Shakespeare and the Allegory of Evil*, 114.
10. Woodes, *The Conflict of Conscience*. Sig. A1r. It is worth noting that this play has two alternative endings, one featuring the damnation of the protagonist and the other his redemptive death-bed conversion.
11. Wager, *Enough*, ll. 34–36, 83–84.
12. Potter, *The English Morality Play*, 57.
13. Streete, *Protestantism and Drama in Early Modern England*, 8; Doran and Durston, *Princes, Pastors, and People*, 25.
14. Rozett, *The Doctrine of Election*, passim.
15. Ibid., 88, 93. Potter, *The English Morality Play*, 117–19.
16. Guinle, 'Where Angels Fear to Tread', 156.
17. Benbow, 'Introduction', xiv.
18. Ibid., xvi.
19. Spivack, *Shakespeare and the Allegory of Evil*, 174, 229, 248; Bevington, *From Mankind to Marlowe*, 163, 183.
20. Tarantino, 'Between Peterborough and Pentecost', 76.
21. Ibid., 75.
22. Wager, *The Longer Thou Livest*, ll. 409, 501, 504.
23. Ibid., ll. 472–76.
24. Ibid., ll. 341, 345, 347, 356.
25. Ibid., ll. 389, 393.
26. Ibid., ll. 379, 1092, 425.
27. Ibid., ll. 1265–68.
28. Tarantino, 'Between Peterborough and Pentecost', 56.

29. Ibid., 81.
30. Ibid., 79–80.
31. Kolve, *The Play Called Corpus Christi*, 139.
32. Ibid., 134.
33. Gilhus, Laughing Gods, Weeping Virgins, 98–102.
34. Ibid., 102.
35. Prescott, 'The Ambivalent Heart', passim; Mallinson, 'Humor', 350.
36. Benbow, *The Longer Thou Livest*, 98 n379. All scriptural references are taken from the Geneva Bible.
37. Wager, *The Longer Thou Livest*, l. 1799.
38. Ibid., ll. 1805–6.
39. Ibid., ll. 1857–58.
40. Benbow, *The Longer Thou Livest*, 141 n1401.
41. Wager, *The Longer Thou Livest*, l. 1415.
42. Marlowe, *Dr Faustus* (A-Text) 5.1.116–18.
43. Ibid., 2.3.80.
44. Ibid., 5.2.113. See also Nuttall, *The Alternative Trinity*, 46–48. In the B-text, the phrase 'My God, my God' was replaced with 'O mercy, heaven!' According to Nuttall, this 'suggests strongly that contemporaries of Marlowe noticed the biblical echo and were made uncomfortable by it' (46n.).
45. Marlowe, *Dr Faustus* (B-Text), 5.3.4, 6–7.
46. Screech, *Laughter at the Foot of the Cross*, 57, 58.
47. Ibid., 307.
48. Spivack, *Shakespeare and the Allegory of Evil*, 248.
49. Berger, *Redeeming Laughter*, 13.
50. Ibid.
51. Ibid., 195.
52. Ibid., 196.
53. Ibid.
54. Ibid.
55. Potter, *The English Morality Play*, 119.
56. Quoted in Cressy and Ferrell (ed.) *Religion and Society in Early Modern England*, 74.
57. Ibid.
58. Stachniewski, *The Persecutory Imagination*, 46.
59. Rozett, *The Doctrine of Election*; Diehl, *Staging Reform*; Streete, *Protestantism and Drama in Early Modern England*; Waldron, *Reformations of the Body*; Mullaney, *The Reformation of Emotions*.
60. Potter, *The English Morality Play*, 117.
61. Morreall, *Comedy, Tragedy and Religion*, 2.
62. Kierkegaard, *Concluding Unscientific Postscript*, 432–33.
63. Lippitt, *Humour and Irony in Kierkegaard's Thought*, 130.
64. Ibid., 130.
65. Ibid., 132–33.
66. Cox, *The Feast of Fools*, 150, 153.

## Bibliography

Amir, Lydia B. *Humor and the Good Life in Modern Philosophy: Shaftesbury, Hamann, Kierkegaard*. Albany: State University of New York Press, 2014.

Anonymous. 'The Second Shepherds' Pageant from Wakefield'. In *Medieval Drama*, edited by David Bevington, 383–408. Indianapolis, Cambridge: Hackett Publishing Company, 2012.

Benbow, R. Mark. Editor. *The Longer Thou Livest* and *Enough Is As Good as a Feast*. London: Edward Arnold, 1968.

Berger, Peter L. *Redeeming Laughter: The Comic Dimension of Human Experience*. Second Edition. Berlin, Boston: De Gruyter, 2014.

Bowers, Rick. *Radical Comedy in Early Modern England: Contexts, Cultures, Performances*. Aldershot: Ashgate, 2008.

Burke, Peter. *Popular Culture in Early Modern Europe*. Third Edition. Farnham: Ashgate, 2009.

Carroll, Noel. *Humour: A Very Short Introduction*. Oxford: Oxford University Press, 2014.

Cox, Harvey. *The Feast of Fools: A Theological Essay on Festivity and Fantasy*. Cambridge, MA: Harvard University Press, 1969.

Cressy, David, and Lori Anne Ferrell. *Religion and Society in Early Modern England: A Sourcebook*. Second Edition. New York: Routledge, 2005.

Diehl, Huston. *Staging Reform, Reforming the Stage: Protestantism and Popular Theater in Early Modern England*. Ithaca and London: Cornell University Press, 1997.

Doran, Susan, and Christopher Durston. *Princes, Pastors, and People: The Church and Religion in England, 1500–1700*. Second Edition. London: Routledge, 2003.

Ghose, Indira. *Shakespeare and Laughter: A Cultural History*. Manchester: Manchester University Press, 2008.

Gilhus, Ingvild Sælid. *Laughing Gods, Weeping Virgins: Laughter in the History of Religion*. London and New York: Routledge, 1997.

Grantley, Darryll. *English Dramatic Interludes, 1300–1580*. Cambridge: Cambridge University Press, 2004.

Guinle, Francis. '"Where Angels Fear to Tread": Allegory and Protestant Ideology in *The Longer Thou Livest, The More Fool Thou Art* (1559) and *Enough is as Good as a Feast* (1560)'. In *Tudor Theatre: Allegory in the Theatre*. Volume 5. 145–58. Bern: Peter Lang, 2000.

'humour | humor, n.'. *OED Online*. December 2019. Oxford University Press. www.oed.com/view/Entry/89416 (accessed January 25, 2020).

Kierkegaard, Søren. *Concluding Unscientific Postscript*, edited and translated by Alastair Hannay. Cambridge: Cambridge University Press, 2009.

Kolve, A.A. *The Play Called Corpus Christi*. London: Edward Arnold, 1966.

Lippitt, John. *Humour and Irony in Kierkegaard's Thought*. Basingstoke: Macmillan, 2000.

Mallinson, Jeff C. 'Humor.' In *Encyclopedia of Martin Luther and the Reformation*, Vol. 2, edited by Mark A. Lamport, 350–51. Lanham etc.: Rowman and Littlefield, 2017.

Marlowe, Christopher. *Doctor Faustus: A Two-Text Edition (A-Text, 1604; B-Text, 1616) Contexts and Sources Criticism*. Edited by David Scott Kastan. New York and London: W. W. Norton, 2005.

Morreall, John. *Comedy, Tragedy and Religion*. Albany: State University of New York Press, 1999.

Mullaney, Steven. *The Reformation of Emotions in the Age of Shakespeare*. Chicago and London: University of Chicago Press, 2015.

Nuttall, A.D. *The Alternative Trinity: Gnostic Heresy in Marlowe, Milton, and Blake*. Oxford: Clarendon Press, 1998.

Potter, Robert. *The English Morality Play: Origins, Influence and History of a Dramatic Tradition*. London and Boston: Routledge & Kegan Paul, 1975.

Prescott, Anne Lake. 'The Ambivalent Heart: Thomas More's Merry Tales'. *Criticism* 45, no. 4 (2003): 417–433.

Rozett, Martha Tuck. *The Doctrine of Election and the Emergence of Elizabethan Tragedy*. Princeton: Princeton University Press, 1984.

Screech, Michael A. *Laughter at the Foot of the Cross*. Chicago: University of Chicago Press, 2015.

Spivack, Bernard. *Shakespeare and the Allegory of Evil: The History of a Metaphor in Relation to His Major Villians*. New York and London: Columbia University Press, 1958.

Stachniewski, John. *The Persecutory Imagination: English Puritanism and the Literature of Religious Despair*. Oxford: Clarendon Press, 1991.

Streete, Adrian. *Protestantism and Drama in Early Modern England*. Cambridge: Cambridge University Press, 2009.

Tarantino, Elisabetta. '"Between Peterborough and Pentecost": Nonsense and Sin in William Wager's Morality Plays'. In *Nonsense and Other Senses: Regulated Absurdity in Literature*, edited by Elisabetta Tarantino with Carlo Caruso, 55–85. Newcastle upon Tyne: Cambridge Scholars, 2009.

Thomas, Keith. 'The Place of Laughter in Tudor and Stuart England'. *Times Literary Supplement*, January 21, 1977. 77–81.

Wager, William. *The Longer Thou Liuest the More Foole Thou Art*. London: Wyllyam How, 1569.

Wager, William. *Inough Is as Good as a Feast*. London: Iohn Allde, 1570.

Waldron, Jennifer. *Reformations of the Body: Idolatry, Sacrifice and Early Modern Theater*. New York: Palgrave Macmillan, 2013.

Woodes, Nathaniel. *The Conflict of Conscience*. London: Richarde Bradocke, 1581.

CHAPTER 18

# Romantic Irony: Problems of Interpretation in Schlegel and Carlyle

*Giles Whiteley*

Irony is always a question of power. It involves registering the differences between denotation and connotation, between the world presented and as it really is, or between its ideal image and reality. Like satire more broadly and with which it is often conflated, irony can be a conservative force, but even at its most radical, irony still presupposes the existence of hierarchical structures, mobilising those differences productively. It plays upon the gap between those who get the joke and those who don't. Indeed, it is this possibility of not getting the joke that is key: potential for confusion constitutes irony, and marks the ironist as elect, separated from those below them who call a spade a spade. Moreover, since anyone that calls 'a spade a spade should be compelled to use one', as Oscar Wilde (1854–1900) once quipped,[1] irony implies, at least structurally, an elitism. The ironist, on the other hand, is happy to say they have 'never seen a spade',[2] and they 'hover' above such pedestrian concerns.[3]

Is irony funny or is it precisely too aloof to trouble itself with humour? And assuming irony is funny, who is it who finds it humorous? From the Latin *ironia*, a witticism in which one says the opposite of what one means, irony is a form of what Cicero called 'pretended ignorance'.[4] Not real ignorance, but only feigned, the humour lying in recognising this pretence. 'Irony' derives etymologically from the ancient Greek *eironeia*, 'dissimulation', and is linked to one historical figure in particular, Socrates. His ironic 'disingenuousness' (*OED*, 'irony', *n.* 2.) is said to have disarmed his philosophical interlocutors

---

G. Whiteley (✉)
Stockholm University, Stockholm, Sweden
e-mail: giles.whiteley@english.su.se

© The Author(s), under exclusive license to Springer Nature
Switzerland AG 2020
D. Derrin, H. Burrows (eds.), *The Palgrave Handbook of Humour, History, and Methodology*, https://doi.org/10.1007/978-3-030-56646-3_18

341

through a kind of studied performance of naivety. According to his champions, Socrates' mode of enquiry was productive, allowing him to call into question seemingly incontrovertible givens. And insofar as it is 'feigned', Socrates seems to be in the position of power, holding all the cards and cajoling his philosophical opponents into compromised positions from which he may bring 'truth' to light. Likewise, those who saw the irony, such as his disciple Plato, who gives Socrates dramatic voice in his dialogues, bask in the philosopher's reflected glory. But that is Plato's portrait, not that drawn by Aristophanes, who, in *The Clouds*, ridicules Socrates' irony as less feigned ignorance than farcical arrogance. The situation is reversed: Aristophanes is now in a position of power and Socrates is subject to it, the comedian's own ironic distance the vantage point from which to criticise the philosopher's lofty claims. Aristophanes shows us that if feigned ignorance is potentially funny, then funnier still is real ignorance that thinks it is clever. In Aristophanes' hands, the philosopher-king becomes nothing other than another sophist amongst the pack.

In its technical meaning in ancient rhetoric, irony is 'the expression of one's meaning by using language that normally signifies the opposite, typically for humorous or emphatic effect' (*OED*, 'irony', *n.* 1.a.). Rhetorically, irony is often characterised by the use of approbative phrasing to signal contempt, and is linked closely to sarcasm. Again, as contemptuous, irony is intrinsically a question of power and who wields it; historically too, rooted in Greek rhetorical discourse, irony is a form of persuasion intimately associated with argumentative 'urbanity', the *polis* and the political.[5] From this rhetorical definition, a more figurative meaning emerged: irony as 'a state of affairs or an event that seems deliberately contrary to what was or might be expected', 'an outcome cruelly, humorously, or strangely at odds with assumptions or expectations' (*OED*, 'irony', *n.* 3.). In both its technical and figurative meanings, then, irony is 'humorous'. But how are we to explain this humour? Appealing to those various 'universalising' theories which have guided so much of humour studies in the twentieth and twenty-first centuries, what becomes clear is that how one explains the humorous effect of irony depends very much on how sympathetic one may be to the politics of the ironist and the hierarchies of power that underwrite it. Irony does not seem to be a particularly benign violation of a norm, since there always has to be a butt of the joke, whether that be an institution or a person. Nor is irony easily accounted for by relief theory, unless by a particularly Freudian version that considers all transgressions libidinal. But as for the other two major universalising theories, incongruity and superiority, things are more complicated, not to say undecidable when it comes to accounting for the humour of irony. On the one hand, irony implies incongruity, so that the audience registers the jarring mismatch between what was expected and what occurred. It is in registering this disorder in the order of things that humour is produced. But on the other hand, this incongruity is precisely a question of power. In *The Clouds*, Aristophanes invites his audience to laugh at Socrates rather than with him, and likewise the humour of irony resides somewhere in the pleasure felt in superiority: the audience sees the dissimulation for what it is, and as such knows that they are better than those that are occluded from the joke.

The respective *OED* definitions highlight the humour of both rhetorical and figurative irony. The dictionary dates the figurative meaning in English to 1833 and Connop Thirlwall's (1797–1833) essay 'On the Irony of Sophocles'. The text is notable for its early analysis of the idea of dramatic irony, and involves the extrapolation from the ancient to the modern. Dramatic irony, of course, can be both tragic and comic—indeed, it precisely calls into question these kinds of divisions—but this is not the subject pursued here. For our purposes, the significance of Thirlwall's essay lies in situating the figurative meaning of irony within the context of late Romanticism. Later Bishop of St David's, Thirlwall was then a leading figure in the intellectual life of Trinity College, Cambridge, friendly with Samuel Taylor Coleridge (1772–1834) and William Wordsworth (1770–1850). He was also a keen reader of German Romanticism, translating Ludwig Tieck (1773–1853) with his close friend Julius Hare (1795–1855). For his part, Tieck is often considered one of the great practitioners of so-called romantic irony,[6] defined by the *OED* as 'an attitude of detached scepticism adopted by an author towards his or her work, typically manifesting in literary self-consciousness and self-reflection' ('romantic irony', *n*.). What is notable from the outset is that, by comparison to the definitions of other kinds of irony, the 'humour' appears to be lacking in 'romantic irony'. The idea of romantic irony itself has proved a particularly tenacious concept and, as a consequence, the origins of modern theories of irony are often traced to the German Romantic movement. According to these over-rehearsed narratives, romantic irony is said to pave the way towards both modernism and postmodernism, not in terms of its humour, but rather in its manifestation of a philosophy of critical detachment and absolute subjectivisim.[7] Associated primarily with Friedrich Schlegel (1772–1829), and with fellow members of the Jena-school such as Tieck, the poet Novalis (Friedrich Freiherr von Hardenberg) (1772–1801) and philosopher Karl Wilhelm Ferdinand Solger (1770–1819), romantic irony has proved a fertile meeting point of the philosophical and the literary. Influentially criticised by Georg Wilhelm Friedrich Hegel (1770–1831), romantic irony has been championed by later writers such as Paul de Man (1919–1983), whose approach has often ended up determining contemporary readings of Schlegel. As a form of supposed proto-poststructuralism, romantic irony casts a long shadow, to the extent that many recent critics have unabashedly suggested that, in its own sense of ironic detachment and determined reluctance to nail its colours to any mast of metanarrativity, the postmodern is intrinsically ironic.

In this chapter, I read Schlegel's comments on irony, focusing on this figure in particular given the significant role he has come to play in later histories of the concept of romantic irony, as the figure generally credited as being the concept's originator. Against a critical heritage that has marginalised the humour in romantic irony, what becomes clear reading Schlegel is that for him, romantic irony is not only humorous, but offers a kind of humour that troubles the subject who experiences it, calling them into question. Then, I turn to consider a work of British late Romanticism contemporaneous with Thirlwall's essay, Thomas Carlyle's (1795–1881) novel, *Sartor Resartus* (1833–1834), reading it through and alongside Schlegel as a work of humorous romantic irony and as a text which problematises the power structures implied in irony. My interest in this chapter lies in teasing out the problem of precisely locating the humour in romantic irony on both contextual and textual grounds.

Joseph A. Dane sums up the issues at stake succinctly: 'what is romantic irony? the irony used by romantics? or an irony envisaged by the romantics and romanticists?'[8] In the context of our current discussion, we may add to his questions further ones: where is the humour in romantic irony? and is it always located in the same place depending on which answer we give to Dane's questions? Indeed, it is not easy to answer these questions, in part because the adjective in 'romantic irony' does not make clear the nature of its qualification. It is also tricky because the various figures of the Romantic Movement do not deploy irony in their own works of fiction consistently, because their theorisations of irony do not always comport with their own practice, and because the idea of romantic irony was popularised after the fact. Part of the methodological issue with reading the humour in romantic irony lies in pinning down precisely just what constitutes romantic irony in the first place.

In its 'detached scepticism' (*OED*, 'romantic irony', *n.*), romantic irony maintains the distance characteristic of irony more broadly. This distance is not least that maintained between the ironist and their object, in which the irony manifests the exercising of power, the recognition of which produces humour, explicable through either superiority or incongruity theory. However, this distancing effect is even more marked than in either rhetorical or figurative irony: in romantic irony, distance is also established between the ironist and their own work. Rather than the ironist exercising power, they themselves become implicated in the irony, distanced from not only the work, but from themselves, so that works of romantic irony manifest a kind of empowered powerlessness, expressed in the form of the work itself. Not simply registered in a moment of humorous pleasure, incongruity has been made conscious of itself as such, where this quality of incongruity is less, or at least only partially, a mark of 'humour', and more a question of form. In this sense, as the *OED* definition cited above makes clear, works of romantic irony are self-consciously literary, and ones where this literariness is linked to an entire philosophical project of Romanticism as the coming-to-self-consciousness of the subject. As Søren Kierkegaard (1813–1855) puts it in *Om Begrebet Ironi* [*The Concept of Irony*] (1841), for 'the expressions: *irony* and the *ironist* [...] I could as easily say *romanticism* and the *romanticist*'.[9] In lieu of an original meaning, then, the *OED* gives as a definition a concentrated history of the concept's reception. Consciously or not, it is written in the shadow cast by Hegel and those who followed him. Romantic irony has come to be considered a meta-textual conceit of the text ironically reflecting back on itself in endless *différance*. Little surprise in this context that, in the hands of some critics, the varied history of romantic irony has come to be collapsed into a too-neat narrative in which Schlegel leads irresistibly to Jacques Derrida (1930–2004).[10]

But in point of fact, as Dane points out, this kind of definition, indeed almost any neat definition of romantic irony, is actually a reading of 'selected romantic literature'.[11] The critical heritage on romantic irony is predicated upon a 'myth of coherence', with Schlegel supposed to be its original source and wellspring. He is made out as though he had a consistent and coherent idea of irony, in spite of the fact that most of his published pronouncements on the subject are to be found in his *Lyceum* (1797) and *Athenaeum* (1798) fragments, and so were, by definition, examples of fragmentary rather than systematic thinking. Schlegel is portrayed as if he had in mind a theory of 'romantic irony', although he never names it anywhere in his published work.[12] Moreover, this critical heritage has read this supposedly coherent theory of 'romantic irony' as constituting a kind of 'progressive, universal poetry', Romanticism as a way of life.[13] But the effect has been to amputate the comedy. As Thomas Hobbes (1588–1679) wrote in a much-quoted line, 'great persons, that have their minds employed on great designs, have not leisure to laugh'.[14] With critics occupied primarily with Schlegel's 'great designs', they have given his laughter little credit, and failed to register the importance of the humour in romantic irony. It is for this reason that I want to pause with the critical reception of Schlegel's fragments on irony in order to trace the ways in which criticism has amputated the comic from its proper place in the theory of romantic irony. This lineage of criticism is Hegelian in spirit, even when his presence remains unacknowledged.

In his lectures on the history of philosophy, Hegel treated Schlegel as a 'follower' of Johann Gottlieb Fichte (1762–1814), Schlegel's concept of romantic irony read as a reflection and literary equivalent of Fichte's idea of the subject. For its part, Fichte's philosophy responded to that of Immanuel Kant (1724–1804), who claimed a radical gulf between our phenomenal experience of the world and the 'things-in-themselves', the noumena of which the experienced phenomena were but the sensory impressions.[15] By contrast, Fichte argued in his *Wissenschaftslehre* [*Science of Knowledge*] (1794) that the subject posits their existence in an auto-genetic *Tathandlung* or act, seeking to bridge Kant's unbridgeable gulf, in an act that in turn founds their knowledge of the world. Reading Schlegelian irony in this light, Hegel argues that his irony is one in which 'das Subjekt weiß sich in sich als das Absolute' [the subject knows itself to be within itself the Absolute].[16] By this, Hegel means that Schlegelian irony is the result of a subject who claims that, through the distancing power of their irony, they have transcended the worldly limitations of the subject, becoming one with the Absolute. This is Hegel's term for the state where the subject and the object are unified, claiming complete knowledge of, and command over, both the ideal world of the things-in-themselves and the real world of the phenomena, history and human activity. In reading Schlegel's comments on irony as a theory of the Absolute, the romantic ironist is figured as the counterpoint of Fichte's aspiring philosophical subject.

Hegel famously preferred the old comedy of Aristophanes and even pantomime to 'modern' humour, positioning himself both politically and in terms of taste on the side of 'low' as opposed to 'high' culture.[17] It is in this context that Hegel accuses Schlegel of intellectual arrogance. In Schlegel, according to Hegel, 'die Ironie weiß ihre Meisterschaft über alles dieses; es ist ihr Ernst mit nichts, es ist Spiel mit allen Formen' [irony knows itself to be the master of every possible content; it is serious about nothing, but plays with all forms].[18] This idea of 'mastery' is, however, a sham, built not on a true appreciation of the nature of the Absolute, which retains difference in itself rather than distancing itself from it. Schlegelian irony, by contrast, was philosophically and politically pernicious. Its 'trick' resided in 'dem Sichvernichten des Herrlichen, Großen, Vortrefflichen' [the self destruction of the noble, great, and excellent]. For Hegel, romantic irony mobilises a nihilistic form of superior laughter, one through which Schlegel represents 'was dem Menschen Wert und Würde hat, als Nichtiges in seinem Sichvernichten zeigen' [what has worth and dignity for mankind as null].[19] Schlegel is charged with superiority, his irony looking 'vornehm auf alle übrige Menschen nieder, die für beschränkt und platt erklärt sind' [down from his high rank on all other men, for they are pronounced dull and limited]. He supposedly treats the rabble as 'pauvre bornierte Subjekte, ohne Organ und Fähigkeit' [deceived, poor limited creatures, without the faculty and ability] to reach his own heights.[20]

For Hegel, Schlegel's irony was purely negative or destructive, expressing its author's elitist disregard for both the 'serious' stuff of life and the unelect at whom it laughed. It is in this sense that Hegel makes one of the most important and influential claims about Schlegel, that romantic irony is not comedy, a claim which subsequent generations of critics have yet to fully free themselves from. 'Es kommt [...] bei diesem Unterschiede des Ironischen und Komischen wesentlich auf den Gehalt dessen an, was zerstört wird' [In this difference between the ironic and the comic what is essentially at issue is the content of what is destroyed], Hegel argues.[21] Whereas true comedy destroys only that which was 'false', so that laughter becomes a moment of recognition of a new 'truth', irony destroys indiscriminately, annihilating true and false alike. Rather than being a vehicle towards the dialectical coming-to-self-consciousness of the subject, which Hegel claims to be the result of true comedy, in irony, the 'transcendental' dialectic that supposedly produces the Romantic subject is undercut. Moreover, in so doing, the very possibility of subjectivity, the entire aim of Hegel's philosophical project, is undermined. For Hegel, romantic irony is comedy's horrific mirror image, its fallen doppelgänger.

One of Hegel's most influential heirs is Paul de Man, even if his own theory of irony differs radically from that of Hegel. Like Hegel before him, although without here acknowledging this heritage, de Man reads Schlegel through Fichte in his influential lecture, 'On the Concept of Irony'. I take up de Man critically in this paragraph, less as a response to his own theory of irony than to the ways in which his deconstructive reading of Schlegel has come to dominate later readings of romantic irony.[22] For de Man, Fichte's *Tathandlung* is not only an act of the intellect, but can be read as founding the kind of philosophy of language which he sees underwriting Schlegelian irony. According to this argument, words, in naming the things of the world, possess an absolute power of self-fashioning. However, de Man also shows that this act of naming is simultaneously catachrestic, necessarily a misnaming, petrifying the plurality of experiential reality into the form of an ideal signifier which is meant to stand in its place.[23] For de Man, irony is the effect of the distancing enacted by this catachresis, one that produces the Romantic subject in its constitutive act. As such, in de Man's hands, romantic irony becomes both a philosophy of Romanticism and a progenitor of post-structuralism. But if de Man's reading of Schlegel through Fichte obviously owes much to Hegel, then reading Schlegel closely reveals that his argument is not so securely based in the fragments themselves. While it is true enough that in one of those fragments Schlegel considered Fichte, alongside Johann Wolfgang von Goethe (1749–1832) and the French Revolution, as one of the defining points of Romanticism, in a fragment that de Man quotes,[24] he does not mention irony in this passage. Nor is de Man's reading justified by those passages in which Schlegel does discuss irony, in which he does not mention Fichte.[25] This is important since, as with Hegel's earlier reading of Schlegel, the effect is to distance romantic irony from comedy. The ways such a philosophical approach tends to marginalise humour is exemplified in de Man's prioritisation of Schlegel's unpublished comment that 'Ironie ist eine permanente Parekbase' [irony is a permanent parabasis].[26] A reference to the interlude in ancient Greek comedy in which the chorus directly addresses the audience, parabasis is an idea clearly rooted in traditions of humour, with the chorus offering ironic commentary on the action of the play, and where humour is produced precisely through this distance. But de Man does not consider the humour, instead emphasising the 'permanence': 'parabasis not just at one point but at all points, […] irony is everywhere'.[27] It globalises Schlegel's comment so that irony becomes a meta-textual philosophy, rather than a humorous effect. Likewise, when de Man argues that another critic, Peter Szondi (1929–1971), conflates Schlegel and Jean Paul (1763–1825) in his reading of romantic irony. For de Man, this means conflating irony and comedy; but 'irony is not comedy, and theory of irony is not a theory of comedy'.[28]

Having established some of the philosophical contexts lying behind the marginalisation of the humorous in romantic irony, I want to reply to this received view. Neither Hegel nor de Man do Schlegel justice, for whom irony is precisely a question of humour. Indeed, when the word 'irony' does appear in his fragments, it is often explicitly in relation to other key terms such as 'parody', 'humour' and 'wit'.[29] After Hegel, these aspects have tended to be marginalised in the discussions of romantic irony. Attempting to recontextualise Schlegel's comments on irony, I want to focus on three passages from the *Lyceum* fragments in particular. Rather than speak of them as the germ of a coherent theory of 'romantic irony', which is not particularly relevant to my interests here, what I want to emphasise is their implications for the ways in which romantic irony produces humour. The first is Schlegel's claim that 'Ironie ist die Form des Paradoxen'.[30] If irony is the form of paradox, then, as romanticists have pointed out, it seems to mime the structure of Romanticism, insofar as the ideal and real coexist in the artwork. But this fragment also tells us something about how irony produces humour: through registering an incongruity, which is precisely a moment of paradox.[31] This point is crucial for understanding the oft-quoted *Lyceum* fragment 42. For Schlegel, 'poetic' irony (an idea which is often read as 'romantic irony', but which is not so named here) breathes 'den göttlichen Hauch der Ironie' [the divine breath of irony] and constitutes 'eine wirklich transzendentale Buffonerie'.[32] As 'transcendental buffoonery', irony marries high and low, the ideal to the jape and the jest. What this means is that, for Schlegel (*pace* Hegel and de Man), irony is less a manifestation of Fichtean *Tathandlung* or an expression of the subject's 'mastery' over the world, than a moment of self-reflection in which the subject recognises precisely its 'transcendental' limitations. It is the incongruity of registering the unbridgeable divide that separates myself as a limited subject from the absolute as the ideal that produces the ironic moment of bathos. As he puts it in *Lyceum* fragment 108, irony precipitates 'ein Gefühl von dem unauflöslichen Widerstreit des Unbedingten und des Bedingten' [a feeling of indissoluble antagonism between the absolute and the relative]. If Romanticism seeks knowledge of the Absolute, and fashions the Romantic subject in a moment of 'communication' with this Absolute, then irony offers at once 'der Unmöglichkeit und Notwendigkeit einer vollständigen Mitteilung' [the impossibility and the necessity of complete communication].[33]

In this same fragment, Schlegel argues that:

> [Ironie] soll niemanden täuschen, als die, welche sie für Täuschung halten, und entweder ihre Freude haben an der herrlichen Schalkheit, alle Welt zum besten zu haben, oder böse werden, wenn sie ahnden, sie wären wohl auch mit gemeint.

> [Irony is meant to deceive no one except those who consider it a deception and who either take pleasure in the delightful roguery of making fools of the whole world or else become angry when they get an inkling they themselves might be included.][34]

This point complicates the initial sketch of irony I presented earlier in this chapter. Schlegel recognises the power and hierarchies implied in irony; which is to say, he recognises the role that superiority plays. But more than this, Schlegel also points out that this subject of irony, precisely since it also serves as its own object, may respond through a kind of 'joy'. Such an experience is not one of superiority or subjective 'mastery', but of an incongruity which paradoxically roots the subject. An experience of 'stete Selbstparodie' [continuous self-parody],[35] irony does not found but confounds the Romantic subject. Or rather, irony constitutes the subject as one built upon an 'unfounded' foundation, what Schlegel's contemporary and another resident of Jena, the philosopher F. W. J. Schelling (1775–1854) calls the 'unground', *das Ungrund*.[36] Precisely in this confounding structure of unfounding, it becomes difficult to know in irony 'den Scherz grade für Ernst, und den Ernst für Scherz halten' [what is meant as a joke seriously and what is meant seriously as a joke].[37]

Three things can be taken from this brief reading of some of Schlegel's fragments on irony: firstly, irony produces humour—it is a 'serious' form of joking, but joking nonetheless; secondly, irony produces humour through a particular kind of incongruity in the moment of paradox; and thirdly, that this incongruity is linked to a radical moment where the subject is called into question. Irrespective of what the critical heritage has maintained, then, Schlegel certainly considered irony humorous. This is not to say that romantic irony is not also a philosophical idea, and in what follows, it will be clear that my reading of romantic irony is deeply indebted to that of both Hegel and de Man. But what I contend is that romantic irony is not simply a philosophical category to the exclusion of its humorous qualities. Indeed, in building upon and complicating earlier traditions of irony, Schlegel's theory complicates any attempt to pin down the ways in which humour is produced through 'romantic irony'. It is not explicable solely through superiority theory, since in this case, the object is also the subject of the irony, not the 'master' of it or the elect, but recognising himself or herself as the butt of the joke. However, nor is romantic irony simply an example of incongruity, since the humour lies not only in recognising the difference between ideal and real, but in recognising the subject as itself paradoxical. In other words, this means that the subject itself is unable to definitively recognise the incongruity, precisely since it itself is revealed to be incongruous, lacking that sort of exterior vantage point with which to see the humour, to control it. This is, after all, the germ of Hegel's theory of comedy, in which the subject is supposedly raised 'durchaus erhaben über seinen eigenen Widerspruch' [altogether above his own inner contradiction]. By contrast to Schlegelian irony, then, in comedy proper the potentially destablising effects of humour are resolved dialectically, with the subject making themselves 'sich [...] dieser Auflösung Meister' [master of this dissolution] and remaining 'unangefochten und wohlgemut' [undisturbed and at ease].[38] It is precisely this quality of 'inner contradiction' that Schlegel's irony mobilises without seeking to resolve it, so that it reveals the subject to be hopelessly divided from itself. In romantic irony, the subject takes itself as both subject and object of the same joke, where the humour relies precisely in laughing at ourselves. Idealist 'transcendence' collapses into a moment of 'transcendental buffoonery'.

In what remains of this chapter, I now turn to consider *Sartor Resartus*, using it as a test case to tease out some of the problems briefly sketched above, and in the interests of space, I will content myself with discussing only the first of the three books of Carlyle's novel. But from the outset, it is important to remember that *Sartor Resartus* is not a work of romantic irony, if by that we mean a work which was consciously crafted as being a part of, or a response to, the tradition of romantic irony discussed above, since at the time of Carlyle's writing, no such tradition existed.[39] Still, for our purposes, the text perhaps constitutes one of the most interesting examples of the genre, certainly in

English, because at its root, Carlyle's novel is not only a work *of* romantic irony, but also a work *about* romantic irony.

The plot runs as follows: an unnamed Scottish editor encounters the work of Diogenes Teufelsdröckh, a radical new voice from the fictional university town of Weissnichtwo, the German translating as 'Know-not-where', where Teufelsdröckh is 'Professor of Things in General'. The editor is fascinated, and aims to publish Teufelsdröckh's magnum opus, *Die Kleider ihr Werden und Wirken* [*Clothes, their Origin and Influence*], to introduce his idealist philosophy to the British public. The Latin *Sartor Resartus* translates as *The Tailor Re-tailored*, so that Carlyle's title both ironises Teufelsdröckh's philosophy of clothes and the editor who seeks to reclothe this philosophy in a manner palatable to his British public. The novel takes the form of ostensible quotations from Teufelsdröckh's text, and passages in which the editor reflects upon his editorial difficulties in making sense of either the work or the life of Teufelsdröckh. If the editor considers Teufelsdröckh's work a moment of Romantic Sublime, 'an "extensive volume", of boundless, almost formless contents, a very Sea of Thought', then his philosophy never reaches any satisfying moment of transcendental revelation.[40] The humour of the novel lies in watching the editor's frustrated attempts to try 'to bring what order we can out of this Chaos' of Teufelsdröckh's philosophy, one which threatens on all sides to overwhelm him.[41]

From the very first paragraph of the novel, constituted from a single sentence, Carlyle's operation is ironic, and humour produced through bathos:

> Considering our present advanced state of culture, and how the Torch of Science has now been brandished and borne about, [...] for five thousand years and upwards; how, in these times especially, not only the Torch still burns, [...] but innumerable Rushlights, and Sulphur-matches, kindled thereat, are also glancing in every direction, so that not the smallest cranny or dog-hole in Nature or Art can remain unilluminated, — it might strike the reflective mind with some surprise that hitherto little or nothing of a fundamental character [...] has been written on the subject of Clothes.[42]

The beginning of the sentence situates the text from the outset within the context of the *Aufklärung* or Enlightenment, figured as a progressive movement towards human and world-historical perfection. But the semi-colon marks a break, with ironic distance already established. This suggests the editor's awareness, on some level, that the idealist narrative of *Aufklärung* is a teleological projection: this same light burns not only in the lofty 'Torch' of truth, but flickers in cheap rushlights, used by the British lower-classes, deployed to illuminate 'dog-holes', places 'unfit for human habitation' (*OED*, 'doghole', *n.*). It speaks, unconsciously, of the editor's arrogance, a 'superiority' that undermines his idealism. And what is the result of this *Aufklärung*? Precisely Teufelsdröckh's *Die Kleider ihr Werden und Wirken*. The very first sentence of the novel is an exercise in romantic irony, then, which from its transcendental first clause, is already buffooned by the final clause.

Context is key to reading the romantic irony of *Sartor Resartus*. Analysing its humour requires critical sensitivity to both the history of the work itself and to the history upon which it comments. Methodologically, the critic must balance an awareness of the contours of early nineteenth-century German literature and philosophy alongside an awareness of the context of the British reception of these German traditions. From the epigraph which appeared under the title onwards, an untranslated quotation in German drawn from Goethe's *Wilhelm Meisters Wanderjahre* [*Wilhelm Meister's Travels*] (1821), a work that Carlyle translated elsewhere, and with whose author he had enthusiastic correspondence, it is clear that Carlyle had a very specific implied reader in mind for *Sartor Resartus*.[43] This implied reader is one who could see the German on the page and recognise it as Goethe's; not simply one of the 'rabble', but an educated, cosmopolitan figure, like Carlyle himself. As such, Carlyle mobilises irony through a sense of superiority, but is also working to ironise this very same implied reader, precisely because Teufelsdröckh is no Goethe. This double-edged nature to the superiority of its irony is confirmed when we read the novel itself, the text peppered throughout with German phrases. Take as an example Diogenes Teufelsdröckh's name, at once an ironic reflection on German idealist philosophy and a paradox. The German translates as Born-of-God Devil's-excrement, a seemingly sacrilegious conjunction of opposites. But only a certain kind of reader could be expected to get the jokes within Carlyle's jokes. Not only must the reader know the language, they must also be keenly aware of the contours of early nineteenth-century German literature. The scatology implied in 'dröckh' plays knowingly on the ways in which many British readers reacted to so much contemporary German 'speculation'. This Anglo-Germanic culture clash is productive in the novel, with the editor suggesting that 'English culture [...] cramps the free flight of Thought'.[44] The implied reader laughs at themselves, recognising themselves in this image of their national philosophic temper, but at the same time, recognises it as hyperbolic, so they also laugh at the editor's inflated opinion of Germany, its philosophy deemed self-indulgent 'dröckh', excessive and untethered from the conditions of the real world. Indeed, if the idea of Teufelsdröckh's philosophy of clothes is deliberately hyperbolic and meant as a joke, those who had been paying attention to the state of post-Kantian philosophy, like Carlyle himself, would not have considered such an *outré* idea to have emanated from Germany: there is a kind of confirmation bias at work in the joke. We are told in the text that Teufelsdröckh is a critic of Hegel's, and on good terms with the 'nature-philosopher' Lorenz Oken (1779–1851), whose ideas were roundly mocked in Britain during the time, as well as contributing anonymously to Oken's journal *Isis*, equally infamous, where his anonymity means that a reader aware of the journal might imagine his authorship behind any of its more outrageous papers.[45] And not only this, but the devilish first noun in Teufelsdröckh's name implies further knowledge on the part of his implied reader. The connotations of his name are played upon throughout the novel, as when a toast is proposed in Teufelsdröckh's honour: 'Die Sache der Armen in Gottes und Teufls Namen (The Cause and the Poor in Heaven's name and —'s)!'[46] Here, the editor's translation marks 'Teufel' as untranslatable, passed over in an aposiopesis.[47] Such puns acknowledge in silence the widely held British preconception that German philosophy was atheistic (a hangover from the *Pantheismusstreit*, 1785–1789). So if only an ironic reader, a 'superior' one who knew German, could have got the scatological joke in Teufelsdröckh's name, then only a romantic ironist, reflecting ironically on this irony, could have got the jokes within Carlyle's jokes. And moreover, such a reader, one who gets this romantic irony, is also one who is aware enough to know that they are part of the joke, that they are being played.

The implied reader, then, is a romantic ironist, and the ostensible subject of the novel, Diogenes Teufelsdröckh and his philosophy of clothes, are also figures of romantic irony. But the situation is more complicated, for both Teufelsdröckh and his editor stand as doppelgängers of Carlyle himself. As with the editor seeking to introduce Teufelsdröckh's philosophy to a British audience, so Carlyle too was a keen reader of Schlegel, a translator of Goethe, Schiller, Tieck and Jean Paul, a tentative advocate of post-Kantian philosophy in Britain, and an authoritative essayist on Novalis and all things German.[48] Carlyle is also bound biographically to Teufelsdröckh, whose moment of 'Spiritual New-birth, or Baphometic Fire-baptism',[49] experienced on the *Rue Saint-Thomas de l'Enfer*, stands allegorically for Carlyle's own moment of revelation, experienced at Leith Walk, Edinburgh, 1821. But just as the editor is both an enthusiastic populariser of Teufelsdröckh and a Scottish sceptic, who maintains ironic distance from his subject, so too Carlyle, the man educated at an Edinburgh University still very much under the shadow of the common sense philosophy of Dugald Stewart (1753–1828). Carlyle is at once the buffooned transcendental philosopher of *Sartor Resartus* and the buffooned editor who seeks to popularise him.

It is this Scottish context that perhaps best explains the editor's constant dissatisfaction with Teufelsdröckh's tome. Even he recognises *Die Kleider* as 'dröckh', for 'there is much rubbish in his Book, though likewise specimens of almost invaluable ore'. As he puts it at the beginning of chapter four, entitled 'Characteristics':

> It were a piece of vain flattery to pretend that this Work on Clothes entirely contents us; that it is not, like all works of genius, like the very Sun, which [...] has nevertheless black spots and troubled nebulosities amid its effulgence, — a mixture of insight, inspiration, with dullness, double-vision, and even utter blindness.[50]

'Selection, order appears to be unknown to the Professor',[51] the editor notes, but Teufelsdröckh's fault is not just structural, insofar as his work shows 'an almost total want of arrangement',[52] but also on the level of style. The editor considers Teufelsdröckh's prose 'marred too often by [...] rudeness, inequality, and apparent want of intercourse with the higher classes'.[53] As such, the editor positions himself as Teufelsdröckh's superior, hovering ironically above his subject, who while a genius, is not able to carry off his task:

> On the whole, Professor Teufelsdrockh, is not a cultivated writer. Of his sentences perhaps not more than nine-tenths stand straight on their legs; the remainder are in quite angular attitudes, buttressed up by props (of parentheses and dashes), and ever with this or the other tagrag hanging from them.[54]

Not only does this passage poke fun at Teufelsdrockh, it also ironises the editor purportedly writing it, for there is obviously something funny in his own effulgent style, 'his prolixity and tortuosity',[55] when criticising the stylistic excesses of his subject. Moreover, the joke is not only on the editor, but a knowing moment of 'romantic irony' on the part of Carlyle, for this 'effulgence' is characteristically 'Carlylean'. James Joyce (1882–1941), famously pastiched Carlyle in the 'Oxen of the Sun' episode of *Ulysses* (1922), finding humour in the excessiveness of his late Romantic style which, precisely in its awareness of being 'late' and embracing anachronism as its stylistic quality, is read as self-ironic.[56] In the first paragraph of 'Characteristics', then, we find that Carlyle's own 'blindness' is as much the subject of this sentence as Teufelsdröckh's is.

At moments like this, the implied reader of *Sartor Resartus* would certainly find its romantic irony funny, the humour operating on a number of different levels simultaneously. But if we recall Hegel's idea that the romantic irony of Schlegel 'annihilates' everything, reading Carlyle's *Sartor Resartus* as a work of romantic irony allows us to understand this point somewhat differently. For Hegel, to recall, romantic irony differs from comedy, insofar as the former annihilates indiscriminately as a manifestation of the superior, nihilistic arrogance of the author, whereas the later annihilates only what is false, as a reparative or dialectical step, producing laughter in a moment of recognition. Laughter supposedly rehabilitates the subject who is as though born afresh into a newly illumined world. But in *Sartor Resartus*, what is annihilated is not just the stable ground that underwrites the world of the implied reader, but the figure of the author himself. Far from being the nihilistic expression of the author's superior or elitist sense of their own self-worth, the novel expresses the moment of ironic joy which Carlyle experiences in annihilating himself as a 'transcendental subject', a moment which produces another kind of laughter.

As the editor exclaims, 'How much lies in Laughter: the cipher-key, wherewith we decipher the whole man!'[57] The point recalls a moment earlier in the novel when the editor had recalled William Whitehead's (1715–1785) definition of man as 'a Laughing Animal' in his *Essay on Ridicule* (1743).[58] Laughter is precisely in question in this novel from the earliest passages of *Sartor Resartus* onwards, or rather, three distinct forms of laughter. The first is a cruel form of laughter, a quality associated with a certain sense of superiority, and the kind of quality Hegel identified at work in Schlegel's irony. The editor sees in the 'sly'

Teufelsdröckh an aloofness, the German writer coming across as being 'imperturbably saturnine' and displaying 'such indifference, malign coolness', betrayed in his 'bitter sardonic humor'.[59] A few chapters earlier, Teufelsdröckh's 'slyness' has been associated with a certain 'satirical edge' to his style.[60] This links to the editor's misgivings that Teufelsdröckh may be playing him for a fool, detecting in *Die Kleider* 'an idle wire-drawing spirit, sometimes even a tone of levity, approaching to conventional satire'.[61] In other words, the editor has the suspicion that he himself may be butt of Teufelsdröckh's jokes, and that the philosophy of clothes is not meant to be taken seriously.

However, alongside this kind of 'superior' irony, which would fit in with the Hegelian critique of the romantic ironist (*Die Kleider* an annihilating pastiche of the pretensions of idealist philosophy to offer an 'transcendental' truths), there are the moments when Teufelsdröckh's humour shows us his humanity, and which, in its generosity, differentiates him from the editor himself, who is distanced from the world. In a telling incident, the editor recalls a moment when Teufelsdröckh himself laughs:

> Here, however, we gladly recall to mind that once we saw him *laugh*; once only, perhaps it was the first and last time in his life; but then such a peal of laughter [...]! It was of Jean Paul's doing: [...] The large-bodied Poet and the small, both large enough in soul, sat talking miscellaneously together, the present Editor being privileged to listen; and now Paul, in his serious way, was giving one of those inimitable 'Extra-Harangues'; and [...] gradually a light kindled in our Professor's eyes and face, a beaming, mantling, loveliest light; [...] and he burst forth [...] — tears streaming down his cheeks, pipe held aloft, foot clutched into the air, — loud, long-continuing, uncontrollable; a laugh not of the face and diaphragm only, but of the whole man from head to heel. The present Editor, who laughed indeed, yet with measure, began to fear all was not right.[62]

Importantly, the context is Teufelsdröckh's conversation with Jean Paul, a key influence on both Carlyle and *Sartor Resartus*, and that figure whom de Man considers truly comic, against which he compares Schlegel and romantic irony. In Carlyle's novel, on the other hand, the romantic ironist is not divided from Jean Paul, but he and Teufelsdröckh are connected precisely through this power of laughter. Whereas the editor laughs 'with measure', marking the second form of laughter identified in these passages of *Sartor Resartus*, Teufelsdröckh laughs in an unrestrained manner, the third form of laughter. A few paragraphs earlier, the editor had remarked that he has 'never fully satisfied' himself whether *Die Kleider* has 'a tone and hum of real Humor, which we reckon among the very highest qualities of genius, or some echo of mere Insanity and Inanity, which doubtless ranks below the very lowest'.[63] According to the editor, real humour is precisely a mark of 'sanity', a healthy rather than a diseased mind, but Teufelsdröckh's laughter by contrast passes beyond 'measure', at once 'insane' and 'inane', the latter suggesting that the madness is a moment of insight into the 'void' (Latin: *inanus*). Moreover, this kind of 'insane' laughter may be linked to romantic irony, as a paradoxical moment of ironic distancing, where the subject itself is revealed not to be whole, stable or 'ideal', but is itself figured as a kind of 'void'. In this sense, Teufelsdröckh's romantic irony anticipates a rich tradition of post-romantic philosophical humour that stretches from Kierkegaard through Friedrich Nietzsche (1844–1900) and on to Georges Bataille (1897–1962).[64] This tradition pits an 'excessive' form of humour against Hegel's system, which constitutes precisely a philosophy that grounds the subject, and for whom true humour is an essential dialectical moment in this grounding, By contrast, with 'the whole man' laughing 'from head to heel', Teufelsdröckh's body is pulled erect, with laughter erupting in what Bataille would call a 'heterological' moment. Man becomes an animal, the subject is called into question in an 'excessive' moment, laughter another form of 'dröckh'.

What is 'characteristic' of Teufelsdröckh is a certain indecideability in his humour, which is precisely a mark of romantic irony. The editor is unable to discern if he is being ironic and, if so, what precisely the nature of his irony is or what its object might be. The editor's suspicion of being played, and of being the butt of the joke links Teufelsdröckh to Socrates, and the editor's experience of reading *Die Kleider* with an older tradition of irony, which manifests the ironist's superiority. But both as a work investigating romantic irony on a philosophical level, and as a work which is itself an expression of romantic irony, *Sartor Resartus* is far from easy to analyse. When the editor considers 'real humour' a mark of 'genius' and differentiates this humour from Teufelsdröckh's 'unmeasured' laughter, should we expect that all or any of Carlyle, his implied reader or his actual readers, are aware that Schlegel links 'genius' to irony in *Lyceum* fragment 42?[65] There, Schlegel is discussing the 'paradoxical' and 'incongruous' quality of romantic irony, which operates simultaneously in both directions, with 'alles treuherzig offen, und alles tief verstellt' [everything guilelessly open and deeply hidden]. Not simply produced by recognising the difference between expression and meaning, irony disturbs the dichotomy of surface and depth. The style is Icarian in its pretensions, 'hovering' above the world; but the result is 'die mimische Maniere eines gewöhnlichen guten italiänische Buffo' [the mimic style of an averagely gifted Italian buffo],[66] precisely in a moment of 'transcendental buffoonery'. It is this destabilising moment that gives power to romantic irony, but also which makes it so hard to pin down, and its humour so radical. It calls into question not just the external values of the world, as Hegel argued, but also the very subject themselves, the one who is reading and the one who is writing, the one who is laughing and who is called to laugh at themselves. If other forms of irony, such as that of Socrates, had used humour to express power, or to 'master' or control the world, fixing things, then in romantic irony, such pretensions are frustrated at every turn. Whenever we try to pin the humour down, it slips from our grasp, and if we laugh, we do not do so from the perspective of a grounded subject, let alone a 'transcendental' one: there is no 'measure' in this kind of madness, with romantic irony holding the seeds of a revolutionary form of humour.

## Notes

1. Wilde, *The Picture of Dorian Gray*, 334.
2. Wilde, *The Importance of Being Earnest*, 2.583.
3. The English term translates the German 'schweben', recalling Schlegel's comment that irony 'hovers' in *Charakteristiken und Kritiken*, 133; Wheeler, *German aesthetic and literary criticism*, 67. See also Schlegel's comments on the 'hovering' of humour in *Athenaeum* fragment, § 305. As Dane comments, after Schlegel, the word 'hover' has become 'part of the standard vocabulary of irony' (*Critical Mythology*, 208 n. 12). Unless otherwise indicated, quotations from Schlegel's fragments are cited by fragment number, with translations from Wheeler's *German aesthetic and literary criticism*.
4. Definitions and etymologies are taken from the *Oxford English Dictionary*, third edition, accessed online at www.oed.com.
5. See Colebrook, *Irony*, 20.
6. See Lussky, *Tieck's Romantic Irony*, and for a critique of Lussky, see Dane, *Critical Mythology*, 75–77.
7. See Booth's *Rhetoric*.
8. Dane, *Critical Mythology*, 73.
9. Kierkegaard, *Concept of Irony*, 275 n.
10. See Colebrook, *Irony*, 47–71.
11. Dane, *The Critical Mythology of Irony*, 73. I am indebted to Dane's excellent work in this and the following paragraphs, particularly on Hegel's reading of Schlegel.
12. While both Schlegel and Novalis do use the phrase in notebook entries, these were not published until the middle of the twentieth century, meaning that they 'played little part in the traceable reception of romantic irony' (Dane, *Critical Mythology*, 74).
13. Schlegel, *Athenaeum* fragment, § 116. For an example of this kind of over-reading, see Newmark, *Irony on Occasion*, 29–40.
14. Hobbes, 'Answer', 454–455.
15. It is worth noting that in this distancing separating phenomena from noumena, Kant's entire project may be read as ironic: see Colebrook, *Irony in the Work of Philosophy*, 109–151.
16. Hegel, *Geschichte der Philosophie*, 18: 64; *History of Philosophy*, 3: 307.
17. See Hegel, *Ästhetik*, 14: 530; *Aesthetics*, 2: 1202. See also Bown, *Event of Laughter*, 87, and more broadly, see 83–96 for Bown's excellent chapter on Hegel.
18. Hegel, *Geschichte der Philosophie*, 19: 642; *History of Philosophy*, 3: 307. The distaste Hegel felt for Schlegel was mutual: see Rush's *Irony and Idealism*.
19. Hegel, *Ästhetik*, 12: 104; *Aesthetics*, 1: 67.
20. Ibid., 12: 102, 101; 1: 66, 65.
21. Ibid., 12: 104; 1: 67.
22. Indeed, de Man's essay is prefaced by a quotation from Schlegel to the effect that interpreting his meaning requires the reader already take up an ironic position with respect to his comments on Schlegel and romantic irony ('Concept of Irony', 163–164, quoting *Lyceum* fragment, § 108). In other words, de Man's reading of Schlegel itself is explicitly ironic, but subsequent critics have not always attended to this fact. Thanks to Magnus Ullén for reminding me of this point.

23. de Man, 'Concept of Irony', 172–175.
24. See *Athenaeum* fragment, § 251, and de Man, 'Concept of Irony', 172.
25. For instance, *Athenaeum* fragment, § 252, where Schlegel develops his Fichtean idea of 'a real aesthetic theory of poetry' which might follow from 'the proposition I = I', but does not use the word 'irony' once.
26. Schlegel, *Philosophische Lehrjahre*, 85, and de Man, 'Concept of Irony', 178–179.
27. de Man, 'Concept of Irony', 179.
28. de Man, 'Concept of Irony', 182, discussing Szondi's 'Friedrich Schlegel und die romantische Ironie'; 'Friedrich Schlegel and Romantic Irony'.
29. See for instance, Schlegel, *Athenaeum* fragments, §§ 253, 305.
30. Ibid., § 42.
31. Schlegel's own understanding of incongruity theory would have been influenced by Kant's *Kritik der Urteilskraft* [*Critique of the Power of Judgment*] (1790), I.ii § 53; *Power of Judgment*, 209–210. Kant does not discuss irony here, however.
32. Schlegel, *Athenaeum* fragment, § 42.
33. Ibid., § 108.
34. Ibid.
35. Ibid.
36. The concept is central to Schelling's so-called positive philosophy. Schelling features as Ludovico in Schlegel's *Gesprach iiber die Poesie* [*Dialogue on Poetry*] (1800), and was read by Carlyle: see my *Schelling's Reception*, 71–88.
37. Schlegel, *Athenaeum* fragment, § 108.
38. Hegel, *Ästhetik*, 14: 528, 531; 2: 1200, 1202. Indeed, we should bear in mind that mastery is always a kind of servitude in Hegel's philosophy, as in the famous master-slave dialectic of his *Phänomenologie des Geistes* [*Phenomenology of Spirit*] (1807).
39. This has not meant that Carlyle's critics have not been keen to read *Sartor Resartus* as a work of romantic irony, however. See for instance, Haney, '"Shadow-Hunting"', and Mellor, *English Romantic Irony*, 109–134.
40. Carlyle, *Sartor Resartus*, 1.2.8. References are to the Oxford Classics edition unless otherwise stated.
41. Ibid., 1.4.27.
42. Ibid., 1.1.3.
43. On Carlyle's immersion in all things German, see Harrold, *Carlyle and German Thought*, Dibble, *Pythia's Drunken Song*, and Vida, *Romantic Affinities*.
44. Carlyle, *Sartor Resartus*, 1.1.5.
45. Ibid., 1.3.12.
46. Ibid., 1.3.12.
47. See Ibid., 1.6.34 and 1.10.54 for further German puns. Likewise, the 'Devil' is a persistent presence throughout the narrative, most notably in a key passage of book two: 'The Everlasting No had said: "Behold, thou art fatherless, outcast, and the Universe is mine (the Devil's)"; to which my whole Me now made answer: "*I* am not thine, but Free, and forever hate thee!" (2.7.129) This kind of splitting of the subject is precisely a mark of romantic irony.
48. On Carlyle and Schlegel, see Vida, *Romantic Affinities*, 9–23. Carlyle had translated Goethe, Schiller, Tieck and Jean Paul in *German Romance* (1827); on Jean Paul, see Vijn, *Carlyle and Jean Paul*, and on Tieck, see Zeydel, *Ludwig Tieck and England*, 114–124. Carlyle was also heavily indebted to Novalis,

whom he had also translated, and regarding whom he had written an important essay 'Novalis' (1829), the influence of which is clearly traceable in the text of *Sartor Resartus*.

49. Carlyle, *Sartor Resartus*, 2.7.129.
50. Ibid., 1.4.22.
51. Ibid., 1.11.60.
52. Ibid., 1.4.26.
53. Ibid., 1.4.22.
54. Ibid., 1.4.24.
55. Ibid., 1.4.22.
56. Joyce, *Ulysses*, 14.402.
57. Carlyle, *Sartor Resartus*, 1.4.26. For more on these passages, see Dunn, '"Inverse Sublimity"'.
58. Carlyle, *Sartor Resartus*, 1.5.32. For Carlyle's source, see Tarr's notes to his edition of *Sartor Resartus*, 269 n.
59. Carlyle, *Sartor Resartus*, 1.4.25.
60. Ibid., 1.3.12.
61. Ibid., 1.6.34.
62. Ibid., 1.4.25–26.
63. Ibid., 1.4.24–25.
64. On Kierkegaard, see Lippitt, *Humour and Irony*. More broadly on these lineages, see Critchley, 'Comedy and Finitude', Morreall, *Taking Laughter Seriously*, and Parvulescu, *Laughter*.
65. See also Schlegel, *Athenaeum* fragment, § 305.
66. Ibid., § 42.

## BIBLIOGRAPHY

Booth, Wayne C. *A Rhetoric of Irony*. Chicago: University of Chicago Press, 1974.

Bown, Alfie. *In the Event of Laughter*. London: Bloomsbury, 2019.

Carlyle, Thomas. *Sartor Resartus*. Edited by Kerry McSweeney and Peter Sabor. Oxford: Oxford University Press, 1989.

Carlyle, Thomas. *Sartor Resartus*. Edited by Roger L. Tarr. Berkeley: University of California Press, 2000.

Colebrook, Claire. *Irony*. London: Routledge, 2003.

Colebrook, Claire. *Irony in the Work of Philosophy*. Lincoln: University of Nebraska Press, 2002.

Critchley, Simon. 'Comedy and Finitude: Displacing the Tragic-Heroic Paradigm in Philosophy and Psychoanalysis'. In *Ethics-Politics-Subjectivity: Essays on Derrida, Levinas and Contemporary French Thought*, 217–238. London: Verso, 1999.

C. T. [Connop Thirlwall]. 'On the Irony of Socrates'. *The Philological Museum* 2 (1833): 483–537.

Dane, Joseph A. *The Critical Mythology of Irony*. Athens: The University of Georgia Press, 2011.

Dibble, Jerry A. *The Pythia's Drunken Song: Thomas Carlyle's* Sartor Resartus *and the Style Problem in German Idealist Philosophy*. The Hague: Martinus Nijhoff, 1978.

Dunn, Richard J. '"Inverse Sublimity": Carlyle's Theory of Humour'. *University of Toronto Quarterly* 40, no. 1 (1972): 41–57.

18 ROMANTIC IRONY: PROBLEMS OF INTERPRETATION IN SCHLEGEL... 359

Haney, Janice L. '"Shadow-Hunting": Romantic Irony, "Sartor Resartus", and Victorian Romanticism'. *Studies in Romanticism* 17, no. 3 (1978): 307–333.

Harrold, C. F. *Carlyle and German Thought, 1819–1834.* New Haven: Yale University Press, 1934.

Hegel, G. W. F. *Aesthetics.* Translated by T.M. Knox. 2 vols. Oxford: Oxford University Press, 1988.

Hegel, G. W. F. *Vorlesungen über die Ästhetik.* Vols. 12–14 of *Sämtliche Werke,* edited by Hermann Glockner, 20 vols. Stuttgart: Fromann, 1927–1940.

Hegel, G. W. F. *Lectures on the History of Philosophy.* Translated by E.S. Haldane and Frances H. Simson. 3 vols. Lincoln: University of Nebraska Press, 1995.

Hegel, G. W. F. *Vorlesungen über die Geschichte der Philosophie.* Vols. 17–19 of *Sämtliche Werke,* edited by Hermann Glockner, 20 vols. Stuttgart: Fromann, 1927–1940.

Hobbes, Thomas. 'Answer to Sir William Davenant'. In *The English Works of Thomas Hobbes of Malmesbury,* 11 vols, edited by Sir William Molesworth, Bart., vol. 4, 441–458. London: John Bohn, 1845.

Joyce, James. *Ulysses: The 1922 Text.* Edited by Jeri Johnson. Oxford: Oxford University Press, 2008.

Kant, Immanuel. *Kritik der Urteilskraft.* Edited by Wilhelm Windelband. Berlin: Georg Reimer, 1913.

Kant, Immanuel. *Critique of the Power of Judgment.* Translated by Paul Guyer and Eric Matthews. Cambridge: Cambridge University Press, 2000.

Kierkegaard, Søren. *The Concept of Irony.* Translated by Howard V. Hong and Edna H. Hong. Princeton: Princeton University Press, 1989.

Lippitt, John. *Humour and Irony in Kierkegaard's Thought.* London: Palgrave Macmillan, 2000.

Lussky, Alfred Edward. *Tieck's Romantic Irony.* Chapel Hill: University of North Carolina Press, 1932.

de Man, Paul. 'The Concept of Irony'. In *Aesthetic Ideology,* edited by Andrej Warminski, 163–184. Minneapolis: University of Minnesota Press, 1996.

Mellor, Anne K. *English Romantic Irony.* Cambridge, MA: Harvard University Press, 1980.

Morreall, John. *Taking Laughter Seriously.* Albany: State University of New York Press, 1983.

Newmark, Kevin. *Irony on Occasion: From Schlegel and Kierkegaard to Derrida and de Man.* New York: Fordham University Press, 2012.

Parvulescu, Anca. *Laughter: Notes on a Passion.* Cambridge, MA: MIT Press, 2010.

Robinson, Henry Crabb. *Diary, Reminiscences, and Correspondence.* Edited by Thomas Sadler, 3 vols. London: Macmillan, 1869.

Rush, Fred. *Irony and Idealism: Rereading Schlegel, Hegel, and Kierkegaard.* Oxford: Oxford University Press, 2016.

Schlegel, Friedrich. *Charakteristiken und Kritiken I (1796–1801).* Edited by Hans Eichner. Munich: Schöningh, 1967.

Schlegel, Friedrich. *Philosophische Lehrjahre (1796–1806), Erster Teil.* Edited by Hans Eisner. Munich: Schöningh, 1963.

Szondi, Peter. 'Friedrich Schlegel and Romantic Irony'. In *On Textual Understanding and Other Essays,* translated by Harvey Mendelsohn, 57–73. Minneapolis: University of Minnesota Press, 1986.

Szondi, Peter. 'Friedrich Schlegel und die romantische Ironie'. In *Schriften,* 2 vols., edited by Wolfgang Fietkau, vol. 2, 11–31. Frankfurt am Main: Suhrkamp, 1978.

Vida, Elisabeth M. *Romantic Affinities: German Authors and Carlyle*. Toronto: University of Toronto Press, 1993.

Vijn, Jacob Peter. *Carlyle and Jean Paul: Their Spiritual Optics*. Amsterdam: John Benjamins, 1982.

Whiteley, Giles. *Schelling's Reception in Nineteenth Century British Literature*. London: Palgrave Macmillan, 2018.

Wilde, Oscar. *The Importance of Being Earnest*. Edited by Joseph Donohue. Oxford: Oxford University Press, 2019.

Wilde, Oscar. *The Picture of Dorian Gray: The 1890 and 1891 Texts*. Edited by Joseph Bristow. Oxford: Oxford University Press, 2005.

Wheeler, Katherine M., ed. and trans. *German aesthetic and literary criticism: the Romantic Ironists and Goethe*. Cambridge: Cambridge University Press, 1984.

Zeydel, Edwin H. *Ludwig Tieck and England*. Princeton: Princeton University Press, 1931.

CHAPTER 19

# Unlocking Verbal-Visual Puns in Late-Nineteenth-Century Japanese Cartoons

*Ronald Stewart*

In general, political cartoons tend to become more difficult to understand as temporal and cultural distance from the societies and circumstances that shaped them increases. Events, the immediacy of which once seemed important enough to warrant cartoon commentary, in time fade from memories and in many cases fail to make the pages of history books. Moreover, cultural understandings and practices once commonplace can also disappear as cultures continue to change. This is particularly true with Japanese cartoons of the late-1870s and 1880s. They differ from modern cartoons in both structure—filling much of the open space within the cartoon frame with text—and content—making heavy use of verbal and visual puns. It is this punning that makes their humour and messages about topical events of the time especially inaccessible today.

The aim of this chapter is to explore a method for unravelling the complex multi-layered puns in cartoons of this period. To do this it will utilise and modify the set of reading cue types developed by pragmatics scholar Hiroko Takanashi for understanding and resolving the double meanings pivoting on puns in the traditional Japanese humorous poetry form *kyōka* (lit. 'crazy verse').[1] The cue types will be expanded and adapted to account for the verbal-visual interplay between caption and cartoon image, and to consider the possible reading circumstances of the time. This will be applied to reading a representative cartoon of the period from Japan's most successful humour magazine of the late-nineteenth century, *Maru-maru Chinbun* 團團珍聞. Created at a time

R. Stewart (✉)
Daito Bunka University, Tokyo, Japan
e-mail: rgstewart@ic.daito.ac.jp

© The Author(s), under exclusive license to Springer Nature
Switzerland AG 2020
D. Derrin, H. Burrows (eds.), *The Palgrave Handbook of Humour, History, and Methodology*, https://doi.org/10.1007/978-3-030-56646-3_19

361

shortly after Japan opened its doors to the outside world and had begun remaking itself as a modern nation-state, the magazine's cartoons can be understood as an important stage in the development of modern Japanese political cartooning. While using modern printing techniques and taking a step towards the foreign cartooning models that they drew inspiration from, they were still firmly seated within the visual and verbal sensibilities of the urban woodblock print culture of Edo Period (1600–1868) and its taste for verse, puzzles and puns. As Peter Duus observes of *Maru-maru Chinbun*'s humour, 'its addiction to outrageous word play and visual punning, was predominantly local, drawing on an older tradition of visual verbal satire'.[2]

Before making an analysis of a cartoon related to a military revolt and its verbal-visual puns, an overview of punning in Japan in general as well as a closer look at the magazine *Maru-maru Chinbun*, its background and place in cartooning history, is in order. A brief discussion regarding relevant research on punning and on cartoon humour will be then given before discussing and modifying Takanashi's approach to reading *Kyōka* puns in order to read the *Maru-maru Chinbun* cartoon.

## PUNS IN JAPAN

Puns and punning are woven into the fabric of everyday life in contemporary Japan. Hinting at their omnipresence are the multiple words for wordplay which can be used as labels for puns in Japanese. One is the literal term for wordplay *kotoba-asobi* ことば遊び, and other traditional terms include *goroawase* 語呂合わせ, *jiguchi* 地口 and/or *share* 洒落. In Japan's literary tradition, puns as a form of poetic rhetoric are called *kakekotoba* 掛詞 (usually translated as 'pivot words'). A general term used in recent decades for puns, often disparagingly, is *dajare* 駄洒落.

Today in Japan puns are encountered in daily conversations, in advertising and product branding, in tabloid newspaper headlines, in the names of calendar and life events, in entertainment forms such as games, comic books, theatre and comic performances, and even in education with puns used as anchoring strategies for remembering information. Puns can be found in collections sold in book form and on websites and blogs devoted to punning. Moreover, visual puns at times also form part of the city and townscapes, such as Statue of Liberty sculptures found on bathhouses indicating bathing *nyūyoku* 入浴 punning on New York (in Japanese *Nyū Yōku*) symbolised by the statue. Puns, of course, also play a major role in Japanese political cartooning today. Though, unlike the tangle of multiple puns found in cartoons of the 1870s and 1880s, these overwhelmingly revolve around single verbal-visual puns.

The Japanese language is particularly well suited to punning. The writing system is made up of four types of scripts, two *kana* syllabaries, *kanji* ideograms (see comparison in Fig. 19.1) as well as Romanised script, the alphabet familiar to English users. Each of the *kana* scripts consist of forty-seven relatively simple characters which are phonetic representations of basic syllables

| Characters | Script features | Example sounds:<br>a ka sa ta ha na<br>ra wa o(wo) i(wi)<br><br>In brackets example of word for<br>'artillery': (hōheitai) |
|---|---|---|
| **Kana**<br>Syllabaries<br><br>2 sets<br>about 47 each | **Hiragana**<br>● simple – rounded<br><br>● Represent basic syllabic<br>sound clusters (or morae) | あ か さ た は な<br>ら わ を ゐ<br><br>(ほうへいたい) |
| | **Katakana**<br>● simple – angular<br><br>● Represent basic syllabic<br>sound clusters (or morae) | ア カ サ タ ハ ナ<br>ラ ワ ヲ 井<br><br>(ホウヘイタイ) or (ホーヘータイ) |
| **Kanji**<br>Sino-Japanese<br>Ideograms<br><br>over 50,000<br>available | ● more complex<br><br>● represent meanings or<br>concepts<br><br>● high lexical density often as<br>compound words<br><br>● can also be used phonetically<br>regardless of meaning | 阿 火 差 他 歯 奈<br>羅 話 遠 意<br><br>(砲兵隊)<br>or homophonous neologism<br>(放屁鯛) |

Fig. 19.1

that make up the Japanese sound system.[3] The most commonly used of the two *kana* is *hiragana* which are rounded characters used for verb conjugations, grammatical articles, and to break up the more complicated *kanji* script. At times they are also used as a gloss above or below *kanji* to indicate their readings. That is to say, their sound-values are used to guide how the meaning-based *kanji* script should be pronounced when read aloud (As we will see in our later cartoon analysis, this reading gloss also becomes another tool in the punster's armoury). The other *kana* script is the more angular *katakana*, today often used to represent foreign (non-*kanji* based) loan words or to give emphasis, but during the 1870s and 1880s the use of both types of *kana* was much more flexible. *Kanji* are Sino-Japanese ideograms, most imported from China, but some were created in Japan. At present the standardised set of everyday use *kanji* (*jōyō kanji*) taught in Japanese primary and secondary schools contains 2136 characters, and the highest-level proficiency exam tests around 6000 characters. However, the number of characters imported from China and created over the centuries is much higher. Japan's most comprehensive dictionary, the *Dai-kanwa jiten*, lists over fifty-thousand characters.[4]

The large number of borrowed terms from China, and later from the West, with their pronunciation refashioned to fit the simple Japanese sound system resulted in a huge pool of homophones. One example is the *kanji* compound *kōshō* 交渉 meaning 'negotiation' which has at least twenty-eight *kanji* compound homophones.[5] In creating imperfect puns using near-homophones the number of possible choices expands greatly. As many individual characters were introduced into Japan more than once within imported concepts during different eras and from different regions of China, they can have multiple *on*-readings, 'Chinese readings'. These readings are in reality approximations of Chinese pronunciations using the Japanese sound system and are mostly used in compound words of two or more ideograms representing abstract or technical terms. Moreover, many have been given one or more *kun*-readings, or Japanese readings, when used to represent existing indigenous words most often as a single character accompanied by *kana*. Take for example the character 生 which has basic meanings of 'birth', 'live', 'fresh' and 'raw', it has two possible *on*-readings and at least eighteen possible *kun*-readings (see Fig. 19.2).

*Kana* can be used to replace *kanji* ideograms with the sound equivalent in a text, or *kana* can be used as a gloss added to *kanji* to indicate how the *kanji* should be read. For example, the word for cartoon, manga, can be written in *kanji* ideogram as 漫畫, or the post-war form 漫画, in kana as either まんが or マンガ or in kanji with kana gloss to guide reading 漫 <sup>カリカチュア</sup>画, in this case with an unconventional reading *karikachua* (the kana rendering of 'caricature') adding another layer of meaning. These methods can be used to aid readers with lower literacy, or to deliberately make meanings more ambivalent or to force unconventional readings onto familiar *kanji*. And either method can be employed to aid the creation of puns and deliberately affect the speed of their processing. The cartoons of *Maru-maru Chinbun* make use of these methods, and as they were produced at a time well before government efforts from around 1902 to rationalise the writing system, cartoonists had a greater pool of resources, more *kanji* and non-standard readings, to draw on when creating written puns in their captions.

Punning has a long and auspicious tradition in Japanese literature. Present in Japan's oldest and most voluminous collection of poetry the *Man'yōshū* (c.759), puns as *kakekotoba* (pivot-words or hitch-words) became established as an integral part of Japanese poetry with the first anthology of royal *waka* poetry, the

| Kanji Character | Reading type | No. of readings | Possible readings |
|---|---|---|---|
| 生 <br><br> (meaning: born, fresh raw, etc.) | *on* reading <br> (Chinese Reading) | 2 | *sei    shō* |
| | *kun* reading <br> (Japanese Reading) | 18 | *ikiru  ikasu  iku  ikeru   umu umareru ki ō  haeru  hayasu  nama  fu  ari  i nari  naru  nō  oki  bu  yo  susumu u  taka ...* |

**Fig. 19.2**

*Kokinshū* (c905). They would remain a central device in Japan's poetic tradition, particularly thirty-one syllable *waka* forms of poetry, such as *tanka* and the comic version *kyōka* 狂歌 which flourished in the seventeenth and eighteenth centuries. According to poetry scholar Kawamoto Koji, in the case of *tanka* these puns were all figurative devices used not for comic effect or as mere 'ornaments', but rather for their poetic function. The creation of excellent puns would stir excitement, winning the author admiration and even fame.[6] Kawamoto argues for a poetics of punning as a scholarly pursuit to explore the complexity and potential of pun usage, and to recover from the bad name given to punning by Western scholars of literature and rhetoric.[7]

The use of puns was also common in the popular literature (*gesaku* 戯作) of the Edo period's (1600–1868) thriving urban print culture. They flowered in the illustrated books known as *kibyōshi* 黄表紙 (yellow-covers) which peaked in popularity in the late eighteenth century. Scholar of *kibyōshi* Adam L Kern describes their content as an 'unsurpassed' vortex of visual and verbal puns, puzzles, parody, allusions to all manner of literature, and that to read them in the 'rapid-fire page-flipping mode' of modern comics 'one would miss half the fun'.[8]

One of Japan's visual punning traditions is *mitate* 見立て bringing two worlds together. In seventeenth- to nineteenth-century popular print culture, *mitate* came to mean 'visual puns' or 'simile pictures'.[9] According to Adam L. Kern, this practice visual intertwining of two worlds in a single image, also known as *naimaze* 綯交ぜ, was widespread, appearing in books for children and adults. Kern proposes that possibly the more divergent the two worlds, the greater the incongruity and hence the greater the resultant mirth.[10] Yet another type of visual punning was the use of rebus in a genre of prints called *share-e* 洒落絵 (punning pictures) or more generally as *hanji-e* 判じ絵 (puzzle pictures) which enjoyed particular popularity in the 1850s and 1860s. These worked like conundrums with sound components of words broken down and represented by pictures of unrelated objects with the same or similar pronunciation. For example, on an 1860s print with rebus puzzles for food types, *ninjin* 人参 (carrot) is represented by a pregnant woman and beside her two small dashes normally used with a kana character to indicate a voiced consonant. Pregnancy in Japanese is *ninshin* 妊娠. By understanding the two dashes mean voicing the sound '*shi*' as '*ji*' the reader arrives at the puzzle answer *ninjin*.[11] In this way, unusual verbal-visual or visual mixtures take on surprise commonplace meanings when combined. In the cartoons of *Maru-maru Chinbun* both *mitate* and *hanji-e* style rebus forms of punning can be seen.

A final area where forms of visual puns can occur is in Japanese orthography, particularly *kanji*, and examples of this form of wordplay can be found dating back more than a millennium to the eighth century.[12] Punning neologisms can be constructed with *kanji* retaining the sound of a word but replacing ideograms to add extra or create new meanings. This type of wordplay common in Edo period popular print culture was used frequently in *Maru-maru Chinbun*. An example of this can be found in a cartoon from the July 1880 issue with the punning title '*Nanjū keisai*' 難獣径犀, a near-homophone of the common expression *nanju keizai* 難渋経済 meaning a 'stagnant economy'. While this meaning reverberates in the sound of the caption, the unusual combination of *kanji* actually means, 'a rhino on a path full of vicious beasts'. This pun works as a metaphor for the difficult challenges ahead with the economy and is reinforced by the cartoon image of a politician on a perilous road surrounded by beasts and coming face to face with a rhino.[13] A further way *kanji*-based puns are created is by manipulating elements within characters to create near-homographs with different meanings. This is practice that has long been used in China too, as Giulia Baccini's chapter in this book shows.

As noted above, *Maru-maru Chinbun* with its love of punning drew on many of the forms of puns mentioned here which had flourished in popular culture though into the nineteenth century. However, they were put to new use, for regular and open satirical attacks on the government and politics in the form of cartoon journalism inspired by Western models.

## Maru-maru Chinbun

*Maru-maru Chinbun* 團團珍聞, known also by the contraction *Maru-Chin*, was founded in 1877 modelled closely after London's *Punch* magazine.[14] It became the most successful humour magazine of late-nineteenth-century Japan. Its weekly circulation reached an impressive, for the time, figure of 15,000 in its first year, and by 1880 it had nationwide distribution with more than half its readers outside of urban Tokyo.[15] As magazines were often read in groups and circulated between readers, its actual readership was doubtlessly much higher. *Maru-chin* ran for thirty years, losing its initial popularity over time and eventually coming to an end in 1907, making way for a new breed of more heavily illustrated humour magazines, such as *Tokyo Puck* (1905–1912), based on US models with less interest in punning.

While *Maru-chin* contained roughly the same number of pages, twelve to fourteen, as *Punch* magazines of the 1870s, it was smaller in dimension. Its compact 23 by 16 cm size pages had a mere three-fifths the area of *Punch*'s larger 28 by 22 cm pages. Consequently, it had less content. It did however retain a text-to-image ratio similar to *Punch*. *Maru-Chin* had three to four cartoons per issue, one or two of which were full-page. The rib-tickling text portions of the magazine were a mixture of political and social satirical articles such as its 'Irresponsible' editorials *chasetsu* 茶説[16] and humorous literature or *kyōbun* 狂文. It also featured humorous poetry forms, *kyōka* and *senryū* 川柳 the comic version of haiku poetry, as well as of *kyōshi* 狂詩 (lit. 'crazy poems') a parody version of Chinese-style poetry. These three poetry forms contributed by readers also filled the inner rear pages of the magazine.

New technology and a smattering of English language gave *Maru-Chin* a modern look. Its cover (Fig. 19.3) was produced with zinc-plate relief printing technology with cross-hatching not possible with traditional Japanese

**Fig. 19.3** *Maru-maru Chinbun*, issue no. 175 (25 August 1885) cover. (Personal collection of the author)

woodblock (or woodcut) prints. Its use of movable type also made it look modern. *Maru-chin* also introduced a mascot character similar to Punch with a large nose who would at times appear in cartoons and offer meta-commentary. When it first appeared, the ideas of news being published periodically, and of directly discussing and criticising the government were both novel.

*Maru-Chin* was founded by Nomura Fumio (1836–1912) part of the country's new educated elite. He was sent at age seven to Nagasaki to study Dutch and medicine. In 1865, a time when it was still illegal for Japanese to leave the country, Nomura with the help of a Scottish merchant secretly travelled to the UK, spending nineteen months in Aberdeen and visiting Paris. By the time he returned in 1868, the year of the Meiji Restoration heralding the start of Japan's modern nation-state building project, he had been enamoured with the British parliamentary system and the role of journalism in keeping an eye on the government. His 1870 published account of his travels marked him as an expert on the West and led to him working for a number of Japanese government departments as a bureaucrat. However, hailing from Hiroshima, he found himself on the outside of the government's power cliques which had coalesced around members of domains directly involved in the overthrow of the old feudal regime and establishment of the Meiji government. In frustration he resigned in 1877 to embark on a career in journalism founding his own magazine *Maru-Chin*. With this magazine he criticised the government's excessive aping of the West, agitated against government domain-cliques and lent support to the nascent 'freedom of popular rights' (*jiyū minken*) movement's call for the introduction of a constitution and elections.

In this new era, it had become much easier to satirise the government. During the Edo period, beginning in the 1780s, restrictions carrying harsh penalties were put in place to prevent publications discussing politics or political leaders. The urge to criticise and satirise never completely disappeared and continued to a small degree, although it was usually disguised, hidden behind *mitate* visual puns and allegory. By the 1830s restraints were eroding and satire became more overt, but never vicious.[17] In 1874, the ban on discussing political affairs was officially lifted and this led to a flowering of 'small newspaper' (小新聞) journalism, offering news and political debate to a broader public.[18] *Maru-Chin* was among these. Unlike the so-called large newspapers (大新聞) broadsheets aimed at the educated elites using *kanbun* 'Chinese-style' writing, these were written in a more vernacular style, and provided phonetic glosses (*rubi* ルビ) in *kana* beside *kanji* to aid the less educated with reading. While literacy in urban areas was relatively high among *bushi* (samurai) and merchant classes, Japan's compulsory education system only began to take shape from 1872, so levels of literacy still varied greatly.

Despite this new relative freedom to discuss politics a series of new inconsistently enforced press and publication laws in the last decades of the nineteenth century would chip away at these freedoms. In 1869, a publication ordinance banned some topics and required prepublication approval. In 1875, the government in reaction to the growing freedom of people's rights movements throughout the country introduced libel laws into their press ordinance. And in 1889, the new constitution subjected all publications to censorship. *Maru-Chin*'s title is itself a tongue-in-cheek allusion to restrictive press laws, hinting at one of the common forms of censorship 'covering characters' *fuseji* 伏字. These characters replaced sections of movable type to 'cover', in effect delete, segments of text found problematic by censors. One of the most common 'covering characters' was a circle. A word for circle in Japanese is *maru*. *Chinbun* means rare tales or news. Thus, the magazine's name, anticipating of future battles with censors, roughly equates to in English, 'Extraordinary XXXXX News'.[19] The two concentric circles framing the image of three reporters in the centre of the cover also echoes this title. Just as anticipated, the magazine would indeed be forced by censors to use 'covering characters' and at times the publication was even banned from sale. For this reason, until the practice was outlawed, *Maru-Chin* ran a parallel publication with a different name *Kibidango* 驥尾団子 (1878–1883) to send to subscribers when sale of *Maru-Chin* was prohibited. After the government promulgation of a constitution 1889 and the death of founder Nomura in 1891 the magazine floundered somewhat losing its political edge, and its readership went into decline.[20]

Playfulness and punning on the magazine's cover go beyond just the title. The three journalists in the centre form a parody of the famous Three Wise Monkeys of Tōshō-gū Shrine, who 'see no evil, hear no evil, speak no evil'.[21] One journalist holds binoculars looking out for evil, one pricks up his ear promising to listen for evil and one with a brush points to his huge nose intending to sniff out evil. Framing the magazine title banner at the top of the cover are a horse and a deer forming a visual wordplay. The *kanji* character for horse, *uma* 馬, when added to the character for deer, *shika* 鹿, combine to form the compound 馬鹿 which in Chinese *on*-reading becomes *baka* meaning idiot. Between these two animals can be seen the magazine's subtitle in *kanji* 於東京繪, which literally means 'Pictures in Tokyo' (in '*o*' 於, *Tokyo* 東京, pictures '*e*' 繪). However, this is turned into a pun by forcing an unconventional reading onto the compound using the phonetic gloss in *kana* to the right of each character. It renders Tokyo as a corrupted and clipped version of one alternate reading of the *kanji* compound name of the country's capital before it became standardised '*Tokei*' とうけい as a near-homophone '*Doke*' どけ. With this it puns with the homophone *odoke-e* (戯け絵) meaning comical pictures. The cover page is a mere taste of the torrent of puns and other visual-verbal wordplay readers are confronted with on entering the magazine's pages.

The magazine was a pioneer in political cartooning in Japan. Its first cartoonist, and artist behind the cartoon we will examine, was Honda Kinkichirō 本田錦吉郎 (1851~1921) a former Hiroshima domain student of the magazine founder Nomura. Honda was invited by Nomura to join the magazine due to his experience in 'Western art' and for seven years he drew all the cartoons for both *Maru-Chin* and *Kibidango*. Cartoon historian Shimizu Isao estimates that Honda drew over a thousand cartoons during this period.[22] While initially using rebus to indicate political figures, he would later be the first to introduce direct likenesses of his satirical targets making use of facial caricatures in his cartoons. For this reason, he is considered important in Japanese cartooning development.[23] With very few models within Japan to draw from occasionally he turned for inspiration to *Punch* magazine as well as cartoons by other overseas artists. Shimizu Isao has demonstrated that Honda's July 1878 cartoon satirising attempts to avoid clashes between the government and the popular rights movement is based directly on *Punch* artist Edward Linley Sambourne's cartoon 'Working the Points'. Published a mere two months earlier in May 1878, Sambourne's cartoon shows German Chancellor Bismarck operating switchable rail tracks in order to avoid a clash between his country and Britain.[24] Another Honda cartoon from July 1880, 'A rhino on a path of vicious beasts' (mentioned above) takes its composition from a 1808 James Gillray political print 'The Valley of the shadow of Death'.[25]

Despite the use of modern Western models, use of modern printing technology and movable type, and its overt satire of the government, the cartoons of *Maru-Chin* during its first decade had changed little in form from late-eighteenth-century *kibyōshi* illustrated books. They had lengthy captions filling the spaces around the cartoon image within the cartoon frame. And just like *kibyōshi* these captions were in poetic metre and littered with puns and allusions. Images of known political figures in cartoons by Honda were initially represented not by likenesses but rebus alluding to their names. The cartoons, just as in Edo period print culture, were designed to be read aloud to enjoy the flavour of the voice and to slowly unravel the verbal-visual puzzles within. The cartoons of this period would become known as *ponchi-e* ポンチ絵, meaning 'Punch-pictures'. From around the late-1880s cartoons in Japanese magazines and newspapers gradually began moving towards a form more recognisable as the modern cartoon manga 漫画 (or 'political cartoons' *seiji manga* 政治漫画) of today. These were more suited to a faster pace of media with short captions, international cartooning symbols and instantly recognisable caricatures of their satirical targets.

By the first decade of the twentieth century when modern cartooning had become commonplace, *Maru-Chin*'s cartooning was considered decidedly old-fashioned, representative of a bygone age. In 1907 the use of puns in cartoons was criticised as 'low-grade' by the artist and critic Yamamoto Kanae 山本鼎 (1882–1946). Cartoonist Kitazawa Rakuten 北澤楽天 (1876–1955), a central figure in Japanese cartooning in the first decades of the twentieth century, attacked the *Maru-chin*'s excessively wordy cartoons and criticised their continued practice of hiding of satirical messages behind puns in an era when it was possible to express things directly.[26]

## Reading Japanese Verbal-Visual Puns

Most research on puns tends to be focused on the verbal[27] and this is also the case with some of the limited research specifically on Japanese puns.[28] One of the more fruitful ways of thinking about the structure and operation of puns is the Script-based Semantic Theory of Humour (SSTH) developed by Victor Raskin and Salvatore Attardo. This focuses on the script opposition (SO) always present in puns and which is seen in this theory as a necessary condition for humour. The SO should contain both oppositeness (surface incompatibility) and overlap to work.[29] The overlap occurs in the punning word triggering a logical mechanism (LM), the understanding of the playful logic allows the scripts to be connected, which allows the opposition be resolved.[30]

One of the few studies that takes into account the visual aspects of puns is Hiroko Takanashi's study of *kakekotoba* in Japanese *kyōka* poetry. While using SSTH as a start point, she examines the orthography of the poems to show how it was used to both hide and reveal meaning. Readers may be tricked into certain understandings by the increased ambiguity (polysemy) of words written in sound-value script *kana* rather than their conventional orthography of *kanji* ideograms which would normally anchor meaning more clearly. Meanings may also be initially hidden or masked from readers by *kanji*, only to have other meanings based on homophones of their conventional reading, or sound-value, revealed as the poem unfolds.[31] As Takanashi points out, Raskin and Attardo's theory sees script opposition, or incompatibility, of two scripts as important but their theory has little to say on the quality of the scripts. In *kyōka* poetry, one script is serious (aesthetic or commonplace) and the other a recognised deviation from the serious script is non-serious (non-aesthetic, playful, surprising or funny).[32] This is similar to the punning captions of *Maru-chin* cartoons in that one script refers to a serious real-world political event and satirical target, and the other script will be a playful surprising script (at times working as a metaphor). Although in the case of the cartoons, the playful script is revealed first and the serious script accessed through resolving puns.

Takanashi in her analysis rejects the use of 'script' for its connotations of linear or chronological events, preferring instead the notion 'frame' to refer to cognitive sets of knowledge, or 'specific unified frameworks of knowledge' built on experience used to decode the texts.[33] This seems important firstly because there is debate over whether the processing of *kanji* and *kana* are done through visual aspects or sound aspects first, or whether, the view supported by Takanashi, the sound and visual aspects are processed simultaneously for familiar orthography.[34] In the captions of *Maru-Chin*'s cartoons the processing of text is complicated even more by use of uncommon orthographic combinations such as punning *kanji* neologisms and unconventional *kanji* readings forced by *kana* glosses. The markedness of this kind of language would draw the attention of an experienced reader flagging locations of puns which need to be resolved. Also for those who could not rely on orthographic hints, that is, for readers with lower literacy levels unable to access all the *kanji* meanings, and for listeners, in cases when the caption was read aloud or performed by someone else during the then common practice of group reading, the processing of the text would have varied.

Another reason why the use of 'fame' over 'script' seems preferable, particularly in the case of *Maru-Chin*'s cartoons, is that there is no set entry point into cartoons. They may be read image first followed by the caption, or vice versa. In addition, the reading of captions may not always be linear. It is not uncommon to preview and review while reading. By skimming ahead and glancing over *kanji* characters and their meanings in the text to come, the reader can glean hints as to what comes next. Readers can also review by going back to retrieve puns missed on first pass, or by referring back to the image for confirmation or for additional contextual clues. In *Maru-Chin* cartoons, some verbal puns within the caption are also reiterated in visual form. Francisco Yus in a rare examination of the multimodal humour of cartoons argues that cartoons are more complex than usually assumed, and the cognition of varying combinations of verbal and visual sources is non-linear.[35] Whether entering the image or caption first as well as the act of referring back to the image or text will depend on the reader and their construction of an interpretive hypothesis based on verbal-visual clues and their own background knowledge of events being referred to.[36] Moreover, the global processing of images and the more-or-less linear processing of text are done at different speeds.[37]

In analysing the cartoons of *Maru-Chin* consideration should also be given to the strength of the puns. Hempelmann points out that puns that work on a single word with no support from a second frame are considered weak, and that recovery of the target pun can be aided (pun strengthened) by semantic support from other contextual factors.[38] Most studies of puns tend to focus on single instances of puns, or see multiple instances of humour as 'overdetermined'.[39] But, in *Maru-chin*'s long cartoon captions a plurality of puns seems to be important for its overall operation. In them a nonsense frame usually contains multiple points of overlap (puns) with an oppositional serious news frame, and these individual instances of puns within the caption work to reinforce adjacent puns. Image interplay with the textual puns also seems crucial to the cartoon's overall comic effect. Ronald Barthes, in his famous 'Rhetoric of the Image' essay, reasons that captions can anchor ambivalent meanings of the image they accompany.[40] Yus expands on Barthes arguing that in cartoons the reverse also occurs with the cartoon images at times anchoring meaning in the captions.[41] In the same way *Maru-Chin* cartoon captions and their textual puns can anchor or reinforce cartoon image visual puns, and vice versa. In addition, a single easily understood pun can work as a key pun in each caption helping to set up the themes of the two frames which in turn aid the discovery of less obvious puns in the text and image. The popularity of the magazine hints that the act of reading and discovering the multiple puns in a single cartoon must have appreciated by the readers in this time when the pace of media was much slower.

In order to explore this type of heavily punning cartoon of the late-1870s *Maru-Chin*, in the next section use will be made of a modified version of the seven cues put forward by Takanashi for resolving the puns in *kyōka*. Takanashi's cues are listed (1) to (7) below. To these I have added two extra cue categories, (8) presentation and (9) performance, in order to account for visual support/ interplay and the possibility of the text being read aloud in a group.

(1) print: the magazine text
(2) sound: as indicated on the page
(3) meaning: semantics and repetition
(4) frames: 'real world' satirical target frame and 'nonsense' (or metaphor) frame
(5) familiarity with orthography: level of literacy
(6) cultural knowledge: culture of period and knowledge of current events
(7) genre knowledge: political cartoons
(8) presentation: visual image support for, and interplay with, text
(9) performance: reading aloud / group interaction

Before beginning the analysis, it is worth reiterating an aspect of reading cartoons that makes them quite different to reading *kyōka* poetry. The more linear reading process of poetry allows Takanashi to assume a garden path effect revealing some meanings to readers earlier than others, and this to a degree dictates the order of her seven clues.[42] However, in the case of reading cartoons with their visual and verbal mix, as well as readers' varied literacy levels and reading practices, all readers may not follow the same processing route. For this reason, processing of the reading cues in this analysis will also be assumed to be non-linear, with many cues working in parallel. However, for clarity the analysis below will be conducted in roughly the same order as the list of cues above.

## CARTOON ANALYSIS

Let us now examine the untitled full-page political cartoon by Honda Kinkichirō published in the 31 August 1878 issue of *Maru-maru Chinbun*. The cartoon relates to the Takebashi Incident which occurred just a week earlier on 23 August 1878. The incident was a rebellion by the artillery corps (*hōheitai* 砲兵隊) of the elite Imperial Guard stationed at Takebashi near the Imperial Palace in Tokyo. Despite playing an important role in the government's victory in the Seinan War of 1877 in Satsuma domain, cuts in military funding saw their salaries reduced and other benefits lost. Boiling dissatisfaction turned into an uprising by 259 members of the corps. They fired on conscript troops sent to resist them and, reportedly, fired on the nearby residence of the Minister for Finance Ōkuma Shigenobu. The uprising resulting in two deaths was quashed within a day. Over 120 of the rebels were sent to jail and 55 were executed for their part. The government shocked by their troops putting monetary compensation before allegiance to the government and country, began lecturing the military using the rhetoric of loyalty. *Maru-chin* took delight in mocking the government over the incident (Fig. 19.4).

We will begin the analysis by focusing on the caption, where the first three reading cues are found: (1) the print, which is the *kanji* and *kana* of the caption; (2) sound, which is indicated by the phonetic *kana* script, by conventional readings (pronunciations) associated with the *kanji* characters, and in

**Fig. 19.4** Untitled cartoon by Honda Kinkichirō (*Maru-maru Chinbun*, 31 August 1878). (Reprinted with the permission of the National Diet Library, Japan)

some cases by *kana* glosses or reading guides on *kanji* forcing them to be read in unconventional ways; and (3) meaning which is found in the semantics, neologisms and repetition of theme-related terms. All of these come together to form cue (4) the frames. These are two oppositional or incompatible frames. The first frame, the initial surface meaning, is a nonsense frame about flatulent fish. The second frame is a serious frame related to the target of satire, the government and its treatment of troops.

These two frames set up by the caption overlap on six occasions. All work to mutually support and reinforce each other, particularly a key pun, *hōheitai* 放屁鯛, made up of the kanji *hō* 放 to release, *he* 屁 to fart, and *tai* 鯛 sea bream, which clearly sets the themes of both frames. This is a neologism 'fart releasing sea bream' coined as a pun for this cartoon. It stands out for its markedness in three ways: it is a fanciful combination of characters, it is an unconventional mixture of *on* (Chinese) and *kun* (Japanese) readings within the same word and lastly the character for fart which has been given a corrupted *kun* reading of '*hei*' rather than the correct '*he*' by the *kana* reading gloss. This novel word is homophonous with the common, and at the time newsworthy, noun *hōheitai* 砲兵隊 meaning 'artillery corps', here pointing to the rebellious artillery corps of the Imperial Guard.

Let us look at the caption's six puns in sequence. The first pun ① *tai* 鯛 works as both pun and metaphor. The word *tai* 鯛 'sea bream' puns on *tai* 隊

'troops/corps'. But it also forms part of a common saying which begins the caption, 'even if sea bream have gone rotten, they are still sea bream'. In Japanese culture sea bream are the most highly prized of all fish, and the saying means that something of great value or quality, even if it has gone bad, dropped in condition or been damaged, it is still a cut above the rest. In this case, the thing of great quality of course alludes to the elite artillery corps. The next pun ② *teppō* 鉄砲 'canon/gun' is an imperfect pun on *seppō* 説法 meaning 'to preach at' or 'to scold', possibly referring to lectures on loyalty given to the military. The third pun ③ *he* 屁 'fart' is understandable as the interjection *he* へ 'huh?'. These first three puns are not marked and only accessible through background knowledge of the incident and as the serious frame develops throughout the caption. The next pun ④ *būi* 武威 'armed force' usually pronounced as *bui* has been given an extended *u* vowel by its *kana* gloss making the reader/listener imagine *bū* ブー the onomatopoeia for a fart sound coupled with the sound *i* 威 meaning power, reinforced by the *kanji*'s ideographic meaning, and creating a humorous new expression 'fart (sound) power'. The fifth pun ⑤ is the key pun explained above *hōheitai* 'farting sea beam' / 'artillery'. The final pun ⑥ is a shortened version of this, *hōhei* 放屁 'break wind' the homophone of *hōhei* 砲兵 'member of the artillery'.

A breakdown of each vocabulary item in the caption and its meaning can be seen in Fig. 19.5 below. There is a column for each item, with the original orthography at the top, followed by its Romanised pronunciation, and below that its possible meanings. In the case of puns, a further row is added at the bottom showing the pun target with its usual orthography, pronunciation and meanings. The six puns ① to ⑥ described above are indicated with the same numbers. Four types of puns A to D are also indicated. Type A puns are simple perfect puns using homophones. Type B is a near-homophonic imperfect pun. Type C uses a forced reading to produce a novel onomatopoeia-based punning compound word. Finally, type D puns are irregular readings forced on neologisms to create punning homophones. The use of poetic metre and lack of punctuation makes breaks in the text somewhat ambiguous.[43] Nevertheless, bracketed sections in the caption are divided in the table by thin empty grey columns. Other apparent breaks in the text are indicated by thin white columns. Approximate translations of the two frames with puns numbered and underlined follow the table.

Frame 1: Nonsense Frame
Though it is said that even when ① sea bream are rotten they are still valuable, the stench from this blast will probably linger for up to a thousand years. Isn't their blast release after all this time, after being told they just should put up with this amount of upset stomach, merely to laugh it away with a single shot of their hundred-day-③ fart ② canon. Possibly due to being forced to only eat vast amounts of Satsuma sweet potatoes, this behaviour using their characteristic ④ 'fart-power' comes from their inability to overcome their upset stomachs. However, because they are ⑤ farting-bream this is a rude fart (fart sound). 'They weren't given a treat so they ⑥ released the fart!' 'Despite appearances, this canon also doubles as a trumpet!'

## Fig. 19.5

| 腐つ (くさ) | ても | **A** 鯛 (たい) | だけあつて | 此 | 一發 (いっぱつ) | 臭気 (しゅうき) | ハ | 千歳 (せんさい) |
|---|---|---|---|---|---|---|---|---|
| *kusat* | *temo* | *tai* | *dake atte* | *kono* | *ippatsu* | *shuuki* | *wa* | *sensai* |
| rot / go bad / become depraved or disheartened | even if | sea bream / ① 隊 (*tai*) troops | merely being | this | one blast / single shot | stench | TOP | thousand years / a long long time |

| までも | 残る (のこ) | だらう | 彼程 (かれほど) | はたらいて | 置いて (お) | 辛抱 (しんぼう) | すれハ |
|---|---|---|---|---|---|---|---|
| *mademo* | *nokoru* | *darou* | *korehodo* | *hataraite* | *oite* | *shinbou* | *sureba* |
| as long as | remain | probably | to this extent | work / to serve / do sth bad | leave (done) | endure / be patient | if done |

| よい | に | 今更 (いまさら) | 放發 (ほうはつ) | とは | 百日 (ひやくにち) | の | **B** 鐵砲 (てっぽう) |
|---|---|---|---|---|---|---|---|
| *yoi* | *ni* | *imasara* | *houhatsu* | *to wa* | *hyaku nichi* | *no* | *teppou* |
| okay / fine | against / towards | after such a long time | fire (shot)/ release blast | TOP (explain) | hundred days | NOM | canon / gun / ② 説法 (*seppou*) preaching / scolding |

| **A** 屁 (へ) | 一つ (ひと) | ただ | 笑ふ (わら) | だらう | 餘りに (あま) | 薩摩 (さつま) | の | 堅芋 (かたいも) |
|---|---|---|---|---|---|---|---|---|
| *he* | *hitotsu* | *tada* | *warau* | *darou* | *amarini* | *satsuma* | *no* | *kataimo* |
| fart / ③ へ (he) huh? | one | just / merely | laugh | probably | excessively | Satsuma (region) | NOM | potatoes (Satsuma "sweet potato") |

| 計り (ばか) | 食せられた (くわ) | せい | か | 腹の虫 (はら むし) | が | 折合ぬ (おりあわ) | 處 (ところ) |
|---|---|---|---|---|---|---|---|
| *bakari* | *kuwasareta* | *sei* | *ka* | *hara no mushi* | *ga* | *oriawanu* | *tokoro* |
| only | made to eat | fault of | ? | aggravation / anger (lit: insects in stomach) | SUB | not come to terms with | point (in time) |

| から | 持前 (もちまえ) | の | **C** 武威 (ブーゐ) | を | 振舞た (ふるまっ) | の | だ | が |
|---|---|---|---|---|---|---|---|---|
| *kara* | *mochimae* | *no* | *buui* | *o* | *furumatta* | *no* | *da* | *ga* |
| from | charateristic | NOM | armed force / ④ ブーゐ (*buui*) "fart" power | OBJ | actions / behaviour | EMPH | COP | but |

| ソコ | ハ | **D** 放屁鯛 (はうへいたい) | だ | から | 失敬 (しっけい) | ブウー |
|---|---|---|---|---|---|---|
| *soko* | *wa* | *houheitai* | *da* | *kara* | *shikkei* | *buuu* |
| that / there | TOP | "fart releasing sea bream" / ⑤ 砲兵隊 (*houheitai*) artillery squad | COP | so / because | disrespectful / bad manners | (fart sound) |

| 彼方 (あっち) | か | 褒美 (はうび) | を | くれぬ | から | **D** 放屁 (はうへい) | だ | ゾ |
|---|---|---|---|---|---|---|---|---|
| *atchi* | *ga* | *houbi* | *o* | *kurenu* | *kara* | *houhei* | *da* | *zo* |
| the other party | SUB | reward | OBJ | not give | so / because | "released fart" / ⑥ 砲兵 (*houhei*) artillery soldier(s) | COP | EMPH |

| こう | 見えても (み) | ラッパ | 兼帯 (けんたい) | の | 鐵砲 (てっぽう) | だ | ゾ |
|---|---|---|---|---|---|---|---|
| *kou* | *mietemo* | *rappa* | *kentai* | *no* | *teppou* | *da* | *zo* |
| this way / like this | even if ~ appears (to be) | trumpet / bugle | dual-use / multi-purpose | NOM | gun / canon | COP | EMPH |

COP=Copula   EMP= Emphasis or Emphatic particle   NOM= nominative
OBJ= object marker   SUB= subject marker   TOP= Topic marker

**Fig. 19.5**

Frame 2: 'Serious' Incident Explanation Frame
They say even when something as esteemed as ① <u>troops (imperial artillery corps)</u> have gone bad they are still a cut above the rest, but the <u>bad smell (taint / fallout)</u> arising from this one outburst of shooting will probably last for many years. In reaction to being told they should just tolerate having been made work to this extent, their outburst of gun/canon fire was no doubt to laugh off, with a <u>single</u> ③ <u>'huh' (simple shrug of the shoulders)</u>, one hundred days of ② <u>being scolded (preached to)</u>. Possibly due to being forced to just eat so many Satsuma sweet potatoes (subjected to such harsh conditions fighting in Satsuma), they acted with their characteristic ④ <u>military force</u> on coming to a point where they could no longer overcome their anger. However, as they are ⑤ <u>artillery corps</u> this was unbecoming conduct. (fart sound) 'We ⑥ <u>fired</u> because they didn't give us compensation for our work!' 'Despite appearances the canon doubles as a bugle!'

Reading cue (5) familiarity with the orthography is dependent on the literacy level of the reader or viewer of the cartoon. As noted above literacy levels at the time varied greatly. For a reader educated enough to be familiar with all of the *kana* and *kanji* used, the markedness of instances of unconventional usage would give rise to humour and/or give cause to intensify focus to resolve any incongruity. For readers with access to *kana* and limited *kanji* knowledge, most puns would require additional contextual support, visual or, if in a group, performative. Another cue for reading the puns is (6) cultural knowledge. Knowledge would be necessary not only of the recent Takebashi incident, but also knowledge that in Japanese culture *satsuma-imo*, sweet potatoes from Satsuma, the region where the artillery corps had fought the Seinan War, are popularly believed to be a cause of flatulence. Cue (7) is genre knowledge. Familiarity with this new genre, political cartoons, means there would be an expectation on the reader's part that the cartoon would contain numerous puns and that the cartoon would be pointing to a real-world event as well as a target of satire. Resolutions to puns bringing the nonsense and real-world frames together would be found with this in mind.

Cue (8) presentation is the viewing or showing of the cartoon image. The cartoon in this case provides support for the puns providing hints for both frames. The anthropomorphised sea bream are pictured breaking wind as in the key pun. They also form a group as they use their flatulence to operate a canon, and are hence both a fish type *tai* and an artillery 'troop' *tai*. So the image visually melds both frames of the pun together. The image also gives additional visual hints for the serious frame. In the centre attached to the cannon is the Emperor's crest, the chrysanthemum, indicating they are imperial troops. The two figures under fire on the right in military uniform allude to the conscript troops sent to quell the uprising. At the bottom left fleeing for its life is a bear, *kuma*, with a *kanji* character for large *ō* 大 on its back. These elements combine to form a rebus for Ōkuma the Finance Minister an alleged target of the corps' gun fire.

As mentioned earlier, in the 1870 and 1880s it was still common to read aloud in groups. Silent and individual reading would only become the norm with the later spread of compulsory education and development of new reading spaces (commuter trains, modern libraries, etc.). So, with *Maru-Chin* cartoons the performance, cue (9), of the cartoon was also important at the time. Beyond enjoying the flavour of the voice in poetic five-seven, four-eight or other timed metre, members of a group with low literacy could access all the sounds of the caption in combination with viewing the image. These audio and visual hints would have allowed them to grasp the key pun and understand much of the frames. Puns such as pun ④ *būi* 'fart power'/'military force' could be grasped more readily by intonation or stress in its performance to mimic the sound of flatulence. Group interaction in discussing the cartoon could also lead to discovery and reinforcement of puns not so easily accessible by the surface sounds and image.

The 1870s and 1880s in Japanese cartooning history represents an interesting convergence of the old with new ideas and technologies that produced relatively short-lived expression forms difficult to understand today. The above was an attempt to read the type of pun-rich cartoon favoured in this period. The analysis began with the premise, drawing on Raskin and Attardo's Script-based Semantic Theory of Humour, that puns work by connecting two incompatible frames of meaning through playful logic. To take into consideration visual aspects of Japanese language and orthography in the cartoon caption, use was made of Takanashi's seven reading cues. Further, to account for image text interplay of the cartoons as well as varying literacy levels and reading practices of the time two more cues were added. While giving the historical context of the cartoon, the background of the magazine *Maru-maru Chinbun* and details of the incident the cartoon refers to, the nine cues were used to understand the two frames of the cartoon and how readers would have found and resolved its multiple verbal and visual puns. It is an approach that is well suited to exploring other late-nineteenth-century cartoons and even earlier illustrated Edo print culture, but could possibly be adapted to examine instances of punning from other cultures and times in which visual aspects play an important role.

## Notes

1. Takanashi, 'Orthographic puns', 235–259.
2. Duus, 'Punch Pictures', 307–335.
3. Before post-war rationalisation there were a slightly greater number of characters.
4. Morohashi, *Dai kanwa jiten*.
5. Gottlieb, *Language and Society*, 130.
6. Kawamoto, 'Pun's Not', 38.
7. Ibid., 37–38, 42–43.
8. Kern, *Manga*, 70–73, 170.
9. Ibid., 170. Duus, 'Punch Pictures', 311.
10. Kern, *Manga*, 170–171.
11. This and many other examples can be found in the exhibition catalogue, Tabacco and Salt Museum, *Kore o hanjite gorōjiro*.
12. For examples see, Kon'no, *Kotoba asobi no rekishi*, 22–27.

13. An examination of recent usage of creative punning using *kanji* neologisms in games can be found in, Robertson, 'Unspeakable puns', 1–19.
14. This magazine is accessible in bound reprint form, Kitane, *Maru-maru Chinbun*. Reprints of some complete issues as well as highlights and explanations of many of the magazine's thirty years of cartoons can be found in Shimizu, *Manga zasshi hakubutsukan*.
15. Duus, 'The *Maru-maru Chinbun*', 49.
16. This is a near-homophonic pun on the usual word for editorial *shasetsu* 社説, literally 'social explanations', which changes the character for society *sha* 社 to the character for tea *cha* 茶 which also means irresponsible or half-hearted.
17. Duus, 'Punch Pictures', 309, 313.
18. Ibid., 326.
19. Duus translates the title as 'blue pencil news'. Ibid., 309, 324.
20. For a more detailed account of Nomura and his magazine *Maru-Chin* see in English, Duus, 'The *Maru-maru Chinbun*', 42–56, and in Japanese Kimoto, '*Maru-maru Chinbun*' '*Kibidango*'', and Shimizu, *Manga zasshi hakubutsukan*, 207–213.
21. This is also based on a pun. One negative inflection of verbs is *zaru* ざる which is homophonic with the word monkey *saru* 猿 when used with compound words leading to the first consonant being voiced, *zaru*. So in the three verbs of the expression 'see not, hear not, say not' (*mizaru, kikazaru, iwazaru* 見ざる, 聞かざる, 言わざる) the word 'monkey' reverberates.
22. Maeda, et al., *Kindai manga II*, 38.
23. Ibid.
24. Ibid., 20–21. Also see Duus, 'Punch Pictures', 313.
25. Maeda et al., *Kindai manga II*, 49–50. For a more detailed biographical essay on Honda, see Ibid., 38–39.
26. For an overview of the early-twentieth-century discourse on the overuse of puns in cartoons and the historical change from *ponchi-e* to a modern form of cartooning called *manga* see, Stewart, 'Manga as Schism', 27–49.
27. For example, Attardo, 'Universals in puns', 91–109; Hempelmann, 'Puns', 612–615; Hempelmann et al., 'Puns: Taxonomy and Phonology', 95–108; and Oswald et al., 'Deceptive Puns', 145–171.
28. Kawahara et al., 'Role of psychoacoustic similarity', 111–138; Kawamoto, 'Pun's', 36–43; Dybala et al., 'Extracting *Dajare* Candidates', 46–51; and Dybala et al., 'Japanese Puns', 7–13.
29. The SSTH is an extension of the General Theory of Verbal Humour (GTVH) framework. See Attardo et al. 'Script Theory revis(it)ed', 293–347.
30. Hempelmann argues that while this is the general understanding, a more complex understanding of the LM is necessary to account for imperfect puns where the sounds are similar but not the same. Hempelmann, 'Script oppositeness', 381–392.
31. Takanashi, 'Orthographic puns', 235–259. Another paper that looks at the visual aspects of text in punning is Katherine Shingler's study of the calligrammes of French poet Apollinaire. Examples she gives, such as the character 'c' in word forming the neck of a bird formed by text and 'o' the mouth of a fountain, are similar to the Japanese *moji-e* puns discussed above. Shingler, 'Mad Puns', 19–34.
32. Takanashi, 'Orthographic puns', 241.
33. Ibid.

34. Ibid., 243–245.
35. Yus, *Humour and Relevance*, 279. Also see Hempelmann, Christian et al. 'Cartoons: Drawn Jokes?', 626. On the importance of modifying humour theory to take into consideration visual aspects of cartoons, see Tsukona, 'Language and image interaction', 1171–1188.
36. See cartoon inferential strategies elaborated by Yus for reading cartoons and first example. Yus, *Humour and Relevance*, 279–283.
37. Ibid., 270.
38. Hempelmann, 'Script oppositeness'; Hempelmann, 'Puns'; and Hempelmann et al., 'Puns: Taxonomy and Phonology'.
39. Or in the terms of Attardo 'hyperdetermination'. An exception to this is appreciation of Shakespeare's sustained conversational punning ('ping-pong punning') matches. See Adamczyk, 'Context-sensitive aspects', 105–123.
40. Barthes, *Image-Music-Text*, 32–51.
41. Yus, *Humour and Relevance*, 268.
42. Takanashi, 'Orthographic puns', 236, 246.
43. The standardised punctuation marks of modern Japanese were not yet in use.

## BIBLIOGRAPHY

Adamczyk, Magdalena. 'Context-sensitive aspects of Shakespeare's use of puns in comedies'. In *The Pragmatics of Humour across Discourse Domains*, edited by Marta Dynel, 105–123. Amsterdam: John Benjamins, 2011.

Attardo, Salvatore and Victor Raskin. 'Script Theory revis(it)ed: joke similarity and joke representation model'. *Humor: International Journal of Humor Research* 4, no.3/4 (1991): 293–347.

Attardo, Salvatore. 'Universals in puns and humorous wordplay'. In *Cultures and Traditions of Wordplay and Wordplay Research*, edited by Esme Winter-Froemel and Verena Thaler, 91–109. Berlin: Mouton De Gruyter, 2018.

Barthes, Roland. *Image-Music-Text*. London: Fontana Press. 1977.

Duus, Peter. 'The *Maru-maru Chinbun* and the Origins of the Japanese Political Cartoon'. *International Journal of Comic Art* 1, no.1 (1999): 42–56.

Duus, Peter. '"Punch Pictures": Localizing Punch in Meiji Japan'. In *Asian Punches: a Transcultural Affair*, edited by Hans Harder and Barbara Mittler, 307–335. Heidelberg: Springer, 2013.

Dybala, Pawel, et al. 'Extracting *Dajare* Candidates from the Web–Japanese Puns Generating System as a Part of Humor Processing Research'. *The Proceedings of the First International Workshop on Laughter in Interaction and Body Movement (LIBM'08)*, June (2008): 46–51.

Dybala, Pawel, et al. 'Japanese Puns Are Not Necessarily Jokes'. *AAA Technical Report FS-12-02 Artificial Intelligence of Humor* (2012): 7–13.

Gottlieb, Nanette. *Language and Society in Japan*. Cambridge: Cambridge University Press, 2005.

Hempelmann, Christian F. 'Script oppositeness and logical mechanism in punning'. *Humor: International Journal of Humor Research* 17, no.4 (2004): 381–392.

Hempelmann, Christian F. 'Puns'. In *Encyclopedia of Humor Studies*, edited by Salvatore Attardo, 612–615. Los Angeles: SAGE Publications, 2015.

Hempelmann, Christian F. and Tristan Miller. 'Puns: Taxonomy and Phonology'. In *The Routledge Handbook of Language and Humor*, edited by Salvatore Attardo, 95–108. New York: Routledge, 2017.

Hempelmann, Christian F. and Andrea Samson. 'Cartoons: Drawn Jokes?' In *The Primer of Humor Research*, edited by Victor Raskin, 609–640. Berlin: Mouton de Gruyter, 2008.

Kawamoto, Koji. 'Pun's Not Just for Fun: Towards a Poetics of *Kakekotoba*'. *Poetica* 52 (1999): 37–43.

Kawahara, Shigeto and Kazuko Shinohara. 'The role of psychoacoustic similarity in Japanese Puns: A corpus study'. *Journal of Linguistics* 45, no.1 (2009): 111–138.

Kern, Adam L. *Manga from the Floating World: Comicbook Culture and the Kibyoshi of Edo Japan*. Cambridge, MA: Harvard University Asia Center, 2006.

Kimoto Itaru. '*Maru-maru Chinbun*' '*Kibidango*' *ga yuku* [Maru-maru Chinbun' and 'Kibidango' go their way]. Tokyo: Hakusui-sha, 1989.

Kitane, Yutaka, ed., *Maru-maru chinbun (fukkoku-ban)*. Reprinted edition. Tokyo: Tōkyō Honhō Shoseki, 1981–1984.

Kon'no Shinji. *Kotoba asobi no rekishi* [The History of Wordplay]. Tokyo: Iwade Bukkusu, 2016.

Maeda, Ai and Shimizu Isao, eds., *Kindai manga II: jiyūminken-ki no manga* [Modern Manga II: Freedom and People's Rights Movement Period Cartoons]. Tokyo: Chikuma Shobō, 1985.

Morohashi, Tetsuji, et al. 'Dai kanwa jiten—shūtei dai 2 han'. *Grand Sino-Japanese Dictionary*. Second revised edition. Tokyo: Daishū Shoten, (1943) 1989.

Nagashima, Heiyō. 'Sha-re: A Widely Accepted Form of Wordplay'. In *Understanding Humor in Japan*, edited by Jessica Milner Davis, 75–83. Detroit: Wayne State University Press, 2006.

Ono, Mitsuyasu. *Kotoba asobi no sekai* [The World of Wordplay]. Tokyo: Shintensha, 2005.

Oswald, Steve and Didier Maillat. 'Deceptive Puns: The pragmatics of Humour in Puns'. In *Perspectivas sobre el significado. Desde lo biológico a lo social*, edited by Cristián Noemi Padilla, 145–171. Editorial Universidad de La Serena, 2018.

Robertson, Wes. 'Unspeakable puns: kanji-dependent wordplay as a localization strategy in Japan'. *Perspectives* (2018): 1–19.

Shingler, Katherine. 'Mad Puns and French Poets: Visual-Verbal Punning and 'L'art des fous' in Apollinaire's Calligrammes'. *Nottingham French Studies* 53, no.1 (2014): 19–34.

Shimizu, Isao. *Manga zasshi hakubutsukan—Meiji-hen: Maru-maru Chinbun (jiyūminken-ki)* 1 & 2 [Comic Magazine Museum—Meiji volume: *Maru-maru Chinbun* 1 & 2]. Tokyo: Kokushokankōkai, 1986.

Stewart, Ronald. 'Manga as Schism: Kitazawa Rakuten's resistance to 'Old-Fashioned' Japan'. In *Manga's cultural crossroads*, edited by Berndt Jaqueline and Bettina Kümmerling-Meibauer, 27–49. New York: Routledge, 2013.

Tabacco and Salt Museum. *Kore o hanjite gorōjiro: Edo no hanji-e* [Try solving this puzzle: Edo Period Puzzle Pictures]. Tokyo: Tabako to Shio Hakubutsukan, 1999.

Takanashi, Hiroko. 'Orthographic puns: The case of Japanese *kyōka*'. *Humor: International Journal of Humor Research* 20, no.3 (2007): 235–259.

Tsukona, Villy. 'Language and image interaction in cartoons: Towards a multimodal theory of humor'. *Journal of Pragmatics* 41 (2009): 1171–1188.

Yus, Francisco. *Humour and Relevance*. Amsterdam: John Benjamins, 2016.

CHAPTER 20

# Popular Humour in Nordic Jesting Songs of the Nineteenth and Twentieth Centuries: Danish Recordings of Oral Song Tradition

*Lene Halskov Hansen*

The vicar's name was Jeppe Knud,
The parish clerk's name was Peter,
She pissed their eyes out.
She never pissed again.[1]

What amused the 'common people' in the nineteenth and the beginning of the twentieth centuries in the Nordic Countries, and how did the elite view their sense of humour?[2] One way to answer these questions is to take a closer look at how the common people expressed humour in their jesting songs, and the interactions between text, tunes and performance. Scholarly interest in these jesting songs has been scant in the Nordic countries. To some extent, the motifs, themes and language have been analysed, but not the way in which they were sung and performed. Nor has the humour been given much attention. New angles and methods are needed. This chapter focuses on the performance of these songs. It views humour as a phenomenon that relates to all aspects of life, relations and interactions,[3] and takes as its methodological framework the tripartition of laughter formulated by the Danish philosopher Peter Thielst: 'Det frie, det distancerende og det frigørende grin' [the free, the distancing and the liberating laugh].[4]

---

Chapter translated by senior researcher, PhD. Peter Hauge.

---

L. H. Hansen (✉)
Royal Danish Library, Copenhagen, Denmark
e-mail: lene.halskov@mail.dk

© The Author(s), under exclusive license to Springer Nature
Switzerland AG 2020
D. Derrin, H. Burrows (eds.), *The Palgrave Handbook of Humour, History, and Methodology*, https://doi.org/10.1007/978-3-030-56646-3_20

383

Thielst acknowledges the value of earlier theorists' dualistic views on laughter, counterposing malicious and good humour: for example, irony versus humour and obscene jokes versus harmless ones.[5] Nevertheless, Thielst suggests a three-part division based on the humour's 'væsensforskellige hensigter og funktioner' [fundamentally different intentions and functions of humour]. 'Hvad er det nemlig latteren vil?' [What does laughter seek to achieve?], Thielst asks. His next three questions refer to each of the three types of laughter mentioned above: does it achieve: 'Nærhed og bekræftelse? Forsvar og distance? Eller genkalde tabt glæde og virke frigørende?' [Nearness and approval? Defence and detachment? Or to recreate lost happiness and to have a liberatory effect?].[6] Thielst's tripartite taxonomy gives us the opportunity to look beyond degradation, vulgarity and traces of the medieval carnival laughter as key features, and from this fresh starting point to pay attention to how the songs were performed in the oral song tradition, and why.

## JESTING SONGS—DEGRADATION AND 'THE WORLD TURNED UPSIDE DOWN'

In the context of this chapter, jesting songs are defined as humorous songs that, regardless of type, age and provenance, were disseminated through an oral singing tradition—a tradition in which songs were learned mainly by listening to other people and performed in everyday life. The characters represented in the jesting songs are largely drawn from the singers' environment and daily life: professionals such as farmers, tailors, millers and beer brewers, men and women—young and old—from the poorest people to the wealthy proprietors, clergy and parish clerks. Animals behaving like humans are also represented. By placing in opposition characters from different social classes and from different power levels in general, the lyrics articulate eroticism, adultery, the power struggle between man and woman, the generation gap, social oppression, stupidity, gluttony, and so on. Often, the characters with low status win the struggle.

At first sight, degradation is a pervasive driving force in the songs as in the commoners' other genres of jesting as well. They are basically about fooling and making fun of each other as well as humiliating people in positions of power, in particular the clergy, parish clerks and squires. Until the 1960s most song collectors and researchers described the lyrics as vulgar, rude, low-comedic and obscene.[7] The humour was characterised in similar terms. Texts recorded during the nineteenth century were analysed in the 1980s and 1990s by means of the Russian Mikhail Bakhtin's theory of the carnivalesque laughter culture of the Middle Ages in which hierarchies are discarded and the world is set upside down with grotesque realism and exaggeration: that is, when high becomes low and low high, the bishop becomes the fool and the fool becomes the bishop.[8] In the jesting songs, we find traces of this inversion, mainly among the earliest examples of the genre: the jocular ballads with roots dating back to the Middle Ages. The first and so far the only large-scale work on the jesting songs in the Nordic countries is Olav Solberg's ground-breaking Norwegian doctoral thesis *Den omsnudde verda*, of 1993. One of its conclusions is that the image of the world turned upside down may stir up 'ingrained habits and practices and current issues, and thereby allow problems to come to the surface; things may happen'.[9] In this sense, the songs produce some sort of social critique.[10] As a result of the influence of Bakhtin's laughter theory, however, the versions of nineteenth-century jesting songs and fairy tales have also been seen as a diluted or even a pornographic version of a bygone heyday. The literary critic and professor, Torben Brostrøm, explains in the Danish Encyclopaedia of 1997 that the popular jest represents an afterlife of carnivalesque laughter; it should therefore not be termed a 'modern' kind of humour. According to Brostrøm, the common main ingredients of the jesting fairy tales are 'orgies of shit[,] open mouth and open womb' wherein all fool each other and humiliate their superiors.[11] The same may be said about many of the jesting songs, no matter how old they are.[12]

## Humour as a Way of Perceiving and Experiencing Life

What, then, is humour? The question has been discussed and examined in countless contexts since Antiquity.[13] Even so, or maybe therefore, there is as yet no consensus on a precise and comprehensive definition of the concept of humour—and perhaps there will never be one, as the American researcher, Amy Carrell, argued in 2008.[14] Carrell regards humour as a universal human phenomenon that relates to all aspects of life, relations and interactions, and refers to the psychologist and humour researcher, Harvey Mindess, for further discussion of the subject. In 1971, Mindess defined humour as a frame of mind, a way of perceiving and experiencing life, a kind of outlook on life and a phenomenon that has great therapeutic potency.[15] Regarding a further issue, the relationship between humour and seriousness, Peter Thielst describes it this way: 'latteren kræver, at smerten og medfølelsen ikke pirres frem i forreste linie, men lever diskret som en nuancerende tragi-komisk resonans' [laughter requires that pain and compassion are not stirred to the forefront, but exist subtly as a nuancing tragi-comical resonance].[16] Mindess' and Thielst's views will be employed in this chapter as a platform for studying the humour connected to the jesting songs. I would argue that their concepts open up a broader understanding of the tonality and variety of the humorous songs than Bakhtin's concept of the carnivalesque which only covers the oldest parts of the songs, the ballads. However, first an introduction to the source material will be provided.

## Text, Tune and Sound Recordings

The first Danish ballad scholar, philologist Svend Grundtvig (1824–1883), thought that the songs ought to be recorded for academic purposes but not to be published.[17] Evald Tang Kristensen (1843–1929), a school teacher and folklore collector, believed, however, that they should be made available, partly in order to be able to get to know every aspect of the people, and partly because he believed that there could be more to the jests than meets the eye.[18] Despite Grundtvig's advice and the criticism from prominent cultural figures for daring to 'touch the filthy stuff',[19] Kristensen published with ten years' delay the first large collection of sources of jesting songs in the Nordic countries: *Et hundrede gamle danske skjæmteviser* (1901). The book was reprinted in 1903 with a selection of eighty-eight tunes. However, the most obscene and blasphemous lyrics were not included, and certain words in the songs were replaced with an ellipsis. Evald Tang Kristensen's texts, tunes and sound recordings of jesting songs will form the main part of the source material of this chapter, in addition to his comments on song performance and humour.

Around one hundred versions of forty-nine different types of jesting song were recorded on a phonograph with wax cylinders during the period 1907–1947: in the first year by Kristensen and the archivist at the Danish Folklore Archives, H. Grüner-Nielsen (1881–1953); in 1909–1910, 1912, 1914, 1927, 1929 and 1935 by Grüner-Nielsen; and in 1922, 1925 and 1929 by Kristensen and the Australian-American composer and pianist Percy Grainger (1882–1961). The recordings from 1947 were made by an unknown collector.[20] Except for a five-year-old boy, all the singers were born in the last part of the nineteenth century (Fig. 20.1).

Especially in the early years of the project only a few stanzas of each song were recorded, mainly because the duration of the wax cylinders is only a few minutes and, in addition, because the purpose was first and foremost to record the tunes and not the melodic variations, performance of the songs or the phrasing of the lyrics.

It was Grüner-Nielsen who encouraged Kristensen to make phonograph recordings of those of his informants who were still alive at the time. Kristensen was highly sceptical of the new-fangled recording device but eventually he agreed to participate. He was worried about whether the performers would agree to sing into the phonograph and, furthermore, he preferred rather to rely on his own transcriptions of lyrics and tunes. Later he admitted that the singers did not seem to be affected by the phonograph as much as he had anticipated. He maintained, however, that it was a 'nasty device and, as a whole, it will never be able to reproduce the song either correctly or accurately'.[21] Kristensen had a point, although today we would rather not be without the recordings.

Already in 1906 and 1908, Grainger had made phonograph recordings in collaboration with The English Folk Song Society in London. On a concert tour in Denmark in 1911, Grainger got in touch with Kristensen, and they planned a field study which, as mentioned above, took place in the 1920s.[22]

Most of the phonograph recordings are available on five CDs, *Viser på Valse* (Songs on Wax Cylinders), and on *Youtube.com*, *iTunes Store*, *Spotify* and *Tidal*, see Tables 20.1 and 20.2. Biographical information on the singers, photos and transcriptions of lyrics (all in Danish) as well as tunes are downloadable at www. forlagetkragen.dk.

**Fig. 20.1** Percy Grainger is instructing crofter Jens Peter Jensen on how to sing into the funnel of the phonograph while Evald Tang Kristensen is ready to transcribe the lyrics, 1922. (Photo: H. P. Hansen. Danish Folklore Archives, The Royal Danish Library)

**Table 20.1** Recordings from *Viser på Valse* mentioned in this chapter. *The Types of the Scandinavian Medieval Ballad* (TSB) classification numbers have been added

| CD:no | First lines | Translation | TSB |
|---|---|---|---|
| 5:38 | Kjællingen var så læk i bag | The hag had a leaky bum | |
| 4:68 | Og da de kørte ad vejen hen | And as they drove along the road | |
| 4:20 | Bispens datter i Pile | The Bishop's daughter in Pile | |
| 2:25 | Mads spændte bøssen | Mads cocked the gun | F 54 |
| 4:35 | Lars han hvisked' hans kon' i ør' | Lars whispered in his wife's ear | F 54 |
| 4:44 | Lasselille sig op ad Lundebakken gik | Little Lasse went up the grove's hill | F 54 |
| 5:79 | Og Mads og Las de gange på råd | And Mads and Las took counsel together | F 54 |
| 4:34 | Her Terkild han holder herude | Mr Terkild is waiting out here | |

By analysing both text and sound recordings we are able to investigate the following questions: How is the common people's humour articulated in the singing? How did the singers stimulate or create the jesting in the songs? Which humorous and performative means did they employ? And of what does their humour consist?

388  L. H. HANSEN

**Table 20.2** The singers on *Viser på Valse* mentioned in this chapter, and the year the song/ballad was recorded

| CD | Singer | Recorded |
|---|---|---|
| 5:38 | Ane Jensen (1865–1932), farmer's wife | 1925 |
| 4:68 | Valdemar Bendixen (1895–?), farmer | 1947 |
| 4:20 | Laust (Laurits) Frandsen (1851–1947), farmer and cattle dealer | 1929 |
| 2:25 | Miss Munk | 1909 |
| 4:35 | Peder Øvig (1852–?), retired farmer | 1929 |
| 4:44 | Selma Nielsen (1887–1954), train conductor's wife | 1929 |
| 5:79 | Thyge Jørgensen | 1927 |
| 4:34 | Anton Fløe (1884–?), farmer | 1929 |

## FREE LAUGHTER AND THE GIBBERISH REFRAIN

According to Thielst, 'free' laughter is first and foremost 'legens grin, den umiddelbare munterhed, den smittende latter uden dobbeltbindinger, garderinger eller motiver ud over sig selv, lysten og fællesskabet' [the laughter of play, the immediate cheerfulness, the contagious laughter without double-binds, protection and motives—except oneself, the pleasure and the sense of community].[23] It is a moment when we in that instant detach ourselves from demands of performance, rules and private hobbyhorses, and have no reservation towards others. We find it in childish games, in the erotic, in dance and when eating. The moment can also arise when words are shared in confidence, or turned into associations, playful digs or good stories. Emotions such as intimacy and acknowledgement are associated with free laughter.[24]

The songs' gibberish refrains may typically be an outlet for free laughter. The gibberish consists of non-semantic expressions possibly with the addition of infrequent conventional words, without the refrain having any opinion-forming significance. Such a type of refrain could make even the otherwise very serious Kristensen laugh when he listened to Iver Pedersen (1798–1875): 'Med en uimodstaaelig Humor sang gamle Iver Visen om "Knud Hyrding"[25] og den naaede sit Højdepunkt, da han sang Slutningen: Hurr byen-ne lovv, sov low low, sow lowlowlow! Man kunde ikke bare sig for at briste i Latter' [With an irresistible humour old Iver sang 'Knud the Shepherd' and reached the climax when he ended by singing: Hurr byen-ne lovv, sov low low, sow lowlowlow! One couldn't help bursting into laughter].[26] The ballad is about the shepherd Knud who was known for having a lot of mistresses, including the queen. In the last stanza the refrain appears as a lullaby sung for the shepherd's fourteen babies. Unfortunately, we do not know how Pedersen performed the refrain, but he had ample opportunity to cultivate the different articulations of the consonants l, s, v and w—that is, the words *lovv*, *low*, *sov* and *sow* (*sov* or *sow* in dialect means 'sleep' in Danish). Emphasising the consonants is a well-known narrative device in traditional singing, both in tragic and humorous songs.[27] It was not, therefore, the refrain itself that provoked laughter, but the way Pedersen sang it.

In another humorous ballad, 'Tord af Havsgaard',[28] the Nordic god Thor has lost his powerful hammer. Here the same singer, Iver Pedersen, included a long series of alliteration in one of the stanzas: 'Jer Hammer den er funden | den kan I ikke faa | for den ligger fulde fire | og fyrretyv' Favn i Jord' [Your hammer has been found | you cannot fix it | for it lies in full four | and forty fathoms of soil].[29] The alliteration provides the song with a distinct rhythm and furnishes the stanza with an additional comical touch—that is, playing with words, sounds and rhythm.

On another occasion, Kristensen describes a situation which provides us with a rare insight into the ways in which the performance and the learning of traditional singing intertwine. The performer was Kristensen's first major informant for the songs, Sidsel Jensdatter (1793–1871), who sang 'Høstpigen' [The Harvest Girl][30] with the gibberish refrain 'Levende brav | strunt o mæ vel en drunt om drej | rager der kat over mark og eng | snuller i godt ja vel aa gi russer aa rirum' [Living brave | strunt o mæ vel | a drunt om drej | the cat rummages on field and meadow | snuller in well oh yes gi russer aa rirum].[31] Kristensen explains that 'Sidsel har tidt fornøjet hyrdedrengene med den vise. De har gærne villet lære det forskrækkelige omkvæd, men Sidsel sang det så hurtigt, at de aldrig fik det lært' [Sidsel has often entertained the shepherd boys with this song. They would very much have liked to learn the difficult refrain, but Sidsel sang it so fast that they never acquired it'.[32] It is conceivable that for both Sidsel Jensdatter and the boys there was a great deal of amusement related to the boys' failed attempt to learn, remember and sing the refrain as fast as Sidsel could. It is great fun to be challenged by strange words and phrases and to make them roll off the tongue, and it is amusing to listen to if the refrain is distinctly articulated and rhythmic. It is not a coincidence that we find both short and, not least, long gibberish refrains in the jesting songs and particularly in the old jocular ballads. On the phonograph recordings we have, for example, the peasant woman Ane Jensen[33] (1865–1932) who sings a refrain between the stanza's two lines: 'for en kopsom smælt hendes syrum'; and then after the stanza: 'for en kopsom smælt hendes syrum | for hun var slagen å rasken bom | hun saj po en guldring å spilt å en knap | kanselirum' [For a kopsom smælt her syrum | for she was hidden on rasken bom | she sat on a golden ring and played on a button | kanselirum] (CD 5:38). However, Ane Jensen does not sing nearly as fast as Sidsel Jensdatter must have done (Fig. 20.2).

## Gibberish Refrains Commenting on the Stanzas

Besides giving rise to 'free laughter', the gibberish refrain may also function as a comment on individual stanzas or the song in general. One good example is the refrain to a song about the drunken tailor who falls into a ditch on his way home from the inn and ends up sleeping arm-in-arm with a sow. The refrain in one of the versions goes 'Lem lem lem fur sig en buk | mek mek mek hejså virri | virri vom bom bæjj'.[34] The word *lem* [limb] is a common term for arms and legs as well as the male organ. *Buk* means both a stag and a lecherous man (i.e.,

**Fig. 20.2** Ane Jensen (1865–1932), 1925. (Photo: Percy Grainger. Danish Folklore Archives, The Royal Danish Library)

he is a goat). The words may be sung with varying weight, pronunciation and articulation from stanza to stanza but, in any case, invariably they refer to and speak ironically of the drunken tailor's fate. When the tailor arrives home, his wife hits him on the forehead with his own iron proclaiming that she will now look for another man who is her equal (CD 4:68).[35]

## Dissociating Laughter. Irony in Different Disguises

In a concise definition, irony is a mode of expression where someone with intentional comic or contemptuous effect says the opposite of what is meant. Peter Thielst discusses dissociating laughter as irony in various disguises, a laugh by which reality is kept at an arm's length as when threatening behaviour takes the form of cynical merriment or when a narcissistic staging of sensuality and nearness in fact intends to interrupt and create distance. Irony has often been contrasted with humour where humour has been seen as having a more conciliatory character.[36] Nevertheless, the range of nuances between comedy and contemptuousness can also include empathy.

'Rammer' or 'Unge Ramund' [Young Ramund][37] [also named Rammur] was one of the very popular ballads in Scandinavia during the nineteenth century. The refrain deals mainly with the young hero, Ramund, and his cynical and scornful comments, in particular regarding those enemies whom he encounters on his way to the emperor's daughter. Reading the stanzas without these scornful remarks, some of the versions appear as pure heroic ballads about a giant who successfully and brilliantly defeats other giants and little trolls. Irony arises in the tension between the stanzas and the alternating refrains. Ramund's replies are dry, declaratory and in stark contrast to the bloody plot in which he is the protagonist. The following two stanzas are from a version sung by a woman, Ædel Thomasdatter, recorded in 1871:

> Rammur drog ud hans brune brand [sværd]
> den, han kaldte Dennemliden røde:
> så hog han de syv risserer djer hoveder af,
> te blodet randt dennem til døde.
> —'Her ligger I alle syv', sagde Rammur.
> 'Jeg står alt lige styv', sagde Rammur til de risserer—.
>
> Rammur gik sig ved den samme havsbred,
> der så han den store kæmp' stande:
> halvfjerdsenstyve alen da vare han bred,
> og hundrede det var hans længde.
> —'Vel er du bred og lang', sagde Rammur.
> 'Har du lyst at kjæmpes med mig en gang?', sagde Rammur til den kjæmpe—.[38]
>
> Rammur took out his brown sword,
> the one he called Dennenlinden the red:
> Then he chopped off the seven giants' heads,
> and the blood ran from them until they died.
> —'Here you lie all seven', Rammur said.
> 'I still stand erect', Rammur said to the giants—.
>
> Rammur went along at the same shore,
> there he saw the great giant standing:
> he was 140 feet broad, and 200 long.
> —'You might be long and broad', said Rammur,
> 'do you fancy a quick fight with me sometime?', said Rammur to the giant.

The irony in 'Unge Ramund' is not aimed at the social conditions or conditions of life but retained within the ballad's own narrative. It may also be understood as a parody of solemn heroic ballads.[39]

A more overt kind of irony is seen in 'Bispens datter i Pile' [The Bishop's Daughter in Pile], consisting of several layers of contrasts. In the first stanza of the version by the farmer and cattle dealer Laust [Laurits] Frandsen (1851–1947), the bishop's daughter pisses 'en lille tår' [a tiny drop] so there is enough to work fifteen water mills. On the mountain, she pisses so that five gilded churches with vicar and parish clerk materialise, and they can preach whenever they want. The third and final stanza tells us that the parish clerk's name is Jeppe Knud and the vicar's is Peter, and then she pisses their eyes out and never pisses again. All this is sung to a sweet tune and in a quiet and calm manner. The daughter's good deeds in the first two stanzas fit well with the mild tune and the performance. In the third stanza, however, when the bishop's daughter pisses the vicar's and parish clerk's eyes out, a sudden contrast occurs between tune and performance on the one hand and plot on the other. Tune and performance understate the story while the plot exaggerates it in all its grotesqueness (CD 4:20).

Kristensen, writing about the tunes of the jesting songs and their performance, explains that they are sung by men and women in such a plain and straightforward fashion that one does not in the least feel repelled by the crudeness as one might have thought. The tunes are usually very pretty and promote, furthermore, the popularity of these songs somewhat.[40] In a draft to this foreword, Kristensen explains that the beautiful tunes assist so that 'the raw is better digested'.[41] I have no doubt that Kristensen's observation is correct; however, the clash between gentleness and roughness in the surprising expression of the final stanza also intensifies the grotesque, the absurd and the hilarious. A surprise may typically both provoke laughter and tease or pinpoint an underlying seriousness: here, apparently, a strong displeasure with the vicar's and the parish clerk's power and interference in the lives of the local population or with the vicar and clerk leading a luxurious life compared to that of the congregations is revealed. The incongruent conflict corresponds to the well-known ironic means by which someone says one thing and yet does another. It is similar to when Ramund in the ballad mentioned above speaks in a calm and measured way while at the same time he challenges, scares or kills his enemies.

Another kind of humorous contrast in the song comes in the different lengths of the stanzas. The first two stanzas each has five lines while the final one has only four. The same irregularity is found in other versions of the song as well, and there are also versions where the first stanza or both the first and final stanzas are shorter. Thus, the differing lengths cannot be explained by arguing that the singers have forgotten part of a stanza, even though such irregularities may have been handed down from one singer to another. It is a small detail that the audience might not necessarily notice; nonetheless, it has an effect. A dramatic plot may be described in detail with additional stanzas— typically in a serious ballad—or the plot may be enhanced by shortening the narration as much as possible. The technique is therefore not an irregularity, but rather a narrative ploy using the abruptness to augment the grotesqueness of the daughter's action, and one which may provoke laughter. Using such a ploy might not be a deliberate choice but rather an intuitive and empirical one based on how to narrate a story, incident or event in daily life.[42]

Kristen Rasmussen Egendal (Kræn Rask, 1825–1906) performed the same song in two different versions. In one of them the daughter wishes rather than urinates, and this is the version on which I will concentrate. Instead of the bishop's daughter, it is Jesper's daughter who wishes churches for herself, grain in the barn for her father, cattle for her mother and boats for her brother—all of it in quantities so that they may be content with only working when they feel up to it—and for her sister, she wishes clothes so that she may be married to whomever she wishes.[43] The stanzas appear as if the desires immediately come true, just as in a dream or fairy tale. The relatively many stanzas in this version of Egendal's provide the opportunity for the audience to be able to enter the fantastic universe of the lyrics. The final and shortened stanza seems yet more shocking when the daughter wishes that the vicar and parish clerk lose their eyes and that she will never wish again. Thus, we see a contrast between the violent wish and a consistently attractive and a seemingly calm tune. In both versions the joyfulness points towards the daughter while the vicar and parish clerk become the butt of the irony revolving around repression or poor social conditions. The jesting songs themselves are not specifically aimed at anyone personally, but in a small society the characters in the songs can easily be associated with neighbours, family members, the local vicar or the squire.

As an intermezzo the following, rather special story must be mentioned. Kristensen had once been told that in a village the vicar's wife, for some odd reason, hummed 'The Bishop's Daughter in Pile' while proceeding up the aisle of the church with a child of one of the peasants, who was to be baptised.[44] One must agree with Kristensen and the person from whom he got the story that it was indeed a surprising choice of song. Kristensen also refers to another source reporting that long after her death the vicar's wife was still living on in people's memory. Apparently, she dealt with things in a high-handed way and sold the hay from the meadow without her husband's knowledge. She took good care of her family and sons-in-law while the vicar, 'en krøbling' [a cripple], had to endure in general. It was said, however, that sometimes he did 'pull himself together and used his power'—presumably physically.[45] Whether the lyrics exposed the wife's innermost desire for her husband, the vicar, or whether she just liked the tune, is an open question.

## Vocal Means. Antiphonal Singing, Speech and Voice Imitations

Antiphonal singing in the oral song tradition is based on alternation within stanzas or within refrains. The frame of the dialogue presents several distinct options for comical contrasts that may comprise different kinds of nuances: features of speech and voice imitations which may be formed, mixed and integrated in the lyrics in various ways.

In the song 'Bjørnejagten' [The Bear Hunt],[46] Las and Mas (or Lars or Lass and Mads or Mass in other versions) go on a bear or deer hunt expedition. They are far from familiar with the mission and indeed they meet with an accident. In some versions, dogs bite the testicles of one of them. They therefore seek out some women who are able to stitch the testicles. The women guffaw at the young men. As a contrast to their mishaps and clumsy deeds, Las and

394  L. H. HANSEN

Mas speak together wryly and affirmatively at the end of each stanza. As an additional contrast, the remarks are not necessarily sung but recited in a serious and declaratory manner which makes the young men appear even more perplexed as to what is going on around them. In some versions, the dialogues float between speech and song. Here Miss Munk sings one stanza (CD 2:25):

> Mads satte bøssen for sit bryst
> for sit bryst.
> —Hejsa for det dages—
> Og så skød han bjørnen af hjertens lyst.
> —[talt:] 'Der ligger han', sagde Mads.
> 'Det gør han dæleme regedere mig osse', sagde Las.
> [sunget] 'Det er godt', sagde Mads.
> 'Det er godt', sagde Las.
> Og så vandrer de så let igennem lunden—.

> Mads cocked the gun at his breast,
> At his breast.
> —Hey for the day is dawning—
> And then he shot the bear to his heart's content.
> —[spoken:] 'There he lies', Mads said.
> 'By the devil, so he does', Las said.
> [sung:] 'It is good', said Mads,
> 'It is good', said Las.
> And then they wandered so easily through the grove—.

Contrary to what happens in the Ramund ballad, here the discrepancy between the dramatic incidents and the stagnant reaction falls back on Las and Mads as a not-too-bright pair. It is an indulgent and playful humour/irony which just as much laughs at them as empathises with them—just as we laugh *at* Don Quixote and his battle against the windmills, and at the same time *with* him in silent identification with his hopelessness.[47]

Another version of 'The Bear Hunt' is at CD 4:35, in which one of the characters' lines is spoken while the other is sung; a third version is at CD 4:44, where it is only Lars who has a line after each stanza which is first spoken and then sung when repeated; and finally at CD 5:79, in which the lines float between speech and singing. In a Norwegian version, the lines are recited 'hurtigt og hemmelighedsfuldt som en Samtale. Mass og Lass hviske i Öret på hverandre' [fast and secretively just as a conversation. Mass and Lass whisper in each other's ear].[48]

A section which is recited may also occur in prose between stanza and refrain such as in 'Cousin Mikkel'. The husband has previously caught his wife several times in an intimate situation with Mikkel; however, this time he also finds them in bed. The related spoken commentary is 'Men jeg skuld vel ikke tro, at Fanden skulde fare I knægten, at han skulde tage et spænd eller to dybere end sædvanlig' [But I should surely not believe that the devil would take the lad, so he should reach a span or two deeper than usual].[49] Spoken passages in a verse or a chorus introduce an effect of surprise, accentuating the current mood, underscore an action or highlighting a particular side of a person. With the prose text in 'Fætter Mikkel' [Cousin Mikkel] the contrast between song and spoken passages is even more obvious. The element of comic surprise is further amplified by the fact that one of the characters—the husband—suddenly steps out of the song and becomes a 'real' person who gives us a first-person account of how appalled he is by Mikkel's behaviour. This spoken passage also employs the well-known comic device—an oblique reference to the erotic: 'tage et spand eller to dybere' [reaching a span or two deeper]. We can both laugh at the poor husband and laugh with him, for lacking the resolve to confront his wife with her infidelity. Instead he asks time and again in the chorous:

> But yet it will not do, and is it right?
> my wife cannot live without cousin Mikkel,
> that gawky underling.[50]

A particular type of jesting song has the so-called *snyderim* [cheating rhyme]—words that rhyme and that, from the context in which they are used, are expected to be naughty but are replaced with an innocent word that also rhymes, though moving the sense of the stanza in an entirely different direction. One version of 'The Madam in Køge' contains a sung section in each stanza asking for the naughty word; however, the reply is a pleasant one. Even if the song is very rude, Kristensen writes, it cannot be denied that it is also very funny: 'A great comical effect is achieved during the song when each vocal part or the chorus joins in with a statement comment that is also sung'.[51]

The stanzas in the jesting songs may be formed as dialogues, as for instance with a single performer imitating the voices of both husband and wife, mother and daughter, or doctor and patient. Thus, the performer's imitation of the daughter, for example, is in a high voice while the mother is given a deeper and a coarser one. In some cases, the structure of the tune supports the distinction. The voice imitations may be exaggerated or be close to ordinary speech (for an example, see CD 4:34).

## Liberatory Laughter

In the words of Thielst, liberatory laughter does not only act as an outlet. Rather than settle on the gravity of protest and objective confrontations this type of laughter chooses 'den punkterende, løsslupne latter, som i ét hug skærer sig igennem absurditet, fremdgørelse og undertrykkelse' [the exploding, unrestrained laughter, which in one stroke cuts through the absurdity, alienation and repression]. Basically, it stems from pain but the liberatory laughter would not get far without the help of free laughter, with its capacity to allow danger and push limits. Its particular purpose is to recall lost joy.[52] The song about the bishop's or Jesper's daughter in Pile might equally be described by the category of liberatory laughter as the ironic and distancing type.

'Husband Plays with Wife' is a clearer example of liberatory laughter—certainly if one is a woman. The song takes up the issue of gender, more so in some versions than in others. The plot of the song corresponds to the well-known storyline of short, comical and clichéd narratives in oral tradition in which two main characters fight in order to take over; however, the instigator ends up as the loser which in this instance is the husband.[53]

The song is based on the premise that it is the man who is the head of the household and from that point of view the plot takes several unexpected turns. Surprise is a recurring humorous effect and, together with the degrading of a superior person, it helps transform a serious subject, in this case changing violence into comedy with a somewhat absurd touch (Fig. 20.3).

In Mette Marie Jensdatter's version, the husband and wife sit happily talking together, whereupon the husband, without warning, accuses his wife of not having been a virgin when they started dating. It is a surprising remark occurring during cheerful conversation although it does not necessarily provoke laughter. The first unexpected twist in the song is the wife's rash and straightforward answer: irrespective of whether she was virgin or not, she is as she is and, by the way, just as good a wife as he is a husband. She knows her true worth. The wife verbally pulls him down from his self-appointed pedestal as the head of the family. And then 'hurrah' for that, as the refrain goes: 'Hurrah for you and me, I say, | and the day will never be forgotten'.[54]

Quick and brazen answers were widespread and appreciated among the common people. This is evident in songs, fairy tales, legends and various stories about people's lives. It is a way to manage both the world of reality and imagination. A brazen remark employs surprise or suddenness as a humorous tool of attack or defence.

**Fig. 20.3** Mette Marie Jensdatter (Mette Skrædder, 1809–1895), 1895. 'A strong memory, a living imagination and a natural, poetic talent'—that is how Kristensen characterised her. Kristensen, *Gamle kildevæld*, 62. (Photo: Peter Olsen. Danish Folklore Archives, The Royal Danish Library)

In the second stanza, the husband tries to regain his position as head of the household, slapping his wife in the face and remarking that any Danish husband should do so when his wife does not obey him. In this one stanza the refrain may be interpreted as the man's voice.

The second unexpected twist arises in stanza three when the wife, on the same premise, replies to the husband's physical outburst with a more powerful blow than his initial smack. She takes her spinning wheel and hits him on the forehead. It is easy to imagine that it must have knocked him to the ground. It is so exaggerated—presumably—that it makes one laugh. It certainly requires strength and speed to get hold of the spinning wheel and hit the husband before he dodges the blow. We must take the song at its word, just as a movie playing in the mind's eye of the singer and audience. In one out of fourteen versions, the wife hits her husband with the distaff (a small stick on the spinning wheel); in two versions, she hits him neither with the spinning wheel nor the distaff. From the plot's point of view, it is not important whether it is the one or the other she is hitting him with; from a comical and humorous angle, it does make a difference, however. There is not so much force in the distaff, and therefore neither in the comical aspect, as if she had used the whole spinning wheel. After having hit her husband, the wife replies that this is what any Danish woman should do when her husband goes mad. And now it is he who has to follow her orders.

In one of Plato's dialogues, Socrates and Protarchus discuss laughter and comedy. Socrates concludes that human beings are ridiculous when they pretend to be something which they are not, or, in particular, more than they are, whether that be in monetary affairs or their own loftiness. Self-deception and self-overestimation provoke laughter of any kind.[55] The husband in the song plunged headlong into a role which he could not fulfil and made a laughing stock of himself. Before giving up, however, he goes out into the woods to cut some sticks in order to beat his wife into line. Nevertheless, after three days of fighting his wife assumes control beating him into line with his own sticks. The increasing violence from stanza one, in which the wife first hits her husband with her spinning wheel, to stanza three in which she beats him with rods, turns the song into a slapstick comedy at the same time as a certain amount of unsentimental realism lurks beneath the surface.

In fifteen of Kristensen's sixteen versions—in addition to four broadside ballads—the song ends when the husband surrenders or leaves the house, meets his neighbour's wife and with great annoyance and self-pity recounts the course of events. However, besides Mette Marie Jensdatter's version, one pamphlet has a final stanza with a third and the most significant and unexpected twist in the plot: the neighbour's wife is so encouraged and inspired by her neighbour's report that she will return home and do the same to her spouse. The neighbour's wife is transformed from a subordinate character to the main character in the final stanza. The reasonableness of a wife not wanting to succumb to her husband is increased—some would be amused and rejoice, and others would probably not:

Og du har leget med konen din i dag,
så begge dine öjne de rinde;
så har hun vist nok banket dig i dag,
og det som en ærlig dannekvinde.
Sådan har jeg hørt, at du har gjort ved din,
og sådan vil jeg hjem at prygle på min.
—Hurra for dig og mig, siger jeg,
og den dag forglemmes aldrig.—[56]

And you have played [so much] with your wife today
that your eyes are running;
so, she has no doubt beaten you today,
and that as an honest Danish woman.
I've now heard that she did that to you,
and I'll return home and flog mine.
—Hurrah for you and me, I say,
and that day will never be forgotten.—

Only the one who has assumed control and has sufficient mental resources can say with irony, 'hurrah for you and me' and with pleasure recall the unforgettable day. For the spouse there is not much reason to say hurrah; he is only able to grieve. The ironic tone in the refrain intensifies the more the quarrel develops.

Is the song pure entertainment or does it make the woman who is singing or listening to the song proud? Does it leave traces in important ways beyond the comical—as, for instance, optimism or a renewed courage to fight? If so, it is more than merely a vent for accumulated dissatisfaction.

## BEHIND THE MIRTH WITH EVALD TANG KRISTENSEN

Evald Tang Kristensen has been chosen as the chapter's central focus—not only because he is regarded as one of the world's greatest personal folklore collectors, but also because he managed to get very close to his informants.[57] He literally went from door to door to seek out singers and narrators, eating and spending the night at their homes. The former senior researcher at the Danish Folklore Archives, Palle Ove Christiansen, names Kristensen as the first Danish field worker.[58]

As Kristensen got to know these often extremely poor people, his national-romantic outlook developed into a more social view focused on the connection between the singers, their manner of singing and their repertoire. His records are more precise, and his points of view and observations are more modern than those of his contemporary collectors and scholars. Kristensen recorded the first songs in 1867 and made his last field study together with Percy Grainger in 1927. In 1928, Grainger wrote that Tang Kristensen was—

> the greatest genius known to me amongst folk-song-gatherers anywhere in the world. None other seem to me to have delved as deep as he to the very roots of

folk-music—to have held as dear as he its every shade of feeling from wistful purity to rankest coarseness.[59]

Kristensen dealt with almost all genres of folklore and of popular jesting such as fairy tales, songs, legends, riddles and sayings. He repeatedly pointed out that behind the jest often more than mirth is hidden. He wrote that one should not regard the jesting legends as merely superficial 'as if they were simply made for amusement'.[60] There is—if not in all then at least in many of them—

> a certain thought, or a certain attitude to life that, through particular images, has been brought to life by the oral narrative and precisely therefore is able to be instilled more clearly and more firmly in the consciousness of the audience than the frankly cold presentation of subjects, rules of conduct, thoughts and so on.[61]

According to Kristensen, even those legends that are told in order to entertain may also have a practical function. They can help to 'avert baseless attacks, to fight back when attacked, to spice up one's whims, to behave towards one's superiors and thus assert one's human rights and so forth'.[62] The legends were, without doubt, instrumental in affirming norms and rules of conduct but at the same time were apparently also a tool for challenging superiors by going against injustices and stating rights. He points out that 'the peasant'—men as well as women—should not be judged according to what they sing or like to listen to. Their way of expression in everyday life is very 'bold' and they use many 'plump phrases'.[63] However, that must not lead us to think that they are crude in their being; rather, the opposite is true. Since 'everything has been said straight out and called by its proper name' they have avoided 'muck in the mind', and as everything went 'quite natural' no one was offended.[64] Children could also listen without difficulty.[65]

## CONCLUSION. HUMOUR, LAUGHTER AND ACTUAL REALITY

The common people of the nineteenth and early twentieth centuries have to a large extent been responsible for their own daily, musical entertainment with a song tradition based on oral and aural practices and informal learning. That has created a foundation of humorous expression in songs that were developed communally as well as individually.

By choosing performance as the overall framework, humour as a phenomenon that relates to all aspects of life, relations and interactions, and Peter Thielst's tripartition of laughter, it has been possible to extend our understanding of the humour of the jesting songs beyond the notion that they merely instantiate the carnivalesque. The present analyses have shown us that common people could deal with different humorous devices and nuances in their song performance and hereby create a free laughter without intentions, a distancing laughter with a sympathetic or sharp irony, and a liberating and unrestrained laughter built on seriousness and a touch of the free. The songs and ballads and the laughter they generate have a more wide-ranging character than the degrading and/or carnivalesque.

Although the jesting songs do not contain the ambiguity and drawn-out suspension of other more contemporary kinds of humour, the comical aspects do challenge social issues, the controversies of everyday life, acts of folly, tragedy, repression and unfairness. We see and hear the underlying seriousness of these challenges in the interaction and contradictions between lyrics, tunes and performance: between sections of speech and singing, between tunes and voice imitations, between different voices in antiphonal singing, or between a calm or solemn expression in contrast to a dramatic plot.

It is well known that laughing at something comical may produce a sudden thought, a reflection in the person laughing. Laughter is very often 'an indication that a new place of observation—perhaps merely for one second—has been born and lets a world of subjects become visible in an unexpected and very appealing way'.[66] Literature, art and music—also including songs of an oral tradition—are often approached with an 'either-or' question: does it preserve society or is it subversive, is it conservative or liberating? The media and performance researcher, Amber Day, argues against the polarised positioning of entertainment and plot as incompatible opposites and maintains that the answer is more likely a 'both-and'.[67] With the wide range of individual expressions of songs which have been presented here, there is reason to believe that jesting songs are entertainment and may, at the same time, have given rise to afterthought influencing everyday life on at least a small scale.

## NOTES

1. DFS 1929/21, 'The Bishop's daughter in Pile', quot. Kresten Rasmussen Egendal (Kræn Rask, 1825–1906).
2. 'Common people' and 'commoners' are used throughout for Danish *almuen*, non-elite, non-clerical poor people, most of whom lived in the countryside and in small villages and towns, comprising most of the population.
3. Carrell, 'Historical views of humor', 306.
4. Thielst, *Det onde og latterens lyst*, 272.
5. For example, Søren Kierkegaard and Sigmund Freud, quot. Thielst, *Det onde og latterens lyst*, 202, 234–235, 271.
6. Thielst, *Det onde og latterens lyst*, 272.
7. Dal, *Nordisk folkeviseforskning*, 223, 225
8. Bakhtin, *Rabelais and his world*.
9. Solberg, *Den omsnudde verda*, 173.
10. Ibid., 169–176.
11. Brostrøm, 'Humor', vol. 9, 63.
12. For example, Jansson, *Den levande balladen*, 203.
13. For example, Carrell, 'Historical views of humor', 303–332; Keith-Spiegel, 'Early Conceptions of Humor', 3–39; Knuutila, 'Humorforskningens teori og praksis', 38–59.
14. Carrell, 'Historical views of humor', 306.

20 POPULAR HUMOUR IN NORDIC JESTING SONGS OF THE NINETEENTH... 401

15. Quot. Ibid., 306.
16. Thielst, *Det onde og latterens lyst*, 193.
17. Letter dated 10 Nov. 1881; quot. Kofod, *Evald Tang Kristensens syn på folke-minderne*, 126.
18. Kristensen, *Et hundred gamle danske skjæmteviser*, 5.
19. Ibid., 5.
20. All the recordings are incorporated in Danish Folklore Archives (DFS), The Royal Danish Library, Copenhagen.
21. Nielsen, 'Evald Tang Kristensens møde med fonografen', 82–90.
22. Grainger, *Danish Folk-Music Settings*, no page numbers; DFS 1929/143, seventy-three letters from Percy Grainger to Evald Tang Kristensen.
23. Thielst, *Det onde og latterens lyst*, 272.
24. Ibid., 272.
25. DgF 427 and TSB D 394. 'Knud the Shepherd' is categorised as a ballad in Grundtvig et al., *Danmarks gamle Folkeviser* (DgF), vol. 7, 313 and vol. 11, 349, and in Jonsson et al., *The Types of the Scandinavian Medieval Ballad* (TSB), 186.
26. Kristensen, *Gamle kildevæld*, 29; a drawing of Iver Pedersen is included.
27. Hansen, *Balladesang og kædedans*, 149–150, 156, 158–167, 177–178, CD nos. 2 and 3.
28. DgF 1.
29. TSB E 126 and DgF 1Ca, in Grundtvig et al., *Danmarks gamle folkeviser*, vol. 4, 581. Neither DgF nor TSB categorises the ballad as a humorous ballad.
30. TSB F 72.
31. Kristensen, *Jyske folkeminder*, vol. 1, xvii, 25.
32. Ibid., 25–26.
33. Alias Ane Nielsen Post.
34. Kristensen, *Et hundrede gamle danske skjæmteviser*, 223.
35. Ibid., 221–224.
36. Thielst, *Det onde og latterens lyst*, 274–276.
37. Categorised as a heroic ballad, DgF 28, but also as a humorous ballad in Kristensen, *Et hundrede gamle danske skjæmteviser*, 9–16.
38. Kristensen, *Et hundrede gamle danske skjæmteviser*, 10.
39. Hansen, "Ironi og forvirring i 1800-tallet", 114, 125–131.
40. Kristensen, *Et hundrede gamle danske skjæmteviser*, 5.
41. DFS 1929/26, [7–8].
42. Hansen, *Balladesang og kædedans*, 18–19.
43. Kristensen, *Et hundrede gamle danske skjæmteviser*, 31–32, tunes, 5–6.
44. Kristensen, 'Levende Kildespring', cols. 7.
45. Ibid., cols. 7–8.
46. TSB F 54. The Nordic designation for the oldest jesting songs—jocular or humorous ballads with roots going back to the Middle Ages—are named TSB F; cf. Jonsson et al., *The Types of the Scandinavian Medieval Ballad*, 269–291.
47. Katz, 'Humor. Humor, psykologisk', 66.
48. M. B. Landstad, *Norsk Folkeviser*, 671.
49. Kristensen, *Et hundrede gamle danske skjæmteviser*, 201.
50. Ibid., 200–201.
51. Ibid., 271.
52. Thielst, *Det onde og latterens lyst*, 276.

402  L. H. HANSEN

53. Bausinger 1967, 126; cf. Solberg 1993, 45–46; Hansen, "Et lystigt slagsmål"; Hansen, "Perspectives on Common People's Humour.
54. Kristensen, *Et hundrede gamle danske skjæmteviser*, 119–120.
55. Plato, *Philebus*, quot. Thielst, *Det onde og latterens lyst*, 189–190.
56. Kristensen, *Et hundrede gamle danske skjæmteviser*, 120.
57. Dal, *Nordisk folkeviseforskning*, 80.
58. Christiansen, "From Collection to Fieldwork".
59. Grainger, *Danish Folk-Music Settings*, no page numbers.
60. Kristensen, *Danske Skjæmtesagn*, [1].
61. Ibid., [1].
62. Ibid., [3].
63. Kristensen, *Et hundrede gamle danske skjæmteviser*, 6.
64. Ibid.
65. Ibid., 4.
66. Nielsen, *Holbergs komik*, 28.
67. Day, *Satire and Dissent*, 3.

## Bibliography

Bakhtin, Michael. *Rabelais and His World*. Cambridge, MA: MIT Press, 1968.

Bausinger, Hermann. 'Bemerkungen zum Schwank und senien Formtypen'. *Fabula* 9 (1967): 118–136.

Brostrøm, Torben. 'Humor. En moderne opfindelse'. In *Digternes paryk. Studier i 1700-tallet. Festskrift til Thomas Bredsdorff*, edited by Marianne Alenius et al., 323–334. Copenhagen: Museum Tusculanum Press, 1997.

Brostrøm, Torben. 'Humor'. In *Den store danske encyklopædi*, edited by Jørn Lund, vol. 9, 62–64. Copenhagen: Gyldendalske Boghandel, Nordisk Forlag, 1999.

Carrell, Amy. 'Historical Views of Humor'. In *The Primer of Humor Research*, edited by Viktor Raskin, 303–332. Berlin: Mouton de Gruyter, 2008.

Christiansen, Palle Ove. 'From Collection to Fieldwork. The Field Research of Danish Folklorist Evald Tang Kristensen, 1870–1890'. In *Scientists and Scholars in the Field: Studies in the History of Fieldwork and Expeditions*, edited by Kristian H. Nielsen, Michael Harbsmeier and Christopher J. Ries, 191–223. Aarhus: Aarhus University Press, 2012.

Dal, Erik. *Nordisk folkeviseforskning siden 1800. Omrids af text- og melodistudiets historie og problemer især i Danmark (Universitets-Jubilæets danske Samfund, 276)*. København: J.H. Schiltz Forlag, 1956.

Day, Amber. *Satire and Dissent. Interventions in Contemporary Political Debate*. Bloomington: Indiana University Press, 2011.

DFS. Unpublished sources from Danish Folklore Archives, The Royal Danish Library. 1929/21, 1929/26, and 1929/143.

Grainger, Percy Aldridge. *Danish Folk-Music Settings. No. 9 Jutish Medley*. London: Schott & Co Ltd., 1928.

Grundtvig, Svend et al., ed. *Danmarks gamle Folkeviser*. 12 vols. Copenhagen: Universitet-Jubilæets Danske Samfund, 1853–1976.

Halliwell, Stephen. *The Poetics of Aristotle. Translation and Commentary*. London: Bloomsbury, 1987.

Hansen, Lene Halskov. 'Et lystigt slagsmål. Perspektiver på almuens humor i 1800-tallet'. In *Lekstugan. Festskrift til Magnus Gustafsson*, edited by Mathias Boström, 111–130. Växjö: Smålands Musikarkiv/Musik i Syd, 2015a.

Hansen, Lene Halskov. 'Ironi og forvirring i 1800-tallet. Perspektiver på viseforskningens alvor og almuens humor'. In *'En alldeles egen och förträfflig National-Musik'. Nio författare om 'Svenska folk-visor från forntiden' (1814–1818)*, edited by Märta Ramsten & Gunnar Ternhag (Acta Academiae Regiae Gustavi Adolphi, 139), (Skrifter utgivna av Svenskt visarkiv, 40), 113–134. Uppsala: Kungl. Gustav Adolfs Akademien för svensk folkkultur, 2015b.

Hansen, Lene Halskov. 'Perspectives on Common People's Humour in Nineteenth-Century Denmark through Comic Songs and Ballads'. In *Ethnic Mobility in Ballads. Selected Papers from the 44th International Ballad Conference of the Kommission für Volksdichtung*, edited by Andrew C. Rouse and David Atkinson, 96–108. Pécs: Spechel, 2017.

Hansen, Lene Halskov. *Balladesang og kædedans. To aspekter af dansk folkevisekultur*. Summary in English, incl. 1 CD. Copenhagen: Museum Tusculanum, Københavns Universitet, 2015c.

Jonsson, Bengt R. et al. *The Types of the Scandinavian Medieval Ballad. A Descriptive Catalogue*. (Skrifter udgivne af Svenskt visarkiv, 5), (Instituttet for sammenlignende kulturforskning, serie B, 59). Oslo: Universitetsforlaget, 1978.

Katz, Benjamin. 'Humor. Humor, psykologisk'. In *Den store danske encyklopædi*, edited by Jørn Lund, vol. 9, 64–66. Copenhagen: Gyldendalske Boghandel, Nordisk Forlag, 1999.

Keith-Spiegel, Patricia. 'Early Conceptions of Humor. Varieties and Issues'. In *The Psychology and Humor. Theoretical Perspectives and Imperial Issues*, edited by Jeffrey H. Goldstein & Paul E. McGhee, 3–39. New York: Academic Press, 1972.

Knuutila, Seppo. 'Humorforskningens teori och praksis'. In *Humor och kultur* (NIF Publication 34), edited by Ulf Palmenfelt, 38–59. Turku: Nordic Institute of Folklore, 1996.

Kofod, Else Marie. *Evald Tang Kristensens syn på folkeminderne*. Copenhagen: Dansk Folkemindesamling, 1984.

Kristensen, Evald Tang. *Jydske Folkeminder, især fra Hammerum Herred. Samlede af Evald Tang Kristensen*, vol. 1, xvii, 35–26. Copenhagen: n.n., 1871.

Kristensen, Evald Tang. 'Levende Kildespring'. *Viborg Stift Tidende* 93 (1877).

Kristensen, Evald Tang. *Danske Skjæmtesagn samlede af Folkemunde af Evald Tang Kristensen*. Aarhus: Forfatterens Forlag, 1900.

Kristensen, Evald Tang. *Gamle danske skjæmteviser. Efter nutidssang samlede og for størstedelen optegnede af Evald Tang Kristensen*. Aarhus: Jacob Zeuners Bogtrykkeri, 1903.

Kristensen, Evald Tang. *Gamle kildevæld. Portrætter af danske eventyrfortællere og visesangere fra århundreskiftet*. n.p.: Nyt Nordisk Forlag, 1981.

Landstad, M. B. *Norske folkeviser samlede og udgivne af M.B. Landstad*. Oslo: Norsk Folkeminnelag, Universitetsforlaget, 1968.

Nielsen, Erik A. *Holbergs komik*. Copenhagen: Gyldendal, 1984.

Rossil, Helen. 'Viser på valse—vokale vinkler'. *Danish Musicology Online* 7 (2015): 83–105. www.danishmusicologyonline.dk.

Solberg, Olav. *Den omsnudde verda. Ein studie i dei norske skjemteballadane*. Oslo: Solum, 1993.

Solberg, Olav. 'Kropp, kjønn og komikk i danske skjemteviser'. In *Svøbt i mår. Dansk folkevisekultur 1555–1700*, edited by Flemming Lundgreen-Nielsen and Hanne Ruus, vol. 2, 161–182. Copenhagen: Reitzel, 2000.

Thielst, Peter. *Det onde og latterens lyst*. Frederiksberg: Det lille Forlag, 2001.

*Viser på Valse* (*DFS 13-17*), Five CDs. Copenhagen: Forlaget Kragen.

CHAPTER 21

# Spanish Flu: The First Modern Case of Viral Humour?

## Nikita Lobanov

'I had a little bird, Its name was Enza, I opened up the window, And in flew Enza'[1] was a popular children's jump rope song during the years of the Spanish flu that shows the social impact of a pandemic that killed an estimated 50 to 100 million people worldwide between 1918 and 1920.[2] Culture, populations and politics were transformed irrevocably by the pandemic wave because, while often forgotten, the Spanish flu matched the extension of changes wrought by the still on-going World War I:

> The Spanish flu was significant—if not more so—as two world wars in creating the modern world; in disrupting, and often permanently altering, global politics, race relations, family structures and thinking across medicine, religion and the arts.[3]

Spanish Flu became the result of 'millions of discrete, private tragedies'.[4] The outcome of a historical pandemic is a social phenomenon as much as it is a biological one, woven 'into the fabric of communal memory'[5] in different layers. The flu itself took its name, erroneously, thanks to the fact that Spain was one of the few states that allowed the free circulation of information during war time.[6]

The world was facing a complex process of globalisation.[7] The counterreaction to this process after the flu and the war was to be significant. These processes of the changing meanings of death, and humour, heavily influenced

---

N. Lobanov (✉)
University of Bologna, Bologna, Italy
e-mail: nikita.lobanov2@unibo.it

© The Author(s), under exclusive license to Springer Nature Switzerland AG 2020
D. Derrin, H. Burrows (eds.), *The Palgrave Handbook of Humour, History, and Methodology*, https://doi.org/10.1007/978-3-030-56646-3_21

405

how cartoons and newspaper articles were framed for the different national audiences.

It looks like humour followed the viral advance of Spanish flu. For example, authorities were ridiculed by intellectuals and civil society as fearmongers. The opposite was true as well, for instance with jingles such as 'Obey the laws And wear the gauze/Protect your jaws From Septic Paws', a warning for US citizens.[8] Spanish flu became a health crisis suspended between dark hilarity and tragedy. Stories, some funny and other simply absurd, such as adverts and 'miraculous' snake-oil merchandise, multiplied in the wake of the first wave of the flu. Everyone suspected everyone:

> Did the German chemical company Bayer lace aspirin—its 'drug of the century'—with a deadly substance? Or had Hun[9] spies spread vials of lethal bacteria in America's water supplies?[10]

Conspiracies became the 'new normal' in societies that had been engulfed by war for years until that point. Survivors reported a hazy mental state as high fever altered their perceptions of reality. Individual stories, cartoons and jabs often encased a feeling of desperation and detachment from reality.

Feasts and art were a frequent response to the pandemic[11] and provided spontaneous instances of catharsis. Boundaries became stretched into, sometimes perverse, non-seriousness. Post-flu rapes are a notable example.[12] On a brighter note, artistic creativity also exploded, for example due to survivor guilt, because 'for decades after, people had a chronic sense of what might have been—of "alternate histories"'.[13] Psychological defence mechanisms functioned through a bitter post-flu irony:

> Whenever anyone asked Samuel about his parents, he would tell them they had died of the Spanish flu. And if someone replied that this was quite impossible, since the Spanish flu epidemic had reached Brazil at the beginning of the twentieth century, he would respond: 'Well, maybe it was Asian flu; I didn't ask it for its passport'.[14]

The impact of the flu would be deeply embedded in every nation hit. Is it possible to trace how the seeds that the Spanish flu left blossomed? This chapter will attempt to deepen the connection between humour, often through cartoons, and Spanish flu in the UK, Italy and Russia.

## METHODS AND TOOLS

The dataset gathered for this inquiry consists of a selection of newspaper articles and cartoons, mostly focused on the first wave of the Spanish flu during October-November 1918. I chose to focus on newspapers and cartoons because these represent a viable compromise between well-preserved items and capture narratives of the period as well as humorous tropes and techniques that were popular for artists and journalists at the time. This selection was conducted by visiting archives and browsing digitalised collections for instances of intersections between flu and humour in four languages: English, Italian, Russian and Ukrainian. The nature of my investigation represents a niche of historiographic research that requires processing great quantities of data. My goal is to provide a wide spectrum of sources and secondary literature to diversify available perspectives of what flu was at the time.

My research was conducted between summer and autumn 2018 and spring and summer 2019. It comprises a sizeable sample of texts/cartoons for each country, each of which required a specific approach. While cartoons and other material were gathered through mostly digitalised archives, the extraction of material regarding Italian events was focused often on individual artists (e.g., Bianchi, Menotti) and independent items (such as poster cards, posters, etc.) as well. Russia represented a unique challenge, due to a general lack of data on humour and the flu, that was resolved through a wider focus on materials that included propaganda and war posters of the Civil War. The focus on each country provided a lucid picture of the flu of 1918 from different angles while maintaining the cohesiveness of the sample.

## Methodological Challenges

Historical research faces staggering complexity. The first challenge is that the researcher has to submerge him or herself into the chosen historic period's values and norms. The second one is in the mistakes that should be avoided: 'narrow sectarianism, narcissism and self-adulation'.[15] In particular, one's ideological and national identity often provides a justification to 'adjust' the results of historical research. Great historical narratives such as the Spanish flu create a shared traumatic memory for historians from Germany, Britain and France, for example.[16] Humour as an unpredictable variable makes historical research even more complex because 'monocausal explanations simply do not work'.[17] Understanding humour requires different perspectives because 'we historians cannot, alas, actually be present, with notebooks, tape-recorders and cameras, at the events we describe'.[18] The narrative form provides the much-needed flexibility to write about humour and historical events through academic rigour and a clearly defined story.

The approach to humour extracted from data depends on 'preferences for various factor analytically-derived humor categories'.[19] Values of the time can be better unlocked through the understanding of symbols and forgotten stories. 'Theoretical absolutism' becomes less relevant in this research process. The 'cultural-evolutionary' potential of a 'set of symbols' used to represent the pandemic, such as the image of a 'hooded reaper', is key to understanding. For example, some historical instances of humour could mirror cartoons, images and metaphors that circulate in contemporary societies. As Polimeni and Reiss state: 'Reviewing the 95 humorous situations led us to the same broad conclusions as previous anthropologists—that humor in traditional societies grossly appears similar to our own'.[20] The wealth of historical material and studies points to the fact that a historian is required to apply the techniques and methodologies of different disciplines to achieve proper comprehension.

Cartoons changed throughout history while conserving common structural features. Use of symbols to create meaning remains a central quality of this art form. Often symbols aimed at clarifying a cartoon's deeper meaning will be delivered in a way that provokes humour.[21] In-culture knowledge capital usually characterises these symbols and allows for a working interpretation.

> Attempting to understand a different culture's humor usually requires a shift in perspective, and recognition that the way reality is viewed depends upon (and varies according to) a set of cultural assumptions, concepts and values.[22]

Exploring the biography and the motives of the author allows for an understanding of his or her moral matrix.

In this analysis, priority is given to understanding the values of the given historical period, country, social class and so on that emerge by 'by linking the content of ironic works with historiographical-social themes'.[23] This priority lay in the capacity of the author to understand biographical details and reconstruct their identities through their art. It is humour that often emerges as a tool in mediating between identities and values. As highlighted in the work of Christie Davies, historical occurrences of humour can be regarded as a fundamentally moral phenomenon.[24] Furthermore, the evolution of cultural items, such as cartoons, newspaper articles, posters and so on should be analysed not only as historical material artefacts but also as signals in the analysed society of an information-psychological layer as proposed by Gramsci.[25] These different perspectives, theories and the consequent collection of methodological strategies will be used together to expand on selected countries impacted by the Spanish flu. This methodological approach is useful for avoiding the dangers of revisionism and misleading historical sources and provides the possibility of fully and innovatively exploring the selected case study.

The consideration of different points of view, methodological approaches and the values of the historical actor diminish the risks of misinterpretation. Theoretical determinism is the first historiographic danger of historical research, regardless of the focus of the given undertaking. Humour throughout history can be explained through successful and daring methodological strategies while avoiding the established dangers of historiography.

## ITALY

The Spanish flu left a lasting mark on Italy. Italy had one of the highest mortality rates in Europe[26] and several regions had neither medical material nor personnel.[27] Nevertheless, Italians joked about the flu, verbally and in cartoon form. It is still possible to hear jokes born during the flu period in some Italian villages today, with Spanish flu being used as a curse for misbehaving children.[28]

At the start of the 'Black October' of 1918, when Spanish flu entered its viral phase, the newspaper *Avanti* portrayed the epidemic as 'the conqueror of Europe'.[29] The virus is dressed as Napoleon in a fierce pose over the European mainland. Doctors and scientists that fought against the disease described it as cowardly, semi-comical, comfortable, for all naïve lazy acts were a source for humour.[30] The different hypotheses about the nature of the flu were also ridiculed because 'un altro parla di peste polmonare, un quarto di meningite, un quinto di malattia coleriforme, un sesto di grippe' [another one talks about lung plague, a fourth person of meningitis, a fifth of choleriformic disease, a sixth of gripe].[31] Sometimes, doctors themselves laughed off this new disease.

The newspaper *Il Mulo*'s rubric 'E—chi (se ne [...] impipa)' [and who gives ... a toss] is an apt example. The first trope of this article was to make fun of the provenance of the flu. The second is to associate Spanish flu with disgust, with toilet humour, through the suggestion that panic results in a 'spontaneous evacuation':

> A proposito della pandemia che serpeggia in Europa e che va sotto il nome di febbre spagnuola, ad onta delle proteste della Spagna che si ostina a chiamarla febbre [...] napoletana; il professore Kulstijon di Chicago ha scoperto che essa ha avuto le sue origini in Bulgaria, e quindi deve denominarsi febbre bulgara. Il malore si manifesta con una tremarella improvvisa, della volgarmente Fifa e con appariscenti disturbi intestinali. Tra i vari rimedi atti a curare il malore, il professore Kulstijon consiglia un paio di pantaloni [...] di ricambio.[32]

> With regard to the pandemic that is spreading around Europe like a snake and goes by the name of Spanish flu, against the protest of Spain that continues to call it a Neapolitan flu; professor Kulstijon from Chicago found out that she originated in Bulgaria, and so it should be called Bulgarian flu [*sic*]. The sickness manifests itself with a sudden tremor, commonly called Fear and visible intestinal problems. Among the various remedies that are useful to heal the sickness, professor Kulstijons suggests a pair of trousers for a [...] change of clothes.

Patriotism is used here to suppress information circulation through humour. Citizens' concerns were downplayed to re-direct the masses towards victory in the Great War.

> Dopo tutto la cittadinanza deve rimanere tranquilla e fiduciosa, e non lascarsi impressionare da voci esagerate a riguardo specialmente della gravità della malattia e della mortalità imputata alla medesima, voci non degne di fede perché messe in giro da persone affatto incompetenti.[33]

> After all that happened citizens should remain calm and trustful, and not be impressed by the over-blown voices regarding in particular the seriousness of the disease and its mortality, voices that are not worthy of trust because put out by people that are totally incompetent.

Journalism aligned with the Italian monarchy used ridicule to suppress news on the flu. A cartoon in *Il Mulo* (20 October 1918) entitled 'La Grippe Spagnola' exemplifies such patriotic graphic art. The patient asks the doctor how he is faring and in the next scene he is dead with a couple at his funeral that comment: 'he was so happy to dodge the draft!' The pandemic is seen as a punishment for people's immoral behaviour. The author is shifting between disease as punishment and the visually humorous seen in the patient's comically overstretched mouth.

On the other hand, another theme for humour were the inaccuracies of the civic authorities. Repression produced 'humorous rebellions' as faulty information was given to readers with clearly ironic elements to strike the point home:

> [...] concetti errati dei quali—proprio noi—abbiamo un tempo imbevuto il pubblico, che è soddisfatto perché la difesa contro i germi è in rapporto diretto col puzzo che emanano i disinfettanti, come se i microrganismi avessero il naso come abbiamo noi.[34]

> [...] erroneous concepts which we gave the public to drink and who is satisfied as if defence against germs is in direct relationship with the stink of the disinfectants, as if microorganisms have a nose like we do.

This trend manifests itself in other stories that I was able to collect. The public health functionary goes on in the interview with a funny story that illustrates the dangers of mass panic. He describes the survivor of a town whose population died from cholera, that berates Death for the great number of victims. Death replies:

> 'Non darmi più colpa di quanto io abbia'—disse la morte.—'Io avevo ordinato al colera di fare un terzo solo delle vittime che si sono avute fra i tuoi concittadini. Gli altri due terzi sono dovute al fatto che la paura mi è venuta, con generosa spontaneità, in aiuto'.[35]

> 'Don't give me more blame than I already have'—said death—'I've ordered cholera to claim only one third of the victims of your fellow citizens. The other two thirds are due to the fear that arrived with me, with generous spontaneity, to help'.

The end of the war and the waning of the flu provided an outlet for a carnivalesque joy that had previously been repressed, similar to the Black Death centuries before. Such was the extravaganza in Milan on 6 October 1918 due to the request of armistice by Austria, as narrated by Anna Kuliscioff, that it engulfed the city in a 'joyful insanity'.[36] The city folk's passivity was equally sudden two days later with 'no soul alive on the central square', a true 'mystery'.[37] Turati also, sadly, jokes about the flu, saying on 13 October that 'trincee di libri non ci possono salvare da questa piaga' [not even trenches of books can save us from this plague].[38] Furthermore, Spanish flu provoked a proliferation of 'snake oil' sellers like elsewhere in the world. 'Health' merchandise and the medicine 'craze', in a country ravaged by a daily struggle to survive, were often wrapped up in irony in newspapers. In the '*Resto del Carlino*', during the first wave of the flu, a reader ironically reports a brief interaction in a Bologna pharmacy about how people have to humiliate themselves to obtain quinine.[39]

Cartoonists exemplified the symbolism of flu in these events. Frate Menotti, the pseudonym of the cartoonist Menotti Bianchi, ironically depicts the arrival of 'Our Lady of Spanish Flu' in a cartoon of September 1918: an ethereal, green skinned woman with skeletons in the background bringing the promise of a cemetery full of coffins. Authorities were mocked too: Menotti tackled the way Baglio, a government official, had tried without much success to fight Spanish influenza in Canosa. He is ridiculed, portrayed as a public cleaner with a giant canister of carbolic acid strapped to his back.[40] The school and the pupils that try to help Baglio represent the mass at the centre of the image, the projection of struggling crowds that meet influenza.

Left-wing newspapers attempted to resist authorities by using humour as a tool of subversion. In the first extract, criticism against the state is structured with a widely encountered trope where authorities are passive and cowardly.

> L'organnizzazione (sic) di difesa dell'epidemia, non esiste, di fatto—[…] da noi, si tira avanti come in tutte le necessità cittadine: quattro parole al pubblico dettate dal momento e poi si lascia correre.[41]

> The organization of defence from the epidemic, factually does not exist—[…] everybody tries to go forward as in all citizen necessities: four words to the public about what happens now and then let it run away.

These newspapers criticised and defended doctors and scientists at the same time. A clear way to oppose the authorities was to underline their passivity regarding the lack of clear communication and the absence of infrastructure, even when the first wave of the flu was weakening in November 1918. The next excerpt is an example of this attitude in ironic form.

> Siamo nel periodo decrescente? Non sappiamo in modo certo. […] La mortalità continua però e non ci consta che l'apertura di uno ospedale, come si era deliberato, sia in via di fatto. Le misure arriveranno, ancora, quando l'epidemia sarà finita?
> Nessuna meraviglia è successo sempre cosi.[42]

> Are we in [the flu's] weakening period? We do not know for sure […] mortality goes on—and there are no clues that the opening of a hospital, as was decided [by the local authority], is under way. Will these measures be applied only when the epidemic is over?
> No wonder, this is the way it always happens.

Humorous criticism towards the state and local authorities in Italy was the main position of left-wing newspapers, their anti-war stance providing a counterbalance to the patriotism of the rest of the press. The humour of these left-wing newspapers was more refined than that aligned with the government. It avoided censorship by using irony and indirect mockery, and became the main channel of resistance for Italian society in the context of Spanish influenza.

## Great Britain

The impact of the Spanish flu in the United Kingdom was widely regarded by newspapers across the country as an issue that originated somewhere foreign, the 'Spanish' flu. The impact of the pandemic was mostly uniform in its mechanics on British soil.[43]

On a local level, often the reaction to the Spanish flu was characterised by the needs of World War cohesion, similarly to Italy. The UK authorities tried to calm the population and there were 'attempts by local health authorities and newspapers to detract from the seriousness of the pandemic the evident effects of influenza'.[44] Local newspapers downplayed the impact of the flu and ridiculed local protests and avoided official figures on the number of the sick and dead citizens. On the other hand, authorities were uncertain on how effectively to communicate instructions to the public to contrast the pandemic's effects.

At the height of the flu, newspapers of the time indicate an increasing need to entertain the population. Some segments of the public did not want to give up going to theatres or races, even in the face of a growing body of sick people. The rhetorical question for cities and villages was that 'members of each community should consider which is of benefit to them, a night of 'Charlie Chaplin' and similar thrills, or the services of a nurse'.[45]

> The column about influenza appears on a back page sandwiched between the motoring news ('a two seater sports car for 100 guineas') and the prospects for the race meeting at Pontefract. One column heading is 'Scarcity of whisky'.[46]

Eventually, in major cities such as Birmingham and Manchester, public authorities started to warn citizens about what was truly happening and acted to some effect.[47] Moreover, the authorities, due to the war effort and the pandemic threat, asked people, even at such dark times, to be openly joyful. This state of mind was required and encouraged on all levels, amongst all 'loyal' subjects of the Crown:

> It is the buoyant man or woman, who sees the bright side of things, who can most easily conquer disease germs, and there is much that is happening, even in the midst of victories, to present dark side of things to many thousands every day.[48]

The reaction to the flu was shaped by the need for collective cohesion, of keeping the social structure intact in the final stages of the war. State and local authorities actively employed ridicule for the task of social management and control.

Those sick with flu acquired a close-to-pariah status. For example, they were ridiculed if they did not segregate themselves at home. The title of this article, in the *Daily Mirror*, contains by itself a surprising ironic take: 'What to do with our influenza heroes?' The first point, after making fun of 'doctorese' language, was that one's class position was the deciding factor for surviving the flu anyway:

21 SPANISH FLU: THE FIRST MODERN CASE OF VIRAL HUMOUR? 413

We conclude, after mouthing such plaguey syllables as 'meningococcic' and 'saprophylic'—oh that doctors had never heard of Greek!—that here is no cure, no remedy, small hope and little help. Usually the advice as to how to keep from any plague is: 'Have a large fixed income'.[49]

The second point is that those who are sick but decide to continue to work and not stay at home should be heavily penalised by society. They, by being sick, are themselves the 'virus incarnate'. The lines of the article have an intentionally funny 'beat':

He spreads the influenza germ. He is the meningococcus rampant. She is the micrococcus passant. Kill her. Try to convince her she is not a heroine. Send her home. Kick him out. [...] We suggest that influenza should be notifiable at least so far as this: That all who notify that they have it on them should be punished with penal servitude, or bed.[50]

The punchline is that these 'influenza heroes' should be punished with penal servitude, or as an equal alternative, bed. Another funny comment in the article's conclusion is that the afflicted themselves should notify the whole of society and authorities of their infection to be removed from the wider society. Lighter comments and cartoons were provided by other newspapers as well.

The *Daily Mirror* published several cartoons about Spanish influenza authored by William Kerridge Haselden. A cartoon entitled 'How to avoid Span'sh influenza' was addressing the first instances of flu in the UK.[51] A worried man is shown on the left of the frame, in various brief caricatures: avoiding crowded streets, walking to avoid public transport, resting, avoiding taxis, acting scared to a lady simply asking 'how do you do Mrs. Jones?'. On the right of the frame a tower touching the sky with a food package, attached with a cord to the highest window of the tower, being delivered with a sign 'Notice to aeroplanes—don't come near' signed: the only solution. The cartoon ridicules the safety advice of 'experts'. The seemingly 'useless' idea to avoid everybody is absurd for the author, who asks 'Don't talk to anyone, don't go near anyone, and you are safe!'[52] The answer is straight forward 'No doubt. But is not this a little difficult?'[53] Doctors and experts faced contempt and were ridiculed in some form or another at the start of the flu. In October, when the Spanish flu had reached its height, the tone of the public did not change. In a cartoon entitled 'The city worker and the influenza plague.—No. 2', a worker asks a self-entitled doctor for an advice.[54] This cartoon shows the routine of a worker in six different scenes, worrying at home before going to work, under the rain while walking to work with an umbrella, at the office with other workers coughing and sneezing, taking a crowded train to go home, the alternative to train pictured as more walking, and finally home again: to start sneezing himself. The omnipresence of the influenza, and the fear of getting sick itself, captured in the cartoon through the repetition of the word 'Achoo!' provide an ironic frame while the numbers of deaths from the flu started to rise. The author writes:

414　N. LOBANOV

he tries to follow doctor's orders and to avoid wet feet, crowds and fatigue. But how is this possible under conditions of modern life? When he gets home he feels the dreaded symptoms.[55]

In this cartoon, while medical authorities are still criticised, the author is now aware of the deadliness of the flu. This awareness can be observed through the 'sound' of sneezing and the visible saliva that provide a disgust-based tag to the disease avoidance behaviour for those that managed to avoid influenza.

The symbolic evolution of this awareness emerges in the archetype of influenza as the Grim Reaper. This cartoon, 'The Passing Enemy', by Gordon Brewster, in the *Irish Weekly Independent*, describes the ironically grim acceptance of the British populace for this new plague.[56] Death with influenza on her scythe marches through the lands reaping lives, something to which you can only resign yourself. The spirit of 'Why should I try to do something about the flu if nothing could be done' was well described by a mayor:

> A heavy sense of anxiety and apprehension like a dismal cloud in midsummer weighs heavily upon us because of the deadly ravages of the so-called Spanish influenza. Funerals jostle one another so the sable procession goes on.[57]

It is from this sense of utter end that communities embraced a pendulum, between desperation and increased excitement with sporadic instances of humour.

## The Russian Empire

The case of the Spanish flu in the Russian Empire, later engulfed in a civil strife between the newly formed Red Army and anti-Bolshevik forces, had unique features compared to other European countries. It seems that the Spanish flu was described and perceived as a component of a wider picture: hunger, death by a bullet and repression, other diseases.[58] Its impact was perceived as just another calamity of that period. That is why some images drawn for newspapers showed the rising epidemic danger of Czarist Russia in an 'ultra-serious' tone. One reads: 'Мы здесь даёмъ зарисковку забольевшаго тифомь вь подваль вь моментахь посьщения больного врашемì [...] Грустная и безтродная картина!' [Here we provide a sketch of a (person) sick by typhus in a basement during the moments of a visit by a doctor. A sad and hopeless image!].[59] The picture is dark, barely sketched and evokes the hopelessness of a terrible disease. The author asks himself: 'is it typhus?' Uncertain medical authorities, which in the Italian and British cases were ridiculed, here are criticised for the dreadful difficulty of understanding the disease. Still, an article in the newspaper above the 'sad and hopeless image' attempts ridicule towards the only aspect that could become funny for readers. Entitled 'Холерой торгують' [Cholera Traded], it makes fun out of sellers at the market using the disease: 'Вь Москвь холерой торгують. Посмотрите на продавцовь моченыхь груш и кваса—вьдь это страшный ядь' [in Moscow they trade in Cholera. Just look at the sellers of marinated pears and kvas—these are (the prices) of the scariest poison].[60] The Spanish flu became a propaganda tool first, but still it was a major topic of grim humour for Russian cartoonists and newspapers.

The population faced a crumbling polity and wide-spread misery. The speed at which Spanish flu and other diseases expanded in different locations in the Russian empire contributed to this feeling of helplessness. This process contributed to an epidemic spiral, especially for smaller towns and villages that lacked professional medical help:

> the overwhelming majority (perhaps as many as 80 percent) died from hunger, cold, and disease (especially the pandemics of typhus and Spanish Flu) that were attendant upon the social and economic Gomorrah of the civil wars.[61]

Old rituals had a new resurgence. Hebrew minorities organised black weddings, in cemeteries that according to tradition, while being incongruous and somewhat ironic, provided protection against diseases:

> Following a wave of black weddings in Kiev and other cities, a group of Odessan merchants had got together in September, when both the cholera and ispanka epidemics were waxing, and decided to organize their own.[62]

The ceremony was meant to encourage participants by celebrating life in a cemetery, a ritual that merged with the absurd to 'slay' the disease. Sometimes, chance and the rituals worked hand in hand: 'on 8 October, Bardakh announced that the epidemic had passed its peak, allowing the organisers of the black wedding to claim that their efforts had paid off'.[63] Moreover, the sense of imminent apocalypse fuelled the desire to live each day as one's last as 'Odessans continued to pursue their pleasure, and in the midst of all the killing and carousing, the Spanish flu returned'.[64] On the other hand, propaganda campaigns to stop and control the sick population were wide spread on a local level, such as in the Zabaykalskoya Oblast.[65] *Svoboda*, the oldest existing Ukrainian newspaper, started to promote 'miraculous' products. While based in the US, Ukrainians in Galicia and Bukovyna, in the Russian Empire, also subscribed to it:[66]

> ІНФЛЮЕНЦА—СЕ СТРАШНА ГИДРА і відрубайте їп голову одним те їп голову одним ЗАМАХОМ. У Ж ИЙТЕ Кальваріиське Вино Лїчниче.
>
> INFLUENZA—THIS SCARY HYDRA and you should cut her heads with one SWING. EVERYONE SHOULD DRINK the Healing Wine from Kalvar.[67]

While this advert is not directly humorous, it includes a colourful metaphor and irony presenting influenza as a mythical monster that can be miraculously defeated.

The response of the population was placed on a scale that went from hysterical mania to suicidal desperation. Placed between group reaction and individual physiology affected by a febrile state, people embraced the unprecedented 'weirdness' of the overall situation.[68] This could explain the response of the population portrayed through cartoons. For instance, the report of the chief of the Communist Mobile Emergency Committee mentions the peasant Pryazhin:

> который подозревался в том, что с женой и тремя взрослыми сыновьями нарочно ходили по улице, будучи в болезненном состоянии и распространяли «испанку» на всех жителей, [...] посему дом расстреляли из винтовок и сожгли со всеми бывшими там людьми[69]

> who was under suspicion, that with his wife and three grown-up sons walked around the alley on purpose while being in a sickened state and spreading the Spanish flu to all inhabitants, [...] therefore the house was shot repeatedly by rifles and then burned down with all the people inside.

These apocalyptic events influenced the aesthetics of cartoons and propaganda of all factions in Russia in this period. Spanish flu in the image of the Grim Reaper was this time projected onto political adversaries. The focus of the nationalist or White propaganda was that 'Bolshevism was depicted not as an adversary for the battle of ideas, but as a some kind of a disease, an evil madness'.[70] In the propaganda poster of 1918, the frame of 'Lenin and Trockij, the doctors of a sick Russia' emerges. The two are depicted looming over Russia as a woman with dark hair with her hands tied and wrists bleeding, armed with knives. The spilling of innocent blood underscores communist brutality. Ultimately, the White attempt to win hearts and minds by using anti-Bolshevik propaganda proved to be too 'anti-' and not 'pro-' enough.[71]

On the other hand, Russian revolutionaries used propaganda as a weapon of the revolution, trying to present a brighter future instead of the miserable present. The massive number of sick, especially in the Red Army, encouraged that shift in toward discussing a brighter future instead of the miserable, sick, present. 'Typhus, influenza, smallpox, cholera, typhoid and venereal diseases were the main killers, but many more men suffered from various skin rashes, stomach bugs, dysentery and toothache'.[72] Pro-Bolshevik authors constantly and 'mercilessly ridiculed capitalists, corrupt politicians and spineless yes-men', often through disease metaphors.[73] Whites (nationalists) were portrayed as a black infection on the body of the healthy nascent Soviet Union and as slaves of the 'Czar-weakling'. A cartoon published in *Petrogradskaya Gazeta* on 14 July 1918 depicts the Tsar as a child, with a crown too big for his head, grabbing the black tunic of Cholera depicted as the Grim Reaper. The disease is used as a tool to ridicule the traditional authority figure, the Tsar, and convince like-minded citizens that loyalty to a toddler holding a woman's gown is misplaced. The whole body of pro-Bolshevik art evokes the contrast between physically broken, sickly looking and ugly enemies of the Proletariat that fought gigantic and healthy soldiers of the Red Army. Ironically, disease and disgust were central to Bolshevik efforts. In a cartoon, a woman carrying a sign saying 'The Party of Essers and Mensheviks' is trying to enter a communist worker's cooperative while a small upright pig dressed up in a smoking jacket is holding her gown: 'Товарищи, не пускайте "эту даму." за хвостикь тетеньки держался!' [Comrades, don't let 'this lady' inside. He was holding his auntie's gown].[74] The class enemy is dehumanised while opposite political currents are 'tagged' as an ideological contagion. The mirroring of the cartoon on the Tsar, with the Mensheviks in place of the Cholera, is uncanny.

Lenin himself, with dark irony typical of his love for humour[75] was writing to one of his collaborators, Inessa Armand, that 'the times are bad: jail-fever, influenza, Spanish flu, cholera. I've just got up and I will not go outside'.[76] It seems that the flu and other diseases became a key dimension for different factions engaged in the civil war. For the citizens of the Russian empire, the *smuta* or 'Time of Troubles' of the seventeenth century returned with a vengeance two centuries later, this time with a contagious laugh.

## ANALYSIS

European societies that emerged after World War I and the Spanish flu as well as other epidemics were deeply changed, especially concerning how they understood progress. Cleanliness became what civilised meant after the horrors of the invalids, sick and dead. For example, in Germany the national relief law of the 1920s[77] guaranteed free healthcare.[78] Moreover, these developments empowered radical political currents across all of Europe, with the lessons learnt during the 1918–1920 period applied to the propaganda of cartoons and disparaging humour. As Narayanaswami underlines: 'The "Us vs. Them" theme became particularly explicit as Germany began its war on aggression, and showed a picture perfect German mother and child, contrasted with an abject poverty-stricken Bolshevik family, with a man who resembles the Nazi Jewish caricatures'.[79] The nascent Nazi movement exploited this kind of ridicule based on disgust towards minorities through images and language to coalesce a national consciousness and accelerate radical political tendencies for concrete electoral gains.

Similarities between the UK, Italy and Russia are evident in the feelings of physical and moral disgust that emerged during pandemics. A sick person was often seen as morally corrupt because of the 'causal relationship between feelings of physical disgust and moral condemnation'.[80] The use of class and race to identify 'repugnant' minorities became the trademark of radical political currents. Schaller and Park's conception of the 'behavioral immune system' identifies 'psychological mechanisms' that:

(a) detect cues connoting the presence of infectious pathogens in the immediate environment, (b) trigger disease-relevant emotional and cognitive responses, and thus (c) facilitate behavioral avoidance of pathogen infection.[81]

This helps to explain the perception of the Spanish flu in those living through it, for example, pathogen presence seemed to shift attitudes towards the conservative end of the political spectrum.[82] Eugenics, an established set of proto-scientific beliefs in 1918, became increasingly popular worldwide because of a 'toxic cocktail of an idea: people who caught infectious diseases only had themselves to blame'.[83]

Carnivals emerged both as a tool for validation to those in power but also to channel discontent. A condition of humour during the flu seems to have been ritualistic ridiculousness, embracing the trickster archetype in the face of adversity.[84] The reaction to Spanish flu was often to mock authority and break rules, embodying the behaviour described by Jung. The newspapers reported that there are cholera, flu and 'in this tiny corner of the peninsula, *fiestas*'.[85] Festivities provided the occasion to unleash this 'unusual surge of excitement'.[86] Apocalyptic laughter resulted in a crescendo through cartoons and carnivalesque rituals.[87] There was an interest in 'the lower things, sexual matters, what is blasphemous and to which it holds while mocking the law'.[88] Darker elements of the carnivalesque surfaced as 'a double stance between disgust and laughter, apocalypse and carnival'.[89] This process is consistent with Bakhtin's definition that carnival was 'the feast of becoming, change, and renewal'.[90] The flu indirectly provided the conditions to unleash 'great changes', which 'even in the field of science, are always preceded by a certain carnival consciousness'.[91] Post-flu writers such as Pirandello, Beckett and Kafka explored absurdity and nonsense humour.[92] The more wicked aspects of this fascination were described by Lovecraft.[93] Smith suggests that 'the equation of immigrants entering a country to disease infesting a body can be observed directly in Lovecraft's fiction', as for instance in 'The Horror at Red Hook'.[94] Journalists and cartoonists were 'characterised by a swing from a mock-serious tone, to the comic or sardonic, providing a malleable space'.[95] While responsibility, fear and information frames[96] were widely present, ideological and disgust frames expanded with the flu's tragedy. Each of the analysed countries had unique quirks and responses to the Spanish flu.

In the UK, suppression of news on the flu by the newspapers and its downplay through ridicule were widespread, often using a polite style. Doctors were targeted through newspapers such as the *Daily Mirror* that, at the time, focused on middle-class audiences. For example, those citizens who were active while sick were ridiculed as if they actively wanted to infect others. There was a transition from behaviour connected to the Spanish flu to humorous art, and cartoon strips were present in great quantities in the UK, a well-established trend. Information was disseminated through graphic art, sometimes with a cartoon series that focused on the influenza for several days.

Italian newspapers and cartoons shared some similarities with the UK. Italian medical personnel were in alliance with the authorities and less subject to ridicule while still criticised. The impact of influenza was assessed as a moral issue, a punishment for bad behaviour or cowardice. In Italy, newspapers and cartoon symbolism were often deeply connected to traditional ritualism and described a carnivalesque response to the flu. Due to more intense left-wing activity in Italy, there was much more opposition to authorities in comparison to the UK.

The Russian Empire is a unique case. Influenza was a part of civil unrest and other epidemics as well as the civil war that followed. The social environment was brutal even in the context of World War I. Such unprecedented suffering resulted in extreme seriousness, dark humour and absurdity. These peculiar conditions were exacerbated by a climate of political polarisation that contributed to mapping ideological adversaries through disease symbolism. Bolshevism became a disease while Whites were feeble parasites. Rituals and carnivals became the easy answer for minorities that took refuge in their own traditions. The memory of the Spanish flu was for Soviet elites a myth of the civil war won.

Does the impact of a pandemic provoke humour? Flu, and the war, provided a new way to reconceptualise humour and tragedy through the idea of masses where 'heroes of cartoons turned into primitive little men in the crowd, the symbols of the absurd world, portrayed as herd animals, duplicates traveling from one cartoon to the next'.[97] Yet, people embraced tragedy through absurdity because 'cartoons thrive in a social environment where the dissatisfaction of the majority creates the need to release the energy of social discontent'.[98] This release manifests itself in a social mechanism in which, in a country afflicted by a pandemic, the opposing sides of the existing political confrontation each capitalise on the situation. Each of the two sides will project the qualities and characteristics of the pandemic, such as death imagery, sickness, weakness and so on, onto the opposition using humour to further ridicule the adversaries. To conclude, I am putting forward a hypothesis about the hidden social essence of widespread diseases that provoke a reaction in the population that is evoked through humorous graphic representations by artists that try to capture feelings of despair and disgust to transform or enhance an emotional response. This process usually results in a back and forth between the wider population and the artists that evoke an effect in the material world by eliciting spontaneous collective action.

## Conclusions

Humour during the Spanish flu is a little-explored aspect of the pandemic. This study attempts to shed light on whether humour through cartoons, newspapers and rhymes can shape the behaviour of the sick and healthy alike, and to establish how. Three different countries provide different but unique perspectives, ideologically and individually, of how people answer to deadly pandemics when humour is involved. The main goal was to capture the 'spectrum of humour' involved when disgust in large groups is heightened by an environmental shift. The proposed cartoons, symbols and newspaper articles' framing allow for new possibilities for interpreting how humour could function as an accelerator of people, groups and nations into concrete action long before the internet revolution. The fascinating aspect of the feedback loop between the Spanish flu and humorous items in the 1918 media and the carnivalesque surge

420  N. LOBANOV

is that increasingly blurred moral boundaries seem to contribute to both jollier and darker aspects of the 'collective intelligence' actions in each country. This results in the interplay between humour, irony, tragedy and disgust that validates a complex perspective on how these elements intermingle:

> by expanding the humour and irony—system and introducing a highest common denominator equivalent to 'The world isn't as it "should" be' which would be something like 'Out of this world', and an equivalent polarity principle consisting of the primary emotional realities of charm (attraction) on the one hand and horror (repulsion) on the other.[99]

Further research on other pandemics with the above-mentioned attraction-repulsion polarity in mind can unlock and elaborate the ways in which the two poles interact with the collective consciousness of the afflicted.

The research process has to adapt and improve from existing research its methods and chosen ways to deliver and interpret the extracted knowledge from archives, newspapers of the time and so on. To use new findings in different fields, for example psychology, and integrate it with traditional historiographic research is an enriching way to elaborate historical data:

> In writing histories of humor, historians may explore how people use humor strategically in diverse contexts as, for example, socially as protest against the conventions of society or individually for self-definition.[100]

Several cohesive frameworks are emerging to generate the necessary complexity for historiographic research.[101] The goal of the modern researcher is to select the appropriate collection of methodological strategies while integrating them into a solid narrative.

The last legacy of the flu was the detached irony of the survivors because 'the story of the Spanish flu is about truth'.[102] The post-flu phase, with the tragedy of World War I still alive and well, becomes the search for truth on how to survive and 'better forget', through humour and cartoons. This process had an impact for decades on different levels: from the obsession with cleanliness and cartoons that portray the Jewish people as corrupt, to the rise of absurdist literature, to the impossibility of the Soviet Union to distance itself from the 'war-communism' conditions that gave birth to its initial structure and values. New diseases such as swine flu and Ebola, and other events that heighten disgust perception such as migration waves, could have similar social and political effects. Understanding humour and other facets during the Spanish flu is the best way to disentangle ourselves from the social and cultural dangers of pandemics. A poem written by Winston Churchill at the age of 15 on the 'Russian' flu, the 1889–1890 predecessor of the Spanish flu, describes the impact of a pandemic:

> For though it ravaged far and wide

Both village, town and countryside,
[...]
Its power to kill was o'er;
And with the favouring winds of Spring
[...]
(Blest is the time of which I sing)
It left our native shore.[103]

Ironically, Churchill would discover, during the 1940 Blitz enacted by Nazis obsessed with purity and cleanliness, that the legacy of flu was to last far longer than he had expected.

## NOTES

1. 123HelpMe.com, 'Children's Songs' Popularity in 1918'.
2. See Poon, 'Remembering'; crucially, she also underlines the vulnerability of current pandemic preparedness.
3. Spinney, 'The flu', 3.
4. Ibid., 5.
5. Ibid., 6.
6. Davis, *More Deadly Than War*, 2.
7. See Daudin, Morys and O'Rourke, 'Europe and Globalization'.
8. Reported in Crawford, '1918 Spanish flu'.
9. A derogatory term for Germans in the Allied countries. It is believed to have originated from a famous speech of Wilhelm II of 1900. See for example Musolff, '*The afterlife*'.
10. Davis, *More Deadly Than War*, 26.
11. See Carrade, 'The Black Death'.
12. Caulfield, *In Defense of Honor*, 2–3.
13. Davis, *More Deadly Than War*, 191.
14. Canetti, *Party in the Blitz*, 240.
15. Stone, 'The Revival', 4.
16. Geremek, 'Common Memory', 37.
17. Ibid., 13.
18. Ibid., 14.
19. Martin, 'Approaches to the sense of humor', 50.
20. Polimeni and Reiss, 'The First Joke', 359.
21. Neighbor, Karaca and Lang, *Understanding the world of Political Cartoons*, 7.
22. Ibid., 21.
23. Barkai, 'Historiographic Irony', 2.
24. Davies, *The Mirth of Nations*, 8.
25. Gramsci, *Note sul Machiavelli, sulla politica e sullo stato moderno*, 41.
26. Percoco, 'Health Shocks', 3.
27. See Magistro, *l'anno della Spagnola*. Magistro underlines that in Basilicata, an Italian region, the lack of state intervention during the Spanish flu did not spark initiatives at a community level, a notable difference from Black Death, with each family left isolated.
28. Ibid.

29. Scalarini, 'Il Conquistatore dell'Europa', 1. Translation by the author. Throughout this is indicated by 'tba'.
30. Bertarelli, '*Rivista d'Italia*', 228.
31. *Il Resto del Carlino*, 'L'influenza', 3, tba.
32. Sprone, "E—Chi (se ne.... impipa)—La febbre spagnuola," 4, tba.
33. *Piccolo*, "La febbre Spagnuola," 2, tba.
34. *Il Resto del Carlino*, 'La salute pubblica', 3, tba.
35. Ibid., tba.
36. Turati and Kuliscioff, *Carteggio*, 1026, tba.
37. Ibid., 1031, tba.
38. Ibid., 1052, tba.
39. *Il Resto del Carlino*, 'L'influenza', 3.
40. For the use of Carbolic Acid for sanitary purposes, see Simpson, *Note on the history of carbolic acid*, 7.
41. *Il Socialista*, 'Cronaca—L'inflnenza' [sic], 17 October 1918, 2, tba.
42. *Il Socialista*, 'Cronaca—L'influenza', 7 November 1918, 2, tba.
43. Johnson, *Scottish'flu–The Scottish Experience Of 'spanish Flu'*, 218.
44. Corfield, *Death and Disease*, 4.
45. Ibid., 19.
46. Butler and Hogg, 'Exploring Scotland's influenza pandemic', 364.
47. He et al., Inferring the causes', 6.
48. *North-Eastern Daily Gazette*, 'The influenza epidemic', 3.
49. 24 Oct. 1918, 3.
50. Ibid.
51. *The Daily Mirror*, 27 Jun. 1918, 6.
52. Ibid.
53. Ibid.
54. *The Daily Mirror*, 17 Oct. 1918, 6.
55. Ibid.
56. Brewster, 'The Passing Enemy', 2 Nov. 1918, 3.
57. NIAID Media Team, 'Video: The Mother (of all Pandemics)'.
58. The executions by shooting were rampant during the Russian Civil War; see Footman, *Civil War in Russia*, 292.
59. *Gazeta Dlya Vseh*, 'Na pochv goloda...', 9 June 1918.
60. *Gazeta Dlya Vseh*, 'Holeroj Torguiut', 9 June 1918. 'Kvas' is a traditional Slavic beverage.
61. Smele, *The 'Russian' Civil Wars*, 40–41.
62. Ibid., 110. 'Ispanka' refers to Spanish flu.
63. Ibid., 111.
64. Ibid., 112.
65. Shalamov, 'Zdravoohranenie v Zabajkalskoj', 163.
66. Petryshyn and Dzubak, *Peasants in the Promised Land: Canada and the Ukrainians*, 46.
67. *Svoboda*, 'Influenca—Se Strashna Gidra', 5, tba.
68. Honigsbaum, 'The Great Dread', 312.
69. As reported in Dobrovolskij, 'Ispanka s traurnym', tba.
70. Berezovaya, 'Krasnyj i belyj', 496.
71. Rogatchevskaia, 'Propaganda in Russian Library'.
72. Figes, 'The Red Army', 193.

73. Novin, 'Chapter 63'.
74. Krasnaya Gazeta, 'V Zhenskom Universitete', tba.
75. Klinge, *Lenin. Samaja pravdivaya biografia Iljicha*, 64.
76. Ibid., 99.
77. What became *Reichsversorgungsgesetz*.
78. Pironti, 'Post-war Welfare Policies'.
79. Narayanaswami, 'Analysis of Nazi Propaganda'.
80. Schnall et al., 'Disgust as Embodied Moral Judgment', 1105.
81. Schaller and Park, 'The Behavioral Immune System', 99.
82. Helzer and Pizarro, 'Dirty Liberals!', 4.
83. Spinney, 'Pale Rider'.
84. Jung, *The Archetypes and The Collective Unconscious*, 259.
85. *El Correo de Zamora* as reported in Spinney, 'The flu', 65.
86. Ibid., 118.
87. On apocalyptic laughter see Kristeva, *Powers of Horror*, 204.
88. Ibid., 204–205.
89. Ibid., 138.
90. Bakhtin, *Rabelais and His World*, 10.
91. Ibid., 49.
92. See Pirandello, *Six Characters'* and Beckett, *Murphy*.
93. See Arnaiz, 'El extraño que surgió del abismo'. The synopsis of the movie: 'Spain, 1918. During the Spanish flu, a landowner loses his beloved wife—and will do whatever it takes to get back to see her alive, even if it means a pact with the devil—literally'.
94. Smith, 'Lovecraft's Otherworldly Xenophobia'.
95. Simonson, 'Bloodli(n)es', 6.
96. Nwabueze et al., 'Framing of Cartoons', 2.
97. Kazanevsky, 'Cartoons', 6.
98. Ibid., 8.
99. Tchamitch, 'On the connection', 6.
100. Swart, 'The Terrible Laughter', 906.
101. See Maldonado, 'History as an increasingly complex system'.
102. Davis, *More Deadly Than War*, 112.
103. Sandys, *From Winston with Love*, 143.

## BIBLIOGRAPHY

Arnaiz, Rubén. Director. 'El extraño que surgió del abismo'. 2015.

Bakhtin, Mikhail. *Rabelais and His World*. Bloomington: Indiana University Press, 1984.

Barkai, Sigal. 'Historiographic Irony, Art, Nationality and In-Between Identities'. *Studies in Visual Arts and Communication*, 3, no. 2 (2016): 1–12.

Beckett, Samuel. *Murphy*. New York: Grove Press, (1938) 1994.

Berezovaya, Lena. 'Krasnyj i belyj plakaty Grazhdanskoj vojny'. In Grazhdanskaja vojna v Rosii. 1917–1922: Lekcii i uchebno-metodicheskie materialy', edited by Mikhail Karpenko, 481–511. Moscow: Izd-vo Ippolitova, 2006.

Bertarelli, Enrico. *Rivista d'Italia Vol. III Fasc. II*. Roma: Biblioteca Nazionale Centrale di Roma, 1918.

Bianchi, Menotti, 'Arrivo della signora febbre spagnuola'. September 1918a, 1418 documenti e immagini della grande guerra. http://www.14-18.it/disegno/BNBA_BAALBUM13/037.

Bianchi, Menotti. 'Il cav. Baglio a Canosa durante l'epidemia'. 1918b, 1418 documenti e immagini della grande guerra. http://www.14-18.it/disegno/BNBA_BAALBUM13/039.

Boyd, D. 'Caretakers'. *The Scots Magazine*, 1 (1924): 215–218.

Brewster, Gordon. 'The Passing Enemy'. *Irish Weekly Independent*, 2 November 1918, National Library of Ireland. http://catalogue.nli.ie/Collection/vtls000515975.

Butler, A.R., and J.L. Hogg. 'Exploring Scotland's Influenza Pandemic of 1918–1919: Lest We Forget'. *Journal of the Royal College Physicians Edinburgh*, 37 (2007): 362–366.

Canetti, Elias. *Party in the Blitz: The English Years*. London: Harvill, 2005.

Carrade, Shirley. 'The Black Death in the Medieval World: How Art Reflected the Human Experience Through a Macabre Lens'. *Senior Theses and Capstone Projects*, 41, 2016.

Caulfield, Sueann. *In Defense of Honor: Sexual Morality, Modernity, and Nation in Early-Twentieth-Century Brazil*. Durham: Duke Press University, 2000.

'Children's Songs' Popularity in 1918'. *123HelpMe.com*, 1 September 2019. https://www.123helpme.com/view.asp?id=43511.

Corfield, Edmund Steven. *Death and Disease: 'Spanish' Influenza in County Durham, 1918–1919*. Victoria: CorfieldHistory, 2010.

Crawford, Richard. '1918 Spanish Flu Epidemic Held San Diego in Its Grip'. *San Diego: San Diego Union–Tribune*, 13 November 2008. http://www.sandiegoyesterday.com/wp-content/uploads/2014/10/flu.pdf

Daudin, Guillaume, Matthias Morys, and Kevin H. O'Rourke, 'Europe and Globalization, 1870–1914'. *Paris: OFCE*, 17, 2008.

Davies, Christie. *The Mirth of Nations*. New Brunswick: Transaction Publishers, 2002.

Davis, Kenneth C. *More Deadly Than War: The Hidden History of the Spanish Flu and the First World War*. New York: Henry Holt and Co, 2018.

Dobrovolskij, Aleksandr. 'Ispanka s traurnym veerom: istoriaja epidemii, zatronuvshej chetvert chelovechestva'. *MKRU*, 15 August 2014. https://www.mk.ru/social/2014/08/15/ispanka-s-traurnym-veerom-istoriya-epidemii-zatronuvshey-chetvert-chelovechestva.html.

Figes, Orlando. 'The Red Army and Mass Mobilization during the Russian Civil War 1918–1920'. *Past & Present*, 129 (1990): 168–211.

Footman, David. *Civil War in Russia*. New York: Frederick A. Praeger, 1961.

*Gazeta Dlya Vseh*, 'Holeroj Torguiut', 9 June 1918, Gazetnye Starosti, sent by Sergey Sokurenko (Gazetnye Starosti curator).

*Gazeta Dlya Vseh*, 'Na pochv goloda...', 9 June 1918, Gazetnye Starosti. http://starosti.ru/archive.php?m=6&y=1918.

Geremek, Bronisław. 'Common Memory and European Identity'. In *Politics of the Past: The Use and Abuse of History*, edited by Hannes Swoboda and Jan Marinus Wiersma, 31–42. Wien: RennerInstitut, 2009.

Gramsci, Antonio. *Note sul Machiavelli, sulla politica e sullo stato moderno*. LiberLiber: Italia, (1932) 2008.

He, Daihai, Jonathan Dushoff, Troy Day, Junling Ma, and David J.D. Earn. 'Inferring the Causes of the Three Waves of the 1918 Influenza Pandemic in England and

Wales'. *Proceedings of the Royal Society*, 7 September 2013. https://royalsocietypublishing.org/doi/full/10.1098/rspb.2013.1345.

Helzer, Erik, and David Pizarro. 'Dirty Liberals! Reminders of Physical Cleanliness Influence Moral and Political Attitudes'. *Psychological Science*, 4 (2011): 517–522.

Honigsbaum, Mark. 'The Great Dread: Cultural and Psychological Impacts and Responses to the 'Russian' Influenza in the United Kingdom 1889–1893'. *Social History of Medicine* 23, no. 2 (2010): 299–319. https://www.123helpme.com/view.asp?id=43511.

*Il Mulo*, 'La Grippe Spagnola'. 20 October 1918. Biblioteca Nazionale Centrale di Roma. http://www.14-18.it/periodico/TO00205532/1918/n.35/3?search=37a6259cc0c1dae299a7866489dff0bd&searchPos=623.

*Il Resto del Carlino*, 'L'Influenza'. 15 October 1918. La Guerra in Prima Pagina 1914–1918. http://badigit.comune.bologna.it/ilrestodelcarlino/index.html.

*Il Resto del Carlino*, 'La salute pubblica a Bologna: Intervista con l'ufficiale sanitario del Comune'. 24 September 1918. La Guerra in Prima Pagina 1914–1918. http://badigit.comune.bologna.it/ilrestodelcarlino/date_open.asp?testo=24%2F09%2F1918&submit=Cerca.

*Il Socialista*, 'Cronaca—L'inflnenza' [sic]. 17 October 1918. Biblioteca digitale faentina. http://manfrediana.comune.faenza.ra.it/index.php?option=com_content&view=article&id=96&Itemid=264.

*Il Socialista*, 'Cronaca—L'influenza'. 7 November 1918. Biblioteca digitale faentina. http://manfrediana.comune.faenza.ra.it/contenuto/Periodici/Il_Socialista/Il_Socialista_1918_n.1-50/index.html.

Johnson, Niall. 'Scottish' Flu–The Scottish Experience of "Spanish Flu"'. *Scottish Historical Review*, 83, no. 2 (2004): 216–226.

Jung, G. Carl. *The Archetypes and the Collective Unconscious*. 2nd edition. London and New York: Routledge, [1959] 2014.

Kazanevsky, Vladimir. 'Cartoons: the Art of Dissenters'. *Amsterdam: Cartoon Movement*, 12 September 2016. https://blog.cartoonmovement.com/2016/09/the-art-of-dissenters.html.

Klinge, Aleksandr. *Lenin. Samaja pravdivaya biografia Iljicha*. Moscow: Jauza, 2017.

*Krasnaya Gazeta*, 'V Zhenskom Universitete'. 21 October 1918. Gazetnye Starosti. http://starosti.ru/archive.php?y=1918&m=10&d=21.

Kristeva, Julia. *Powers of Horror: An Essay on Abjection*. New York: Columbia University Press, 1982.

Lebedev, Alexander. 'Probuet'. *Petrogradskaya Gazeta*, 14 July 1918, Gazetnye Starosti. http://starosti.ru/archive.php?m=7&y=1918.

'Lenin i Trockij, vrachi bolnoj Rossii', 1918. In Bibliotechnaya Sistema Gosudarstvennogo Universiteta 'Dubna'. *Rodina* 3 (2008): 3. https://lib.uni-dubna.ru/biblweb/search/bibl.asp?doc_id=141292&full=yes.

Magistro, Cristoforo. *1918, l'anno della Spagnola*. Montescaglioso: Montescaglioso Web Community, 2007. https://www.montescaglioso.net/node/1862.

Maldonado, Carlos. 'History as an Increasingly Complex System'. In *History and Cultural Identity*, edited by John Hogan, 129–151. Washington: Council for Research in Value and Philosophy, 2011.

Martin, A. Rod, 'Approaches to the Sense of Humor: A Historical Review'. In *The Sense of Humor: Explorations of a Personality Characteristic*, edited by Willibald Ruch, 15–60. Berlin: Mouton De Gruyter, 1998.

Miletic, Alexander. '1914 Revisited. Commemoration of the WWI centenary in Serbia'. *Múltunk: Journal of Political History*, special issue, *Memory and memory and Memorialization of WWI in Eastern and Southeastern Europe*, edited by Gábor Egry (2016): 5–32.

Musolff, Andreas. 'The Afterlife of an Infamous Gaffe: Wilhelm II's 'Hun Speech' of 1900 and the Anti-German Hun Stereotype during World War I in British and German Popular Memory'. *Pragmatics and Society* 9, no. 1 (2018): 75–90.

Narayanaswami, Karthik. 'Analysis of Nazi Propaganda: A Behavioral Study'. Harvard Law blog, 2011. http://blogs.law.harvard.edu/karthik/files/2011/04/HIST-1572-Analysis-of-Nazi-Propaganda-KNarayanaswami.pdf.

Neighbor, Tese, Capri Karaca, and Kate Lang. *Understanding the World of Political Cartoons: Understanding the World through the Eyes, Ears and Pens of Editorial Cartoonists*. Seattle: World Affairs Council of Seattle, 2003. http://hhssocialstudies30. weebly.com/uploads/5/1/9/2/5192923/understanding_the_world_of_political_cartoons.pdf

NIAID Media Team. *Video: The Mother (of All Pandemics) and Her Naughty Children*. Bethesda, MD: National Institute of Allergy and Infectious Disease, 13 April 2018. https://www.niaid.nih.gov/news-events/video-mother-pandemics-her-naughty-children.

*North-Eastern Daily Gazette*. 'The Influenza Epidemic'. 31 October 1918, The British News Archive. https://www.britishnewspaperarchive.co.uk/search/results/1918-10-31/1918-10-31?basicsearch=north-eastern%20daily%20gazette&somesearch=north-eastern%20daily%20gazette&retrievecountrycounts=false&newspapertitle=daily%2b gazette%2bfor%2bmiddlesbrough.

Novin, Guity. 'Chapter 63: Posters of the Russian Civil War of 1917–1921 and Soviet Propaganda Posters'. *A History of Graphic Design: The Online Textbook*. 2016. http://guity-novin.blogspot.com/2012/12/chapter-63-posters-of-russian-civil-war.html.

Nwabueze, Chinenye, Chinedu Igboeli, and Ugochukwu Ubah. 'Framing of Cartoons on Ebola Virus Disease in Selected Nigerian Dailies: A Content Analysis'. *Journal of Healthcare Communications* 2, no. 1 (2017): 1–6.

Percoco, Marco. 'Health Shocks and Human Capital Accumulation: The Case of Spanish Flu in Italian Regions'. *Regional Studies* 50, no. 9 (2015): 1–13.

Petryshyn, Jaroslav, and Luba Dzubak. *Peasants in the Promised Land: Canada and the Ukrainians*. Toronto: James Lorimer & Company, 1985.

*Piccolo*, 'La febbre Spagnuola'. 6 October 1918. Biblioteca digitale faentina. http://manfrediana.comune.faenza.ra.it/contenuto/Periodici/Il_Piccolo/Il_Piccolo_1918_n.1-52/index.html.

Pirandello, Luigi. *Six Characters in Search of an Author*. New York: Signet Classic, (1921) 1998.

Pironti, Pierluigi. 'Post-war Welfare Policies'. *1914–1918 Online—International Encyclopedia of the First World War*. 2017. https://encyclopedia.1914-1918-online. net/article/post-war_welfare_policies.

Polimeni, Joseph, and Jeffrey P. Reiss. 'The First Joke: Exploring the Evolutionary Origins of Humor'. *Evolutionary Psychology*, 4 (2006): 347–366.

Poon, Linda. 'Remembering the 'Mother of All Pandemics,' 100 Years Later'. *CityLab*, 2018.

*Resto del Carlino*, 'L'influenza'. 12 October 1918, La Guerra in Prima Pagina 1914–1918. http://badigit.comune.bologna.it/ilrestodelcarlino/date_open.asp?te sto=12%2F10%2F1918&submit=Cerca.

Rogatchevskaia, Katia. 'Propaganda in Russian Library'. The British Library, 2018. https://www.bl.uk/russian-revolution/articles/propaganda-in-the-russian-revolution.

Sandys, Celia. *From Winston with Love and Kisses: The Young Churchill*. College Station: Texas A&M University Press, 2013.

Scalarini, Giuseppe. 'Il Conquistatore dell'Europa'. *L'Avanti*, 13 October 1918. Biblioteca del Senato. https://avanti.senato.it/avanti/controller.php?page=archivio-pubblicazione-anno-edizione-mese&anno=1918&edizione=Edizione%20 Nazionale&mese=10.

Schaller, Mark, and Justin Park. 'The Behavioral Immune System (and Why It Matters)'. *Current Directions in Psychological Science* 20, no. 2 (2011): 99–103.

Schnall, Simone, Jonathan Haidt, Gerald L. Clore, and Alexander H. Jordan. 'Disgust as Embodied Moral Judgment'. *Personality and Social Psychology Bulletin* 34, no. 8 (2008): 1096–1109.

Shalamov, Vladimir. 'Zdravoohranenie v Zabajkalskoj oblasti vo vremja rezhima atamana G. M. Semenova (Osen 1918–Vesna 1919 ye.)'. *Vestnik Tomskogo gosudarstvennogo universiteta*, 414 (2017): 156–166.

Simonson, Sheila. 'Bloodli(n)es: Carnivalizing Narratives of Illness: Breathing Bakhtinian Life into the Compromised and/or Dying Body'. *InTensions Journal* 3 (2009).

Simpson, James Young. 'Note on the History of Carbolic Acid and Its Compounds in Surgery Prior to 1867 on First Medical Uses of Carbolic Acid'. *U.S. National Library of Medicine*, 1867. https://collections.nlm.nih.gov/bookviewer?PID=nlm: nlmuid-101502846-bk#page/1/mode/2up.

Smele, Jonathan. *The 'Russian' Civil Wars, 1916-1926: Ten Years That Shook the World*. Oxford: Oxford University Press, 2015.

Smith, Zachary Snowdon. 'Lovecraft's Otherworldly Xenophobia'. *Areo*, 2019. https://areomagazine.com/2019/03/05/lovecrafts-otherworldly-xenophobia/.

Spinney, Laura. *Pale Rider: The Spanish Flu of 1918 and How It Changed the World*. New York: Public Affairs, 2017.

Spinney, Laura. The Flu That Transformed the 20th Century. BBC, London, 2018. http://www.bbc.com/future/story/20181016-the-flu-that-transformed-the-20th-century.

Sprone, 'E—Chi (se ne.... impipa)—La febbre spagnuola'. *Il Mulo*. 13 October 1918. Biblioteca Nazionale Centrale di Roma. http://www.14-18.it/periodico/ TO00205532/1918/n.34/4?search=37a6259cc0c1dae299a7866489dff0bd& searchPos=615.

Stone, Lawrence. 'The Revival of Narrative Reflections on a New Old History'. *Past & Present* 85, no. 1 (1979): 3–24.

*Svoboda*, 'Influenca—Se Strashna Gidra'. 11 December 1918, Svoboda Digital Archive. http://www.svoboda-news.com/arxiv/pdf/1918/Svoboda-1918-148.pdf

Swart, Sandra. 'The Terrible Laughter of the Afrikaner—Towards a Social History of Humor'. *Journal of Social History* (2009): 889–917.

Tchamitch, Peter. 'On the Connection between Humour, Irony, Tragedy and Enchantment, the Intellect and the Emotions, and Consciousness'. 2006. www. petertchamitch.se.

Ter Braake, Serge, and Antske Fokkens. 'How to Make It in History. Working towards a Methodology of Canon Research with Digital Methods'. In *Proceedings of the first conference on Biographical Data in a Digital World (BD2015)*, edited by Serge ter Braake, Antske Fokkens, Roderick Sluijter, Thomas Declerck, and Eveline Wandl-Vogt. *CEUR*. 2015. 85–93.

*The Daily Mirror*, 'How to avoid Span'sh Influenza'. 27 June 1918. The British News Archive. https://www.britishnewspaperarchive.co.uk/search/results/1918-06-27/1918-06-27?basicsearch=daily%20mirror%201918&somesearch=daily%20mirror%201918&exactsearch=false&retrievecountrycounts=false&newspapertitle=daily%2bmirror.

*The Daily Mirror*, 'The City Worker and the Influenza Plague. No. 2'. 17 October 1918. The British News Archive. https://www.britishnewspaperarchive.co.uk/search/results/1918-10-17?NewspaperTitle=Daily%2BMirror&IssueId=BL%2F0000560%2F19181017%2F&County=London%2C%20England.

*The Daily Mirror*, 'What to Do with Our Influenza Heroes?'. 24 October 1918. The British News Archive. https://www.britishnewspaperarchive.co.uk/search/results/1918-10-24/1918-10-24?basicsearch=daily%20mirror%201918&somesearch=daily%20mirror%201918&exactsearch=false&retrievecountrycounts=false&newspapertitle=daily%2bmirror.

Turati, Filippo, and Anna Kuliscioff. *Carteggio IV 1915–1918 La Grande Guerra e La Rivoluzione Tomo Secondo*. Torino: Einaudi, 1977.

PART III

# Humour of the Past in the Present

CHAPTER 22

# Translating Humour in *The Song of Roland*

## *John DuVal*

A fourth of the way into the 4002-line twelfth-century Anglo-Norman *Song of Roland*, Marsille, king of the Spanish Saracens at the most western reach of the ninth-century Islamic Empire, leading two armies of 100,000 knights each, ambushes Charlemagne's 20,000-knight rearguard, led by Roland, at Roncevals in the Pyrenees mountains. As soon as Roland knows the Saracens are about to attack, Roland exhorts his troops to strike hard, 'Que malvaise cançun de nus chantet ne seit' [lest a malicious song be sung about us.][1] After Roland's rearguard has destroyed Marsille's first army and Marsille has thrown his second huge army against the weary and depleted French forces, Roland repeats his allusion to malicious songs, reminding his friend Oliver that after all the great fights they have fought together, they must 'granz colps l'empleit, / Que malvaise cançun n'en deit cantee' [strike great blows / lest a malicious song be sung about this one].[2] A few lines later, realizing that the French forces cannot survive this second wave of Saracen knights, the fighting Archbishop Turpin exhorts the French knights with reminders of their rewards in heaven; but first he warns them not to run away, 'Que nuls prozdom malvaisement n'en chant' [lest some man sing maliciously about it].[3]

The kinds of songs Roland and Turpin refer to belong to a long tradition of soldier humour from ancient through modern times, composed by low-ranking soldiers to report stinginess, incompetence, unmanliness, pettiness, or cowardice in superior officers or by rival companies to claim superiority for themselves by right of comedy, such as the verses Julius Caesar's soldiers made up about Caesar's amours with King Nicomedes[4] or the verses Hernando Cortés'

---

J. DuVal (✉)
University of Arkansas, Fayetteville, AR, USA
e-mail: jduval@uark.edu

© The Author(s), under exclusive license to Springer Nature
Switzerland AG 2020
D. Derrin, H. Burrows (eds.), *The Palgrave Handbook of Humour, History, and Methodology*, https://doi.org/10.1007/978-3-030-56646-3_22

431

432   J. DUVAL

soldiers scribbled about Cortés' stinginess on the walls of his palace.[5] Even so, in my verse translation of *The Song of Roland* in 2012 for Hackett Publishers, I was perhaps over-zealous in writing the dreaded songs not just as malicious, but explicitly humorous, for I translated the above phrases successively as 'comic rhymes',[6] 'sarcastic little songs',[7] and 'refrains / making fun of those who ran away'.[8] Nevertheless, Roland's and Turpin's fear is of being laughed at, because in *The Song of Roland*, being laughed at is a fearful thing.

Roland himself laughs very early in the poem. That is when his stepfather, Ganelon, threatens him. This laughter occurs emphatically at the end of one of the shortest of the poem's verse paragraphs (*laisses*), with the word *rire* [laugh] as the last word.[9] The seven-line *laisse* ends with Ganelon's threat and Roland's response:

> 'Einz i ferai un poi de legerie
> Que jo n'esclair ceste meie grant ire'.
> Quant l'ot Rollant, si cumençat a rire[10]

which my verse translation expresses as,

> 'I swear I'll do some rash
> And reckless deed. I must appease my wrath!'
> When Roland hears these words, he laughs.[11]

Nobody else laughs, and Roland does not laugh good-humouredly. Is Roland's laughter a mean-spirited attack, a Hobbesian expression of the 'sudden glory' of apprehending 'some deformed thing' in Ganelon?[12] Or is he laughing à la William Hazlitt, at the incongruity of the high regard Ganelon has for his threat as it 'disconnects' and 'jostles' against Roland's disregard for any threat at all.[13] Regardless of how critics may interpret Roland's laughter, for Ganelon, Roland is glorifying himself by belittling Ganelon's threat and thereby belittling Ganelon himself. Roland's laughter has attacked him, and he will attack back. Not with laughter, but with betrayal. He will be avenged. Fifty lines later on, he is conspiring with a Saracen king to arrange the death of Roland at the fatal ambush of Roncevals.

Now, on the field of Roncevals in the Pyrenees Mountains, having spied the huge Saracen army led by Marsille, King of Spain, riding in full armour towards them, Roland and Turpin shout warnings against malicious comic songs. It is therefore curious—one might even say funny—that they themselves, more than any of the other warriors in this epic poem not noted for its comedy, have their comic side. Their comedy arises not from any cowardice in these incredibly brave heroes, but from the incongruities of their generous but flawed human characters. Part of my responsibility in translating *The Song of Roland* was to reveal this comedy without hinting any malicious intent on the part of the author, because however much the author wanted to shed the light of humour on his characters, he did not want to make them essentially ridiculous.

My greatest temptation in that respect occurred when Roland was the last man standing on the battlefield, dying a protracted death and trying to destroy his sword, lest some unworthy knight possess it after his death. The sword has a name, Durendal, and Roland has wielded it through many a victorious battle. Now, in a moment of intense feeling, he speaks to it, reminding it of the battles they have fought together, praising it for the precious jewels imbedded in its hilt, and for the precious relics. Relics! Protracted deaths are risky enough when the author is striving for pathos (witness the death of Pyramus as 'authored' by Peter Quince, Shakespeare's comic director in *A Midsummer Night's Dream* 5.1.284–295), but relics? Who can forget the relic that Chaucer's Host declared the Pardoner would have him kiss[14] or that he threatened the Pardoner he would cut off and have 'Shryned in an hogges toord'?[15] Or Friar Cipolla's catalogue of relics, recorded by Boccaccio in the *Decameron*, including a 'finger of the Holy Spirit', 'a cherub's fingernail', 'an ampulla containing the sweat of St. Michael', and 'the Angel Gabriel's feather'.[16]

The translation that follows the French below is my literal translation of the description of the sword Durendal's relics rather than the corresponding lines of verse I wrote to be published by Hackett.

> [...] assez y a reliques;
> La dent seint Perre e del sanc seint Basilie
> E des chevels mun seignor seint Denise,
> Del vestement i ad seinte Marie.[17]

> [...] lots of relics,
> St Peter's tooth, some of St Basil's blood
> and some of my lord St Denis's hairs;
> there's some of St Mary's clothing.

A translator has lots of ticklish phrasing in this literal translation that it were better to avoid. 'Some of' sounds too casual. 'Lots of relics' sounds worse, like something from Friar Cipolla's sales pitch. The English genitive apostrophe s ('s) is less weighty and more subject to humorous reading than the 'of' construction: 'blood of St Basil' sounds less silly than 'St Basil's blood'. First year French students are taught to translate *cheveux* as hair, not hairs, but the *des* that precedes *chevels* does indeed suggest that these hairs be considered precious one by one in an age when relics are taken seriously, which today they are not. 'Some of' is even more ticklish with St Mary's clothing than with St Basil's blood, as it invites the reader to wonder what particular items of clothing might have been stuffed into the hilt of the sword. Here is the less literal, more formal translation that I wrote for Hackett:

> A tooth of St Peter, a vial of St Basil's blood,
> A lock of St Denis' hair, and with all those,
> A precious patch of holy Mary's robe[18]

which, if read without lifting the eyebrows and rolling the eyes, should not evoke laughs that the Roland poet never intended.

Intentional humour, however, occurs earlier when Oliver pokes grim fun at his friend Roland, chiding him for wanting, all too late, to blow his ivory horn Olifant and warn their lord Charlemagne that they are being slaughtered. At the beginning of the battle of Roncevals, Oliver begged his friend, each time more urgently, to sound the warning to Charlemagne's main army that they must turn around in the Pyrenees mountains and ride to rescue Roland and Oliver and their 20,000 ambushed knights. Each time Roland refused more obstinately, insisting on displaying his personal glory and even implying that his friend's requests were cowardly and deriding them by reducing the honourable action of sounding the ivory war horn to a single hapax legomenon, *cornant*,[19] whose derisive humour I think I managed to keep with:

> God forbid that it be said
> By any man alive that infidels
> Drove me to horn blowing.[20]

—although I might have better suggested the hapax-legomenonality with the spelling hornblowing.

Henri Bergson, in his essay on the nature of comic characters in *Laughter* (*Le Rire*), claims that comedy begins:

> avec ce qu'on pourrait appeler le raidissement contre la vie sociale. Est comique le personnage qui suit automatiquement son chemin sans se soucier de prendre contact avec les autres. Le rire est là pour le tirer de son rêve.[21]

> with what might be called a glowing callousness to social life. Any individual is comic who automatically goes his own way without troubling himself about getting into touch with the rest of his fellow beings. It is the part of laughter to reprove his absentmindedness.[22]

That is, absentmindedness of other people's feelings. Roland's 'social life', in widening circles, includes Oliver and the 20,000 French knights serving under Oliver and him, Charlemagne and all of Charlemagne's army, and the French nation, whose well-being he sacrifices for the sake of personal glory. Bergson elaborates that, 'Un vice souple serait moins facile à ridiculiser qu'une vertu inflexible'.[23] [A flexible vice may not be so easy to ridicule as a rigid virtue].[24] Roland's defining characteristic, valour, is rigid and puts limits on the wisdom of his battle strategy. Oliver is not cowardly, but he is also wise; his strategic mind is flexible.

Although none of Bergson's comic plot patterns fit the pattern of repetition that enforces a sense of Roland's rigidity, Bergson himself, in his preface to the 23rd edition of *Le Rire*, exclaims that comic patterns abound so multiplicitously that no scholar could ever chart them all. 'Le rebondissement du comique', he writes, 'est sans fin'[25] [Comic reboundability is endless].[26] In the first of a series of three *laisses* (verse paragraphs), Roland rejects Oliver's wise advice and refuses to blow his horn. A second, similar *laisse*, establishes the rigidity of his refusal. This doubling half-prepares for audience laughter in the third *laisse* when, despite Oliver's reasonable and passionate arguments, Roland still insists on his own, disastrous decision. At this point, however, too many other, attractive sides of Roland's character have already been developed for these three *laisses* to define him, and the consequences of Roland's refusal to call for help are too catastrophic for his rigidity, including his derisive *cornant*, to be funny. As if to explain why Roland's rigidity is not yet funny, Bergson writes, 'Peignez-moi un défaut aussi léger que vous voudrez: si vous me le présentez de manière à émouvoir ma sympathie, ou ma crainte, ou ma pitié, c'est fini, je ne puis plus en rire'[27] [Depict some fault, however trifling, in such a way as to arouse sympathy, fear, or pity; the mischief is done, it is impossible for us to laugh].[28] Instead of eliciting laughter, the author concludes with a character summation: 'Rollant est proz e Oliver est sage'[29] [Roland is valiant. Oliver is wise].[30]

But late in the battle, as the hugeness of his mistake begins to dawn on him, his rigidity transmogrifies. With all but a few dead, he turns to Oliver and addresses the absent Charlemagne—absent because he refused to blow his horn. He asks, 'E! reis amis, que vos ice nen estes?'[31] [Charlemagne, why aren't you with us now?].[32] Then Roland addresses Oliver: 'Oliver, frere, cumment le purrum nus faire? / Cum faitement li manderum nuveles?'[33] ['Oliver, Brother, how can we hold out? / How can we let him know we've been pinned down?].[34] That, the incongruity of asking questions of the very person who has three times already answered them, is beginning to sound funny.

Even funnier, in the next *laisse* Roland ignores Oliver's sarcastic replies and answers his own question: 'Cornerai l'olifant'[35] [I'll blow my horn].[36] Somehow his refusal to acknowledge that not blowing the horn was a mistake 'jostles' so noticeably against his proposal to blow the horn that not even the seriousness of his mistake can smother the humour. (I was so taken by the humour of that sentence, that, in order to underline it, in an early draft I added two words: 'I know!' I wrote, 'I know! I'll blow my horn', but then revised back closer to the original author's nuanced humour). In the third *laisse*, Roland repeats his determination to blow his horn, and the repetition manifests a new kind of rigidity as he clings to the illusion that horn blowing is his idea. To conclude this *laisse*, Oliver, who recognizes the incongruity but is not amused, loses patience altogether:

> Ne sereit vasselage!
> Quant jel vos dis, cumpainz, vos ne deignastes.
> S'i fust li reis, n'i ousum damage.
> Cil ki la sunt n'en deivent aveir blasme.
> [...] Par ceste meie barbe,
> Se puis veeir ma gente sorur Alde,
> Ne jerreiz ja mais entre sa brace![37]

436    J. DUVAL

> That wouldn't show much valor.
> You wouldn't blow your horn when all this started,
> Although I asked. If Charles were here, no harm
> Would come to us. It's not their fault they're far
> And riding ever farther. By my heart,
> If I could see my noble sister Alda,
> She'd never lie with Roland in her arms.[38]

The ultimate threat between male friends, 'You'll never get to sleep with my sister', finally wakes Roland to the fact that Oliver is irked, so he asks, 'Por quei me portez ire?'[39] [Why are you mad at me?].[40] An English friend of mine reminded me that the correct adjective was angry; mad, he said, was too informal for Roland, and, yes, too American. He had to admit though that his wife, also English, preferred mad. My own wife, my best critic, tended to side with him. But I was reaching for a diction that I had used before any adult had told me that mad could only mean insane, as in, mad dog. I was reaching for the plain, direct language of two boys who have been friends since childhood, reaching for an almost but not quite childish diction since there is something a little childish in the confrontation between these two friends on the bloody field of Roncevals, where the poet allows himself to ridicule his complex hero's lack of self-knowledge. We, too, may feel justifiable amusement, though in this case Roland and Oliver do not. And unlike Roland, we may appreciate the paradox (first cousin to incongruity) that Roland's love of personal glory, through which Charlemagne gained so much of his empire, is now the reason for Roland's death and Charlemagne's loss of his best knights.

Ridiculing Roland, the 'wise' Oliver has shown himself to be rigid, too, in his ill humour. After all, scolding Roland (three times!) for wanting to blow his horn too late is no more helpful than blowing the horn too late. As their deaths approach, Oliver's repetitive complaint threatens to solidify the judgement of ridicule against his friend. The archbishop, however, hears Oliver chiding Roland, rides up, and prepares for Christian forgiveness between the two friends by resolving the argument: horn blowing, he explains, may not save their lives, but it will bring Charlemagne's main army back to avenge their deaths.

The renewed bonds of friendship between Roland and Oliver prepare for one last dialogue between the two warriors who have been friends since childhood—and one last opportunity for the poet to make fun of the incongruity between Roland's success as a leader of men and his occasionally childish behaviour. To characterize the ridicule to which our poet sometimes subjects his hero Roland, I have so far referred to classical theorists of the nature of comedy, such as Hobbes, Hazlitt, and Bergson; but it was only recently, while I was reading an unpublished paper of mine about *The Song of Roland*, 'Roland the Hero', at Wolfson College, Cambridge, that I discovered this last touch of ridicule. Describing the admirable generosity of Roland and Oliver's friendship, I read, 'Oliver loves Roland, and their last farewell to each other is touching in a way that only the Roland poet can be touching. Roland has fainted and is slumped upon his horse. Oliver is dying and blinded by his own blood but still fighting'. To illustrate the pathos of that last farewell, I read from my translation, with a tiny, two-word change from my published translation:

> There slumps Roland, fallen on his horse,
> And there is Oliver, whose wound is mortal.
> So much more blood from his back-wound pours,
> He can't see far or near to know the form
> Or face of any man that comes before him,
> Not even Roland, his friend through countless wars.
> Blinded, he strikes out upward with his sword
> At Roland's gold, gemmed helmet. The blade stops short
> In the steel noseguard, then cuts up past his forehead.
> Roland looks, and in language sweet and courtly,
> Asks, 'Oliver, are you doing that on purpose?'[41]

At that point, my listeners at Wolfson laughed.

Instead of lashing out at them, Ganelon-like, for laughing, ruining the pathos of the moment, I made a mental note that that line might be another instance, like Roland's praise of his relics, where the translator needed to avoid translating into humour where humour was not intended. The meaning of the original French, 'Faites le vos de gred?' is indeed 'Are you doing that on purpose?' For the version that would be published, I had written, 'Are you hitting me?' instead of, 'Are you doing that?' because hitting was a stronger English verb than doing. For the Wolfson reading, I read the literal, 'Are you doing that?' to capture the pathos of a grown man reverting to a child-like phrasing when speaking to a childhood friend. I had constructed the whole *laisse* in English with *ur* or *or* assonance because I thought, 'Are you hitting me on purpose', was the most powerful line of the *laisse*. I did not realize, however, until I thought about the laughter after the reading, that the humour probably was intended and that the power of the line contributed to its humour. I now believe the original author made Roland's language so 'sweet' that audiences had to laugh at the incongruity of such sentimentality on the field of carnage, and at the rigidity of Roland's mind, which could imagine that his friend could ever strike him on purpose. But I stick by my phrase from the Wolfson talk, 'touching in a way that only the Roland poet can be touching', because embedded in the incongruity of the great leader talking like a child is the recognition that the friendship that has endured past childhood, and that death will soon end, still survives in the child language that Roland addresses to his dear friend Oliver: 'Are you doing that on purpose?' But now the part Roland has played of the rigid and risible commander is over, simply folding into our understanding of this complex and generous hero as we experience the pathos of Oliver's, Turpin's, and finally his own death.

438    J. DUVAL

Archbishop Turpin's comic side is altogether different from Roland's, because Turpin himself, unlike everybody else in *The Song of Roland*, has a sense of humour. At the beginning of the poem, several of Charlemagne's knights volunteer for a very dangerous mission to go alone to meet the treacherous and bad-tempered enemy king Marsille, but Turpin alone adds a soldier's comic bravura to his offer, remarking, 'E jo irai al Sarazin en Espaigne, / Sin vois vesdeir alques de sun semblant'[42] [I'll go to the Saracen in Spain. I'd love / To get a look at him].[43]

It is he, a Christian priest, who not only solves an argument between friends by calling for vengeance (not a Christian virtue), but even preaches to the Christian knights that they must fight hard, has them kneel and pray for forgiveness of their sins, and tells them that for their penance they must strike their enemies.[44]

When almost all the French are dead, but Roland is still delivering mighty blows, Archbishop Turpin praises Roland's violent deeds.

> 'Well struck!'
> The Archbishop cries, 'The way a good knight must
> Who rides a steed!'[45]

For a man of God to be defining goodness in terms of how one person (knight or no knight) kills others is incongruous to his Christian profession; Turpin must realize this, because here, knowing that his own life will not last many minutes longer, he cannot resist making a little joke out of the incongruity. Here is the original French, followed by a literal translation rather than the published verse translation:

> Dist l'arcevesque: 'Asez le faites ben!
> Itel valor deit aveir chevaler
> Ki armes portet e en bon cheval set;
> En bataille deit estre forz e fiers,
> U altrement ne valt .IIII. deners;
> Einz deit monie estre en un de ces mustiers,
> Se prierat tuz jurz por noz pecez'.

> The archbishop says, 'You do that very well.
> Such valor a knight ought to have,
> who carries arms and sits on a good horse.
> In battle he should be strong and fierce,
> or otherwise he is not worth four deniers.
> Rather, he ought to be a monk in one of those monasteries,
> and he will pray every day for our sins'.[46]

The first thing a translator has to do, even when translating into verse, is to make sure the words accord with the rules of the new language. 'And he will pray' has to be changed for parallelism with be or subordination to ought: 'he ought to be a monk / and pray' or 'he ought to be a monk, praying', keeping sharp the contrast between fighting and praying. If the translator thinks Turpin is being funny, as I do, he has to keep the dismissive 'one of those'. I also hoped to work in the dismissive English idiom, 'He might as well be'. I had a lot of trouble cramming all that into my standard pentameter line, which is the nearest equivalent in English to the French decasyllabic. I finally settled on:

> 'Well struck!'
> The Archbishop cries, 'The way a good knight must
> Who rides a steed and bears a lance and buckler!
> If he's in battle and he isn't tough,
> He's not worth dirt, might as well be a monk
> In one of those cloisters, muttering prayers for us
> For all our sins'.[47]

I thereby lost the financial comparison, 'four deniers', which I would have translated, if I had had room, 'He's not worth two cents'. A worse loss was the phrase, 'every day', emphasising the quotidian tedium of praying as opposed to the excitement of fighting. As I was translating, I got it into my head that to pray for one's sins doesn't make sense in English. We pray for the sinner, not the sins. I've decided since that though the phrase is logically wrong, it is clear and forceful in its intention and might have allowed me to get 'every day' back into the lines, as in,

> If he's in battle and he isn't tough,
> He's not worth dirt, might as well be some monk
> In one of those cloisters, every day muttering
> Prayers for our sins.

As with Roland, one source of the humour is incongruity, but with Turpin, it is more blatant. 'Our sins' are the sins of warriors, bloody and cruel. Turpin's humorous dismissal of the church at prayer reminds us of the uneasy discrepancy between his vocations of knighthood and priesthood. The poet himself was likely a priest, and his general glorification of Christian warfare in *The Song of Roland* suggests that, of all his characters, he identifies most with Turpin, who probably comes in second after Roland for the most killings on the field of Roncevals. To write *The Song of Roland* he had to glorify cruelty and killing, or otherwise he might as well have been some other monk in one of those cloisters writing dreary lives of the saints.

But not all of the great saints' lives are dreary. Maybe some of them have nuances of humour waiting to be discovered, and a translator working with a powerful and complex classic hopes to convey the power of the original work, not miss any of its many meanings, and maybe discover, under the weight of its famous old seriousness, nuances that critics and other translators have missed. *The Song of Roland* is a deadly serious epic, but the author knew the uses of

440   J. DUVAL

humour: to arouse anger or fear in his characters, to critique and humanize his heroes, and maybe even to laugh at himself for composing such a bloodthirsty poem.

Tone is crucial to a literary work, and the slow business of translating a great work of literature permits the translator to reflect its varieties of tone, including its humour. With the case of translating *The Song of Roland*, key problems encountered in doing so were the loss of meaning sometimes tied up with preserving the humour of the original, as in Turpin, and the tension between humorous potential and author-intentionality, as in Roland's Durendal. In considering Roland's speeches, I judged how many times (two times? three?) Roland had to subject himself to mockery before the reader should find him laughable, and then made sure the translation prepared for the laughter. In considering the comic side of the Archbishop Turpin, I strove for the best phrasing in English that would express his awareness of the comic incongruity between his soldierly and priestly professions. For me the last, sometimes painful, stage of translation is to look back at the translation after it is published and discover shades of meaning, character, or humour I might have missed, such as the sentimentally comic last conversation between Roland and Oliver. On the other hand, in considering holy relics, I chose the least humorous possible phrasing to convey the author's reverence for those mystical objects, a reverence that later authors such as Chaucer and Boccaccio rejected comically.

## NOTES

1. DuVal and Staines, 157, l. 1014. Subsequent citations from the original Old French of *The Song of Roland* will give the page number in DuVal and Staines followed by the line number of the French poem (as in this citation) so that readers can refer to any edition of *La Chanson de Roland*. For a similar reason, references to Chaucer's Middle English will also include the line numbers.
2. DuVal and Staines, 169, 1466.
3. DuVal and Staines, 171, 1516.
4. Singleton, 634–635, quoting Suetonius, *De vita Caesarum* I (I, xlix, 1–4).
5. Díaz, 411.
6. DuVal and Staines, 30.
7. DuVal and Staines, 43.
8. DuVal and Staines, 44.
9. DuVal and Staines, 137, 302.
10. DuVal and Staines, 137, 300–302.
11. DuVal and Staines, 9–10.
12. Hobbes, I, 6.
13. Hazlitt, 12.
14. Chaucer, 154, 948–949: 'Thou woldest make me kisse thyn olde breech, / And swere it were a relyk of a seint'.
15. Chaucer, 154, 955.
16. Boccaccio, 389.
17. DuVal and Staines, 193, 2345–2348.

18. DuVal and Staines, 67.
19. DuVal and Staines 159, 1075.
20. DuVal and Staines, 85.
21. Bergson, *Rire*, 102–103.
22. Bergson, *Laughter*, 134. *Rigidification* would be a better translation of *raidissement* than Brereton and Rothwell's *callousness*, if only *rigidification* were a word. On the other hand, their *absentmindedness* to translate *rêve* is probably closer to Bergson's intent than the more literal *dream*.
23. Bergson, *Rire*, 106.
24. Bergson, *Laughter*, 138.
25. Bergson, *Rire*, 156.
26. My translation. Brereton and Rothwell do not include this preface.
27. Bergson, *Rire*, 106.
28. Bergson, *Laughter*, 139.
29. DuVal and Staines, 159, 1093.
30. DuVal and Staines, 32.
31. DuVal and Staines, 176, 1697.
32. DuVal and Staines, 49.
33. DuVal and Staines, 176, 1698–1699.
34. DuVal and Staines, 49.
35. DuVal and Staines, 176, 1702.
36. DuVal and Staines, 49.
37. DuVal and Staines, 176, 1715–1721.
38. DuVal and Staines, 49–50.
39. DuVal and Staines, 176, 1722.
40. DuVal and Staines, 50.
41. The Old French for the last two lines quoted is, 'Si li demandet dulcement e suef: / "Sire cumpain, faites le vos de gred?"' DuVal and Staines 184, 1999–2000.
42. DuVal and Staines, 136, 269–270.
43. DuVal and Staines, 8.
44. DuVal and Staines, 34; 160, 1138.
45. DuVal and Staines, 54.
46. DuVal and Staines, 180–181, 1876–1882.
47. DuVal and Staines, 54.

## Bibliography

Bergson, Henri. *Laughter*. Translated by Cloudesley Brereton and Fred Rothwell. New York: Macmillan, (1911) 1937.

Bergson, Henri. *Le Rire: Essai sur la signification de la comique*. Paris: Presses Universitaires de France, (1911) 1979.

Chaucer, Geoffrey. *The Works of Geoffrey Chaucer*. Edited by F. N. Robinson. Boston: Houghton Mifflin, 1961.

Díaz, Bernal. *The Conquest of New Spain*. Translated by J. M. Cohen. Middlesex, UK: Penguin, 1967.

Boccaccio, Giovanni. *The Decameron*. Translated by J. G. Nichols. New York: Everyman's Library, 2008.

442  J. DUVAL

DuVal, John (translator) and David Staines (introducer). *The Song of Roland*. Cambridge, Massachusetts: Hackett, 2012.

Hazlitt, William. *Lectures on the English Comic Writers*. Garden City and New York: Doubleday, 1819, 1951.

Hobbes, Thomas. *Hobbes's Leviathan, reprinted from the ed. of 1651; with an essay by the late W. G. Pogson Smith*. Oxford: Clarendon Press, 1958.

Singleton, Charles S. *Dante Alighieri: The Divine Comedy, Purgatorio 2: Commentary*. Princeton: Princeton University Press, 1973.

Shakespeare, William. *The Norton Shakespeare*. Edited by Stephen Greenblatt et al. Second Edition. New York: Norton, 2008.

CHAPTER 23

# Intercultural and Interartistic Transfers of Shandean Humour in the Twentieth and Twenty-First Centuries

*Yen-Mai Tran-Gervat*

In the last pages of Laurence Sterne's *The Life and Opinions of Tristram Shandy, Gentleman* (nine volumes published between 1759 and 1767), Tristram, the narrator, recounts an anecdote that took place in Shandy Hall around the time of his birth, when his father Walter's servant Obadiah came into the Shandys' kitchen to complain about his cow, that was covered by Walter's bull repeatedly over the last few months but was still far from bearing a calf, while, in the meantime, Obadiah's wife had been pregnant and had given birth to a healthy child. Everyone started pondering the family bull's ineffectiveness, then Tristram's mother, who had not heard the whole story, asked: 'what is all this story about?' To which parson Yorick who, along with Tristram, carries the author's voice within the fiction, gives the following witty answer, which is also the last line in the novel: 'A cock and a bull, said Yorick—and one of the best of its kind I ever heard'.[1]

These famous last words perfectly encapsulate Sterne's humour throughout the nine volumes of *Tristram Shandy*. In context, it is a double pun referring to the discussion that has just taken place: playing with the expression 'a cock and bull story' meaning 'nonsense', Yorick's reply manages to allude at the same time to Walter's bull, that was the subject of Obadiah's complaint, and to his poor performance as a reproductive male, by dissociating the animal from its sexual appendage—or 'cock'. By doing so, Sterne adds a last instance of

Y.-M. Tran-Gervat (✉)
Université Sorbonne Nouvelle – Paris 3, Paris, France
e-mail: yen-mai.tran-gervat@sorbonne-nouvelle.fr

© The Author(s), under exclusive license to Springer Nature Switzerland AG 2020
D. Derrin, H. Burrows (eds.), *The Palgrave Handbook of Humour, History, and Methodology*, https://doi.org/10.1007/978-3-030-56646-3_23

443

sexual innuendo to the long list of similar occurrences of ironic understatement throughout the book, one of the most effective devices of his tongue-in-cheek humour: the narrator regularly accuses his reader of seeing sexual references in various 'innocent' details, such as the Shandy family's obsession with long noses or Uncle Toby's interest in a crevice in a wall. Yorick's wit also gently mocks Mrs Shandy's difficulty in following the men's banter in her kitchen, which points to the way the narrative has created a houseful of ridiculous but attaching characters in the various members of the Shandy family: each character is eccentric in his or her own way, through his or her specific 'hobby horse'. Walter, Tristram's father, and Toby, his uncle, are the most humorous characters in this sense, which is close to the etymological, physiological meaning of 'humour': each character's 'hobby horse' is the distinctive symptom of his humour or idiosyncratic eccentricity; Toby is obsessed with facts and words related to war and the army, since he has been wounded at the battle of Namur; Walter is always trying to build systems and principles in order to explain, control, and predict every event in his life, only to have them ruined by facts: his bull's ineffectiveness is one catastrophic element among many others, that contradicts all his theories about the Shandy males' virility and grandeur.

On a metafictional level, the last lines of the novel are also significant: Tristram's mother's question, 'what is all this story about?', could legitimately be asked by any reader discovering *Tristram Shandy*, and Yorick's answer would be an accurate reflection of Sterne's book: 'A cock and a bull—and one of the best of its kind I ever heard!'. One could be tempted to substitute 'read' for 'heard' but 'heard' also accurately applies to this 'odd' book, as Samuel Johnson considered it, since its narrator (and through him, the author himself) regularly states within the narrative that his 'progressive digressive' writing is like a conversation.[2] The metatextual aspect of the book—which will be studied as 'metalepsis' but also by means of parody in this chapter—is one of the main features of Sterne's humour in *Tristram Shandy*.

The preceding pages were a lengthy but necessary reminder of some of the main aspects of Sterne's humorous masterpiece: this necessity in itself shows that humours of the past, as eternal and universal as they may appear to the specialist of literary history, can be forgotten in later centuries or can seem ineffective to today's audiences, both in the country of their original reception and in other languages and cultures.

In contributing to this part of the volume, this chapter centres on adaptations and translations of *Tristram Shandy*, in order to examine how some of the main aspects of this 'book of books' of eighteenth-century humour can be effectively transferred through time, languages, and media.[3] This chapter will study the following works: the last two French translations of *Tristram Shandy*, one by Charles Mauron in 1946 (republished in 1982) and the other by Guy Jouvet in 2004; Martin Rowson's graphic novel, *The Life and Opinions of Tristram Shandy, Gentleman* (1996); and the 2005 motion picture by Michael Winterbottom, *[Tristram Shandy:] A Cock and Bull Story*.

Following some of the previously highlighted aspects of Sterne's novel, the chapter will first examine the general principle of 'metalepsis' as humour and how it is rendered, from the eighteenth-century novel into the twentieth- and twenty-first-century versions of it. In a second part, it will deal with the specific devices of anachronism and parody and conclude with discussion of ironic understatement.

## Metalepsis as Humour

Two film posters simultaneously circulated in the English-speaking world when Michael Winterbottom's film was released in 2005. The one that accompanied the film in the theatres of Australia, New Zealand, and the United States bears the complete title: *Tristram Shandy: A Cock and Bull Story*. Visually, it is predominantly white and shows a rear view of the actor playing both Tristram and his father Walter (Steve Coogan) in his costume and wig, seated in his movie star chair in the courtyard of a seventeenth or eighteenth-century mansion, with a mobile phone in his right hand and flashy running shoes on his feet.[4] On the back of the canvas chair are engraved the following words: 'Steve Coogan/ STAR'; they refer to the opening sequence of the film, in which 'Steve Coogan' and co-star 'Rob Brydon' are behind the scenes, being made up for their roles and arguing about who should be considered the star of the film according to the importance of his character in the book.[5] The time gap between Sterne's time and ours is clearly shown through the contrast between the eighteenth-century set and costume and the twenty-first-century real life props.

In the UK and in Ireland, the film poster was very different: attracting the eye with flashy pink heading and letters, it shows, in its lower half, a close shot of the two main 'actors'; 'Steve Coogan', with a rooster in the background, is throwing a complicit look at the audience, while 'Rob Brydon' is uneasily eyeing a black bull touching his right shoulder. The pink heading and writing occupy the upper half of the poster and quote enthusiastic critics: 'The best film ever ever ever', 'Brilliantly inventive, smart and very funny' and 'Hilarious', followed by Steve Coogan's name (in black letters) and the shortened title: *A Cock and Bull Story*, in black and pink letters. The insistence here is less on the time gap between the novel and its adaptation than on the filmmaker's success at creating a humorous story that is not explicitly that of *Tristram Shandy*.[6]

Both 'Steve Coogan's' look to the camera in the British poster and the canvas star chair in the non-British one, point to one of the main humorous aspects of Sterne's *Tristram Shandy* wittily rendered in the film: metalepsis. The notion, which is close to what is called in the context of theatre studies 'breaking the fourth wall', is defined by John Pier as follows: 'In its narratological sense, metalepsis, first identified by Genette, is a deliberate transgression between the world of the telling and the world of the told'.[7] Although the link between metalepsis and humour has not been clearly established by humour studies theories—the following development will try to give a few elements of reflection—it is a fact that, through the centuries, metalepsis has been widely used in comedy (e.g. the craftsmen's rehearsed tragedy of *Pyramus and Thisbe* in Shakespeare's *A Midsummer Night's Dream*, 1598) and in comic fiction (e.g. Cervantes' *Don Quixote*, 1605, pretending to be the translation of an old Arab manuscript). Metalepsis not only makes the audience reflect on what they are watching or reading, but it also elicits their laughter, for reasons we shall try to determine. Because the device was particularly favoured by postmodern writers and artists in the last quarter of the twentieth century, 'Steve Coogan' quite pedantically declares, in Winterbottom's film, when giving an on-set interview and answering the journalist's question 'Why *Tristram Shandy*?': 'This is a postmodern classic before there was any modernism to be post about'.

## WHY IS METALEPSIS HUMOROUS?

In the historical meaning of humour, the one that was established by the first theorists of the notion in eighteenth-century England, at the exact time when Sterne was writing *Tristram Shandy* and his first readers in and outside of England discovered it, 'humour' includes a self-conscious dimension, which was at the time defined as a 'sense of humour'.[8] Paradoxically, that conception is more present in the lasting French understanding of what was quickly considered 'English humour' than it is in the present uses of the word in English.[9]

The reflexive dimension of humour is summed up by Michael Critchley in his analysis of Freud's sense of humour in the last chapter of his essay *On Humour*, entitled 'Why the Super-Ego is your Amigo': 'in humour, the superego observes the ego from an inflated position, which makes the ego look tiny and trivial. [...] I find myself ridiculous and I acknowledge this in laughter or simply in a smile. Humour is essentially self-mocking ridicule'.[10]

When a work of art reflects on itself by representing or exhibiting its own devices, it points to the inner reflexivity of humour, through something that resembles *mise en abyme*. But metalepsis is also humorous in other ways: by creating at least an illusion of personal complicity between the author and the audience, it flatters a paradoxical collective sense of superiority: each one of us feels privileged when directly addressed by a fictional instance breaking the fourth wall, temporarily forgetting that every reader or spectator is getting the exact same treatment.[11] But that effect converges with the self-mocking attitude identified by Critchley as being part of the sense of humour: respectfully parodying the above quotation, we could say that the meta-reader observes the mere reader from an inflated position, which makes the mere reader—that we all are or were—look tiny and trivial. Thus, in *Tristram Shandy*, each time Tristram alludes to his writing within the narrative, we become a 'meta-reader', the one the narrator—and through him, the author—addresses, the one who is a privileged witness to the making of the book, so much superior to the 'mere reader' of fiction, who is contented with following the story that is being told.

Of course, the humorous effect of metalepsis can also be explained through the incongruity theory, since incongruity is part of the definition for metalepsis: breaking the fourth wall creates a voluntary and obvious incongruity with the standards and expectations of fiction and narrative, leading the audience from one surprise to the other, each one marked by outward laughter or inner smile.

In Sterne's book, various elements within the fictional narrative (Tristram telling his family history and his own) regularly point to the materiality of the book that we hold in our hands, thus blurring the distinction between fictional first-person narrator and actual author. As Wayne C. Booth clearly summarised in 1952, and since then been extensively studied:[12] 'Our attention must be centered on the self-conscious narrator who intrudes into his novel to comment on himself as writer, and on his book, not simply as a series of events with moral implications, but as a created literary product'.[13] These elements are well-known: Sterne's play with the conventions of a printed book (blank, black and marbled pages, dashes of different lengths...),[14] Tristram's regular allusions to the act of writing or to the volumes he has already written, his efforts to visually outline the digressive progression of his narrative.[15] All these instances point to the book as 'a created literary product' and disrupt the fictional illusion created by the narrative.

This aspect of Sterne's humour should present no real problems for the translators, since the enunciative status (narration or commentary) of the text is not affected by the language it is written in. The typographic fantasies could have been a bother for the printers of the first eighteenth-century translations (1776 and 1785), but they were always reproduced, at least as best as they could be at the time. In the last two French translations, it is interesting to note, though, that the translators adopt different attitudes towards Sterne's uncommon use of dashes; this typographic detail reflects the tendencies of those two translations regarding the rendering of Sterne's disruptive humour: over-translation for Jouvet, who uses his own brand of fancy dashes in the narrative,[16] and a general faithfulness with a slight attenuation for Mauron,[17] whose dashes are reproduced from the original, but without any variation in length, they are much less disruptive.

In the film as well as in the graphic novel, the authors did not lack specific means related to their respective media to adapt the metaleptic devices of the original. Michael Winterbottom's film is a pseudo-documentary on the set of a film adaptation of *Tristram Shandy*. From the very first sequence, 'Steve Coogan' addresses the audience as the narrator of the book the film is adapted from: approaching from the seventeenth-century mansion that represents Shandy Hall, he is facing the camera and after quoting Groucho Marx states: 'I'm Tristram Shandy [...] The main character of this story. The leading role'. The anachronic quotation is incongruous and precludes the immersion in the period film that the setting and costume should allow to take place; the declaration and the opening credits that follow ('in order of appearance') are a direct allusion to the mock-quarrel from the pre-credits sequence with 'Rob Brydon', who insisted he was 'co-lead' and wanted to be the first name mentioned in the credits, due to his alphabetical advantage: in the opening sequence, 'Steve Coogan' is making a statement and his narcissistic speech is much more than the mere cinematic version of the novel's first-person narrative; it is part of the realistic and satirical depiction of the war of egos that is supposed to take place in the 'real world' of the film set. This is further illustrated in the following sequence, supposedly the 'cock' part announced by the title and by 'Tristram' himself, that shows when young Tristram is accidentally circumcised, due to the malfunctioning sash-window through which he was peeing.[18] 'Steve Coogan' addresses the audience here to comment on the poor job of the child actor playing Tristram as a (suffering) five year-old, and a childish 'did not-did too' debate is started: the young boy stops shrieking in order to defend himself against his elder's cheap attacks, defying him to do better, then commenting on his performance: 'I was told it was a comedy, not a pantomime', before going on shrieking as young Tristram.

Be it in Sterne's book or in Winterbottom's film, metalepsis is never just a modern or postmodern playful device: without losing its humorous effect, it can be linked with a more serious meaning. In *Tristram Shandy*, it serves both an aesthetic statement about fiction itself as a complex creation by the human mind and an existential reflection on such common experiences as the passing of time, love, freedom, and death. In *A Cock and Bull Story*, 'Steve Coogan's' amusing egoticism as an actor allows the development of the main story of the frame-narrative (the events on the film set), which is about an insecure male living among strong women (the two 'Jennys' of the film, a very literate script girl who *has* read *Tristram Shandy*, and his own girlfriend, who has just given him a son; 'Gillian—Scully—Anderson', the real star on the film set) and who is uncertain about how to go through the 'commitment' moment of his life, when he has just become a father. It is a strong feature of the film to include an echo that works like a *mise en abyme*, between the paternity theme present in Sterne's novel (through Walter Shandy's obsessions) and the-actor-who-plays-Tristram-and-Walter's obsessions. The fictional set is not only a humorous reflection on cinema: it succeeds in creating substantial characters who, like their Shandean models, are humorously flawed or, in other words, at the same time ridiculous *and* attaching.

In Martin Rowson's 1996 graphic novel, metalepsis is also prominent: the book is, in many respects, a meta graphic novel. The author-drawer himself is represented in the book, accompanied by a talking dog who is much more knowledgeable than he is. The author-drawer does not replace Tristram as the narrator of Sterne's story: the latter is represented by a character in eighteenth-century garter with a long black hat, who leads his eighteenth-century readers through doors that allow them to transition from one volume to the other.

One of the most hilarious of the metaleptic moments of the graphic novel is the page where the author-drawer and his dog encounter a group of French deconstructionists. Dressed in clichéd striped shirts and berets, they hop into the comics frame armed with carpenter tools and a French accent and start to deconstruct the frame itself, the speech bubbles and eventually the characters that are drawn within the frame, leaving a heap of lines on the ground and departing with a satisfied '*Voilà mes amis! C'est déconstructé! 'ave a nice day!*'. The added comic effect produced by that page is nonsense, mixed with satire (through caricature) on one of the main movements in the academic criticism of the twentieth-century Anglophone world.

That page also points to the other main metaleptic feature of the film and of the graphic novel: they both explicitly deal with what it means to read *Tristram Shandy* today, including as academics. A caricature of the actual curator of Shandy Hall (played by Stephen Fry) gives a filmed interview on *Tristram Shandy* in the film. Rowson devotes many satiric pages to academic interpretations of Sterne's novel: at the end of Volume II of the drawn version, in a Leviathan-like allegory (referred to by the author-drawer's talking dog as a 'Moby Dick metaphor'), the author-drawer and his dog are lost at sea on a rowing boat, approaching 'the legendary lost wandering ship of critics' and hope that 'they will doubtless afford [them] further insight', but the speech bubble coming out of the vessel is just 'Blah blah blah blah'! The vessel and the rowing boat are then both gulped down by a giant whale and, inside its stomach, Rowson juxtaposes Tristram's delayed Preface from Volume III and critical discourses of different periods, from Samuel Johnson's famous erroneous prognosis 'Nothing odd will do long'[19] to various satiric caricatures of contemporary critical trends, including what we would now call 'digital humanities': 'Of course, since Le Prout's pioneering work in abstracting all the punctuation onto floppy disk, one actually no longer has to read the actual text'.[20] Aside from the amusing caricature, this example makes a good point about 'reading the actual text' being a problem.[21] In Rowson's graphic novel, the author-drawer orders his dog to read a heap of Shandean criticism for him; later, when the drawn version of Volume V should be starting, he discovers that 'some dangerous nerd has bloody downloaded the entire text of *Tristram Shandy* into sodding cyberspace' and exclaims: 'now I've got to hack into the system to find out what happens next', revealing that he has not read the book—'who has ????', he asks his dog.[22] The irony of addressing an adaptation of *Tristram Shandy* to contemporary readers who may not have read the original is not there to mock these readers, but rather, to take into account the difficulty of such a reading nowadays outside academia. Similarly, in *A Cock and Bull Story*, the question of who can read or has read *Tristram Shandy* today is also a recurring theme: 'Steve Coogan' realises while filming that he should have read it to better understand the characters he is playing; Jenny the script girl shares her opinions on the novel and her enthusiasm for Walter's *Tristrapaedia*. The graphic novel and the film, which are more familiar media for the twentieth and twenty-first-century audiences than 'the most typical novel of world literature', are self-conscious about their role in making it more accessible, through their own—equivalent—expressive means.[23]

## Assumed Anachronism

The authors show their awareness of the time and cultural difference they are dealing with by adapting Sterne's many references, some of which are explored hereafter, to some that are better known in our own time. That results in anachronism because in the film as well as in the graphic novel, the modern references voluntarily clash with the eighteenth-century context of the story that is preserved.

I have already commented on the non-British film poster clearly playing on anachronism; the same clash between historical costume and contemporary references or context appears throughout *A Cock and Bull Story*, each time the 'actors', on set, are 'themselves' instead of their characters.

In Rowson's graphic novel, there are numerous instances of humorous anachronism. I shall study one that is both really amusing and perfectly effective at rendering Sterne's humour through obvious actualisation: it is the moment in Tristram's narrative, when the narrator describes Walter's obsession about first names. As a man of systems and principles, Walter is convinced that a man's first name determines his future life and place in history, with a clear hierarchy between noble names and despicable ones. The whole anecdote is fundamentally ironic, because the purpose of this part of the story is to present Walter's arguments in favour of 'Trismegistus' as his soon-to-be-born son's name, and his abhorrence of 'Tristram', which would, according to him, be a curse for his child. The irony is underlined by the narrator himself: 'When this story is compared with the title-page,—will not the gentle reader pity my father from his soul?—to see an orderly and well-disposed gentleman, who though singular,—yet inoffensive in his notions,—so played upon in them by cross purposes [...]'.[24] The storyline reappears in Volume IV, Chapters 11 to 14, to tell—at last—how it so happened that the child's name ended up not as the intended 'Trismegistus' but as the despised 'Tristram' (I am keeping a bit of suspense here, so that the reader can go and read it for himself or herself!).

In the graphic novel, Walter's dissertation on first names as it is summed up by Tristram takes place in 'The Grand Hall of ye Nonentities': the drawn Tristram character quotes extracts from Volume I, Chapter 19 of *Tristram Shandy* in his speech bubbles, while guiding his eighteenth-century 'gentle readers' through a succession of monumental statues of historical or artistic figures who were all forgotten because they bore the wrong first name. The statues are burlesque parodies of their glorious homonyms, perched on pedestals that bear their ill-chosen names: failed doubles of glorious references, like Michelangelo's *Ian*, Alec the Great, Julian Caesar, Monica Lisa, and Lionel Da Vinci; ridiculous alter egos of historical tyrants like Ambrose Hitler, Gervase Khan, Jolyon Stalin, and Chris Borgia; deformed versions of artistic geniuses, like Wilbur Shakespeare, Simon Rushdie, Walter Aloysius Mozart, Adrian Einstein, Nigel Bonaparte—this one being out of his supposed series!—Cyril Freud; not-so-great inspirations, like Jeremy Christ and the Virgin Maureen; and finally, two more near celebrities of all times, Leroy Sterne and Jason Bach.

While the presence of Sterne's text in the speech bubbles gives the reader an opportunity to read the original anecdote, simultaneously, he or she can immediately catch the burlesque principle at work in Sterne's references through Rowson's drawings of the successive parodic statues: the graphic narrative completes the literary one and guarantees that its humour passes from past to present.

## PARODY

Parody is indeed another humorous device that is very effective, both at underlining the time gap between Sterne's work and our time, and at filling this gap by allowing the modern audience to experiment with a similar kind of humour as in the original. As I have studied elsewhere how pastiche is used in Rowson's graphic novel and how this example is useful to differentiate between pastiche and parody, I will here centre my analysis on parody.[25]

*Tristram Shandy* as a whole was considered by Viktor Schklovsky as the perfect example of parody as a genre.[26] It is also a goldmine for examples of parody as a trope, which can be defined as: 'the playful rewriting of a recognisable literary system (text, style, stereotype, generic norm…), that is exhibited and transformed in order to create a comic contrast, with an ironic or critical distance'.[27]

In various instances that are not always mocking, Sterne rewrites multiple literary, philosophical, scientific, or religious references,[28] usually through what Linda Hutcheon studies as 'transcontextualization'.[29] For instance, when in Volume V, Chapters 28 and 29, Yorick wishes to illustrate what he calls 'a polemic divine', he takes a book from his pocket and reads the battle between Gymnast and Tripet from chapter 35 in Rabelais's first volume of *Gargantua*. 'Refunctioning'[30] the (translated) Rabelaisian extract within the fictional conversation between the Shandy brothers and Parson Yorick is enough to technically create a parody: the original context of the comic narrative from *Gargantua* was the Pichrocolian war episode and it served Rabelais's satire on the absurdity of war; it is used here to satirise vain religious quarrels. Rabelais is far from being ridiculed by such a parody, which is here a respectful use of the device: it serves a playful literary homage from Sterne to one of his avowed masters. Similarly, as early as Volume I, Chapter 10, Yorick's horse was presented as the brother of Don Quixote's Rossinante, in an equine parody that illustrates Sterne's admiration for Cervantes; as in the case of the respectful parody of Rabelais, it also identifies one of the main landmarks of the humorous tradition to which he now belongs to, thanks to the very book we are reading.

Rabelais is a strong influence in Guy Jouvet's translation of *Tristram Shandy*. When the new translation of *Vie et opinions de Tristram Shandy* came out in 2004, its publishers, self-consciously named Editions Tristram, argued that, at last, the French readers would have access to the original humour of Sterne's book, after centuries of bland, academic, and un-inventive versions, among which they included Jouvet's predecessor, Mauron's. Taking on the eternal debate between the translator's fidelity to the letter or to the spirit of the translated text, Jouvet decidedly chose the second option, but Sterne's spirit here is clearly interpreted, for a French reader, as a Rabelaisian spirit, to the point that the letter is sometimes hard to recognise under the over-enthusiastic Rabelaisian invention of the translator.[31]

An example of that tendency is how Jouvet decided to translate the 'cock and bull' double pun that closes *Tristram Shandy* and that opened this chapter:

Une CHAPONNADE en trop et une RATACONNICULADE en moins, fit Yorick; l'histoire sans queue, mais non sans tête, d'un taureau flapi du bas, d'une vache qui n'avait pas eu d'andouille après souper, et d'une femme peut-être trop tôt vannée en sa grange—et une des meilleures que j'aie jamais entendues dans le genre.

Yorick's tongue-in-cheek summary ('A cock and bull') of how Walter's bull could not inseminate Obadiah's cow, when at the same time, Obadiah's wife had no problem being pregnant becomes an added Rabelaisian lexical invention (marked by the capital letters), which is followed by a rather convincing attempt at translating the pun by parodying a well-known French expression: Jouvet's '*l'histoire sans queue, mais non sans tête*' plays with the French expression '*Une histoire sans queue ni tête*', which means a nonsensical story, and also on the double meaning of '*queue*', which is similar to 'cock'. But Jouvet is not satisfied with this translation of the letter and he goes on developing the Rabelaisian spirit of his version, by adding a succession of transparent sexual metaphors referring to the said story. By transforming Sterne's sexual innuendo into explicit lexical invention and sexual explanation, Jouvet in a way creates a Rabelaisian pastiche, where Mauron in 1946 had tried to keep the short, Sternian implicit form of Yorick's pun: '*Une histoire à NE PAS dormir debout*', which parodies the French expression '*une histoire à dormir debout*' (a nonsense story) by inverting it; the sexual meaning of the resulting play-on-words is here very discreet: either '*NE PAS*' is about '*dormir*' and implies that one does not sleep well when experiencing virility problems, or it is about the impossibility of 'debout', thus alluding to impotence.

In Rowson's and Winterbottom's adaptations, Sterne's literary references are no longer present: introducing the audience to one pre-twentieth-century author is already enough of a challenge! Instead, they both chose to parody references within their own artistic worlds: visual arts and cinema. In doing so, they explore personal artistic issues that are not strictly equivalent to what was at stake in *Tristram Shandy*, but that still produce a similar form of mild humour, alongside harsher satiric moments.

For Rowson, one of the issues at stake in his graphic version of *Tristram Shandy* is how a graphic novel, as it is now called but which is also known under the less dignified names of 'comic book', 'comics', or 'cartoon', stands within the hierarchy and history of arts: is it a lesser form of visual art than engraving or painting? The story of Slawkenbergius, the long-nosed traveller, at the beginning of Volume IV of *Tristram Shandy*, gives Rowson the opportunity to show that, although he chose caricature and the graphic novel genre as his forms of artistic expressions, he is still a respectable and talented artist.

Sterne wrote the story of Slawkenbergius as a mock ancient narrative, giving his reader a pseudo Latin version and its English translation; he also adopted the typical structure of seventeenth-century 'exemplary novels', in imitation of Cervantes. His own novel being partly a reflexion on how to write a story, his use of a parodic Cervantic *novela ejemplar* at the start of Volume IV is both a playful fantasy (the bilingual text and the long nose theme) and a homage to a literary model that is now part of the book we are reading.

Rowson transposes this playful homage to glorious artistic models through 'plates' that illustrate the story of long-nosed Slawkenbergius: in plates II to IV, he successively parodies Albrecht Dürer's *Knight, Death and the Devil* (1513), William Hogarth's *Southwark Fair* (1733/1734) and Aubrey Beardsley (1876–1898)'s *The Eyes of Herod*, the main comic transformation for each of them being the introduction of and insistence on the long nose theme or representation. Plates I and V, respectively identified as 'Anonymous German Woodcut' [...], 1658' and 'George Grosz. Artwork for a poster of Erwin Piscator's production of Bertold Brecht "Slawkenbergissimus". Berlin 1922', are pastiches more than parodies, as are the accompanying texts, which tell the story of Slawkenbergius through different narrative styles corresponding with the visual style of each plate.

In Winterbottom's case, part of his film is about how to adapt an eighteenth-century literary puzzle like *Tristram Shandy*. Sterne's novel was already atypical among eighteenth-century novels: Winterbottom transposes this unfitting aspect of Sterne's work in his own unclassifiable film. One of the references he plays with is the genre of period films anchored in the seventeenth or eighteenth century: visually, when 'Tristram' appears in the film in his eighteenth-century costume, everything points to a typical period film, including the music. But instead of having its own soundtrack, *A Cock and Bull Story* recycles well-known period film musics that are parodied through what Linda Hutcheon identified as one of the technical elements of parody: 'transcontextualization'. The opening scene uses the Purcell pastiche that Michael Nyman wrote for Peter Greenaway's 1982 *The Draughtman's Contract*.[32] In another sequence adapted from Sterne, when Walter and his wife are coming back from London after a false alert concerning Tristram's birth, their whole carriage trip on some Yorkshire countryside road is accompanied by Handel's *Saraband*, transcontextualised from Kubrick's *Barry Lindon*.

As was the case in Sterne's respectful parodies of Rabelais or Cervantes, parody here is not satirical, but humorous, in the historical, 'amiable', and reflexive sense of 'humour' discussed earlier.[33] Sterne's book was first intended as a general satire, and genuine satire is still very much present throughout it, but what makes its specific 'sense of humour' is its ability to laugh at characters, situations and references that are sometimes ridiculous, but that, at the same time, excite our interest and empathy: my uncle Toby is the best example to understand that, and in Volume III, chapters xiii and xv the reversal of the word 'parody' illustrates it perfectly.

In those chapters, Shandy Hall is preparing at last to welcome Walter's new born son. In Chapter xiii, Doctor Slop, a proud obstetrician, has 'not digested' that the midwife has been 'put over [his] head' and in his vexed state of mind, decides to 'parody' Toby by using a military metaphor to describe what is supposedly happening in the patient's room. 'Parody' here is of the mocking kind, used by a pompous character to debase a likable although hobby-horsical gentleman: Dr Slop 'happened to have his green bays bag upon his knees, when he began to parody my uncle Toby'.[34] But Sterne returns the device against the ridiculous doctor, and in favour of Toby: Slop's intention was to triumphantly take his forceps out of his bag to mark his superiority, which was supposed to have been prepared by his satiric parody of Toby's hobby-horse. What really happens is an anti-climax, when, while brandishing his obstetrical tool, a squirt comes along, and Toby has the final witty repartee: 'Good God! Cried my uncle Toby, are children brought into the world with a squirt?' Slop started to crush Toby through parody, but his own clumsiness resulted in a burlesque parody of his intended noble gesture, which 'threw the advantage of the argument quite on my uncle Toby's side'. Here, Sterne's humour returns the aim of parody in favour of the gentle eccentric character.

Although 'humour' in English now has a very broad meaning, the eighteenth-century reflexive, empathetic form of humour is what this chapter has been mostly centred on, because it is one of the most remarkable features in Sterne's *Tristram Shandy*, one that some would be quick to consider a specific form of 'English humour', as Sterne's French contemporaries tended to do.[35] Showing that the idea of an 'English humour' is mostly fabricated by French eighteenth-century thinkers, sometimes in order to argue against such a specificity, is another subject altogether, that I intend to explore in other papers. But it is clear that British contemporary authors Winterbottom and Rowson would be proof that that kind of humour successfully passes through time. Jouvet's Rabelaisian over-translation could let us think that a French twenty-first-century reader needs a transposition from English humour to French humour to better appreciate it; however, the empathy for the ridiculous eccentrics of Shandy Hall is intact, even through an over-translation, since the invention of characters, their hobby-horse, their speeches and actions are not affected by a stylistic change in narration.

The effect is quite different concerning Sterne's stylistic taste for understatement and ambiguity, particularly in sexual innuendo, as exemplified by the final tongue-in-cheek wordplay on 'a cock and a bull'. As we have seen, Jouvet chooses to over-explain the pun. Winterbottom actually does the same: not only does he choose that pun as a title for his film, he underlines the sexual meanings in the first minutes, through 'Steve-Coogan'-Tristram's presentation: 'this is the bull [showing a bull in a field]; you'll see the cock in a minute', followed by the film adaptation of young Tristram's accidental circumcision. Finally, at the very end of the film, the final scene in Sterne's novel is also adapted on screen. Jouvet transforms one short pun in a whole long paragraph; Winterbottom multiplies the same pun by three occurrences.

Compared to the twenty-first-century authors, the twentieth-century translator and caricaturist seem more restrained: Mauron is very careful to render every comic device used by Sterne, with the same tongue-in-cheek tendency, which in a way could be seen as his effort to respect Sterne's 'humour of the past'; his sobriety may be one of the reasons why his translation, that was the reference for French readers from 1946 to 2004, was blamed for being weak or bland: when reading it closely, those accusations are mostly unfair.

In the specific case of the 'cock and bull' pun, Rowson also chose sobriety: he just illustrated the anecdote from Volume IX of *Tristram Shandy* at the end of his own graphic version, but metalepsis has the last word, when the 'author-drawer' decides to end his narrative on his own pun: flattening his dog's nose, he proudly presents him to 'Tristram Shandy' by insisting that 'My dog has no nose!' and, on the 'FINIS' page, explains his pun: he created a 'shaggy dog', which is a twentieth-century synonym for the eighteenth-century 'cock and bull', without the sexual connotation.

Although it is an important part of Sterne's eighteenth-century humour, in the age of visual abundance and non-stop communication, ironic understatement is harder to preserve with a similar effect than metalepsis, obvious incongruity, parody, and humorous characterisation.

## NOTES

1. Sterne, *Tristram Shandy*, Volume IX, Chapter xxxiii.
2. Samuel Johnson is quoted as saying 'Nothing odd will do long. *Tristram Shandy* did not last', by Boswell, *The Life of Samuel Johnson*, volume II, 27.
3. Sterne, *Tristram Shandy*, Volume I, Chapter xxxi.
4. The filming locations are listed on the Internet Movie Database (IMDb): https://www.imdb.com/title/tt0423409/locations.
5. As the actors play their own roles as actors playing in a film adaptation of *Tristram Shandy*, I shall use inverted commas to distinguish between the actors' actual names (e.g. as it appears in the film credits) and their fictional alter egos.
6. Unless it is supposed that the British audience will immediately identify 'a cock and bull story' as a quotation from Sterne's masterpiece.
7. See Genette, *Métalepse*; Pier, 'Metalepsis'.
8. See Morris, *An Essay*.
9. See Noonan, 'Reflecting Back, or What can the French tell the English about humour'.
10. See Critchley, *On Humour*, 94.
11. Woody Allen gave a fictional life to that impression in *The Purple Rose of Cairo* (1984), when during one of the multiple times she has watched the film, Cecilia (played by Mia Farrow) is suddenly specifically addressed by the film character she admires (played by Jeff Bridges), who then comes out of the screen to interact with her.
12. See for example the third part of: Pier, 'Composition and Metalepsis in *Tristram Shandy*'.
13. Booth, 'The Self-Conscious Narrator in Comic Fiction before *Tristram Shandy*', 165.
14. See Sterne, *Tristram Shandy*, respectively Volume VI, Chapter 38; Volume I, Chapter 12; and Volume III, Chapter 36.
15. See Sterne, *Tristram Shandy*, Volume VI, Chapter 40.
16. See Bandry, 'Tristram in French Garb', 74: 'The twenty first century has its own *Tristram* in French, showing that the comic and zany perception of Sterne is

thriving on both sides of the Channel. Guy Jouvet's version, with its burlesque vocabulary and systematic over-translation, revitalises Sterne in a manner worthy of Rowson's comic strip *Shandy* and Winterbottom's film *A Cock and Bull Story*. Les Editions Tristram have managed to render faithfully or transpose efficiently most visual effects. The translation teems with dashes of all sizes, almost *ad nauseam*. Added to the inflation of Tristram's original lists, this often stifles Sterne's playfulness. A reading at random flashes with brilliant renderings, studded with archaisms and occasional neologisms which give the text a distinct Rabelaisian flavour, but the excess of dashes and of accumulations definitely strains the text. This hobby horsical translator often gets carried away and out-sternes Sterne in a version for post post modernist times'.

17. See Bandry, 'Tristram in French Garb', 74: 'Mauron, the translator of Woolf, Mansfield and Forster, made it possible for *Shandy* to be seen as a precursor of *Ulysses* and surrealist objects, a laboratory where metafiction was first brewed'.

18. See Sterne, *Tristram Shandy*, Volume V, Chapters 17–23.

19. See note 2.

20. Rowson, *The Life and Opinions of Tristram Shandy, Gentleman*, Vol. III, double page (no page number).

21. See De Voogd, 'How to read *Tristram Shandy*'.

22. The hacking is a clever device that derails the narrative and allows half of the book to be 'lost', so that after a series of literary and film pastiches that zap through Books V and VI, the drawn narrative can go directly to Volume VII then, in a few pages, to the end of Volume IX and the 'cock and bull story' quote and *FINIS*.

23. See Shklovski, 'The Novel as Parody', conclusion sentence.

24. Sterne, *Tristram Shandy*, Volume I, Chapter 19.

25. See Tran-Gervat, 'Pastiche'.

26. See Shklovsky, 'The Novel as Parody'.

27. See Tran-Gervat, 'Pour une définition opérationnelle de la parodie littéraire': 'réécriture ludique d'un système littéraire reconnaissable (texte, style, stéréotype, norme générique…), exhibé et transformé de manière à produire un contraste comique, avec une distance ironique ou critique'.

28. See Hawley, '*Tristram Shandy*, learned wit and Enlightenment knowledge', 35: '*Tristram Shandy* does incorporate a parodic survey of the branches of knowledge. In its whimsical and haphazard way, Sterne's fiction covers the field from ancient to modern, Renaissance to Enlightenment'.

29. See Hutcheon, *A Theory of Parody*, 11.

30. See Rose, 'Parody'.

31. See Bandry, '*Tristram* in French Garter' as quoted above, note 13.

32. That reference is also present in the French version of Winterbottom's film, whose title parodies Greenaway's French title *Meurtre dans un jardin anglais* into *Tournage dans un jardin anglais*.

33. See also Tave, *The Amiable Humorist*.

34. Sterne, *Tristram Shandy*, Volume III, Chapter xv.

35. On the broad meaning of 'humour', see Attardo, *Encyclopaedia of Humor Studies*, Introduction: 'a common understanding has been reached in the field [of humor studies] of using the word *humor* as an umbrella term to cover all the synonyms'.

## BIBLIOGRAPHY

Attardo, Salvatore, ed. *Encyclopaedia of Humor Studies*. Thousand Oaks, CA: Sage Publishing, 2014.

Bandry, Anne. 'Romantic to Avant-Garde: Sterne in Nineteenth and Twentieth Century France'. In *The Reception of Sterne in Europe*, edited by Peter de Voogdt and John Neubauer, 32–67. London and New York: Thoemmes, 2004.

Bandry, Anne. 'Tristram in French Garb: The French Translations of *Tristram Shandy*'. In *Through Other Eyes. The Translation of Anglophone Literature in Europe*, edited by Richard Trim and Sophie Alatorre, 67–76. Newcastle: Cambridge Scholars Publishing, 2007.

Boswell, James. *The Life of Samuel Johnson, LL. D. [...] in Two Volumes*. London: Printed by Henry Baldwin for Charles Dilly, in The Poultry, 1791.

Critchley, Simon. *On Humour*. London: Routledge, 2002.

De Voogd Peter. 'How to read *Tristram Shandy*'. In *XVII–XVIII. Revue de la société d'études anglo-américaines des XVIIe et XVIIIe siècles* 63 (2006), 7–17, open edition.

Escarpit, Robert. *L'Humour*. Paris: Presses universitaires de France, 1960.

Genette, Gérard. *Métalepse. De la figure à la fiction*. Paris: Seuil, 2004.

Hawley, Judith. '*Tristram Shandy*, learned wit and Enlightenment knowledge'. In *The Cambridge Companion to Laurence Sterne*, edited by Thomas Keymer, 34–48. Cambridge: Cambridge University Press, 2009.

Hutcheon, Linda. *A Theory of Parody. The Teachings of Twentieth Century Art forms*. New York and London: Methuen, 1985.

Morris, Corbyn. *An Essay towards Fixing the True Standards of Wit, Humour, Railery, Satire, and Ridicule*. London: Printed for J. Roberts and W. Bickerton, 1744.

Noonan, Will. 'Reflecting Back, or What can the French tell the English about humour'. *Sydney Studies in English*, (2011): 92–115.

Pier, John. 'Composition and metalepsis in *Tristram Shandy*'. In *Usure et rupture – Breaking points*, edited by Claudine Raynaud and Peter Vernon, 87–104. Tours: Presses universitaires François-Rabelais, 1995. Web. http://books.openedition.org/pufr/4487

Pier, John. 'Metalepsis'. *The Living Handbook of Narratology*. https://www.lhn.uni-hamburg.de/node/51.html

Rose, Margaret. 'Parody'. In *Encyclopaedia of Humor Studies*, edited by Salvatore Attardo, 553–54. Thousand Oaks, CA: Sage Publishing, 2014.

Schkovsky, Viktor. 'The Novel as Parody'. In *Theory of Prose*. Available online: http://www.tristramshandyweb.it/sezioni/novel/critical_studies/sklovsky.htm

Tave, Stuart M. *The Amiable Humorist. A Study in the Comic Theory and Criticism of the Eighteenth and Early Nineteenth Centuries*. Chicago: Chicago University Press, 1960.

Tran-Gervat, Yen-Mai. 'Pastiche'. In *Encyclopaedia of Humor Studies*, edited by Salvatore Attardo, 554–57. Thousand Oaks, CA: Sage Publishing, 2014.

Tran-Gervat, Yen-Mai. « Pour une définition opérationnelle de la parodie littéraire: parcours critique et enjeux d'un corpus spécifique ». In *Cahiers de Narratologie* 13 (2006): [Online] http://journals.openedition.org/narratologie/372

CHAPTER 24

# *The Scholars, Chronique indiscrète* or *Neoficial'naja istorija*? The Challenge of Translating Eighteenth-Century Chinese Irony and Grotesque for Contemporary Western Audiences

*Anna Di Toro*

## RULIN WAISHI: A NOVEL THAT 'RESISTS CLOSURE'

*Rulin waishi* «儒林外史» ('The Unofficial History of the Forest of the Literati', from here on RLWS), by Wu Jingzi 吳敬梓 (1701–1754), represents one of the highest achievements of the *literati* novel, written by the intellectual élites of late imperial China for a limited number of readers from the same social background.[1] The novel is a satirical representation of the *literati* class, the intellectual and political élite of the country, from among which the government officials were selected through a complex examination system. The scholars in RLWS are for the most part hideous creatures, corrupted by a reality that disfigures human beings and by instincts hidden behind the Confucian virtues

---

My thanks to David Walthall for the accurate linguistic revision and to Igor Dorfmann-Lazarev for his valuable advice on the passages in Russian. I would also like to thank the editors of this volume, Daniel Derrin and Hannah Burrows, for their suggestions and support.

---

A. Di Toro (✉)
Università per Stranieri di Siena, Siena, Italy
e-mail: ditoro@unistrasi.it

© The Author(s), under exclusive license to Springer Nature Switzerland AG 2020
D. Derrin, H. Burrows (eds.), *The Palgrave Handbook of Humour, History, and Methodology*, https://doi.org/10.1007/978-3-030-56646-3_24

459

they preach; the few positive characters are *literati* whose pure ideals are challenged by reality. The characters often have real models. Some of the positive ones have been identified in close friends and relatives of the author, and one of them, Du Shaoqing 杜少卿, is even modelled on the author himself.[2] RLWS is not only a satirical novel: it envisages also a solution for the corruption of society and its values, but this solution, represented by a proposal of reform of Confucian rituality and by the virtue of withdrawal from power and career, does not offer a final answer: the novel 'resists closure'.[3]

RLWS is a satirical and ironic account of the inconsistency between reality and ideal. From this incongruity emerge all the absurdities and paradoxes governing both human beings and society, often expressed by a humorous tone. This chapter introduces the novel, some of its humorous themes and registers, and, rooted as they are in the highly ritualised social codes of the *literati*, how they have been reproduced in the English, Russian and French versions of the novel. Moreover, I shall observe the strategies adopted by the translators in order to give a new life to eighteenth-century Chinese satire. In a final section, I will consider the broader contexts in which the different versions were made.

Devoid as it is of a narrative plot, RLWS' structure has been often criticised as evasive, especially by the scholars of the May Fourth Era (1920s), probably because of the influence of the model of nineteenth-century European fiction on the Chinese intellectuals of the time.[4] As a matter of fact, while innovative, RLWS follows a pattern that was already consolidated in the vernacular novel.[5]

The Prologue (Chapter 1) of RLWS introduces Wang Mian, an artist who, by refusing to serve the government, represents the model of the ideal 'true' scholar. Living in the Yuan period (thirteenth-fourteenth centuries), Wang foresees the spiritual decay of the *literati*. Part I (Chapters 2–30) is centred on the decline predicted by the artist, narrating the hypocrisy and greed for power and riches of a series of scholars of the Ming time (fourteenth–seventeenth centuries). Part II (Chapters 31–37) depicts a group of *literati* who try to resist moral decay by proposing a reformed Confucian ritual, the Wu Taibo ceremony. Part III (Chapters 38–55) follows the path of these virtuous Confucians who try to spread their vision throughout society, but, in the end, fail. The only alternative solution seems to be a lyrical vision of existence, as represented by four eccentrics in Chapter 55. The Epilogue (Chapter 56) commemorates the participants of Taibo ceremony and is concluded by a poem. The authenticity of the last chapter has been questioned for a long time; it was removed from the twentieth-century editions of the novel and reintroduced only since the 1980s.[6]

In his *Brief History of Chinese Fiction* (1925), Lu Xun 魯迅 (1881–1936) thus defines the style of RLWS: '*The Scholars* is the first novel in which a writer criticises social abuses without any personal malice [...]. The style is warm and humorous, gentle and ironic'.[7] Although RLWS indeed presents situations and characters that can be called 'warm and gentle', the novel at moments is cruelly sarcastic or coarsely grotesque.

At first, RLWS was criticised as a cynical book offering a negative image of the world.[8] Qing literary critics replied to these allegations, defending the moral purpose of the novel. Huang Anjin 黃安謹 remarked that Wu Jingzi's intention was to write a book 'in order to awaken the world, and not to curse it' ('爲醒世計, 非爲罵世也').[9] The interpretation of RLWS as a novel imbued with benignity was shared by many intellectuals of the twentieth century. Tian Liaosheng 天僇生 (1880–1913) placed RLWS among the novels that '[express] pain for the turbid [aspects] of society' ('痛社會之渾濁').[10] In 1968, Chih-tsing Hsia wrote: 'Confucianism [in RLWS] is tinged with melancholy over the futility of government action or social reform'.[11]

In the last decades, critics have also developed an intense interest towards an aesthetic and narratological analysis of Wu Jingzi's masterpiece.[12] However, this analysis was already present, and related to the moral issue, in one of the first stems of RLWS criticism, that is the Preface, by Xianzhai laoren 閑齋老人 ('Old Man of Leisure Studio'), and the Chapter comments included in the earliest extant version of the novel.[13]

The Preface places RLWS in the tradition of 'ancient and modern unofficial historical records' ('古今稗官野史'), with the aim: 'to be prone to good and loath evil (*shan shan wu e* 善善惡惡) [...], in order to [...] preserve uncorrupted hearts and customs [in the readers]'.[14] Xianzhai laoren then connects the moral issue to the structural one, observing that *gong ming fu gui* 功名富貴 ('success, fame, riches and rank') are the 'skeleton' (*gu* 骨) of the book.[15]

The prevailing voice in RLWS is perhaps the one of irony, directed to the characters, but also to the readers themselves, as clearly pointed out by the author of the Preface: 'The number of characters who appear in the novel is beyond counting [...]. No matter what sort of personality the reader may have, he can be sure to find [a character] who will mirror [the reader] himself'.[16]

## Expression of Humour in Chinese Literature Before the Modern Era

In 1924 Lin Yutang 林語堂 (1895–1976) coined the Chinese neologism *youmo* 幽默 ('humour', from the English term), implying that the concept was new to China.[17] Later, Lin further explained his idea, asserting that something similar to the 'Western' type of humour (in fact, 'English' type) had existed in ancient China, especially in the Daoist tradition, to find later expression only in unorthodox literary traditions, including the vernacular novel.[18] Lin Yutang fostered English-style humour as a 'civilizing tool for the modernization of Chinese society': in his opinion 'humour should have a didactic purpose'.[19] Among the few literary works quoted to illustrate the humoristic tradition in Chinese literature, Lin also mentioned RLWS, which 'presents a form of worldly wisdom (*shigu renqing* 世故人情) and, in addition to humour, provides a mixture of satire as well'.[20] Lin Yutang, in line with his contemporaries mentioned above, like Lu Xun and Hu Shi, finds in RLWS a soft tone of humorous wisdom, that mingled with the sharper satirical one. In order to be able to comprehend the manifold comic devices used by Wu Jingzi to highlight the evils and absurdities of his contemporaries, I briefly describe some aspects of the Chinese humorous tradition.

As observed by Jocelyn Chey, who prefers to speak of 'humour "with Chinese characteristics"', rather than of a 'peculiarly Chinese sense of humour', one of its main features is represented by the influence of Confucian etiquette in many aspects of social life and mentality.[21] Confucianism, however, does not only have a role of cultural background: it has also developed its own idea and ideal of humour. In the Confucian tradition, being associated with *xi* 喜 ('joy') and *le* 樂 ('delight'), humour has to undergo the process of refinement and culturalisation involving all the emotions. As stated by Xu Weihe, 'in accordance with the spirit of the Rites (*li* 禮), proper humour should be moderate, private, tasteful, useful and benign'.[22] Not only does humour have to be 'proper', but it should also have a 'proper usage', with a certain amount of compassion and a didactic purpose.[23]

As far as Daoism is concerned, one of the main texts of this tradition, the *Zhuangzi* 莊子 (fourth-third centuries BCE), makes large use of humour. Funny anecdotes, playful remarks, witticisms and self-irony all contribute to questioning the value we usually give to social conventions, hierarchies, language (which is limited in its nature) and to all the categories that prevent our comprehension of, or union with, the Dao. In some passages, humour is refined and highly intellectual, while in others it is rude, farcical and sometimes almost shocking.[24] As we shall see, all the forms and nuances of humour briefly illustrated here appear in RLWS.

## Aspects of Humour in RLWS and in the English, Russian and French Translations of the Novel

As stated by Shang Wei, the class of Chinese *literati* is an 'elusive category [...], held together by a collective ethos as well as by cultural prestige and socio-political status'.[25] During the eighteenth century, however, many of these educated men, prepared specifically in order to be able to serve in the administration, found themselves in possession of a degree, but without an office, thus deprived of financial means. At the same time, despite their claim of a moral superiority, corruption was a real plague among Qing bureaucrats. This situation catalysed an intellectual crisis that, having originated already in the Ming period, found full expression during the eighteenth century, when literature and thought were pervaded with 'a very profound sense of epistemological uncertainty'.[26] In this context, *literati* novels represent an intellectual laboratory in which the 'conflicting forces' of the society were absorbed: although 'characterised by a serious, conservative Confucian tone, [...] yet irony constantly creeps in, with the free play of intellectual fancy, wit, and humorous observation that produces caricature'.[27]

Being a novel of self-representation, the readers of RLWS shared with the author the same formation, the same values, codes and language: the main ingredients of Wu's satire and irony, albeit so complex, were clear to his public. The use of refined codes that were shared by the Chinese intellectual *élite* of the eighteenth century represents a serious challenge to the translators.[28]

After a series of partial translations, realised since the 1930s, the novel in its entirety was translated in a few European languages between the 1950s and the 1970s.[29] The first complete translated version of the novel is the English one, by Gladys Yang and Yang Xianyi, and published by Beijing Foreign Languages Press in 1957 with the title *The Scholars*.[30] The Yangs' version, like all the translations I analyse, follows the 55-chapter edition of the novel. *The Scholars* is extraordinarily readable, but the language is elegant and never shallow. The rare footnotes are extremely agile, there is neither Preface nor Introduction, only a 'List of Principal Characters' and an appendix on the examination system and official ranks.[31]

The first edition of the Russian version of RLWS was published in Moscow in 1959, translated by Dimitrij N. Voskresenskij, with the title *Neoficial'naja istorija konfuciancev* ('Unofficial History of the Confucians').[32] While footnotes are reduced to the essentials, the translator adds an extensive introduction to the novel and Wu Jingzi's life and an appendix on the examination system. When he approached the novel, Voskresenskij was still a young translator: while he is extremely precise, his Russian sometimes seems affected by Chinese syntax. The rendering of the lyrical passages, however, is extremely elegant, and the dialogues sound vivid and rich in nuance.[33]

The French version (*Chronique indiscrète des Mandarins*, 1976), translated by Tchang Fou-jouei, is a very learned version, with detailed footnotes, an appendix, consisting of a 'List of Principal Characters', a bibliography of studies related to RLWS and a brilliant introduction by André Levy (1925–2017).[34] Although being extremely adherent to the original text, Tchang Fou-jouei succeeds in reformulating it in an elegant French prose. At moments, however, the translation lacks incisiveness, especially in some dialogues.

In order to better appreciate the creative solutions of the different versions of the novel, we should turn back to the expression of humour in RLWS. The writer shows an accomplished mastery of different comic devices and satirical strategies, and this skill requires an equal ability in translators.[35]

According to Mo Chunxing 莫純星, one of the most used satirical strategies in the novel is that of contrast.[36] As an example, we could observe the moment of Wang Mian's definitive 'conversion' or, better still, 'diversion', from official service to art (Chapter 1). Wang Mian is a brilliant boy who earns his living by looking after the buffalo of a neighbour. One day, while he is contemplating the lovely view of the lake after a summer shower, three *literati* enter the scene and begin a conversation concerning money, relations and privileges. From that moment on, the boy decides to devote himself to painting and to give up any idea of a bureaucratic career. This moment is particularly meaningful, since Wang Mian represents, in the novel, the model of the ideal scholar.

464   A. DI TORO

那日正是黃梅時候，天氣煩躁。王冕放牛倦了，在綠草地上坐着。須臾，濃雲密布，一陣大雨過了。那黑雲邊上鑲着白雲，漸漸散去，透出一派日光來，照耀得滿湖通紅。湖邊上山，青一塊，紫一塊，綠一塊。樹枝上都像水洗過一番的，尤其綠得可愛。湖裏有十來枝荷花，苞子上清水滴滴，荷葉上水珠滾來滾去。王冕看了一回，心裏想道：「古人說：『人在畫圖中』，其實不錯。可惜我這裏沒有一個畫工，把這荷花畫他幾枝，也覺有趣。」又心裏想道：「天下那有個學不會的事，我何不自畫他幾枝。」 [37]

One sultry day in early summer, tired after leading the buffalo to graze, [Wang Mian] sat down on the grass. Suddenly dense clouds gathered, and there was a heavy shower of rain. Then the black storm clouds fringed with fleecy white drifted apart, and the sun shone through, bathing the whole lake in crimson light. The hills by the lake were blue, violet and emerald. The trees, freshly washed by the rain, were a lovelier green than ever. Crystal drops were dripping from a dozen lotus buds in the lake, while beads of water rolled about the leaves.

As Wang Mien watched, he thought, 'The ancients said, "In a beautiful scene a man feels he is part of a picture". How true! What a pity there is no painter here to paint these sprays of lotus. That would be good'. Then he reflected, 'There's nothing a man can't learn. Why shouldn't I paint them myself?'[38]

All the translators are acutely aware of the importance of these lines that, by a rhythmical change, interrupt the account of the life of the young Wang Mian in a moment of suspension. The original version contains a rhyme ('湖邊上山, 青一塊 *kuài*, 紫一塊 *kuài*, 綠一塊 *kuài*。樹枝上都像水洗過一番的, 尤其綠得可愛 *ài*')[39] and pauses and repetitions that contribute to the musicality of the description ('苞子上*shàng*—清水滴滴, 荷葉上*shàng*—水珠滾來滾去。')[40] Although the translators do not reproduce the rhymes, and only Voskresenskij tries an assonance (*izumrud*, 'emerald', and *žemčug*, 'pearl'),[41] all the three versions use the peculiarities offered by their own languages in order to re-create the lyrical atmosphere of the landscape. To offer an example, the rendering of '樹枝上都像水洗過一番的, 尤其綠得可愛' with 'The trees, freshly washed by the rain, were a lovelier green than ever', by Yang and Yang, is a very vivid translation, where 'lovelier' perfectly matches, even etymologically, *ke'ai* 可愛 ('lovable; lovely').

The more lyrical the rendering of the passage, the stronger the ironical effect of contrast pursued by Wu Jingzi with the apparition of three anonymous *literati* who, very dignified in appearance, move towards the shore to admire the landscape, but strike the reader with their vulgarity as soon as they open their mouth:[42]

吃了一回，那胖子開口道：「危老先生回來了。新買了住宅，比京裏鐘樓街的房子還大些，值得二千兩銀子。因老先生要買，房主人讓了幾十兩銀賣了，圖個名望體面。前月初十搬家，太尊、縣父母都親自到門來賀，留着吃酒到二三更天。街上的人那一個不敬。」 [...]

「他 [危老先生]若肯下鄉回拜，也免得這些鄉戶人家，放了驢和豬在你我田裏吃糧食。」[...]。[王冕]自此，聚的錢不買書了，託人向城裏買些胭脂鉛粉之類，學畫荷花。[43]

They began eating. After a while, the fat man said, 'Mr. Wei has come back. His new house is even bigger than the one in Bell Tower Street in the capital. The price was two thousand taels of silver, but, because the purchaser was so distinguished, the owner allowed him several dozen taels discount for the sake of the credit he would get from this transaction. On the tenth of last month Mr. Wei moved in. The prefect and the county magistrate called to congratulate him, and stayed there feasting until nearly midnight. There is nobody who does not respect him.

'[...] if Mr. Wei condescends to come to the village to return the visit, the villagers won't dare to turn their donkeys and pigs loose to eat the grain in our fields any more'. [...] After that, Wang Mien no longer spent his savings on books, but asked somebody to buy paints for him in the city, and learnt to paint lotus flowers.[44]

In a few lines, the conversation reflects the betrayal of more than one fundamental Confucian value: the use of power in order to obtain advantages, boast of one's position and relations, disdain towards common people (the villagers) and uninhibited talk of money. The passage is typically caricatural, aiming at the effect of ironical contrast with the lyricism of the landscape in front of the three *literati*, who, immersed in their mundane talk, completely neglect the scenery. Unconcern about the beauty of nature is recurrent in the novel and is undoubtedly a litmus test to distinguish true and false Confucians.[45] This indifference is perhaps the paradigm of the 'death of poetic consciousness' painfully felt by Wu Jingzi, who, in Shang Wei's opinion, envisaged in the lyric vision of life the possible, albeit ephemeral, home for the spiritually homeless intellectuals of his time.[46]

The versions analysed here use different devices to achieve the effect of contrast. Lack of material interest should be ingrained in Chinese intellectuals, but among European cultural élites, this issue is probably not as sensitive as in China, so the passage requires a particular care. Materialism here, as in many other places of the novel, is symbolised also by gluttony. While the Russian translator renders literally *chijiu* 吃酒 [to eat/drink alcohol; to eat and drink generously] with 'пили вино' [(they) drank wine], the English and the French versions use 'to feast', thus underlying the self-indulgence of Mr. Wei and his guests.[47] Voskresenskij, however, stresses more another moral deficiency of the false Confucians, that is the abuse of power, caricaturally expressed by the idea of making use of the connection between one of the three *literati* and Mr. Wei in order to prevent the villagers pasturing their animals on the fields of the three gentlemen. The Russian translator emphasises the contempt towards the farmers, using the derogatory term 'деревенщина' [a country bumpkin] to render *xianghu renjia* 鄉戶人家 [village people].

466 A. DI TORO

Wang Mian's choice to shrink from *gong ming fu gui* 功名富貴 [success, fame, riches and rank] and to turn towards the ideal of *Tian ren heyi* 天人合一 literally, 'Heaven and man form a unity' recalls the theme, typical of the Daoist school of thought, of 'Preserving one's life by retiring from official title'.[48] However, the indifference to bureaucratic career in RLWS is substantially different from the one pursued by Daoists. Daoist indifference to position is an existential choice deriving from the stress 'upon the individual in nature rather than the individual in the society',[49] while the indifference to career shown by the 'real' scholars in RLWS derives from their disgust towards the betrayal of Confucian ideals among the bureaucratic class and, at the same time, the value given to modesty and withdrawal and the attraction towards the lyrical level of existence.[50] We can notice a similar attitude in Du Shaoqing, when a Magistrate calls to inform him about the announcement of an extraordinary examination session and Du fakes an illness in order to avoid it.[51] The passage has a farcical nuance:

小廝進來說: 「鄧老爺來了[...]」杜少卿叫兩個小廝攙扶着, 做個十分有病的模樣, 路也走不全, 出來拜謝知縣; 拜在地下, 就不得起來。知縣慌忙扶了起來, 坐下就道: 「朝廷大典, 李大人專要借光, 不想先生病得狼狽至此。不知幾時可以勉強就道?」杜少卿道: 「治晚不幸大病, 生死難保, 這事斷不能了。」[52]

Just then the servant-boy came in. 'Magistrate Teng [Deng] is here', he announced. [...] Ordering two servants to support him, Tu [Du] tottered out looking desperately ill to greet the magistrate. He knelt down, then failed to get up again. The magistrate hastily helped him to his feet, and they sat down. 'The court has issued an important decree [...]', said Magistrate Teng [Deng], 'I had no idea you were so ill. How soon do you think you will be able to travel?' 'I'm afraid my illness may prove incurable, hence what you ask is impossible,' replied Tu.[53]

The way in which Du Shaoqing receives his visitor, stressing his indisposition, clearly shows that he wants to make fun of magistrate Deng. The question of whether Du Shaoqing is acting according to proper or improper (Confucian) humour remains ambiguous. Du Shaoqing is not, in fact, a model of virtue, even though he catalyses the fondness of both the author and the reader: he is rather inconstant, indulges in idle occupations, he does not always abide by etiquette in his relationship with his wife and, most importantly, he is incorrigibly and naively extravagant with his money.

The translators make different choices in interpreting Du's jest. In the Yangs' version, the description of the illness given by Du as '治晚不幸大病, 生死難保'—literally, 'unfortunately, the disease of this "late-born" [self-reference formula used when reporting to a superior] is serious, I do not know whether I am going to live or to die'—is rendered 'I'm afraid my illness may prove incurable', avoiding the use of 'to die' and opting for the immediacy of the cue. The French version reads: 'Moi, votre surbodonné (*zhiwan* 治晚), je suis par malheur gravement malade, je ne suis pas sûr de pouvoir vivre' [Unfortunately,

I, your subordinate, am seriously ill, and I am not sure whether I am going to live].[54] We may observe that, in rendering the self-derogatory formula used when talking to a superior, Tchang Fou-jouei underlines the scorn poured by Du Shaoqing upon his interlocutor. Du Shaoqing, here, is only apparently gentle: we could recall the traditional formula of *xiao zhong dao* 笑中刀 [a knife (concealed) in laughter].[55] The French version does justice to the sharpness of Du's humour.

The scene in which the scholar discusses the question with his wife is, on the contrary, an example of Du Shaoqing's gentle irony:

娘子笑道:「朝廷叫你去做官，你為甚麼粧病不去?」杜少卿道:「你好呆!放着南京這樣好頑的所在，留着我在家，春天秋天，同你出去看花吃酒，好不快活! 為甚麼要送我到京裏去?假使連你也帶往京裏，京裏又冷，你身子又弱，一陣風吹得凍死了，也不好。還是不去的妥當。」[56]

'When you are invited to court to become an official, why refuse on the pretext of illness?' asked Mrs. Tu [Du] with a smile. 'Don't be absurd! What! Leave an amusing place like Nanking? Don't you enjoy having me at home, to go out with you in the spring and autumn to look at the flowers and drink wine? Why do you want to pack me off to Peking? Suppose I take you along too? It's a cold place, the capital, and you're so delicate that one gust of wind there would freeze you to death! That would never do. No, no, I'd better not go'.[57]

The passage sounds like a parody of a *topos* in Chinese traditional fiction, the one of the virtuous wife who exhorts her husband to study hard and take part in the official examinations. Usually, either the husband abides by these sensible words, thereby commencing a successful career, or he does not listen to his wise spouse, thus ruining himself and his family. Here the situation is completely different: Du refuses because he has another ideal of life, and he knows that his wife shares his ideals. The refusal is expressed in a playful and intimate manner that is finely conveyed in the Yangs' translation, by the spontaneous rendering of Du's answer '為甚麼要送我到京裏去?' [why do you want to send me to the capital?] with 'Why do you want to pack me off to Peking?' and with the ironical but delicate concern for his spouse's health: 'It's a cold place, the capital, and you're so delicate that one gust of wind there would freeze you to death!'. In order to express the intimacy of the couple, Voskresenskij exploits the richness of affective nuances typical of Russian, using 'ты' [you (singular)], in 'Эх ты, глупая!' [O you, silly!], and by the familiar 'Там холодно, а ты у меня слабенькая' [It is cold there, and you, mine (possessive form conveying affection), are so delicate (diminutive-endearment form)].[58] The translators make here an effort to render a peculiarity of Chinese culture, where love is usually not explicitly communicated by passionate words, but rather by concern for the wellbeing of the partner and by the level of informality in the relationship.[59] While Du's humour sounds sharp and even disdainful with

468    A. DI TORO

superiors that, in his opinion, do not deserve his respect, he is extremely gentle with his wife and friends.[60]

Many scenes of RLWS take place during banquets or similar social gatherings, ideal arenas for display of power. One of these episodes offers a remarkable example of improper and high-handed humour. Chapters 2 and 3 tell the rise of Zhou Jin 周進, a poor and unsuccessful scholar who, already in his sixties, becomes at last a powerful mandarin. When we first meet him, he is not even in possession of the lowest degree, the one of *xiucai* 秀才, 'licentiate', literally, 'fine talent'. Guest of honour in a banquet organised to celebrate his election as the new teacher of a village school, he is the victim of a series of humiliating pranks by Mei Jiu 梅玖, a younger scholar, who is, instead, a *xiucai*. Noticing that Zhou Jin abstains from meat, Mei Jiu recites a joke in verses:

「我因先生吃齋, 倒想起一個笑話, 是前日在城裏我那案伯顧老相公家聽見他說的。有個做先生的一字至七字詩。」眾人都停了箸, 聽他念詩。他便念道:
「呆, 秀才, 吃長齋, 鬍鬚滿腮, 經書不揭開, 紙筆自己安排, 明年不請我自來。」[61]

'Your fasting reminds me of a joke I heard the other day from Mr. Ku [Gu] in the county town', said Mei Chiu [Jiu]. 'It is a one character to seven character verse about a teacher'. The villagers put down their chopsticks to listen, while he recited: *A foolish scholar / Fasted so long, / Whiskers covered his cheeks; / Neglecting to study the classics, / He left pen and paper aside. / He'll come without being invited next year.*[62]

To be exposed to public scorn is a painful experience for its victim in any culture, but in Chinese culture, characterised by the centrality of the concept of face (*mian* 面 or *lian* 臉) linked to the dignity of the person, it is all the more distressing.[63] Humour in this passage is thus particularly aggressive, and the poem sounds rather disdainful than playful. While both the English and the French versions opt not to render the metrical form of the jocular verses, the Russian one tries a re-creation of the metrical form by a calligram:

Один
глупец–сюцай
постился так усердно,
что бородою длинною оброс,
[…].[64]

In spite of Zhou Jin's embarrassment after this joke, in order to add to his scorn, Mei Jiu, when criticised by a guest, comments: '但這個話不是為周長兄, 他說明了是個秀才。' [But these words were not about Mr. Zhou. They were about a licentiate (*xiucai*)], underlying once more Zhou's inferior position. It is worth underlining here the choice made by the Yang couple, who use the term 'scholar', instead of 'licentiate', for *xiucai*, thus giving emphasis to the fact that Mei Jiu does not even recognise Zhou Jin as a scholar.[65]

To conclude the discussion I will turn to a final example that draws more clearly on the farcically grotesque and on caricature. Caricature and grotesque, rooted in Chinese folklore and traditionally rejected in lofty literary genres, are present in many vernacular Ming-period novels and, among the *literati* novels, appear not only in RLWS, but also in another eighteenth-century masterpiece, *Honglou Meng* 紅樓夢 (*Dream of the Red Chamber*).[66]

One of the main caricatural characters of the novel is Butcher Hu, father-in-law of another unfortunate and miserable scholar, Fan Jin 范進. Disappointed by the constant failures of his son-in-law in the examinations, Butcher Hu abuses him in any possible way, and criticises his obstinacy when, after having passed the first level, Fan Jin asks him for money in order to be able to attend the second level:

范進因沒有盤費, 走去同丈人商議, 被胡屠戶一口啐在臉上, 罵了一個狗血噴頭道:「不要失了你的時了!你自己只覺得中了一個相公, 就『癩蝦蟆想吃起天鵝肉』來! [...] 如今痴心就想中起老爺來!這些中老爺的 [...]都有萬貫家私, 一個個方面大耳。像你這尖嘴猴腮, 也該撒拋尿自己照照!不三不四就想天鵝屁吃!趁早收了這心, 明年在我們行事裏替你尋一個館, 每年尋幾兩銀子, 養活你那老不死的老娘和你老婆是正經!」 [67]

[...] he had no money for the journey. He went to ask his father-in-law to help. Butcher Hu spat in his face, and poured out a torrent of abuse. 'Don't be a fool!' he roared. 'Just passing one examination has turned your head completely—you're like a toad trying to swallow a swan! [...] Now, like a fool, you want to pass the higher examination and become an official. [...] All those officials have pots of money, dignified faces and big ears. But your mouth sticks out and you've a chin like an ape's. You should piss on the ground and look at your face in the puddle! You look like a monkey, yet you want to become an official. Come off it! Next year I shall find a teaching job for you with one of my friends so that you can make a few taels of silver to support that old, neverdying mother of yours and your wife—and it's high time you did!'[68]

Through Butcher Hu's words, Wu Jingzi displays his mastery in the construction of dialogues and also the peculiar modernity of his narrative.[69] The rendition of this character requires mimetic ability and a daring attitude.

Butcher Hu's colourful language is rich with idioms. An example is the proverb '癩蝦蟆想喫起天鵝肉', literally, 'a leprous toad that wants to eat swan's meat', meaning a preposterous desire, used twice, with a foul variation '想天鵝屁喫', 'to desire to eat a swan's arse'. Yang and Yang's version renders the idiom with 'a toad trying to swallow a swan' (not wanting to translate *lai* 癩, 'leprosy'), and censors its variation by substituting it with 'You look like a monkey, yet you want to become an official', compensating the loss by repeating the parallel between Fan Jin and a monkey, not repeated in the original. The Russian translator softens both the idiom and its variation, with different solutions. The idiom is rendered with 'Ты [...] стал похож на глупую жабу, которая собиралась полакомиться лебединым мясом' [you begin to look like a foolish (глупый, for *lai*) toad, that is going to treat itself to swan's meat], and its variation as 'Тоже, лебединого мяса захотел!' [And still, you would like (to eat) swan's meat!].[70] Tchang Fou-jouei's translation reads 'un crapaud lépreux qui pense se nourrir de chair de cygnet céleste' [a leprous toad who thinks to feed on the flesh of a celestial swan] adding a chapter note.[71] The French translator is the only one not to censor the coarseness of the second expression, by rendering it with: 'Comment avec une tête pareille peux-tu penser manger du pet ['fart'] de cygne?' [How with that head can you think of eating a swan's fart?].[72] Adding colour to Butcher Hu's insult, his son-in-law is not even worthy of dreaming about eating a swan's fart.

From the different choices made in rendering this passage, we could envisage some cultural differences regarding the potential foreign readers of the novel. From the translators' point of view, Russian and Anglophone readers were likely not prepared to find such vulgarity in a classical novel. By comparison, the French reader living in the post-1968 period was probably much more accustomed to expressions of coarseness, and even scatology, in literature.

## Translation and Context

In this brief journey through RLWS and some of its Western translations, we have observed a few examples of how the different translators have rendered the nuances of some of the expressions of humour present in the novel. Besides personal taste and style, differences in time and space between the versions and the audiences to whom they were intended may explain different attitudes of the translators.

Every translation implies a 'Model Reader, who is different from the reader of the original text'.[73] Wu Jingzi's Model Reader, a member of the eighteenth century's Chinese cultural élite, is very distant from twentieth-century readers, who, not having much competence in the cultural context of RLWS, very likely are 'encyclopedically inadequate readers'.[74] Moreover, the socio-political, cultural and editorial contexts in which these translations appeared present some peculiarities that may have contributed to the concept of the Model Readers that the translators had in mind. The Yang-Yang translation was made for an imagined international reader of the middle of the last century, a potential friend of China, maybe not particularly interested in Qing culture, but rather in gaining a general knowledge of the traditions of the Middle Kingdom. Behind the activity of the state-sponsored publishing house of *The Scholars* (the Beijing Foreign Languages Press, from here on FLP) stood a precise political agenda: to use outward translation for 'nation branding and promoting Chinese communism abroad'.[75] Moreover, FLP controlled the whole translation process: selection of texts, original text editing, translating, revising, publishing and distributing.[76] Besides the rendering of 'revolutionary literature', the necessity of asserting Chinese national identity and some aspects of its traditional legacy in the international scene led to many translations of masterpieces of classical and vernacular literature of the past. Although translations of classical literature had less political implications, they could also be susceptible to criticism. Thus, Yang Xianyi describes his activity for the Foreign Languages Press in the 1950s:

> I only translated classical Chinese literature, so I was often lucky with my choices. However sometimes even classical poems were chosen for their 'ideological' or political content, and we often argued with the editors about their choices, reaching a compromise only after lengthy discussion. [...] There was a very nice [Ming] story called 'The Pearl Vest'. The original edition contained some exquisitely written erotic passages. Though we were using the original unexpurgated edition, our English edition was censored and these passages were deleted.[77]

As we have seen, Butcher Hu's foul language was censored in *The Scholars*. Although we do not have any evidence about the phase of the translating-editorial process in which censorship was exerted (self-censorship by the translators, revision by an editor or 'sanitization' by some political authority?), the translating choice is however coherent with the 'need to preserve China's "face"'[78] and the concern of presenting China as a civilised country, which were central aspects of FLP's policy.[79] The readability of the Yangs' version is also very much in tune with the aims of the publishing house, that is to reach Anglophone readers from the capitalist world and even to act as vehicular versions, as happened with many of these English translations, that led to renditions in yet other languages.[80] The use of mother-language translators was crucial to reach high quality standards in order to guarantee the international circulation of the books: as stated by Yang Xianyi in reference to his wife, 'Without her, I could have not rendered them into good English'.[81]

Ni Xiuhua has placed FLP's activity in the background of the cultural diplomacy fulfilled by the main actors of the Cold War.[82] Interestingly enough, the almost contemporary translation by Voskresenskij was conceived in a similar atmosphere. As in China, also in the USSR translation (both outward and inward) was considered a powerful means for self-empowerment and prestige and was promoted as a fundamental part of a project of cultural internationalisation.[83] Moreover, the Russian version has its roots in the brief decade of mutual friendship between the Soviet Union and China (1950–1960) and in the climate of renovated vigour of translation activity and of partial openness that followed Stalin's death (1953).[84] The Model Russian reader of the RLWS of Chruščëv's time was probably a well-educated person with a strong interest in the neighbouring country. Although RLWS was historically remote, and thus ideologically harmless (in spite of the partial openness after 1953, foreign culture was still considered a potential threat), as a matter of fact, the novel deals with subjects (especially the hypocritical use of ideology in function of power) that could perhaps have been too sensitive in the USSR a few years before. It should also be remembered that the literary translator, in the Soviet Union of 1950s and 1960s, was considered as a 'pedagogical agent', with the precise duty to educate readers.[85] The translator, together with the editors, was also responsible for 'puritanical' censorship, concerning sex, foul language, offensive odours, uncleanliness and certain parts of the body.[86] Some of the choices made by Voskresenskij (or by the editors), such as censoring the coarse vocabulary of Butcher Hu, may be an example. If the translation choice of the passage is similar to the one made in *The Scholars*, the motivation is however different: in this case the translator was not a Chinese intellectual representing his own culture, but a sinologist who had to contribute to creating a positive image of China, a friendly socialist nation, among Soviet readers.

As far as the French edition is concerned, the back cover of the book may help us to imagine the French reader of the 1970s at whom the translation is aimed: 'Qui veut connaître la sociétè chinoise d'avant la Révolution, c'est [...] Wou King-tseu [Wu Jingzi] qu'il devra lire de toute urgence' [Whoever wants to know Chinese society preceding the Revolution, should immediately read Wu Jingzi]. The link to the present is strongly underlined, since in France the interest in China at the time was linked to the attraction towards contemporary, post-Revolutionary China. The French reader, in the mind of the publishing house, must have been a very motivated intellectual with the desire to acquire a deep knowledge of Chinese traditional culture, and the style of the translation, as well as the rich apparatus of chapter notes, reflects that idea of the Model Reader. The idea of a well-educated reader is stressed again in the back cover by comparing *Dead Souls* with RLWS posing a provoking question: '[Wu...], celui qu'on appelle souvent le «Gogol chinois». Pourquoi ne pas dire de Gogol qu'il est le Wou King-tseu [Wu Jingzi] russe?' [Wu... who is called the 'Chinese Gogol'. But why couldn't we say of Gogol that he is the Russian Wu Jingzi?]. The French Model Reader of 1970s is thus expected to be acquainted with the classics of world literature and to be able to read the novel through the lens of cultural relativism. The adequacy-oriented translation approach adopted in rendering, as we have seen, *realia*, idioms and also the vulgarity of some passages of RLWS, reflects this idea of a mature, aware and unprejudiced reader.[87]

All three versions, with their various peculiarities, make an effort to render the nuances of RLWS' humour and to communicate to Western readers the deep meaning of the novel, that is:

> to expose hideousness neither in order to exhibit hideousness, nor to derive ephemeral solace from giving impulsively vent to [the author's] feelings: it stems from a 'grief for the world' (*youshi* '憂世'), with the aim of transforming society and human heart.[88]

Seen together, the three versions reveal both the difficulty and the possibility of translating historical humour into a tone that suits the particular Model Reader in view.

## NOTES

1. On the *literati* novel, see Shang, 'The Literati Era'.
2. Since the Qing period, much has been written about the real models for RLWS' characters: see Li, 'RLWS yanjiu shilüe', 538–40.
3. Shang, *RLWS and Cultural Transformation*, 160ff.
4. See Lin, 'Ritual and Narrative Structure in RLWS', 248, and Shang, *RLWS and Cultural Transformation*, 179.
5. The main innovation is the minimisation of the role of the simulated storyteller-narrator, thus depriving the reader of the guidance of the author (see Shang, 'The Literati Era', 276).
6. The first editions of the novel (the *Woxian caotang* 臥閑草堂 edition, published in 1803, and the following editions of the nineteenth century), all include Chapter 56, but some Qing scholars began already to question its authenticity (see Li, 'RLWS de banben'). Shang Wei demonstrates its coherence with the general plan of RLWS (*RLWS and Cultural Transformation*, 163 and ff.).
7. Lu, *Brief History of Chinese Fiction*, 273.
8. Li, 'RLWS yanjiu shilüe', 520.
9. Huang Anjin 黃安謹, 'Rulin waishi ping' 儒林外史評 ('Commentary to RLWS', *Bao wen ke* 寶文閣 ed. of RLWS, Shanghai, 1885), in Wu Jingzi, *RLWS*, 695.
10. Tian Liaosheng 天僇生, 'Zhongguo lidai xiaoshuo lun' 中國历代小說史論 ('Essay on the History of the Chinese Novel of the Past Dynasties'), *Yueyue xiaoshuo* 月月小说 (*Monthly Fiction*), 1907, Vol. 1, N. 11, quoted in Li, 'RLWS yanjiu shilüe', 520. Hu Shi 胡適 (1891–1962) wrote that RLWS 'satirises the world from devotion to public good' ('用公心諷世'; Idem, '*Guanchang xianxing ji xu*' 官場現形記序 ('Preface to *Observations on the Current State of the Official Circles*'), 1927, quoted in Ibid., 527.
11. Hsia, *The Classic Chinese Novel*, 209.
12. See Li, 'RLWS yanjiu shilüe', 540 ff.; see also Shang, *RLWS and Cultural Transformation*.
13. Scholars disagree on whether behind the pseudonym of Xianzhai laoren could lie Wu Jingzi himself (see Shang, *RLWS and Cultural Transformation*, 312 ff.). The Preface is dated 1736, a watershed year in Wu Jingzi's life, when he decided not to take part in the imperial examinations and withdraw from the bureaucratic career. Both Preface and chapter comments of the *Woxian caotang* edition are published in the Appendix of Li Hanqiu's edition and have been translated into English by David Rolston in *How to read the Chinese Novel*, 249 ff. In this article, I follow this translation with slight changes.
14. Wu Jingzi, *RLWS*, 687–88. The expression '*shan shan wu e*' is a quotation from Sima Qian's *Shiji* (*Records of the Historian*, first century B.C.), see Rolston, *How to read the Chinese Novel*, 249, n. 1. I express my gratitude to the anonymous referee for the valuable advice concerning the first part of the quotation.
15. Wu Jingzi, *RLWS*, 687; translation in Rolston, *How to read the Chinese Novel*, 250.
16. Ibid.
17. The term was first used in Lin Yutang's article entitled 'Zheng yi sanwen bing tichang '*youmo*'' 徵譯散文並提倡'幽默' ('Soliciting the translation of essays and promoting humour'), *Chenbao fukan* 晨報副刊 (Supplement to the *Morning Post*), 1924, NN. 3–4 (Rea, *The Age of Irreverence*, 133).

18. Lin Yutang, 'Lun youmo' 論幽默 (*Lunyu banyue kan* 論語半月刊, January and February, 1934; translated by Joseph C. Sample in 'Contextualizing Lin Yutang's Essay "On Humour"'). To convey the Chinese concept of humour, Lin preferred to use the existing terms of *fengci* 諷刺 ('satire') and *huaji* 滑稽 ('laughable'), not finding it perfectly adherent to the English idea of 'leisurely humour' he was promoting (Ibid., pos. 4162). The 'artificial distinction' between Daoist and Confucian humour made by Lin, has been the centre of many debates ever since (see Chey, '*Youmo* and the Chinese sense of humour', pos. 281).

19. Chey, '*Youmo* and the Chinese sense of humour', pos. 260 and 281.

20. Sample, 'Contextualizing Li Yutang's Essay 'On Humour", pos. 4210, with slight changes by the author of this article.

21. Chey, '*Youmo* and the Chinese sense of humour', pos. 827 and 696.

22. Xu, 'The Classical Confucian Concepts of Human Emotion', pos. 1196. The Rites denote both the canonical texts, *Li* 禮, and the 'ritual propriety', deriving from the rules, discipline and social attitude conveyed by the Confucian teachings. The term *Lǐ* 禮 is used for *Sānlǐ* (三禮, *Three [Books on] Rites*), a corpus centred on Ritual, formed by *Zhōulǐ* 周禮, *Yílǐ* 儀禮 and *Lǐjì* 禮記, whose origins date back to the Eastern Zhou dynasty (eighth-third century BCE) and early Han period (206 BCE–220 CE).

23. Xu, 'The Classical Confucian Concepts of Human Emotion', pos. 1671.

24. In James Sellmann's opinion, smile and laughter in *Zhuangzi* represent a 'vehicle of transformation and liberation, [...] the means to awaken (*jue* 覺) and loosen (*jie* 解) us from the fetters of convention' (Idem, 'Transformational Humour in the Zhuangzi', 169), while Wolfgang Schwabe, in 'Is Life but a Joke? Who is Laughing in the Zhuangzi?', underlines in the book the presence of coarse humour (especially in front of pious Confucians), or of laughter out of 'helplessness', when facing the impermanence of all things (329).

25. Shang, 'The Literati Era', 249.

26. Roddy, *Literati Identity*, 20.

27. Shang, *RLWS and Cultural Transformation*, 9.

28. On the question of the 'implicit knowledge', upon which humour often relies, and the difficulty it poses to translators, see Vandaele, 'Humour in Translation'.

29. Li, '*RLWS* waiwen yiben'.

30. Gladys Yang (*née* Tayler; Chinese name: Dai Naidie 戴乃迭, 1919–1999) and her husband Yang Xianyi (楊憲益, 1915–2009) contributed enormously in introducing the main masterpieces of Chinese literature to Anglophone readers.

31. In this essay, I refer to the third edition of *The Scholars*, published in Beijing in 1973. The Yangs' version is not truly an integral one, since the translators choose to synthesise parts of Chapter 37, considered by many critics as the climax of RLWS (see Shang, *RLWS and Cultural Transformation*, Part IV, 'The Taibo Myth and its Dilemma').

32. In this essay, I refer to the new edition of Voskresenskij's translation published by Nauka, Moscow, in 2014. A scholar of Chinese literature, Dimitrij Voskresenskij (1926–2017) translated more than 200 literary works.

33. In an interview released in 2014, Voskresenskij declared that he did not feel completely satisfied with his juvenile translation of *RLWS* (http://old.russ.ru/krug/20011011_voskr.html, retrieved in Jan. 2020).

34. Tchang Fou-jouei (Zhang Furui 張馥蕊, 1915–2006) was born in Anyi (Shanxi). He taught Chinese literature in France and has been a prolific translator.

35. However, whatever Wu's mastery, some of the comic passages of the novel have not escaped criticism from C.T. Hsia, who finds them over-disdainful and excessively farcical (Idem., *The Classic Chinese Novel*, 221 and ff.).

36. Mo, 'RLWS renwu duibi', 83.

37. Wu Jingzi, *RLWS*, 3.

38. Yang-Yang, *The Scholars*, 3.

39. 'The hills by the lake were blue, violet and emerald. The trees, freshly washed by the rain, were a lovelier green than ever' (Yang-Yang, *The Scholars*, 3).

40. 'Crystal drops were dripping from [...] lotus buds [...], while beads of water rolled about the leaves' (Ibid.).

41. Voskresenskij, *Neoficial'naja istorija*, 29.

42. One of the early Qing critics of the novel, Huang Fumin 黄富民 (1750–1841), thus comments the three men: 'Unexpectedly, as soon as they open their mouth, they sound vulgar, but this is exactly the real intention of the Master [Wu] in writing the book' (Wu Jingzi, RLWS, 3).

43. Wu Jingzi, RLWS, 3–4.

44. Yang-Yang, *The Scholars*, 3–4.

45. See, for example, the episode of the trip to Hangzhou made by Ma Chunshang 馬純上, who visits all the sites of the West Lake, famous for their beauty and for their synthesis of nature and culture, without really seeing anything, except, maybe, beautiful women, noisy crowds and food sold at the stalls (Chapter 14).

46. Shang, *RLWS and Cultural Transformation*, Epilogue: 'RLWS and Literati Nostalgia for the Lyrical World', 287 ff. On the subject of the quest for a spiritual home in RLWS, see also Li Hanqiu, 'Daolun' 導論 (Introduction), in Idem et al., *RLWS jianshang cidian*, 10 ff.

47. Voskresenskij, *Neoficial'naja istorija*, 29, and Tchang, *Chronique indiscrète*, Vol. 1, 3.

48. See Chan, 'Identifying Daoist Humour', pos. 1958. The notion of unity of man and nature is common to the main philosophical schools of ancient China and found a definition with the ideological re-elaboration made by Dong Zhongshu 董仲舒, in the second century BCE.

49. Ibid., pos. 2103.

50. Wang Mian himself, model of the disinterested scholar, is 'not entirely free of concern for the wider world' (Roddy, *Literati Identity*, 116). On the relation between the Taibo Ritual, at the centre of the novel, and the motif of withdrawal, see Shang, *RLWS and Cultural Transformation*, 74 ff.

51. The episode has been the object of many discussions, since, as we have seen above (n. 13), it is the fictional re-narration of a crucial moment of Wu Jingzi's life. See Li Hanqiu, 'Daolun' 導論 (Introduction), in Idem et al., *RLWS jianshang cidian*, 8 ff. and Li, 'RLWS yanjiu shilüe', 536 ff.

52. Wu Jingzi, *RLWS*, 419–20.

53. Yang-Yang, *The Scholars*, 373.

54. Tchang, *Chronique indiscrète*, Vol. 2, 492.

55. Xu Weihe compares this formula with Shakespeare's 'There's daggers in men's smiles' (*Macbeth*, Act III; Idem, 'The Classical Confucian Concepts of Human Emotion', pos. 1575).

56. Wu Jingzi, *RLWS*, 419.

57. Yang and Yang, *The Scholars*, 372.
58. Voskresenskij, *Neoficial'naja istorija*, 453–54.
59. Another issue of the passage is peculiar to the world of RLWS: the contrast between Beijing and Nanjing, respectively the centre of political power and the centre of rituality and of a possible lyrical existence (see Shang, *RLWS and Cultural Transformation*, 72 and 291).
60. 'Although humour is (generally) inappropriate in public, a Confucian gentleman could indeed lighten up in private', but his humour had to be 'mild. [...] After all, a supreme Confucian virtue is *ren* 仁 ('humaneness'), which connotes human fellowship' (Xu, 'The Classical Confucian Concepts of Human Emotion', pos. 1485). Christoph Harbsmeier finds this form of 'light-hearted jocularity' in Confucius' *Analecta* (Idem, 'Humour in Ancient Chinese Philosophy', 292).
61. Wu Jingzi, *RLWS*, 22.
62. Yang-Yang, *The Scholars*, 19.
63. For a discussion on the subject, see Mao, 'Beyond politeness theory'.
64. Voskresenskij, *Neoficial'naja istorija*, 49; as pointed out in the title page, the translation of the poems is made by S. Severcev.
65. Yang-Yang, *The Scholars*, 19.
66. See Chey and Davies, *Humour in Chinese Life and Letters*, 23. Lu Shengyang argues that RLWS shows its debt towards the tradition of comic performances (Idem, 'Qi er neng xie, wan er duo feng').
67. Wu Jingzi, *RLWS*, 37–38.
68. Yang-Yang, *The Scholars*, 32.
69. As underlined by critics, RLWS is one of the first novels to reduce to the minimum the rhetoric of storyteller and to present events without the mediation of the narrator, using a direct prose with realistic effects. See Shang, 'The Literati Era', 276 and Pu, *Pu Jiangqing jiang Ming Qing wenxue* (Chapter on RLWS).
70. Voskresenskij, *Neoficial'naja istorija*, 64–65.
71. It is interesting to observe, here, the choice to translate *tian'e* 天鹅 ('swan'), with 'cygne céleste' (rendering also *tian* 天, 'heaven'), with the effect of emphasising the contrast between the two animals of the metaphor.
72. Tchang, *Chronique indiscrete*, Vol. 1, 39–40. *Pi* 屁 means also 'fart'.
73. Osimo, *Manuale del traduttore*, 39. On the concept of 'Model Reader', see Eco, *Lector in Fabula*, 50 ff.
74. Ibid., 55.
75. Ni, 'Translating the Socialist Nation', 28.
76. Ibid., 32.
77. Yang, *White Tiger*, 202–3.
78. Lau, 'More Than Putting Things Together', 226.
79. Ni, 'Translating the Socialist Nation', 34.
80. Ibid.
81. Yang, *White Tiger*, 202.
82. Ni, 'Translating the Socialist Nation', 31.
83. See Sherry, *Discourses of Regulation and Resistance*, Introduction.
84. See Friedberg, *Literary Translation in Russia*, 4. The openness was, however, not free from anxiety, among the authorities, about negative influences of foreign culture (see e.g. the restrictions in translating activity issued in 1958 by the

Committee Commission on Questions of Ideology, Culture and International Party Contacts; Sherry, *Discourses of Regulation and Resistance*, 3 and 26).
85. Ibid., 92.
86. Sherry, *Discourses of Regulation and Resistance*, 8.
87. We adopt the conception developed by Gideon Toury. A translation is called 'adequate' when the linguistic and cultural norms of the source-text are reflected in the target-text, without however breaking the norms of the target language. The translation is called 'acceptable' when the translation is subject to norms originated in the target culture. Actual translation decisions, however, 'involve some ad-hoc combination of, or compromise between the two extremes' (Idem, *Descriptive Translation Studies and Beyond*, 57).
88. Jin He 金和 (1818–1885) synthesised by Li Hanqiu (Idem, '*Rulin waishi* yanjiu shilüe', 520).

## BIBLIOGRAPHY

Chan, Shirley. 'Identifying Daoist Humour: Reading the *Liezi*'. In *Humour in Chinese Life and Letters: Classical and Traditional Approaches*, edited by Jocelyn Chey and Jessica Milner Davis, 73–88. Hong Kong: Hong Kong University Press, 2011. Quotations from Kindle edition.

Chey, Jocelyn and Jessica Milner Davis, eds. *Humour in Chinese Life and Letters: Classical and Traditional Approaches*. Hong Kong: Hong Kong University Press, 2011.

Chey, Jocelyn. '*Youmo* and the Chinese sense of humour'. In *Humour in Chinese Life and Letters: Classical and Traditional Approaches*, edited by Jocelyn Chey and Jessica Milner Davis, 1–30. Hong Kong: Hong Kong University Press, 2011. Quotations from Kindle edition.

Eco, Umberto. *Lector in fabula. La cooperazione interpretativa nei testi narrativi.* Milano: Bompiani, (1979) 2016.

Friedberg, Maurice. *Literary Translation in Russia: A Cultural History.* Pennsylvania: Pennsylvania State University Press, 1997.

Harbsmeier, Christoph. 'Humour in Ancient Chinese Philosophy'. *Philosophy East and West* 39, no. 3. Philosophy and Humour (1989): 289–310.

Hsia, Chih-tsing. *The Classic Chinese Novel. A Critical Introduction.* Ithaca: Cornell University Press, (1968) 1996.

Lau, Joseph. 'More Than Putting Things Together. The Anthologizing of Chinese Literature in Translation'. In *Translating Chinese Literature*, edited by Eugene Eoyang and Lin Yao-fu, 221–30. Bloomington and Indianapolis: Indiana University Press, 1995.

Li, Hanqiu, 李漢秋. '*Rulin waishi* de banben ji qi yandi' 儒林外史的版本及其沿遞 (*RLWS*'s editions and their transmission). In 李漢秋: *Rulin waishi: huijiao huiping* 儒林外史:彙校彙評 (*Rulin waishi. Critical Edition*), edited by Li Hanqiu, 1–13. Shanghai: Shanghai Gujichubanshe, 2010.

Li, Hanqiu 李漢秋, Zhang Guofeng 張國風, and Zhou Yueliang 周月亮. '*Rulin waishi jianshang cidian*' 儒林外史鑒賞辭典 (*Rulin waishi Appreciation Dictionary*). Shanghai: Shanghai Cishu chubanshe, 2011.

Li, Hanqiu 李漢秋. '*Rulin waishi* yanjiu shilüe' 儒林外史研究史略 (Brief History of *RLWS* Studies). In Li Hanqui et al., '*Rulin waishi jianshang cidian*' 儒林外史鑒賞辭典 (*Rulin waishi Appreciation Dictionary*), 517–46. Shanghai: Shanghai Cishu chubanshe, 2011.

Li, Hanqiu 李漢秋. '*Rulin waishi* waiwen yiben' 儒林外史外文譯本 (Foreign Translations of *Rulin waishi*). In '*Rulin waishi ziliao huibian*' 儒林外史資料彙編 (Collected Materials on *Rulin waishi*), edited by Zhu Yixuan 朱一玄 and Liu Yuchen 劉毓忱, 240–46. Tianjin: Nankai Daxue chubanshe, 2012.

Lin, Shuen-fu. 'Ritual and Narrative Structure in RLWS'. In *Chinese Narrative: Critical and Theoretical Essays*, edited by Andrew H. Plaks, 244–65. Princeton: Princeton University Press, 1977.

Lu, Shengyang 盧聲揚. 'Qi er neng xie, wan er duo feng' 戚而能諧, 婉而多諷 (Expressing Sorrow with a Smile, Satirizing with Tact'). In '*Anhui zhiye jishu xueyuan xuebao*' 安徽職業技術學院學報 6, no. 3 (2007): 50–53.

Lu, Xun 魯迅. '*Zhongguo xiaoshuo shilüe*' 中國小說史略 (*Brief History of Chinese Fiction*). Translated by Hsien-yi Yang and Gladys Yang. Beijing: Foreign Languages Press, (1959) 1982.

Mao, Robert Luming. 'Beyond politeness theory: 'Face' revisited and renewed'. *Journal of Pragmatics* 21 (1994): 451–86.

Mo, Chunxing 莫純星. '*Rulin waishi* renwu duibi fengci tan' 儒林外史人物對比諷刺談 (About Comparative Satirical Representation of Characters in RLWS). *Guangdong Haiyang daxue xuebao* 廣東海洋大學學報 27, no. 2 (2007): 83–86.

Ni, Xiuhua. 'Translating the Socialist Nation. Exporting Chinese Literature under the People's Republic of China (1949–1966)'. *Revue Internationale d'interprétation et de traduction* 15, no. 1 (2017): 27–49.

Osimo, Bruno. *Manuale del traduttore: Guida pratica con glossario*. Milano: Hoepli, 2011.

Pu, Jiangqing 浦江清, Pu Hanming 浦漢名, Peng Shulin 彭書麟, eds. '*Pu Jiangqing jiang Ming Qing wenxue*' 浦江清講明清文學 (Lessons on Ming and Qing Literature by Pu Jiangqing). Beijing: Beijing Chubanshe, 2014.

Rea, Christopher. *The Age of Irreverence: A New History of Laughter in China*. Oakland: University of California Press, 2015.

Roddy, Stephen J. *Literati Identity and its Fictional Representations in Late Imperial China*. Stanford: Stanford University Press, 1998.

Rolston, David L., ed. *How to read the Chinese Novel*. Princeton: Princeton University Press, 1990.

Sample, Joseph C. 'Contextualizing Li Yutang's Essay "On Humour": Introduction and Translation'. In *Humour in Chinese Life and Letters: Classical and Traditional Approaches*, edited by Jocelyn Chey and Jessica Milner Davis, 169–90. Hong Kong: Hong Kong University Press, 2011. Quotations from Kindle edition.

Santangelo, Paolo, ed. *Laughing in Chinese*. Rome: Aracne, 2014.

Schwabe, Wolfgang. 'Is Life but a Joke? Who is Laughing in the Zhuangzi?'. In *Laughing in Chinese*, edited by Paolo Santangelo, 319–34. Rome: Aracne, 2014.

Sellmann, James. 'Transformational Humour in the Zhuangzi'. In *Wandering at Ease in the Zhuangzi*, edited by Roger Ames, 163–74. New York: State University of New York Press, 1998.

Shang, Wei. *Rulin waishi and Cultural Transformation in Late Imperial China*. Cambridge, MA: Harvard University Asia Center, 2003.

Shang, Wei. 'The Literati Era and its Demise'. In *The Cambridge History of Chinese Literature, Volume 2. From 1375*, edited by Kang-I Sun Chang and Stephen Owen, 245–342. Cambridge: Cambridge University Press, 2010.

Sherry, Samantha. *Discourses of Regulation and Resistance: Censoring Translation in the Stalin and Khrushchev Era Soviet Union*. Edinburgh: Edinburgh University Press, 2015.

Tchang, Fou-jouei, transl. *Chronique indiscrète des Mandarins*. Paris: Gallimard, 1976.

Toury, Gideon. *Descriptive Translation Studies and Beyond*. Amsterdam and Philadelphia: John Benjamins, 1995.

Vandaele, Jeroen. 'Humor in Translation'. In *Handbook of Translation Studies, volume 1*, edited by Yves Gambier and Luc van Doorslaer, 147–52. Amsterdam and Philadelphia, John Benjamins, 2010.

Voskresenskij, Dimitrij N. transl. *Neoficial'naja istorija konfuciancev*. Moscow: Nauka, (Gosudarstvennoe Izdatel'stvo Chudožestvennoj Literatury, 1959) 2014.

Wu, Jingzi 吳敬梓. *Rulinwaishi* 儒林外史. Edited by Li Hanqiu李漢秋, '*Rulin waishi: huijiao huiping*' 儒林外史:彙校彙評 (*Rulin waishi. Critical Edition*). Shanghai: Shanghai Gujichubanshe, 2010.

Xu, Weihe. 'The Classical Confucian Concepts of Human Emotion and Proper Humour'. In *Humour in Chinese Life and Letters: Classical and Traditional Approaches*, edited by Jocelyn Chey and Jessica Milner Davis, 49–72. Hong Kong: Hong Kong University Press, 2011. Quotations from Kindle edition.

Yang, Gladys and Hsien-yi Yang, transl. *The Scholars*. Beijing: Foreign Language Press, (1957) 1973.

Yang, Xianyi. *White Tiger: An Autobiography of Yang Xianyi*. Hong Kong: Chinese University Press, 2002.

CHAPTER 25

# Putting Humour on Display

*Laurence Grove*

## INTRODUCTION: EXHIBITING ART

Exhibitions can, maybe should, be like humour itself: they bring together disparate and unlikely elements; they depend on the interpretation of the receiver; and they often belong to a specific time and place. Bringing visual humour from the past into the present through exhibitions is an opportunity not merely to explain jokes, but in effect to create new humour by means of unexpected juxtapositions—just as humour itself has been understood to do—and to encourage varied reactions to what is 'past'.

This chapter aims to consider some of the issues raised when curating exhibitions that relate to humour, and in particular to the humour of the past. To that end I will draw specifically on two recent Glasgow exhibitions—*Comic Invention* (2016, Hunterian Art Gallery) and *Frank Quitely: The Art of Comics* (2017, Kelvingrove Art Gallery and Museum)—both of which focussed upon the culture of comics, including elements of humour (comics are of course not always funny) from present and past.[1]

Initially it is worth setting the scene with some background on the notion of the exhibition of art.[2] The eighteenth century saw the public display of princely collections throughout Europe, with notable examples being the Uffizi Galleries in Florence and those of Dresden. The *Salons* that took place in Paris from 1667 onwards were displays of contemporary art that reached prominence in the latter half of the eighteenth and throughout the nineteenth centuries. In England and in Scotland it was the years 1850 to 1914 that saw the spread of museums and art galleries. This was partly as a result of the

---

L. Grove (✉)
University of Glasgow, Glasgow, UK
e-mail: laurence.grove@glasgow.ac.uk

© The Author(s), under exclusive license to Springer Nature
Switzerland AG 2020
D. Derrin, H. Burrows (eds.), *The Palgrave Handbook of Humour, History, and Methodology*, https://doi.org/10.1007/978-3-030-56646-3_25

481

482  L. GROVE

requirements of the commercial artworld—images of crowds gathering before Georgian print shop windows are now well known—but also in response to social and political encouragement of learning.[3] In addition, the Victorian and Edwardian ages saw the rise of the Universal Exhibition and with it the creation of an all-encompassing learning experience. To take the example of the Glasgow International Exhibition of 1901, visitors could not only enjoy the artwork in the newly built Kelvingrove museum, but also industrial and scientific displays with associated electric lighting, the nature-based attractions of the park and the river Kelvin, theatrical and sporting performances, and amusements such as a switchback railway and gondola rides.[4]

Temporary art exhibitions grew from a marketplace role underpinned by the need to promote artists commercially, later to become narratives—such as that of the life of a chosen artist—although the notion of selected as opposed to universal inclusion was more of a twentieth-century phenomenon, and so scholarly exhibitions would draw upon photographs and electrotypes as an accepted way of completing displays. As temporary exhibitions developed and took an increasingly prominent role in gallery and museum activities, so did the conflict between financial objectives—the need for a display to make money both for practical purposes and as a mark of success—and those of instruction and entertainment.[5] As an aside—a discussion that is beyond the scope of this chapter—we might also remember the critical view put forward by Michel Foucault and Pierre Bourdieu whereby museums and exhibitions might be viewed as agents of social control and manipulation by the ruling classes.

## Exhibiting Comics

What then is the role of comics or indeed humour in the display of art? There have been numerous comics, or at least cartoons, of exhibitions, best known of these perhaps being offerings from *Punch*, such as a George Morrow cartoon from 1914 mocking the reception of Cubism (Fig. 25.1). Although there is some debate surrounding claims of a first ever exhibition of comics being at the Lucca Salone Internazionale del Comics in 1965 (which was in fact in Bordighera), the landmark comic exhibition was that of 1967, *Bande dessinée et figuration narrative*. It was this display that lent legitimacy to the form, if only by dint of the fact that it took place in Paris' prestigious Musée des Arts Décoratifs. The display itself nowadays appears less than forward-looking, based largely on reproductions of single pages of comic artwork and examples of Pop Art (in particular by Roy Lichtenstein), but its existence was in itself ground-breaking.

Indeed, from then onwards the norm has been and remains the framing of comics artwork on walls or in cases. Such was largely the format of the Bibliothèque nationale de France's 2001 *Maîtres de la bande dessinée europée-nne*, or, slightly more recently, the Hammer Museum in Los Angeles' 2005–2006 *Masters of American Comics*. There are, however, exceptions. The 1991–1992 *Opéra bulles*, that took place at various venues including the Grande Halle de la Villette in Paris, was the work of Lucie Lom, the

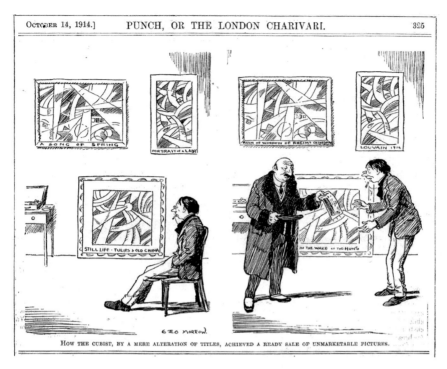

**Fig. 25.1** George Morrow. 'How the Cubist, by a Mere Alteration of Titles, Achieved a Ready Sale of Unmarketable Pictures'. *Punch* (October 14, 1914), 32

production company headed by Marc-Antoine Mathieu, the *bande dessinée* artist known for his black humour in experimenting with the comic-book form. *Opéra bulles* allowed the visitor to enjoy a campsite toilet, with reference to the humour of comics that take place on holiday, for example, Binet's *Les Bidochon* or Reiser's *Vive les vacances*.[6] Further sections of the exhibition—similarly walk-though three-dimensional experiences—involved wandering within René Goscinny's studio or entering the science-fictional *cités obscures*.

The British Library's *Comics Unmasked* in 2014 did have artwork in cases, but also a recreation of Dave McKean's artist's studio, masked dummies for the *V for Vendetta* display, or for the erotica section a behind-the-red-curtain sex-shop. Comics that are not intrinsically funny were taking on black humour through the ludic interactive displays. Nonetheless, most of the numerous exhibitions of comics—indeed too numerous to list—are still essentially artwork on walls, as a quick Google search will show, or, perhaps more reliably, a flick through the increasingly substantial exhibitions reviews section of the *International Journal of Comic Art*.

A reaction to the phenomenon of exhibitions that principally display artwork on walls might be to ask why, in a world of digital scans and on-line graphic novels, should such events present comics—for our purposes humorous ones, but the question also applies more broadly—in a way that a computer screen in a comfortable armchair could also do? Furthermore, and perhaps more importantly, how can such exhibitions serve a purpose beyond that of explaining jokes?

Firstly, not everything is on the web. Our modern tendency is increasingly to use Google as a first resort of broad knowledge but also specific scholarship. Much is to be gleaned and connections can be made, but resources remain less than systematic, as an attempt, for example, to find the full contents of the exhibitions cited above might show. The reader of this volume will be able to find individual images and extracts from, say, *Opéra bulles* or *Masters of American Comics*, but universal coverage will not be available.

More importantly, I refer here to Walter Benjamin, who in *The Work of Art in the Age of Mechanical Reproduction* (reproduced in the collected volume *Illuminations*) underlines the importance of the original creation, noting that 'Even the most perfect reproduction of a work of art is lacking in one element: its presence in time and space' (214). The notion here is that to see the original is not only perfect in terms of aesthetic clarity, but, moreover, that we live a connection by being in the presence of the hand of the artist-creator, or even of a reproduced engraving that dates from the time of the artist. This is a view echoed without exception by students taking classes in the Special Collections Department of Glasgow University Library, when they are asked whether seeing the originals adds anything to the learning experience. A key aspect of exhibitions, whatever the subject matter, and indeed like concerts or sporting events, remains the privileged *frisson* at being in the presence of 'the real thing'.

## EXHIBITING THE HUMOUR OF THE WORLD'S FIRST COMIC

Exhibitions allow us to escape to different worlds and to create the stories that go with our adventures. In this case stories are also what comics are all about, and within the present discussion of how we exhibit stories there is also the story of the world's first comic, albeit in this case a slight diversion or sub-plot.

Most scholars, traditionally but also to some extent still today, attribute the title of world's first comic to Rodolphe Töpffer's *Histoire de Mr. Jabot*, composed in 1833 but not published until 1835.[7] The 'real' world's first modern comic is however the *Glasgow Looking Glass* (Fig. 25.2), largely the brainchild of William Heath and which ran for 17 issues from June 11, 1825, until April 3, 1826, with two further issues in May and June 1826 as an attempt to revive the initial publication.[8] Number 6 (August 18, 1825) saw the change of title to *Northern Looking Glass*, an indication that the publication had broadened its audience, as was also confirmed by the increasing list of selling points at the end of each number. It was, however, Heath's satirical humour that made enemies for him—[9]he eventually fled back to London—as attested by William Strang in his *Glasgow and its Clubs*: the publication 'for many months during the year 1825, kept the members of the Police Board in hot water and the

25 PUTTING HUMOUR ON DISPLAY 485

**Fig. 25.2** *Glasgow Looking Glass.* No. 1, June 11, 1825, front cover. Glasgow University Library

citizens in roars of laughter'.[10] The end rubric on the final issue of the *Looking Glass* (April 3, 1826) likewise points to potential offense through satire:

> The Editor of the *Northern Looking Glass* regrets the necessity of announcing to his Friends and the Public, the discontinuance of his paper: and can only console himself that this circumstance cannot fail of adding to its novelty, at least one other attraction—that of wit:—For, since brevity is the soul of wit, and tediousness the limbs and outward flourishes—it has been brief. Whilst his warmest

thanks are due for the kind patronage he has received, during its short career, he trusts he will be forgiven, if in any instance whatever he may have accidently touched too roughly individual feeling—nothing was farther from his intention than to offend.

Until the end of the twentieth-century the *Glasgow Looking Glass* had been overlooked by virtually all historians of the graphic novel, despite the fact that as well as holding claim to the title of first modern comic, it also contained the world's first comic strip, *History of a Coat*, which over three episodes told the humorous adventures of the eponymous object as it transferred from owner to owner. Within the pages of the *Glasgow Looking Glass* we also find examples of speech bubbles, 'before and after' sequences, political and social cartooning, and panoramas—for example a view of the Glasgow Fair on the back cover of issue 4 (July 23, 1825)—that might be compared to the 'Pilotoramas' of *Pilote* or *Eagle*'s 'Cutaways'. In all of these cases the comparison with the workings of comics as we know them is striking.[11]

Why then did a journal that was noted for its biting humour, and that has since been identified as fitting the characteristics of the modern comic, go unnoticed for so long? Central to the status of comics and to their display has been the notion of comics as 'low culture' not worthy of attention, indeed Töpffer himself had referred (albeit potentially tongue-in-cheek) to his *Mr. Jabot* as 'un livre amusant, médicorement imprimé, fort cher, et à sa place dans un salon surtout' ['an amusing book, of mediocre print quality, that is rather expensive and above all at home in a *salon*'].[12] With the evolution of scholarship and with comics now bursting into the canon, attracting the attention of learned conferences, societies, and networks—or alternatively with the collapse of the traditional canon—a history is needed, or has been needed. Scholars have turned erudite attention to Geneva, Paris, and New York—which is how canons work—but no one thought, understandably enough, to look for the world's first comic in the vaults of a medieval Scottish university.

Figure 25.3 shows how the Hunterian Art Gallery, Glasgow, displayed the world's first comic for a key section of its *Comic Invention* exhibition. The background casing gave the central display a comics-style theme, with speech bubbles forming a chronology and interacting with the 'pictures', in this case including the objects themselves. The *Glasgow Looking Glass* (1825), in the Glasgow section, was placed alongside the *Mr. Jabot* manuscript (1833) and first edition (1835) representing Geneva, then the pirated *Obadiah Oldbuck*, America's first comic (New York, 1842), and finally reworkings of Töpffer's strips for the mass-selling journal *L'Illustration* (Paris, 1845).

Although there was enough there to make any comics historian tingle, it was nonetheless still a case of comics in cases. In addition, one could ask, why should the *Glasgow Looking Glass* be the world's first comic, and not a slab of Egyptian hieroglyphs, a bawdy medieval text/image manuscript, or the side-splitting offerings of Thomas Rowlandson, William Hogarth, or Isaac Cruickshank, all pre-dating 1825?

25 PUTTING HUMOUR ON DISPLAY 487

**Fig. 25.3** *Comic Invention.* Hunterian Art Gallery, Glasgow. March 18 to July 17, 2016. Display panel for 'The World's First Comic' section

488    L. GROVE

The answer is that a comic in the modern sense needs to be mass-produced, fold-up and take-home. For this to be possible, the large-scale reproduction of images is needed, and the earliest western technology to that end was lithography, invented by Alois Senefelder in Munich in 1796, but not commonly understood until the publication of his *Vollstandiges Lehrbuch der Steindruckerei* in 1818. Although an unknown comic dating from between 1818 to 1825 may be lurking in an archive somewhere, the window is slim, and the chances are that the title of world's first belongs to the *Glasgow Looking Glass*.

Alternatively, one might say in the broader sense that the numerous examples of text/image humour from hieroglyphs to Hogarth are all valid possibilities, in that everything depends on definitions. The important thing is to raise the question. The next question then, of relevance to the current discussion, is how do we make a display of such questions?

## COMIC INVENTION

The answer in this instance is the *Comic Invention* exhibition that ran from March 18, 2016 to July 17, 2016 (Fig. 25.4). In addition to the *Glasgow Looking Glass*, the exhibition also included, as current readers might have guessed, examples of humour from hieroglyphs to Hogarth.[13] Surrounding the display of 'the world's first comic' (to the left of the central round stairwell on the plan, Fig. 25.5) a timeline took the visitor from Ancient Egypt, via the Middle Ages, up to the nineteenth century. Nonetheless, at the planning stages of *Comic Invention* it was also suggested that in order for the visitor experience to match expectations given by the title, then contemporary comics, with touches of humour, should feature in the display. The solution came via the work of Frank Quitely.

Frank Quitely was born in Glasgow in 1968 as Vincent Deighan. It was in the early 1990s that he spoofed family favourites for the underground comic *Electric Soup*, and realising that, quite frankly, his work might offend his family, he hid behind the spoonerism penname. In 1996, he started working for Detective Comics (DC), initially on *Flex Mentallo*, before going on to *The Sandman*, *Pax Americana*, and *We3*. Frank Quitely's output is vast and varied, but for many it is the *Superman* and *Batman* duo that makes him the boy wonder of comics. He has worked with many of the icons of the graphic novel, including Alan Grant, Bruce Jones, and Neil Gaiman, but it is his partnerships with fellow Glaswegians Grant Morrison and Mark Miller that are best known. Stylistically, Frank Quitely is noted for his irreverent humour, be it the large lady emptying the buffet (*Batman: The Scottish Connection*), the cookie jar holding up the rocket (*All Star Superman*), or the townscape with buttocks at a skylight window (*Flex Mentallo*).

For *Comic Invention*, a system of thematic matching was used, whereby adjacent podia would allow a Frank Quitely work to be viewed next to each timeline artefact (Fig. 25.6). For example, the bawdy comedy of the fifteenth-century *Cent Nouvelles Nouvelles*, with framed-off scenes of bedhopping

25 PUTTING HUMOUR ON DISPLAY    489

**Fig. 25.4** Sha Nazir. *Two Hipsters in the Car*. 2015. Poster for *Comic Invention*

between merchants, their wives, and three lusty friars, was complemented by the dark pathos of a bed-sharing episode from *Flinch*. Still with sexy humour of dubious taste, Rowlandson's *The Connoisseurs* (1799), in which four leering elder gentlemen 'appreciate' the artistic nude, was placed against a nerve-tingling moment of misplaced youthful voyeurism from *Heart Throbs*. Social observation through physiognomy dominated the caricature studies of Hogarth or Cruickshank, placed against the pretty young things of Frank Quitely's world of social must-haves in *The Authority* and *Jupiter's Legacy*. In all of these cases, and others, the aim was for the visitor to make unexpected connections, via an active but personal process that could potentially create a different experience for each individual. Nonetheless a clear conclusion was that through the

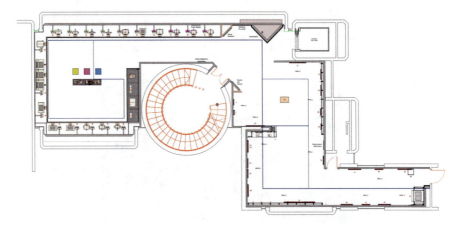

**Fig. 25.5** *Comic Invention*. Hunterian Art Gallery, Glasgow. March 18 to July 17, 2016. Design plan

**Fig. 25.6** *Comic Invention*. Hunterian Art Gallery, Glasgow. March 18 to July 17, 2016. A system of podia allows the juxtaposition of a comics timeline with contemporary works by Frank Quitely that share the same themes. Centre-left is the series of six engravings for William Hogarth's A Harlot's Progress (1732)

timeline we might see the timelessness of 'comics'—we have always told stories with pictures—whilst noting that certain themes span the ages.

Building on this synchronic aspect a linked section explored 'Comics and Culture' (Fig. 25.7), presenting a range of art works united by their ability to tell stories through the visual, be it the consumerism of everyday life inherent to Andy Warhol's *Campbell's Soup* (1969), or Hervé Télémaque's take on the world of advertising in *Boîte d'allumettes* (1963). Key to the effect once again was the placing of the objects so as to create curious and humorous juxtapositions leading to individual reflection: a Rembrandt within eyeshot of a Lichtenstein, in turn next to a Frank Quitely; an icon of 'high art', Pablo Picasso, but with a comic strip version of the Guernica story marked by comedic phallic symbols mocking Franco (*Sueño y mentira de Franco*, 1937), placed adjacent to a felt pen drawing of *Scooby Doo and Shaggy* (1997) by Iwao Takamoto. Overall vistas created in themselves tongue-in-cheek stories, for instance the Edward Paolozzi *Broken Head* (1984) that appeared to be kissing the female character from Lichtenstein's *In the Car* (1963), or the latter viewed through Martin Boyce's *Everything Passes Through* (2016) with the holes in the mask playing upon the pop artist's Ben Day dots.

In short, the associations underpinning the visitor's experience depended very much upon the overall scenography, which was intuitive and visitor-driven, and indeed the final experience was that no one asked the questions that might have been expected, namely 'what has all this got to do with comics?' or 'is it

**Fig. 25.7** *Comic Invention*. Hunterian Art Gallery, Glasgow. March 18 to July 17, 2016. The 'Culture of Comics' section

492    L. GROVE

*deliberately* playful and humorous?' Other twists included the effect of Superman 'flying out' from his position at the end of a long corridor section, the subliminal creation of the atmosphere of the world of comics through the use of the CMYB (cyan, magenta, yellow, and black) printing colours, and the palimpsest exchanges with the layers of *In the Car*. These came through the large-scale iconic painting itself, but also the play upon the displayed extract from *Girls Romance*, and the updating by Sha Nazir's poster version showing two Glasgow hipsters (Fig. 25.4). The key motif for the exhibition was therefore part of a playful layering, an echo of the very nature of comics, or indeed of humour.

A larger-scale display a year later at Glasgow's Kelvingrove Art Gallery and Museum drew inspiration from *Comic Invention* and applied two of its key techniques: the mixing of past with present, and comedy through juxtaposition. Whereas the 2016 exhibition had displayed the humour of past whist giving it a contemporary connection, *Frank Quitely: The Art of Comics* focussed on contemporary work but gave it a twist via connections with the past. The *Glasgow Looking Glass* and George Wither's 1635 *A Collection of Emblems* gave the background of text/image cultures in Glasgow, whilst looking onto *The Broons* and Frank Quitely's Batman and Superman productions. The poster itself (Fig. 25.8) juxtaposed Superman with the Edwardian splendour of Kelvingrove museum and its architectural references to Spanish baroque. Again, the effect of the display was achieved by going beyond the objects themselves.

## Conclusion: Beyond Walls

One of the key attractions of *Comic Invention*, Hogarth's *A Harlot's Progress* (1732) encapsulates the potential openness of a visual reading of humour.[14] Hogarth's series of six plates tells the story of Moll Hackabout: her arrival in London; her high-life within the keeping of a rich Jew; the downfall in her life of prostitution with imminent arrest; her time in prison; her devastation by disease; and her wake attended by fellow prostitutes. Although a grim story, the tone is that of a satirical attack on the foibles and hypocrisies of society, also marked with farcical comedy such as the arguing doctors (plate 5) or the extra lover sneaking out behind the servant (plate 2).

How we read the series of prints depends on the viewer, with numerous very different approaches possible. Each picture can be read as a single entity— indeed in pirate versions they could originally have been purchased individually. Within each frame, we see the character portrayal, such as Moll's wistful cheekiness as she pushes over the table to distract attention away from her lover, whilst smiling out to the viewer (plate 2). Background details tell part of the story, for example the overturned tin pot to suggest her fallen status (plate 3), or the vicar 'spilling his liquid' as he fondles the prostitute (plate 6). Within each plate references to contemporary characters—Justice John Gonson is seen

**Fig. 25.8** Frank Quitely. *Frank Quitely: The Art of Comics.* 2017. Exhibition Poster

in plate 3 about to arrest Moll—allow us to weave the static image into the movement of early-Georgian London.

Alternatively, or perhaps additionally, the plates can be read individually, but within a network of references between them. The wigs of highwayman James Dalton—assumed to be Moll's lover—above the bed (plate 3) prefigure the hangman scribble in plate 4, a possible reference to Dalton's fate, or the desired ending for John Gonson, whose initials are above the drawing. Moll's hat, central to the first image, is to be seen hanging on the wall in plate 6, an anchor for an object narrative (to be compared with the *Glasgow Looking Glass' History of a Coat*) drawing attention to the fact that we all must inevitably 'hang up our hat'. Nonetheless, the final scene sees the prostitutes continuing to ply their trade, with the range of ages reflecting the ages we have seen of Moll Hackabout,

494    L. GROVE

and the notion that even in death life goes on reminding us of the cyclic nature of human existence.

Alternatively, the six plates can be read directly as the frames of a comic, in sequence, with the reader's imagination providing the missing action that takes place in the 'gutters' between each image. The story thus advances chronologically with character and plot development. This was the reading implied, but not imposed, by the set-up of *Comic Invention*, whereby *A Harlot's Progress* was displayed in a three-by-two grid (Fig. 25.6).

Like the humour of Hogarth, the *Comic Invention* exhibition had several pathways, with each reader/viewer/visitor creating their own experience, their own beginning, middle and ending, for instance starting with the 'Culture of Comics' and then the timeline, or vice versa, or dipping between the two picking up on connections, such as the copy of *L'Illustration* that had influenced Martin Boyce, or *The Hypnotist* (1963) by David Hockney, playing upon the notion of influences at the very time when Hockney was himself inspired by Hogarth. A comparison can be made here with Marshall McLuhan's view of 'hot' and 'cool' media, whereby comics would be 'cool' as they are a form whose reception has a high level of dependency on the input of the receiver.[15] With a comic, the reader may bolt towards a central image and then read outwards, read in sequence from top left to bottom right, or mix the two approaches. Humour of the past—particularly visual humour—likewise tends to have a high level of 'reader participation', depending on whether the individual concentrates, for example, on the artistry, the depiction of folly, potential word-plays, or the deciphering of social satire that may be blurred in the now-forgotten front-pages of the past.

But we should not forget that comics have 'gutters', like the plates of a Hogarth satirical series, that is to say the gaps between the frames in which key actions happen but are not seen. When we are creating exhibitions we should likewise be aware of the 'gutters', or the points that are being made by what is absent. Hogarth's *A Harlot's Progress* is about the plight of a woman, but it remains the work of a dead white male based in the metropolis of London, and as such the unnamed protagonists in the 'gutters' remain the women, the minorities, and those from beyond the English capital.

Accordingly, a final example of visual humour and the unexpected is that of Christine Borland's *To be Set and Sown in the Garden* (2001, Fig. 25.9), an outdoor interactive sculpture that draws inspiration from manuscript additions to the 1549 Glasgow University Library copy (Bl3-k.20) of Leonhard Fuch's *De Historia stirpium*, including the line, referring to a listing of plants, 'To be sett and sawin in ye garding'. The sculpture, at the foot of the University Library, plays on the palimpsest of the past by suggesting that the seeds of the future are those who sit on the sculpture's benches. Indeed, it is in keeping with Borland's style of mixing past with present—another example is her *Family Conversation Piece* (1998), a set of painted skulls referring to the slave trade of Liverpool's past—so as to challenge the viewer with unexpected connections tinged with wry humour.

**Fig. 25.9** Christine Borland. *To Be Set and Sown in the Garden*. 2001. University of Glasgow

In the context of *Comic Invention*, *To be Set and Sown in the Garden* was flagged as the last artwork to be seen by the visitor upon leaving, one which might have been overlooked upon entering, with the final narrative therefore being that created by each visitor as they intermingle on the anatomy-style benches, chatting, playing, and looking around. The inclusion of Borland's work addressed another issue, that of the exclusion of women in the exhibition, and in the world of comics. By presenting her as the final piece, the implication was that the future might lie with women, or potentially that women remain on the periphery. Alternatively, with reference to those on the sculpture's benches, in answer to the potential question of 'where is the exhibition's last word', one might reply with flippant comedy, 'under people's arses'.

In short, how do we display the humour of the past rather than simply placing prints on walls and explaining the joke in the label? The answer, it seems to me, is to create a 3-D interactive experience that challenges the visitor to put together their own connections, creating their own emphasis and messages, and in so doing deliver an enjoyable, challenging, and hopefully humour-laden experience for each individual. Humour is based on unexpected connections, often on incongruity. Modern-day exhibitions should be likewise.

## Notes

1. For this section in particular, but throughout more generally, I am grateful to Daniel Derrin for his careful reading and subsequent input.
2. For an examination of the process of the creation of exhibitions in the context of contemporary art, with reference to the viewpoints of artists, but also curators, audience, and managers, see Afterall Books, 'Exhibition Histories'.
3. See in particular Waterfield, The People's Galleries, passim.
4. A glimpse of the Exhibition is given in the Official Guide (Glasgow International Exhibition 1901), which is presented by Julie Coleman as the University of Glasgow Special Collections' Book of the Month 2009 (Coleman, 'Glasgow International Exhibition 1901').
5. See Waterfield, The People's Galleries, in particular 175–95.
6. Some images of the exhibition are available on the Lucie Lom website.
7. See, for example, Groensteen, M. Töpffer invente.
8. For an overview of the context of the Glasgow Looking Glass with specific reference to its satirical content, see Grove, 'La Caricature comme pilier'. For the context of the Glasgow Looking Glass within the debate surrounding the title of 'world's first comic', see Grove and Black, Comic Invention.
9. See Grove, 'La Caricature comme pilier'.
10. Strang, Glasgow and its Clubs, 339.
11. Again, for examples of these techniques, see Grove, 'La Caricature comme pilier'.
12. See Grove, Comics in French, 94.
13. For full details, see the exhibition's box-publication catalogue: Grove and Black, Comic Invention. This work also includes illustrations of items displayed. For a further illustrated overview see Gravett, 'Comic Invention'.
14. Full reproductions of the plates are available via the Hunterian's online catalogue: http://collections.gla.ac.uk/#view=list&id=67d0&what=Harlot's%20 progress. Accessed September 12, 2019.
15. See McLuhan, Understanding Media, 22–32.

## Bibliography

Afterall Books. 'Exhibition Histories'. Accessed August 16, 2019. https://www.afterall.org/books/exhibition.histories/

Benjamin, Walter. Illuminations. Edited by Hannah Arendt. Translated by Harry Zohn. London: Fontana, 1973.

Bibliothèque nationale de France, Paris. Maîtres de la bande dessinée européenne. October 10, 2000–January 7, 2001.

Borland, Christine. Family Conversation Piece. 1998. Glasgow, Hunterian Art Gallery.

Borland, Christine. To Be Set and Sown in the Garden. University of Glasgow, 2001.

Boyce, Martin. Everything Passes Through. Private collection, 2016.

British Library, London. Comics Unmasked: Art and Anarchy in the UK. May 2, 2014–August 19, 2014.

Brother Jonathan Extra no. IX, Containing The Adventures of Mr Obadiah Oldbuck. New York: Wilson, 1842.

Les Cent Nouvelles Nouvelles. Paris, c. 1480. Glasgow University Library. Ms Hunter 252.

Fuch, Leonhard. *De Historia stirpium*. Lyon: Balthazar Arnollet, 1549. With manuscript additions. Glasgow University Library Bl3-k.20.

Gardham, Julie. '*Glasgow International Exhibition 1901*: Glasgow University Library Special Collections October 1999 Book of the Month'. Accessed August 16, 2019. http://special.lib.gla.ac.uk/exhibns/month/oct1999.html

*Girls' Romances* 78 (1961).

Glasgow International Exhibition *1901: Official Guide*. Glasgow: Chas. P. Watson, 1901.

Grande Halle de la Villette, Paris. *Opéra bulles*. November 26, 1991–January 5, 1992.

Gravett, Paul. 'Comic Invention: Interview with Co-Curator Laurence Grove'. Accessed September 10, 2019. http://www.paulgravett.com/articles/article/comic_invention

Groensteen, Thierry. *M. Töpffer invente la bande dessinée*. Brussels: Les Impressions Nouvelles, 2014.

Grove, Laurence. 'La Caricature comme pilier du premier *comic* du monde: *The Glasgow Looking Glass* (1825)'. In *L'Image railleuse: La Satire visuelle du XVIIIe siècle à nos jours*, edited by Laurent Baridon, Frédérique Desbussions and Dominic Hardy. Paris: Institut National d'Histoire de l'Art, 2019. On-line publication housed on INHA website. Accessed August 26, 2014. https://journals.openedition.org/inha/8213

Grove, Laurence. *Comics in French*. Oxford: Berghahn, (2010) 2013.

Grove, Laurence and Peter Black. *Comic Invention*. Glasgow: BHP Comics, 2016.

Hammer Museum, Los Angeles. *Masters of American Comics*. November 20, 2005–March 12, 2006.

Hockney, David. *The Hypnotist*. 1963. Glasgow, Hunterian Art Gallery.

Hogarth, William. *A Harlot's Progress*. 1732. Glasgow, Hunterian Art Gallery.

Hunterian Art Gallery, Glasgow. *Comic Invention*. March 18, 2016–July 17, 2016.

Lichtenstein, Roy. *In the Car*. 1963. Edinburgh, Scottish National Gallery of Modern Art.

Lucie Lom. 'Opéra bulles'. Accessed August 23, 2019. http://www.lucie-lom.fr/site/scenographies/opera-bulles/

McLuhan, Marshall. *Understanding Media*. London: Routledge, 1964.

Morrow, George. 'How the Cubist, by a Mere Alteration of Titles, Achieved a Ready Sale of Unmarketable Pictures'. *Punch* (14 October 1914), 32.

Musée des Arts Décoratifs, Paris. *Bande dessinée et figuration narrative*. April 7, 1967–June 5, 1967.

Nazir, Sha. *Two Hipsters in the Car*. 2015. Collection of the artist.

Paolozzi, Edward. *Broken Head*. 1984. Glasgow, Hunterian Art Gallery.

Picasso, Pablo. *Sueño y mentira de Franco*. 1937. Glasgow, Hunterian Art Gallery.

Picasso, Pablo. *Frank Quitely: The Art of Comics*. Exhibition Poster. 2017.

Quitely, Frank. *Sandman Endless Knights*. Retail Poster. 2003. Original artwork. Collection of the artist.

Quitely, Frank and Alan Grant. *Batman the Scottish Connection*. New York: DC Comics, 1998.

Quitely, Frank and Bruce Jones. *Watching You. Flinch* 12 (2000). Original artwork (page 11). Collection of the artist.

Quitely, Frank and Grant Morrison. *Flex Mentallo* 2 (1996).

Quitely, Frank and Mark Miller. *The Authority* 22 (2001). Original artwork (cover art). Collection of the artist.

498 L. GROVE

Quitely, Frank and Mark Miller. *Jupiter's Legacy* 1 (2013). Original artwork (page 7). Collection of the artist.

Rembrandt Harmensz van Rijn. *A Sketch of the Entombment.* c.1639–c.1655. Glasgow, Hunterian Art Gallery.

Senefelder, Alois. *Vollstandiges Lehrbuch der Steindruckerei.* Munich: K. Thienemann, 1818.

Strang, John. *Glasgow and its Clubs: Or Glimpses of the Condition, Manners, Characters, and Oddities of the City, During the Past and Present Centuries.* London/Glasgow: Richard Griffin, 1856.

Takamoto, Iwao. *Scooby Doo and Shaggy.* 1997. Glasgow, Glasgow Museums.

Télémaque, Hervé. *Boîte d'allumettes.* 1963. Glasgow, Hunterian Art Gallery.

Töpffer, Rodolphe. *Histoire de Mr. Jabot.* Geneva: Freydig, [1835].

Töpffer, Rodolphe. *Histoire de Mr. Jabot.* 1833. The Gourary Manuscript. Los Angeles, Kunzle Collection.

Warhol, Andy. *Campbell's Soup.* 1969. Glasgow, Glasgow Museums.

Waterfield, Giles. *The People's Galleries: Art Museums and Exhibitions in Britain, 1800–1814.* New Haven: Yale University Press, 2015.

Wither, George. *A Collection of Emblems.* London: A. M. for Robert Allot, 1635.

CHAPTER 26

# Building *The Old Joke Archive*

*Bob Nicholson and Mark Hall*

In 1892, the writer Sarah Butler Wister went before the American people and made a heartfelt 'Plea for Seriousness'.[1] In an article for the *Atlantic Monthly*, she complained that her countrymen had developed an unhealthy obsession with humour. The greatest vice of the age, she argued, was a 'constant craving for the ludicrous' and an incessant desire to make 'a joke of everything'.[2] Worst of all, it was the 'dismal jocosity' of the period's published humour that troubled her most:

> Does the column of newspaper facetiae add to the average of daily cheerfulness? Do the funny books on railway stalls lift the burden and heat of the day, or warm the cockles of the heart against its chill? If people take comfort in exchanging such pleasantries among themselves, well and good, but to see them in print recalls Macaulay's outburst—"A wise man might talk folly like this by his fireside, but that any human being, having made such a joke, should write it down, copy it out, transmit it to the printer, correct the proof, and send it forth to the world, is enough to make us ashamed of our species".[3]

At the heart of Wister's objection to printed humour was her belief that 'nothing is more volatile and evanescent than the essence of a joke'.[4] A good jest might burst forth naturally in conversation, but its spirit could evaporate just as quickly. While more serious works of art and literature could be passed from one generation to the next, comedy, for Wister, was condemned to decay; even

B. Nicholson (✉)
Edge Hill University, Ormskirk, UK
e-mail: bob.nicholson@edgehill.ac.uk

M. Hall
The Open University, Milton Keynes, UK

© The Author(s), under exclusive license to Springer Nature Switzerland AG 2020
D. Derrin, H. Burrows (eds.), *The Palgrave Handbook of Humour, History, and Methodology*, https://doi.org/10.1007/978-3-030-56646-3_26

the best jokes were destined to become 'weary, stale, flat, and unprofitable for merriment'.[5] The humours of the past, she concluded, were destined to be forgotten.

We shudder to think what Wister would make of *The Old Joke Archive* [*TOJA*]—a project that aims to recover, catalogue, and explore the very same jests that she so vociferously denounced. *TOJA* is an open access digital archive of historical jokes, developed in partnership between a historian, a computer scientist, and the British Library Labs. Our core mission is to make historical humour more accessible to both academic researchers and members of the public alike. All of the jokes in *TOJA* are keyword searchable and have been tagged with richly descriptive metadata, thereby allowing users to identify and filter material using categories such as a joke's place of publication, date, subject, format, and the identities and relationships of characters that appear within them. For instance, a user might search for <u>conundrums</u> featuring <u>milkmen</u> that were published in <u>Liverpool</u> during the <u>1860s.</u> Alternatively, they might request all <u>dialogue</u> jokes printed in <u>newspapers</u> featuring a <u>husband</u>, a <u>wife</u> and the word <u>'hat'</u>. As the collection grows, these tags will also allow us to 'distant read' the archive and quantitively track joke-telling trends, such as the emergence and decline of particular comic subjects, regional variations in taste, or stylistic and editorial differences between comic periodicals. *TOJA* will eventually contain hundreds of thousands of jokes from a wide range of historical sources, periods, and locations. However, for now, the pilot phase of the project focuses on recovering English-language, textual humour from the nineteenth century. Our research into the history of joke-telling in this period is still ongoing and our preliminary findings form the basis of other publications.[6] This chapter examines the construction of *The Old Joke Archive* and reflects on the methodological challenges involved in building a repository of historical humour.

While Wister would doubtlessly disapprove of our endeavours, her 'Plea for Seriousness' neatly highlights the key challenges and opportunities faced by our project. Firstly, her frustrations speak to the pervasiveness of humour, as well as its social, cultural, and political significance. A society that seeks to 'make a joke of everything' offers rich pickings for a collector of jests, but there are challenges involved in systematically documenting a practice that was apparently so ubiquitous and diffuse. Secondly, and rather more ominously for an archival project, Wister rightly highlights the transient nature of joking. After all, most of the folly talked by our firesides is never transmitted to a printer, and even publication is no guarantee of a joke's long-term survival. All of which leads us to the question at the heart of this chapter: how do we build an archive devoted to a historical practice that was apparently so pervasive, *and yet* so ephemeral? We begin by reflecting on the process of finding new sources of old jokes and by outlining the main forms in which they have—and have not—survived. Then, the chapter considers the curation of jokes and the challenges involved in determining and cataloguing their subjects and genres.

## FINDING JOKES

The word 'joke' is a nebulous term that encompasses a wide variety of comic practices, texts, and expressions. In its broadest sense—a thing intended to cause amusement or laughter—we might use it to describe a prank, a cartoon, a funny passage in a novel, a line of stand-up comedy, a comic detail in a painting, a conversational quip, a piece of graffiti, and countless other humorous expressions. In the fullness of time, *The Old Joke Archive* may expand in order to include several of these comic forms. For now, however, we have adopted a narrower set of criteria that define a joke in the following terms: a <u>short, self-contained, comic text or expression</u> that typically <u>terminates in a punchline</u>. This definition is best exemplified by the short gags published in joke books and comic papers, but our criteria are expansive and flexible enough to cover other modes of publication, as well as second-hand evidence of jokes which were performed on stage or shared with friends. Our stipulation that jokes must be self-contained excludes those that were contextually dependent on their place within a wider text or performance; a funny quip, or call-back, in the middle of a narrative stand-up routine would probably not meet our criteria, but a one-liner told by the same comedian might. Our guidelines also exclude comic short stories, although the line between these texts and some of the longer jokes in our archive is ambiguous and rests on whether the story builds to a punchline. We have not implemented a strict word-count for our shortness criteria, chiefly because some gags derive their humour from a tortuously extended set-up. Similarly, while most jokes in our archive finish on a clear punchline, there are some exceptions to this rule. Victorian joke writers often explained pun-based punchlines using a parenthetical postscript, while accounts of the jests told by famous wits sometimes describe how these immortal quips were received by their audiences. Our punchline criteria also leave room for the anti-jokes and shaggy dog stories that comically subvert joke-telling conventions by ending anticlimactically. Finally, our focus on textual jokes (or spoken jokes that can be rendered, or described, textually) also excludes cartoons, caricatures, comic strips, and slapstick routines. While visual humour is a fascinating and important element of many historical cultures of joke-telling, a different archival infrastructure and interface is needed to curate and display this material.

Historical jokes, as we define them, have survived in an eclectic range of places and formats. The jokes in *TOJA* come from historical sources that fall into one of four main categories, each of which present us with different curatorial and technical challenges. In each case, our goal is first to *find* a prospective source of old jokes, then to *extract* the individual jokes contained within it, and finally to *annotate* each of these jokes with descriptive metadata. The end result is a record in *TOJA* for each instance of a joke, featuring: (1) an image of the joke as it appeared in its original publication; (2) a digital transcription of the joke's text in order to make it keyword searchable; and (3) a range of metadata categories which are discussed later in this chapter. While this might seem like a relatively straightforward workflow with a consistent output, the haphazard ways in which jokes have been preserved means that the tasks and tools involved in this process vary considerably depending on the nature of documents involved.

## JOKE BOOKS

Existing research on the history of jokes typically concentrates on joke-focused publications, the most obvious examples being historical jest books.[7] The great advantage of these sources is that they contain a large quantity of jokes, the vast majority of which fit the criteria for our archive. The most substantial books in our collection contain thousands of jests, while even their smallest counterparts usually have dozens of items that are eligible for inclusion in *TOJA*. In many cases, these publications also have titles and bibliographic metadata that make them discoverable using library and archival catalogues. The British Library catalogue, for instance, immediately returns 203 results for nineteenth-century publications featuring the words 'jokes' or 'jests' in their title, almost all of which are joke books. Follow-up searches for terms like 'wit', 'humour', 'comic', 'laugh', and 'fun' reveal thousands more. While these basic catalogue searches have proven fruitful, it is important to stress that many historical joke books are not so easily traced. For instance, one late-nineteenth-century anthology named *How To Set The Table In A Roar!* features 256 pages packed with jokes, but does not have an obviously comic keyword in its title.[8] Moreover, even though the book was published by a company based in London and Yorkshire, it does not appear in the British Library's catalogue or, for that matter, the catalogues of other major UK libraries. A search on WorldCat returns just one result for a copy of the book held by Cornell University in New York State. This is not an uncommon problem. While joke books were theoretically subject to the same laws of legal deposit as other publications, many seem to have slipped through the net and evaded systematic preservation. This is particularly true of titles released by minor, short-lived publishing houses and flimsy texts such as chapbooks and pamphlets. This is, perhaps, a reflection of the perceived ephemerality and disposability of jokes; it may also stem from the fact that many of these anthologies were heavily based on unattributed reprints and were not identified with a specific author or editor, placing them in an ambiguous relationship with copyright. In any case, it is likely that many historical joke books have been lost forever. Many of those that have been preserved are now scattered across the globe, buried in uncatalogued special collections or held in private hands. Finding these texts requires lengthy detective work and a dash of good fortune. We only discovered *How To Set The Table In A Roar!* when it was listed on eBay with the word 'jokes' in the description. As a result, while it is unlikely that *TOJA* will ever feature *all* of the jest books printed in a particular place or period, some of the holes in our collection will gradually be plugged as more publications are discovered.

While some historical jest books are hard to track down, others were so frequently reprinted that they present an entirely different curatorial problem.

Dozens of eighteenth and nineteenth-century jest books were named *Modern Joe Miller*, *New Joe Miller*, or *Joe Miller Up To Date* in homage to the celebrated *Joe Miller's Jests* of 1739. Some were straightforward reprints, either of the original text or one of its earlier imitators; others borrowed selectively from previous incarnations of Joe Miller while adding their own material; and several of these self-appointed sequels shared no content with the 'original' texts whatsoever. In all cases, we aim to add the book's contents to *TOJA*, even if it is a word-for-word reprint of a text that we have already processed. There are two reasons for this apparent duplication of effort. Firstly, it is almost impossible to conclusively determine the 'original' source of most jokes; even the ones in an ostensible foundation-text such as the first *Joe Miller* were probably borrowed from other texts, both ancient and modern, or plucked from oral culture. To include only the earliest instance of each joke would give a misleading impression as to their authorship and require us to assess and cross-reference the date of each individual joke before deciding whether to include or reject it. Secondly, we consider each reprint and retelling of a joke to be a meaningful historical act with its own distinctive purpose and context. Capturing this data gives historians a better understanding of how, where, when, and why particular jokes were told. As *TOJA* grows, so too will our ability to trace the origins, evolution, and circulation of individual jests. In an earlier project, Nicholson tracked the life of a single nineteenth-century joke from its apparent origins in a New York comic periodical, through its international circulation across dozens of English-language books and newspapers, to its eventual status as a stock jest used by British politicians.[9] This was accomplished by keyword searching multiple digital archives for a phrase in the joke's punchline and then trawling through thousands of irrelevant hits. *TOJA* will simplify this process by automatically suggesting connections between similar jokes in its collection, even if they are not word-for-word reprints of one another.

## COMIC PERIODICALS

Jest books are the most concentrated source of material for *TOJA*, but they represent only a small fraction of the total number of jokes that have survived within the historical record. Comic periodicals are, potentially, an even richer source of jokes, particularly for the Victorian Era. *Punch* magazine, founded in 1841, is the most famous of these publications and is routinely cited by historians seeking to discover what made the Victorians laugh. However, while it was certainly an influential title, it is important to stress that *Punch* was not the only humorous paper in wide circulation. Donald J. Gray's bibliography of comic periodicals lists nearly 400 titles published in Britain between 1800 and 1900, and this list is unlikely to be exhaustive.[10] The majority of these papers were very short-lived, some only lasting for a single issue, but many appeared on a weekly or monthly basis for years at a time, and some endured for decades. As well as supplying a large amount of material for our archive, these long-running titles make it possible to explore how, and why, jokes changed over time, or, alternatively, to pinpoint jests that arose at a very specific historical moment. Indeed, the periodicity of comic periodicals—their weekly and monthly rhythms, their ability to respond rapidly to current events, and their expected disposability—means that they were produced and consumed in very different ways to one-off jestbooks and carried different types of comic material as a result. A witty pun about a recent parliamentary speech by Gladstone might appear in a weekly paper like *Punch*, but the topicality of this joke would make it too short-lived for inclusion in a hardbound jestbook designed to sit on bookshelves long after the Prime Minister's speech had been forgotten.

The titles in Gray's bibliography vary enormously in style, content, and target audience: from expensive, high-brow, satirical periodicals aimed at middle-class literary gentlemen, to more accessible halfpenny weeklies whose social jokes and slapstick cartoons were more suited to a popular audience. By studying key aspects of these periodicals—their price, title, branding, circulation, adverts, tone, and political position—it is possible to make tentative observations about the class, gender, age, and politics of the readers who were expected to enjoy and understand the jokes within them. While similar techniques can be used to reconstruct the implied readers of jestbooks, these texts typically feature fewer contextual clues as to their intended audience. Comic periodicals are also more effective for exploring geographical variations in joke-telling. Some titles enjoyed a national circulation, but others were focused on serving and satirising a particular town or region, such as Liverpool's long-running *Porcupine* and Edinburgh's shorter-lived *Mac Punch*. In these publications, jokes about well-known local people, places, and events were far more common. Integrating a wide range of comic periodicals into *TOJA*, therefore, is desirable not simply because they increase the overall size of our archive, but because their jokes reflect different aspects of the period's comic culture and enable us to contextualise it with greater precision.

Unfortunately, the vast majority of comic papers have yet to be digitised, and some of the rarest surviving titles are in fragile condition. While it is relatively cost-effective and practical for us to digitise joke books, particularly those already owned by researchers on the project, our current budget does not stretch to the large-scale digitisation of hundreds of comic periodicals spread across multiple libraries and archives. Each page of a jest book typically yields between five and fifteen jokes, but periodicals contain a wide range of other comic genres that do not fit *TOJA's* current selection criteria. Satirical political commentary, comic verse, parodies, burlesques, short stories, and cartoons all fall outside our purview. A typical Victorian comic periodical, modelled on *Punch's* successful formula, usually featured a handful of jokes (as we define them) in each weekly issue, but scattered them throughout the paper as column-filers that need to be identified and extracted one-by-one. This is a task that Victorian sub-editors knew only too well. Every week, in newspaper offices around the country, they combed the pages of newly released comic periodicals in search of jokes. Soon after, they reprinted them in dedicated humour columns with titles such as 'Wit and Humour' and 'Pickings from the Comic

Press'. Just like us, these Victorian newspaper editors needed to identify self-contained, short pieces of humour that would survive the decontextualising process of being transplanted into a new publication. Observing their well-honed technique helped to sharpen our curatorial practices and also pointed to an unexpected source of new material. Curiously, most of the jokes reprinted from *Punch* were lifted from the captions that appeared underneath the magazine's cartoons, many of which functioned surprisingly well in the absence of any visual component. This kind of copying was quicker, cheaper, and technologically simpler than reproducing magazine's woodcuts, and it also seems to have lessened the risk of legal disputes; *Punch* litigiously defended the copyright of its illustrations, but generally turned a blind eye to persistent, low-level textual plagiarism.[11] *TOJA* operates in a different legal and technical context, but the extraction of jokes from the captions of some cartoons is also a viable option for our archive.

In practice, the most efficient way for us to gather material from comic periodicals is also inspired by the practices of nineteenth-century editors. While some publications clipped jokes directly from *Punch*, others seem to have bypassed this task and copied the selections made by other newspapers. *TOJA* adopts a similar approach and piggy-backs on the work of Victorian editors by collecting material from comic periodicals that was reprinted in daily and weekly newspapers. These jokes were often published with attributions, which allows us to trace them to an original publication. As *TOJA* grows, it will also become increasingly capable of pinpointing the sources of unattributed jokes—the work of one diligent sub-editor is sometimes enough to reveal the uncredited borrowings made by dozens of his rivals. There are clear pros and cons to this second-hand curation of the comic press. On the plus side, newspapers have been digitised more extensively than comic periodicals and are therefore much cheaper and easier for us to access and process. As Nicholson has explored elsewhere, one of the most efficient ways to build a new digital archive is to creatively 'remix' material that has already been scanned by other projects, but which is not well-served by their interfaces and metadata schema.[12] Importing newspaper joke columns also bypasses the manual task of reading through the comic press and picking out the jokes ourselves, allowing us to add material to the archive more quickly. Outsourcing our curatorial judgement to Victorian sub-editors is an unconventional strategy, but our experiments suggest that their choices closely mirror our own. Crucially, we do not rely on the selections of a single editor, but on the collective clippings made by dozens of papers. In the process, we also gain valuable new datapoints that help to reveal the true popularity, circulation, and audience of these jokes. The unavoidable downside of this approach is that Victorian editors typically focused their attention on a narrow range of publications—*Punch* looms large, closely followed by other London-based weeklies like *Judy*, *Fun*, and *Ariel*. At present, the pilot stage of *TOJA* replicates this focus because it offers the most efficient method of harvesting jokes, but also because it captures the most widely circulated jests of the age. However, as the archive develops, we aim to address this imbalance and manually process jokes from obscurer Victorian periodicals that were left undisturbed by the scissors of the period's editors.

## Newspaper Humour

Newspapers are arguably the most promising source of nineteenth-century jokes, and not just because they grant us second-hand access to the highlights of comic periodicals. More jokes have been preserved in these publications than in all comic periodicals and joke books put together. Jokes and other comic clippings appeared sporadically in newspapers from the earliest days of the press, where they functioned as useful column-fillers. However, from the 1870s onwards, organised humour columns became a staple feature of provincial and national newspapers alike. A typical column, such as 'Jokes of the Day' in *Lloyds' Weekly News*, featured approximately 20 jests in each weekly instalment—this quickly adds-up to 1000+ jokes in a year or 10,000+ over the course of a decade. Dozens, possibly even hundreds, of Victorian newspapers published columns of this nature every week, sometimes for several decades. Bestselling penny magazines, such as *Tit-Bits* and *Answers*, made even more extensive use of jokes; they often devoted their front page entirely to jests and routinely sprinkled more of them inside. It was not uncommon for papers like this to feature between 50 and 100 jokes in each weekly issue. Only a small portion of the press has been digitised. Nevertheless, if we process two decades of material from 20 of the most prolific digitised newspapers, we might expect to harvest something in the region of half-a-million jokes. Of course, many of them will be reprints—but, as previously explained, we consider the repetition of a joke to be a significant act, and each reprint gives valuable contextual data for interpreting its meaning and significance.

This does not mean that *TOJA* will be swamped by half a million reprints from *Punch*. Newspaper editors populated their joke columns from a variety of sources, including newspapers and magazines published overseas. In particular, imported American jokes were hugely popular in Victorian Britain.[13] Editors gathered them into dedicated columns of 'Yankee Humour' which appeared everywhere from the biggest national papers to the smallest provincial weeklies. *Tit-Bits* magazine included plenty of transatlantic jokes, but also looked across the channel for fresh material; its weekly page of 'Continental Tit-Bits' featured jokes clipped, and translated, from papers in mainland Europe. Other papers, such as the *Dundee Weekly News*, sourced material directly from their readers via long-running weekly joke competitions. The results for these competitions often printed the name and address of winning participants. When cross-referenced with the census, it is often possible to discover the age, occupation, and marital status of the people who submitted them—a rare, and extremely valuable insight into the public's joke-telling preferences.[14] In short, even though Victorian newspapers might not seem particularly humorous at first glance, they hold the greatest volume and variety of preserved jokes for this period *and* provide us with the richest contextual metadata.

Unfortunately, extracting jokes from newspapers presents the biggest curatorial and technological challenge. After all, the vast majority of the articles in these publications are not suitable for our archive—jokes appeared alongside news stories, editorials, adverts, letters, stock prices, gardening columns, serialised stories, sports results, and dozens of other journalistic genres. At present, this is one of the chief obstacles faced by researchers who might want to explore the history of joke-telling in nineteenth-century Britain. It is not difficult to find Victorian jokes, once you know where to look, but it is much more challenging to find jokes about a specific pre-determined topic. Searching a digital archive of Victorian newspapers for the term 'Gladstone' will return plenty of jests about him, but these results will be overwhelmed by thousands of hits from other journalistic genres. Similarly, if we wanted to explore Victorian jokes made at the expense of lawyers or doctors, we would need to wade through millions of other articles that cite these professions. For instance, a search for the word 'doctor' in one nineteenth-century newspaper archive returns more than five million hits; if ten thousand doctor jokes appeared in these results, they would represent no more than 0.2% of the total. Moreover, our search would only find doctor jokes in which the word 'doctor' appears; a jest that signals its topic by naming a character 'Dr Sawbones' would remain undiscovered. This approach is also vulnerable to errors in an archive's Optical Character Recognition (OCR) data, where the word 'doctor' is often mistranscribed by the software as 'dactor' or 'docton'. It is possible to construct complex queries that increase the percentage of useful hits, but the success of this approach is heavily dependent on an archive's search tools and requires a detailed understanding of how joke columns were formatted. We developed *TOJA* to solve this problem and make historical humour more accessible to non-expert researchers, but to accomplish this we needed to develop a strategy for extracting hundreds of thousands of jokes from millions of pages of digitised newspapers.

The easiest jokes to extract are those which were organised into consistently titled, long-running, weekly humour columns. Our dataset of nineteenth-century newspapers includes a 'document title' field in its metadata, which allows us to isolate individual columns based on the words that appear in their headers. For instance, we can extract all columns titled 'Jokes of the Day' that appeared in *Lloyd's Weekly News*—a total of 340 columns, each containing between 10 and 30 jokes. The same approach nets us 180 instalments of 'Jonathan's Jokes' from the *Hampshire Telegraph*, 798 columns of 'Wit and Humour' from the *Lancaster Gazette*, 102 editions of 'Clippings from the Comic Papers' published by the *Hull Packet*, and many more. Once the title of a long-running column has been discovered, it is relatively straightforward to extract all of its instalments from our newspaper dataset; at this stage of the curatorial process, a batch of 500 columns is no more difficult to gather than a set of five. Things become trickier for newspapers with a less settled format. The *Hampshire Telegraph*, for instance, changed the name of its imported American humour column on an almost weekly basis and resorted to the use of increasingly obscure transatlantic reference points; a column titled 'Buckwheat Cakes' sounds more like a recipe than a collection of jokes and is unlikely to be discovered via keyword searching. In cases like this, we have to gather columns manually at a slower pace. We also resort to manual methods in order to plug gaps caused by OCR errors. If a column was mistranscribed as being titled 'Jakes of the Doy' then its absence is often easy to identify simply by looking for unexplained interruptions in a column's weekly pattern.

Focusing on the titles of long-running columns is the most efficient way to extract jokes from nineteenth-century newspapers, but we know that this will not find *all* of the jokes hidden in our dataset. Many of them were printed outside of dedicated humour columns, sometimes in broader collections, and often as isolated column-fillers with no identifying title or recurring pattern. While it would technically be possible to browse through each newspaper, page by page, in search of every joke, this would be a laborious process for our small team to undertake. We are currently experimenting with two potential solutions. The first involves a crowdsourcing platform discussed in more detail in part two of this chapter. In brief, users of the archive and a team of volunteer 'joke detectives' can find and submit potential new sources to *TOJA*—subject to copyright, and the approval of the project team—in return for being credited as the joke's discoverer. The results of this process are unpredictable, and dependent on the unpaid labour of volunteers, but they have already identified viable new collections. Our second experiment uses a combination of Computer Vision (CV) and Natural Language Processing (NLP) to automatically identify potential jokes. The underlying algorithms are relatively complex but, in layman's terms, we feed a 'training corpus' of verified jokes into the system and instruct it to find articles that it thinks share similar visual and linguistic properties. Humour columns of the type discussed earlier tend to have characteristic visual patterns, such as shorter paragraphs and a repetitive layout. This visual search provides an initial filter, which results in a significant number of incorrectly identified blocks of text. In the second step, word and punctuation patterns characteristic to humour columns are used to filter out most of the incorrectly identified text blocks. For instance, if the characters '—*Punch*' or '—*Fun*' appear nearby, then a body of text is likely to be part of a joke column (the italics and dash were typically used to signal an attribution). The resulting list of potential humour columns is then manually verified before being ingested into the system. The quality of the process and the amount of manual intervention needed depends heavily on the amount of training data available. As the archive grows, the amount of training data also grows, thereby gradually training the system to recognise jokes more effectively. Nevertheless, the manual verification step will always be required, as the algorithms are tuned to fish with a wide and fine net, as we believe it is preferable to discover as many jokes as possible, at the cost of finding and filtering out a lot of incorrect data. Both of these approaches are still under development but, when used in combination, we are optimistic that crowdsourcing and automatic identification will allow us to find and extract hundreds of thousands of long-forgotten jokes that would otherwise remain hidden.

## Manuscripts and Other Fragments

The majority of jokes in *TOJA* come from published sources—chiefly jest books, comic periodicals, and newspapers. However, traces of historical humour have also survived in an eclectic range of other documents and objects. Some people recorded jokes in their diaries, others jotted them down on postcards, and some scrawled them on toilet walls. The most exciting one-off sources we have discovered so far include the extensive and carefully organised files of Cliff Dean, a comedian from Lancashire operating in the 1940s, and a Victorian notebook filled with 91 pages of handwritten jokes assembled from a range of printed and oral sources. Our archive is receptive to this kind of evidence, but it is almost impossible to develop a systematic strategy for finding and processing it. We perform regular searches of auction sites, second-hand bookshops, manuscript dealers, and archive catalogues. However, our best sources have so far been brought to us by people who learned about the project and wanted to contribute. We suspect there must be many joke-filled scrapbooks, notepads, postcards, and other ephemeral fragments sitting in people's attics all over the world. Over time, we hope that *TOJA* will continue to act as a magnet for this material and allow us to make it accessible to researchers for the first time.

## Cataloguing Jokes

Once jokes have been located and extracted from their original documents, they must be processed and catalogued. This process consists of the following steps: splitting apart the individual jokes in an image; transcribing the image into text; and annotating the text. The workflow always uses an automate-first, manually check/correct-after approach. An initial version of the output for each step is generated automatically. The result is then presented to volunteers through our purpose-built crowdsourcing tools. Depending on the quality of the automatic result, the volunteer may only have to verify its correctness. However, if the output contains errors, they may have to correct these manually or, in the worst-case scenario, repeat the whole step themselves. A detailed account of each step in this process lies beyond the scope of this chapter. However, in brief, images featuring multiple jokes—such as newspaper columns—are first broken down into clippings of individual jokes. This work is performed using a web-based tool which prompts users to draw a box around every joke; a similar approach is used by many citizen science projects, including those hosted on the industry-standard Zooniverse platform.[15] Next, each of these clippings is automatically processed using OCR software, and these digital transcriptions are manually corrected by project volunteers whose contributions are automatically cross-checked for discrepancies and errors. Finally, volunteers and members of the core project team annotate each joke with metadata describing aspects of its format and focus. This metadata falls into three main groups: (1) the subject(s) of a joke; (2) the genre, or format, of a joke; and (3) subject/format specific details, such as information about a joke's characters and locations. Figure 26.1 outlines the metadata captured for a typical nineteenth-century 'dialogue' joke.

Our project is not the first to wrestle with the challenge of categorising and organising jokes. Once again, we looked to the past for inspiration. The editors of the jestbooks in our collection all had to decide how their anthologies would be structured, and they reached a range of contrasting conclusions. Many, including the aforementioned *How To Set The Table In A Roar!*, eschewed any kind of organisation and printed their jokes in a seemingly random order. These unstructured books are well-suited to casual browsing, but do not function very successfully as reference works; if we want to find a joke about a particular subject, we have to skim through the book until we find one. At the other end of the spectrum, some jokebooks organised their material thematically by subject. For instance, *Bennett Cerf's Vest Pocket Book of Jokes* (1957) is arranged into 135 alphabetised categories; under 'd' in the contents page we find dentists, department stores, dinner parties, doctors, dogs, and drink. The specificity of these categories varies greatly from one collection to another. Geoff Tibballs' *Mammoth Book of One-Liners* (2012) features separate categories for cats, dogs, ducks, and even turtles; in the personal joke files of the Lancashire comedian, Cliff Dean, this material was grouped under the broader category of 'Animals'.[16] At a more conceptual level, critics and comedians throughout history have asserted, with varying degrees of seriousness, that every joke can be placed within a small handful of broader, universal categories—unfortunately, each version of this theory confidently asserts a different set and number of categories. In short, there is no universally agreed system for classifying jokes, and we had to develop a robust taxonomy that would best fit the data and curatorial processes involved in the archive.

We attempted to establish a subject classification system at the start of our project, but it became apparent that no amount of forward-planning could anticipate all the jokes we later discovered. Wister's complaint that her contemporaries were happy to 'make a joke of anything' rings true. Some categories— marriage, lawyers, doctors, mothers-in-law, and so on—loom consistently large, but others ebb and flow in response to historical events and societal changes. A taxonomy developed and tested using Victorian humour would struggle to represent the comic culture of other periods and locations. However,

---

**FORTUNE-TELLER :** " You will be very poor until you are thirty-five years of age."
**OUR IMPECUNIOUS POET (eagerly) :** " And after then ? "
**FORTUNE-TELLER :** " You will get used to it."

| | | | |
|---|---|---|---|
| Source Title: *The Sketch* | Format: dialogue | Character 1: 'Fortune-Teller' | Character 2: 'Impecunious Poet' |
| Source Type: Newspaper | Subjects: Poetry; Poets; | Gender: Unknown | Gender: Unknown |
| Pub Date: 10 Oct 1894 | Fortune Telling; Poverty. | Ethnicity: Unknown | Ethnicity: Unknown |
| Pub Location: London | Location: Unknown | Life-stage: Adult | Life-stage: Adult |
| Archive: BNA | | Profession: Fortune-Teller | Profession: Poet |

**Fig. 26.1** A nineteenth-century dialogue joke with metadata

one of the true benefits of digital archives is that it is easily possible to expand any categorisation and to categorise objects in multiple ways at the same time. To that end, our classification model is capable of expanding in response to the discovery of new jokes. If a volunteer cannot find an appropriate classification in our system when they are annotating a joke, they can propose a new one, subject to the approval of the archive's curators. In many cases, these emergent topics can be flagged as sub-categories of existing subjects; jokes about motor-cars, for instance, are a distinctive new presence at the turn of the twentieth century and deserve their own subject classification, but this sits within a broader topic of 'Transportation' which includes earlier gags about railways and cyclists. Crucially, each joke in *TOJA* can be annotated with multiple topic keywords, which solves a problem faced by the editors of printed jestbooks who usually needed to place a joke in a single category. Should a gag about airline food appear in the food section or in the air travel section? In a digital archive like *TOJA*, it can be assigned to both. This also makes it possible for jokes within *TOJA* to be re-classified with new layers of descriptive metadata, perhaps in response to the development of alternative joke taxonomies, or in order to answer the research questions of other projects.

The jokes in *TOJA* are also categorised by genre/format. This was a common organisational strategy used by editors of joke books. Some, such as *Four Hundred Laughs* (1901), did not sort by subject, but devoted separate chapters to conundrums, verses, and witty sayings. Similarly, Cliff Dean's joke folders feature separate sections for comic songs and humorous newspaper advertisements. Devising an exhaustive taxonomy of joke genres presents the same methodological problems as categorising subjects; new genres and sub-genres emerge as our search broadens to new periods and locations, and many jokes do not fit into a single distinctive format. Once again, we have adopted a flexible approach that will allow us to expand, and refine, our categories as *TOJA* develops. We begin by flagging the presence of a particular comic format or element—what might be termed its stylistic building blocks. For instance, most of the jokes in our Victorian pilot corpus currently feature one, or more, of the following elements: puns, dialogue, prose, verse, and questions and answers (Q&As). Next, we identify whether a joke belongs to a specific identifiable genre, such as a 'conundrum' or a 'knock-knock' joke. At present, this classification work is performed manually by volunteers using the project's crowd-sourcing tools. However, we have begun to experiment successfully with computer-assisted classification. Genres with a very specific format, or distinctive linguistic markers (such as the quotation marks in a dialogue joke), can be identified automatically. For now, this works as a prompt to human users of the archive who are asked to verify the accuracy of the automated classification.

Finally, the metadata attached to each item in *TOJA* is shaped by the genre and content of the joke in question. For instance, the joke in Fig. 26.1 was categorised as featuring 'dialogue', and so its cataloguer was prompted to provide additional information about the joke's characters. Annotations like this are particularly important for improving the discoverability of jokes. Vital

512    B. NICHOLSON AND M. HALL

elements of a joke's subject are often implied by context, or communicated playfully, instead of being signalled by a straightforward keyword. An undertaker might be referred to simply as 'Mr Freshgrave;' a man might refer to his mother-in-law as 'your grandmother' in conversation with his children; and an Irishman's nationality might be signalled through dialect. None of these would be returned by a simple keyword search for 'undertaker', 'mother-in-law', or 'Irish'. The richer we make this character metadata, the more nuanced our search queries can become. For instance, by capturing (wherever possible) the gender, profession/role, life-stage, and nationality of characters in a dialogue joke, we can focus a keyword search on passages of dialect spoken by adult women or identify gags in which a man converses with a child. However, there are limits to the depth of detail we can achieve. At present, we can only capture unambiguous aspects of a character's identity. We initially hoped to record the social class of a character, but found that this could not be inferred reliably by non-expert volunteers; fortunately, the 'profession/role' category acts as an alternative way to explore this issue. Similarly, if a joke published in London features a man speaking Standard English, then we might reasonably assume that he was Englishman—but we do not record this character's nationality unless it is signalled more directly. In all cases, if no evidence exists to support an annotation—if a character's gender, for instance, is not stated or very strongly implied—then it is left blank. For instance, the implied genders of the characters in Fig. 26.1 are female (fortune-teller) and male (poet), but this is not signalled decisively enough to become part of the joke's factual metadata.

Built on top of the images, texts, and metadata is an interface for searching and exploring the archive, which aims to support both focused search and open-ended exploration and browsing in the archive. The search interface uses a standard faceted-search interface, which enables the researcher to input keyword searches or construct more complex queries such as all <u>verse</u> jokes printed in <u>books</u> featuring a <u>teacher</u>, a <u>pupil</u> and the word <u>'apple'</u>. It also provides access to the annotated texts in a Text Encoding Initative (TEI) format, which enables offline working with the joke corpus and integration with other Digital Humanities research tools.[17] While *TOJA* is partly intended to facilitate complex, academic research queries, we also recognise that jokes have a leisure life; that users might browse them for pleasure in a much less focused or analytical way. To support this, the archive provides an interface that allows the user to choose from a range of automatically and manually curated topics and then explore, read, and enjoy the jokes.

## CONCLUSION

At the time of writing, the first prototype of *The Old Joke Archive* is nearing completion and will soon be ready for public testing. Once launched, it will be possible for researchers to access tens of thousands of long-forgotten jokes and explore them with a newfound precision. It is too early to predict what impact this might have on the ways that we explore and understand the history of joke-telling. However, the construction and design of the archive has already helped us to understand the complex place of jokes in the historical record. Despite their inherent ephemerality, it turns out that nineteenth-century jokes *have* survived in remarkably large numbers—and the same is likely true of many other historical periods and places. Millions of jokes have been preserved in archives and personal collections around the world. They have been captured in the pages of jestbooks, comic periodicals, newspapers, and manuscripts. Sometimes this preservation was deliberate and systematic but, more often, it was haphazard and accidental. Many jokes have survived as stowaways in the margins of more valued texts; as column-fillers that were used to plug gaps between newspaper articles, or throwaway quips in diaries. The diffuse nature of this historical record has long been an obstacle to researchers and has tended to direct our attention to the most prominent and accessible sources of material. *TOJA* aims to redress this imbalance, but gathering and cataloguing jokes from such a wide array of unidentified sources presents significant curatorial challenges. As this chapter has outlined, the solution involves a combination of historical expertise, computer science, and the generous help of volunteers. There is much more work to be done in each of these areas, and millions more old jokes to be found. Over the coming years, we hope that fellow researchers in the field of humour studies will join us to expand the temporal, linguistic, geographical, and curatorial limits of *The Old Joke Archive* and uncover new insights into the forgotten humours of the past.

## Notes

1. Wister, 'A Plea for Seriousness'. This article was initially published anonymously, but it was subsequently attributed to Wister in the *Atlantic Monthly's* annual index.
2. Ibid., 628.
3. Ibid., 628.
4. Ibid., 625.
5. Ibid., 627.
6. See Nicholson, 'Capital Company'.
7. See, for example: Dickie, *Cruelty and Laughter*; Verberckmoes, *Laughter, Jestbooks and Society*; Reinke-Williams, 'Misogyny, Jest-Books and Male Youth Culture'.
8. Anon., *How To Set The Table in A Roar!*
9. Nicholson, 'You Kick the Bucket'.
10. Gray, 'A list'.
11. Nicholson, 'Capital Company'.
12. Nicholson, 'The Victorian Meme Machine'.
13. Nicholson, 'Jonathan's Jokes'.
14. Nicholson, 'Capital Company'.
15. The Zooniverse Project, www.zooniverse.org.
16. The joke files of Cliff Dean are privately held by the Dean family.
17. Text Encoding Initiative, https://tei-c.org.

## BIBLIOGRAPHY

Anon. *How To Set The Table In A Roar! The jester's, punster's and humourist's guide.* London: Miller and Co., c.1880s.

Cerf, Bennet. *Bennett Cerf's Vest Pocket Book of Jokes.* London: Hammond, Hammond & Company, 1957.

Dickie, Simon. *Cruelty and Laughter: Forgotten Comic Literature and the Unsentimental Eighteenth Century.* Chicago: Chicago University Press, 2011.

Gray, Donald J. 'A List of Comic Periodicals Published in Great Britain, 1800–1900, with a Prefatory Essay'. *Victorian Periodicals Newsletter* 5, no. 1 (1972): 2–39.

Kemble, John R. *Four Hundred Laughs: or Fun Without Vulgarity.* New York: A. L. Burt, 1901.

Nicholson, Bob. 'The Victorian Meme Machine: Remixing the Nineteenth-Century Archive'. *19: Interdisciplinary Studies in the Long Nineteenth Century* 21 (2015).

Nicholson, Bob. '"You Kick the Bucket; We Do the Rest!": Jokes and the Culture of Reprinting in the Transatlantic Press'. *Journal of Victorian Culture* 17, no. 3 (2012): 273–286.

Nicholson, Bob. 'Capital Company: Writing and Telling Jokes in Victorian Britain'. In *Victorian Comedy and Laughter: Conviviality, Jokes and Dissent*, edited by Louise Lee. London: Palgrave, 2020.

Nicholson, Bob. 'Jonathan's Jokes: American Humour in the late-Victorian Press'. *Media History* 18, no. 1 (2012): 33–49.

Reinke-Williams, Tim. 'Misogyny, Jest-Books and Male Youth Culture in Seventeenth-Century England'. *Gender and History* 21, no. 2 (2009): 324–339.

Tibballs, Geoff. *The Mammoth Book of One-Liners.* London: Constable & Robinson, 2012.

Verberckmoes, Johan. *Laughter, Jestbooks and Society in the Spanish Netherlands.* London: Palgrave, 1999.

Wister, Sarah Butler. 'A Plea for Seriousness'. *Atlantic Monthly* (May, 1892): 625–630.

# INDEX[1]

**A**

Absurdity, 4, 20, 113, 192, 233, 281, 294, 392, 395, 396, 406, 413, 415, 418, 419, 451, 460, 461, 467

Abuse, 54, 56, 58, 227, 280, 282, 328, 329, 460, 465, 469

Adaptation, 190, 314, 444, 445, 447, 449, 452, 454, 455n5

Advertisement/s, 406, 415, 504, 507, 511

Aggression, 24, 25, 33, 190, 216n36, 265, 299, 320, 417, 468

Alighieri, Dante, 261
  *Divina Commedia*, 261

Allegory, 3, 321, 368, 449

Alterity, 183, 185–186, 223, 240, 241, 280, 281

Ambiguity, v, vi, 6, 26, 52, 53, 83, 155, 202, 204, 261, 278, 283, 288n1, 371, 375, 400, 454, 466, 501, 502

Amusement, v–vii, 4, 6, 7, 26, 30, 46, 47, 49–51, 53, 55, 63, 64, 78, 100, 133–135, 137, 140, 141, 153, 155, 159, 167n27, 180, 186, 192, 214, 233, 250, 251, 260, 269, 313, 320, 321, 327, 389, 399, 436, 448–450, 467, 482, 486, 501

Anachronism, 9, 14, 23, 29, 140, 144, 146, 147, 202, 275, 283, 353, 445, 449–450

Anecdote, 76, 79, 86n24, 88n87, 204–211, 213–215, 216n28, 216n30, 217n52, 217n61, 227, 234, 263, 264, 443, 450, 455, 462

Animals
  animality, 194
  boar, 181, 182, 303
  cicada, 209
  deer, 369, 393
  fish, 252, 374, 375, 377, 508
  goat, 213, 214, 390
  horse, 4, 26, 213, 267, 268, 369, 437, 451
  mantis, 209
  monkey, 81, 85n2, 88n86, 98, 184, 214, 379n21, 469
  pig, 330, 417, 420, 465
  Reynard the Fox, 314, 319
  swan, 469, 470, 476n71
  whale, 246–248, 254n28, 449

Anthropology, 128, 156, 159–161, 240, 241, 251

Antiquity, 20, 24, 25, 34, 190–191, 196n33, 332, 385

---

[1] Note: Page numbers followed by 'n' refer to notes.

© The Author(s), under exclusive license to Springer Nature
Switzerland AG 2020
D. Derrin, H. Burrows (eds.), *The Palgrave Handbook of Humour, History, and Methodology*, https://doi.org/10.1007/978-3-030-56646-3

515

516    INDEX

Apte, Mahadev, 159–161
Arabic, 297, 298
Aristophanes, 178, 191, 342, 345
   *Clouds, The*, 342
   *Wasps*, 191
Aristotle, 12, 23, 25, 32, 33, 37n85, 72,
   75, 85n6, 86n36, 97, 136, 145,
   175, 176, 190, 250, 294
   *Poetics*, 25, 136, 176
   *Rhetoric*, 32
Art/s, visual, 255n42, 305, 452
Attardo, Salvatore, 15n8, 15n12, 111,
   371, 378, 380n39
Attractiveness, 54, 140, 146, 278, 280,
   282–288, 393, 435
Audience, vi, vii, 7, 8, 10, 15, 31–34, 48,
   58, 60, 61, 63, 73, 76, 77, 96, 97,
   99, 104n28, 110, 113–115,
   119–123, 125–128, 130n39,
   130n41, 133, 134, 138, 140–142,
   213, 214, 228, 229, 233, 241, 242,
   244–246, 255n40, 264, 275–279,
   281, 282, 284–288, 314, 326, 327,
   330, 332, 335, 336, 342, 347, 352,
   392, 393, 397, 399, 418, 435, 437,
   444–449, 451, 452, 455n6,
   459–472, 484, 496n2, 501,
   504, 505
Avarice, 124, 126, 136, 142–144, 320,
   332, 460

## B

Bakhtin, Mikhail, 7, 8, 12, 13, 25,
   87n54, 113, 124, 126, 127, 166,
   224, 228, 269n2, 275, 276, 295,
   304, 384, 385, 418
   bodily lower stratum, 8, 295
   carnival, 7, 87n54, 126, 127, 166, 418
   carnivalesque, 13, 25, 113, 124,
      269n2, 384, 385
   *Rabelais and His World*, 7,
      87n54, 269n2
Ballad/s, 57, 384, 385, 388, 389, 391,
   392, 394, 397, 399, 401n46
Banter, 53, 444
Barthes, Roland, 31, 372

Bawdy, 5, 74, 287, 330, 486, 488
Beard, 178, 179, 184, 188, 189, 226
Bergson, Henri, 9, 12–14, 97, 109–128,
   128n1, 128n4, 128n10, 129n14,
   129n20, 129n22, 129n23, 130n38,
   182, 183, 188, 224, 295,
   434–436, 441n22
   comic devices, 115–119, 127, 128n1
   indifference, 294
   *Le Rire (Laughter)*, 109–114, 127,
      128n1, 129n23, 434
   mechanical, 97, 110–112, 116,
      120–125, 127
   rigidity, 9, 114, 122, 123, 125, 127
   *Time and Free Will*, 113,
      128n5, 129n23
Bible, 9, 157, 158, 275–279, 282–284,
   288n1, 318, 330, 331, 333,
   337n36, 337n44
Billig, Michael, 20, 249
Bitter, 4, 47, 55, 215n9, 222, 223, 225,
   230, 354, 406
Black humour, gallows humour, 25, 53,
   323, 483
Blasphemous, 287, 329, 386, 418
Boccaccio, Giovanni, 74, 433, 440
   *The Decameron (the heliotrope)*, 433
Body, human
   abjection, 295, 296
   bodily humours (*see* Humoral theory)
   disfigurement (*see* Deformity)
   embodiment, 295
   scatology, 276
Bourdieu, Pierre, 103n13, 177, 482
Bracciolini, Poggio, 73
Bremmer, Jan, 10, 11, 19, 63
Britain, 23, 57, 71, 80, 85, 94, 101,
   254n28, 263, 267, 275, 277, 279,
   280, 283, 327, 334, 351, 352, 370,
   407, 445, 446, 481, 503, 507
Buddhism, 156–159, 164
   *See under* Religion
Burke, Peter, 10, 86n19
Burlesque, 177, 180–182, 278, 450,
   454, 456n16, 504
Butt, of joke, *see* Target, of humour
Byzantium/Byzantine Empire, 262

**C**

Caricature, 73, 118, 176, 183, 185, 186, 323, 364, 370, 413, 417, 448, 449, 452, 462, 469, 489, 501

Cartoon/s, 178, 211, 361–378, 406–409, 411, 413, 414, 416–420, 452, 482, 501, 504, 505

Categorisation, 5, 11, 12, 15n3, 16n27, 19, 27, 62–64, 72, 97, 98, 111, 116, 119, 130n36, 136, 144, 145, 147, 152, 153, 157, 160, 161, 165, 201–207, 211, 214, 216n15, 228, 233, 248–251, 261, 265, 293, 349, 372, 387, 395, 407, 462, 500, 501, 510–512

Censorship, 74, 84, 369, 411, 469–472

Cervantes, 221, 222, 446, 451–453
*Don Quixote*, 222, 225, 446

Chaucer, Geoffrey, 261, 277, 278, 433, 440, 440n1
'The Miller's Tale,' 277
*Troilus and Criseyde*, 261

Child/ren, 31, 78, 80, 100, 109, 141–143, 146, 155, 160, 176, 183, 211, 217n56, 232, 278, 282, 285, 286, 313, 315–317, 320–323, 325, 332, 365, 393, 399, 405, 408, 416, 417, 437, 443, 448, 450, 454, 512

China
Confucius, 202, 204, 210, 216n15, 225, 228, 459, 460, 462, 465, 466, 474n18, 474n22, 474n24, 476n60
Daoist, 158, 204, 216n15, 223, 224, 230, 461, 462, 466, 474n18
Han, period of, 205, 213, 474n22
*literati*, 202, 206, 214, 215, 228, 459, 460, 462–465, 469, 473n1
May Fourth Movement, 201, 203, 460
Ming, period of, 226, 462, 469
Qing, period of, 226, 473n2
Song, period of, 204, 208
Tang, period of, 212–214
*wenyan*, 205, 228, 229, 236n31
Yuan, period of, 460

Cicero, 24, 25, 32, 33, 72, 75, 97, 98, 145, 341
*De Oratore (Orator)*, 72, 75, 97

Classical, 21, 33, 72, 75, 96–98, 104n25, 115, 145, 151, 162, 176, 183, 190, 195n9, 205, 230, 259, 281, 289n28, 293, 332, 436, 470, 471

Classification, *see* Categorisation

Class, social, 159, 250, 384, 408, 512

Clowns, 73, 96, 139, 152, 157, 160, 194, 239, 245, 313, 332, 333

Cognition, vi, vii, 5, 94–97, 102, 103n11, 112, 137, 161, 240, 241, 244, 250, 252, 258, 276, 335, 371, 372, 417

Comedy, 5, 20, 21, 23, 72, 74, 76–79, 93–102, 109–128, 138, 141, 156–159, 165, 180, 182, 188, 189, 224, 249, 261, 262, 270n16, 298, 306, 322, 325, 327, 329, 330, 332, 334–336, 336n9, 345–347, 349, 353, 390, 396, 397, 431, 432, 434, 436, 446, 448, 488, 492, 495, 499, 501

Comic character, 12, 94, 99, 101, 114, 123, 125, 133–147, 277, 287, 289n41, 434

Comic hero, 157, 314, 317

Comics, viii, 24, 57, 71, 94, 109–128, 133–147, 152, 156–157, 176, 202, 221, 261, 275, 294, 313, 326, 343, 362, 390, 418, 432, 446, 461, 481, 500

Congreve, William, 27, 99–101

Contempt, 24, 49, 63, 79, 234, 247, 320, 331, 342, 390, 413, 465

Context, vii, 4, 5, 7–15, 20, 23, 27–28, 30, 31, 33, 34, 43–47, 49, 52–54, 56, 58, 60, 62, 64, 72, 73, 85, 94, 102, 111, 113, 114, 126–128, 133, 136, 139, 140, 143–147, 160–162, 164, 165, 176–178, 185, 190, 194, 196n26, 201, 203, 226, 229, 251, 254n28, 257–269, 276, 288n1, 293, 295, 299, 305, 332, 333, 343, 344, 346, 347, 350–352, 354, 372, 377, 378, 384, 385, 395, 411, 419, 420, 443, 445, 450, 451, 460, 462, 470–472, 495, 496n2, 496n8, 503–506, 512

518 INDEX

Contradiction, 154, 166, 225, 243, 329, 335, 349, 400
Corruption, 26, 265, 416, 417, 420, 460, 462
Courtesy, 5, 117, 118, 230
Cowardice, 26, 136, 139, 142, 144, 181, 182, 189, 319, 409, 411, 418, 431, 432, 434
Criticism, humour as, 11, 12, 133, 152, 161, 265, 411
Cruelty, 61, 104n41, *277*, 353, 439
Cue/cues, 5, 123, 322, 361, 372–374, 377, 378, 417, 466

**D**

Death, humour and, 405
Deformity
  moral, 176
  physical, 135
Democritus, 24
Derision, 47, 52, 72–74, 152, 157, 162, 225, 230, 249, 250, 276, 287, 288, 331, 335, 434
Didactic function, 204, 208, 210, 214, 228, 230, 241, 247, 282, 326, 327, 329, 335, 461, 462
Disgust, 315, 409, 416–420, 466
Distance, viii, 8, 9, 11, 72, 112, 135, 148n31, 222, 283, 332, 342, 344, 347, 350, 352, 361, 390, 420, 451
Double entendre, 242
Drama, 84, 115, 125, 159, 194, 275–288, 305, 325–327, 329, 330, 332, 334, 336
Drunkenness, 210, 263, 270n16, 313, 318, 321, 323

**E**

Elias, Norbert, 10, 94, 96, 97, 189–191, 194
  *Civilizing Process*, 94, 189
Emotion/s
  affect, 95
  affection, 78, 101, 210, 318, 467
  affect theory, 94–96
  anger, 32
  courage, 32
  delight, 462

embarrassment, vi, 233, 468
fear, 123, 240
history of, 44, 94, 95, 103n13
humiliation, 49, 54, 73, 84, 117, 247, 295, 300, 303, 306, 384, 385, 411, 468
joy, 462
merriment, 9, 25, 30, 32, 34, 50–52, 57, 58, 258, 263, 327, 390, 500
mirth, 25, 33, 46, 59, 80, 84, 99, 100, 117, 327, 330, 365, 398–399
mood, 21, 63, 260, 306, 314, 395
pity, 32
pleasure, 285
pride, 3
revulsion, 285
sadness, 83, 84, 225, 307, 414
theory of, 93
Empathy, 110, 125, 223, 230–232, 234, 300, 301, 305, 323, 390, 453, 454
Enigma, *see* Riddle
Entertainment, 3, 12, 46, 49–52, 55, 61, 99, 128n1, 207, 210, 212, 213, 277, 278, 282, 284–287, 302, 303, 362, 398–400, 482
Ephemera/l/ity, 63, 465, 472, 500, 502, 509, 513
Equivocation, 138, 139
Erasmus, Desiderius, viii, 5, 9, 24, 34, 77, 80, 82, 85n2, 314, 330
  *Praise of Folly*, 5, 77
  *stultitia*, 5
Ethics, 111, 133, 134, 138, 140, 144, 146, 147, 151, 300, 301
Europe, 13, 22, 24, 71–85, 275, 276, 302, 309n45, 408, 409, 417, 481, 506
Exaggeration, 56, 74, 121, 154, 159, 177, 186, 188, 261, 278, 300, 316, 319, 384, 392, 395, 397

**F**

Fabliau/x, 258, 261, 264, 267
Face, v, 12, 24, 33, 46, 55, 119, 121, 147, 176, 180, 186, 188, 242, 265, 280, 297, 299, 303, 306, 320, 321, 330, 333, 354, 366, 397, 407, 412, 418, 468, 469, 471

Fantastic, 71, 154, 241, 242, 251, 260, 280, 281, 393
Farce, 20, 35n15, 43, 56, 101, 113, 116–119, 122, 298, 325, 342, 462, 466, 475n35, 492
Fart, 82, 130n43, 330, 374, 375, 470, 476n72
Festivity, 10, 25, 51, 59, 77, 84, 275, 330, 418
Fiction, 163, 202, 204, 222, 223, 258, 261, 267, 307, 323, 344, 418, 443, 446, 448, 456n28, 460, 467
Film, 147, 278, 299, 305, 445–450, 453, 454, 455n5, 455n11, 456n16, 456n22, 456n32
Folk humour, 10, 295
Folklore/folk literature, 151, 158–160, 203, 206, 211, 216n42, 243, 314, 316, 385, 398, 399, 469
Folly, viii, 5, 9, 46, 164, 279, 294, 322, 400, 494, 499, 500
   *stultitia* (*see* Erasmus, Desiderius)
Fool/s
   foolishness, 25
   in *King Lear*, 3, 8
Foucault, Michel, 95, 302, 482
France, 21, 22, 31, 71, 73, 74, 76, 78, 80, 82, 83, 85, 113, 115, 128n1, 128n4, 128n5, 141, 260, 283, 298, 302, 407, 431, 433, 434, 437–439, 440n1, 444, 446–448, 451, 452, 454, 455, 455n9, 455n16, 456n32, 460, 462–470, 472, 475n34, 482
Freud, Sigmund, 9, 12, 13, 82, 147, 224, 294, 295, 446
Fun, 35n14, 51–54, 192, 212, 230, 263, 307, 323, 329, 353, 365, 389, 434, 502, 505, 508
   make/ing fun of, 57, 181, 185, 187, 194, 213, 384, 409, 412, 414, 432, 436, 466
Funny/funniness, vii, 4, 5, 8, 11, 22, 24, 46, 48–51, 53, 59, 62–64, 75, 79, 93, 97, 102, 119, 123, 133–135, 137, 144, 153, 202, 206, 246, 258, 259, 261, 262, 266, 325, 330, 332, 341, 342, 353, 371, 395, 406, 410, 413, 414, 432, 435, 439, 445, 462, 481, 483, 499, 501

**G**
Game/s, 12, 49, 50, 52, 77, 109, 114, 189, 192, 213, 263, 313, 332, 333, 362, 379n13, 388
Gender, *see* Sex and sexuality
Government, 101, 190, 196n26, 209, 364, 366, 368–370, 373, 374, 411, 459–461
Greece, ancient, 10, 62, 175, 183, 190
Grotesque, 76, 78, 154, 177, 179, 183, 185, 186, 188, 192, 228, 239, 243, 252, 288, 315, 328, 330, 332, 384, 392, 459–472

**H**
Hazlitt, William, 261, 293, 294, 432, 436
Health, wellbeing, 297, 305
   mental illness, 305
   *See also* Medical humanities
Hebrew, 321, 322, 415
Hierarchy, social, 194, 341, 462
Historicism, 11–13, 23, 94, 95, 103n7, 103n13
Hoax, 31
Hobbes, Thomas, 12, 20, 23, 25, 29, 31–35, 37n70, 37n75, 72–74, 111, 345, 432, 436
   *The Elements of Law*, 31
   *Leviathan*, 32, 34, 72
Holy Land, 280
Honour, viii, 62, 74, 133, 134, 138–141, 143–146, 176, 233, 319, 352, 468
Huizinga, Johan, 35n1, 154
   *Homo Ludens*, 35n1, 154
Humanist, 71, 72, 79, 80, 84, 316, 330, 335
   *See also* Erasmus, Desiderius
Humoral theory, 21, 33, 82, 110, 223, 240, 335
Humourist/s, vi, 24, 97, 157, 221, 224, 234, 314

**I**
Ideology, 12, 94, 160, 202, 203, 275, 471
Imagination, 9, 110, 112, 153, 248, 253, 259, 281, 396, 494

520    INDEX

Incongruity, vi, 11, 12, 20, 32, 71,
    78–80, 84, 94, 97, 110, 111, 121,
    126, 130n46, 137, 151, 152, 154,
    155, 158, 159, 162, 164–166,
    166n5, 207, 223, 224, 231, 232,
    234, 240, 246, 247, 249–251, 258,
    342, 344, 348, 349, 357n31, 365,
    432, 435–440, 446, 455, 460, 495
  *See under* Theory/ies of humour
Innocence, 25, 26, 30, 34, 36n37, 84,
    120, 142, 258, 278, 327, 395,
    416, 444
Innuendo, 78, 444, 452, 454
Insult, 46, 51, 56, 62, 63, 76, 79, 213,
    260, 470
Intention, vi, 7, 10, 19, 28, 29, 31, 33,
    34, 44, 46, 47, 53, 56, 58, 63, 64,
    73, 75, 78, 88n86, 96, 113, 142,
    163, 224, 227, 242, 276, 279, 283,
    285, 288, 295, 296, 306, 307, 319,
    384, 399, 434, 437, 439, 450, 453,
    454, 461, 470, 475n42, 486, 501,
    504, 512
  intentional/ity, 7, 23, 28–30, 33, 34,
    176–183, 390, 434
Interpersonal dynamics, 264
Intimacy, 22, 94, 165, 232, 265, 266,
    328, 388, 394, 467
Inversion, 110, 118–121, 123, 125,
    126, 181, 189, 192, 301,
    303, 384–385
Irony, 29, 33, 55, 56, 125, 241, 249,
    277, 341–355, 384, 390–394, 398,
    399, 406, 410, 411, 415, 417, 420,
    449, 450, 459–472
  romantic irony, 341–355
Islam, 154, 158, 159, 168n48, 283
Italy, 22, 27, 71, 73, 74, 76, 78–80, 82,
    83, 85, 145, 221, 224, 262, 297,
    355, 406–412, 414,
    417–419, 421n27

**J**

Japan
  Edo, 115, 130n43, 362, 365, 368,
    370, 378
  kyōgen, 115, 116, 121, 122, 126–128,
    129n30, 129n32, 130n35, 130n38,
    130n39, 130n46, 130n51

  *kyōka*, 361, 362, 366, 371–373
Jest
  jest book/s, 71, 73, 76, 80, 86n18,
    201–215, 225–227, 229, 230,
    234, 235n25, 235n29, 502–504,
    509–511, 513
  jester/s, 8, 81, 82, 152, 184, 210,
    212, 227, 230
  jesting, 4, 5, 8–10, 25, 28, 36n37,
    86n36, 383–400
Jibe/s, 74, 258
Johnson, Samuel, 444, 449, 455n2
Joke/s, 6, 20, 45, 73, 97, 109, 134,
    166, 178, 201–215, 225,
    231–234, 248, 257–269, 276,
    293, 325, 341, 342, 384, 408,
    438, 468, 481, 499,
    501–503, 509–512
  joke book, 27, 206, 226, 299,
    501–504, 506, 510, 511
Jonson, Ben, 98, 100
  *Every Man Out of His Humour*, 98
Joubert, Laurent, 73, 79–84, 87n66,
    88n86, 104n22, 294, 298, 299,
    305, 332
  *Treatise on Laughter*, 73, 104n22,
    294, 298

**K**

Kant, Immanuel, 12, 32, 78, 97, 345,
    356n15, 357n31
  *Critique of Judgement*, 97

**L**

Language game, 5
Laughter
  laughable, 7, 9, 71–73, 76, 77, 79, 84,
    85n13, 88n86, 113, 128n4, 134,
    136, 139, 140, 143, 144, 175,
    184, 221, 223, 225, 229, 230,
    277, 278, 282, 288, 294,
    440, 474n18
  laugh/s, vii, 8, 10, 12, 19, 24, 26, 34,
    50, 61–63, 72, 73, 75–83, 85n4,
    85n7, 85n10, 97, 110, 114, 120,
    125, 126, 140, 157, 182, 183,
    206, 207, 221–223, 226, 233,

234, 239–253, 258, 261, 284, 286, 293, 294, 300, 301, 313, 320, 329, 331, 333, 335, 342, 345, 351, 354, 355, 383, 388, 390, 394, 395, 397, 417, 432, 434, 435, 437, 440, 453, 502, 503

Law, 19, 31, 47, 50, 51, 56, 58, 62, 63, 74, 113, 177, 191, 231, 282, 293, 297, 317, 368, 369, 406, 418, 502, 505

Levi-Strauss, Claude, 155, 162

Libel, 56, 369

Liberation, 12, 13, 114, 153, 155, 326, 474n24

Locke, John, 99, 100
  *Essay Concerning Human Understanding*, 99

Logical mechanism (LM), 6, 7, 371, 379n30

Lucian, 24, 34

Ludicrous/ness, 4, 97, 100, 144, 154, 161, 169n88, 239, 499

**M**

Machiavelli, Niccolò, 73, 133, 134, 141–147, 149n38
  *Mandragola* (The Mandrake), 133, 141, 149n38

Maggi, Vincenzo, 76, 78, 83, 88n98, 176
  *De Ridiculis (On the Ridiculous)*, 76, 78, 83, 88n98, 176

Malice, vii, 53, 58, 72, 73, 78–80, 84, 85n7, 99, 110, 288, 320, 384, 431, 432, 460

Marginalia, 239, 253n1

McGraw, Peter, 126, 127, 133–136, 139, 144

Medical humanities, 14, 293–308
  *See also* Health, wellbeing

Merleau-Ponty, Maurice, 95, 103n13, 295, 296, 299, 304, 305, 307
  phenomenology, 95, 295

Merriment, 9, 25, 30, 32, 34, 50–52, 57, 58, 258, 263, 327, 390, 500

Methodology, v, vii, 10, 11, 13–15, 23, 27, 34, 44, 62, 64, 84, 94, 95, 102,

161, 201, 295, 344, 383, 407–408, 420, 500, 511

Mockery, 20, 46–48, 52–59, 61–64, 67n92, 76, 81, 83, 109, 110, 135, 152, 157, 161, 162, 177, 183, 189, 210, 213, 242, 277–280, 282, 287, 288, 303, 314, 315, 328, 330, 331, 373, 411, 418, 444, 449, 451–453, 482, 491

Modes, of humour, 85

Molière, 109, 113, 122, 320

Money, 30, 33, 209, 258, 285, 319, 463, 465, 466, 469, 482

Monstrosity, 86n16, 98, 165, 181, 239–253, 253n2, 303, 415

Morality, 4, 8, 13, 24, 30, 32, 74, 76, 77, 85, 93, 98, 99, 102, 112, 113, 121, 125–127, 134, 135, 137, 141–144, 146, 147, 176, 181, 184, 189–190, 194, 214, 228, 249, 260, 293, 408, 417, 418, 420, 447, 460–462, 465

More, Thomas, 24, 28, 74, 76

Morreall, John, 12, 35n6, 72, 157–159, 162, 165, 168n48, 168n49

Myth
  myth-making, 23
  mythology, 179, 192

**N**

Neologism, vi, 21, 27, 35n13, 365, 371, 374, 375, 379n13, 456n16, 461

Neoplatanism, 240, 253

Neurology, 299

Newspaper, magazines, 361, 362, 366, 368–370, 372, 378, 379n14, 379n20, 406, 408–415, 418–420, 499, 500, 503–509, 511, 513

Nonsense, 5, 20, 28, 50, 318, 328, 329, 372, 374, 377, 418, 443, 448, 452

Non-serious, vi, 128, 156, 258, 371, 406

Nordic countries
  Denmark, 45, 47, 383–400
  Iceland, 46, 51, 54, 56–58, 60, 63
  Norway, 47, 48, 50, 54, 55, 57, 384, 394
  Scandinavia, 63, 64, 67n96, 391

522 INDEX

Norm/s
affirmation of, 399
normative, 134, 144
violation of, 8, 127, 135, 140, 141, 147, 342
North America
USA, 9, 31, 366, 385, 406, 415, 436, 499, 506, 507
Yankee humour, 506
Nostalgia, 316, 317

**O**

Obscene, 58, 62, 228, 282, 293, 295, 316, 321, 384, 386
Offence, 34, 53, 56, 62, 63, 73, 75, 78, 485
Oring, Elliott, 12, 136, 137, 142, 143, 146
Otherness, *see* Alterity

**P**

Pain, 9, 48, 82, 136, 164, 176, 285, 294, 295, 299, 306, 331, 332, 335, 385, 395, 461
Paradox, 9, 30, 31, 34, 72, 136, 249, 278, 329, 330, 334, 347–349, 351, 355, 436, 446, 460
Parody, 14, 30, 56, 57, 130n36, 139, 155, 166, 184, 192, 194, 283, 285, 313–323, 347, 365, 369, 391, 444, 445, 450–455, 456n28, 456n32, 467, 504
Pastiche, 354, 451–453, 456n22
Pastime, 49, 50, 52, 316
Performance/s, v, 3, 4, 26, 28, 29, 57, 84, 97, 101, 102, 109, 115, 117–119, 125–127, 129n32, 130n43, 138, 165, 191, 206, 210, 212–214, 275–280, 282–287, 296, 315, 319, 329, 330, 335, 342, 362, 371, 372, 378, 383, 384, 386, 388, 389, 392, 399, 400, 443, 448, 476n66, 482, 501, 509, 511
Performativity, 46, 48, 114, 127, 298, 377, 387

Persuasion, 75, 76, 84, 146, 342
*Philogelos*, 178, 208
Physicality, 8, 25, 82–84, 113, 115, 121, 123, 124, 127, 135, 146, 176, 177, 181, 183–187, 189–190, 194, 210, 228, 244, 251, 264, 295, 296, 298, 299, 303, 305, 306, 319, 330, 331, 397, 417
Plato, 23, 32, 37n85, 72, 175, 342, 397
Play, viii, 3, 20, 52, 71, 94, 109, 133, 154, 182, 205, 223, 246, 260, 275, 276, 294, 313, 325, 343, 362, 388, 447, 462, 492
Poetry, 23, 28, 29, 46, 55–59, 62, 64, 99, 206, 244, 345, 357n25, 361, 364–366, 371, 373
Popular culture, 175–194, 239, 366
Postmodernism, 343, 446, 448, 456n16
Power, 9, 13, 21, 29, 32, 63, 74–76, 83–85, 93, 98, 118, 140, 141, 143, 145, 147, 148n33, 152, 154, 160, 166, 177, 182, 190, 213, 257–269, 277, 279–283, 286, 287, 316, 322, 335, 341, 342, 344, 345, 347, 348, 354, 355, 368, 375, 384, 392, 393, 418, 437, 439, 460, 465, 468, 471, 476n59
Prank, 52, 63, 126, 301, 468, 501
Propaganda, 23, 314, 407, 415–417
Prudence, 134, 145–147
Psychology, v, 8, 9, 14, 22, 94, 112, 128n9, 135–138, 161, 164, 222, 224, 250, 258, 264, 269, 298, 301, 406, 417, 420
Punchline/s, 6, 208, 226, 230, 232, 233, 258–260, 266, 413, 501, 503
*Punch*, magazine, 366, 370, 482, 483, 503–506, 508
Puns and punning, 12, 22, 48, 78, 123, 134, 192, 213, 229, 241, 331, 352, 361–378, 443, 504
*See also* Wordplay
Puttenham, George, 24

**Q**

*Qur'an*, 158

**R**

Rabelais, François, 7, 71, 82, 293–308, 313–323, 451, 453
  *Gargantua*, 295, 299, 303, 304, 307, 308n2, 318, 319, 451
  *Le Quart Livre*, 298
  *Pantagruel*, 294, 295, 297, 300–304, 306, 308n2, 316, 317, 319
  *Rabelais and his World* (*see* Bakhtin, Mikhail)
  *Tiers livre*, 303, 308n2, 319
Raskin, Victor, 6, 251, 371, 378
Rationality, 29, 100, 112, 191, 253
Recognition, vi, 6, 8, 13, 32, 34, 94, 126, 127, 159, 166n5, 245, 287, 296, 299, 316, 319, 344, 346, 353, 408, 437
Redemption, 113, 157, 162–164, 328, 336n10
Relief, *see* Theory/ies of humour
Religion
  Buddhism, 116, 130n41, 156–159, 164, 212
  Christianity, 25, 29, 30, 74, 77, 134, 144, 146, 152, 154, 156–158, 162, 163, 240, 241, 244, 252, 278, 281–285, 287, 325, 326, 330–332, 334, 335, 436, 438, 439
  indigenous, 160
  Islam, 158, 159, 168n48, 283, 284
  Judaism, 154, 158, 164, 321, 322, 415, 420, 492
  theology/theological, 156, 163, 326
Rhetoric, 7–10, 13, 14, 24–26, 33, 72, 73, 76, 79, 80, 84, 138, 142, 143, 146, 212, 214, 239–253, 260, 284, 285, 342–344, 362, 365, 373, 412, 476n69
Riddle, 3, 4, 30, 60, 154, 191, 240, 243–249, 254n12, 254n13, 399
Ridicule, 31, 46, 47, 53, 54, 56, 57, 73, 74, 76, 77, 79, 85n13, 96–98, 100, 111, 113, 125, 161, 162, 177, 182, 185, 213, 227, 239, 243, 250, 331, 342, 409, 412–414, 416–419, 434, 436, 446

ridiculous, 7, 14, 16n27, 76, 85n2, 85n7, 85n13, 97, 99, 177, 184, 186, 190, 278, 279, 294, 316, 397, 432, 444, 446, 448, 450, 453, 454
*Rig Veda*, 154, 167n18
Risible, 21, 437
Ritual, 151, 152, 155–162, 165, 166, 212, 415, 418, 419, 460
Rome, ancient, 10, 141
Roodenburg, Herman, 10, 11, 63
Russia, 406, 407, 416, 417
  USSR (Soviet Union), 25, 416, 420, 471

**S**

Sarcasm, vi, 56, 331, 342
Satire, 20, 22–24, 27, 30, 31, 34, 43, 46, 54, 56, 58, 59, 66n82, 74, 75, 98, 99, 105n59, 130n36, 152, 157, 161, 164, 202, 227, 228, 235n25, 258, 306, 313, 314, 316, 318, 320–323, 329, 354, 362, 366, 368, 370, 371, 373, 374, 377, 447–449, 451–454, 459–461, 463, 473n10, 474n18, 484, 485, 492, 494, 496n8, 504
Satyr, 176, 189–194, 197n59
Scandinavia, *see* Nordic countries
Schadenfreude, 63, 72
Scorn, 46–48, 50, 53, 63, 64, 73, 77, 78, 82, 231, 278, 288, 331, 391, 467, 468
Scriblerian/s, 30, 31
Script, 6, 7, 213, 335, 362, 363, 371, 373, 448, 449
  script opposition, 6, 7, 371
Scurrility, 330
Self
  self-awareness, 9, 22, 114, 125, 318
  self-deprecation, 63, 266
  self-fashioning, 347
  selfhood, 93
  self-mockery, 32, 34, 316
  self-reflection, 343, 348

524 INDEX

Semantic/s, 6, 20, 23–27, 29, 35n14, 43, 44, 62, 64n8, 240, 248, 249, 251, 372–374
Sense of humour, viii, 19, 21–22, 24, 26, 27, 30, 35n11, 43–64, 93, 100, 102, 155, 157, 230, 234, 330, 335, 383, 438, 446, 453, 462
Serious, v, vi, 7, 11, 20, 28, 30, 50, 58, 63, 75, 76, 114, 115, 148n31, 152, 153, 155, 156, 179, 192, 239, 240, 246, 252, 257–269, 276, 284, 288, 299, 306, 314, 322, 326, 328, 331, 332, 346, 349, 354, 371, 372, 374, 375, 377, 385, 388, 392, 394, 396, 399, 400, 409, 412, 419, 435, 439, 448, 462, 463, 466, 499, 510
Sermon/s, 75, 77, 260, 326
Sex and sexuality, 159, 160, 266, 269, 396, 504, 512
  erotic/sexual humour, 5, 49–51, 135, 160, 185, 189, 194, 228, 231, 232, 248, 251, 265, 388, 395, 418, 443, 444, 452, 454, 455, 471, 483
  gender, 151, 159, 160, 266, 269, 396, 504, 512
  genitalia, 228
  marriage, 50, 231, 233, 264, 268, 321, 510
Shadwell, Thomas, 26, 98, 99
Shaftesbury, Lord, Earl of (Anthony Ashley-Cooper), 20, 31, 100
Shakespeare, William, 3–5, 8, 9, 15n2, 26, 29, 77, 79, 122, 130n42, 133, 134, 138–140, 142–146, 148n1, 148n26, 278, 329, 380n39, 433, 446, 475n55
  Comedy of Errors, The, 122
  Falstaff, 26, 130n42, 133, 134, 138, 139, 148n31
  Hamlet, 278
  Julius Caesar, 29
  King Lear, 3, 15n2
  Macbeth, 139, 148n26
  A Midsummer Night's Dream, 433, 446
  Much Ado About Nothing, 29
  1 Henry IV, 26, 133, 138
  Taming of the Shrew, The, 122

  Twelfth Night, 77, 329
  2 Henry IV, 26
Shame, 46, 58, 62, 63, 72, 136, 139, 140, 176, 228, 263, 316, 318
Sheridan, Thomas, 30, 31, 37n63
Slapstick, 135, 299, 397, 501, 504
Smiling, vi, 11, 12, 159, 242, 492
Social
  cohesion, 183–185
  correction, 110, 125, 126
  laughter, 183
Sociology, 258, 264–266, 269
Socrates, 341, 342, 355, 397
Solidarity, 265, 266
Song/s, 57, 58, 115, 203–206, 208, 215, 227, 261, 383–400, 431, 432, 511
Sound, 30, 32, 110, 118, 125, 214, 298, 363–366, 371, 373, 375, 377, 378, 379n30, 385–390, 414, 433–435, 463, 467, 468, 475n42, 508
  homophone, 363, 364, 366, 369, 371, 375
Spain, 405, 409, 423n93, 432, 438
Spontaneity, 25, 294, 406, 409, 410, 419, 467
Spoof/s, 300
Status, social, 62, 126, 384, 412
Stereotypes, 54, 114, 122, 125, 130n41, 214, 276, 451, 456n27
Stinginess, 210, 228, 431, 432
Stock character/s, 109, 115, 118, 121, 123, 130n42, 332
Subjectivity, of viewpoint, 10
Subversion, 25, 29, 177, 240, 400, 411
Superiority, 350
  See under Theory/ies of humour
Surprise, vi, 4, 26, 32, 34, 46, 78, 79, 84, 104n28, 121, 127, 176, 178, 182, 192, 239, 240, 248, 268, 269, 275, 293, 332, 344, 350, 365, 392, 395, 396, 447
Sympathy, 26, 110, 111, 113, 125, 259, 314, 316, 320, 332, 342, 399, 435

T
Taboo/s, 62, 228, 265, 299
Takanashi, Hiroko, 361, 371–373, 378

Target, of humour, 44, 57, 97, 207, 266, 296
Taunt/s, 47, 60, 61, 210, 264
Teasing, 49, 50, 53, 184, 209, 210, 240, 244, 344, 349, 392
Terminology, v, 9, 14, 23, 43, 45, 50, 144, 146, 147, 201, 202
Theory/ies of humour, 11–13, 16n26, 20, 24, 32, 34, 71–78, 80, 84, 85, 85n4, 94, 96, 97, 111, 125, 126, 128n8, 128n10, 136, 156, 157, 162, 166n5, 182, 188, 223, 234, 240, 249, 250, 264, 282, 287, 342, 346, 348, 351, 353, 355, 431, 446, 454, 462
  aggression, 313
  appropriate incongruity, 137
  Bakhtin, Mikhail (*see* Bakhtin, Mikhail)
  Benign Violation Theory, 126
  Bergson, Henri (*see* Bergson, Henri)
  Billig, Michael (*see* Billig, Michael)
  false beliefs, 13, 284
  Freud, Sigmund (*see* Freud, Sigmund)
  General Theory of Verbal Humor (GTVH), 6, 7, 12–14
  Hazlitt, William (*see* Hazlitt, William)
  Hobbes, Thomas (*see* Hobbes, Thomas)
  incongruity, vi, 11, 12, 20, 32, 71, 78–80, 84, 94, 97, 110, 111, 121, 126, 137, 151, 152, 154, 155, 158, 159, 162, 164–166, 166n5, 207, 223, 224, 231, 232, 234, 240, 246, 247, 249–251, 258, 285, 326, 335, 342, 344, 348, 349, 365, 377, 432, 435–440, 446, 455, 460, 495
  Ontological Semantic Theory of Humor, 6, 13
  Pirandello, the opposite, 13
  Play Theory, 127
  relief, release, 11–13, 20, 71, 80–84, 94, 162, 166n5, 240, 246, 249, 250, 342
  reversal, 258
  Semantic Script-base Theory of Humor, 6, 371
  superiority, 11–13, 20, 24, 32–34, 37n85, 71–78, 80, 84, 85, 85n4, 94, 96, 97, 111, 125, 126, 128n8, 156, 157, 162, 166n5, 182, 188, 223, 225, 234, 240, 249, 250, 264, 276, 278, 279, 285–287, 331, 342, 344, 346, 348–351, 353, 355, 431, 446, 454, 462
  Terror Management Theory, 258
  Thielst, Peter (*see* Thielst, Peter)
  universalising, vii, 13, 84–85, 94, 133, 134, 147, 152, 342
Therapy (therapeutic), 82, 295, 297, 299–301, 305–308, 385
Thielst, Peter, 383–385, 388, 390, 395, 399
Thomas, Keith, 10
Threat, 120, 126, 130n51, 135, 187, 239, 244, 265, 282, 283, 286, 288, 390, 412, 432, 436, 471
Tickling, 83, 113, 134, 135
Tone, 48, 49, 52, 54, 98, 142, 241, 245, 247, 259, 261, 265, 266, 354, 398, 413, 414, 418, 440, 460–462, 472, 492, 504
Tragedy, 5, 76, 98, 100, 101, 115, 156–159, 165, 166, 223, 225, 233, 261, 270n16, 279, 285, 321, 327, 328, 330, 333–336, 343, 388, 400, 405, 406, 418–420, 446
Transgression, 192, 243, 258, 342, 445
Translation, 14, 15, 22, 27–30, 34, 45, 48, 52, 55, 58, 115, 116, 128n1, 130n35, 202, 205, 229, 230, 236n41, 294, 352, 375, 432, 433, 437, 438, 440, 441n22, 444, 446, 447, 451, 452, 454, 456n16, 462–472, 477n87
  Model Reader, 470, 472
Trauma, 407
Trickery, 50, 57, 79, 116, 121, 123, 139, 244, 258, 294, 332, 346
  trickster figure, 151
Trigger, 97, 222, 231, 417
Triviality, 114, 259, 262, 446
Truth, 3, 6, 7, 9, 53, 94, 100, 121, 127, 151, 240–242, 251, 257–264, 266–269, 278, 284, 286, 319, 321, 326, 342, 346, 354, 420
Types, of humour, 261

## U

Ugliness, 14, 72, 73, 76, 78, 83, 85n8, 99, 175–194

Understatement, 64, 444, 445, 454, 455

Universality, 11, 12, 19–23, 27, 29, 30, 102, 114, 135, 140, 151, 152, 160, 164, 194, 215, 249, 335, 345, 385, 444, 482, 484, 510

## V

Values, 8, 9, 22, 28, 33, 44, 46, 75, 77, 103n13, 119, 121, 126, 139, 141, 143–147, 157–159, 161, 162, 177, 183, 184, 187, 190, 191, 194, 203, 210, 214, 228, 239, 242, 252, 266, 288, 294, 314, 318, 321–323, 355, 375, 384, 407, 408, 420, 460, 462, 465, 466

Veatch, Thomas, 133, 136
  *See under* Theory/ies of humour
Victim, of joke, *see* Target, of humour
Violation, of norms, 8, 9, 127, 134–136, 138, 140, 144, 145, 147
  *See under* Norm/s

Visual humour, 8, 30, 123, 175–194, 243, 305, 306, 361, 362, 365, 368, 369, 371–373, 377, 378, 452, 453, 455, 456n16, 481, 491, 492, 494, 501, 505, 508

Vulgar, 27, 226–228, 242, 329, 384, 464, 470, 472, 475n42

## W

Warren, Caleb, 126, 133–136, 143, 144
Wellbeing, 298–300, 308, 467
  *See also* Health, wellbeing; Medical humanities
Wisdom, 3, 8, 9, 141, 145, 146, 183, 239–244, 253, 434, 461
Wit, 4, 20, 22, 23, 25–27, 30, 33, 43, 48, 74, 75, 99, 100, 113, 123, 125, 152, 164, 211, 251, 264, 267, 269, 294, 347, 444, 462, 485, 502
  witticism, 48, 60, 75, 266, 341, 462
Wordplay, vi, 48, 59, 64, 209, 214, 229, 241, 362, 365, 369, 454

## Y

Yutang, Lin, 202, 229, 230, 234, 461

Printed in the United States
By Bookmasters